McGRAW-HILL MATHEMATICS

Math in my World

DOUGLAS H. CLEMENTS

KENNETH W. JONES

LOIS GORDON MOSELEY

LINDA SCHULMAN

McGraw-Hill School Division

New York   Farmington

PROGRAM AUTHORS

Dr. Douglas H. Clements

Kenneth W. Jones

Lois Gordon Moseley

Dr. Linda Schulman

CONTRIBUTING AUTHORS

Christine A. Fernsler

Dr. Liana Forest

Dr. Kathleen Kelly-Benjamin

Maria R. Marolda

Dr. Richard H. Moyer

Dr. Walter G. Secada

MULTICULTURAL AND EDUCATIONAL CONSULTANTS

Rim An

Sue Cantrell

Mordessa Corbin

Dr. Carlos Diaz

Carl Downing

Linda Ferreira

Judythe M. Hazel

Roger Larson

Josie Robles

Veronica Rogers

Telkia Rutherford

Sharon Searcy

Elizabeth Sinor

Michael Wallpe

Claudia Zaslavsky

COVER PHOTOGRAPHY Jade Albert for MMSD; t. m. Photri; t. l. Gary D. Landsman/The Stock Market; b.l. MMSD.

PHOTOGRAPHY CREDITS All photographs are by the McGraw-Hill School Division (MMSD), Clara Aich for MMSD, and Scott Harvey for MMSD except as noted below.

1: © James Kozyra/Liaison International. • 6: © Robert Ginn/PhotoEdit. • 9: m. © Walter Bibikow/FPG. • 12: t.l. © Vince Pierri/Daily Herald Photo. • 20: © Aaron Haupt/Stock Boston. • 23: © Salomon Collection/ ET Archive, London/Superstock. • 25: b.r. © D. Young-Wolff/PhotoEdit. • 26: © Mary Kate Denny/PhotoEdit. • 28: t. Sid Avery/MPTV . • 30: © Tony Freeman/PhotoEdit. • 31: Courtesy, Giselle Cruz. • 32: m.r. © F.O.S. Inc.. t.l. © S. Dooley/Liaison International; t.r. © L. Van Der Stockt/Gamma-Liaison; • 33: © Ellen B. Senial/Photosynthesis. • 38: both © Scala/Art Resource, NY. • 40-41: © Lionel Isy-Schwart/The Image Bank; • 40: m. © Stephen Ogilvy for MMSD. • 42: l. © A.B. Dowsett/Science Photo Library/Photo Researchers; r. © Ian Shaw/Tony Stone Images. • 46: © Gamma-Liaison. • 48: b. © Jonathan Blair/Woodfin Camp & Associates. • 53: t.r. © Lee E Battaglia/Photo Researchers. • 56: © Focus on Sports. • 59: © U.S. Naval Historical Center. • 61: © Sovfoto/Eastfoto; b. © Tim Flach/Tony Stone Images. • 65: © Robert Frerck/Woodfin Camp & Assoc. • 68: © Ed Bock/The Stock Market. • 74: © Bernard Wursig. • 76: Woodfin Camp & Assoc. • 78: b.l. © N.W. Quinto/U.S. Navy. m.r. © Jeff Cadge/The Image Bank. • 84: b.l. © Thomas J. Abercrombie, National Geographic Society. • 85: © Bill Morson /Liaison International; © Jack S. Grove/Liaison International. • 86: i. © Charles O'Rear/Westlight. • 86-87: © W. Cody/Westlight. • 91: Courtesy, Chase Manhattan Bank. • 92: © Patrick Aventurier/Gamma-Liaison. • 94: t.r. © D. Young-Wolff/PhotoEdit. • 96: © D. Ogust/The Image Works. • 97: b.l. © 1995 Smithsonian Institution; b.r. Courtesy, Bank of Canada; t.r. © 1995 Smithsonian Institution. • 106: r. © Michael S. Thompson/Comstock; t.l. Courtesy, Sandy Pandiscio. • 110: r. © Lance Nelson/The Stock Market. • 118: m. © Myrtly V. Lytle; t. © Charles O'Rear/Westlight. • 120: © Ken Graham/Tony Stone Images. • 122: © Charlie Westerman/Liaison International. • 122-3: © Tom Tracey. • 127: © Culver Collection/Superstock. • 128: t.r. Rick Noyle/Visual Impact. • 130: © David Young-Wolff for MMSD / PhotoEdit. • 131: © John Coletti for MMSD / The Picture Cube. • 134: © Tony Stone Images. • 135: © D. & J. Heaton/Westlight. • 138: © Archive Photos. • 142: b. © Alan Schein/The Stock Market; l. © Randa Bishop/Uniphoto; r. © Busch Entertainment Corp. • 144: © Ron Kimball.• 154: Courtesy, Patrick Hong; © Bill Losh/FPG. • 155: © Steve Elmore/The Stock Market. • 160: b.r. StockMarket/Alan Schein; t.r. © David Parker/Science Photo Library/Photo Researchers. • 161: l. © Nancy J. Pierce/Photo Researchers; r. Courtesy, Amy Schoffler. • 162: m.r. Walter Bibikow/The Image Bank; b.l. © William James Warren/Westlight; b.r. © Saab-Scania/Photo Researchers; b.m.r. © Walter Bibikow 1991; t.l. © Tony Stone Images; t.r. © Aneal Vohra/Unicorn; t.m.r. © Bob Daemmrich/The Image Works. • 168: l. © The Granger Collection; r. © Mark Richards/PhotoEdit. • 169: © Cindy Lewis. • 170-171: © Superstock; • 170: m. © Steve Dunwell/The Image Bank. • 172: © Joe Sohm/Chromosohm. • 176: Joan Marcus. • 180: © Bill Ross/Woodfin Camp & Associates. • 186: © Joan Marcus. • 187: Ken Lax/MMSD. • 188: t.r. Darius Rucher. • 190: © David Lassman-Syracuse Newspapers/The Image Works. • 191: Liaison/Bob Torrez. • 194: t. © Tom McCarthy / Photo Edit. • 196: © Evan Agostini/Gamma-Liaison. • 198: © The Kobal Collection. • 203: © Tom Hurst/Nickelodeon. • 205: Courtesy, Srean Van. • 206: b.l. © W. Anthony/West Stock; t.l. © John P. Kelly/the Image Bank; t.r. © The Stock Market. • 212: t.m. © David Weintraub/Photo Researchers; t.r. © David Weintraub/Photo Researchers. • 214: © Lori Adamski/Tony Stone Images. • 220: t.r. © Hiroyuki Kaijo/Bliss. • 224: t.r. © Michael Melford/The Image Bank. • 229: © H. De Marcillac/GLMR. © Patricia Martinez/PhotoEdit. • 235: © Private Collection/The Bridgeman Art Library, London/Superstock. • 242: © Galen Rowell; t.l. © Superstock. • 254: © Photo Researchers; © Don Smetzer/Tony Stone Images. • 254-5: PhotoDisc. • 256: © Billy E. Barnes/Stock Boston. • 258: © Nancy Sheehan/The Picture Cube, Inc.. • 260: © Susan Van Etten/PhotoEdit. • 262: Uniphoto. • 266: © Daemmrich/The Image Works. • 272: © Esto Photographics. • 278: Courtesy, Plimouth Plantation, Inc.. • 281: © 1995 Chromo/Sohm/Photo Researchers. • 282: © 1991 Frank Siteman/The Picture Cube. • 287: © Kindra Clineff/The Picture Cube; Courtesy, Crystal Stribling. • 288: © Camerique/The Picture Cube; © Bruce Hands/The Image Works; © Superstock; © Murray Alcosser/The Image Bank. • 294: © Walter Choroszewski/FPG; © Gamma-Liaison. • 295: © 1996 Chuck Pefley/Stock Boston. • 296-297: © Hans Neleman/The Image Bank; • 297: m. Thomas Heinz. • 298: © Tate Gallery, London/Art Resource, NY. • 300: © Joanne Ciccarello. • 303: © Bryan F. Peterson/The Stock Market. • 305: m. © Giraudon/Art Resource, NY. • 306: © Glen Allison/Tony Stone Images. • 309: © Scott Frances/Esto Photographics. • 316: t. © Steve Casimiro/Liaison International. • 318: © Scala/Art Resource, NY. • 322: © Gary Payne/Gamma-Liaison. • 325: © Photofest. • 326: m. © The Lowe Art Museum, University of Miami/Superstock; m.r. © Paul Steel/Stock Photos. • 328: © Everton/The Image Works; t. © David Young-Wolff. • 331: Courtesy, Naomi Malette. • 332: b.l. © Travelpix/FPG International; m.l. © Superstock. • 338: b.r. © Photograph Chun Y. Lai; t.l. © Lee Boltin. • 340-341: © Morgan Fisher/Photonica; • 340: m. © D. Young-Wolff/Photo Edit. • 345: © Martin Westero/Comstock. • 346: John Burgoyne. • 349: © Roger Wyeth/Woodfin Camp & Assoc. • 350: Kevin Sprouls. • 354: © Robert Burke/Liaison International.• 355: © John Cancalosi/Stock Boston. • 360: © R. & S. Michaud/Woodfin Camp & Assoc. • 364: Courtesy, Sherilyn Brannon. • 365: © Wildlife Conservation Society. • 368: t. © NASA/Photo-Researcher. • 369: © NASA/ Westlight. • 372: t. © SYGMA. • 373: m.r. Courtesy, Corrine Hamilton. • 374: b.l. © Joe Carini/The Image Works; m.l. © Etienne de Malglaive/Gamma-Liaison; t.l. © Stuart Cohen/Comstock • 380 : b.r. © SCALA/Art Resource; t.l. © Lien/Nibauer Photography Inc./Liaison International; t.r. © The Ancient Art & Architecture Collection. • 381: b.r. © Don Mason/Stock Market. • 382: m. © Chris Marona/Photo Researchers. • 384: t.r. © W. Cody/Backgrounds for Advertising. • 385: © Stephen Ogilvy for MMSD • 388: © Karl Weatherly/Tony Stone Images. • 397: © Sebastien Dufour/Gamma-Liaison. • 398: t. © PhotoEdit/Myrleen Ferguson. • 400: © Hank DeLespinasse/The Image Bank. • 402: t.r. © Gary Braasch/Woodfin Camp & Assoc. • 404: © Brownie Harris/The Stock Market; © Brownie Harris/The Stock Market. • 407: m.r. © M. Paganelli/LGI Photo Agency. • 408: Courtesy, Pat Kambesis. • 409: m.r. © Max & Arne Hodalrc/Saola/Gamma-Liaison. • 411: Courtesy, Tim Asher. • 412: m.l. © Kim Robbie/The Stock Market; t.l. © Richard Elkins/Liaison International; t.r. © Mark Junak/Tony Stone Images. • 418: t. © Mehau Kulyk/Science Photo Library/Photo Researchers. 422: © Techmap/Westlight; m. © Jeff Zaruba/Tony Stone Images. 424: m.r. © Erich Lessing/Art Resource. 426: t.r. © Melanie Carr/Uniphoto. • 427: t.r. © Ed Malitsky/Liaison International. • 430: t.r. © M. Benjamin/The Image Works. • 432: © John Pinderhughes/The Stock Market. 439: t.r. © Alan Klehr/Liaison International. 440: © Susanne Buckler/Liaison International. 445: b.r. © Sam Sargent/Liaison International. • 446: © Bonnie Kamin/PhotoEdit. © Llewellyn/Uniphoto. • 451: Courtesy, Kandie Bennett. • 452: © Busch Entertainment Corp. 458: b.r. © BPL; m. NASA; m.r. © Comstock. t.r. © Loren McIntyre/Woodfin Camp & Assoc. 459: b.r. © BPL; t.l. © Lee Boltin. 460: © Pablo Bartholomew/Liaison International; • 460-461: © Mark Romine/Liaison International. • 465: b.r. © James Carmichael/The Image Bank. • 465: m.r. © Giraudon/Art Resource, NY. • 469: b.r. © Joe Traver/Gamma-Liaison. • 474: © Bob Daemmrich/The Image Works. • 482: m.l. © Comstock; m.l. © Gerard Vandystadt/Photo Researchers. • 488: © Bob Daemmrich/Stock Boston. • 489: © Comstock. • 490: © Marvin E. Newman/The Image Bank; © Wesley Hitt, 1994. 494: t.r. Courtesy, Steve Crockett. • 490–1: PhotoDisc. • 500: © Comstock. • 502: t.r. © Robert V. Eckert JR. / Stock Boston. • 504: © Superstock. • 505: © Superstock. • 506: © D. Donne Bryant. • 510: © R. Sheridan/Ancient Art & Architecture Collection Ltd. © Jason Hawkes/Tony Stone Images. • 512: © Dallas & John Heaton/WestLight. • 513: Stephen McBrady/PhotoEdit. 514: © Joseph Nettis/Photo Researchers. • 516: © Charles Feil/Stock Boston. • 522: © Uniphoto. • 528: © Grant Heilman Photography, Inc. © Superstock. • 533: Stephen Ogilvy. for MMSD • 534: © FPG International; t.r. © Corbis-Bettmann. • 535: © Uniphoto. • 536-537: © G. Brad Lewis/Liaison International; • 536: m. © Art Wolfe/Tony Stone. • 541: m.r. © John P. Kelly/Image Bank. • 542: t. © Culver Pictures. • 546: t.r. © Del Mulkey/Photo Researchers. • 550: t.r. © Andy Sacks/Tony Stone. • 551: © B. Daemrich for MMSD / The Image Works. • 553: t.r. © Photri/Stock Market, NY. • 554: b.r. © Chris Sorenson/The Stock Market. • 556: © Courtesy D2 Peter Mays. • 557: © Jeff Amberg/Gamma-Liaison; t.r. © Frank P. Rossotto/Stock Market, NY. • 558: b.r. © Cheryl Graham/Tony Stone. • 572: t.l. The Granger Collection, New York. • 573: b. © Art Brewer/Tony Stone Images; m. © Frozen Images. • 636: Peter Saloutos/Stock Market. • 637: David R. Frazier/Tony Stone. • 686-687: © Mark Harwood/Tony Stone Images.

ILLUSTRATION CREDITS: John Burgoyne 163, 215, 232, 249, 251, 268, 305, 310, 313, 315, 321, 327, 328, 329, 331, 333, 344, (t.) 348, 353, 364, 367, 372, 390, (b., b.m.) 407, 499, 545, (b.m.l., t.m.l.) 566, (t.r.) 572; • Leslie Evans 15, (b.) 17, (b.r.) 32, 54, (t.r.) 78, (b.r.) 78, (b.) 99, 107, (m.r.) 113, 125, (b., t.) 186, 219, 223, 231, 272, 314, (b.r., t.r.) 339, 341, 394, 403, 408, 464, 465, 466, 467, 468, 470, 475, 477, 482, 484, 486, 488, 500, 507; • Mark Fisher 332, 342, 373, (b.l.) 386, 421, 492, 524, 528; • Ruth Flanigan 79, (b.) 109, 450, 461, 472, 485, 487; • Beverly Goldschmidt 111, (t.) 117, (b.) 119, 288, 452, 482, 554, (t.r.) 567, 574; • John Hart 2, (b.l.) 5, 47, 91, (t.) 99, 100, (t.r.) 113, 133, (b.) 181, 225, (t.) 238, 245; • Mark Herman 123, 139, (t.r.) 142, 146, 148, 153, 177, 234, 235, (t.r.) 244, 291, 295, (b.m.r.) 374, (t.) 395, (t.) 407, 412, 497; • Ken Jacobsen 42, 63, 69, 343; • Chris LaValle 77, 126, 255, 265, 284, 348, 528, 529, 531, (t.r., t.m.r.) 529, 531, (t.r., t.m.r.) 566; • Joni Levy-Liberman 22, 228, 241, 289, 354, 384; • David Lund 37; • Peg Magovern (b.) 101, 102; • John Margeson 60, 74, 78, 102, (m.r.) 112, 124, (m.l., b.r., t.l.) 206, 419, 457, 484, 564; • Jim O'Brien 81; Roberto Osti 41, 66, 83, 87; • Jim Owens 28, 29, 101; • Julie Pace 159, (m., b.) 162; • Chris Reed (b.r.) 7, (m.l., b.r., b.l.) 32, 130; • Paul M. Rudolph 1, (t.l.) 78, 95, 205, 321, 528; • Kevin Sprouls 72, (m.l.) 112, 185, 190, 265, 282, 289, 370, 371, 379, 401, 424, 444, 445, 447, 448, (t.) 538; • Darryl Stevens 75, 147, 435, 441, 471; • Matt Straub 93, TCA Graphics (b.r.) 5, 47, (r.) 88, 97, (r.) 133, (m.) 181, 193, (r.) 225, 265, 321, 367, (b.r.) 407, 449, 465, 505, 563; • Ray Vella 3, 4, 117, 179, (t.) 188, 196, 303, 361, 362, 363, (b.r.) 386, 393, 411, 423, 443, 445, 452, 455, 479, 542, 560, 561, 562, (t.) 563, (b.m.r.) 566, (t.l.) 567; • Catherine Wilcox-Schnurr (b.r.) 395, 410, (b.l.) 563

McGraw-Hill School Division

A Division of The McGraw-Hill Companies

McGraw-Hill School Division
1221 Avenue of the Americas
New York, New York 10020

Printed in the United States of America
ISBN 0-02-110321-6 / 6
4 5 6 7 8 9 043/027 04 03 02 01 00

Contents

1 | **Data, Statistics, and Graphs**

xiv THEME: The Average Sixth Grader

1 What Do You Know?
2 Collect, Organize, and Display Data *Explore Activity*
6 Bar Graphs
10 Range, Median, Mode
12 Mean *Explore Activity*
16 Problem-Solving Strategy Make a Table
18 Midchapter Review
19 Developing Technology Sense Comparing Graphs
20 Real-life Investigation:
       Applying Statistics **Scatter Plots and Basketball**
22 Line Graphs
26 Stem-and-Leaf Plots
28 Sampling and Predicting *Explore Activity*
30 Problem Solvers at Work Choose the Appropriate Graph
34 Chapter Review
36 Chapter Test
37 Performance Assessment • What Did You Learn?
38 Math • Science • Technology Connection

2 | **Add and Subtract Whole Numbers and Decimals**

40 THEME: Water, Water Everywhere

41 What Do You Know?
 42 Exponents *Explore Activity*
46 Understanding Place Value: Whole Numbers
48 Place Value: Decimals

 These lessons develop, practice, or apply algebraic thinking through the study of patterns, relationships and functions, properties, equations, formulas, and inequalities.

52 Compare and Order Decimals

54 Estimate Sums and Differences *Mental Math*

a **56** Add Decimals

a **60** Subtract Decimals

64 Midchapter Review

65 Developing Number Sense   Front-End Estimation

66 Real-life Investigation:

Applying Addition and Subtraction   **Splash Relay**

68 Problem-Solving Strategy   Guess, Test, and Revise

a **70** Addition and Subtraction Expressions

72 Applying Decimals: Metric Units of Length

74 Applying Decimals: Metric Units of Mass and Capacity

76 Problem Solvers at Work

Use Estimation

80 Chapter Review

82 Chapter Test

83 Performance Assessment • What Did You Learn?

84 Math • Science • Technology Connection

3   Multiply Whole Numbers and Decimals

86 THEME: Money

87 What Do You Know?

a **88** Patterns and Properties   *Mental Math*

92 Estimate Products   *Mental Math*

94 Multiply Whole Numbers

96 Multiply Decimals by Whole Numbers

98 Problem-Solving Strategy   Solve Multistep Problems

100 Midchapter Review

a **101** Developing Number Sense

Use Properties to Multiply Mentally

102 Real-life Investigation:

Applying Multiplication   **Make Money Decisions**

104 Multiply Decimals by Decimals   *Explore Activity*

106 Multiply Decimals

110 Problem Solvers at Work
    Underestimates and Overestimates

. . . .

114 Chapter Review

116 Chapter Test

117 Performance Assessment • What Did You Learn?

118 Math • Science • Technology Connection

120 Cumulative Review

4 | Divide Whole Numbers and Decimals

122 THEME: Transportation

123 What Do You Know?

a **124** Estimate Quotients *Mental Math*

a **128** Whole Number Division: 1-Digit Divisors

130 Whole Number Division: 2-Digit Divisors

a **134** Multiplication and Division Expressions

a **136** Order of Operations

138 Problem-Solving Strategy Use a Formula

a **140** Midchapter Review

141 Developing Technology Sense Use a Spreadsheet

142 Real-life Investigation: Applying Division Plan a Trip

144 Divide Decimals by Whole Numbers

a **148** Multiplication and Division Patterns *Mental Math*

a **150** Divide by Decimals *Explore Activity*

a **154** Divide by Decimals

158 Changing Metric Units

160 Problem Solvers at Work
    Interpret Quotients and Remainders

. . . .

164 Chapter Review

166 Chapter Test

167 Performance Assessment • What Did You Learn?

168 Math • Science • Technology Connection

a These lessons develop, practice, or apply algebraic thinking through the study of patterns, relationships and functions, properties, equations, formulas, and inequalities.

5   Number Theory and Fraction Concepts

170   **THEME: Entertainment**

171   What Do You Know?

172   Divisibility   *Mental Math*

a **174**   Prime Factorization   *Explore Activity*

178   Common Factors and GCF

180   Common Multiples and LCM

182   **Problem-Solving Strategy**   Make an Organized List

184   **Midchapter Review**

a **185**   **Developing Algebra Sense**   Another Way to Find the LCM

186   **Real-life Investigation:**
        Applying Divisibility   **Design a Stage Set**

188   Understanding Fractions

190   Equivalent Fractions   *Explore Activity*

194   Simplest Form

196   Compare and Order Fractions

198   Understanding Mixed Numbers

200   Connect Fractions, Mixed Numbers, and Decimals

204   **Problem Solvers at Work**   Expressing Quotients

208   **Chapter Review**

210   **Chapter Test**

211   **Performance Assessment • What Did You Learn?**

212   **Math • Science • Technology Connection**

6   Add and Subtract Fractions and Mixed Numbers

214   **THEME: Leisure Time**

215   What Do You Know?

216   Estimate Sums and Differences   *Mental Math*

a **220**   Add and Subtract Like Fractions

222   Add Unlike Fractions

 224 Subtract Unlike Fractions

226 Add Mixed Numbers *Explore Activity*

 228 Add Mixed Numbers

230 Midchapter Review

231 **Developing Spatial Sense** Spatial Visualization

232 Real-life Investigation:

Applying Fractions **Hikers' Guide**

 234 Problem-Solving Strategy Find a Pattern

236 Subtract Mixed Numbers *Explore Activity*

238 Subtract Mixed Numbers

242 Problem Solvers at Work

Missing or Extra Information

 246 Chapter Review

248 Chapter Test

249 Performance Assessment • What Did You Learn?

250 Math • Science • Technology Connection

252 Cumulative Review

7 Multiply and Divide Fractions and Mixed Numbers

254 THEME: Getting It Built

255 What Do You Know?

 256 Find a Fraction of a Whole Number *Mental Math*

258 Multiply Fractions *Explore Activity*

 262 Multiply by Fractions

 266 Estimate Products *Mental Math*

 268 Multiply Mixed Numbers

270 Midchapter Review

 271 **Developing Algebra Sense**

Properties of Addition and Multiplication

272 Real-life Investigation:

Applying Multiplication **Blueprints**

 274 Problem-Solving Strategy Work Backward

276 Divide Fractions *Explore Activity*

 These lessons develop, practice, or apply algebraic thinking through the study of patterns, relationships and functions, properties, equations, formulas, and inequalities.

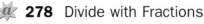

a **278** Divide with Fractions

a **280** Divide with Mixed Numbers

282 Apply Fractions: Customary Units of Length

284 Apply Fractions: Customary Units of Capacity and Weight

286 **Problem Solvers at Work**
Choose Whether to Use Fractions or Decimals

290 **Chapter Review**

292 **Chapter Test**

293 **Performance Assessment • What Did You Learn?**

294 **Math • Science • Technology Connection**

8 Geometry

296 **THEME: Art and Design**

297 **What Do You Know?**

298 Classify 2-Dimensional Shapes *Explore Activity*

300 Angles *Explore Activity*

304 Lines

a **306** Triangles and Quadrilaterals

310 Sums of Angles *Explore Activity*

a **312** **Problem-Solving Strategy** Make a Model

314 **Midchapter Review**

315 **Developing Spatial Sense** Möbius Strips

316 **Real-life Investigation:**
Applying Geometry **Reflection of Light**

318 Constructions

322 Circles

324 Translations and Rotations

326 Reflections and Line Symmetry

328 Tessellations *Explore Activity*

a **330** **Problem Solvers at Work** Find a Pattern

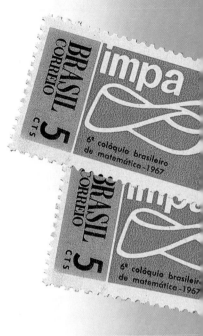

334 Chapter Review

336 Chapter Test

337 Performance Assessment • What Did You Learn?

338 Math • Science • Technology Connection

9 Introduction to Algebra

340 THEME: Science and the World Around Us

341 What Do You Know?

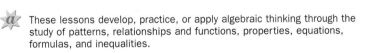 **342** Functions *Explore Activity*

344 Graph Functions

348 Describe Change

350 Use Graphs to Solve Problems

354 Problem-Solving Strategy Solve Simpler Problems

356 Midchapter Review

357 Developing Technology Sense
Use Graphs to Make Predictions

358 Real-life Investigation:
Applying Algebra **Bouncing Balls**

360 Solve Equations *Explore Activity*

364 Solve Addition and Subtraction Equations

368 Solve Multiplication and Division Equations

372 Problem Solvers at Work Work Backward

376 Chapter Review

378 Chapter Test

379 Performance Assessment • What Did You Learn?

380 Math • Science • Technology Connection

a These lessons develop, practice, or apply algebraic thinking through the study of patterns, relationships and functions, properties, equations, formulas, and inequalities.

10 Ratio and Proportion

382 THEME: Travel and Vacations

383 What Do You Know?
384 Understanding Ratios *Explore Activity*
a **388** Equal Ratios
a **390** Rates
394 Better Buys
a **396** Midchapter Review
a **397** Developing Algebra Sense Bottle Functions
398 Real-life Investigation: Applying Ratios
A Wave Around Your School Gymnasium
a **400** Proportions *Explore Activity*
a **402** Problem-Solving Strategy Write an Equation
a **404** Similar Figures *Explore Activity*
408 Scale Drawings
a **410** Problem Solvers at Work Solve Multistep Problems
a **414** Chapter Review
a **416** Chapter Test
417 Performance Assessment • What Did You Learn?
418 Math • Science • Technology Connection
420 Cumulative Review

11 Percent

422 THEME: Buying and Selling

423 What Do You Know?
424 Percent *Explore Activity*
a **426** Percent, Fractions, and Decimals
430 Percent of a Number *Explore Activity*

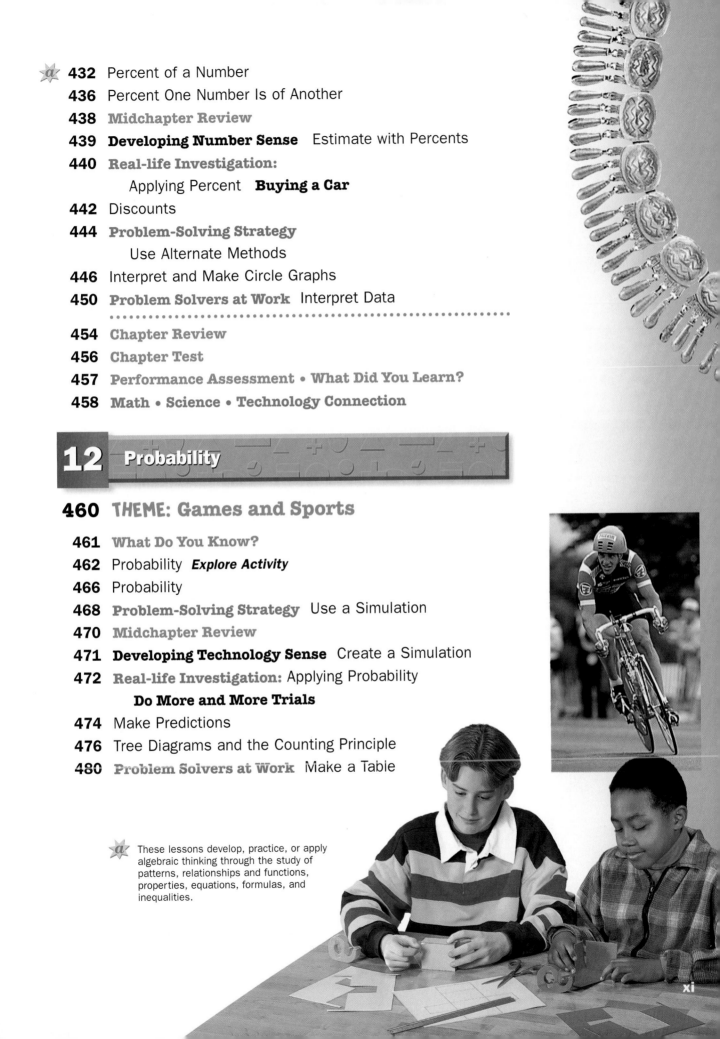

a **432** Percent of a Number

436 Percent One Number Is of Another

438 Midchapter Review

439 **Developing Number Sense** Estimate with Percents

440 Real-life Investigation:

        Applying Percent **Buying a Car**

442 Discounts

444 Problem-Solving Strategy

        Use Alternate Methods

446 Interpret and Make Circle Graphs

450 Problem Solvers at Work Interpret Data

454 Chapter Review

456 Chapter Test

457 Performance Assessment • What Did You Learn?

458 Math • Science • Technology Connection

12 Probability

460 THEME: Games and Sports

461 What Do You Know?

462 Probability *Explore Activity*

466 Probability

468 Problem-Solving Strategy Use a Simulation

470 Midchapter Review

471 **Developing Technology Sense** Create a Simulation

472 Real-life Investigation: Applying Probability

        Do More and More Trials

474 Make Predictions

476 Tree Diagrams and the Counting Principle

480 Problem Solvers at Work Make a Table

a These lessons develop, practice, or apply algebraic thinking through the study of patterns, relationships and functions, properties, equations, formulas, and inequalities.

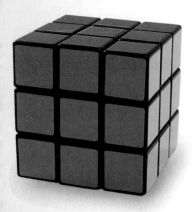

484 Chapter Review

486 Chapter Test

487 Performance Assessment • What Did You Learn?

488 Math • Science • Technology Connection

13   Perimeter, Area, and Volume

490 THEME: Interesting Buildings

491 What Do You Know?

a **492** Perimeter and Area

a **494** Enlarging Rectangles *Explore Activity*

a **496** Area of Parallelograms and Triangles

500 Circumference of a Circle *Explore Activity*

a **502** Area of a Circle *Explore Activity*

506 Area of Compound Figures

508 Midchapter Review

509 Developing Spatial Sense   Pentominoes

510 Real-life Investigation:

     Use Perimeter and Area   **Area Usage**

512 Problem-Solving Strategy   Make a Diagram

514 Classify 3-Dimensional Figures

516 Different Views of 3-Dimensional Figures *Explore Activity*

a **518** Surface Area: Prism *Explore Activity*

a **522** Volume *Explore Activity*

526 Problem Solvers at Work   Make a Model

530 Chapter Review

532 Chapter Test

533 Performance Assessment • What Did You Learn?

534 Math • Science • Technology Connection

14 Integers

536 THEME: Earth Science

537 **What Do You Know?**

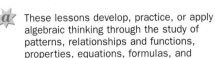 538 Integers *Explore Activity*

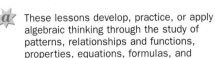 540 Compare and Order Integers

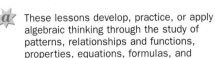 542 Add Integers *Explore Activity*

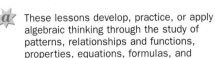 546 Subtract Integers *Explore Activity*

550 **Problem-Solving Strategy** Use Logical Reasoning

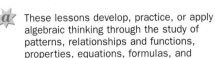 552 **Midchapter Review**

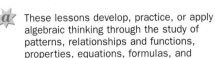 553 **Developing Number Sense** Multiplication of Integers

554 **Real-life Investigation:**

Apply Integers **Effects of Salt on Water and Ice**

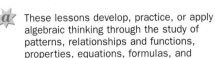 556 Coordinate Graphing in All Four Quadrants

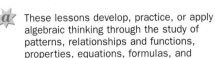 560 Addition and Subtraction Equations *Explore Activity*

564 **Problem Solvers at Work** Interpret Data

 568 **Chapter Review**

 570 **Chapter Test**

571 **Performance Assessment • What Did You Learn?**

572 **Math • Science • Technology Connection**

574 **Cumulative Review**

576 **Extra Practice**

632 **Databank**

643 **Glossary**

653 **Table of Measures**

654 **Index**

 These lessons develop, practice, or apply algebraic thinking through the study of patterns, relationships and functions, properties, equations, formulas, and inequalities.

DATA, STATISTICS, AND GRAPHS

THEME

The Average Sixth Grader

You probably already know a lot about what sixth graders like. In this chapter you'll explore what activities they like best, what they watch on TV, and what they listen to on the radio. Then you'll show your data in a graph.

What Do You Know ?

In 1994, the following questions were asked of 12- to 13-year-olds across the United States:

a. Do you ever fix your own breakfast?
b. Do you ever fix your own lunch?
c. Do you ever fix your own dinner?

Here are the results.

12- to 13-Year-Olds Who Make Their Own Meals	
Meal	**Number**
Breakfast	157
Lunch	120
Dinner	74
Total Surveyed: 197	

SOURCE: NICKELODEON/YANKELOVICH YOUTH MONITOR™

1 How can you tell that not all the 12- to 13-year-olds surveyed answered *yes* to question A?

2 Make a bar graph or a pictograph to show the data. Write at least two statements about what your graph shows.

 Ask Questions **Ben did a survey. This is the summary he wrote: The average sixth grader in my school is 11 years old, 57 inches tall, and has a pet.**

As you read, ask yourself questions to see if you understand what you are reading and to figure out what you want to know.

1 What questions do you have about how Ben did his survey?

Vocabulary* *partial list

frequency table, p. 3	**mode,** p. 10	**stem-and-leaf plot,** p. 26
line plot, p. 3	**mean,** p. 12	**population,** p. 28
pictograph, p. 3	**average,** p. 12	**sample,** p. 28
double-bar graph, p. 6	**scatter plot,** p. 20	**random sample,** p. 28
range, p. 10	**line graph,** p. 22	**biased data,** p. 28
median, p. 10	**double-line graph,** p. 23	**representative,** p. 29

Collect, Organize, and Display Data

What does it mean to call something "typical"? How would you find out if you're a "typical" sixth grader? Collecting, analyzing, and displaying data, such as a census or the likes, dislikes, and habits of sixth graders, is a part of mathematics called statistics.

Cultural Note

A census is a count of all the people living in a country, city, or other region. The Babylonians recorded census data on clay tablets more than 5,000 years ago.

Work Together

Work in a group to conduct a survey. Use the questionnaire to the right. Decide whom to survey and be sure to save your results.

Talk It Over

▶ How did you keep track of the responses from the people surveyed?

▶ How do you want to present the results of your survey?

QUESTIONNAIRE

Name: _____

Male: ___ Female: ___   Age: ___

1. How many hours a night do you spend doing your homework?

2. On the average weekday, about how many hours a day do you watch TV?

3. On the average weekend day, about how many hours a day do you watch TV?

4. Which activities do you do between the time you get out of school and the time you eat dinner? You can choose more than one.

   A. Do homework
   B. Watch TV
   C. Play outside
   D. Talk on the phone
   E. Play on a sports team

Make Connections

You can organize and display data in several ways. Students in one class used a **frequency table** to organize their data for the first question of the questionnaire on page 2. They made a **line plot** and a **pictograph** to display the data.

FREQUENCY TABLE

Hours Spent on Homework Each Night

Hours	Tally	Frequency
0	//	2
1	〽️ ////	9
2	〽️ ///	8
3	〽️ //	7
4		0
5 or more	/	1

PICTOGRAPH

Hours Spent on Homework Each Night

Hours	Students
0	
1	
2	
3	
4	
5 or more	

Key: = 2 students

LINE PLOT

Hours Spent on Homework Each Night

```
      x
      x    x
      x    x    x
      x    x    x
      x    x    x
      x    x    x
      x    x    x
 x    x    x    x
 x    x    x    x              x
 0    1    2    3    4    5 or more
```

Hours

▶ Find the most common number of hours spent on homework.

▶ Most of the data in this line plot groups, or *clusters,* around three particular numbers. What does that tell you?

▶ One of the numbers in this line plot has no data for it. It has a *gap.* Find the number. Explain what the gap means.

Check Out the Glossary
frequency table
line plot
pictograph
See page 643.

Check for Understanding

1 Make a frequency table to show your data for Question One of the questionnaire on page 2.

2 Make a line plot or a pictograph from your data in ex. 1. What conclusions can you draw from the graphs?

Critical Thinking: Generalize   Explain your reasoning.

3 Why is it helpful to use graphs to display data from surveys?

4 *Journal* Create a survey question of your own about sixth graders. Ask ten classmates your question. Tell how you would organize and display the data.

Practice

Use the frequency table and pictograph for ex. 1–4.

Hours Spent Watching TV Each Weekday		
Hours	**Tally**	**Frequency**
0	卌	5
1	卌 卌 卌 卌 卌 卌 卌	35
2	卌 卌 卌 卌 卌	25
3	卌 卌	10
4 or more	卌	5

Hours Spent Watching TV Each Weekday	
Hours	**Students**
0	
1	
2	
3	
4 or more	

Key: = 10 students

1 How many students were surveyed in all?

2 Which number of hours did the most students say they watched TV?

3 **What if** 20 students watch TV for 2 hours. How would the pictograph change?

4 Which display is easier to use, the frequency table or the pictograph? Explain why.

Use the line plot for ex. 5–7.

5 If you make a pictograph from the data in the line plot, what symbol will you use to represent the number of students? Explain your choice.

Baseball Caps Owned by Students

```
        x           x
        x     x     x
        x     x     x
        x     x     x
        x     x     x
        x     x     x     x
  x     x     x     x     x
  x     x     x     x     x     x           x
  0     1     2     3     4     5     6     7
                    Caps
```

6 Analyze the line plot at the right. Identify any clusters or gaps in the data. What conclusions can you draw?

7 **What if** among the students surveyed, 8 students like caps that have mixed colors, 5 students like blue, 4 students like purple, 3 students like orange, and 2 students like red. Explain how you would organize and display the data.

Solve.

8 **Ask Questions** List two situations in which you might conduct a survey using a questionnaire. Tell what questions you might include in the questionnaire.

Problem Solving

9 A pictograph in a newspaper shows the types of music teens prefer. The key for the graph is 🎵 = 100 teens. How many 🎵 are needed for 500 teens?

10 During a survey, 489 phone calls were made the first week, 508 were made the second, and 505 were made the third. About how many phone calls were made in all?

Use the data sheets for problems 11–12.

11 Sixth-grade students conducted a survey to decide on patterns and colors for T-shirts. Tell how you would display the data.

12 What color and pattern do you think the class should choose for the T-shirt based on the conclusions of their survey?

Choices of Pattern and Color				
Pattern		**Color**		
★	𝍷𝍷𝍷𝍷 //	red	𝍷𝍷𝍷𝍷 ///	
✳	𝍷𝍷𝍷𝍷 //	blue	𝍷𝍷𝍷𝍷 ///	
✛	𝍷𝍷𝍷𝍷 𝍷𝍷𝍷𝍷 //	white	𝍷𝍷𝍷𝍷 ///	
✳	𝍷𝍷𝍷𝍷 ///	green	𝍷𝍷𝍷𝍷 𝍷𝍷𝍷𝍷	

13 Data Point Graph the data you collected for questions 2–4 of the questionnaire on page 2. What conclusions would you draw based on the graphs?

14 Maria cut a piece off a 12-inch-long pipe to fix a sink. That left a $3\frac{1}{2}$-inch-long piece. How long was the piece she cut off?

Cultural Connection Quipu

Different cultures have been recording and displaying data for centuries. The Inca recorded numbers on a kind of knotted cord called a *quipu* (KEE-poo).

The picture below shows how 354, 0, and 102 are recorded on a quipu.

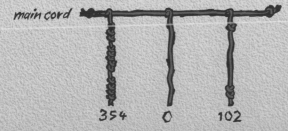

SOUTH AMERICA

Inca Empire

The closer to the main cord the higher the value of the knots.

To represent 0, the cord was left blank.

The ones place was located at the free end of the cord.

Draw a quipu to represent the following numbers.

1 56 **2** 902 **3** 195 **4** 400 **5** 996

Bar Graphs

"Which activities do you do between the time you get out of school and the time you eat dinner?" This question was asked of more than 100 girls and 100 boys in a national survey of 11- to 13-year-olds.

After-School Activities for 11- to 13-Year-Olds		
Activity	Percent of Girls	Percent of Boys
Do homework	95	92
Watch TV	86	80
Play outside	75	80
Talk on the phone	65	43
Play on a sports team	26	49

SOURCE: NICKELODEON/YANKELOVICH YOUTH MONITOR™

You can use a **double-bar graph** to display the data. This kind of graph helps you compare the two sets of data.

Follow these steps to make a double-bar graph.

> **Check Out the Glossary**
> double-bar graph
> scale
> axes
> key
> See page 643.

▶ Decide on a **scale** for the bars.

▶ Write labels for the horizontal and the vertical **axes.**

▶ Draw bars for each set of data. Use a different color for each.

▶ Make a **key** that shows what each type of bar represents.

▶ Write a title for your graph.

After-School Activities for 11- to 13-Year-Olds

(bar graph showing PERCENT on vertical axis from 0 to 100, ACTIVITIES on horizontal axis: Home-Work, Watch TV, Play Outside, Phone, Sports Team; Girls and Boys bars)

Talk It Over

▶ What are some comparisons you can make based on this graph?

▶ Why is it sometimes easier to make comparisons when data is presented in a graph instead of a table?

The table at right shows how some sixth graders responded to a survey that asked about their after-school activities. Both single-bar graphs below display the data from the table. Which graph shows the difference better? Why?

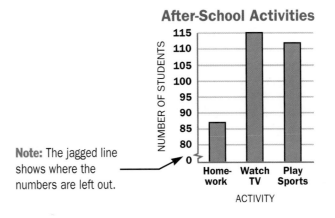

After-School Activities	
Activity	Number of Students
Do homework	87
Watch TV	115
Play sports	112

After-School Activities

NUMBER OF STUDENTS — ACTIVITY: Home-work, Watch TV, Play Sports (intervals 0–120 by 20)

Note: The jagged line shows where the numbers are left out.

After-School Activities

NUMBER OF STUDENTS — ACTIVITY: Home-work, Watch TV, Play Sports (intervals 80–115 by 5)

The graph on the right shows the difference in the data better because the intervals are 5 instead of 20.

Check for Understanding

1 Use the data from the table at right to make a double-bar graph. Write a short paragraph to report about the after-school activities for the two classes in the survey.

After-School Activities		
Activity	Mr. Garcia's Class	Ms. Nagy's Class
Do homework	13	11
Watch TV	30	21
Play sports	21	30

2 Change the double-bar graph by using a different interval. Tell how it is different from the original graph.

Critical Thinking: Generalize Explain your reasoning.

3 Explain whether it makes sense to display the data for problems 1 and 2 using a line plot or a pictograph.

4 List two situations in which you would use a single-bar graph to display data. List two situations in which you would use a double-bar graph to display data.

Practice

Use the bar graph for problems 1–3.

1 Which messy supply did the TV show use the greatest amount of? About how many gallons did they use?

2 About how much more pudding was used than eggs?

3 How would you change the scale to make the graph smaller?

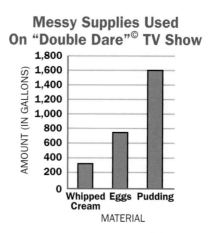

Messy Supplies Used On "Double Dare"© TV Show

Make bar graphs for the data in the tables.

4

Average Number of School Days	
Countries	**Days Each Year**
United States	180
Canada	185
England	195
Israel	215
China	240
Japan	245

SOURCE: CENTER FOR EDUCATION STATISTICS

5

Celebrity Types Teens Prefer in Ads		
Celebrity Type	**Boys**	**Girls**
Sports stars	42	16
Music stars	12	33
Movie stars	8	16
Animated characters	11	11
TV stars	4	12

6 Change the graph below to better show the difference between data.

Favorite Type of Book	Fifth Graders	Sixth Graders
Fiction	278	289
Biography	185	198
Nonfiction	201	211
Poetry	123	132

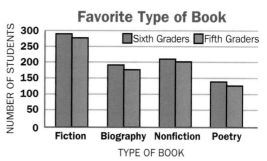

Favorite Type of Book

······················· **Make It Right** ·······················

7 Tell what the error is in the vertical scale of this graph. How would you fix it?

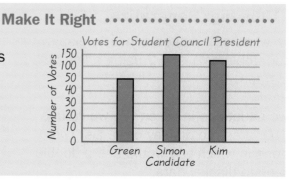

Votes for Student Council President

Problem Solving

Pencil & Paper | Calculator | Mental Math

Use the graph for problems 8–10.

8 In which of the three grades do the most boys own bikes? the most girls? Explain how you know.

9 Based on this graph, what comparisons and conclusions can you make about bicycle ownership as students get older?

10 **Write a problem** that can be solved by using information from the graph. Solve it and have others solve it.

11 **Data Point** Use the Data Bank on page 632 to make at least two double-bar graphs. Write a short paragraph to describe each graph.

12 What is the fastest bicycle speed rounded to the nearest tenth? SEE INFOBIT.

Students Who Own Bikes By Grade

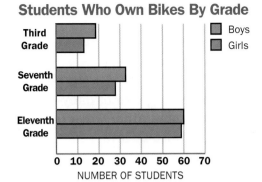

NUMBER OF STUDENTS

INFOBIT
According to *The Guinness Book of Records*, the fastest speed ever achieved on a bicycle is 152.284 miles per hour.

more to explore

Histograms

A *histogram* is a bar graph that shows the frequency of data in various intervals.

Typing Speed (number of words per minute)	Frequency
21–25	5
26–30	8
31–35	14
36–40	9
41–45	3

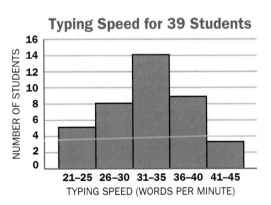

Typing Speed for 39 Students

TYPING SPEED (WORDS PER MINUTE)

1 Among the 39 students taking computer typing class, which is the most common speed? the least common?

2 Would you use a bar graph or a histogram to show the ages of 50 people? Explain.

Range, Median, Mode

Do you baby-sit? Here's the record of the ages for a group of baby-sitters. What are some other ways to describe and summarize data?

You can use the **range**, **median**, and **mode** to describe and summarize data.

First, list the ages in order from least to greatest:
11, 12, 12, 12, 12, 13, 13, 13, 14, 15

Ages of Baby-Sitters		
Age	Tally	Frequency
11	/	1
12	////	4
13	///	3
14	/	1
15	/	1

The **range** is the difference between the greatest number and the least. It is one way to show the spread of a set of data.

15 − 11 = 4

There is a 4-year difference in ages. The range is 4.

The **mode** is the number that occurs most often.

11, 12, 12, 12, 12, 13, 13, 13, 14, 15

The most common age is 12. The mode is 12.

The **median** is the middle number. Since the data has 10 numbers, there are two middle numbers. You can find the median by adding the two middle numbers and then dividing by 2.

> **Check Out the Glossary**
> For vocabulary words, see page 643.

The two middle numbers
▼ ▼
11, 12, 12, 12, 12, 13, 13, 13, 14, 15

Half the ages are older than 12.5, and half are younger.

The median is 12.5.

12 + 13 = 25   ← Sum of the two middle numbers.

25 ÷ 2 = 12.5 ← Divide the sum by 2.

Check for Understanding

1 The table shows the number of hours Andrew spent baby-sitting during the summer. What is the range of the hours? the median? the mode? What does each number tell you?

Baby-Sitting Hours				
Week	1	2	3	4
Hours	8	9	7	8

Critical Thinking: Generalize   **Explain your reasoning.**

2 Why do you think the range, median, and mode are good ways to describe and summarize a set of data?

Practice

Find the range, median, and mode for each set of data.

1 32, 47, 34, 34, 33

2 9, 13, 13, 8, 12

3 58, 24, 36, 67, 29, 58

4 17, 3, 28, 45, 28

5 72, 40, 35, 72, 60

6 2, 7, 4, 2, 7

7 29, 32, 40, 29, 34, 44

8 275, 315, 188, 190

9 11, 8, 12, 7, 9, 11, 8, 6

10 124, 235, 68, 157, 98, 88

11 37, 28, 45, 21, 21, 36, 21

12

Class	A	B	C	D
Students	34	35	42	38

13

Game	1	2	3	4	5
Scores	123	99	134	117	108

14

Month	1	2	3	4	5	6	7	8	9	10
Income	$200	$155	$167	$200	$178	$178	$200	$167	$155	$178

MIXED APPLICATIONS
Problem Solving

15 The range of Tyler's 5 math scores is 5. The two highest scores are 85 and 87, the median score is 84, and the mode is 84. Name the 5 scores.

16 Sara bought a CD player for $360. She will pay for it in equal monthly payments for 12 months. How much does she have to pay each month?

17 Ramona surveyed 18 other students on the number of video tapes they watched and displayed the data in a line plot. What are some other ways you can describe and summarize Ramona's data?

Videotapes Watched in a Month

```
              x
              x     x
        x     x     x
        x     x     x     x     x
  x     x     x     x     x     x                 x
  0     1     2     3     4     5     6     7     8
```

18 Amy scored 109, 118, 125, 68, 121, 117, and 109 points when bowling. Is the mode or the median better for summarizing these scores? Explain.

19 **Number sense** David is 13 years old. He estimated that his age is about 50,000 in days. Does his estimation make sense? Explain.

mixed review • test preparation

1 Make a frequency table for these ages: 12, 13, 15, 12, 11, 15, 13, 15, 14, 15, 15, 13, 16, 13, 16, 16.

2 Make a bar graph and a pictograph of the data in ex. 1.

Mean

IN THE WORKPLACE

**Marla Grossberg,
Market Researcher,
Northbrook, Illinois**

How would you find the mean time sixth graders spend listening to music? That is the sort of thing that Marla Grossberg must know so she can better understand teen preferences.

Time Spent Listening to Music						
Sixth Grader	Tony	Bain	Connie	Susan	Yoshi	Francis
Hours per Month	72	107	90	86	77	68

You can find the **mean** by finding the **average** time for the 6 sixth graders. You can use the mean to represent a set of data.

Here is how to find the mean for the time spent listening to music:

► Add the times.
► Divide the sum by the number of sixth graders in the group.

 $72 + 107 + 90 + 86 + 77 + 68 =$ **500.**

$500 \div 6 =$ **83.333333**

The mean listening time is 83 hours per month, rounded to the nearest hour.

mean (average) The mean of a set of numbers is found by adding the numbers and dividing their sum by the number of addends.

Work Together

Work in a small group to find the mean of the data for your group.

► Survey to find the number of hours everyone listens to music, watches TV, and reads each week.

► Find the mean time spent on each activity for your group. Round to the nearest whole number.

► Discuss other ways to describe and summarize data.

Talk It Over

► What is the mean of each activity time for your group? How did you find each mean?

► What are some other ways your group used to describe and summarize the data? What are those numbers?

Make Connections

Here is how John's group found the mean and median of the music listening time of its members.

Music Listening Time Each Week (in hours): 12, 21, 17, 10, 13

The mean of the listening time:

12 + 21 + 17 + 10 + 13 = 73

 73 ÷ 5 = **14.6**

The mean for the group is 14.6 hours.

The median of the listening time:

The middle number
▼
10, 12, **13**, 17, 21

The median for the group is 13 hours.

▶ Does the mean or the median better represent the time spent listening to music for John's group? Explain.

▶ How do you think the mean will change if 21 is removed from the data of the listening times? Explain.

Check for Understanding

Use a calculator to find the mean to the nearest whole number.

1 84, 78, 79   **2** 12, 15, 9, 13, 14   **3** 45, 56, 48, 43, 52

4 89, 101, 97, 98, 85, 103   **5** $21, $25, $18, $26, $31

6 245, 231, 238, 242, 239   **7** 75, 90, 100, 0, 81, 65

Tell whether you would use the mean, median, or mode to represent each set of data. Explain.

8

Time Watching TV Each Week	
Student	**Hours Watching TV**
Amy	8
Luca	11
Kai	9
Shienchi	12
Jake	10

9

Paul's Scores for 5 Math Tests	
Test	**Score**
1	67
2	66
3	98
4	68
5	99

Critical Thinking: Analyze

Explain your reasoning.

10 Look at ex. 9. **What if** each of Paul's test scores was increased by 5 points. How will it change the mean and the median?

Turn the page for Practice. ▶

Practice

Use a calculator to find the mean to the nearest whole number.

1 23, 25, 31, 29, 32 **2** 71, 65, 70, 69, 68 **3** 37, 40, 42, 39, 44

4 $42, $51, $48, $45, $49 **5** 87, 119, 131, 128, 125 **6** 501, 519, 521, 518

7 78, 42, 50, 90, 0, 85, 75, 60 **8** 356.2, 751, 240, 850, 546.6

Find the range, mean, median, and mode for each set of data.
Round answers to the nearest whole number.

9 20, 85, 11, 7, 71 **10** 33, 30, 31, 38, 33 **11** 94, 92, 83, 83, 97

12 13, 11, 10, 7, 8, 11 **13** 13, 28, 27, 13 **14** 62, 68, 63, 62, 65

15 38, 12, 4, 68, 51 **16** 2, 9, 7, 1, 4, 1, 2, 3 **17** 321, 334, 328, 345

Tell whether you would use the mean, median, or mode
to represent each set of data. Explain.

18

Ages of a Karate Team	
Name	Age
Cathy	11
Bob	11
Rosa	13
Jeffrey	9

19

School Attendance	
Month	Students Absent
January	10
February	22
March	10
April	16

20

Test Scores	
Test	Score
1	98
2	56
3	89
4	84
5	88

21

Shoe Sizes of 5 Sixth Graders	
Name	Size
Alice	5
Bonnie	6
Chen	6
Julian	8
Latoya	4

Tell if the mean for each set of data will become greater
or less if the boldfaced number is included. Explain.

22 18, 19, 17, 16, 15 **42** **23** 36, 35, 28, 41, 30, 29 **12**

24 121, 108, 119, 132, 125 **99** **25** 40, 35, 50, 30, 44, 57 **60**

26 99, 75, 88, 76, 82, 100, 94 **75** **27** $2.95, $3.04, $5, $6.85 **$5.95**

28 Scott earns $4.25 each hour running errands for a radio station. If he works from 1 P.M. to 5 P.M., how much will he earn?

29 In the standing broad jump, Cody's jumps were 113 cm, 107 cm, and 123 cm. What was the mean of his jumps to the nearest tenth?

30 The Computer Club has 37 members. There are 5 more girls than boys. How many girls and boys are members of the club?

31 Elena wants her average to be at least an 88. Her scores so far are 91 and 78. What must her next test be to get the average she wants?

32 A sixth-grade class decided to recycle cans to raise money. The chart shows how many cans they collected each month. About how many cans can they expect to collect in a 10-month school year? Explain.

33 Why do you think the number of cans collected in January was so much greater than the number in December?

Month	Cans Collected
September	173
October	231
November	166
December	166
January	297

Use the table for problems 34–38.

34 What was the mean number of children's tickets sold each week?

35 In which week was the greatest number of tickets sold? What conclusion can you draw?

36 For which type of ticket is the mean number of tickets sold each week the least? What conclusion can you draw?

37 **Write a problem** that you can solve by using multiplication. Use information from the table. Solve it and ask others to solve it.

Amusement Park Ticket Sales			
Week	Children	Adults	Seniors
1	562	321	119
2	437	294	92
3	486	185	86
4	450	229	110

Children's Ticket: $2.50   Adult's Ticket: $3.50
Senior's Ticket: $3.00

38 **Make a decision** A group ticket is $15 for 6 people. A family has 4 children and 2 adults. Should they buy a group ticket? Explain.

mixed review • test preparation

1 Make a line plot showing these quiz scores: 5, 6, 8, 5, 5, 6, 7, 6, 7, 10, 3, 4, 0, 5, 7, 5, 4, 8, 4, 5, 10, 6.

2 Using the line plot that you made for ex. 1, find the median and the mode of the quiz scores.

Make a Table

A class took a survey to find how much time they spend at a sport each week. Do more students spend from 6 to 10 hours or from 11 to 15 hours?

Answering the checklist questions can help you solve problems.

Survey Results				
2	6	10	6	5
10	9	12	0	8
8	0	14	7	15
10	14	11	9	20
7	12	10	19	20
	15	6		

Read | **What do you know?** | the number of hours spent each week

What do you need to find? | Do more students spend from 6 to 10 hours or from 11 to 15 hours?

Plan | **How can you solve the problem?** | Make a table to organize the data.

Solve | **How can you carry out your plan?** | Make a table by sorting the data into 4 categories:

Hours	0–5	6–10	11–15	16 or more
Students	4	13	7	3

More students spend from 6 to 10 hours than from 11 to 15 hours.

Look Back | **How can you check if your answer is reasonable?** | Make sure that the total number of items of data matches the total number of students in the table.

$4 + 13 + 7 + 3 = 27$

Yes, 27 students are being surveyed.

Check for Understanding

1 Conduct a survey about the amount of time other students in your class spend at a sport each week. Show your results in a table and compare with the results above.

Critical Thinking: Analyze   **Explain your reasoning.**

2 **What if** you surveyed all sixth graders in your state. How might your data change or stay the same?

Problem Solving

1 Gail conducted a survey of all the cars in the school parking lot. She found the year each car was made. Were more cars made between 1986 and 1990 or between 1991 and 1995? Explain.

> **Years Cars Were Made**
> 1988, 1996, 1994, 1993, 1987, 1993, 1995, 1996, 1989, 1990, 1986, 1982, 1994, 1993, 1987, 1980, 1992, 1991, 1985, 1992, 1986, 1996, 1995, 1994

2 The CD Music House has a promotion. Each customer will get a free CD if their purchases total more than $30. Tom bought 2 CDs for $12.99 each and one CD holder for $5.50. Did he get the free CD? Explain.

3 **Spatial sense** What three-dimensional figure will this net form when it is cut out and folded on the dashed lines?

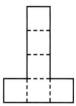

4 **Logical reasoning** A is greater than B, C is greater than A, and C is 5 less than D. What if D is 103, and A and B are both odd numbers. What is C? What are possible numbers for A and B?

5 Jan scores 86, 96, 107, 113, and 98 in 5 bowling games. Tom scores 123, 74, 109, 77, and 72. Who has a greater average? Explain.

Use the prices at right to solve problems 6–7.

6 Marco and Ralph each had $5 to spend. They both bought at least one of each item. Marco purchased 6 items and Ralph purchased 5 items. If neither received any change, what did each purchase?

7 What is the least number of items you could purchase for $10? the greatest number of items?

Use the table for problems 8–10.

8 What conclusions can you draw from the information from the table?

9 **Write a problem** in which you must find the mean using the data in the table. Solve it. Have others solve it.

10 **Data Point** Conduct a survey about other students' favorite lunch drinks. Decide the categories to use. Show your results in a table.

Lunch Drinks Sold at a Cafeteria				
Grade Levels	Whole Milk	Fruit Juice	Sport Drink	Chocolate Milk
K–2	77	65	6	22
3–4	58	62	19	69
5–6	67	43	46	75

Find the range, mean, median, and mode for each set of data. Round to the nearest tenth if necessary.

1 30, 51, 37, 42, 30

2 28, 13, 36, 12, 17

3 142, 178, 142, 164

4 5, 7, 2, 4, 1, 8, 8, 10

5 832, 654, 787, 832

6 5, 9, 1, 1, 4, 5, 7, 3

7 9, 15, 27, 8, 11, 65

8 1,000, 500, 500

9 $1, $1, $1, $5, $10

10 80, 75, 95, 100, 100, 100

11 72, 72, 73, 76, 74, 72, 75

12 64, 64, 68, 72, 60, 58, 60, 61

13 2, 1, 3, 3, 1, 2, 3, 1, 2

Use the results of the survey for problems 14–15.

14 Make a double-bar graph to show the data.

15 What are the most and the least popular brands of jeans among the boys? the girls?

Favorite Brands of Jeans		
Brand of Jeans	Boys	Girls
Levi's	35	24
Gap	21	36
Guess	11	38
Other	42	10

Solve. Use the survey results at right for problems 16–17.

16 The table shows the favorite in-line skate colors among students. Make a pictograph to display the data. Write two problems based on the graph.

17 How would your pictograph change if 8 more students chose purple and 4 more students chose pink?

Favorite In-Line Skate Colors	
Color	Number of Students
Black	40
Lime	68
Purple	32
Pink	8

18 Gail went shopping at a gift shop. She had $5.38 left after buying a stuffed animal for $12.45, a card for $2.95, and a balloon for $5.99. How much money did Gail start with?

19 Your math test scores are 89, 85, 97, 62, and 93. Your teacher is using the average score based on four tests only. Which score should you remove to get a higher average? Explain.

20 Journal Survey at least 10 other students to find their favorite brand of sneakers. Use a graph to display the data. Write conclusions about your data.

Comparing Graphs

For one week Ana's group tracked the sources of the calories they ate.

Using a computer, you can link a table to a graph. Then you can choose the type of graph that best describes the data.

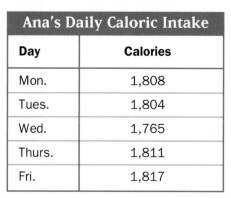

Ana's Daily Caloric Intake	
Day	**Calories**
Mon.	1,808
Tues.	1,804
Wed.	1,765
Thurs.	1,811
Fri.	1,817

Ana's Daily Caloric Intake

▶ Why do you think Ana chose a line graph to display the total calories she ate each day for a week?

Average Daily Calories					
			Carbohydrates		**Total**
Student	**Fat**	**Protein**	**Simple**	**Complex**	**Calories**
Ana	414	216	144	1,027	1,801
Sam	270	108	371	1,062	1,811
Bob	630	216	396	542	1,784
Li	144	576	360	720	1,800

Use the table. Choose the best graph for the situation and make the graph using a computer graphing program.

1 Compare the total calorie intake for each of the members in Ana's group.

2 Show how the number of calories Ana ate from each source varied during the week.

3 Compare the number of calories from each source for each member of the group.

4 Explain the differences between the graphs you made. How did you decide which type of graph to use?

Scatter Plots and Basketball

Scatter plots are useful for exploring the relationship between two sets of data. In this activity you will work in teams to investigate basketball.

Here are the results when one team shot 20 baskets from various distances.

Distance (in feet)	5	10	15	20	25	30
Baskets Made	17	12	8	9	6	4
Baskets Missed	3	8	12	11	14	16

Check Out the Glossary
scatter plots
See page 643.

The scatter plot at the right shows the relationship between the distance from the basket and the number of baskets made. As the distance from the basket increases, the number of baskets made tends to decrease. This relationship is called a negative correlation.

The scatter plots below show the types of relationships two sets of data may have.

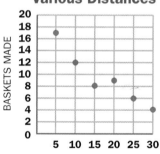

20 Shots from Various Distances

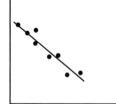

Positive correlation
As the values of one set of data rise, the values of the other set of data tend to increase also.

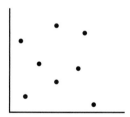

Negative correlation
As the values of one set of data increase, the values of the other set of data tend to decrease.

No correlation
The values of one set of data show no relationship with the values of the other set.

Explore Relationships

1 Separate into teams to play Trash Basketball. Players take turns standing 2, 4, 6, 8, 10, and 12 feet from a trash can that is at least 4 feet from a wall. Each player throws 4 crumpled paper balls at the trash can from each position. Combine your team results and record in a table.

2 Then play a version of the game with the trash can against the wall. Record the results in another table.

3 For each game make a scatter plot that shows the relationship between the distance from the trash can and the number of baskets made.

4 Repeat step 3 for the number of baskets missed.

Report Your Findings

5 **Portfolio** Prepare a report on what you learned. Do the following:

▶ Show the tables and the scatter plots you made for each game.

▶ Describe the type of correlation shown in each scatter plot and explain why you think it happened.

▶ Describe the conclusions you can draw from the scatter plots.

▶ Decide which way you would play the game to get the best score and explain why.

Revise your work.
▶ Are your graphs accurate?
▶ Is your report clear and well organized?
▶ Did you proofread your work?

PREDICT what the results would be if the best shots in the class shot baskets with a real basketball on a basketball court.

EXPLORE how well the best shots in the class shoot baskets from 4, 8, 12, 16, and 20 feet. Make a table and a scatter plot to show the data. What conclusions can you draw?

FIND the world record distance for a basketball shot.

Line Graphs

When researching a report for health class, you may find this data about the average heights of boys and girls. What graph would you use to display the data?

A **line graph** can be used to show the change in data over time.

First, make a single-line graph to show the average heights of boys from 10 to 18 years old.

Average Heights (in centimeters)									
Age	**10**	**11**	**12**	**13**	**14**	**15**	**16**	**17**	**18**
Boys	138	143	150	157	163	169	174	176	177
Girls	138	145	152	157	160	162	162	163	164

Follow these steps to make a line graph:

▶ Decide on a scale for the vertical axis.

▶ Draw and label the vertical and horizontal axes.

▶ Plot each point on the graph.

▶ Connect the points with a line.

▶ Give the graph a title.

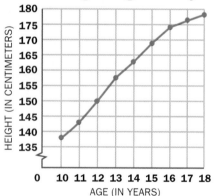

Average Height of Boys

Talk It Over

▶ How does a line graph show an increase over time? a decrease? no change?

▶ What are some conclusions you can make based on this graph?

A **double-line graph** can be used to compare two sets of data.

Make a double-line graph to compare the average heights of boys and girls.

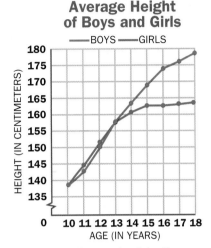

Average Height of Boys and Girls

Follow these steps to make a double-line graph:

▶ Begin the way you would for a single-line graph.

▶ Plot the second set of data using a different color or type of line to connect the points.

▶ Make a key to show what each type of line represents.

▶ Give the graph a title.

Cultural Note
Over generations, people have gotten taller. In colonial America, 18-year-old males were about 4 in. shorter than they are today.

Check for Understanding

Use the double-line graph above to answer questions 1–2.

1 At the age of 12, do girls or boys have a greater average height? How did you know?

2 After which age is the average height of boys greater than the average height of girls?

3 The table at right shows the number of students at Palos Verdes Middle School in various years. Make a double-line graph for the data. What are some conclusions you can make based on the graph?

Palos Verdes Middle School		
Year	Boys	Girls
1970	459	423
1980	481	483
1990	516	535

Critical Thinking: Generalize **Explain your reasoning.**

4 How do you know when to use a double-line graph or a double-bar graph? Give an example for each.

**C
H
E
C
K**

Turn the page for Practice. ▶

Data, Statistics, and Graphs **23**

Practice

Use the double-line graph for problems 1–3.

1 About how many more boys than girls were in the school soccer program in 1990?

2 In which year were the number of boys and girls in the soccer program the same?

3 What other conclusions can you make based on the graph?

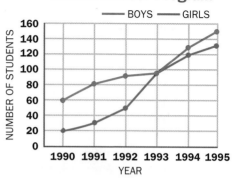

Students in the School Soccer Program

— BOYS — GIRLS

Use the table for problems 4–6.

4 Make a graph. Explain why you think the graph you chose best displays the data.

5 How many more Super Computers than ACE Computers were sold during this week?

6 Between which two days was the decrease in sales for each computer greatest?

Computer Sales		
	Sales	
Day of the Week	**Super Computer**	**ACE Computer**
Monday	58	42
Tuesday	11	23
Wednesday	13	5
Thursday	25	12
Friday	37	29

Use the tables for problems 7–10.

Prices for Movie Tickets	
Year	**Price**
1975	$2.00
1980	$2.50
1985	$3.50
1990	$4.00
1995	$5.50

Enrollment of Students		
Year	**Boys**	**Girls**
1991	243	229
1992	256	278
1993	281	299
1994	276	286
1995	307	284

7 Make a single-bar graph to show the change in movie prices.

9 Would intervals of $0.50, $1, or $2 be best for a scale to show the change in movie prices? Explain.

8 Make a double-line graph to show how student enrollment has changed.

10 Is it easier to find the years when there were more girls than boys enrolled by looking at the table or the graph? Explain.

Problem Solving

Pencil & Paper *Calculator* *Mental Math*

11 Darcy has grown 3 inches in the past year. If she is $56\frac{1}{2}$ inches now, how tall was she a year ago?

12 Four weeks before a recital, Eric will practice 2 hours each weekday and 3 hours each Saturday and Sunday. How long will he practice in 4 weeks?

Use the graph for problems 13–16.

13 Which are the two driest months of the year?

14 In which month is there an average of about 3 inches of rain? Explain how you know.

Average Monthly Rainfall: Honolulu, HI

(Line graph with RAINFALL (IN INCHES) on the y-axis from 0 to 4.5, and MONTH on the x-axis: Jan., Feb., Mar., Apr., May, June, July, Aug., Sept., Oct., Nov., Dec.)

15 Which three months have the most rainfall?

16 **Make a decision** If you were planning a vacation to Honolulu, during which months would you go and why?

17 **Data Point** Interview at least 20 sixth graders in your school. Ask them which sport they like the most. Use a graph to display your data.

18 About how many soccer participants are boys? **SEE INFOBIT.**

INFOBIT
According to a 1996 report, 7.2 million of the 18 million U.S. youth soccer participants are girls.

mixed review • test preparation

1 Make a pictograph and a bar graph of the data in the table.

2 Compare the two graphs you made in ex. 1. How are they alike? How are they different?

Number of Eggs Laid at a Time	
Reptile	**Average Number**
Agama lizard	17
Python	29
Nile crocodile	60
Green turtle	104

Stem-and-Leaf Plots

Here are the results of a test in a sixth-grade class. How would you use a stem-and-leaf plot to show the data?

83, 74, 85, 90, 62, 92, 77, 86, 54, 79, 89, 88, 96, 70, 64, 88, 74, 85, 73

A **stem-and-leaf plot** is another way to organize data. It helps you see the shape for a set of data.

> **Check Out the Glossary**
> stem-and-leaf plot
> See page 643.

You can follow these steps to make a stem-and-leaf plot for the scores.

Step 1	Step 2	Step 3
Make the stems by listing the tens digits from least to greatest.	Make the leaves by listing the ones digits in order to the right of their tens digit. Draw a line to separate the stems and leaves.	Add a title and key.

Step 1

5
6
7
8
9

Step 2

5	4
6	2 4
7	0 3 4 4 7 9
8	3 5 5 6 8 8 9
9	0 2 6

Step 3

Test Scores

5	4
6	2 4
7	0 3 4 4 7 9
8	3 5 5 6 8 8 9
9	0 2 6

Key: 5|4 = 54

Check for Understanding

Make a stem-and-leaf plot for each set of data. Draw conclusions based on the plot you made.

1 quiz scores:
86, 79, 78, 85, 97, 89, 84, 90, 80, 87, 87, 88, 82, 89, 92, 82, 81, 83

2 push-ups per student in a minute:
13, 14, 17, 20, 14, 19, 25, 18, 15, 23, 28, 14, 30, 16, 32, 19, 15, 18, 19, 21, 25, 14, 10, 33

Critical Thinking: Generalize

3 When would you use a stem-and-leaf plot instead of a line plot? Give an example.

Practice

Make a stem-and-leaf plot for each set of data. Draw conclusions based on the plot you made.

1 number of library books borrowed:
4, 12, 25, 13, 42, 5, 28, 15, 3, 7, 30, 8, 2, 1, 7, 41, 8, 16, 16, 12, 11, 10

2 arm spans in inches:
56, 48, 57, 58, 62, 50, 53, 67, 58, 51, 46, 59, 55, 57, 52, 51, 56, 60

3 candy bars sold:
34, 23, 54, 34, 67, 34, 54, 56, 67, 32, 61, 69, 12, 34, 28, 42, 65, 14, 51, 66, 42, 31, 37, 38, 47, 45, 60, 21, 13, 52, 43, 19, 23

4 test scores of Mr. Callahan's class:
98, 77, 42, 81, 96, 75, 82, 94, 67, 71, 82, 88, 72, 74, 66, 91, 59, 79, 90, 93, 48, 63, 86, 92, 79, 67, 89, 71, 73, 62, 87, 83, 91

MIXED APPLICATIONS

Problem Solving

Use the stem-and-leaf plot for problems 5–7.

5 What is the range, median, mean, and mode of the data?

6 How many students spent 30 min on math homework?

7 Why is a stem-and-leaf plot a better display for this data than a line plot?

8 **Number sense** Karen bought 10 items for her party at a local market. The mean price of the items was $2.85. What is a reasonable estimate for her purchases?

Minutes Spent on Math Homework

1	2 5 5
2	0 0 5 5 5 5
3	0 0 0 0 0 0 5 5
4	0 5 5

Key: 1|2 = 12

9 Each game of bowling is $4.95 for adults and $2.50 for children. Isabel went bowling with her father. She bowled 3 games and her father bowled 4 games. How much did they spend?

---

more to explore

Double Stem-and-Leaf Plots

A double stem-and-leaf plot shows two sets of data side by side.

Test 1 Scores	Test 2 Scores
78, 84, 75, 86,	70, 96, 85, 83,
92, 80, 71, 91,	90, 87, 74, 93,
76, 90, 85, 79	85, 76, 89, 84

Test 1		Test 2
9 8 6 5 1	7	0 4 6
6 5 4 0	8	3 4 5 5 7 9
2 1 0	9	0 3 6

Key: 71 → 1|7|0 ← 70

1 What was the most common score on the two tests?

2 Find the range for each test.

Sampling and Predicting

In the 1950s, the *I Love Lucy* show was a consistent Nielsen winner. It had a 31.6 average for the decade.

Check Out the Glossary
For vocabulary words,
see page 643.

Who finds out if a TV show is a success? From the earliest days of television, the Nielsen Media Research Company has conducted surveys to find out which TV shows are popular among people in the United States.

Market research companies can't survey everyone, so they survey samples of the whole population.

The **population** is the entire group of people about whom information is gathered.

The **sample** is the part of the population that is used to get information about that population.

The people in a **random sample** are chosen by chance in order to avoid **biased data.** For example, you would not use professional basketball players as your sample to find the average height of an adult.

Work Together

Work in a group to create your random sample.

Have each person in the class write his or her name on a piece of paper. Put all the names in a bag. Pick 15 names out of the bag.

Ask each person whose name is chosen how many hours of TV they watch each day and if they watch the commercials.

You will need
- *a bag*
- *a notebook*

▶ Do you think that your sample's average hours of TV watching and average number of commercial watchers are close to the averages for the entire class? Explain.

▶ **What if** the people in the sample were the 15 people who watched the most TV in the whole class? Explain how you think this average would compare to the class average.

Make Connections

A school newspaper conducted a survey to see which TV game shows were the most popular with students. The paper selected a random sample of 100 students from a list of all the students.

The population of this survey is all of the students in the school. The random sample is the 100 students surveyed.

In this survey, the random sample is **representative** of the population. It can be used to make predictions about the whole population.

Based on the survey results, you may generalize that *Carmen Sandiego* was the most popular TV game show with students in the school.

▶ Give examples of what kinds of samples would not be representative for the above survey.

Favorite TV Game Shows for Students in the School	
Game Show	**Students**
Guts!	29
Double Dare	8
Carmen Sandiego	51
Treasures of the Lost Temple	7
What Would You Do?	3
Others	2

representative A sample of a population that is typical of the population, so that it is valid to draw conclusions from the sample about the population as a whole.

Check for Understanding

Identify the population and sample in each situation. Tell if you think the sample is representative.

1 In a school of 600 students, pick the names of 50 students out of a box to find which TV show is the most popular.

2 Sample a few parents you know to find out which TV shows all parents prefer their children to watch.

Critical Thinking: Generalize   **Explain your reasoning.**

3 What are some ways to choose a sample randomly?

Practice

Identify the population and sample in each situation. Tell if the sample is representative.

1 Survey sixth graders to find out which subjects all students like best.

2 Survey sixth graders to find out what playground equipment they would use.

3 In a school of 348 students, pick 100 names from a bag to see how popular video games are.

4 Survey 12 computer club members to find the most popular software for sixth graders.

Problem Solvers at Work

Read
Plan
Solve
Look Back

PART 1   Choose the Appropriate Graph

A sixth-grade class is having a science fair. Here is the data for the total points awarded to each project. How many more projects are awarded between 80 and 90 points than between 70 and 80 points? How would you display the data so it will help you solve this problem?

Total Points Awarded to Each Project			
Project #	Scores	Project #	Scores
1	78	14	78
2	82	15	69
3	90	16	85
4	69	17	86
5	87	18	93
6	89	19	94
7	85	20	85
8	83	21	77
9	84	22	93
10	95	23	94
11	89	24	95
12	94	25	82
13	98	26	84

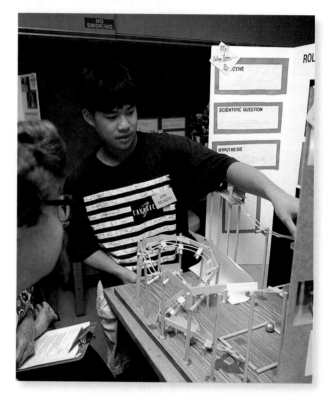

Work Together

Solve. Be prepared to explain your methods.

1 Discuss the type of graph that your group would choose to display the data.

2 Make the graph. Compare your graphs with those of other groups.

3 How many more projects are awarded 80 to 90 points than 70 to 80 points?

4 **Ask Questions** What are some other questions that could be asked based on the graph you made?

5 Would you be able to find out what the top five projects are from the graph you made? Why?

6 Find some graphs that are used in newspapers, magazines, or almanacs. Explain why you think the graphs were chosen.

Giselle did a science project on cat families. She recorded some information about the project in different tables. She made a graph for the first table and wrote this problem.

Weight (in pounds)		
Month	**My Cat**	**Tom's Cat**
Sept.	0.8	1.3
Oct.	2.0	2.6
Nov.	2.7	3.4
Dec.	5.7	6.6
Jan.	6.8	9.8
Feb.	10.9	11.7

Average Weight	
Cat	**Weight (in pounds)**
Jaguar	225
Cheetah	100
Tiger	420
Cougar	200
Lion	375
House cat	10

Favorite Pets	
Pets	**Number of Students**
Dog	13
Cat	12
Fish	8
Bird	5

During which month were the weights of the cats the farthest apart? the closest?

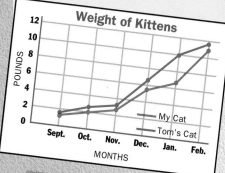

Giselle Cruz
Luis Munoz Marin School
Bridgeport, Connecticut

7 Solve Giselle's problem.

8 What type of graph would you choose to display the data on Average Weight and what graph to display Favorite Pets? Make the graphs.

9 **Write a problem** that can be solved by using information from one or two of the tables.

10 Trade problems. Solve at least two problems written by other students.

11 What was the most interesting problem you solved?

Turn the page for Practice Strategies.

Menu

Choose five problems and solve them. Explain your methods. Use the tables for problems 1–3.

Big Box Office Movies		
Film	Domestic (in millions)	Worldwide (in millions)
E.T. The Extraterrestrial	$400	$641
Jurassic Park	$357	$875
Forrest Gump	$327	$657

Tanker Oil Spills	
Tanker	Oil Spill (in millions of gallons)
Exxon Valdez	10
Amoco	68
Argo Merchant	7
Braer	25
Torrey Canyon	37

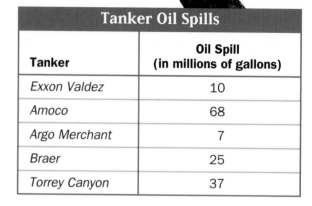

1 Make a graph to show how much money each movie made. Write a conclusion based on the data.

2 Suppose that an average movie ticket cost $5. Create a graph of ticket sales for the movies listed in the table.

3 Several major oil spills have damaged the environment. Make a graph to show the data. Write a conclusion based on the data.

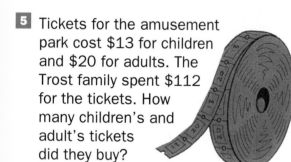

4 In the 1961–1962 NBA season, Wilt Chamberlain set a record average of 50.4 points a game playing 80 games. About how many points did he score that season?

5 Tickets for the amusement park cost $13 for children and $20 for adults. The Trost family spent $112 for the tickets. How many children's and adult's tickets did they buy?

6 To save $500 for a trip, you start by saving $65 the first month. Then you increase that amount by $5 each month. How many months will you need to save $500?

7 You have 5 test scores. The mean is 90, the range is 25, the median is 92, and there is no mode. What are the possible scores?

8 Andrea recorded her last 5 standing broad jumps as 48, 32, 50, 55, and 52 in. Should Andrea use the median or the mean to show the average length of her jumps? Explain.

Choose two problems and solve them. Explain your methods.

9 Write at least three conclusions based on the graph at right.

10 Use the information in the bar graph at right and design a questionnaire for a similar survey. Tell how you would collect and organize your data.

What Will Be Most Important to You as an Adult?

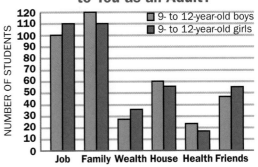

11 Spatial reasoning How many triangles do you see in the shape? In how many of the triangles is the number of dots divisible by 4?

12 Explain why it would be misleading for the Fun Land Company to say their sales were twice as much as Gameco in October and November.

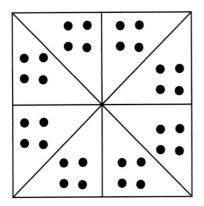

Fun Land and Gameco Sales in October and November

13 At the Computer The table shows how much forest land there was in the United States in 3 different years. Use a graphing program to create two graphs: one using intervals of 10, with a jagged line indicating the numbers between 0 and 700 are left out, and one using intervals of 100. Compare the two graphs. Which graph would you use if you were representing an environmental organization? a logging company? Explain why.

Forest Land (in millions of acres)			
Year	1970	1987	1992
Forest Land	754	731	737

Language and Mathematics

Complete the sentence. Use a word in the chart. (pages 2–29)

1 The ■ is the middle number of a set of data.

2 To find the ■, you subtract the least number from the greatest number in a set of data.

3 A ■ is the part of the population that is used to get information about the population.

4 You use a ■ to show a change in data over time.

5 The item that occurs most often in a set of data is the ■.

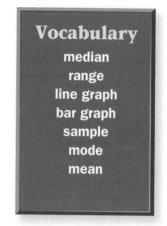

Vocabulary

median
range
line graph
bar graph
sample
mode
mean

Concepts and Skills

Find the range, mode, median, and mean for each set of data.
Round to the nearest tenth if necessary. (pages 10, 12)

6 25, 37, 12, 46

7 52, 63, 17, 31, 52

8 75, 64, 98, 86, 64

9 5, 5, 7, 2, 9, 2, 2, 8

10 28, 13, 84, 16, 84

11 132, 145, 176, 129

12 20, 11, 91, 68, 20, 46, 11

13 11, 15, 12, 19, 16, 15, 17

Make a graph to display the data. Write two statements about the data. (pages 2, 6, 22)

14

Favorite Fruit	
Fruit	Frequency
Apple	12
Banana	10
Orange	4

15

Population of Two Cities		
Year	Fairlawn	Lexington
1970	102,000	134,000
1980	112,000	156,000
1990	125,000	178,000

Solve. (page 22)

16 Between which two years was the increase in Peach Computer's net income the greatest?

17 When did Peach Computer start making more than Micro Systems?

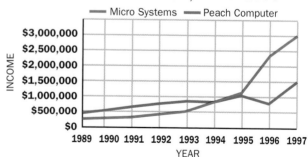

Net Incomes, 1989–1997

Think critically. (pages 7, 22)

18 Analyze. Yoshi's line graph shows how much she has grown. How should she change the graph to show her change in height more clearly?

My Height	
Year	**Height (in inches)**
1994	51
1995	53
1996	56
1997	57

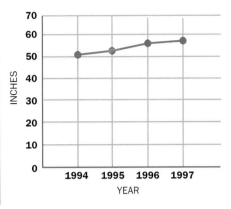

MIXED APPLICATIONS
Problem Solving
Pencil & Paper   Calculator   Mental Math

(pages 16, 30)

19 In a club, 7 members are 12 years old and 4 are 13 years old. The rest are 9, 10, 11, 15, and 17. What are the range, mode, median, and mean of the ages of the members?

20 Karen wants to make $500 from baby-sitting this summer. She is paid $5.25 each hour for baby-sitting. About how many hours does she have to baby-sit this summer?

21 The stem-and-leaf plot at right shows the number of raisins found in 15 boxes. What are the range, mode, and median number of raisins per box?

Number of Raisins

```
2 | 8  9
3 | 5  7  8  8  8  8  9  9
4 | 0  0  1  2  3
```
Key: 2|8 = 28

Use the line plot to solve problems 22–24.

22 What is the median number of cavities in Roger's class? Identify any gaps or clusters in the data.

23 Create a pictograph using the data from the line plot.

24 Does the mean, median, mode, or range best describe the data? Explain your choice.

Cavities in Roger's Class

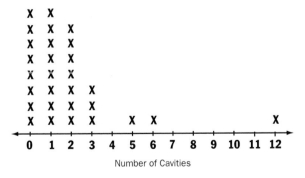

Number of Cavities

25 Brent wants to have a test average of 90. He scored 77 and 98 on his first two tests. What does he have to score on his next test to reach the average he wants?

Use the graph for problems 1–3.

1 How many gallons of buttermilk are made?

2 How many more gallons of 2% milk than skim milk are produced?

3 What is the total number of gallons of milk produced each month?

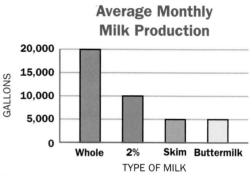

Average Monthly Milk Production

Make a graph to display the information in the table.

4

Favorite Drink	
Drink	**Frequency**
Milk	15
Soda	11
Juice	8
Water	3

5

Voters in Milltown		
Year	**Democrat**	**Republican**
1984	4,300	4,200
1988	5,300	3,300
1992	4,500	5,200
1996	5,400	5,000

6 Write a sentence about the graph you made in ex. 5.

Use the data set: 88, 59, 68, 78, 88, 75. Find each of the following. Round to the nearest tenth if necessary.

7 range   **8** mode   **9** median   **10** mean

Use the data set: 755, 625, 660, 573, 625. Find each of the following. Round to the nearest tenth if necessary.

11 range   **12** mode   **13** median   **14** mean

Make a stem-and-leaf plot of the data.

15 Students' weights in pounds: 88, 98, 73, 75, 82, 81, 90, 66, 68, 72, 84

Make a line plot of the following data.

16 Phone-call lengths in minutes: 3, 3, 6, 4, 5, 8, 6, 8, 8, 6, 3, 3, 5, 4, 8, 6

Solve.

17 The heights in inches of ten students are 61, 58, 60, 59, 60, 67, 69, 58, 63, and 65. Are more students less than 64 in. or more than 62 in.?

18 Find the range, mode, median, and mean for the heights in problem 17.

19 Would you use a frequency table, bar graph, line plot, or stem-and-leaf plot to help you find the mode of the data in problem 17?

20 Sarah has three things to do after school: return books to the library, do her homework, and call her grandmother. Make a table to show the possible orders in which she can get her activities done.

What Did You Learn?

Twelve- to seventeen-year-olds, as you can see in the table below, are a sizeable portion of our population.

12- to 17-Year-Olds in the United States	
Year	**Amount**
1970	23,000,000
1975	24,700,000
1980	22,800,000
1985	21,400,000
1990	20,042,000

▶ Choose an appropriate type of graph for the data in the table. Draw and label your graph.

▶ Write a paragraph describing why you chose that type of graph and how you decided on the scale. What do you think is the most important information your graph tells someone?

You will need
- *calculator*
- *graph paper*

• • • • • • • • • • • • • • • • • A Good Answer • • • • • • • • • • • • • • • • • •
- includes an appropriate graph and scale.
- includes the parts of the graph correctly labeled.
- includes explanations to support your work.

You may want to place your work in your portfolio.

What Do You Think

1 Are you able to decide which kind of graph is best for the data you are given? Why or why not?

2 When you need to organize data to make comparisons, which display are you likely to use? Explain.

- Frequency table
- Line graph
- Bar graph
- Line plot
- Pictograph
- Stem-and-leaf plot

Data, Statistics, and Graphs   **37**

Average Sixth Grader

Cultural Note

Leonardo da Vinci was born in Tuscany, Italy, in 1452 near the town of Vinci. His notebooks are filled with drawings showing his understanding of art, anatomy, architecture, machines, mechanics, flight, mathematics, and nature.

To make his paintings more realistic, Leonardo da Vinci studied the human body. His drawings of the body's internal organs and systems were very precise. They are considered to be the first truly scientific drawings of human anatomy.

Da Vinci made careful measurements of different parts of the body and compared them. He looked for relationships between these measurements.

One way to express these relationships is to compare them to a shape. In this activity, you are going to compare the heights of students in your class to their arm spans. Is the average sixth grader a tall rectangle, a wide rectangle, or a square?

▶ Work with a partner to measure and record each other's height and arm span. Combine your data with the measurements from the rest of your class.

▶ Find the class average for each measurement. Are the averages reasonable? How do they compare?

▶ How do you think artists use this relationship in their work?

What's Average?

Make the measurements necessary to answer the questions. Find the class average for each measurement.

1 Measure your hand span by stretching your hand as far as you can and measuring the distance covered from the end of your thumb to the end of your little finger. How tall are you in hand spans?

2 What is the relationship between the distance around your neck and the distance around your leg at the knee?

3 How does the length of your foot compare to the length of your forearm, measured from the crook of your elbow to your wrist joint?

4 About how many times greater is the distance around your neck than the distance around your wrist?

5 For each of the relationships above, compare your results to the class average for each measurement.

At the Computer

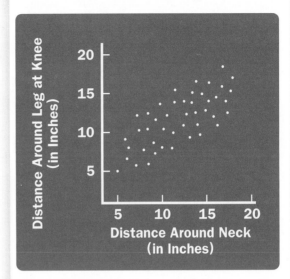

6 Choose one of the relationships you investigated. Choose the most appropriate graph to use to display your data for the class. Use a computer graphing program to create your graph.

7 Write two statements about your class based on this graph.

ADD AND SUBTRACT WHOLE NUMBERS AND DECIMALS

THEME Water, Water Everywhere

About 70% of the earth is under water, but less than 3% of that water is fresh. In this chapter you'll study connections between water and your life.

What Do You Know?

1 What is the range in length of the sharks?

2 A science museum has a 10-meter-long wall for the display of life-size models of sharks. What is the greatest number of different sharks the museum could display if they were placed end to end? Explain your reasoning.

3 Plan a display to feature three sharks. What is their total length?

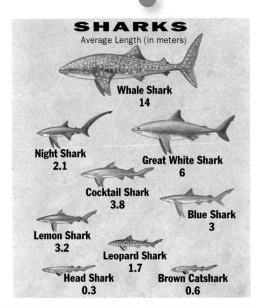

SHARKS
Average Length (in meters)

Whale Shark
14

Night Shark
2.1

Great White Shark
6

Cocktail Shark
3.8

Blue Shark
3

Lemon Shark
3.2

Leopard Shark
1.7

Head Shark
0.3

Brown Catshark
0.6

READING ARITHMETIC WRITING

Use Tables Sailors at sea use nautical measurements. A nautical mile is longer than a mile measured on land.

When you write, you can use tables to present data.

1 Write a paragraph describing the information in the table. How does the paragraph compare to the table?

Nautical Measurements	
Name	**Length**
Fathom	6 feet
Nautical mile	about 6,076 feet, which is about 1.1508 miles

Vocabulary*

*Partial list

factor form, p. 43
base, p. 43
exponent, p. 43
standard form, p. 43
place value, p. 46
expanded form, p. 46
decimal, p. 48

mixed number, p. 49
fraction, p. 48
estimate, p. 54
Commutative
  Property, p. 56
Associative
  Property, p. 57

Identity Property,
  p. 57
perimeter, p. 68
algebraic
  expression, p. 70
variable, p. 70
evaluate, p. 70

numerical
  expression, p. 70
value, p. 70
meter (m), p. 72
gram (g), p. 74
liter (L), p. 74

Exponents

L
E
A
R
N

Bacteria are the most abundant forms of life. One way bacteria reproduce is by splitting in two. Suppose a type of bacteria that lives in the ocean splits in two every hour. Starting with one bacterium, how many bacteria will there be after 6 hours?

Bacteria splitting

Work Together

Work with a partner. Use a sheet of paper to model the bacteria splitting.

Fold the paper in half to show the first split. Then fold the paper in half again to show the second split, and so on.

At the beginning

After 1 h, first split

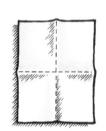

After 2 h, second split

Cultural Note

In the mid-1600s, Anton van Leeuwenhoek (LAY-vun-hook), a Dutch merchant and amateur scientist, was one of the first to build a simple microscope. His microscope enlarged objects up to 270 times.

Record the results on a table like this.

Hours	1	2			
Number of bacteria	2	4			

Look for patterns in your table. Find the number of bacteria there will be after 6 hours. Then determine the number of bacteria there will be after 12 hours.

Talk It Over

a ▶ **ALGEBRA: PATTERNS** What patterns did you see in your table?

▶ How could you use a calculator to help you find the number of bacteria after 20 hours? How many bacteria would there be?

Make Connections

Look at these patterns.

Hours	1	2	3	4	5	6
Number of bacteria	2	4	8	16		

Think: 2 2×2 $2 \times 2 \times 2$ $2 \times 2 \times 2 \times 2$

You can use exponents to show the number of bacteria.

$2^1 = 2$

$2^2 = 2 \times 2 = 4$

$2^3 = 2 \times 2 \times 2 = 8$

factor form

exponent
$2^3 = 8$ **Read:** 2 to the third power is 8.

base   standard form

Check Out the Glossary
exponent
base
standard form
factor form
See page 643.

In the bacteria problem, the base is 2. In other problems you may use other bases. For example $3^4 = 3 \times 3 \times 3 \times 3$.

Here is how to use a calculator to find the standard form of 3^4.

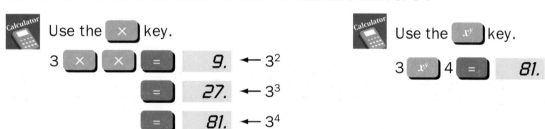

Use the ⨯ key.

3 ⨯ ⨯ =   9. ← 3^2

=   27. ← 3^3

=   81. ← 3^4

Use the x^y key.

3 x^y 4 =   81.

▶ **What if** the bacteria split into 4 every hour. How many bacteria would there be after 5 hours? after 7 hours?

Check for Understanding

Write using an exponent.

1 $5 \times 5 \times 5$

2 7×7

3 $9 \times 9 \times 9 \times 9 \times 9 \times 9$

Write in standard form.

4 7^3 **5** 13^2 **6** 10^2 **7** 10^3 **8** 10^4 **9** 10^5

Critical Thinking: Analyze

10 Look at your answers for ex. 6–9. How is the number of zeros in the standard form related to the exponent?

Turn the page for Practice. ➡

Practice

Write using an exponent.

1 $3 \times 3 \times 3 \times 3$ **2** $7 \times 7 \times 7 \times 7$ **3** 364×364

4 $10 \times 10 \times 10$ **5** $13 \times 13 \times 13 \times 13$ **6** $5 \times 5 \times 5 \times 5 \times 5$

7 $10 \times 10 \times 10 \times 10 \times 10$ **8** $4 \times 4 \times 4 \times 4$

Write in standard form.

9 10^6 **10** 22^2 **11** 3^6 **12** 4^5 **13** 2^8 **14** 9^3

15 5^3 **16** 1^7 **17** 11^3 **18** 17^2 **19** 12^2 **20** 8^2

Copy and complete the tables.

	Exponent Form	Factor Form	Standard Form
21	6^2	6×6	▪
22	6^3	▪	216
23	▪	$6 \times 6 \times 6 \times 6$	1,296

	Exponent Form	Factor Form	Standard Form
24	▪	1×1	1
25	1^6	$1 \times 1 \times 1 \times 1 \times 1 \times 1$	▪
26	▪	$1 \times 1 \times 1 \times 1 \times 1 \times 1 \times 1 \times 1 \times 1$	1

	Exponent Form	Factor Form	Standard Form
27	100^2	▪	10,000
28	100^3	$100 \times 100 \times 100$	▪
29	▪	$100 \times 100 \times 100 \times 100$	100,000,000

Use the tables above for ex. 30–31.

30 What conclusion can you make about the number 1 and exponents?

31 How is the number of zeros in the standard form related to the exponent if the base is 100?

• • • • • • • • • • • • • • • • • **Make It Right** • • • • • • • • • • • • • • • • •
32 Tim wrote: $4^3 = 4 \times 3 = 12$.
Explain what the error is and correct it.

Problem Solving

Pencil & Paper   Calculator   Mental Math

33 There are 10 boxes of jumbo shrimp. Each box contains 10 bags. Each bag contains 10 shrimp. How many jumbo shrimp are there?

34 Mary worked 3 hours and earned $15. Yukio worked 6 hours and earned $30. Do they earn the same amount each hour? Explain.

35 On her last five math tests Dot scored 98, 94, 86, 69, and 88. Hector's scores were 87, 92, 100, 63, and 78. Who had a greater average? By how much?

36 **Write a problem** about an underwater creature that doubles in size every hour. Solve it. Ask others to solve it too. Make up an interesting name for your underwater creature!

37 **Make a decision** In a story the hero is offered a choice. He can take $100,000, or he can take $1 the first day, $2 the second day, $4 the third day, $8 the fourth day, and so on, for 20 days. Decide which you would choose and explain why.

38 Bakers put yeast into dough to make it rise. Some yeast cells reproduce by splitting in two. Suppose there are 1,000 yeast cells to start and each yeast cell splits in two every hour. How many yeast cells will there be after 8 hours?

39 Tony bakes 59 cookies and puts them into bags. Each bag holds 8 cookies. How many bags does he fill? How many cookies are left?

40 José wants to show the amount of rainfall each month over 6 months for two different countries. Which kind of graph should he use? Why?

41 **Data Point** Write a statement about how the population shown in the graph increased. If the same pattern continues, what would you expect the population to be in the year 2000? in the year 2010?

Population of Metropolis

mixed review • test preparation

1 Make a line graph for this population data.

2 Make a stem-and-leaf plot of these heights (in inches): 63, 47, 66, 54, 66, 48, 55, 66, 61, 58, 45.

U.S. Population	
Year	Population
1950	151,325,798
1960	179,323,175
1970	203,302,031
1980	226,542,199
1990	248,718,301

Understanding Place Value: Whole Numbers

Did you know that an oil-eating bacteria helped save Alaskan beaches after the tanker *Exxon Valdez* spilled about 10,080,000 gal of oil?

You can use a **place-value** chart to help you read whole numbers.

Millions			Thousands			Ones		
H	T	O	H	T	O	H	T	O
	1	0	0	8	0	0	0	0

⌐──── **Think:** The place of the digit 8 is ten thousands.
The value of the digit 8 is 80,000.

Read: ten million, eighty thousand   **Short Word name:** 10 million, 80 thousand

Standard form: 10,080,000

Expanded form: $1 \times 10{,}000{,}000 + 8 \times 10{,}000$ or $(1 \times 10^7) + (8 \times 10^4)$

The cleanup from the spill cost more than $2,500,000,000.

Billions			Millions			Thousands			Ones		
H	T	O	H	T	O	H	T	O	H	T	O
		2	5	0	0	0	0	0	0	0	0

> **Check Out the Glossary**
> place value
> expanded form
> See page 643.

Read: 2 billion, 500 million   **Standard Form:** 2,500,000,000

Expanded form: $(2 \times 10^9) + (5 \times 10^8)$

Check for Understanding

Write in standard form.

1 87 million

2 250 thousand

3 $(7 \times 10^4) + (6 \times 10^2) + 7$

4 1 billion, 20 million, 72

5 $(6 \times 10^6) + (2 \times 10^5) + (3 \times 10^2) + 7$

Critical Thinking: Analyze   **Explain your reasoning.**

6 How is the place value of each digit in a number related to the place value of the digit on its right?

Practice

Write the place and the value for each underlined digit.

1 43,698

2 234,321,008

3 2,485,098

4 $1,321,345,587

5 2,549,098,341

6 63,987,076

7 $45,083,331,407

8 40,000,456,210

Write the number in standard form.

9 32 thousand 405

10 14 million, 200 thousand, 30

11 $(5 \times 10^3) + (3 \times 10^2) + (6 \times 10) + 4$

12 1 billion, 19 million, 80

13 2 billion, 10

14 $(9 \times 10^7) + (5 \times 10^5) + (4 \times 10)$

MIXED APPLICATIONS
Problem Solving

Pencil & Paper   Calculator   Mental Math

Use the table for problem 15.

15 Write the expanded form and the word name for the number of gallons in these North American oil spills.

16 Estimates of the world's worst oil spills range from twenty-five million to one hundred thirty million gallons of oil spilled. Write these numbers in standard form.

| Oil Spills in North America | |
Place	Gallons
Galveston Bay, TX	10,700,000
Off Massachusetts	8,820,000
Sewaren, NJ	8,400,000
Nantucket, MA	7,700,000
West Delta, LA	6,720,000

Cultural Connection Ancient Egyptian Numerals

The ancient Egyptians used the following symbols to name their numbers.

| 1 | 10 | 100 | 1,000 | 10,000 | 100,000 |

Egypt —
AFRICA

Here is how the number 124 could be written in this system.

Write these numbers in our system.

1 (Egyptian numeral)

2 (Egyptian numeral)

3 (Egyptian numeral)

4 (Egyptian numeral)

Write these numbers in the Egyptian system.

5 43

6 125

7 241

8 60

9 Compare the ancient Egyptian number system with the system we use today. How are they alike? different?

Place Value: Decimals

Divers are searching the bottom of the ocean for Spanish gold coins. They have divided up the area they are searching into 100 square meters. The shading shows the part they have already searched.

They searched $\frac{40}{100}$ or 0.40 of the area.

You can use a place-value chart to help you read the **decimal.** The word name of a decimal is determined by the place of the digit in the last place at the right.

Ones		Tenths	Hundredths
0	.	4	0

↑
Think: The value of the digit 4 is four tenths.

Read	forty hundredths
Decimal	0.40
Fraction	$\frac{40}{100}$
Short word name	40 hundredths

Look at the two models below. The same amount is shaded in each.

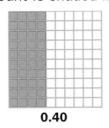
0.40

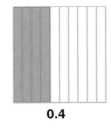
0.4

Decimals that represent the same amount are called **equivalent decimals.**

0.40 and 0.4 are equivalent decimals. 0.40 = 0.4

Check Out the Glossary
decimal
equivalent decimals
mixed number
fraction
See page 643.

Talk It Over

▶ How could you model 1.06? 2.3?

▶ How could you use dollars, dimes, and pennies to model 2.68? 3.7?

▶ Name three other pairs of equivalent decimals and explain why they are equivalent.

Scuba divers see many amazing creatures. The dwarf goby is the smallest freshwater fish in the world. It weighs as little as 0.00007 ounce. How do you read this decimal?

The place-value chart can be extended to the right for decimals.

Ones		Tenths	Hundredths	Thousandths	Ten-Thousandths	Hundred-Thousandths
0	.	0	0	0	0	7

Think: The value of the digit 7 is seven hundred-thousandths. ⟶

Read Decimal   seven hundred-thousandths   0.00007

Short word name   7 hundred-thousandths

Fraction $\frac{7}{100,000}$

More Examples

A 2.375

Decimal	2.375
Mixed number	$2\frac{375}{1,000}$
Short word name	2 and 375 thousandths

B fifty-four thousandths

Decimal	0.054
Fraction	$\frac{54}{1,000}$
Short word name	54 thousandths

Check for Understanding

Write the decimal represented by each model.

1    **2**   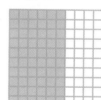   **3**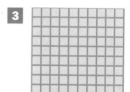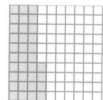

Write the place and the value of each underlined digit.

4 2.7<u>5</u>

5 43.<u>6</u>

6 0.61<u>2</u>5

7 17.815<u>3</u>

Write the short word name.

8 0.5   **9** 6.001   **10** 12.14   **11** 0.0002

Critical Thinking: Analyze   Explain your reasoning.

12 Why doesn't placing a zero to the right of the digit 6 change the value of 0.6?

13 Why does placing a zero between the decimal point and the digit 6 change the value of 0.6?

Turn the page for Practice. ⮞

Practice

Write the place and the value of each underlined digit.

1 73.<u>7</u>

2 91.6<u>2</u>

3 0.00<u>3</u>

4 <u>4</u>8.516

5 1.00<u>2</u>3

6 0.0376<u>5</u>

7 21.0<u>9</u>7

8 2.<u>1</u>000

Write the decimal as a fraction or mixed number.

9 0.6

10 0.35

11 0.7

12 0.582

13 0.63

14 5.2

15 3.843

16 63.9

17 41.625

18 3.7589

19 0.82

20 5.769

21 14.8215

22 6.915

23 0.0005

Write the number in standard form.

24 $\frac{2}{10}$

25 $\frac{17}{100}$

26 $\frac{3}{100}$

27 $4\frac{9}{10}$

28 $3\frac{2}{10}$

29 $4\frac{3}{1000}$

30 35 hundredths

31 28 thousandths

32 2 and 80 hundredths

33 121 thousandths

34 62 thousandths

35 5 and 9 tenths

Write each amount in dollars, using a decimal.

36 1 penny

37 1 dime

38 6 pennies

39 4 dimes

40 2 dimes and 4 pennies

41 5 dimes and 9 pennies

Identify the equivalent decimals.

42 0.8
0.08
0.80

43 0.705
0.75
0.750

44 1.6
1.60
1.06

45 0.33
0.3300
0.330

46 6.0
6.01
6.00

47 0.070
0.007
0.07

48 5.41
5.4100
5.410

49 4.62
4.620
4.602

Estimate the decimal represented by each model.

50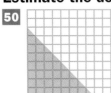

51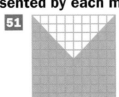

52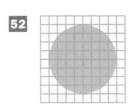

Decimal Concentration Game!

2 players

First, each player writes 6 different decimals between 0.01 and 2.99, one on each of 6 index cards.

Next, each player makes a card showing a model for each of the decimal numbers he or she made.

Play the Game

▶ Shuffle the 24 cards. Place them facedown in 6 rows of 4 cards each.

▶ Take turns turning over two cards from the pile. If the cards match, keep them. If the cards do not match, turn them facedown.

▶ Continue playing until all the possible pairs are made. The player with more cards wins.

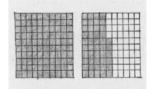

---

mixed review • test preparation

Use the pictograph to answer problems 1–3.

1. In which season were the most lobsters harvested?

2. About how many lobsters were harvested in the summer?

3. About how many lobsters were harvested in the winter?

Lobsters Harvested in a Year

Seasons	Number of Lobsters Harvested
Spring	🦞🦞
Summer	🦞🦞🦞🦞
Fall	🦞🦞🦞🦞🦞🦞
Winter	🦞🦞

🦞 = 5,000 lobsters

Write using an exponent.

4. $6 \times 6 \times 6 \times 6 \times 6$

5. $10 \times 10 \times 10$

6. 462×462

Compare and Order Decimals

Some shells are natural works of art. How would you list the length of these shells from greatest to least?

Snipe's Bill

Spider Conch

Nautilus

Lengths of Some Shells	
Shell	**Length**
Spider Conch	14 cm
Nautilus	12.1 cm
Snipe's Bill	12.6 cm

You can order numbers by comparing them two at a time.

Step 1	Step 2	Step 3
Line up the decimal points. Starting at the left, find the first pair of digits that are not equal.	Compare two more numbers.	Compare the final pair of numbers.

Step 1

14.0
12.1

Think: 4 > 2
14 is equivalent to 14.0.

14 > 12.1

Step 2

14.0
12.6

Think: 4 > 2

14 > 12.6

Step 3

12.1
12.6

Think: 6 > 1

12.6 > 12.1

The order from the greatest to the least is Spider Conch (14 cm), Snipe's Bill (12.6 cm), and Nautilus (12.1 cm).

Another Example
Order from least to greatest: 22.098; 22.1; 20.95; 20.8321; 21

Least → 20.8321   20.9500   21.000   22.0980   22.1000   ← Greatest

(0 < 1 between 20.8321 and 20.9500; 8 < 9; 0 < 1 between 21.000 and 22.0980; 1 < 2)

Check for Understanding
Write >, <, or =.

1 8.7 ● 8.65

2 4.983 ● 5.11

3 1.063 ● 1.067

4 0.8 ● 0.80

Order the numbers from least to greatest.

5 12.8; 11.932; 12.691; 12

6 6.607; 6; 6.7; 6.618

Critical Thinking: Analyze

7 When you compare numbers, why do you start at the left?

8 How do you compare and order these decimals? Explain.
1.052; 1.05; 0.952; 1.1; 1.056

Practice

Write >, <, or =.

1 8.4 ● 8.1

2 72.5 ● 71.381

3 3.126 ● 12.6

4 3,286 ● 348

5 0.019 ● 0.19

6 9.396 ● 9.4

7 4 ● 4.00

8 4.834 ● 4.8333

9 1.1 ● 1.01

10 5.62 ● 56.2

11 0.075 ● 0.07

12 15.05 ● 15.050

Order the numbers from least to greatest.

13 32.12; 23.78; 23.085

14 1.8; 1.82; 1; 1.651

15 $50; $50.25; $51.05; $500

16 4.123; 4.321; 4.0123; 4.0321

17 99.01; 98.991; 99.011; 100.991

18 123.01; 1.2301; 12.302; 12.3021

Solve.

19 10.7 ■ 6 < 10.756
What digits can ■ stand for?

20 99.81 ■ > 99.814
What digits can ■ stand for?

21 Name two whole digits between 19.1 and 21.1.

22 Name three whole digits between 5.01 and 8.1.

MIXED APPLICATIONS
Problem Solving

Use the table for problems 23–25.

23 Which shell has the greatest cost?

24 Which shell has the least cost?

25 Explain what you think is the best way to organize the price list.

Harp Shell

Tiger Cowrie

Fox's Nose

Seashell Price List	
Fox's Nose	$4.69
Harp Shell	$4.99
Tiger Cowrie	$1.39

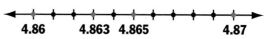

more to explore

The Density Property

There are decimals between 4.86 and 4.87.

4.86   4.863 4.865   4.87

Name two decimals between each pair of numbers.

1 6 and 7

2 5.3 and 5.4

3 8.79 and 8.8

4 3.217 and 3.218

5 Do you think there is always another decimal between any two unequal decimals? Explain your reasoning.

Estimate Sums and Differences

Our bodies lose 3 to 4 L of water each day. Athletes, especially, lose water through perspiration. A biker logs in the water she drinks during practice. Her two water bottles contain 0.5 L and 0.35 L. About how much water does she have?

BIKING LOG

Date	Time	Distance	Water Intake
Sun.	45 min	6 mi	0.5L
Mon.			
Tues.			
Wed.			
Thurs			
Fri.			
Sat.			

Estimate: 0.5 + 0.35

Round each number so you can find the sum mentally.

0.5 + 0.35   **Think:** Round to the
 ↓   ↓   nearest one.
1 + 0 = 1

The biker has about 1 L of water.

You can also estimate when you subtract. Estimate 9.25 − 5.8.

9.25 − 5.8   **Think:** Round to the nearest
 ↓   ↓   whole number.
9 − 6 = 3

estimate To find a number that is close to the exact number.

More Examples

A Estimate. Round to the nearest whole number.

8.43 + 1.5 + 11.62
 ↓   ↓   ↓
8 + 2 + 12 = 22

B Estimate. Round to the nearest ten.

688.7 − 74.8
 ↓   ↓
690 − 70 = 620

Check for Understanding

Estimate the sum or difference by rounding.

1 3.9 + 1.3

2 58.2 − 16.007

3 3.12 + 1.98 + 4.621

4 793.01 − 82.5

5 9.18 − 2.4897

6 \$32.97 + \$21.23 + \$1.90

Critical Thinking: Analyze

7 To estimate 24.73 − 15.96, why is rounding to the nearest whole number more helpful than rounding to the nearest ten?

Practice

Estimate the sum or difference by rounding.

1 7.89 + 4.32

2 13 + 24.7

3 8.67 − 5.239

4 42 − 7.8

5 32.654 − 8.5

6 17.25 + 14.7

7 8 − 5.826

8 24.55 + 7.3

9 28.3 + 43.12 + 21.6

10 921.9 − 64.12

11 53.56 − 9.82

12 6.732 − 0.909

13 $41.23 − $6.58

14 $789.65 − $39.95

15 12.8 + 99.99 + 7.451

16 9.098 + 1.07904 + 1.011 + 9.87

Estimate the cost.

17 a toy seal and a poster

18 a mug and 5 postcards

19 a poster, 10 postcards, and a mug

20 **What if** you bought a toy seal and 3 stickers. About how much change should you get from a $20 bill?

Aquarium Souvenirs			
Item	**Price**	**Item**	**Price**
Toy Seal	$10.98	Mug	$7.25
Button	$0.89	Poster	$4.25
5 Postcards	$2.00	3 Stickers	$0.99

MIXED APPLICATIONS
Problem Solving

21 In training for a triathlon, a biker rides 25.5 mi, 18.4 mi, and 35.75 mi. About how far has he ridden so far?

22 The shark tank at an aquarium holds 28,000 gallons of water. If there are 17,675 gallons in the tank, about how many more gallons can it hold?

23 **Make a decision** Which attraction at right would cost less for a family of two adults and two children? Use estimation to decide.

Ticket Prices	
Maritime Museum	**Aquarium**
Adults: $6.75	All: $5.75
Children: $4.25	

mixed review • test preparation

Write the place and the value for the underlined digit.

1 4,<u>3</u>67

2 731.2<u>6</u>

3 5<u>6</u>2.05

4 73.79<u>8</u>

Write <, >, or =.

5 2,634 ■ 2,642

6 7.46 ■ 7.5

7 0.546 ■ 0.5460

8 8.030 ■ 8.003

Add Decimals

In the 1996 Olympics Women's Freestyle Relay race, Angel Martino swam first for the U.S. team, coming in at 55.34 seconds. She was followed by Amy van Dyken, who completed the course in 53.91 seconds. What was their total time?

Add: 55.34 + 53.91

Estimate the total time.

$$55.34 + 53.91$$
$$\downarrow \qquad \downarrow$$

Think: 60 + 50 = 110

Step 1	Step 2
Line up the decimal points.	**Add. Place the decimal point in the answer.**
55.34 + 53.91	¹ 55.34 + 53.91 109.25

You can also use a calculator to find the exact answer.

 55.34 + 53.91 = **109.25**

Their total time was 109.25 seconds.

Talk It Over

▶ How is adding 55.34 and 53.91 like adding 5,534 and 5,391? How is it different?

▶ Add 0.25 and 0.35 using pencil and paper. Then add the same numbers using a calculator. How are the answers different? the same? Explain.

▶ Do you think the Commutative Property of addition is true for decimals? Give examples to support your reasoning.

> **Commutative Property**
>
> The order of the addends does not change the sum.
>
> Example: 15 + 20 = 35
> 20 + 15 = 35

Add: 45.08 + 52.7 + 44.92

Estimate the sum. **Think:** 50 + 50 + 40 = 140

Step 1	**Step 2**
Line up the decimal points. Write an equivalent decimal if necessary.	**Add. Place the decimal point in the answer.**
45.08 52.70 + 44.92	45.08 52.70 + 44.92 142.70

 45.08 + 52.70 + 44.92 = *142.7*

Check Out the Glossary
For vocabulary words
See page 643.

Associative Property

The way the addends are grouped does not change the sum.

Example: (17 + 42) + 8 = 67
17 + (42 + 8) = 67

Identity Property

The sum of any number and zero is the number.

Example: 12 + 0 = 12
0 + 12 = 12

▶ Do you think the Associative Property and the Identity Property are true for decimals? Use 45.08, 52.7, and 44.92 to show your reasoning.

More Examples

A
0.45
+ 0.30
0.75

B
21.567
+ 4.900
26.467

C 7.3 + 14.52 + 100.08 = *121.9*

Check for Understanding

Add. Estimate to see if your answer is reasonable.

1
51.42
+ 43.05

2
2.6
+ 7.9

3
1.12
+ 3.097

4
$34.79
+ 58.43

5
3.8
12.023
+ 59.56

6 46.21 + 3.74

7 7.904 + 8.999

8 1.1 + 3.8 + 4.9 + 1.2

Critical Thinking: Analyze

9 When adding decimals using paper and pencil, why is it helpful to line up the decimal points?

Turn the page for Practice. ➡

Add and Subtract Whole Numbers and Decimals **57**

Practice

Add. Remember to estimate first.

1 0.7
+ 0.8

2 4.23
+ 2.15

3 0.18
+ 0.74

4 $48.59
+ 57.35

5 4.306
+ 8.104

6 7.8
+ 0.91

7 438
+ 89.6

8 45.67
+ 33.8

9 $0.56
+ 45.83

10 7.83
+ 0.3569

11 160.18
+ 255.24

12 43.123
+ 163.17

13 $2.69
3.25
+ 4.00

14 6.41
12.12
+ 13.43

15 261.15
34.45
+   7.1392

16 2.07 + 19.15

17 $3.38 + $29.62

18 45 + 23.218

19 $2.99 + $234.45

20 14.05 + 0.8391

21 7.0124 + 3.2318

22 8.32 + 1.0011 + 42.6

23 16 + 3.765 + 1.84

24 $14.99 + $100.34 + $0.78

25 0.2 + 3.3 + 0.8 + 3.7

Add mentally. Explain your methods.

26 37 + 21

27 400 + 285

28 58 + 32

29 125 + 64

30 98 + 36

31 $3.42 + $1.99

32 27 + 36

33 $3.01 + $4.83

ALGEBRA: PATTERNS Write a rule for the pattern. Complete the pattern.

34 (5, 5.1), (5, ■), (5, 5.5), (5, 5.7)

35 (1.1, 1.1) (1.2, 1.2) (1.3, 1.3) (■, ■)

Solve.

36 How can you tell that 8.3 + 0.9899 is about 9 without adding?

37 How can you tell that 5.5 + 0.32 is not 8.7 without adding?

Use the table to find the total cost in ex. 38–40.

38 snorkel and face mask

39 snorkel and goggles

40 snorkel, face mask, and flippers

Item	Snorkel	Face mask	Goggles	Flippers
Price	$9.95	$15.00	$8.99	$21.00

·························· **Make It Right** ··························

41 Vernon added 34.5 and 1.78 this way.
Explain what the error is and correct it.

34.5
+ 1.78
‾‾‾‾‾
5.23

Problem Solving

Pencil & Paper | Calculator | Mental Math

42 Mary scored 238.30 points in the compulsory dive. Then she scored 313.96 points in the optional dive. How many points did she score altogether?

43 John has $28. He will spend half of the money on the ticket for a swim meet. He wants to spend the rest of the money for film. Can he buy 3 rolls of film at $2.99 each? Explain.

44 The oil-carrying capacity of the *Pierre Guillaumat* is equal to the gas tanks of about ten million average-sized automobiles. Write this number at least two different ways.

45 Pablo bought a pair of sandals for $6.99, a bottle of sunscreen for $4.25, a beach towel for $10.00, and a pair of sunglasses for $6.29. How much did he spend altogether?

46 Rita is driving from Fairfax to Cade. After she drove 70 miles from Fairfax, she saw a road sign that showed Cade was 250 miles ahead. How many more miles does she have to drive to be halfway between Fairfax and Cade?

47 **Write a problem** that can be solved by adding decimals. Solve it. Have others solve it.

48 How much longer did it take the *Trieste* to descend than to ascend? **SEE INFOBIT.**

INFOBIT
The *Trieste*, a U.S. Navy bathyscaphe, reached the depth of 35,813 ft on Jan. 23, 1960. It took the *Trieste* 4 hours 48 minutes to descend and 3 hours 17 minutes to ascend.

---

more to explore

Using Properties to Add Mentally
You can use properties of addition to add mentally.

Add: $0.91 + $0.38 + $0.09
Think: $0.91 + $0.09 + $0.38   ← Commutative Property
($0.91 + $0.09) + $0.38   ← Associative Property
$1.00 + $0.38
$1.38

Add mentally.

1 $37 + $128.56 + $3

2 $132.25 + $12.11 + $0.75

3 $129.05 + $12.25 + $0.95 + $5.75

4 $49.10 + $18.50 + $1.50 + $0.90

Subtract Decimals

Suppose you caught a bass that weighed 2.7 pounds. What is the most the next fish you catch can weigh?

Subtract: 5 − 2.7

Estimate. **Think:** 5 − 3 = 2

You can subtract using pencil and paper or a calculator.

Step 1	**Step 2**	
Line up the decimal points. Write an equivalent decimal if necessary.	Subtract. Place the decimal point in the answer.	**Check.**
$$\begin{array}{r} 5.0 \\ -\ 2.7 \end{array}$$	$$\begin{array}{r} \overset{4\ \ 10}{\cancel{5}.\cancel{0}} \\ -\ 2.7 \\ \hline 2.3 \end{array}$$	$$\begin{array}{r} 2.3 \\ +\ 2.7 \\ \hline 5.0 \end{array}$$

 5 − 2.7 = **2.3**

You can catch a fish that weighs up to 2.3 pounds.

Talk It Over

▶ How would you subtract 1.28 from 3.4? How could you check your answer?

▶ Cynthia uses a calculator to find 15 − 1.25. The display shows 2.5. How can you tell whether the answer is reasonable or not? If it is not, what might she have done wrong?

Marlins are mighty fish. Think about landing a 181.875-lb white marlin, or a 494-lb striped marlin. Both are record catches. What is the difference in weight of these record fish?

Subtract: 494 − 181.875

Estimate first.   **Think:** 500 − 200 = 300

Step 1	Step 2
Line up the decimal points. Write an equivalent decimal if necessary.	**Subtract. Regroup if necessary. Place the decimal point in the answer.**

Step 1
$$494.000$$
$$-181.875$$

Step 2
$$\overset{3\ \ 9\ 9\ 10}{49\cancel{4}.\cancel{0}\cancel{0}\cancel{0}}$$
$$-181.875$$
$$312.125$$

Check.
$$\overset{1\ \ 1\ 1}{312.125}$$
$$+181.875$$
$$494.000$$

 494 − 181.875 = **312.125**

The difference in the weights is 312.125 lb.

More Examples

A
$$\overset{2\ 10}{\cancel{3}.\cancel{0}79}$$
$$-0.310$$
$$2.769$$

B
$$\overset{3\ 12\ 6\ 9\ 10}{\cancel{4}\cancel{2}.\cancel{7}\cancel{0}\cancel{0}}$$
$$-\ \ 8.289$$
$$34.411$$

C 68.3 − 45.7921 = **22.5079**

Check for Understanding
Subtract. Estimate to see if your answer is reasonable.

1
$$5.89$$
$$-2.63$$

2
$$7.2$$
$$-1.05$$

3
$$10$$
$$-\ 4.412$$

4
$$\$197.25$$
$$-\ 102.99$$

5
$$4.894$$
$$-1.9$$

6 42.2 − 34.076   **7** 104.01 − 19.7   **8** 0.4 − 0.2875

Critical Thinking: Generalize

9 How is subtracting 60.75 from 180 like subtracting 6,075 from 18,000? How is it different?

10 Is there an associative property for subtraction of decimals? Give examples.

CHECK

Turn the page for Practice. ➡

Practice

Subtract. Remember to estimate first.

1
  8.76
− 7.43

2
  12.45
− 9.13

3
  4.05
− 3.7

4
  $17.25
−   9.23

5
  0.84
− 0.38

6
  25.79
− 16.83

7
  14.72
− 3.891

8
  20
− 5.062

9
  6.021
− 3.912

10
  14.6
− 9.35

11
  70.671
− 8.211

12
  100
− 12.542

13
  $930.75
−   29.08

14
  8.9
− 4.0085

15
  711.12
− 401.95

16
  0.96
− 0.78

17
  1.4
− 0.8

18
  0.38
− 0.259

19
  0.9
− 0.726

20
  1.04
− 0.86

21 $61.84 − $39.42

22 2.05 − 0.9

23 3.75 − 0.43

24 4.01 − 3.016

25 84.5 − 28

26 9.71 − 0.546

27 2 − 0.3219

28 303 − 24.61

29 0.321 − 0.3198

30 1.13 − 0.65

31 0.3 − 0.222

32 0.64 − 0.55

α ALGEBRA: PATTERNS Find the output.

Rule: Subtract 0.125.	
Input	**Output**
33 1.01	■
34 48.00	■
35 7.923	■

Rule: Subtract 0.099.	
Input	**Output**
36 0.9	■
37 0.99	■
38 0.9999	■

Rule: Subtract 11.31.	
Input	**Output**
39 50	■
40 150	■
41 1,000	■

Find the length of $\overline{AB}$ in each picture.

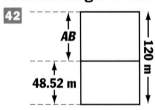

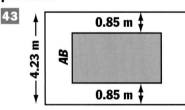

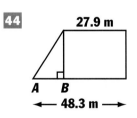

·················· **Make It Right** ··················

45 Here is how Daniel found
100.23 − 0.9. Explain what
the error is and correct it.

   100.23
−   0.9
――――――
   100.33

Problem Solving

46 At a recent "Halibut Derby" about 60 million pounds of halibut were caught in 2 days. What if 10 million more pounds of fish were caught. How many pounds of fish would have been caught altogether?

47 Write a paragraph to tell what the stem-and-leaf plot could be about.

Stem	Leaf
6	0 0 1 8 9
7	0 1 1 2 3 5 8
8	1 1 2 2 4 5 5 7 7 9
9	0 1 1 3 8

48 **Spatial reasoning** If the pattern of the staircase at the right continues, how many toothpicks are needed for the staircase where the tallest step is 5 steps high? 10 steps high?

Use the table to answer problems 49–51.

49 **Use Tables** How does the information being in a table help you find the difference between the longest and shortest lengths? What is the difference?

50 Which two sea giants differ by 2.1 m?

51 Do Kronosaurus and Carcharodon differ in length more than Geosaurus and the Elasmosaurus? Explain your reasoning.

Prehistoric Sea Giants	
Animal	**Average Length**
Kronosaurus Queenslandicus	16.8 m
Carcharodon Megalodon	24.4 m
Elasmosaurus	15.2 m
Tylosaurus	6.7 m
Geosaurus	4.6 m

52 Two basic fishing tools are the rod and the reel. An 8-foot rod and one spinning reel cost $69.29. If the rod costs $34.65, what is the price of the reel?

53 **Data Point** Use the Databank graph of swimming speeds on page 633. Find a different way to display the data.

---

mixed review • test preparation

Make a line plot for each set of fish weights (in pounds).

1 3, 5, 8, 5, 2, 4, 5, 7, 4, 5, 7

2 4, 7, 5, 6, 5, 4, 6, 5, 2, 4, 5, 6, 7, 6

3 Write a statement comparing the two line plots.

Write in standard form.

4 2^5 **5** 10^4 **6** 11^2 **7** 3^4 **8** 10^6 **9** 5^4

Complete the table.

	Factor Form	Exponent Form	Standard Form
1	4 × 4 × 4	4^3	■
2	■	12^5	248,832
3	9 × 9 × 9 × 9	■	6,561
4	10 × 10 × 10 × 10 × 10	■	100,000

Write the number in standard form.

5 three billion, thirty-two million, six

6 two and fourteen thousandths

7 $(3 \times 10^4) + (6 \times 10^2) + (3 \times 10)$

8 $(9 \times 10^9) + (9 \times 10^4) + (2 \times 10^2)$

Order the numbers from least to greatest.

9 5.234; 5.233; 5.34; 5.09

10 1.4; 1.389; 0.989; 1.41

11 0.0017; 0.001; 0.1; 0.0201

12 2; 1.97; 2.01; 2.0008

Add or subtract. Remember to estimate.

13	**14**	**15**	**16**	**17**
7.18	6.6	$100.59	50	$23.45
+ 3.62	− 5.7	+ 89.25	− 7.081	− 4.99

18 4.08 + 23.65

19 18 − 7.981

20 25.744 + 32.51

Solve.

21 Jacy bought a model boat kit for $15.99. She also bought a glue gun for $5.25, a ruler for $0.99, and a screwdriver for $6. How much did she spend altogether?

22 If your swimming times are 34, 35, 39, 42, and 35 seconds, is your median time better than your mean time? Explain.

23 **Logical reasoning** Order the decimals from greatest to least.
Decimal A < D
Decimal B > C and B < A
Decimal E is the greatest number.

24 The Guairá Waterfalls in Brazil and Paraguay flows at a rate of about four hundred seventy thousand cubic feet per second. Write the rate in standard form.

25 Journal How would you explain to a friend how to find the sum and difference of 12.023 and 2.49? You may draw a diagram or use models to explain. Include estimation to support the reasonableness of your answer.

Front-End Estimation

You buy a fish tank filter for $3.25, fish for $4.49, and fish food for $2.25. About how much is the total cost?

You can use front-end estimation to find the approximate cost.

Step 1

Add the front digits.

Write zeros for the other digits.

$3.25
4.49
+ 2.25

$9.00

Step 2

Adjust the estimate.

$3.25
4.49
+ 2.25

$10.00

Think:
$0.25 + $0.49 + $0.25 is about $1.

$9 + $1 = $10

The cost is about $10.

What if you buy only the filter and pay for it with a $10 bill. About how much change should you receive?

Use front-end estimation to subtract.

Subtract the front digits: $10.00 − $3.25 ≈ $7   **Note:** ≈ means approximately equal to.

You should receive about $7.

Estimate. Use front-end estimation with or without adjustment.

1 A restaurant ordered 5.4 lb of trout, 7.2 lb of flounder, and 11.75 lb of sole from a fish market. About how many pounds was the order?

2 Flounder costs $5.39 per pound. Shrimp costs $8.55 per pound. About how much more does shrimp cost than flounder?

3 You buy a fish tank for $14.50, a minicastle for $4.49, and marbles for $1.25. You pay with a $50 bill. About how much change should you get?

4 You jog 0.75 mi on Monday, 1.4 mi on Tuesday, 0.25 mi on Wednesday, and 2.1 mi on Thursday. About how many miles did you jog in all?

5 You have $5. You want to buy tropical fish for your tank. An angel fish costs $3.89; a fancy guppy costs $1.75. Do you have enough money to buy one of each? Explain.

6 One day you drove 20.5 mi to the beach, then 32.75 mi to the lake. From the lake you drove 4.5 mi into town. About how far did you drive?

real-life investigation

ADDITION AND SUBTRACTION

SPLASH RELAY

The Splash Relay is a race with a twist. You run a Splash Relay just like other relays except you don't pass a baton. Instead you pass a cup filled with water!

Your team will need
- *500 mL measuring cup*
- *stopwatch*
- *recording sheets*

GET READY
▶ Work outside on the playground as a team. Take turns being the timekeeper who records race times of each runner.

RACE COURSE
▶ Lay out a race course. Make it so each runner will run back and forth about 20 yd in all.

POUR
▶ Start the race with 500 mL in the cup for each team.

GO!
▶ Run the relay. Time each runner separately. Have the timekeeper record the times.

AFTER
▶ Find the sum of all your recorded times. Then measure how much water is left in the measuring cup. Round to the nearest 100 mL.

You can lower your team's time (and have a better chance of winning) by not spilling water. Make a table like the one below to find the bonus seconds you earned based on the water you have left at the end of the race. The lowest final time wins.

Finish (mL in cup)	500	400	300	200	100	0
Bonus Subtract this number of seconds from your time	15	12.5	9.5	6.5	3.5	0

DECISION MAKING

Splash Relay Results

1 Run several Splash Relays. Make a chart or table to record your times like the one shown.

Race	mL in Cup	Recorded Times (seconds)	Seconds Subtracted	Final Time (seconds)
1	**Start:** 500	José 12.41 Sue 17.05 Bob 14.35		
2	**Finish:** 300	Pat 16.82 Total 60.63	9.5	51.13

2 Decide how you can change your running style to improve your team's final time. Should runners on your team run faster? Should they slow down so they spill less water? Describe the running style that you choose.

3 By how much did your new running style change your final time?

4 How fast do you think your team could run the relay without spilling any water? Does this strategy give you the best final time? Explain.

Report Your Findings

5 **Portfolio** Prepare a report on what you learned. Include the following:
▶ The table made to list your race results.

▶ Your calculations to determine your final times.

▶ Your decision on a running style that worked best for your team.

6 Compare your findings to those of other teams.

▶ How did your times and running style compare to other teams'?

Revise your work.
▶ Did you include all the data you needed and check all calculations?
▶ Did you give reasons to support your decisions?
▶ Did you proofread and edit your report carefully?

MORE TO INVESTIGATE

PREDICT how much water you think would spill if the whole class participated in a giant Splash Relay.

EXPLORE changing the Splash Relay rules to make the relays more fun, easier, or harder.

FIND out about ways in which people can cut down on the amount of water they waste.

Problem-Solving Strategy

Read
Plan
Solve
Look Back

Guess, Test, and Revise

L E A R N

Read

A new pool for the aquarium will be rectangular. It will have a perimeter of 44 meters so that many people can stand around the pool. The architect wants the long sides of the pool to be only 1 meter longer than the short sides. What should the pool's width and length be?

Plan

You can use the guess-and-test strategy to find the width and length of the pool.

The length should be 1 m longer than the width. The **perimeter** should be 44 m.

Solve

Guess: Try 10 m and 11 m.
  Test: 10 + 11 + 10 + 11 = 42
      42 < 44   Try a greater number.

Guess: Try 11 m and 12 m.
  Test: 11 + 12 + 11 + 12 = 46
      46 > 44   Try a smaller number.

Guess: Try 10.5 m and 11.5 m.
  Test: 10.5 + 11.5 + 10.5 + 11.5 = 44

The perimeter is the right length, so the sides should be 10.5 m wide and 11.5 m long.

11.5 m

10.5 m

> **perimeter** The perimeter of a figure is the distance around it.

Look Back

Does this answer make sense?

Yes, 11.5 m is 1 m longer than 10.5 m. The perimeter is 44 m.

C H E C K

Check for Understanding

1 **What if** the perimeter of the pool will be 36 m instead. What should the width and length of the pool be?

Critical Thinking: Analyze

Solve. Tell how you used the guess-and-test strategy.

2 Jewel is filling a fish tank with fancy guppies and black mollies. She wants to have 50 more guppies than mollies. If she wants a total of 100 fish, how many will be guppies? black mollies? Explain.

Problem Solving

1 There are 4 more seals than sea lions at the Seal Pond. Altogether, there are 28 seals and sea lions. How many are there of each?

2 You have to display 15 pictures on 4 walls. No two walls can have the same number of pictures. How many different ways can you display them?

3 The chart at the right shows the times in a swimming relay race with 4 swimmers. Each of the swimmers swam a different style for 50 meters. What was the total time for the four swimmers?

Style	Time (in seconds)
Backstroke	45.16
Breaststroke	52.7
Butterfly	44.78
Freestyle	38

4 **Spatial reasoning** How would you move only two of the toothpicks below so that there will be six squares?

5 Jason mailed some letters and postcards. The total cost was $2.48. Each letter had a 32¢ stamp and each postcard had a 20¢ stamp. How many of each did he mail?

6 Dan poured 0.25 liters of juice from a 1.5-liter container. How much juice is left in the container?

7 Your friend drew a map. To get to his house, you must travel 1.7 mi after your next turn. At 4 mi before that turn, the odometer reads 46,724.9 mi. What will it read when you arrive?

8 Delores had $100 to spend on clothes. She spent $12.50 on Monday, $19.75 on Tuesday, and $27.43 on Wednesday. About how much did she have left?

9 Find 5 consecutive odd numbers that have a sum of 65.

10 In a family, Michael is the youngest. Kim is four times older than Michael, while Sarah, at age 11, is 5 years younger than Kim. How old is each child in the family?

11 **Write a problem** that can be solved by subtracting decimals. Solve it. Have others solve it.

12 Place one of the numbers 1, 2, 3, 4, 5, or 6 in each of the circles at the right so that the sum of the numbers on each side of the triangle is 12.

Addition and Subtraction Expressions

Water has weight, but how do you weigh it? Suppose you need to find the weight of water in a 1.2-oz container.

You can write an **algebraic expression** to find the weight of the water.

The letter x is called a **variable** because it can have various values. Since the total weight depends on the amount of water and the container, let x represent that total weight.

Then $x - 1.2$ is an algebraic expression representing the total weight less the weight of the container.

What if the scale reads 6.8 oz for the total weight of a container with the water. What is the weight of the water?

You **evaluate** an expression by substituting values for the variable.

Check Out the Glossary
For vocabulary words
see page 643.

Evaluate: $x - 1.2$ for $x = 6.8$
Replace the variable: $6.8 - 1.2$ ← This is a **numerical expression.**
Compute: $6.8 - 1.2 = 5.6$ ← 5.6 is the **value** of the expression.

The weight of the water is 5.6 oz.

Check for Understanding
Write an expression for the situation.

1 The total number of people on a jet with x passengers and a crew of 12

2 The number of bowling pins left after y pins of the 10 are knocked down

Evaluate each expression.

3 $x + 3$ for $x = 5$ **4** $13.2 - y$ for $y = 3$ **5** $a - 0.34$ for $a = 8.9$

Critical Thinking: Analyze

6 Write a situation that could be represented by the expression $y + 5$.

Practice

Evaluate each expression.

1 $y + 8$ for $y = 1.8$ **2** $t - 6$ for $t = 15$ **3** $4.2 + x$ for $x = 5$

4 $15 - a$ for $a = 5.7$ **5** $b + 7.34$ for $b = 6.9$ **6** $12.3 - c$ for $c = 5.89$

7 $12.321 - m$ for $m = 5.7$ **8** $1.098 - n$ for $n = 0.089$

ALGEBRA: PATTERNS **Find the output.**

Rule: 0.123 + w	
Input *w*	Output
9 1.2	■
10 2.091	■
11 3.9	■

Rule: 1.999 + c	
Input *c*	Output
12 0.1	■
13 0.01	■
14 0.001	■

Rule: k – 11.111	
Input *k*	Output
15 12	■
16 12.11	■
17 12.111	■

Write an expression for the situation.

18 7.9 miles more than an unknown number of miles

19 Your weight if you weighed 104.5 lb and then you gained x lb

20 Your weight if you weighed 104.5 lb and then you lost y lb

21 Cost of repair of equipment: $45 plus the cost of parts (p dollars)

MIXED APPLICATIONS
Problem Solving

22 Suppose your height with your sneakers on is 158.5 cm and the bottom of your sneaker is 1.7 cm thick. What is your actual height?

23 You draw a 4-in. line. Then you draw a line 4 times its length. Finally you draw a line 4 times the length of your second line. How long is the third line?

24 **Make a decision** Mount Everest is 29,028 ft tall. The bottom of Mauna Kea is 19,669 ft below sea level. It rises 13,796 ft above sea level. Which mountain would you say is higher? Why?

mixed review • test preparation

Find the range, median, and mean for the data.

1 23, 10, 45   **2** 35, 42, 12, 57, 44   **3** 77, 77, 77, 75   **4** 85, 88, 88, 75

Make a bar graph for the number of sixth graders each year.

5 1994: 137; 1995: 150; 1996: 148; 1997: 154; 1998: 157

Applying Decimals: Metric Units of Length

The blue whale is the largest of all mammals. The longest ever recorded was 33.6 meters long.

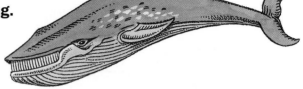

Recall that the **meter (m)** is the basic unit of length in the metric system.

Metric Units of Length
1,000 meters (m) = 1 kilometer (km)
1 meter (m) = 100 centimeters (cm)
1 centimeter (cm) = 10 millimeters (mm)

Check Out the Glossary
meter
See page 643.

You might walk about
1 km in 20 min.

A bat is about
1 m long.

The width of your
fingernail is about 1 cm.

The thickness of a
dime is about 1 mm.

centimeters

The length of the line is:
▶ 9 cm to the nearest centimeter.
▶ 8.7 cm or 87 mm to the nearest millimeter.

Check for Understanding
Choose an appropriate unit. Write *mm, cm, m,* or *km.* Explain.

1 length of an envelope   **2** height of a flagpole   **3** thickness of a wire

4 length of a pencil   **5** distance a train travels in a day

Draw lines of these lengths.
6 2 cm   **7** 57 mm   **8** 16 cm   **9** 2.5 cm   **10** 0.8 cm

Critical Thinking: Analyze
11 Why is it more reasonable to measure the length of a swimming pool in meters instead of millimeters?

Practice

Choose an appropriate unit. Write *mm, cm, m,* or *km*. Explain.

1 distance a ball is thrown

2 thickness of a computer disc

3 length of your foot

4 distance from Texas to New York

Estimate. Then use a metric ruler or tape measure to measure.

5 the height of a drinking glass

6 the length of your index finger

7 thickness of a quarter

8 the width of your math book

Write the letter of the most reasonable estimate.

9 the distance a car travels in an hour   **a.** 60 cm   **b.** 60 mm   **c.** 60 km

10 the width of a door   **a.** 10 cm   **b.** 1 m   **c.** 100 mm

11 the length of a fishing pole   **a.** 200 cm   **b.** 2 km   **c.** 20 m

Use the table for ex. 12–15.
Find the difference in length.

12 St. Lawrence Seaway and Suez Canal

13 Panama Canal and Albert Canal

14 Suez Canal and Albert Canal

15 St. Lawrence Seaway and Panama

Famous Shipping Canals		
Name	**Location**	**Length (km)**
St. Lawrence Seaway	U.S. and Canada	3,862.3
Suez	Egypt	161.9
Panama	Canal Zone	81.6
Albert	Belgium	128.7

MIXED APPLICATIONS
Problem Solving

16 Spatial sense Whales have been seen at depths of 2,400 m. This depth is about the height of a
a. 10-story building.   **b.** tree.
c. mountain.   **d.** horse.

17 Logical reasoning A is a 5-digit number between 2 and 4. It has no tenths or hundredths, and has a 6 in the ten thousandths place. The sum of its digits is 17. Find A.

mixed review • test preparation

Identify the equivalent decimals.

1 0.7, 0.07, 0.70

2 2.03, 2.30, 2.3

3 5.3, 5.300, 5.30

a **ALGEBRA Evaluate each expression.**

4 $x + 6$ for $x = 3$

5 $8 - y$ for $y = 3.4$

6 $2.3 + n$ for $n = 9.87$

Applying Decimals: Metric Units of Mass and Capacity

Dolphins are intelligent and beautiful animals. Marine biologists like Suzanne Yin study these mammals. Dolphins range in mass from 45 kilograms to 9 metric tons. How many kilograms are there in 9 metric tons?

Mass is the amount of matter in an object. Recall that the **kilogram (kg)** and the **gram (g)** are metric units of mass.

Metric Units of Mass
1 metric ton (t) = 1,000 kilograms (kg)
1 kilogram (kg) = 1,000 grams (g)
1 gram (g) = 1,000 milligrams (mg)

about 1 g

about 1 kg

about 9 t

IN THE WORKPLACE
Suzanne Yin, Marine Biologist,
Earth Watch

Since 1 t = 1,000 kg, then 9 t is 9 × 1,000 or 9,000 kg.

Biologists must also understand metric units of capacity.

Check Out the Glossary
For vocabulary words
See page 643.

The **capacity** of a container is the amount that the container can hold. The **liter (L)** and the **milliliter (mL)** are metric units of capacity.

Metric Units of Capacity
1 liter (L) = 1,000 milliliters (mL)

There is 1 milliliter of water in this eyedropper.

This bottle of water holds 1 liter.

Check for Understanding
Name an appropriate unit of capacity or mass. Explain.

1 capacity of a gas tank

2 capacity of a teaspoon

3 mass of a truck

4 mass of a dog

5 mass of a quarter

6 capacity of a pail

Critical Thinking: Analyze

7 When might you need to measure the exact amount of milk in a container? When might you need just an estimate?

Practice

Name an appropriate unit of capacity or mass. Explain.

1 capacity of a cup **2** capacity of a bathtub **3** mass of a pencil

4 mass of a computer **5** capacity of a glass **6** mass of a shark

Write the letter of the most reasonable estimate.

7 A sink can hold about ▮ of water. **a.** 20 mL **b.** 4 L **c.** 20 L

8 A telephone has a mass of about ▮. **a.** 25 g **b.** 1 kg **c.** 20 kg

9 A can of soda has a capacity of about ▮. **a.** 1 L **b.** 300 mL **c.** 10 L

Use the chart for ex. 10–13. Find the total amount of fat.

Nutrition Facts						
Food	Cheese-burger	Fishburger	Chicken-burger	Chef Salad	Milk Shake	Low-fat Milk
Fat per Serving	28 g	16.5 g	25 g	9.5 g	4.5 g	2.5 g

10 one cheeseburger, one chef salad, and one milk shake

11 two fishburgers, one chef salad, and two milk shakes

12 two chef salads and one milk

13 one fishburger and one low-fat milk

MIXED APPLICATIONS
Problem Solving
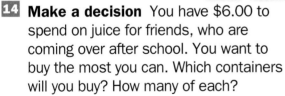

14 Make a decision You have $6.00 to spend on juice for friends, who are coming over after school. You want to buy the most you can. Which containers will you buy? How many of each?

Containers Of Juice Available	
Price	Size
$1.75	1.5 liters (small)
$2.10	1.75 liters (medium)
$4.00	3.75 liters (large)

15 What if you could buy one of each size. How much juice would you get?

16 Data Point Collect food labels. List metric measures in a table.

---

mixed review • test preparation

1 10 − 5.5

2 1.3 + 0.789 + 2.7

3 45.7 + 0.2 + 0.8

4 14.23 − 9.876

5 29.4 + 156 + 0.6

6 32 + 247 + 68

PART 1 Use Estimation

Jane just opened a boat rental business. These are her records for the first week. She estimates to find out if she has made enough money to pay her bills.

Income	
Canoes	$55.75
Rowboats	$40.00
Pedal boats	$28.75
Motorboats	$135.75

Expenses	
Rent for building	$55.00
Gasoline	$25.75
Part-time helpers' salaries	$142.75
Insurance (weekly cost)	$52.80

Work Together

Solve. Be prepared to explain your methods.

1. To underestimate a sum, you replace the addends with numbers that are less than the actual numbers. Should Jane underestimate her income or her expenses? Why?

2. To overestimate a sum, you replace the addends with numbers that are greater than the actual numbers. Should Jane overestimate her income or her expenses? Why?

3. Estimate her income and expenses to see if she made enough to pay her bills.

4. **What if** Jane's income is $500 each week. Do you think that is enough to pay her expenses? Explain your reasoning.

5. **Make a decision** José wants to buy three records. Should he underestimate or overestimate the total cost to make sure he has enough money?

James used the information in the table below to write this problem.

Sandy's Gift List		
Uncle Al	Belt	$11.25
Mom	Wallet	$13.15
Dad	Shirt	$17.25

Sandy's Funds Available	
Allowance	$5.75
Savings	$32.50
Birthday money	$22.50

Sandy wants to buy a belt for her uncle Al, a wallet for her mom, and a shirt for her dad. To see if she has enough money, should she underestimate or overestimate the total cost of the gifts? Should Sandy underestimate or overestimate how much money she has?

6 Solve James's problem.

7 Estimate to figure out whether Sandy has enough money.

8 **READING ARITHMETIC WRITING** **Use Tables** **Write a problem** of your own that can be solved by estimating using information from a table.

9 Solve your problem. Then, exchange problems with other students and check each other's problems and solutions.

James Mundy
Raymond Park Middle School
Indianapolis, IN

Turn the page for Practice Strategies. ➡

Menu

Choose five problems and solve them. Explain your methods.

1 Sal works part-time. His earnings for the last 3 weeks were $24.75, $21.50, and $32.71. He wants to buy a CD player for $90. Should he overestimate or underestimate his earnings? Why? Did he earn enough? How do you know?

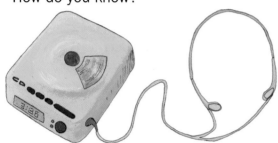

2 Sharon walked 0.75 mi from her home to the store and then walked back home. Jason walked 0.25 mi from his home to his aunt's house, then another 0.3 mi to the store. He walked 0.4 mi from the store back home. Who walked more and by how much?

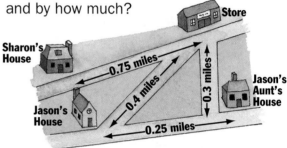

3 The animal shelter has twice as many dogs as cats. There are 93 animals in the shelter. How many are dogs? How many are cats?

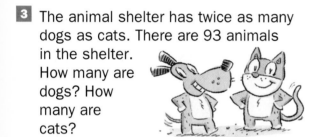

4 There are 119 sixth graders in Central School. There are 13 more boys than girls. How many boys are there?

5 Ship speeds are measured in knots, or nautical miles per hour. A knot is about 1.1508 mi per hour. The record for a U.S. Navy hovercraft is 91.9 knots. The *Alpha* submarine record is 45 knots. How much faster can the hovercraft go than the submarine?

6 You have $50. You want to buy a CD for $12.95, a T-shirt for $18.95, and two $15 videos. Should you overestimate or underestimate the total cost of the items to see if you have enough money? Why? Do you have enough money?

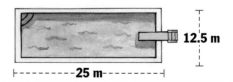

7 Find a pattern. Draw the next figure.

8 What is the perimeter of the pool?

12.5 m

25 m

Choose two problems and solve them. Explain your methods.

9 John, Pat, and Carla are friends. They have different jobs: writing, cooking, and selling, and different hobbies: reading, boating, and bowling. John likes boats but not cooking. Neither Pat nor Carla sell. Carla's hobby is active. Pat's job and hobby are related. Name each person's job and hobby.

11 Replace the letters with digits so the sum is correct. Always replace the same letter by the same digit.

$$\begin{array}{r} \text{SEND} \\ + \text{MORE} \\ \hline \text{MONEY} \end{array}$$

12 Make a table to show all the different ways you can make change for a quarter.

Dimes	Nickels	Pennies
2	1	0

10 Mr. Warren earns $1,100 each month. Each month he spends $375 on rent, $35 on electricity, and $18 for a phone bill. Use this information to complete a monthly budget for Mr. Warren.

Monthly Budget	
Rent	◼
Clothes	◼
Food	◼
Entertainment	◼
Savings	◼
Electricity	◼
Phone	◼

13 **At the Computer** Use the data in the table and make a double-bar graph to compare the skaters' performances.

Use graphing software. Enter Alice's, Cindy's, Joan's, and Lin's scores to make a double-bar graph. Write at least three conclusions based on the graph.

Name	Artistic Performance	Technical Performance
Alice	4.8	5.3
Cindy	5.1	5.7
Joan	5.4	4.6
Lin	5.2	5.0

Language and Mathematics

Complete the sentence. Use a word in the chart. (pages 42–75)

Vocabulary

variable
exponent
sum
thousandths
base
expression
hundredths

1 In 7^3 the 3 is the ■.

2 $x + 7$ is an example of an ■.

3 The place of 5 in 0.3456 is ■.

4 The ■ of 5 and 2 is 7.

5 The y in $235 - y$ is the ■.

6 The ■ in 5^2 is 5.

Concepts and Skills

Write the number in standard form. (pages 42, 46, 48)

7 5^3

8 10^4

9 5 and 17 hundredths

10 four billion, two thousand, six

11 nine and twenty-two thousandths

12 $(3 \times 10^5) + (4 \times 10^2) + 1$

13 $(6 \times 10^4) + (7 \times 10^2) + (9 \times 10)$

Complete. Write >, <, or =. (page 52)

14 0.789 ● 0.798

15 0.101 ● 0.1011

16 1.9 ● 1.0999

17 1.0076 − 0.8 ● 0.2076

18 45.78 + 9 ● 54.9

19 0.801 − 0.29 ● 0.05

Add or subtract. (pages 56, 60)

20
$$\begin{array}{r} \$12.65 \\ + \ 7.25 \\ \hline \end{array}$$

21
$$\begin{array}{r} 1.19 \\ - 0.9 \\ \hline \end{array}$$

22
$$\begin{array}{r} 34.05 \\ + 28.97 \\ \hline \end{array}$$

23
$$\begin{array}{r} 254.14 \\ - \ 98.391 \\ \hline \end{array}$$

24
$$\begin{array}{r} 47.6 \\ 28.978 \\ + 11.008 \\ \hline \end{array}$$

25 4.53 − 2.43

26 $12.19 − $0.25

27 0.1001 + 0.012 + 0.5

Write the letter of the best estimate. (pages 72, 74)

28 the distance a car travels in 5 hours **a.** 30 cm **b.** 300 mm **c.** 300 km

29 the capacity of a soup bowl **a.** 400 mL **b.** 40 L **c.** 400 L

Think critically. (page 60)

30 Analyze. Explain what the error is and correct it.
$$\begin{array}{r} 99.6 \\ - \ 27.25 \\ \hline 72.45 \end{array}$$

Analyze. Write *true* or *false*. Support your answer with an example or explanation. (pages 56, 60)

31 The sum of two decimals that are less than 1 is always less than 1.

32 The difference between two decimals that are less than 1 is always less than 1.

- -

MIXED APPLICATIONS
Problem Solving

(pages 68, 76)

33 A local fishing law forbids catching more than 10 lb of fish in one day. If you caught a 5.75 lb trout and a 3.7 lb bass, did you go over the limit? Explain.

34 Rachel has 127 baseball cards. Her brother has 69 cards. How many cards should Rachel give her brother so they each have the same number of cards?

35 Ann plans to buy a CD for $11.95, a postcard for $0.25, and a cassette tape for $8.75. About how much money will she spend?

36 A theater holds 456 seats. Suppose *x* represents the number of people sitting in the theater. Write an expression for the number of seats in which no one is sitting.

Use the heights given in the table for problems 37–40.

Heads		Middles		Bottoms	
A	2.6 cm	A	3.7 cm	A	1.2 cm
B	3.1 cm	B	4.6 cm	B	2.7 cm
C	3.5 cm	C	3.75 cm	C	3.25 cm

37 Sara made a monster with Head A, Middle B, and Bottom C. How tall is the monster?

38 Bill made a monster with Head B, Middle B, and Bottom B. How much shorter than Sara's is it?

39 Which parts will make the shortest monster? the tallest?

40 If you wanted a monster exactly 9 cm tall, which parts would you use?

Write using an exponent.

1 $9 \times 9 \times 9$

2 $20 \times 20 \times 20 \times 20$

Write in standard form.

3 6^2

4 three and sixteen thousandths

5 five million, four thousand

6 $(8 \times 10^5) + (6 \times 10^3) + (7 \times 10) + 3$

Compare. Write >, <, or =.

7 23,070 ● 23,007

8 0.023 ● 0.203

9 4.62 − 4.6 ● 0.02

Add or subtract.

10
$$\begin{array}{r} 117{,}560 \\ + \ 23{,}018 \\ \hline \end{array}$$

11
$$\begin{array}{r} 4.26 \\ - 1.8 \\ \hline \end{array}$$

12
$$\begin{array}{r} 17.62 \\ - \ 9.548 \\ \hline \end{array}$$

13
$$\begin{array}{r} 4.6 \\ 2.38 \\ + 11.15 \\ \hline \end{array}$$

14 $6.2 - 3.28$

15 $17.95 + 1.80

16 $544{,}009 - 516{,}992$

Evaluate the expression.

17 $x + 4$ for $x = 5$

18 $8.7 - y$ for $y = 3$

19 $a - 3$ for $a = 25.4$

Write the letter of the best estimate.

20 mass of a dog

a. 30 g **b.** 30 kg **c.** 300 kg

21 distance a plane travels in 3 hours

a. 2,400 km **b.** 2,400 m **c.** 24 cm

Solve.

22 Keandra spent $24 for a boat ride, $8.50 for dinner, and $4 for parking. If she had $50, how much does she have left?

23 On the two days before a swim meet, Troy swam a total of 1,836 meters. The first day, he swam 200 meters more than the second day. How many meters did he swim each day?

Use the table to answer problems 24–25.

24 What is the mean area of the Great Lakes?

25 Find the range in depth of the Great Lakes.

The Great Lakes		
	Area (in square meters)	Depth (in meters)
Superior	82,414	406
Huron	59,596	229
Michigan	58,016	281
Erie	25,719	64
Ontario	19,477	237

What Did You Learn?

To keep the fish healthy in an aquarium, you need to give them enough room to swim around. It is suggested that for every 2.5 cm of fish, there should be 3.8 L of water. Suppose you have a fish tank that holds 38 L of water. Plan the types of fish for your aquarium.

▶ What fish would you put in your aquarium? Show two different plans.

▶ Explain the math you used to create your plans. Tell how you could use addition, subtraction, and estimation to create a plan.

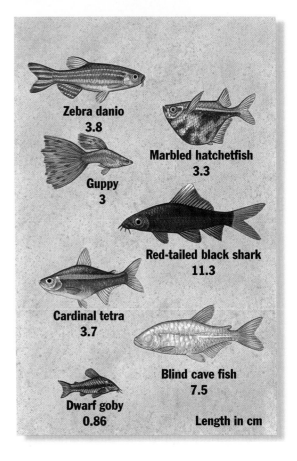

Zebra danio
3.8

Marbled hatchetfish
3.3

Guppy
3

Red-tailed black shark
11.3

Cardinal tetra
3.7

Blind cave fish
7.5

Dwarf goby
0.86

Length in cm

························ A Good Answer ·················
• clearly describes the reasons for each plan.
• includes accurate calculations.

 You may want to place your work in your portfolio.

What Do You Think

1 How would you tell someone else how to add and subtract decimals?

2 When do you check the reasonableness of your answer?
• After using a calculator
• After solving a problem
• Other. Explain.

OCEANS

The oceans represent a very important resource to all of us. All seawater is a solution of salt water. There are many different salts dissolved in the oceans, including a large amount of familiar table salt, known to chemists as sodium chloride (NaCl).

Because there is salt in seawater, ships that are in seawater can be loaded more heavily than those in fresh water. To see why, do this experiment.

You will need
- *golf ball or egg*
- *cup*
- *salt*
- *teaspoon*

Step 1   Put the golf ball into a cup half filled with water. Does it float or sink?

Step 2   Add a teaspoon of salt and stir until it dissolves. Test the golf ball again.

Step 3   Repeat Step 2 until no more salt will dissolve. Check to see if the golf ball floats after dissolving each spoonful. Can you make the ball float?

Step 4   Repeat Step 2 after the ball floats. What do you notice about the ball?

▶ What conclusions can you draw from your experiment?

▶ Why can a ship be loaded with more weight when it is in seawater than when it is in fresh water?

Cultural Note

In some cultures, salt was so valuable that it was used as money. The early Chinese used coins made of salt. In many areas around the Mediterranean Sea, salt cakes were used as money.

How Big Are the Oceans and Seas?

Oceans and seas cover vast areas. The United States covers 3.62 million (3,620,000) square miles. By comparison, the Pacific Ocean, the largest body of water on Earth, covers 69.4 million square miles! (That is 69,400,000 square miles.)

The table below lists some of the major oceans and seas in the world.

Sizes of Some Oceans and Seas (in millions of square miles)	
Ocean/Sea	**Area**
Aegean Sea	0.08
Atlantic Ocean	41.10
Arctic Ocean	5.44
Caribbean Sea	0.97
East China Sea	0.29
Gulf of Mexico	0.62
Indian Ocean	28.40
North Sea	0.22
Pacific Ocean	69.40

1 Make your own table like the one above and list the oceans and seas from largest to smallest in area.

2 How much larger is the North Sea than the smallest body of water listed in the table?

3 What is the total area of the world covered by the oceans and seas listed above?

4 How many square miles larger is the Caribbean Sea than the Gulf of Mexico?

At the Computer

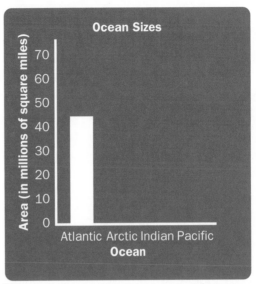

5 Use a graphing program to make a bar graph comparing the sizes of the four oceans in the table.

6 Write two statements based on your graph.

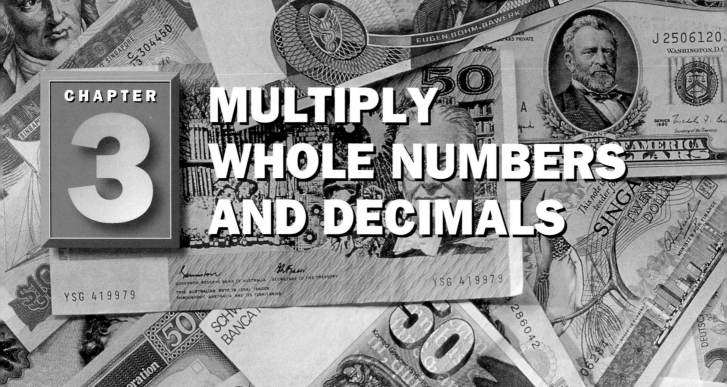

CHAPTER 3

MULTIPLY WHOLE NUMBERS AND DECIMALS

Money

Many sixth graders are thinking about earning money, both for now and for the future. This chapter's activities will help you think about money in your lives, and money in a much wider world.

What Do You Know ?

1 Does it cost more to buy 2 pounds of trail mix or 1.5 pounds of salt water candy? How would you find out?

2 Will a $10 bill be enough to pay for 2.5 pounds of dried fruit and 0.5 pound of mixed nuts? Explain.

3 Suppose you have $15 to spend on the snacks. What would you buy? List the amount of each snack that you would buy and find the total of your purchase.

$1.59 per pound   **$2.50 per pound**

$2.99 per pound   **$3.59 per pound**

Reread **Suppose you take 354 one-dollar bills to the bank and trade as many one-dollar bills for ten-dollar bills as you can. How many ten-dollar bills should you get?**

Sometimes you need to reread a problem one or more times to make sure that you understand the problem.

1 Reread the problem. How did your understanding of the problem change?

2 How can you solve the problem?

Vocabulary

patterns, p. 88
factor, p. 88
product, p. 89
Distributive
   Property, p. 89

Commutative
   Property, p. 89
Associative
   Property, p. 89

Identity
   Property, p. 89
Zero Property, p. 89

Patterns and Properties

Every country issues its own money. How many Zimbabwe dollars are 1,000 Zimbabwe $5 bills worth? 3,000 Zimbabwe $20 bills?

AFRICA

Zimbabwe

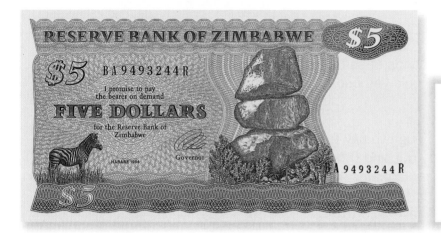

Cultural Note

Zimbabwe (zimh-BAHB-way) is a country in south central Africa. The currency in Zimbabwe, as in the United States, is named in dollars and cents.

You can use basic facts and **patterns** to find products mentally.

$5 \times 1 = 5$ $20 \times 3 = 60$
$5 \times 10 = 50$ $20 \times 30 = 600$
$5 \times 100 = 500$ $20 \times 300 = 6,000$
$5 \times 1,000 = 5,000$ $20 \times 3,000 = 60,000$

1,000 Zimbabwe $5 bills are worth 5,000 Zimbabwe dollars.

3,000 Zimbabwe $20 bills are worth 60,000 Zimbabwe dollars.

You can use similar patterns to multiply decimals by powers of ten.

Pattern A
$1 \times 2.9 = 2.9$
$10 \times 2.9 = 29.$
$100 \times 2.9 = 290.$
$1,000 \times 2.9 = 2,900.$

Pattern B
$1 \times 0.007 = 0.007$
$10 \times 0.007 = 0.07$
$100 \times 0.007 = 0.7$
$1,000 \times 0.007 = 7.$

Talk It Over

▶ **ALGEBRA: PATTERNS** What happens to the product of two whole numbers when you attach a zero to one of its **factors?** Why?

▶ What went wrong if you multiplied 42.09×100 on your calculator and got 420.9 for your answer?

▶ Explain where to place the decimal point in the product of a decimal times a power of ten.

In addition to patterns, you can use the **Distributive Property** to multiply mentally.

> **Distributive Property:** To multiply a sum by a number, you can multiply each addend by the number and add the products.

$$
\begin{aligned}
3 \times 46 &= 3 \times (40 + 6) \\
&= (3 \times 40) + (3 \times 6) \leftarrow \textbf{Distributive Property} \\
&= 120 + 18 \\
&= 138
\end{aligned}
$$

Check Out the Glossary
For vocabulary words, see page 643.

Here are four more multiplication properties to help you.

Commutative Property	**Associative Property**
The order of the factors does not change the product.	The way factors are grouped does not change the product.
$2 \times 8 = 8 \times 2$	$(3 \times 4) \times 5 = 3 \times (4 \times 5)$
Identity Property	**Zero Property**
The product of any factor and 1 equals the factor.	The product of any factor and zero equals zero.
$23 \times 1 = 23$	$87 \times 0 = 0$

More Examples

A
$$
\begin{aligned}
4 \times 58 &= 4 \times (50 + 8) \\
&= (4 \times 50) + (4 \times 8) \\
&= 200 + 32 \\
&= 232
\end{aligned}
$$

B
$$
\begin{aligned}
5 \times 7 \times 20 &= 5 \times 20 \times 7 \\
&= 100 \times 7 \\
&= 700
\end{aligned}
$$

Check for Understanding

⭐ **ALGEBRA: PATTERNS Multiply mentally. Explain your methods.**

1 8×34 **2** 50×200 **3** $50 \times 12 \times 2$ **4** $3,456 \times 0$ **5** 100×0.03

Critical Thinking: Generalize   Explain your reasoning.

6 How can the Distributive Property help you multiply mentally? Give an example.

7 How can the Commutative Property help you multiply mentally? Give an example.

CHECK

Turn the page for Practice. ➡

Practice

✦ ALGEBRA: PATTERNS Complete the patterns.

1
$47 \times 1 = 47$
$47 \times 10 = \blacksquare$
$47 \times 100 = \blacksquare$
$47 \times 1,000 = \blacksquare$

2
$4 \times 6 = 24$
$4 \times 60 = \blacksquare$
$4 \times 600 = \blacksquare$
$4 \times 6,000 = \blacksquare$

3
$5 \times 4 = 20$
$50 \times 4 = \blacksquare$
$500 \times 4 = \blacksquare$
$5,000 \times 4 = \blacksquare$

4
$3.12 \times 1 = 3.12$
$3.12 \times 10 = \blacksquare$
$3.12 \times 100 = \blacksquare$
$3.12 \times 1,000 = \blacksquare$

5
$1 \times \$0.05 = \$0.05$
$10 \times \$0.05 = \blacksquare$
$100 \times \$0.05 = \blacksquare$
$1,000 \times \$0.05 = \blacksquare$

6
$7.5 \times 1 = 7.5$
$7.5 \times 10 = \blacksquare$
$7.5 \times 100 = \blacksquare$
$7.5 \times 1,000 = \blacksquare$

✦ ALGEBRA Complete. What property of multiplication did you use?

7 $67 \times \blacksquare = 43 \times 67$

8 $4 \times (\blacksquare + 7) = (4 \times 50) + (4 \times 7)$

9 $(194 \times 5) \times \blacksquare = 194 \times (5 \times 2)$

10 $8 \times (50 + 6) = (\blacksquare \times 50) + (8 \times 6)$

11 $\blacksquare \times 8 = 0$

12 $(4 \times 6) \times \blacksquare = 4 \times (6 \times 8)$

13 $564 \times 1 = \blacksquare$

14 $49 \times 5 = \blacksquare \times 49$

Multiply mentally.

15 6×100

16 7×80

17 $30 \times \$50$

18 60×900

19 $1,000 \times 43$

20 50×60

21 4×23

22 $5 \times \$34$

23 $817 \times 0 \times 7$

24 9×52

25 $5 \times 13 \times 2$

26 7×42

27 $30 \times \$40$

28 23×8

29 $5 \times 693 \times 2$

30 $543 \times 1 \times 10$

31 $4 \times 8 \times 5$

32 $6,000 \times 30$

33 $30 \times 20 \times 50$

34 $800 \times \$600$

35 6.4×10

36 $\$5.95 \times 100$

37 $4.82 \times 1,000$

38 100×3.05

39 $1,000 \times 0.4$

40 10×0.08

41 10×0.106

42 1.3×100

• Make It Right •

43 Jean mentally multiplied 6×45 and got 54. Here is how she explained her answer. Explain what the error is and correct it.

$$6 \times 45 = (6 \times 4) + (6 \times 5)$$
$$= 24 + 30$$
$$= 54$$

44 There are 42 students in each of 3 buses going to an exhibition of Central African art. How many students are going to the exhibition?

46 A traveler has 20 Zimbabwe $50 bills, 30 Zimbabwe $20 bills, and 40 Zimbabwe $2 bills. How many Zimbabwe dollars does she have?

47 **Write a problem** that you can solve by multiplying mentally. Solve the problem. Then give it to other students to solve.

48 In 1992, Zimbabwe exported 1.5 billion dollars' worth of gold, sugar, and other products. It imported 1.8 billion dollars' worth of goods. What is the difference in billions of dollars between their exports and imports?

49 A coin club has 12 members. Five members are 12 years old, four members are 13 years old, and the other members are 9, 10, and 11 years old. What is the mean age of the members?

50 How many coins were 299 bamboo sticks worth in China? **SEE INFOBIT.**

45 **Make a decision** Sam was given the bill below at the end of his dinner. Should he pay the total amount shown? Tell why or why not.

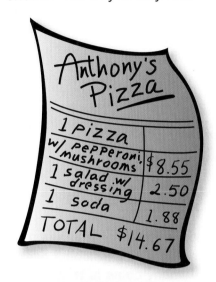

Anthony's Pizza

1 Pizza w/ pepperoni, w/ mushrooms	$8.55
1 salad w/ dressing	2.50
1 soda	1.88
TOTAL	$14.67

INFOBIT
During the 19th century in China, a bamboo stick was worth 100 coins.

---

mixed review • test preparation

Use the stem-and-leaf plot for problems 1–2.

1 How many of the students surveyed read at least 20 hours a week?

2 What conclusions can you draw from the plot?

Reading Hours per Week

0	4 7 9
1	0 2 3 4 5 6 7 9
2	0 0 1 1 2 3 3 4 5 5 6
3	1 2

Key: 1 | 2 = 12

Estimate the sum or difference.

3 5.67 + 8.21   **4** 23.894 − 14.9   **5** 686 − 85.76   **6** 4,356 + 894.33

Estimate Products

Washington, D.C. has great places to visit. You can even watch as sheets of dollar bills are printed at the Bureau of Printing and Engraving. If 29 students pay $18.50 each for a trip to Washington, about how much did the trip cost?

You can estimate products to solve this problem. Round both factors and multiply mentally.

29 × $18.50
↓   ↓
30 × $20 = $600

The class needs about $600.

The Philadelphia Mint can make 12 billion coins in a year. That's 381.52 coins every second. About how many coins is that in one minute?

Estimate the number per minute.   381.52 × 60
↓   ↓
400   × 60 = 24,000

The Mint can make about 24,000 coins per minute.

More Examples

A Estimate: 4 × 4,923
↓   ↓
4 × 5,000 = 20,000

B Estimate: 14.2 × 237.467
↓   ↓
10 ×   200 = 2,000

Check for Understanding

Estimate the product.

1 3 × 812   **2** 18 × $8.95   **3** 7,835 × 7   **4** 427.89 × 3.2

5 75 × 82.9   **6** 97.865 × $98.54   **7** 462 × 521.97   **8** 12 × 765.92

Critical Thinking: Analyze   **Explain your reasoning.**

9 Look at the estimate of the amount of money the class needs for the trip. How would an estimate found by using only the front digits compare with the estimate shown?

10 Look at Example B. How will the exact answer compare to the estimate?

Practice

Estimate the product.

1 7 × 341

2 12 × $5.87

3 712 × 431

4 172 × $43.65

5 13.532 × 41.7

6 230 × 1,254

7 71 × $821.65

8 56 × 92

9 9.134 × 23.4007

10 18 × $357.65

11 32 × 75.12

12 9 × 543.78

Estimate. Write > or <.

13 38.7 × 47.4 ● 2,186.25

14 24 × $31.25 ● $582.25

15 126 × $41.75 ● $3,862.20

16 2.4 × 107.12 ● 186.25

Estimate the cost.

17 32 magnifying glasses

18 20 magnifying glasses

19 28 tweezers and 28 brushes

20 36 bottles of rubbing alcohol and 18 bags of cotton balls

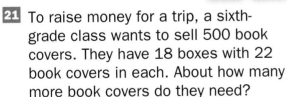

MIXED APPLICATIONS
Problem Solving

21 To raise money for a trip, a sixth-grade class wants to sell 500 book covers. They have 18 boxes with 22 book covers in each. About how many more book covers do they need?

22 **Reread** The Mint spends 5.78 cents to make a half-dollar. About how much does it cost to make $100 in half-dollars? Reread the problem. List the steps needed to solve the problem. Then solve.

more to explore

Estimating Products Using Compatible Numbers

Estimate: 26.75 × 4.25

Think: 26.75 is about 25 and 4.25 is about 4.

25 × 4 = 100

Use compatible numbers to estimate the product. Explain your thinking.

1 14.41 × 2.13

2 26.28 × $3.21

3 6.7 × 17.8

4 26.87 × 12.324

5 51.178 × 8.976

6 1.78 × 16.1

Multiply Whole Numbers

Suppose you have a job mowing lawns from May through September. If you earn $48 per week for each of those 23 weeks, how much will you earn?

Multiply: 23 × $48

Estimate the product.

Think: 20 × $50 = $1,000

To find the exact number use pencil and paper or a calculator.

Step 1	Step 2	Step 3
Multiply by the ones.	**Multiply by the tens.**	**Add the products.**

Step 1:
$$\begin{array}{r} \overset{2}{48} \\ \times 23 \\ \hline 144 \end{array} \leftarrow \textbf{3} \times \textbf{48}$$

Step 2:
$$\begin{array}{r} \overset{1}{\underset{}{\overset{2}{48}}} \\ \times 23 \\ \hline 144 \\ 960 \end{array} \leftarrow \textbf{20} \times \textbf{48}$$

Step 3:
$$\begin{array}{r} \overset{1}{\underset{}{\overset{2}{48}}} \\ \times 23 \\ \hline 144 \\ 960 \\ \hline 1,104 \end{array}$$

Calculator   23 × 48 = **1104.**

You will earn $1,104.

More Examples

A
$$\begin{array}{r} \overset{5\,5}{7,078} \\ \times \quad 7 \\ \hline 49,546 \end{array}$$

B
$$\begin{array}{r} \overset{1}{83} \\ \times 40 \\ \hline 3,320 \end{array}$$

C
$$\begin{array}{r} \overset{2}{\underset{}{\overset{4}{\overset{5}{608}}}} \\ \times 367 \\ \hline 4\,256 \\ 36\,480 \\ 182\,400 \\ \hline 223,136 \end{array}$$
$\leftarrow \textbf{7} \times \textbf{608}$
$\leftarrow \textbf{60} \times \textbf{608}$
$\leftarrow \textbf{300} \times \textbf{608}$

Calculator   367 × 608 = **223136.**

Check for Understanding

Multiply. Remember to estimate.

1 3,452 × 7
2 47 × 27
3 567 × 18
4 629 × 384

Critical Thinking: Analyze   **Explain your reasoning.**

5 Explain how to use the Distributive Property to multiply 23 × 48.

6 How many digits can be in the product if you multiply a 3-digit whole number by a 2-digit whole number? two 3-digit whole numbers?

Practice

Multiply. Remember to estimate.

1   37   × 5

2 $283   × 6

3   906   × 7

4   3,987   × 5

5   1,063   × 4

6   95   × 87

7   42   × 58

8   809   × 86

9   2,391   × 70

10 $529   × 84

11 $755   × 62

12   645   × 203

13   1,009   × 45

14 $299   × 312

15   6,008   × 42

16 742 × 72

17 4,507 × 6

18 93 × 34

19 603 × $483

20 785 × 37

21 982 × 6

22 8,347 × $695

23 708 × 29

MIXED APPLICATIONS
Problem Solving

24 What if you charge $15 to mow a lawn, and $20 to both mow and trim the lawn. How much will you earn if you mow 12 lawns, and both mow and trim 5 lawns?

25 Data Point Survey 10 or more students in your class to find out what hobbies they have. Display the data on a chart or graph. Write a conclusion about the data.

26 Logical reasoning Find the hidden digits in the problem at the right. Explain your methods.

$$1\,\blacksquare4\blacksquare \times 8 = 8{,}368$$

27 Make a decision Would you prefer to have 312 five-dollar bills or 72 twenty-dollar bills? Explain your reasoning.

more to explore

Estimating Sums by Clustering

Sometimes several numbers *cluster,* or group, around one number. You can use *clustering* to estimate sums.

Estimate: 4.7 + 6.1 + 5.2 + 4.9   **Think:** All of the numbers are about 5.
           4 × 5 = 20   The sum is about 20.

Estimate the sum. Explain your reasoning.

1 8.9 + 11.1 + 9.7 + 10.2

2 24.7 + 26.867 + 25.009

3 98.76 + 101.438 + 99.75 + 102.07

4 9.501 + 8.987 + 9.0075 + 8.7

Multiply Decimals by Whole Numbers

If you ever get to travel in another country, you'll pay for items in its currency. Suppose you are in Portugal. The eight 2.5-escudo coins in your pocket are too bulky. How many 10-escudo coins could you exchange them for?

First find out how many escudos you have.

Multiply: 8 × 2.5

Estimate the product.   **Think:** 8 × 3 = 24

To find the exact product, use paper and pencil.

Step 1	**Step 2**
Multiply as with whole numbers.	**Use your estimate to place the decimal point in the product.**
2.5 × 8 — 200	2.5 **Think:** The product is about 24. × 8 Place the decimal point — between the zeros. 20.0

Cultural Note
Like the United States, Portugal has coins of different values. Three of the coins are worth 2.5 escudos (e-SKOO-dohs), 10 escudos, and 20 escudos.

You could exchange the 20 escudos for two 10-escudo coins.

More Examples

A
```
  2 54
  5.487      Estimate to place
×      6     the decimal point.
32.922   Think: 6 × 5 = 30
```

B
```
    3
  0.4      Estimate to place
×   8      the decimal point.
  3.2      Think: 1/2 of 8 is 4.
```

Check for Understanding

Multiply. Use an estimate to place the decimal point.

1 3.05 × 16   **2** 0.7 × 12   **3** 6 × $4.25   **4** 0.484 × 9

Critical Thinking: Generalize   **Explain your reasoning.**

5 How is the number of decimal places in the product of a whole number and a decimal related to the number of decimal places in the decimal?

6 **Journal**   **What if** you multiply a whole number by a decimal less than 1. Will the product be less than or greater than the whole number? Give examples.

Practice

Multiply. Remember to estimate.

1   5.7
    × 6

2 $4.21
    × 9

3   6.4
    × 0.6

4   7.03
    × 7

5   543
    × 0.08

6 $5.24 × 8

7 0.875 × 6

8 563 × 0.7

9 $0.23 × 8

10 6 × 0.417

11 43 × 2.41

12 9 × $0.65

13 52 × 0.184

14 9.74 × 65

15 74 × 0.067

16 2.104 × 33

17 46 × $0.34

18 38 × $0.80

19 68 × 13.06

20 $5 × 0.25

21 28 × 0.02

MIXED APPLICATIONS
Problem Solving

22 Cole has three 20-escudo coins, four 10-escudo coins, and five 2.5-escudo coins. How many escudos is that?

23 Kari buys two postcards for $1.25 each, a gift for $14.95, and film for $4.89. How much did she spend?

24 Does the Swedish copperplate money weigh about as much as a math book, a car, or a dog? **SEE INFOBIT.**

> **INFOBIT**
> In the 18th century, Sweden issued the largest coins ever made—copperplate money. These coins could weigh up to 19 kg.

Cultural Connection Australian Money

Australia's first coins were made from Spanish silver dollars during the 19th century. They were called "holey dollars" because a small plug was punched from the center of the coins. How many shillings was the plug and the "holey dollar" worth in Australia?

Think: (4 × 1.25) + 1.25 = 5 + 1.25 = 6.25 shillings

The outer ring was worth four times as much as the plug. The plug was worth 1.25 shillings.

Write the value in shillings of each combination of coins.

1 3 plugs

2 1 outer ring and 6 plugs

3 5 plugs and 2 whole coins

Multiply Whole Numbers and Decimals   **97**

Solve Multistep Problems

L E A R N

Read Suppose there are two part-time jobs available at a local market. One pays $11.75 per day for 5 days per week. The other pays $5.25 per hour for 11 hours each week. Which job pays more per week? How much more?

Plan To solve this problem, you need to answer several questions:

▶ How much does the first job pay each week?
▶ How much does the second job pay each week?
▶ What is the difference between the weekly earnings?

Solve **Step 1** Find how much the first job pays each week.   Note: **Per** means for each.

$$
\begin{array}{ccccc}
5 & \times & \$11.75 & = & \$58.75 \\
\text{number of days} & & \text{pay each day} & & \text{pay each week}
\end{array}
$$

Step 2 Find how much the second job pays each week.

$$
\begin{array}{ccccc}
11 & \times & \$5.25 & = & \$57.75 \\
\text{number of hours} & & \text{pay each hour} & & \text{pay each week}
\end{array}
$$

Step 3 Subtract to find the difference. $58.75 - $57.75 = $1

The first job pays $1 more each week.

Look Back Could you have solved the problem in a different way? Explain.

C H E C K

Check for Understanding

1 What if the hourly pay is changed to $5.50? Which job will pay more? How much more?

Critical Thinking: Analyze   Explain your reasoning.

2 What questions did you answer to solve problem 1?

3 How could you solve problem 1 in another way?

1 Mary earns $5.75 per hour and works 12 hours a week. José earns $5.25 per hour and works 14 hours a week. Who earns more weekly? Explain.

2 The oldest known records of the use of money are from ancient Mesopotamia, about 2500 B.C. About how long ago was that?

3 Miko jogs 4.5 miles, then walks 2.75 miles. Her brother walks twice as far and jogs 1.25 fewer miles. How many miles does Miko's brother jog and walk altogether?

4 A shop is having a sale on T-shirts. If you buy 3 T-shirts at $6.00 each, you get one free. Mrs. Smith bought $36 worth of T-shirts for her family. How many T-shirts did she get?

5 Use the digits 1, 2, 3, 4, 5, 6 to form three 3-digit numbers with the sum of 999. Use each digit at least once.

6 Al has $5 more than Joe. Joe has $2 less than Terry, who has $22.50. How much do Al and Joe each have?

Use the table for problems 7–8.

7 **Make a decision** Use the sign to decide which is worth more: two 1879M Australian sovereign gold pieces and one 1903M Australian sovereign gold piece or two 10 pesos gold pieces from Chile dated 1853S.

8 **Data Point** Draw a graph that also shows the data in The Coin Shop sign. Explain why the type of graph you chose fits this data.

— THE COIN SHOP —

Country/Denomination	Date	Price
AUSTRALIA		
SOVEREIGN GOLD	1886M	$150
SOVEREIGN GOLD	1879M	$150
SOVEREIGN GOLD	1903M	$135
CHILE		
10 PESOS GOLD	1853S	$240
FINLAND		
10 MARKKA	1882	$120

9 **Write a problem** that needs more than one step to solve. Solve your problem and then exchange it with another student. Compare the steps you each followed to solve each other's problems.

10 Steve has a $5 coupon from a bookstore. He must spend more than $25 to use the coupon. He buys 3 books for $6.75 each and 2 books for $2.95 each. Will he be able to use the coupon? Explain.

11 You need 18 lb of flour to bake cookies. How many of each bag of the two bags at right would you buy? What would be your total cost? Explain.

FLOUR 5lb $3.80

FLOUR 3lb $2.35

Multiply mentally.

1 70 × 500 **2** 37 × 4 **3** 23 × 2 × 5 **4** 62 × 1,000

5 80 × $50 **6** 2 × 97 × 50 **7** 47 × 10,000 **8** 8 × $55

Estimate the product.

9 3 × 678 **10** 28 × $11.43 **11** 4 × 6,838 **12** 6 × 521.897

13 3 × $286.65 **14** 9 × 983 **15** 23 × 754 **16** 47 × 305.924

Multiply.

17
```
  6,103
×     9
```
18
```
   72
× 46
```
19
```
  0.342
×     9
```
20
```
  $25.49
×     18
```
21
```
  53.05
×    12
```

22 14 × $10.65 **23** 7 × 0.69 **24** 643 × 831 **25** 5.091 × 1,000

Use the sign for ex. 26–28.

26 How much does it cost to buy 1 T-shirt and 10 postcards?

27 You buy 2 maps, 12 postcards, 2 mugs, and 1 T-shirt. How much change should you receive from $50?

28 **What if** you have $20. Do you have enough to buy 2 mugs and 6 postcards? Explain your reasoning.

```
INFORMATION                Tourist
                           CENTER

MAP      - $5.95
HAT      - 12.99
T-Shirt  - 15.25
MUG      - 7.69
Postcard - 0.50
```

Solve. Use mental math when you can.

29 A cashier's drawer has ten $20 bills, twenty-five $10 bills, ten $5 bills, and forty $1 bills. How much money is in the drawer altogether?

30 The first 600 people into the soccer stadium will get a free hat. About how many more hats are needed if 21 boxes with 24 hats in each box have been given away?

31 Gary's Electronic Store is selling blank video cassettes at $3.95 each. Anne's Video sells the same cassettes in packages of 4 for $14.40 each package. If you want 4 cassettes, which is cheaper? By how much?

32 At the Super Saver Market, flour costs $0.26 per pound and brown sugar costs $0.37 per pound. How much does it cost to buy 3 lb of flour and 4 lb of brown sugar?

33 Describe how you would find the product 48 × 0.82.

developing number sense
MATH CONNECTION

Use Properties to Multiply Mentally

Sometimes you can use the properties of multiplication to find the product of whole numbers and decimals mentally.

Multiply: 4 × $3.50

Think: 4 × ($3 + $0.50) = (4 × $3) + (4 × $0.50)
$$= \quad \$12 \quad + \quad \$2$$
$$= \quad \$14$$

Here is a way to use another Distributive Property.

3 × $1.95 = 3 × ($2 − $0.05)
$$= (3 \times \$2) - (3 \times \$0.05)$$
$$= \quad \$6 \quad - \quad \$0.15$$
$$= \quad \$5.85$$

Other multiplication properties:

3 × 4.5 = 4.5 × 3 ← **Commutative Property**   1 × 0.9 = 0.9 ← **Identity Property**

3 × (2 × 0.2) = (3 × 2) × 0.2 ← **Associative Property**   1.2 × 0 = 0 ← **Zero Property**

Use properties of multiplication to multiply mentally.

1 3 × $2.10   **2** 8 × $2.50   **3** 4 × $1.99   **4** 4 × 9.5

5 4 × $2.99   **6** 6 × $4.95   **7** 5 × $3.05   **8** 6 × $3.20

9 2 × $1.99   **10** (6 × 3.2) × 1   **11** (7 × 0.5) × 2   **12** 10 × 10.9

13 4 × 37.9   **14** 6.5 × 4.3 × 0   **15** 1 × 0.9 × 1

Solve. Use mental math when you can.

16 How much would it cost 6 adults to see an 8 P.M. movie?

17 How much would it cost 3 adults and 3 children to see a 3 P.M. movie?

18 How much more would it cost 2 adults and 2 children to see a 7 P.M. movie instead of a 5 P.M. movie?

TICKETS	PRICE
Adult	$6.50
Children under 12	$4.50

Tickets for all shows before 6 PM

$5.50 for Adults
$3.50 for Children

MAKE MONEY DECISIONS

Congratulations! You have won the grand prize. You can choose either a check for $50,000 or a stack of $1-bills as tall as you are. Which should we send you?

To make this decision, work in a group to answer the following questions:
a. How tall are you?
b. How many dollar bills are in a stack that is as tall as you are?

You will need
• *ruler or measuring tape*

Make Money Decisions

1 Assume that the thickness of a dollar bill is about the same as the thickness of a sheet of paper. Use sheets of paper to figure out the value of a stack of $1 bills the height of each group member.

2 For each group member, decide which is worth more, the $50,000 or the stack of $1 bills equal to his or her height.

3 **What if** the bills were $5 bills? $10 bills? $20 bills? How would that change your decisions for each group member?

Report Your Findings

4 Prepare a report on your findings. Include the following:

▶ Explain what you were trying to find out.

▶ Show a table or graph displaying the data you collected.

▶ Explain the reasons for your choices (check or stack of bills) for each group member when the bills are $1 bills, $5 bills, $10 bills, or $20 bills.

5 Compare your conclusions with those of other groups.

Revise your work.
▶ Is your table or graph clearly labeled and accurate?
▶ Do your conclusions make sense based on your data?

MORE TO INVESTIGATE

PREDICT how much money would be in a stack of each of the following coins as tall as you: quarters, dimes, nickels, pennies.

EXPLORE how checks, bank cards, and credit cards are used.

FIND *money, the U.S. Mint,* or another money-related topic in an almanac, encyclopedia, or on-line computer service. Find other interesting facts about money and bring them in to share with the class.

Multiply Decimals by Decimals

You can use models to help you multiply decimals.

Multiply: 0.2×0.8

Estimate.   **Think:** 0.8 is about 1, and 1 times 0.2 is 0.2.

Use models to find 0.2×0.8.

Step 1	**Step 2**	**Step 3**
Shade the grid to show one factor.	Use a different color and shade the grid for the second factor.	Count the squares that were shaded twice.
0.8 is yellow.	Shade 0.2 of 0.8 blue.	16 hundredths is shaded twice.

Work Together

Work in a group. Use models to help you fill in the products in the table.

You will need
- *graph paper*

▶ How are the products alike? different?

▶ Are the products always less than their factors? Explain in terms of the models.

×	0.4	0.7	0.9
0.2			
0.5			
0.8			

Make Connections

Models can help you find 0.4×0.7. Use the model to place the decimal point.

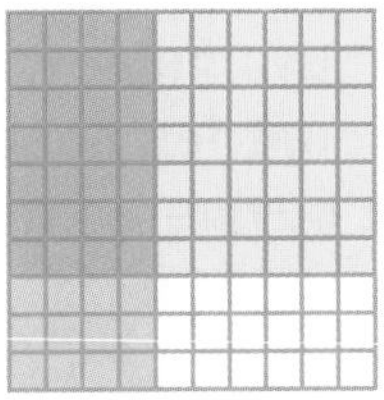

Think: 28 hundredths is shaded green.

$0.4 \times 0.7 = 0.28$

▶ How could an estimate have helped you place the decimal point?

Check for Understanding

Find the product.

1 0.6×0.7

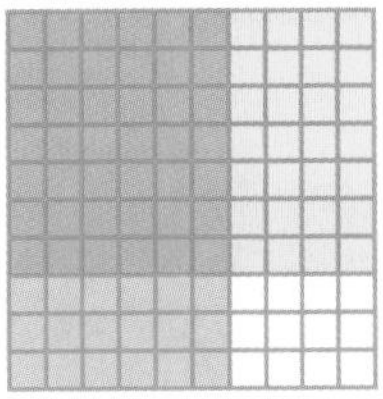

2 0.2×0.3

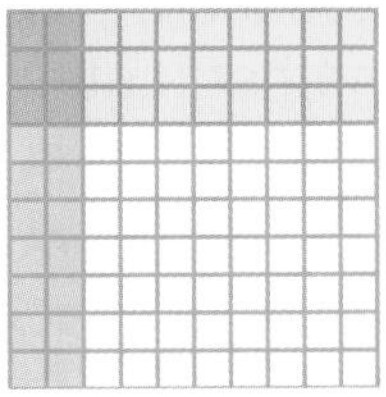

3 0.1×0.8

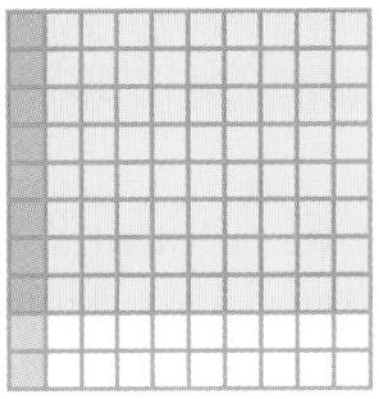

Critical Thinking: Generalize **Explain your reasoning.**

4 When multiplying a tenth by a tenth, how are the number of decimal places in the factors related to the number of decimal places in the products?

5 What rule can you state about where to place the decimal point when multiplying a tenth by a tenth?

Practice

Find the product. You may use models to help you multiply.

1 0.9×0.7 **2** 0.7×0.3 **3** 0.4×0.3 **4** 0.1×0.5

5 0.3×0.3 **6** 0.6×0.8 **7** 0.5×0.2 **8** 0.6×0.9

9 Find the product of 0.6 and 0.2.

10 Find the product of 0.8 and 0.5.

11 The factors are 0.8 and 0.3.

12 The factors are 0.6 and 0.5.

Compare. Write <, >, or =.

13 0.3×0.5 ● 0.2×0.7 **14** 0.4×0.9 ● 0.8×0.5 **15** 0.5×0.5 ● 0.9×0.1

16 0.8×0.8 ● 0.6 **17** 0.1×0.3 ● 0.3×0.1 **18** 0.9×0.8 ● 1

Extra Practice, page 586

Multiply Decimals

Sandy Pandiscio has a great job—she buys money. Companies that do business in other countries need currency for each country. Think about buying an item for 0.9 pesos when one peso is worth $0.15 in U.S. money. What is its cost in U.S. money?

Multiply: $0.9 \times \$0.15$

Estimate. **Think:** 0.9 is about 1.
So $0.9 \times \$0.15$
is about $0.15.

In the last lesson, you used models to multiply decimals. Here is another method.

To place the decimal point in the product, use the estimate or count decimal places.

Step 1	Step 2
Multiply as with whole numbers.	**Write the decimal point in the product.**
$\begin{array}{r} \$0.1\ 5 \\ \times\quad 0.9 \\ \hline 1\ 3\ 5 \end{array}$	$\begin{array}{r} \$0.1\ 5 \leftarrow \textbf{2 decimal places} \\ \times\quad 0.9 \leftarrow \textbf{1 decimal place} \\ \hline 0.1\ 3\ 5 \leftarrow \textbf{3 decimal places} \end{array}$

Rounded to the nearest cent, the item costs $0.14.

Multiply: 6.8×3.79

Estimate. **Think:** $7 \times 4 = 28$

Step 1	Step 2
Multiply as with whole numbers.	**Write the decimal point in the product.**
$\begin{array}{r} 3.7\ 9 \\ \times\quad 6.8 \\ \hline 3\ 0\ 3\ 2 \\ 2\ 2\ 7\ 4\ 0 \\ \hline 2\ 5\ 7\ 7\ 2 \end{array}$	$\begin{array}{r} 3.7\ 9 \leftarrow \textbf{2 decimal places} \\ \times\quad 6.8 \leftarrow \textbf{1 decimal place} \\ \hline 3\ 0\ 3\ 2 \\ 2\ 2\ 7\ 4\ 0 \\ \hline 2\ 5.7\ 7\ 2 \leftarrow \textbf{3 decimal places} \end{array}$

Cultural Note

The eagle, the snake, and the cactus pictured on all Mexican coins are part of an ancient Aztec legend. This legend tells of the place where Mexico City was built.

Talk It Over

▶ Kim used a calculator to multiply 0.5×0.6. The display showed 0.3 instead of 0.30. Explain why.

Sometimes you may need to insert a zero in the product to place the decimal point.

Multiply: 0.06 × 0.456

Estimate.   **Think:** 0.456 is about a half. Half of 0.06 is 0.03.
                      So 0.6 × 0.456 is about 0.03.

Use paper and pencil or a calculator to find the exact answer.

Step 1	**Step 2**
Multiply as with whole numbers.	**Write the decimal point in the product.**

Step 1:
```
  0.4 5 6
×   0.0 6
───────────
  2 7 3 6
```

Step 2:
```
  0.4 5 6  ← 3 decimal places
×   0.0 6  ← 2 decimal places
──────────────
0.0 2 7 3 6  ← 5 decimal places
```

 0.06 × 0.456 = **0.02736**

More Examples

A
```
  0.0 4 2  ← 3 decimal places
×     0.9  ← 1 decimal place
──────────────
  0.0 3 7 8  ← 4 decimal places
```

B
```
    3.0 4  ← 2 decimal places
×  2.3 5  ← 2 decimal places
──────────
  1 5 2 0
  9 1 2 0
6 0 8 0 0
──────────
7.1 4 4 0  ← 4 decimal places
```

 2.35 × 3.04 =   **7.144**

Check for Understanding

Multiply. Round money amounts to the nearest cent. Estimate to check.

1
```
  0.7
×0.9
```

2
```
  0.47
× 0.5
```

3
```
42.087
×   0.01
```

4
```
$1.75
× 2.47
```

5
```
  0.123
× 0.54
```

6 0.5 × 0.37   **7** 6.8 × 7.2   **8** 0.12 × 0.7   **9** 8.9 × $93.75

Critical Thinking: Generalize   Give examples.

10 What rule could you state about placing the decimal point in a product of a decimal times a decimal?

11 If you multiply a number by a decimal less than 1, how does the product compare with the original number?

12 Without multiplying, how can you tell that 6.5 × 0.2 > 6.5 × 0.02?

Turn the page for Practice.
Multiply Whole Numbers and Decimals   **107**

Practice

Multiply. Round money amounts to the nearest cent. Remember to estimate.

| **1** | 0.4
 × 0.7 | **2** | 5.7
 × 9.2 | **3** | 4.21
 × 1.6 | **4** | $1.84
 × 2.3 | **5** | 0.18
 × 0.07 |

| **6** | 3.9
 × 0.78 | **7** | 41.05
 × 6.82 | **8** | $12.15
 × 4.7 | **9** | 0.532
 × 4.7 | **10** | 2.4
 × 4.5 |

11 2.1 × 0.37

12 0.71 × 0.002

13 $5.12 × 0.067

14 25.075 × 0.2

15 0.19 × 0.3

16 7.4 × 3.69

17 0.23 × $5.46

18 0.1 × 0.5

19 5.3 × $8.25

20 1.76 × 0.7

21 0.009 × 0.1

22 0.04 × $2.43

23 8.32 × 4.7

24 4.32 × 3.78

25 0.316 × $5.37

26 0.002 × 6.7

27 2.75 × 2.4

28 3.008 × $2.71

29 5.07 × 2.3

30 6.6 × 0.147

Multiply mentally. Explain your methods.

31 6 × 0.20

32 0.5 × 10

33 50 × 0.08

34 100 × 0.4

35 0.3 × 0.6

36 0.8 × 0.7

37 3 × 4.01

38 4 × $0.99

• • • • • • • • • • • • • • • • • **Make It Right** • • • • • • • • • • • • • • • • • • •

39 Tomás multiplied 0.8 × 0.5 and said the product is 0.04. Tell what the error is and correct it.

MIXED APPLICATIONS

Problem Solving

40 Suppose a roll of film costs 3.29 British pounds. What if a British pound is worth $1.61 in U.S. money that day. How much does the roll of film cost in U.S. money?

41 A U.S. dollar was worth 6.75 Mexican pesos on Monday, and 6.84 on Tuesday. How many more pesos would you get for $10 on Tuesday than on Monday?

42 **Make a decision** Driving to work costs $17.50 in tolls, $25 for gas, and $11.75 for parking each week. Per week, the train costs $35.80 and the bus from the train station costs $15.50. Which would you choose?

43 **Data Point** Use the table on page 634 of the Databank to make a line graph of the value of the U.S. dollar in Japanese yen over the ten-year period. Draw two conclusions from the graph.

Travel Around the World Game!

You will need
- *1 number cube*
- *1 marker for each player*

Play the Game

▶ Two or more players take turns.

▶ Put your marker on **Go Abroad.** Roll the number cube to decide the number of steps to move.

▶ Find the amount of U.S. dollars you get when you land on a country. Keep track of all the money you get.

▶ Play until each player arrives **Home**.

▶ Each player should take three trips.

▶ Find the total amount you have at the end of your trips.

Foreign Exchange

Country	Currency (1 unit)	U.S. Dollar
Brazil	Cruzeiro Real	$1.18
Ethiopia	Birr	$0.20
Germany	Mark	$0.68
Great Britain	Pound	$1.49
Jordan	Dinar	$1.44
Morocco	Dirham	$0.11
Saudi Arabia	Riyal	$0.27
Singapore	Singapore Dollar	$0.69
Thailand	Baht	$0.04

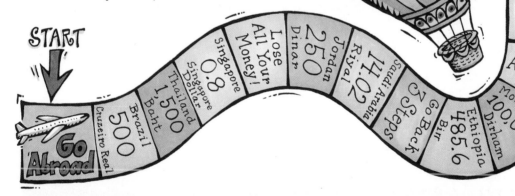

If you land on a country, you get the amount of foreign currency shown.

---

mixed review • test preparation

ALGEBRA Evaluate each expression for *n* = 12.

1 $n + 2$ **2** $15 - n$ **3** $0.5 + n$ **4** $n - 9$ **5** $n + 0$

Find the range, mean, median, and mode for the data.

6 46, 47, 46, 51, 72, 44   **7** 82, 77, 84, 83, 84   **8** 5, 4, 5, 8, 20, 5, 9

PART 1 Underestimates and Overestimates

Mario wants to buy 9 coins that cost $14.75 each. He has saved $24 a month for 5 months. Use estimation to determine if he has enough to buy the coins.

Work Together

Work in a group to answer the following. Explain your reasoning.

1 To overestimate a product, round the factors so that the estimate is greater than the exact product. Would you overestimate the cost of the coins or the amount he has saved?

2 To underestimate a product, round the factors so that the estimate is less than the exact product. Which amount in problem 1 would you underestimate?

3 Estimate the two amounts in problem 1 to determine if Mario has saved enough money.

4 **What if** Mario had saved $41 for the 5 months instead. Would he have saved enough to buy the coins?

5 **Reread** Jason used estimation as shown below to decide whether Mario has enough money. Jason decided that Mario has saved enough money to buy the coins. Reread the problem at the top of the page. Do you think Jason was correct?

> Cost of coins: $9 \times \$10 = \$90$ ← underestimate
> Amount saved: $5 \times \$25 = \$125$ ← overestimate

PART 2 Write and Share Problems

Stacy wrote this problem that can be solved by using data in the table below.

Name	Job	Salary
Alex	Mows lawns	$12.50 each lawn
Jenny	Baby-sits	$4.75 each hour
Cara	Washes cars	$6.25 each car

6 Solve Stacy's problem and explain your reasoning.

7 Change Stacy's problem so that it is harder to solve. Do not change any of the data in the table.

8 Solve the new problem and explain why it is harder to solve than Stacy's problem.

9 **Write a problem** that can be solved by using data from the table.

10 Solve your problem. Then, trade problems with at least three other students and check each other's problems and solutions.

STUDENT TO STUDENT

If Alex mows 2 lawns, and Jenny baby-sits for 7 hours, and Cara washes 6 cars, who makes the most money?

Stacy Allen
Raymond Park Middle School
Indianapolis, IN

Turn the page for Practice Strategies. ➡

Multiply Whole Numbers and Decimals **111**

Menu
**Choose five problems and solve them.
Explain your methods.**

1 Kathy wants to buy 4 stamps that cost $0.45 each. She has 10 quarters.
Does she have enough money?
Explain.

2 You have $13. You want to buy 3 tapes that cost $3.45 each. Do you have enough money?

3 It costs $0.20 to mail a postcard and $0.32 to mail a letter. Suppose you send postcards and letters to 9 friends and spent $2.16. How many postcards and letters did you send?

4 **Spatial reasoning** If the coin on the left is rolled around the coin on the right, in which direction will the head be facing when it reaches the opposite side?

5 In China, the basic unit of money is the yuan. One yuan equals 100 fen. If you have one hundred fifty-four 5-fen coins and one hundred five 2-fen coins, how many fen do you have?

6 The total number of coins in two jars is 42. The difference in the number of coins in the jars is 6. How many coins are in each jar?

7 Tom wants to buy a bamboo pencil holder that costs 150 Taiwanese dollars in Taiwan. One U.S. dollar is worth 27.314 Taiwanese dollars on that day. He estimates the price of the holder to be about 5 U.S. dollars. Is he correct? Explain.

8 A mistake was made on some $10 Canadian silver coins issued in 1973 for the 1976 Olympics. Instead of *1973*, the date *1974* was used on the other side of the coin. These rare coins are worth almost 30 times their original value. Estimate the worth of 12 of these coins.

**Choose two problems and solve them.
Explain your methods.**

9 Use the menu at the right. Plan two different lunches for yourself and three friends. Suppose you could spend a total of $25. Each lunch must include a main course, salad, and drink.

10 **Spatial reasoning** Shade as many squares as you can without shading 3 squares in a row horizontally, vertically, or diagonally.

11 Suppose you are sightseeing in Montreal, Canada. You want to buy a guidebook in a book shop. The cover of the book lists two prices: $3.75 (in Canadian currency) and $3.00 U.S. Suppose one U.S. dollar is worth 1.3 Canadian dollars that day. Would you pay for this book in Canadian currency or U.S. currency?

Country (unit of currency shown in parentheses)	1 Unit of Foreign Currency in U.S. Dollars
Australia (dollar)	0.7545
Brazil (real)	1.0225
Canada (dollar)	0.7247
China (yuan)	0.1206
Israel (shekel)	0.3183
Norway (krona)	0.1557

12 **At the Computer** Use a spreadsheet program to create a table like the one below to investigate currency exchange rates. You may use the information from the chart above or find data in your newspaper. A sample is done in the chart using data from February 14, 1996.

Country, Date, Name of Currency	One Unit of Foreign Currency in U.S. Dollars	Amount of Foreign Currency You Have	Amount of U.S. Dollars You Get in Exchange
Brazil 2/14/96 real	1.0225	234 real	$239.27

Think: Remember to write a formula for column 4 so the computer can calculate the products for you.

Language and Mathematics

Complete the sentence.
Use a word in the chart. (pages 88–109)

1 $6 \times (70 + 2) = (6 \times 70) + (6 \times 2)$
is an example of the ■ Property.

2 The ■ of two numbers is found by multiplying them.

3 An example of the ■ Property of multiplication is $273 \times 0 = 0$.

4 Numbers such as 2.3, 45.01, and 0.091 are called ■.

5 $5 \times 47 = 47 \times 5$ is an example of the ■ Property.

Vocabulary

product
sum
Commutative
Associative
Distributive
Zero
decimals
fractions

Concepts and Skills

Multiply mentally. (page 88)

6 $45 \times 1,000$
7 $12 \times 20 \times 5$
8 50×40
9 70×200

10 6.8×100
11 600×50
12 100×0.5
13 1.5×10

Estimate the product. (page 92)

14 8×234
15 42×99
16 76.54×27.54
17 65×0.89

18 362×250
19 1.6×4.25
20 9.4×9.5
21 1.488×64

Multiply. (pages 94, 96, 104, 106)

22 $\begin{array}{r} 624 \\ \times\ 84 \\ \hline \end{array}$
23 $\begin{array}{r} 307 \\ \times\ 28 \\ \hline \end{array}$
24 $\begin{array}{r} 76.98 \\ \times\ \ \ \ 8 \\ \hline \end{array}$
25 $\begin{array}{r} 0.158 \\ \times\ \ 0.6 \\ \hline \end{array}$
26 $\begin{array}{r} 342.1 \\ \times\ \ \ 4.5 \\ \hline \end{array}$

27 43×59
28 35×105
29 $18 \times 4,624$
30 3.4×1.89

31 0.05×0.09
32 6.8×3.96
33 0.08×1.06
34 17.3×21.02

35 276.4×3.25
36 0.675×1.5
37 3.1417×7.8

38 $\$94.75 \times 365$
39 $6,000 \times 2.04$
40 $\$342.99 \times \$52$

Think critically. (pages 104, 106)

41 Analyze. Explain what the error is and correct it.

846
× 10.4
3384
8460
118.44

42 Analyze. Gina multiplied and found the product of 0.98 × 0.432 as 0.45076. How could you tell this product is incorrect without doing any calculations?

MIXED APPLICATIONS
Problem Solving

(pages 98, 110)

43 In one class, 22 students ordered craft books for $5.95 each, 12 ordered basketball posters for $3.95 each, and 6 ordered bookmarks for $0.99 each. Estimate the total order.

44 Algerian paper bills have a value of 200, 100, 50, 20, and 10 dinar. If you had 50 Algerian 200-dinar bills and 80 Algerian 50-dinar bills, how many Algerian dinar would you have?

45 The stem-and-leaf plot shows the age of people who attended a workshop on coin collection. Chris says that most of the people who attended the workshop were under 30. Do you agree or disagree with him? Explain.

Ages of Workshop Attendees

0	9 9
1	0 1 2 2 5 7 8
2	0 2 3 5 9
3	1 5 6
4	2

Key: 2 | 3 = 23

46 Tickets for the school play are on sale now for $5.00 each. If you buy a ticket on the night of the play, the cost is $6.00. How much would a family save by buying 4 tickets now?

Use the table to answer problems 47–50.

47 How many more Mexican pesos would you receive for $10 U.S. on Oct. 13, 1995, than on Oct. 13, 1994?

48 How many fewer French francs would you receive for $150 U.S. on Oct. 13, 1995, than on Oct. 13, 1994?

49 **What if** you exchanged $237.69 U.S. dollars for Canadian dollars on October 13, 1995. How many Canadian dollars would you get?

Value of One U.S. Dollar		
Foreign Currency	**Oct. 13, 1994**	**Oct. 13, 1995**
Mexican peso	3.41	6.76
French franc	5.26	4.96
Canadian dollar	1.35	1.34

50 Pang went to a bank on October 13 and asked exactly how many Canadian dollars he could get for $5.50 U.S. The teller told him 7.425 Canadian dollars. Was this in 1995 or 1994? Explain.

Estimate the product.

1 9 × 547

2 87 × 52

3 58.36 × 18.9

4 88 × 0.91

Multiply.

5 83 × 10,000

6 15 × 4 × 7

7 900 × 40

8 250 × 400

9
```
  6,021
×    58
```

10
```
  6,409
×    43
```

11
```
  15.86
×     3
```

12
```
  421.9
×    4.6
```

13
```
  0.06
×0.08
```

14
```
  104
×  74
```

15
```
  0.196
×   0.4
```

16
```
  16.5
×7.04
```

Solve.

17 Mr. Fram bought 4 ties for $7.99 and a shirt for $16.99. How much change should he receive from $50.00?

18 There are 100 centimes in 1 franc. How many centimes does Reynaldo have if he has 345.90 francs?

19 Bus tickets cost $49 for adults and $24.50 for children. How much will it cost to buy tickets for one adult and three children?

20 Toni wants to buy 4 coin books that cost $11.75 each. She has saved $9 a month for 6 months. Use estimation to determine if she has enough to buy the coin books.

Use the table for problems 21–25.

21 If you bought 25 shares of Sun stock on August 24, how much money did you spend for the stock?

22 If you sold 100 shares of Sun stock on November 2, how much money would you receive?

23 How much more would it cost to buy 50 shares of stock on September 28 than on September 22?

Sun Microsystems Selected Stock Prices	
Date	**Price Per Share**
Aug. 24, 1996	$54.500
Sept. 22, 1996	$61.750
Sept. 28, 1996	$63.250
Oct. 19, 1996	$60.000
Nov. 2, 1996	$61.875

24 If you paid $3,412.50 for 75 shares of Sun stock and sold those shares on November 2, how much profit did you make?

25 Suppose you bought 125 shares of stock on September 28 and sold them on November 2. How much money did you lose?

What Did You Learn?

Have you seen a table of foreign exchange rates in a newspaper? The table below shows that on September 12, 1996, 1 British pound was worth 1.5545 American dollars and 1 American dollar was worth 0.6433 British pound.

▶ Take a tour of the countries listed. Your travel budget allows you to spend $7.00 for lunch. In each country, how much in foreign currency will you need to buy lunch?

Round the values to the hundredths place to solve the problems.

Foreign Exchange	September 12, 1996	
Currency	Foreign Currency in Dollars	Dollars in Foreign Currency
Australia (Dollar)...... 0.7975		1.2539
Brazil (Real).............. 0.9833		1.0170
Britain (Pound)......... 1.5545		0.6433
Canada (Dollar)........ 0.7292		1.3714
Germany (Mark)....... 0.6612		1.5125
Japan (Yen).............. 0.009074		110.20

· · · · · · · · · · · · · · · · · · A Good Answer · · · · · · · · · · · · · · · · · ·
- includes a written explanation of strategies and reasoning.
- includes accurate calculations.

 You may want to place your work in your portfolio.

What Do You Think ?

1 What are some mistakes that you tend to make when you multiply decimals?

2 How do you check the accuracy of your product when you multiply two decimals?
- Use estimation.
- Use models.
- Make a diagram.
- Use a calculator.

Today, the United States government makes the coins we use. The process of making coins is called *minting*.

Large bars of metal are rolled to the proper thickness. Then, a press punches out blank coins, called blanks. The blanks are treated and cleaned. Then, they pass through a machine called a die that stamps the design onto the coin.

In the past, coins were usually made of gold and silver. Today, very few coins are made of these precious metals. If they were, the metal would be worth more than the value of the coin!

Almost all coins today are made of mixtures of metals called *alloys*. An alloy has different properties than either material from which it is made. Mixing gold with copper results in a harder coin.

Nickels, dimes, quarters, and half dollars are made from copper and nickel. Pennies are made from zinc coated with copper.

Cultural Note

In colonial America, coins from different countries were used. British coins were the most common, but Spanish coins made in Mexico were also popular. To make change, people would often cut these coins into pieces.

▶ Why do you think it is better to make coins from hard alloys rather than soft metals?

▶ Why are alloys of copper, nickel, and zinc used instead of pure silver or copper?

What Is It All Worth?

The table below shows the number of pennies, nickels, dimes, quarters, and half dollars minted in a recent year by the United States Mint.

Coins Minted in One Year	
Coin	**Number**
Penny	12,837,140,368
Nickel	1,497,523,652
Dime	2,240,355,488
Quarter	1,417,290,422
Half dollar	41,196,188

1 How many coins were minted by the United States Mint during that year?

2 What was the total value of each type of coin minted? Explain how you found the answers.

3 What was the total dollar value of the coins minted during that year?

4 Which type of coin had the greatest total value? the least? Why do you think the coins were minted in these amounts?

At the Computer

Coin	Number	Value
Penny		
Nickel		
Dime		
Quarter		
Half dollar		
	Total Value	

5 Use a spreadsheet program to create a spreadsheet that will tell you the total value of a given number of coins of each type.

6 Use reference works to find the number of each type of coin minted last year. Create a table to show the value of these coins.

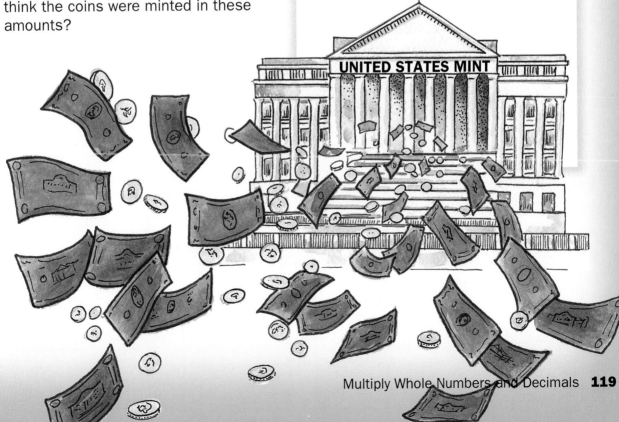

UNITED STATES MINT

Choose the letter of the best answer.

1 Allen scored 104, 111, 99, and 106 in 4 bowling games. Which of the statements below is correct?

  A The mean for his scores is 108.
  B The median for his scores is 105.
  C The range for his score is 111.
  D The mode for his scores is 99.

2 Which shows how to find $9 \times (50 + 4)$ using the Distributive Property?

  F $(9 \times 50) \times (9 \times 4)$
  G $(9 \times 50) + 4$
  H $(9 \times 50) + (9 \times 4)$
  J $(9 + 50) \times (9 \times 4)$

3 Which conclusion can you draw from the bar graph?

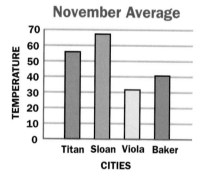

November Average

  A Among the four cities, every day in November was warmer in Sloan.
  B Sloan is the most popular city.
  C Sloan's temperature never goes below 40° F.
  D Among the four cities, the average temperature in Viola was the coldest in November.
  E The average temperature in Baker was 20° warmer than the average temperature in Viola.

4 Round 568.3 to the nearest ten.

  F 560
  G 568
  H 570
  J 600

5 Which number will make the statement true?

$43 \times 5 < 52 \times$ ■

  A 0
  B 1
  C 2
  D 3
  E 5

6 Which of the following is less than 9.0089?

  F 9.009
  G 9.0111
  H 9.1001
  J 9.00809

7 Jose bought 3 shirts. The prices of each were between $18 and $25. Before tax is added, which is a reasonable cost for the 3 shirts?

  A Less than $30
  B Between $30 and $54
  C Between $54 and $75
  D Between $75 and $86
  E More than $86

8 Rose pays a $50 registration fee for a 6-week class on origami. For each week, she pays an extra $5 for the materials. How much does she spend altogether for the class?

  F $50   **G** $55
  H $60   **J** $80
  K Not Here

9 What is the next number in this pattern?
3.8, 4.1, 4.4, 4.7

A 4.9
B 5
C 5.1
D 5.7

10 Suppose you buy a CD for $14.95 and a tape for $11.95. Which is the best estimate for the total, including $1.68 for sales tax?

F $17
G $25
H $29
J $31
K $40

11 $(6 \times 10^4) + (5 \times 10^2) + (7 \times 1)$ is not equivalent to:

A 60,507.
B sixty thousand, five hundred seven.
C 60,507.0.
D 600,507.

12 If you want to bake a dozen cupcakes, about how much milk will you need?

F 300 mL
G 30 L
H 300 L
J 3,000 L

13 Marva's goal is to swim 100 meters in one minute. She swims the first 50 meters in 32.25 seconds. What is the longest it can take her to swim the remaining 50 meters?

A 26.75 seconds
B 27.75 seconds
C 28.75 seconds
D 28.85 seconds
E Not Here

14 The distance from Westville to Clarktown is 19.2 miles. The distance from Clarktown to Bovina is 5.25 miles. How far is it from Westville to Bovina, via Clarktown?

F 7.16 miles
G 14.35 miles
H 24.35 miles
J 71.6 miles
K Not Here

15 Sandy bicycles 13 miles to school. After school, she bicycles 5 miles to work and then another 12 miles home from work. If she does this every weekday, how many miles each week does she bicycle?

A 30 miles
B 125 miles
C 150 miles
D 210 miles

16 Which of the following is not equivalent to 0.001?

F $\frac{1}{1,000}$
G 0.0010
H one thousandth
J $\frac{1}{100}$

17 Which number will make the following statement true?
19.■ < 19.56

A 8
B 7
C 6
D 5

DIVIDE WHOLE NUMBERS AND DECIMALS

Transportation

In this chapter, you will travel by car, plane, train, or boat to places you might like to go. You will divide to find measurements and costs that are important when deciding how to get from here to there.

What Do You Know ?

Aircraft	Passengers	Top Cruising Speed (mph)	Weight in pounds
Piper PA-31P Navajo	6	266	7,800
Douglas DC-7C	99	354	140,000
McDonnell Douglas DC-9	125	561	114,000
Boeing 747B	490	625	775,000

1 How many PA-31P airplanes are needed to seat all the passengers of a 747B? a DC-9?

2 About how many times greater is the seating capacity of the 747B than the DC-7C?

3 Compare the distance traveled by each aircraft in one hour when compared to a car traveling at 65 miles per hour. Write statements that tell about how many times greater the aircraft distance is than the car's distance.

 Make Generalizations Using the table, you can find the average number of miles per gallon that the car got each week by dividing the number of miles for the week by the number of gallons.

A generalization is a general conclusion based on particular facts.

1 Make a generalization about the average number of miles per gallon that the car got.

Record of Gas Used			
Week	1	2	3
Gallons	10	8	9
Miles	280	232	243

Vocabulary

dividend, p. 124
quotient, p. 124
divisor, p. 124

compatible numbers, p. 125
remainder, p. 128
order of operations, p. 136

formula, p. 138
powers of 10, p. 148
metric system, p. 158

Estimate Quotients

Before you know it, you'll think about getting your driver's license. Registry offices in Texas process about 100,000 license renewals or applications each 5-day week. How many renewals or applications do workers process each day?

You can use patterns to find quotients mentally.

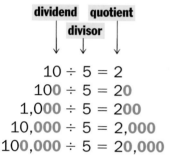

dividend   quotient
| divisor |

$$10 \div 5 = 2$$
$$100 \div 5 = 20$$
$$1,000 \div 5 = 200$$
$$10,000 \div 5 = 2,000$$
$$100,000 \div 5 = 20,000$$

Workers process about 20,000 renewals or applications each day.

You can use similar patterns to divide when both the dividend and divisor are multiples of 10, 100, or 1,000.

$$28 \div 7 = 4$$
$$280 \div 70 = 4$$
$$2,800 \div 70 = 40$$
$$28,000 \div 70 = 400$$

$$30 \div 6 = 5$$
$$300 \div 6 = 50$$
$$3,000 \div 6 = 500$$
$$30,000 \div 6 = 5,000$$

Check Out the Glossary
dividend
divisor
quotient
compatible numbers
  See page 643.

Talk It Over

▶ **ALGEBRA: PATTERNS** Describe the patterns you see above.

▶ Generalize about how to find quotients like the ones above by crossing out zeros.

If it is easy to divide one number by another mentally, the numbers are **compatible numbers.** For example, 12,000 and 40 are compatible numbers: 12,000 ÷ 40 = 300.

You can use patterns and compatible numbers to estimate quotients.

Estimate: 26,895 ÷ 73

Change the divisor and the dividend to compatible numbers.

Think: 26,895 ÷ 73
           ↓   ↓
        28,000 ÷ 70 = 400

More Examples

A Estimate: 335 ÷ 8

Think: 320 ÷ 8 = 40

B Estimate: 3,526 ÷ 42

Think: 3,600 ÷ 40 = 90

C Divide: 20,000 ÷ 500

Think: 20,0ØØ ÷ 5ØØ = 200 ÷ 5 = 40

Check for Understanding

⭐ **ALGEBRA: PATTERNS Use mental math to complete the pattern.**

1
56 ÷ 8 = 7
560 ÷ 8 = 70
5,600 ÷ 8 = ■
56,000 ÷ 8 = ■

2
400 ÷ 50 = 8
4,000 ÷ 50 = 80
40,000 ÷ 50 = ■
400,000 ÷ 50 = ■

3
63,000 ÷ 9 = 7,000
63,000 ÷ 90 = 700
63,000 ÷ 900 = ■
63,000 ÷ 9,000 = ■

Divide mentally.

4 3,500 ÷ 70

5 1,600 ÷ 40

6 36,000 ÷ 400

7 70,000 ÷ 1,000

Use compatible numbers to estimate.

8 470 ÷ 8

9 29,375 ÷ 43

10 439 ÷ 6

11 835 ÷ 9

12 2,631 ÷ 51

13 10,091 ÷ 13

14 28,435 ÷ 890

15 11,561 ÷ 48

Critical Thinking: Analyze   Explain your reasoning.

16 Why is it easier to estimate 26,895 ÷ 73 using compatible numbers than by using rounding?

17 Sometimes there is more than one set of compatible numbers you can use to estimate a quotient. Use compatible numbers and find more than one way to estimate 35,624 ÷ 68. Name the estimates.

Turn the page for Practice. ➡

Practice

ALGEBRA: PATTERNS Use mental math to complete the patterns.

1
$35 \div 7 = 5$
$350 \div 7 = 50$
$3{,}500 \div 7 = \blacksquare$
$35{,}000 \div 7 = \blacksquare$

2
$450 \div 50 = 9$
$4{,}500 \div 50 = 90$
$45{,}000 \div 50 = \blacksquare$
$450{,}000 \div 50 = \blacksquare$

3
$32{,}000 \div 8 = 4{,}000$
$32{,}000 \div 80 = 400$
$32{,}000 \div 800 = \blacksquare$
$32{,}000 \div 8{,}000 = \blacksquare$

Divide mentally.

4 $540 \div 9$

5 $2{,}400 \div 60$

6 $240{,}000 \div 300$

7 $42{,}000 \div 6{,}000$

8 $7{,}200 \div 90$

9 $56{,}000 \div 700$

10 $27{,}000 \div 3{,}000$

11 $100{,}000 \div 10{,}000$

12 $9\overline{)810}$

13 $600\overline{)36{,}000}$

14 $50\overline{)35{,}000}$

15 $60\overline{)540{,}000}$

Estimate by replacing the highlighted number.

16 $\mathbf{3{,}741} \div 90$

17 $3{,}200 \div \mathbf{78}$

18 $\mathbf{44{,}821} \div 700$

19 $240 \div \mathbf{65}$

20 $\mathbf{725} \div 90$

21 $6{,}400 \div \mathbf{75}$

22 $\mathbf{23{,}462} \div 300$

23 $5{,}629 \div \mathbf{90}$

Use compatible numbers to estimate each quotient.

24 $624 \div 8$

25 $205 \div 3$

26 $1{,}478 \div 2$

27 $5{,}571 \div 9$

28 $29{,}521 \div 60$

29 $43{,}510 \div 70$

30 $6{,}400 \div 90$

31 $3{,}456 \div 60$

32 $65{,}624 \div 73$

33 $26{,}201 \div 86$

34 $45{,}103 \div 931$

35 $708{,}431 \div 835$

Use the table for problems 36–39.

36 About how many packs of grape drink can be made?

37 About how many packs of root beer can be made?

38 A vendor needs 470 cans of orange drink. About how many packs should he order?

39 About how many times more cans of root beer were made than grape drink?

Soda Production		
Flavor	**Number of Cans**	**Number per Pack**
Grape	5,359	6
Lemon-Lime	3,427	4
Orange	4,100	12
Root Beer	15,814	24

•••••••••••••••• **Make It Right** ••••••••••••••••

40 Jane divided 40,000 by 50 and got 8,000. Tell what the error is and correct it.

41 A DC-8 airplane cruises at a speed of 550 mi per hour. If you are in a car traveling at 65 mi per hour, about how many times faster than your car is the airplane going?

42 The three states with the most drivers are California with 20,431,000, Texas with 11,619,000, and Florida with 10,705,000 drivers. About how many drivers are there altogether? Explain how you estimated.

43 A truck that hauls automobiles held 5 cars costing $18,428 each and 5 cars costing $21,506 each. What is the total value of the cars?

44 **Write a problem** that you can solve by estimating a quotient. Solve the problem and then give it to other students to solve.

45 **Spatial reasoning** Each box in the diagram holds 2.4 kilograms of fruit. How many kilograms of fruit are there in all?

46 A shipping company bought 10,000 cups to hand out to customers. If each cup costs $2.18, how much will 10,000 cups cost?

47 Write a paragraph describing how you can use compatible numbers to estimate a quotient.

48 On a recent flight, the Concorde crossed the Atlantic in 3 hours 40 min. How much longer did it take Lindbergh to cross the Atlantic? SEE INFOBIT.

INFOBIT
In 1927, Charles Lindbergh made the first solo flight across the Atlantic. He flew 3,610 mi in 33 h 30 min.

mixed review • test preparation

1 How much more did it cost to make a movie in 1996 than in 1992?

2 The average cost in 1996 for advertising and making prints of a movie was $19.8 million. What was the total average cost of making, advertising, and making prints of a movie?

3 Make a bar graph of the data in the table.

Making a Movie				
Average Cost by year (in millions of dollars)				
1992	1993	1994	1995	1996
28.9	29.9	34.3	36.4	39.8

SOURCE: MOTION PICTURE ASSOCIATION OF AMERICA

Whole Number Division: 1-Digit Divisors

Giving helicopter tours of Hawaii's volcanoes is an exciting job. To get a commercial pilot's license, you'll need at least 150 hours of flight time. How many hours per month must you average to get a license in 8 months?

Divide: 150 ÷ 8

Estimate to place the first digit of the quotient.

$$\begin{array}{r} 20 \\ 8\overline{)160} \end{array}$$ **Think:** The first digit of the quotient will be in the tens place.

Step 1	**Step 2**	
Divide the tens.	**Divide the ones.** **Write the remainder.**	**Check: Multiply, then add.**

Step 1

Divide the tens.

$$\begin{array}{r} 1 \\ 8\overline{)150} \\ -8 \\ \hline 7 \end{array}$$
$$\begin{array}{r} 1 \\ 8\overline{)15} \end{array}$$ **Think:**
Multiply: $1 \times 8 = 8$
Subtract: $15 - 8 = 7$
Compare: $7 < 8$

Step 2

Divide the ones.
Write the remainder.

$$\begin{array}{r} 18\ R6 \\ 8\overline{)150} \\ -8\downarrow \\ \hline 70 \\ -64 \\ \hline 6 \end{array}$$
$$\begin{array}{r} 8 \\ 8\overline{)70} \end{array}$$ **Think:**
Multiply: $8 \times 8 = 64$
Subtract: $70 - 64 = 6$
Compare: $6 < 8$

Check: Multiply, then add.

$$\begin{array}{r} 18 \leftarrow \text{quotient} \\ \times\ 8 \leftarrow \text{divisor} \\ \hline 144 \\ +\ \ 6 \leftarrow \text{remainder} \\ \hline 150 \leftarrow \text{dividend} \end{array}$$

— **Note:** To get a whole number remainder when dividing, use this key.

 150 ÷R 8 = **18** *R6*

You will need over 18 hours per month.

Check Out the Glossary
remainder
See page 643.

More Examples

A
$$\begin{array}{r} 109 \\ 3\overline{)327} \\ -3\downarrow\downarrow \\ \hline 27 \\ -27 \\ \hline 0 \end{array}$$
Think: $2 < 3$. Not enough tens to divide. Write 0 in the quotient.

B 625/6 or $\frac{625}{6}$
$$\begin{array}{r} 104\ R1 \\ 6\overline{)625} \\ -6\downarrow\downarrow \\ \hline 25 \\ -24 \\ \hline 1 \end{array}$$

Check for Understanding

Estimate. Divide and check.

1 $8\overline{)736}$ **2** $4\overline{)4,036}$ **3** $7\overline{)737}$ **4** $5\overline{)4,271}$ **5** 620/8

Critical Thinking: Analyze   **Explain your reasoning.**

6 When you divide, why do you compare at each step?

Practice

Divide. Remember to estimate.

1 $8\overline{)788}$ **2** $5\overline{)358}$ **3** $3\overline{)1,345}$ **4** $9\overline{)738}$ **5** $7\overline{)630}$

6 $3\overline{)65}$ **7** $5\overline{)109}$ **8** $8\overline{)168}$ **9** $9\overline{)959}$ **10** $4\overline{)556}$

11 $6\overline{)3,624}$ **12** $4\overline{)3,795}$ **13** $5\overline{)6,570}$ **14** $2\overline{)4,681}$ **15** $7\overline{)21,703}$

16 $5,440 \div 8$ **17** $4,026 \div 4$ **18** $6,006 \div 6$ **19** $53,625 \div 5$ **20** $243,901 \div 8$

21 $1,011 \div 5$ **22** $192 \div 2$ **23** $62,907 \div 9$ **24** $34,900 \div 6$ **25** $4,376 \div 8$

26 $217/2$ **27** $4,104/9$ **28** $34,892/7$ **29** $76,409/9$ **30** $28,027/7$

31 $\dfrac{3,934}{7}$ **32** $\dfrac{2,715}{4}$ **33** $\dfrac{56,235}{6}$ **34** $\dfrac{23,877}{9}$ **35** $\dfrac{2,893}{8}$

⭐ **ALGEBRA Find the missing number mentally. Explain your methods.**

36 $60 \times \blacksquare = 6,000$ **37** $\blacksquare \div 10 = 300$ **38** $2000 \div 100 = \blacksquare$

39 $\blacksquare \div 6 = 700$ **40** $7 \times \blacksquare = 280$ **41** $630 \div \blacksquare = 70$

MIXED APPLICATIONS
Problem Solving

42 Many schoolyards have fences around them. What is the perimeter of the schoolyard at the right?

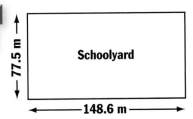

Schoolyard — 77.5 m · 148.6 m

43 Fred has to wait 98 days to apply for his driver's license. How many weeks does he have to wait?

44 An auto transporter holds 8 cars. How many transporters will it take to haul 24,000 cars?

45 Kayla's ferry leaves at 3:15. She needs to be there at least 1 hour before departure time. If it takes her 45 minutes to get to the ferry, what is the latest she should leave?

46 Suppose it costs $17,760 to operate a plane for 8 hours. About how much does it cost to operate the plane per hour? per minute?

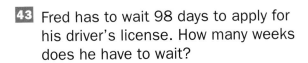

mixed review • test preparation

Use mental math. Explain your methods.

1 $36 + 42$ **2** $50 - 18$ **3** $70 + 42$ **4** $\$3.01 - \$1.99$ **5** $28 + 17$

6 $452 - 98$ **7** $264 + 310$ **8** $823 - 220$ **9** $\$6.14 + \$1.99$ **10** $718 - 316$

Whole Number Division: 2-Digit Divisors

Domino's Pizza started a trend. Now most pizza places offer home delivery. If a pizza delivery person puts 5,363 mi on his car in a year, how many miles per week is that?

Note: There are 52 weeks in a year.

Divide: 5,363 ÷ 52

Estimate to place the first digit of the quotient.

$$50)\overline{5,000} \quad 100$$

Think: The first digit of the quotient will be in the hundreds place.

Step 1	Step 2	Step 3
Divide the hundreds.	**Divide the tens.**	**Divide the ones. Write the remainder.**
$52)\overline{5,363}$ -52 1 **Think:** $50)\overline{50}$ Try 1. Multiply: $1 \times 52 = 52$ Subtract: $53 - 52 = 1$ Compare: $1 < 52$	$52)\overline{5,363}$ $-52\downarrow$ 16 **Think:** $16 < 52$ Not enough tens to divide. Write 0 in the quotient.	$52)\overline{5,363}$ **103 R7** $-52\downarrow\downarrow$ 163 -156 7 **Think:** $50)\overline{150}$ 3 Try 3. Multiply: $3 \times 52 = 156$ Subtract: $163 - 156 = 7$ Compare: $7 < 52$

 5363 ÷R 52 = **103** *R7*

Check: $52 \times 103 = 5,356$
$5,356 + 7 = 5,363$

His average weekly mileage is a little more than 103 mi.

Talk It Over

▶ How do you know that the new digit you write in the quotient for each step is correct?

▶ Will the remainder in a division problem always be less than the divisor?

A pizza delivery person makes 85 deliveries in one week. In checking the records with her supervisor, she finds total receipts of $1,615. What was the average cost of her deliveries?

Divide: $1,615 ÷ 85

Estimate to place the first digit of the quotient.

$$\begin{array}{r} 20 \\ 90\overline{)1,800} \end{array}$$

Think: The first digit of the quotient will be in the tens place.

Step 1

Divide the tens. Change the estimate if necessary.

$$\begin{array}{r} 1 \\ 85\overline{)\$1,615} \\ -85 \\ \hline 76 \end{array}$$

Think: $90\overline{)180}$
Try 2.
Multiply: 2 × 85 = 170
Compare: 170 > 161
Too much!

Try 1.
Multiply: 1 × 85 = 85
Subtract: 161 − 85 = 76
Compare: 76 < 85

Step 2

Continue dividing. Change the estimate if necessary.

$$\begin{array}{r} 19 \\ 85\overline{)\$1,615} \\ -85\downarrow \\ \hline 765 \\ -765 \\ \hline 0 \end{array}$$

Think: $90\overline{)720}$
Try 8.
Multiply: 8 × 85 = 680
Subtract: 765 − 680 = 85
Compare: 85 = 85
Too small.

Try 9.
Multiply: 9 × 85 = 765
Subtract: 765 − 765 = 0

 1615 ÷R 85 = *19* ᴿ⁰

The cost of an average delivery was $19.

Another Example

$$\begin{array}{r} 5 \\ 26\overline{)130} \\ -130 \end{array}$$

Think: $30\overline{)120}$
Try 4.
Multiply: 4 × 26 = 104
Subtract: 130 − 104 = 26
Compare: 26 = 26
Too small.

Try 5.
Multiply: 5 × 26 = 130
Subtract: 130 − 130 = 0

Check for Understanding

Estimate. Divide and check.

1 47)289

2 54)5,955

3 19)1,995

4 64)65,024

5 640 ÷ 32

6 1,620 ÷ 36

7 26,362 ÷ 85

8 36,200 ÷ 93

Critical Thinking: Generalize   Explain your reasoning.

9 If you divide a 4-digit number by a 2-digit number, what is the greatest number of digits the quotient can have? the least?

CHECK

Turn the page for Practice.
Divide Whole Numbers and Decimals **131**

Practice

Divide. Remember to estimate.

1 $86\overline{)7{,}912}$ **2** $24\overline{)610}$ **3** $38\overline{)2{,}698}$ **4** $32\overline{)1{,}997}$ **5** $47\overline{)5{,}623}$

6 $54\overline{)2{,}116}$ **7** $73\overline{)73{,}498}$ **8** $62\overline{)12{,}200}$ **9** $34\overline{)\$19{,}142}$ **10** $6\overline{)12{,}030}$

11 $15\overline{)1{,}396}$ **12** $46\overline{)18{,}630}$ **13** $57\overline{)766}$ **14** $63\overline{)8{,}604}$ **15** $12\overline{)48{,}116}$

16 $526 \div 59$ **17** $1{,}295 \div 34$ **18** $11{,}352 \div 28$ **19** $54{,}834 \div 78$

20 $93{,}466 \div 34$ **21** $8{,}742 \div 93$ **22** $3{,}500 \div 57$ **23** $35{,}916 \div 56$

24 $4127 \div 41$ **25** $1059 \div 80$ **26** $25{,}564 \div 77$ **27** $36{,}178 \div 32$

28 $7{,}814/36$ **29** $16{,}447/79$ **30** $29{,}422/58$ **31** $18{,}718/49$

Find the missing number.

	Dividend	Divisor	Quotient
32	264	■	66
33	■	5	1,041
34	4,375	24	■

	Dividend	Divisor	Quotient
35	381	6	■
36	4,817	■	602 R1
37	■	35	24

Use the table for problems 38–41.

38 Find the number of full boxes of cheese breadsticks produced in January.

39 How many full boxes of garlic bread were produced in February?

40 Find the number of full boxes of cheese breadsticks produced in all three months.

41 Find the number of full boxes of garlic bread loaves produced in all three months.

Frozen Foods: Number Produced		
Month	Garlic Bread Loaves*	Cheese Breadsticks**
January	868	2,358
February	542	17,641
March	387	3,536

*Garlic bread loaves are packaged 12 to a box.
**Cheese breadsticks are packaged 24 to a box.

•••••••••••••••••• **Make It Right** ••••••••••••••••••

42 Billy Joe divided this way. Tell what the error is and correct it.

$$63\overline{)14{,}506} \quad \begin{array}{r} 23 \text{ R16} \end{array}$$

Use the table to answer problems 43–47.

43 Frozen Delite's yearly shipping budget is $56,875. How many 1-lb packages can they send for that amount using Air Express's priority service?

44 How many more 3-lb packages can Frozen Delite send for $56,875 if they use Air Express's economy service instead of using Air Express's priority service?

45 What will Frozen Delite pay altogether for these express packages sent using Air Express's priority service?
- 2-lb package delivered at 10:09 A.M.
- 1-lb package delivered at 8:15 A.M.
- 3-lb package delivered at 9:55 A.M.

47 **Write a problem** Use the information at right and write a problem about this situation. Solve it and have others solve it.

Air Express Delivery Service Rates			
Weight	Economy (2-day)	Standard (next afternoon)	Priority* (next morning)
1 lb	$15	$18	$24
2 lb	$16	$19	$25
3 lb	$17	$20	$26

*Delivery of priority packages guaranteed by 10 A.M. or you do not pay.

46 **Make a decision** Julie wants to send a 2-lb book and a 1-lb game to the same address. She wants them to arrive at 11 A.M. tomorrow. What is the cheapest way to send them by Air Express? Explain your reasoning.

Traveling to Work	
Bus	Train
$1.50 each way per day	$25 per week
Closer to home	faster

Cultural Connection Ancient Egyptian Division

Ancient Egyptians based their division on doubling. The table below shows how they would have divided 60 by 12.

The symbol **/** means 1, **∩** means 10, and **𝟗** means 100.

Egyptian	
i	∩ ii
i	∩ iiii
iiii	∩∩ iiii ∩∩ iiii
iiii iiii	∩∩∩∩∩ iii ∩∩∩∩ iii

Indo-Arabic	
1	12
2	24
4	48
8	96

Start with 1 group of 12. Double the numbers in each column until the right column reaches or is greater than 60. Look for numbers that add to 60: 12 + 48 = 60. Add the numbers on their left. The quotient, 60 ÷ 12, is 1 + 4, or 5.

Use this ancient Egyptian method to find the quotient.

1 64 ÷ 8   **2** 96 ÷ 6   **3** 126 ÷ 14   **4** 144 ÷ 4

Multiplication and Division Expressions

Transportation may be very different in 20 yr. Many city planners are investigating high-speed monorail trains. Suppose each car of a monorail holds 40 people. How can you represent the number of people the train can hold? How many people can a five-car train hold?

Since the number of cars can vary on each train, let the variable c represent the number of cars. That means that $40 \times c$ represents the number of passengers the train can carry.

Evaluate $40c$ for $c = 5$: $40 \times 5 = 200$

Note: The times sign is sometimes confused with the variable x, so the most common way to write the product is $40c$.

The monorail can carry 200 passengers.

A city planner knows that the number of people to be transported changes throughout the day. How many monorail cars are needed to transport 1,000 people during rush hour?

Let x represent the number of people to be transported.

Evaluate $\frac{x}{40}$ for $x = 1,000$. $\frac{1,000}{40} = 25$

The train needs 25 cars to transport 1,000 people.

Check for Understanding

Evaluate each expression.

1 $3x$ for $x = 1.2$

2 $y/7$ for $y = 49$

3 $\frac{x}{16}$ for $x = 80$

Write an expression for each situation.

4 the total weight of n monorail brochures if each brochure weighs 4.8 oz

5 the number of bicycles if you count n tires

Critical Thinking: Analyze

6 Describe a situation that the expression $\frac{z}{2}$ might represent.

Practice

Evaluate each expression.

1 $4x$ for $x = 20$

2 $6b$ for $b = 12$

3 $7x$ for $x = 19$

4 $t/12$ for $t = 24$

5 $m/11$ for $m = 121$

6 $x/15$ for $x = 420$

7 $2.5a$ for $a = 6.4$

8 $1.5t$ for $t = 4$

9 $3.2c$ for $c = 1.5$

10 $\frac{50}{b}$ for $b = 10$

11 $\frac{y}{4}$ for $y = 40$

12 $\frac{16}{z}$ for $z = 8$

Write an expression for the situation.

13 the number of people n cars can hold if each car holds 5 people

14 the cost of n shirts if each shirt costs $16

15 the number of tricycles if altogether they have n tires

16 the number of cookies for n people to have 3 cookies per person

17 the number of feet in a measurement of y inches

18 the total weight of g grapefruits if each grapefruit weighs 1.2 pounds

MIXED APPLICATIONS
Problem Solving

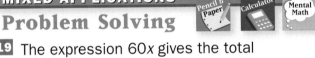

19 The expression $60x$ gives the total dollars in round-trip fares paid by x passengers on a train. Find the total fares collected from 120 passengers.

20 Kara used the Internet 3 hours last week. The average Internet use is 5 h 28 min per week. How much less than the average time did Kara spend?

21 To the nearest thousand, what is the average number of passengers per day on the Bullet Train between Tokyo and Osaka? SEE INFOBIT.

INFOBIT
Bullet Trains (*Shinkansen*) can travel up to 165 miles per hour. About 134 million passengers per year use the Bullet Train between Tokyo and Osaka, Japan.

mixed review • test preparation

Use mental math. Explain your methods.

1 300×40

2 80×50

3 60×700

4 21×4

Write in standard form.

5 8^4

6 10^6

7 14^3

8 $(2.4)^2$

Order of Operations

Two students were asked to evaluate $8^2 + 4 \times 6$ using their calculators. Here is what their calculators displayed.

Julia's calculator shows 88.   Rob's calculator shows 408.

$8^2 + (4 \times 6) = 88$ $(8^2 + 4) \times 6 = 408$

Some calculators add 8^2 to the product of 4 and 6. Some calculators add 8^2 and 4 and then multiply the sum by 6. What does your calculator do?

To decide which answer is correct, mathematicians agree on the following **order of operations:**

Order of Operations

▶ Do all operations in **P**arentheses first.   **P**urple

▶ Evaluate all expressions with **E**xponents.   **E**lephants

▶ **M**ultiply and **D**ivide in order from left to right.   **M**arching **D**own

▶ **A**dd and **S**ubtract in order from left to right.   **A S**treet

Note: This memory device may help you remember the rules.

Use order of operations to simplify $8^2 + 4 \times 6$.
$$8^2 + 4 \times 6 = 8^2 + 24$$
$$= 64 + 24$$
$$= 88$$

> **Check Out the Glossary**
> For vocabulary words, see page 643.

More Examples

A Simplify.
$(11 - 5) \times 4 + 12 \div 2$
$6 \times 4 + 12 \div 2$
$24 \quad + \quad 6$
30

B Simplify.
4×2^3
4×8
32

C Evaluate.
$13 - 2x$ for $x = 4$
$13 - 2 \times 4$
$13 - 8$
5

Check for Understanding

Simplify using order of operations.

1 $250 - 25 + 19$

2 $(50 + 110) \div 4$

3 $0.5 \times 4 + 25 \div 5$

Evaluate the expression.

4 $8x - 3$ for $x = 2$

5 $4 + \frac{x}{2} - 1$ for $x = 12$

6 $3(x + 2) - 6$ for $x = 4$

Critical Thinking: Analyze

7 Make up your own memory device for the order of operations.

Practice

Simplify using order of operations.

1 $60 - 4 \times 10$

2 $(60 - 4) \times 10$

3 $64.2 - (25.4 + 19)$

4 $100 + 45 \times 20 - 10$

5 $55 - 8 \times 2 + 38 \div 2$

6 $(20 + 4) \times 8$

7 $12 \times 4.5 + 8 \div 2$

8 $(16 - 8) \div 4 + 6$

9 $75 - 25 \div 25 + 10$

10 $(3 + 4) \times 5^2$

11 $18 - 25 \times 0.04$

12 $8.2 + (5 - 3)^2$

Evaluate the expression.

13 $125 - x + 13$ for $x = 43$

14 $200 + 32a$ for $a = 20$

15 $28 + 3a - 2$ for $a = 6$

16 $19 - (a - 4)$ for $a = 8$

17 $4x \div 2 + 9$ for $x = 5$

18 $14 - (3 + 2x)$ for $x = 3$

Copy and place parentheses to make the sentence true.

19 $15 + 9 \times 2 = 48$

20 $36 - 45 \div 9 + 27 = 4$

21 $76 - 40 \div 4 = 9$

22 $9 + 2 \times 7 - 3 = 44$

23 $318 - 6 + 3^2 = 303$

24 $81 + 9 \times 10 = 900$

MIXED APPLICATIONS
Problem Solving

25 Last year 23 busloads and 152 carloads of tourists visited a local park. If each bus held 34 people and each car held 5 people, write an expression for the total number of tourists. What is the number?

26 According to *The Guinness Book of Records,* a world tap-dancing record is held by Roy Castle. He did 1 million taps in 23 hours and 44 minutes. About how many taps was that per hour?

27 Use each of the numbers 2, 3, 4, and 5 exactly once to write an expression that equals 5.

28 A school bought 24 books for $3.95 each. They paid $4.00 for shipping. What was the total bill?

29 **Logical reasoning** Each pane in the window at right can be red or blue. How many possible windows are there?

---

mixed review • test preparation

Write the expanded form.

1 352

2 1,006

3 703

4 98

5 32,400

6 Make a stem-and-leaf plot of these race times (in seconds):
34, 36, 41, 43, 38, 52, 40, 47, 61, 39, 43, 50, 45, 53

Use a Formula

Read If an ocean liner sails at a speed of 30 miles per hour, how far can it sail in 5 hours?

Cultural Note
Between 1820 and 1940, about 6 million people immigrated to the United States from Germany, more than from any other country. Most of them arrived during that time by ocean liner.

L
E
A
R
N

Plan To solve this problem, you can use the first of these three related **formulas.** In these formulas, *rate* means "average speed."

distance = rate × time
$d = r \times t$

time = distance/rate
$t = d/r$

rate = distance/time
$r = d/t$

Solve Substitute the values you know from the problem.

$d = r \times t$
$d = 30 \times 5$
$d = 150$

formula An equation which shows a mathematical relationship between the variables in the equation.

The liner can sail 150 miles in 5 hours.

Look Back How could you solve the problem in a different way?

C
H
E
C
K

Check for Understanding

1 **What if** the ocean liner sails at an average speed of 40 miles per hour. How far could it sail in 7 hours?

Critical Thinking: Analyze **Explain your method.**

2 A sea plane flies 1,280 miles in 4 hours. What is its average speed?

3 An ant walked 42 feet at an average speed of 6 feet per minute. How long was it walking?

Problem Solving

1 If an ocean liner sails 864 mi in 24 hours, what is its average speed?

2 A ship sails at 32 mi per hour. About how long will it take to go 670 mi?

3 If a glacier moves 600 feet in 3 years, what is its average speed in feet per year?

4 How many even numbers are there between 101 and 199? Explain how you solved the problem.

Use the table for problems 5–10.

5 How far can a DC-10-10 fly in 4 hours?

6 How much farther can a DC-10-30 fly in 5 hours than a DC-9-10?

7 About how many more passengers does the DC-10-10 carry than the DC-9-10?

Jet Information			
Jets	**Number of Seats**	**Flying Speed (mi per hour)**	**Cost per Hour to Operate**
DC-10-10	282	500	$4,056
DC-10-30	265	520	$4,595
DC-9-50	122	370	$1,640
DC-9-30	102	383	$1,658
DC-9-10	77	380	$1,439

8 **READING ARITHMETIC WRITING** **Make Generalizations** How does the cost of operating a plane change as the average speed increases?

9 Fifty seats on a DC-9-50 on a flight from Seattle to San Francisco sell for $98 each. The remaining seats sell for $198 each. How much are ticket sales when all seats are sold?

10 **Write a problem** using data in the table. Solve your problem. Give your problem to others to solve.

11 You can find the Perimeter P of a rectangle of length ℓ and width w by using the formula $P = 2\ell + 2w$. Find the perimeter of a rectangle of length 5.32 meters and width 0.75 meters.

12 LeRoy drove 100 miles in 2 hours. How fast would he have to drive the next 2 hours in order to travel 220 miles in all? What would his average speed be for the 4-hour trip?

13 **Data Point** Here are the numbers of sixth-grade students who rode the bus to one school in 3 weeks.
56, 78, 65, 68, 62, 58, 55, 48, 59, 62, 53, 45, 72, 81, 69
Make a stem-and-leaf plot of these data. What conclusions can you make?

ALGEBRA: PATTERNS Use mental math to complete the pattern.

1
$21 \div 7 = $ ■
$210 \div 7 = $ ■
$2,100 \div 7 = $ ■

2
$40 \div 5 = $ ■
$400 \div 5 = $ ■
$4,000 \div 5 = $ ■

3
$350 \div 70 = $ ■
$3,500 \div 70 = $ ■
$35,000 \div 70 = $ ■

Estimate the hourly wages.

4 Tara worked 31 hours.

5 Danoi worked 38 hours.

6 Martha worked 28 hours.

Driver	Weekly Wages
Tara	$325
Danoi	$779
Martha	$244

Divide.

7 $2\overline{)618}$

8 $3\overline{)7,936}$

9 $9\overline{)1,982}$

10 $8\overline{)76,000}$

11 $47\overline{)289}$

12 $62\overline{)12,200}$

13 $54\overline{)5,995}$

14 $54\overline{)2,160}$

Evaluate the expression.

15 $21n$ for $n = 18$

16 $\frac{x}{5}$ for $x = 110$

17 $\frac{w}{30}$ for $w = 2,700$

18 $2n + 4$ for $n = 1.6$

19 $\frac{15}{n} - 1$ for $n = 3$

20 $6 - \frac{4}{n}$ for $n = 2$

Simplify.

21 $24 \div 4 \times 3$

22 $24 \div (4 \times 3)$

23 $3 \times 6 + 4 \div 2$

24 $17 + 9 \times 7$

25 $6^2 \times 3 + 2$

26 $640 \div (8 \times 2)$

Solve. Use mental math when you can.

27 A bus holds 45 people. How many buses are needed to transport 810 people?

28 If a car drives an average of 40 miles per hour, how far can it drive in 4 hours?

29 Rick drives a total of 288 miles each week to and from work. How far does he drive each way if he works 6 days every week?

30 Lucas delivers packages to stores. In 8 months he drove 21,672 miles. What is the average number of miles he drove each month?

31 The expression $6.25n$ gives the total amount of pay for n hours of work. Find the total pay for 35 hours worked.

32 If you pay $4,950 for a used car over 3 years, how much would your monthly payments be?

33 Explain the steps you would use to simplify this expression: $(3 + 7)^2 - 12 \times 2 + 12 \div 6$.

Use a Spreadsheet

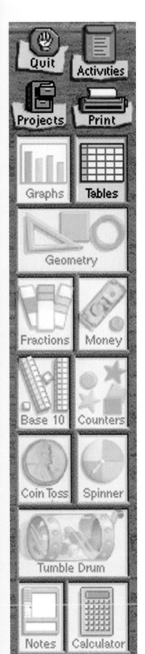

Many things can change as you plan a party. The number of people coming affects how much food and drink you need, which affects your costs. When you need to do calculations using repeated or changeable data, you can use a computer to create a special table known as a spreadsheet.

Look at the spreadsheet below. There are three kinds of information in it: labels, data entries, and calculated values.

Food	Number of Guests	Servings per Unit	Number of Units Needed[1]	Unit Cost	Cost[2]
Chips	25	5		$1.99	
Dip	25	5		$0.79	
Soda	25	10		$0.89	
Pizza	25	5		$5.00	
Ice cream	25	10		$2.29	
				Total Cost	SUM[3]

Labels → Food

Data Entries → Soda 25

Calculated Values → Total Cost / SUM[3]

[1]Column 1 ÷ Column 2   [2]Column 3 × Column 4   [3]Column 5

▶ Explain each of the formulas used to find the calculated values.

▶ Complete the spreadsheet. What do you notice about the values given for the number of units needed?

1 **What if** 15 more people are coming to the party. Enter this data in the spreadsheet. How did the spreadsheet change?

2 **What if** the price of soda went up to $1.39. Enter this data in the spreadsheet. How did the spreadsheet change?

3 Use the spreadsheet to plan your own party. Compare your results with those of others.

Critical Thinking: Generalize   Explain your reasoning.

4 When is it better to use a computer to do calculations? When do you think it is better to use another method?

real-life investigation

APPLYING DIVISION

PLAN A TRIP

Work Together

Plan a round trip from Miami that includes Sea World, Busch Gardens, and Everglades City. Your trip should take no longer than two weeks.

▶ Assume you will average 50 miles per hour as you drive.

▶ Assume your car will get 30 miles per gallon of gas.

▶ Assume gas will cost $1.30 per gallon.

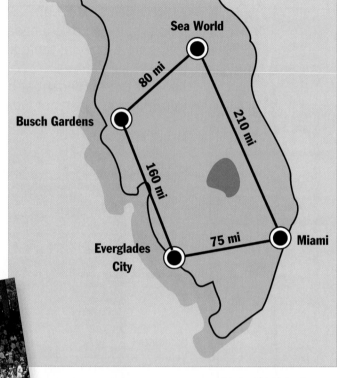

Sea World

80 mi

210 mi

Busch Gardens

160 mi

Everglades City

75 mi

Miami

Sea World

Busch Gardens

Everglades City

You will need:
- *map of Florida*

DECISION MAKING

Plan a Trip

1 Work in a group to plan the trip. Use a Florida map and the travel information on page 142.

2 Decide on the route for your trip. Make it a round trip.

3 Record your travel information in a table like the one below.

4 Record your conclusions about the total distance traveled and the total cost of gasoline.

5 Estimate the time you will spend driving and the time you will spend sightseeing.

Report Your Findings

6 Prepare a report on your trip that includes:

► what you will see and what route you will take.

► your travel information recorded in a table or spreadsheet.

7 Compare your trips with trips of other groups.

Revise your work.
► Are your conclusions about the total distance traveled and the total cost of gasoline reasonable?
► Are your calculations correct?
► Is your report clear and organized?
► Did you proofread your work?

Day	From	To	Distance (in miles)	Time (in hours)	Sightseeing
1	Miami	Orlando			
2					Sea World
3					
4					

MORE TO INVESTIGATE

PREDICT the total cost of the trip, including hotels, meals, and admission to Sea World and Busch Gardens.

EXPLORE the idea of camping out on your trip instead of staying in motels. How much money do you think camping out would save you?

FIND out more about the Florida Everglades.

Divide Decimals by Whole Numbers

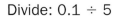

Have you ever seen a prototype of a car of the future? Suppose an experimental car can travel 5 mi on 0.1 gal of gasoline. How many gallons does it use traveling 1 mi?

Divide: $0.1 \div 5$

You can use a model to show how to divide 0.1 by 5.

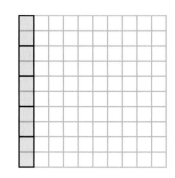

Represent 0.1 by shading. Divide the shaded area into 5 pieces of the same size. Each piece is 0.02.

$0.1 \div 5 = 0.02$

The car uses 0.02 gal of gas to travel 1 mi.

You can also use pencil and paper or a calculator to divide decimals.

Divide: $42.2 \div 4$

Estimate: $40 \div 4 = 10$

Step 1	Step 2	
Place the decimal point above the decimal point in the dividend.	**Divide as with whole numbers.**	**Check.**

Step 1:

$$4\overline{)42.2}^{\,.}$$

Step 2:

$$
\begin{array}{r}
10.55 \\
4\overline{)42.20} \\
-4 \\
\hline
2\,2 \\
-2\,0 \\
\hline
20 \\
-20 \\
\hline
0
\end{array}
$$
← Write a 0 so you can keep dividing.

Check.

$$
\begin{array}{r}
10.55 \\
\times \quad 4 \\
\hline
42.20 = 42.2
\end{array}
$$

 $42.2 \div 4 =$ **10.55**

Note: To get a decimal quotient, use the ÷ key.

Talk It Over

▶ When you are dividing 42.2 by 4, why can you place 0 to the right of the tenths place in 42.2?

▶ How can you use compatible numbers to estimate the reasonableness of your answer?

Sometimes you don't need all the decimal places that are in a quotient. You can round the quotient to a particular place.

Divide: 18.5 ÷ 15. Round to the nearest tenth.

Estimate the quotient. **Think:** 20 ÷ 20 = 1

Step 1	Step 2	Step 3
Place the decimal point.	**Divide to one more place than the place to which you are rounding.**	**Round the quotient.**

Step 1:
$$15\overline{)18.5}$$

Step 2:
```
       1.23
 15)18.50      Write a 0 so you
  − 15 ↓       can continue to
     3 5       divide to the
   − 3 0 ↓     hundredths.
       50
     − 45
        5
```

Step 3:
1.23 → 1.2

Rounded to the nearest tenth, the quotient is 1.2.

 18.5 ÷ 15 = **1.2333333**

More Examples

A $36\overline{)\$26.64}$

B 12 ÷ 5

C Divide: 2.6 ÷ 6.
Round to the nearest hundredth.

A
```
      $0.74
 36)$26.64
  − 25 2 ↓
    1 44
  − 1 44
       0
```

B
```
     2.4   ← Write a zero
 5)12.0      so you can
  −10 ↓      keep dividing.
    20
  −20
    0
```

C
```
     0.433
 6)2.600
  − 2 4 ↓
     20
   − 18 ↓
      20
    − 18
       2
```
Rounded to the nearest hundredth, the quotient is 0.43.

Check for Understanding
Divide. Remember to estimate. Round to the nearest hundredth, if necessary.

1 $3\overline{)\$6.72}$

2 $7\overline{)2.1}$

3 $8\overline{)26}$

4 $24\overline{)12.096}$

5 6.054 ÷ 6

6 324.7 ÷ 16

7 0.306 ÷ 4

8 18.5 ÷ 5

Critical Thinking: Analyze

9 Check example C by multiplying 0.43 by 6. Then multiply 0.433 by 6. Explain why you don't get the exact dividend.

C
H
E
C
K

Practice

Divide. Remember to estimate.

1 5)3.5 **2** 31)$4.34 **3** 36)0.108 **4** 16)76 **5** 69)165.6

6 64)2,707.84 **7** 9)9.945 **8** 44)0.9108 **9** 9)32.22 **10** 8)$3.84

11 0.072 ÷ 3 **12** $27.25 ÷ 25 **13** 6.02 ÷ 28 **14** 0.0825 ÷ 25

15 120 ÷ 25 **16** 0.288/36 **17** 790.4 ÷ 26 **18** 245.7 ÷ 35

19 9.081 ÷ 18 **20** 250.8 ÷ 12 **21** 1,038.94/82 **22** 0.29 ÷ 58

Divide. Round to the nearest tenth, if necessary.

23 43.25 ÷ 8 **24** 17.42 ÷ 16 **25** 28.9 ÷ 9 **26** 11 ÷ 6

27 35.88 ÷ 6 **28** 238.5 ÷ 45 **29** 20.6/17 **30** 12.5 ÷ 7

Divide. Round to the nearest hundredth or cent, if necessary.

31 13.3 ÷ 8 **32** 5.7 ÷ 22 **33** $65.10 ÷ 13 **34** 263.4 ÷ 32

35 $27.78 ÷ 6 **36** 56.3 ÷ 18 **37** $4.82 ÷ 7 **38** 3.2 ÷ 82

Simplify.

39 20 − 12.6 ÷ 2 **40** 4.5 × 3 + 1.5 **41** 3 + 2.5 ÷ 5

42 1.6 + 3.6 ÷ 6 **43** 12 − 7.2 ÷ 9 **44** 6.4 ÷ 8 + 1

Complete the table.

	Vehicle	Distance traveled (in miles)	Time (in hours)	Average Speed (to the nearest mile per hour)
45	Car	332.6	7	s
46	Boat	658.4	34	s
47	Airplane	3,148.8	6	s
48	Train	268.5	3	s
49	Helicopter	675.6	5	s

· · · · · · · · · · · · · · · · **Make It Right** · · · · · · · · · · · · · · · ·
50 Tom divided 0.32 ÷ 8 and got 0.4 for the quotient.
What did Tom do wrong?

51 If a car travels 726.8 mi on 20 gal of gas, how far can it go on 1 gal?

52 If gas costs $24.48 for a 400-mi trip, what is the cost per mile?

53 At a college rowing event, there are 12 eight-person boats and 9 four-person boats on the water. How many people are in the boats?

54 The total weight of a team of 7 sled dogs is 523.5 pounds. What is the average weight of a dog to the nearest pound?

Use the table for problems 55–56.

55 Telecommuters are people who work at home part of the time and use telephones or computers to communicate with their offices. How many telecommuters would you estimate for the year 2000? Explain.

Telecommuters	
Year	Number
1992	6.6 million
1993	7.6 million
2000	n

56 **Write a problem** that can be solved using the table. Solve it and have three other students solve it.

57 In 1977 a Boeing 747 set a world speed record by traveling around the world over both poles, a distance of 26,382 mi. About what was its average speed for the 54-hour trip?

58 In the Philippines coconuts are lashed together and transported by raft. If a raft contains 400 coconuts, how many rafts are needed to transport 16,000 coconuts?

59 A train travels 1,608 miles from Minneapolis to Seattle in 2 days 10 hours. What is the average speed of the train to the nearest tenth of a mile per hour?

60 The total weight of a truck that hauls 10 cars is 66,403 pounds. The weight of the truck without the cars is 44,563 pounds. What is the average weight of a car?

61 **Data Point** Use the graph on page 634 in the Databank. Write a paragraph to describe what the graph shows of the U.S. fleet of railroad freight cars. Explain any trends.

62 **Logical Reasoning** I am a whole number. If you divide 12.8 by me five times you will get 0.0125. Am I 2, 4, 6, or 8? Explain how you know.

mixed review • test preparation

1 6.8 + 1.3

2 3.46 − 2.817

3 89 × 36

4 $64 + $18.62

5 14.8 − 9.93

6 13 × 2.04

7 $20 − $9.75

8 56.3 × 13.5

Multiplication and Division Patterns

Millions of commuters take the train to work each day. Some day you may be one of them. How much will the Commuter Rail collect for 1,000 tickets for travel in two zones?

The **powers of 10** are the numbers 10, 100, and 1,000. You can use patterns to multiply decimals by powers of 10 mentally.

$1.75 \times 1 = 1.75$
$1.75 \times 10 = 17.5$
$1.75 \times 100 = 175.$
$1.75 \times 1,000 = 1750.$

> **power of 10** a number obtained by raising 10 to an exponent.

Commuter Rail Fares

Zones Traveled	One-Way Fare
1	$1.50
2	$1.75
3	$2.00
4	$2.25

The Commuter Rail will collect $1,750.

ALGEBRA: PATTERNS You can also use patterns to divide decimals by powers of 10 mentally.

$26.7 \div 1 = 26.7$
$26.7 \div 10 = 2.67$
$26.7 \div 100 = 0.267$
$26.7 \div 1,000 = 0.0267$

$0.4 \div 1 = 0.4$
$0.4 \div 10 = 0.04$
$0.4 \div 100 = 0.004$
$0.4 \div 1,000 = 0.0004$

More Examples

A $0.013 \times 100 = 1.3$ **B** $6.8 \div 1,000 = 0.0068$ **C** $234 \div 1,000 = 0.234$

Check for Understanding

Use mental math to find each product or quotient.

1 0.02×10 **2** $7.502 \times 1,000$ **3** $26.4 \div 10$ **4** $0.6 \div 100$

Critical Thinking: Generalize   Explain your reasoning.

5 **ALGEBRA: PATTERNS** What seems to happen to the decimal point when you multiply by 10? 100? 1,000?

6 **ALGEBRA: PATTERNS** What seems to happen to the decimal point when you divide by 10? 100? 1,000?

7 In Example B why were zeros placed to the left of the 6?

8 In Example C where is the decimal point in 234 understood to be, even though it is not written?

Practice

Write the letter of the correct answer.

1 46.8×10 **a.** 4,680   **b.** 468   **c.** 4.68   **d.** 0.468

2 0.6×100 **a.** 600   **b.** 60   **c.** 0.06   **d.** 0.006

3 $487.1 \div 10$ **a.** 4,871   **b.** 48,710   **c.** 48.71   **d.** 0.4871

Find the product or quotient mentally.

4 35.8×10 **5** $40.1 \times 1,000$ **6** 100×78.35 **7** $0.02 \times 1,000$

8 $388.9 \div 10$ **9** $2.713 \div 100$ **10** $53.9 \div 10$ **11** $5,476 \div 1,000$

12 $32.75 \times 1,000$ **13** $7.349 \div 1,000$ **14** 43×10 **15** $0.8756 \div 10$

16 $9,431 \div 1,000$ **17** 0.3×100 **18** $7.1 \div 100$ **19** $0.22 \div 1,000$

ALGEBRA Find the missing number.

20 $50 \times n = 5,000$ **21** $b \div 10 = 0.045$ **22** $6 \div 100 = a$

23 $c \div 1,000 = 0.00378$ **24** $0.073 \times n = 73$ **25** $2.8 \div n = 0.028$

MIXED APPLICATIONS
Problem Solving

26 Suppose 100 sixth graders go on a field trip. They each pay the half-fare rate of $0.75 for zone 1 tickets. How much do they pay in all?

27 How many zeros are in the product $10^3 \times 10^2$? the product $10^4 \times 10^5$? Do you see a pattern?

28 Otto bought a $99.99 train ticket. His hotel cost $134 for one night and $49 each night for two more nights. He spent $24.95 per day for a 3-day car rental. How much did the trip cost?

29 The Liberty Bell hung in the State House in Philadelphia for 93 years. If it was rung 24 times a day every day, about how many times was it rung in those 93 years?

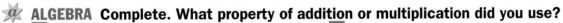

mixed review • test preparation

ALGEBRA Complete. What property of addition or multiplication did you use?

1 $37 + 24 = \blacksquare + 37$

2 $8 \times (40 + 5) = (8 \times \blacksquare) + (8 \times 5)$

3 $643 \times 1 = \blacksquare$

4 $16 + (20 + 8) = (16 + \blacksquare) + 8$

Divide by Decimals

You can use models to help you divide by decimals.

Divide: 1.2 ÷ 0.3

Represent 1.2 by shading grids.

Find the number of groups of 0.3 in 1.2.
Since there are 4, 1.2 ÷ 0.3 = 4.

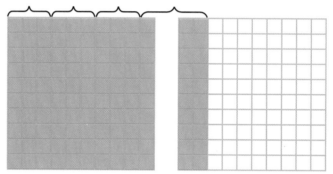

Work Together

Work in a group to find these quotients. Use models to find the quotients only when the divisor is a decimal.

▶ 1.6 ÷ 0.2	16 ÷ 2	160 ÷ 20
▶ 0.32 ÷ 0.08	3.2 ÷ 0.8	32 ÷ 8
▶ 2 ÷ 0.4	20 ÷ 4	200 ÷ 40

You will need
- *graph paper*

Talk It Over

 ▶ **ALGEBRA PATTERNS** What patterns do you see in the quotients?

▶ How are the dividends in each row above related?

▶ How are the divisors in each row above related?

Make Connections

If you multiply both the dividend and divisor of any division problem by a power of 10, the new quotient is the same as the original quotient.

Therefore, to divide a decimal by a decimal, multiply the divisor and the dividend by a power of 10. Then the new divisor will be a whole number.

Divide: 1.6 ÷ 0.2
× **10** ↓   ↓ × **10**
    16 ÷ 2 = 8

Divide: 0.56 ÷ 0.08
× **100** ↓   ↓ × **100**
      56 ÷ 8 = 7

▶ Multiply the divisor and the dividend by a power of 10 to find 4.2 ÷ 1.4. Then use models to find the quotient. Do you get the same answer?

▶ Find 1.32 ÷ 0.12 using both methods.

Check for Understanding

Find the quotient using the model.

1 0.6 ÷ 0.2 = n

2 0.35 ÷ 0.05 = a

3 1.92 ÷ 0.16 = d

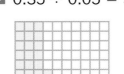

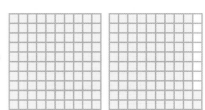

Find the quotient. You may use models.

4 0.27 ÷ 0.09

5 4.5 ÷ 1.5

6 3 ÷ 0.25

7 7.2 ÷ 0.8

8 2.4 ÷ 0.6

9 0.56 ÷ 0.07

10 0.81 ÷ 0.09

11 0.8 ÷ 0.2

Critical Thinking: Analyze

12 If the dividend and the divisor are greater than 1, is the quotient always less than the dividend? Give an example to support your reasoning.

13 Journal If a dividend greater than 1 is divided by a divisor less than 1, could the quotient be less than the dividend? Give an example to support your answer.

14 How is dividing with decimals the same as dividing with whole numbers?

Turn the page for Practice. ➡

Practice

Find the quotient using the model.

1 0.09 ÷ 0.03

2 0.8 ÷ 0.4

3 $1.25 ÷ $0.25

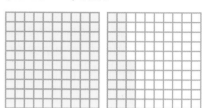

Find the quotient using any method.

4 $0.5\overline{)7.5}$

5 $0.05\overline{)0.75}$

6 $0.36\overline{)0.72}$

7 $3.6\overline{)7.2}$

8 $0.2\overline{)3.2}$

9 $0.37\overline{)1.48}$

10 $3.2\overline{)25.6}$

11 $0.25\overline{)4}$

12 5.5 ÷ 0.5

13 0.84 ÷ 0.07

14 2.99 ÷ 0.23

15 4.9 ÷ 0.7

16 6 ÷ 0.2

17 3.92 ÷ 0.56

18 4.8 ÷ 1.6

19 8.4 ÷ 4.2

20 0.36 ÷ 0.03

21 5.6 ÷ 0.7

22 0.16 ÷ 0.04

23 6.3 ÷ 0.7

24 0.81 ÷ 0.09

25 2.5 ÷ 0.5

26 7.2 ÷ 0.8

27 0.48 ÷ 0.06

28 3.6 ÷ 1.2

29 3.3 ÷ 1.1

30 3.9 ÷ 1.3

31 1.25 ÷ 0.05

☆ ALGEBRA PATTERNS Complete the tables. Look for patterns to help.

Rule: Divide by 6.	
Input	Output
420	n
42	n
4.2	n

32 (420)
33 (42)
34 (4.2)

Rule: Divide by 0.6.	
Input	Output
420	n
42	n
4.2	n

35 (420)
36 (42)
37 (4.2)

Rule: Divide by 0.06.	
Input	Output
420	n
42	n
4.2	n

38 (420)
39 (42)
40 (4.2)

MIXED APPLICATIONS

Problem Solving

41 Suppose a jar weighs 450 g empty and 1,770 g with marbles in it. If each marble weighs 4.5 g, how many marbles are in the jar?

42 Suppose subway tokens cost $1.40 each. You just bought $7 worth of tokens, but you forgot how many you bought. How many did you buy?

43 If a wooden beam weighs 40 kg per meter, what is the weight of a beam 2.4 meters long?

44 A wheel makes a revolution in 0.9 seconds. About how many revolutions will the wheel make in 9 hours?

Finding-a-Path Game!

Label 6 index cards as *divisors* and copy one divisor on each card. Then label 7 cards as *dividends* and copy one dividend on each card.

Divisors:
0.2, 0.02, 0.5, 0.05, 0.4, 0.04

Dividends: 8.2, 16.4, 2.4, 20.4, 10.4, 1.2, 6.8

Play the Game

▶ Form two teams.

▶ Teams choose a color for their counters and take turns. When it is your team's turn, choose a dividend and a divisor. If the quotient appears on the game board, put one of your team's counters on it.

▶ If you find a quotient that is not on the game board or is already covered with a counter, your team loses a turn.

▶ The first team to get a path of counters connecting the team's two sides wins.

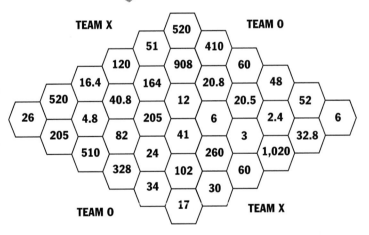

---

mixed review • test preparation

Estimate each product.

1 82 × 51

2 7,016 × 49

3 11.6 × 1.7

4 24.7 × 2.6

5 Make a line graph for the average price of a loaf of white bread in the United States: 1990: 70¢; 1991: 72¢; 1992: 74¢; 1993: 76¢; 1994: 75¢; 1995: 84¢

Divide by Decimals

IN THE WORKPLACE

Patrick Hong of Newport Beach, CA, road tests cars for *Road & Track* magazine.

Once you start buying your own gas, you'll care about mpg—miles per gallon. Patrick Hong tests mpg for *Road & Track*. Suppose a car uses 14.5 gal of gas to go 423.4 mi. How many miles per gallon did the car get?

Divide: 423.4 ÷ 14.5

Estimate the quotient.   **Think:** $400 ÷ 10 = 40$

In the last lesson you learned that to divide a decimal by a decimal, you can multiply the divisor and the dividend by a power of 10.

Step 1	Step 2
Multiply the dividend and the divisor by the same power of 10.	**Place the decimal point in the quotient. Divide as with whole numbers.**

Step 1:

$$14.5 \overline{)423.4}$$

Step 2:

```
        29.2
  145)4234.0
      -290↓
       1334
      -1305
        290
        -290
          0
```

Write a decimal point and a zero so you can keep dividing.

  $423.4 ÷ 14.5 =$ **29.2**

The car gets 29.2 miles per gallon.

Talk It Over

▶ Is 29.2 miles per gallon a reasonable answer for the question? Explain.

▶ **What if** you are dividing 16.25 ÷ 6.5. You multiply the divisor and the dividend by 100 instead of 10. Would you get the same answer? Explain.

Remember that you don't always need all the decimal places in the quotient. You can round the quotient to a particular place. Divide 19.75 ÷ 0.37 and round the quotient to the nearest tenth.

MPG
HWY 28
CITY 22

Divide: 19.75 ÷ 0.37

Step 1	Step 2
Multiply the dividend and the divisor by the same power of 10 so the new divisor is a whole number.	**Place the decimal point in the quotient. Write zeros in the dividend. Continue to divide.**

Step 1:

$$0.37\overline{)19.75}$$

Step 2:

```
         53.37
  37)1,975.00
    − 1 85↓
        125
      − 111
        14 0
      − 11 1↓
          2 90
        − 2 59
            31
```

Divide until there is no remainder, or if rounding, to one more place than you are rounding to.

Calculator 19.75 ÷ 0.37 = **53.378378**

When rounded to the nearest tenth, both quotients equal 53.4.

More Examples

A Divide: 0.1 ÷ 0.3.
Round to the nearest hundredth.

```
      0.333 ← Round to 0.33
  0.3)0.1 000
    − 9↓
      10
    − 9↓
      10
    − 9
       1
```

B Divide: 9 ÷ 12

```
      0.75
  12)9.00   ← Write a decimal point
   − 84↓       and two zeros to
     60        complete the division.
   − 60
```

Check for Understanding

Divide. Remember to estimate. Round to the nearest tenth, if necessary.

1 $4.3\overline{)7.869}$ **2** $0.002\overline{)0.24}$ **3** $0.14\overline{)3.7}$ **4** $8\overline{)4}$

Critical Thinking: Analyze   **Explain your answer.**

5 Divide 261 by 4 on your calculator in two ways:
261 ÷R 4 = and 261 ÷ 4 =.
Compare the answers. How are they related?

C
H
E
C
K

Divide Whole Numbers and Decimals **155**

Practice

Divide. Remember to estimate.

1 $0.8\overline{)136}$ **2** $3.2\overline{)192}$ **3** $0.5\overline{)1.2}$ **4** $0.041\overline{)4.92}$

5 $5\overline{)12}$ **6** $4.2\overline{)2.037}$ **7** $0.143\overline{)0.0572}$ **8** $6.5\overline{)132.6}$

9 $12.6 \div 1.5$ **10** $9.177 \div 0.21$ **11** $8.75 \div 0.35$ **12** $2.88 \div 7.2$

13 $0.399 \div 0.007$ **14** $13.65 \div 0.065$ **15** $0.6405 \div 0.15$ **16** $8.28 \div 2.3$

Divide. Round the quotient to the nearest tenth, if necessary.

17 $0.23\overline{)7.8}$ **18** $2.6\overline{)85.5}$ **19** $6.8\overline{)19.72}$ **20** $0.54\overline{)63.3}$

21 $0.027 \div 0.006$ **22** $7 \div 3$ **23** $6.35 \div 0.07$ **24** $22 \div 7$

25 $19 \div 6$ **26** $0.236 \div 0.5$ **27** $141.6 \div 6$ **28** $0.0036 \div 0.012$

Divide. Round the quotient to the nearest hundredth or cent, if necessary.

29 $3.7\overline{)0.1554}$ **30** $0.9\overline{)8}$ **31** $7\overline{)\$9}$ **32** $6.2\overline{)21.39}$

33 $\$22.76 \div 0.3$ **34** $6.074 \div 3$ **35** $78.8 \div 7.6$ **36** $0.567 \div 25$

Divide mentally. Explain your methods.

37 $0.6\overline{)2.4}$ **38** $0.9\overline{)7.2}$ **39** $0.22\overline{)0.88}$ **40** $0.05\overline{)0.4}$

41 $63 \div 2.1$ **42** $0.75 \div 0.25$ **43** $0.16 \div 0.8$ **44** $0.54 \div 0.6$

α ALGEBRA Evaluate each expression.

45 $\frac{1.25}{x} + 4$ for $x = 0.25$ **46** $0.5b - 1$ for $b = 10$ **47** $4 \times \frac{z}{1.5}$ for $z = 3$

48 $7 - \frac{16.4}{a}$ for $a = 4$ **49** $5r \div 1.2$ for $r = 1.2$ **50** $\frac{t}{1.8} - 5$ for $t = 36$

Find the missing number.

	Dividend	Divisor	Quotient
51	8.46	n	1.8
52	n	0.76	2.8

	Dividend	Divisor	Quotient
53	89	0.05	n
54	7.2	n	45

• • • • • • • • • • • • • • • • • • • Make It Right • • • • • • • • • • • • • • • • • • •

55 Pat divided 12 by 2.4 this way.
Tell what the error is and correct it.

$$\begin{array}{r} 0.5 \\ 2.4\overline{)12.0} \\ -12\ 0 \\ \hline 0 \end{array}$$

Problem Solving

56 Tim used 28 gallons to drive his car 905 miles. What gas mileage did his car get, rounded to the nearest mile per gallon?

57 Jan bought $12.85 worth of gas. The gas cost $1.339 per gallon. How many gallons did he buy, to the nearest tenth of a gallon?

Use the table to answer questions 58–60.

58 Find the gallons of gas used during a 350-mi trip for the Saturn. Round your answer to the nearest tenth.

59 What is the difference between the most expensive vehicles and the least expensive vehicles? Of those two vehicles, which gets more miles per gallon? How much more?

Vehicle Comparison Shopping			
Make and Model	**Base Price**	**Stopping Distance***	**Fuel mpg****
Chevrolet Blazer	$23,252	157 ft	17.4
Saturn	$10,995	149 ft	31.0
Toyota Camry	$21,878	145 ft	23.0
Volvo 850 Turbo Sportwagon	$30,985	130 ft	23.5

*Stopping distance is at 60 mi per hour.
**miles per gallon

60 Which vehicle has the shortest stopping distance? About how many yards is that?

61 **Write a problem** that can be solved by dividing by a decimal. Solve your problem and then ask three other students to solve it.

more to explore

Repeating Decimals

Sometimes when you divide one whole number by another, the digits in the quotient repeat. For example,

$1 \div 9 = 0.1111...$
$24 \div 99 = 0.24242424...$

When the digits repeat like this, the decimals are called *repeating decimals*. The three periods (...) mean that the digits continue to repeat in the same pattern.

Look for a pattern. Predict the answers. Divide to check.

1 $3 \div 9$ **2** $4 \div 9$ **3** $5 \div 9$ **4** $8 \div 9$

5 $53 \div 99$ **6** $13 \div 99$ **7** $86 \div 99$ **8** $2 \div 99$

Changing Metric Units

One of the big advantages of the metric system is that it is easy to change from one unit to another. This is because the metric system is based on 10 just like our place-value system for naming numbers.

Changing a metric measurement from one unit to another is like moving from one place-value position to another.

To change larger units to smaller units, multiply.
To change smaller units to larger units, divide.

Cultural Note
The metric system was developed by a group of French scientists and adopted in France in 1795. It is used by nearly all countries.

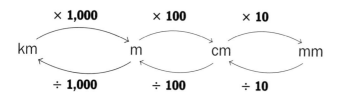

× 1,000	× 100	× 10
km	m	cm	mm
÷ 1,000	÷ 100	÷ 10

Change 0.2 m to centimeters.

Think: 1 m = 100 cm
0.2 × 100 = 20
0.2 m = 20 cm

Change 750 m to kilometers.

Think: 1 km = 1,000 m
750 ÷ 1,000 = 0.75
750 m = 0.75 km

Check Out the Glossary
metric system
See page 643.

More Examples

A 85.4 mg = ■ g
85.4 ÷ 1,000 = 0.0854
85.4 mg = 0.0854 g

B 105 mL = ■ L
105 ÷ 1,000 = 0.105
105 mL = 0.105 L

C 0.62 cm = ■ mm
0.62 × 10 = 6.2
0.62 cm = 6.2 mm

Check for Understanding
Complete.

1 48.9 cm = ■ m

2 17.3 L = ■ mL

3 735 g = ■ mg

4 2 cm = ■ mm

5 4000 mL = ■ L

6 400 g = ■ kg

Critical Thinking: Generalize   **Explain your reasoning.**

7 Explain why you multiply when changing from larger to smaller units, and divide when changing from smaller to larger units.

8 Make a diagram like the one above to show how to change kiloliters to milliliters. How is it the same, and how is it different from the diagram above?

Practice

Complete.

1 20 mm = ■ cm **2** 8 kg = ■ g **3** 1.5 kL = ■ L **4** 8.4 km = ■ m

5 0.4 g = ■ mg **6** 5.1 km = ■ m **7** 4,300 m = ■ km **8** 15 mL = ■ L

9 800 L = ■ kL **10** 924 mL = ■ L **11** 13.52 m = ■ cm **12** 2.4 m = ■ cm

13 3 g = ■ mg **14** 6.5 cm = ■ mm **15** 2400 g = ■ kg **16** 639 cm = ■ m

17 200 cm = ■ m **18** 500 mg = ■ g **19** 3 L = ■ mL **20** 75 g = ■ kg

21 0.5 m = ■ cm **22** 55 g = ■ kg **23** 10 mL = ■ L **24** 1.5 cm = ■ mm

Compare. Write >, <, or =.

25 1.6 m ● 16 cm **26** 500 cm ● 0.5 m **27** 0.07 mg ● 95 g

28 0.008 kg ● 8 g **29** 308 mL ● 0.261 L **30** 400 cm ● 5 m

MIXED APPLICATIONS
Problem Solving

31 The longest train known in the U.S. had 500 coal cars and 6 locomotives. If each coal car was 13 m long and each locomotive was 20 m long, how many kilometers long was the train?

32 In September Maria bought a camera for $80. She made 4 equal payments to pay for the camera. How much was each payment?

33 A stack of unfolded boxes for carrying pizza is 12.5 cm high. The thickness of each box is 2.5 mm. How many boxes are in the stack?

34 **Write a problem** that can be solved by changing meters to centimeters. Solve your problem and then ask three other students to solve it.

more to explore

More Metric Relationships

1 A cube that is 10 cm on a side holds 1,000 cm³ of water. How many milliliters will it hold? liters? What is its mass?

2 How many milliliters of water will a container with a capacity of 600 cm³ hold?

3 How much mass does 900 mL of water have?

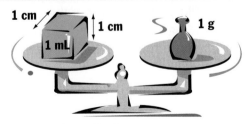

1 cubic centimeter
(1 cm³) holds 1 mL of water.

1 mL of water has a mass of 1 g.

Problem Solvers at Work

Read
Plan
Solve
Look Back

PART 1   Interpret Quotients and Remainders

Ms. Gonzales is planning a field trip to a planetarium for 257 students. The buses she plans to use hold 40 students.

Work Together

Use the work at the right to answer problems 1–3.

1 How many buses can be filled?

2 How many buses will be needed altogether? Explain.

$$\begin{array}{r} 6\ \text{R}17 \\ 40\overline{)257} \\ -240 \\ \hline 17 \end{array}$$

3 **What if** the extra students were accommodated on a smaller bus. How many passengers would that bus need to hold? What number do you use to answer the question?

Solve.

4 Could you find the number of buses needed altogether by dividing to get a decimal and then rounding to the nearest whole number? Explain.

5 **What if** there were 294 students. How many buses would be needed altogether?

6  **Make Generalizations** Sometimes you can divide and use the quotient. Other times you must add 1 to the quotient. Generalize about when to use the quotient and when to add 1 to the quotient.

Amy wrote this problem.

7 Solve and explain Amy's problem.

8 Change Amy's problem so that it is either easier or harder to solve. Do not change any of the data in the graph.

9 Solve the new problem and explain why it is easier or harder to solve than Amy's problem.

10 **Create a problem** by replacing the blanks with different numbers. Roberto has ■ bus tokens. He divides the tokens evenly among the ■ students in his class. How many are left over? Solve your problem.

11 Trade problems. Solve at least three problems written by other students.

Mr. Kim is planning a nature walk for 80 students. He is dividing the students into groups of 12. How many groups will there be?

Amy Schoffler
McPherson Middle School
Howell, MI

Turn the page for Practice Strategies.
Divide Whole Numbers and Decimals   **161**

Menu

Choose five problems and solve them.
Explain your methods.

1 Suppose a sightseeing helicopter holds 8 people and 102 people want to go on it. If the helicopter will be filled every time it goes out except the last time, how many people will be on the last flight?

2 Kendra works for a company that builds roads. Her regular rate is $8 per hour and $12 per hour for overtime. How much does she earn if she works 40 hours at a regular rate and 3.5 hours overtime?

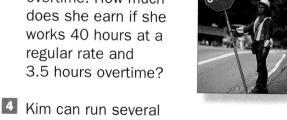

3 There are 3 more books than games to be given away as prizes. Altogether there are 15 books and games. How many are there of each?

4 Kim can run several miles at 0.1 mile per minute. If she runs for 1 hour 10 minutes, how many miles has she run?

5 Each railroad car holds 12 compact cars. There are 795 compact cars to be shipped, but only full railroad cars are sent out. How many railroad cars will be sent out?

6 There are 135 cars waiting in line at a car ferry across the Columbia River. If the ferry holds 16 cars, how many trips will it have to make to ferry all the cars across?

7 Lee bought a coat for $56 and a cap for $10.88. How much change will she get from 4 twenty-dollar bills?

8 A bus used 85 gallons of gas in one day to go 344 miles. About how many miles to the gallon did the bus get?

Choose two problems and solve them. Explain your methods.

9 You plan to arrive at an amusement park at 1 P.M. and leave at 5 P.M. Use the following list of rides to make a schedule for yourself. Allow 20 minutes for walking between rides and allow yourself a 30-minute break for a snack.

Today's Times for Waiting in Line and Taking the Ride			
Haunted Castle	25 minutes	Walk the Plank	15 minutes
Ferris Wheel	10 minutes	Swing to the Sky	9 minutes
Dragon Drop	8 minutes	Flume Mountain	10 minutes
Yesterday Village	32 minutes	Scrambler	5 minutes
Bumper Cars	12 minutes	Roller Coaster	8 minutes

10 **Spatial reasoning** Show how you can remove two toothpicks and leave two equilateral triangles. (A triangle is equilateral if all its sides have the same length.)

11 **Write a problem** Write a possible newspaper headline for this graph and then write a problem using the data in it.

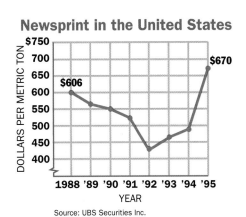

Newsprint in the United States

Source: UBS Securities Inc.

12 **At the Computer** Suppose you want to design several cars that can drive 300 miles without stopping for gas. Make a spreadsheet like the one on the screen to show how many gallons the gas tank will need to hold for cars that get from 15 to 35 miles per gallon. Round the tank capacity to the nearest tenth of a gallon.

Gas Mileage in miles per gallon	Tank Capacity in gallons
15	20.0
16	18.8
17	17.6

Language and Mathematics
Complete the sentence. Use a word in the chart. (pages 124–159)

1 In 48 ÷ 3 = 16, the number 48 is the ■.

2 When you divide one whole number by another, the remainder is always less than the ■.

3 To make estimating quotients easier to do mentally, you can use ■.

4 You can ■ an algebraic expression by substituting a value for the variable.

> ### Vocabulary
> compatible numbers
> divisor
> dividend
> quotient
> evaluate
> divide
> remainder

Concepts and Skills
Divide mentally. (page 124)

5 200 ÷ 5

6 800 ÷ 40

7 1,000 ÷ 20

8 1,800 ÷ 600

Estimate each quotient using compatible numbers. (page 124)

9 473 ÷ 71

10 1,298 ÷ 51

11 368 ÷ 8

12 7,924 ÷ 97

Evaluate the expression. (page 134)

13 $5n$ for $n = 16$

14 $\frac{n}{6}$ for $n = 12$

15 $\frac{n}{8}$ for $n = 640$

Simplify. (page 136)

16 $2 \times 8 - 3 \times 5$

17 $12 \div 6 + 8$

18 $63 \div (3 \times 7) + 5$

Divide. Round to the nearest tenth, if necessary. (pages 128, 130, 144, 150, 154)

19 $6\overline{)642}$

20 $5\overline{)13.5}$

21 $48\overline{)61,584}$

22 $3\overline{)811}$

23 $0.4\overline{)3.5}$

24 $0.36\overline{)1.321}$

Divide. Round to the nearest hundredth, if necessary. (pages 144–157)

25 $1.36\overline{)119}$

26 $100\overline{)4}$

27 $3\overline{)0.8226}$

Solve. (page 148)

28 $14.6 \times 1,000$

29 0.2×100

30 3.06×10

31 $0.04 \times 1,000$

32 $1.82 \div 10$

33 $3.6 \div 1,000$

34 $14 \div 100$

35 $724.8 \div 100$

Complete. (page 158)

36 1.7 m = ■ cm

37 1,300 g = ■ kg

38 75 mL = ■ L

Think critically. (pages 144–157)

39 Analyze. Explain what went wrong. Then correct it.

40 Generalize. Write *always, sometimes,* or *never.* Give examples to support your answers.

  a. If you divide a number greater than 1 by a number greater than 1, the quotient is less than the dividend.

  b. If you divide a number greater than 1 by a number less than 1, the quotient is less than the dividend.

  c. When you estimate using compatible numbers, the estimate is less than the exact quotient.

MIXED APPLICATIONS
Problem Solving

(pages 138, 160)

41 Pat has to ship 322.6 pounds of salmon. The maximum he wants to put in each box is 8.5 pounds. How many boxes will he need?

42 The amount of money George has in the bank, rounded to the nearest $10,000, is $10,000. What is the most and the least money George could have in the bank?

43 Tony drove 600 miles on 20 gallons of gas. What was his average number of miles per gallon?

44 Rita made 6.2L of root beer. How many full 350-mL bottles will she get from this root beer?

45 The cost, in dollars, of the airline tickets that Rosemary bought can be represented by 289*n*, where *n* represents the number of tickets she bought. What is the cost if *n* = 3?

46 Class 101 bought 58 train tickets to Washington, D.C., for $3,509 from ABC Travel. Class 108 bought 44 tickets to Washington, D.C., for $2,783 from XYZ Travel. Which class paid less for each ticket? Explain.

Use the information in the table for problems 47–50.

47 Find the average number of passengers per day in January to the nearest whole number.

48 Find the average number of passengers per month for the four months.

Airport Traffic Bay City Regional Airport	
Month	**Number of Passengers**
January	23,610
February	43,742
March	38,276
April	52,408

49 Which month has the greatest daily number of passengers?

50 The airport has 12 gates. What is the average number of passengers who left through each gate in April?

Evaluate the expression.

1 $12n$ for $n = 8$

2 $\frac{n}{7}$ for $n = 49$

3 $\frac{n}{4}$ for $n = 800$

Simplify.

4 $15 \times 3 \div 5$

5 $15 - 2 \times 6$

6 $15 \div (2 + 3) + 8$

Estimate the quotient using compatible numbers.

7 $521 \div 67$

8 $4,623 \div 91$

9 $60,251 \div 61$

Divide. Round to the nearest hundredth if necessary.

10 $600 \div 3$

11 $10,000 \div 50$

12 $141.6 \div 1,000$

13 $73.6 \div 8$

14 $38\overline{)8,550}$

15 $6\overline{)743}$

16 $32\overline{)628.7}$

17 $0.54\overline{)1.66}$

Complete.

18 $4.2\ L = \blacksquare\ mL$

19 $40\ mm = \blacksquare\ cm$

20 $1,800\ L = \blacksquare\ kL$

21 $0.3\ g = \blacksquare\ mg$

Solve. Show your work.

22 The number of cars that can leave airport parking in an hour can be represented by $45n$, where n is the number of toll booths open. How many cars can leave per hour if 8 toll booths are open?

23 A city bus averages 8 miles per gallon of gas. About how many gallons of gas will the bus use in a day if it travels 731 miles?

24 Devon spends $19 on bus travel. She buys some round-trip tokens for $1.50 each and some one-way tokens for $0.80 each. How many of each kind does she buy?

25 An orange grove produces 11,895 oranges one week. The oranges are packed into bags. Each bag holds 2 dozen oranges. How many full bags are packed?

What Did You Learn?

Three students are discussing the two division problems below.

> $0.6 ÷ 0.45 =$ _____
>
> $0.45 ÷ 0.6 =$ _____

Joe thinks the two problems will have the same answer because they have the same digits and the same operation.

▶ Use graph paper, place-value models, or play money to model the two problems and show their solutions.

▶ Explain to Joe why his thinking is incorrect and show him how to solve the problems using paper and pencil.

You will need:
- *graph paper*
- *place-value models*
- *play money*

················ A Good Answer ····················
- includes a picture, model, or diagram of each problem.
- includes a written explanation of why the two problems would not have the same answer.
- shows accurate steps and correct answers.

 You may want to place your work in your portfolio.

 # What Do You Think

1 Which do you find easier, dividing whole numbers or dividing decimals? Explain why.

2 How do you check your answer to a division problem?
- Use an estimate.
- Use multiplication and division.
- Use models.
- Other. Explain.

Auto Emissions

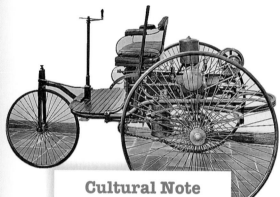

Cultural Note

Karl Benz, a German engineer, invented the first car in 1885. He used an internal combustion engine developed a few years earlier by Nikolaus Otto, another German engineer.

The basic design of a car engine has not changed since Otto invented it. Gasoline is mixed with air and then ignited inside a cylinder. The expanding gas produced by the burning fuel pushes a piston. The force of all of the moving pistons is used to turn the wheels of the car.

Unfortunately, the chemicals in the exhaust made by this burning fuel are a major part of air pollution. Different chemicals cause different problems.

One way carmakers try to reduce emissions is by putting *catalytic converters* on the exhaust system of cars. These devices change the chemicals in the exhaust into less harmful forms.

Emission	Problem Caused
Nitrogen oxides	Acid rain
Carbon monoxide	Breathing difficulties
Carbon dioxide	May cause global warming
Hydrocarbons	Irritate eyes and lungs and damage plant life
Soot, smoke	May cause cancer

▶ What other sources of air pollution do you know about?

▶ What other methods of reducing air pollution can you think of?

How Many Miles?

One obvious way to reduce air pollution is to burn less fuel.

Car manufacturers have significantly improved fuel economy (miles per gallon) since 1970.

Fuel Economy	
Year	Average Mileage (in miles per gallon)
1970	13.5
1975	13.5
1980	15.5
1985	18.2
1990	21.0
1994	21.5

SOURCE: ENERGY INFORMATION ADMINISTRATION

Explain how you found your answer.

1 How much greater to the nearest tenth was the average gas mileage in 1994 than it was in 1970? in 1980?

2 How many more miles can a car built in 1980 go than one built in 1970 if the gas tanks on both cars hold 15 gallons each?

3 How much fuel can be saved if a carpool of 4 people rides 50 miles in a car that gets 25 miles to the gallon rather than each of them riding in separate cars getting the same mileage?

At the Computer

The table below shows the average number of gallons of gas used in cars in different states.

State Fuel Economy		
State	Average Number of Miles Driven per Car per Year	Gasoline Used (in gallons)
California	11,825	688
Texas	12,793	780
Florida	11,172	667
New York	11,236	641
Ohio	10,545	606
Pennsylvania	10,906	675
Illinois	10,980	677
Michigan	11,520	657
Georgia	13,205	745
North Carolina	12,726	734

4 Use a spreadsheet program to create a table that lists the states in order from the best to the worst in fuel economy.

5 Extend your spreadsheet to include the cost of buying the average amount of gasoline used in each state, if gas costs $1.29 per gallon.

6 Write two statements based on your spreadsheet.

Divide Whole Numbers and Decimals **169**

Entertainment

While you're listening to a concert or the radio, or even cheering a live show, numbers are behind the scenes. As you will see in this chapter, whether you enjoy or create entertainment, you need to understand numbers.

What Do You Know

Use this data from a survey of 40 sixth graders for these questions.

1 What fraction of those surveyed voted for watching TV? Write the fraction in simplest form.

2 Which activities got more than $\frac{1}{4}$ of the votes? How do you know?

3 When seventh graders were surveyed, the fraction for the students who voted for dancing was equivalent to the sixth grade fraction. How many possible seventh graders could there be? How many voted for dancing? Explain.

Favorite Activity at a Birthday Party	
Activity	**Number of People**
Going to movies	14
Playing video games	12
Watching TV	8
Dancing	4
Other	2

Draw Conclusions The Creatures band has four members. Jada always wears a red hat, plays the piano, and sings. Kirk plays the drum, wears yellow hats, but never sings. The guitarist Tammy sings and always wears a red hat. Albert plays the bass, sings, but never wears a hat.

You can draw conclusions from paragraphs you read.

1 What conclusions can you state about the band using fractions?

Vocabulary

whole number, p. 172
divisible by, p. 172
divisibility rule, p. 172
composite number,
  p. 175
prime factorization,
  p. 175

prime number, p. 175
factor tree, p. 175
common factor, p. 178
greatest common
  factor, p. 178
common multiple,
  p. 180

least common
  multiple, p. 180
fraction, p. 188
numerator, p. 188
denominator, p. 188
equivalent fractions,
  p. 190

simplest form, p. 194
common
  denominator, p. 196
mixed number, p. 198
improper fraction,
  p. 198
rename, p. 198

Divisibility

Aren't marching bands great fun to watch at parades and football games? It's entertaining to see the musicians arrange themselves into different formations. Can a marching band with 216 musicians form equal rows of 3? of 6? of 9?

To decide, find out if 216 is divisible by 3, by 6, or by 9.

A **whole number** is **divisible by** another number if the quotient is a whole number and the remainder is 0.

 216 ÷R) 3 = 72 *RO*

You can also use a **divisibility rule** to see if 216 is divisible by 3.

If the sum of the digits of a whole number is divisible by 3, then the number is divisible by 3.

Think: 2 + 1 + 6 = 9
9 ÷ 3 = 3
216 is divisible by 3.

Cultural Note
The U.S. has more than 35,000 high school bands and 1,000 college bands.

Check Out the Glossary
For vocabulary words, see page 643.

Divisibility Rules—A whole number is divisible by:	
2 if the ones digit is 0, 2, 4, 6, or 8.	**6** if it is divisible by 2 and by 3.
3 if the sum of the digits is divisible by 3.	**9** if the sum of the digits is divisible by 9.
5 if the ones digit is 0 or 5.	**10** if the ones digit is 0.

You can mentally test if 216 is divisible by 6 or by 9.

216 ÷ 6 **Think:** 216 is divisible by 2.
216 is divisible by 3.
216 is divisible by 6.

216 ÷ 9 **Think:** 2 + 1 + 6 = 9
9 ÷ 9 = 1
216 is divisible by 9.

The marching band can form equal rows of 3, 6, and 9.

Check for Understanding
Tell whether the number is divisible by 2, 3, 5, 6, 9, or 10.

1 78 **2** 63 **3** 201 **4** 700 **5** 336 **6** 8,190

Critical Thinking: Analyze Explain your reasoning.

7 Are numbers divisible by 10 also divisible by 5? Are numbers divisible by 3 always divisible by 9? Give examples.

Practice

Tell whether the number is divisible by 2, 3, 5, 6, 9, or 10.

1 38   **2** 48   **3** 57   **4** 66   **5** 93

6 126   **7** 486   **8** 505   **9** 770   **10** 858

11 9,378   **12** 8,730   **13** 7,965   **14** 10,005   **15** 22,287

16 19,467   **17** 999,999   **18** 1,000,001   **19** 2,001,006   **20** 4,211,122

Use mental math to find the missing digit. Give all possible answers.

21 5 is a factor of 47,58■

22 47,58■ is divisible by 10.

23 123,4■2 is divisible by 9.

24 123,4■2 is divisible by 6.

Solve.

25 What is the least 3-digit number that is divisible by 3?

26 What is the greatest 4-digit number that is divisible by 6?

MIXED APPLICATIONS
Problem Solving

Pencil & Paper   Calculator   Mental Math

27 **Draw Conclusions** Here are the numbers of students in a high school band in recent years. 1995: 96; 1996: 90, 1997: 88; 1998: 84. What conclusion can you draw about the band?

28 **Logical reasoning** A band marches onto the field in 10 rows. The number of students in each row is less than 40, and is divisible by 2, 3, 4, 6, 9, 12, and 18. How many students are there in the band?

29 Name the number of the next calendar year that is divisible by 2, 3, 6, and 9.

30 **Write a problem** that can be solved by dividing whole numbers. Solve it and have others solve it.

more to explore

Divisibility by 4

Is 324 divisible by 4? You can use a divisibility rule to find out.

A whole number is divisible by 4 if the number formed by the last two digits is divisible by 4.

3̲2̲4̲ ÷ 4
Think: 24 ÷ 4 = 6
324 is divisible by 4.

Use the divisibility rule to find if the numbers are divisible by 4.

1 298   **2** 916   **3** 1,720   **4** 2,054   **5** 9,741

Prime Factorization

How many different rectangles can you make with 1 square tile? 2 square tiles? 3 through 20 square tiles?

The diagrams at right show all the different rectangles you can make with 4 square tiles.

Work Together

Work in a small group to find ways to make various rectangles.

1 Make as many rectangles as possible with the tiles for the numbers 1 through 20.

You will need
• *20 square tiles*
• *graph paper*

2 Record the dimensions of the rectangles you made. For example:

2 × 2, or 2 by 2

Number	Dimensions of Rectangles
1	
2	
3	
4	
5	
6	
7	

Rectangles with the same dimensions such as a 2-by-3 rectangle and a 3-by-2 rectangle are not different rectangles.

3 Copy the table at the right to keep track of the rectangles you make.

4 Make a sketch on graph paper of each different rectangle that you make with the tiles. Label each with its dimensions.

Talk It Over

▶ For which numbers was it possible to make only one rectangle?

▶ What do you notice about the dimensions of the rectangles when only 1 rectangle could be made?

▶ Sketch the rectangles you can make with 30 tiles. How would you make sure that you have all possible rectangles?

Make Connections

A **prime number** is a whole number greater than 1 that has two **factors**, 1 and itself.

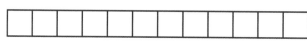

$1 \times 7 = 7$

The factors of 7 are 1 and 7. Seven is a prime number.

▶ Which numbers in your table are prime numbers?

A **composite number** is a whole number that has more than two factors.

$1 \times 12 = 12$

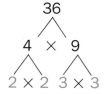

$2 \times 6 = 12$

$3 \times 4 = 12$

The factors of 12 are 1, 2, 3, 4, 6, and 12. Twelve is a composite number.

▶ Which numbers in your table are composite numbers?

Note: Neither 0 nor 1 is a prime number.

You can write a composite number as the product of prime numbers. This is called a **prime factorization** of the number. You can use a **factor tree** to find the prime factors of a composite number.

28
7 × 4
2 × 2

36
4 × 9
2 × 2   3 × 3

Check Out the Glossary
For vocabulary words, see page 643.

$28 = 7 \times 2 \times 2 = 7 \times 2^2$ $36 = 2 \times 2 \times 3 \times 3 = 2^2 \times 3^2$

Check for Understanding

Make a factor tree, and write a prime factorization. Use exponents if you can. Is the number prime or composite?

1 17   **2** 24   **3** 29   **4** 33   **5** 41   **6** 57

7 63   **8** 67   **9** 73   **10** 88   **11** 95   **12** 105

Critical Thinking: Summarize

13 In ex. 1–12, how could you use divisibility rules to help you decide if a number is prime or composite?

14 Write a paragraph describing how to find the prime factorization of a number. Use examples to illustrate.

Turn the page for Practice. ➡

Practice

Make a factor tree, and write the prime factorization. Use exponents if you can. Is the number prime or composite?

1 11   **2** 23   **3** 39   **4** 47   **5** 51

6 54   **7** 61   **8** 87   **9** 91   **10** 119

11 8   **12** 22   **13** 28   **14** 30   **15** 36

16 44   **17** 51   **18** 63   **19** 72   **20** 100

ALGEBRA Find the missing prime factor.

21 $210 = 2 \times 3 \times 5 \times n$

22 $450 = 2 \times n \times 3 \times 5 \times 5$

23 $770 = 2 \times 5 \times n \times 11$

24 $2^3 \times n = 56$

25 $n \times 5^2 = 50$

26 $2^2 \times n = 44$

MIXED APPLICATIONS

Problem Solving

27 Ms. Tucker's class raised $918.47 for a trip to Radio City Music Hall in New York City. It will cost $26 per student to go. If there are 28 students in the class, do they have enough money? Explain.

28 *A Chorus Line* was one of the longest-running Broadway shows in New York City. It was performed 6,137 times from 1975 to 1990. About how many times was it performed each year?

29 Gregory's bowling score is a 2-digit number. Both digits are prime. The difference between the digits is 4. What was his bowling score?

30 **Data Point** Survey your classmates about their favorite kind of entertainment. Decide how you would display the data.

The Prime or Composite Game!

Make a game board like the one at the right.

2 players or 2 teams of players

Play the Game

▶ The first player starts by circling any number on the game board with a red pencil. The number picked is the number of points the first player scores.

▶ The second player uses a blue pencil to circle all of the factors of that number that have not already been circled. The sum of those factors is the number of points the second player scores. All numbers can be circled only once.

▶ Take turns. Repeat first and second steps for all uncircled numbers.

▶ Continue taking turns this way. Play until there are no numbers left. The player with the most points wins.

1	2	3	4	5	6
7	8	9	10	11	12
13	14	15	16	17	18
19	20	21	22	23	24
25	26	27	28	29	30

Malik gets 14 points.
Sarah gets 1 + 2 + 7 = 10 points.

Score Chart

Rounds	Malik	Sarah
Round 1	14	10
Round 2		

If you played this game again, would you use the same strategy or try a different one? Explain your choice.

mixed review • test preparation

1 34.2×2　　**2** $4.05 \div 3$　　**3** 3.12×2.6　　**4** $9.5 \div 5$　　**5** $7.44 \div 2.4$

6 20.8×5.2　　**7** $48.5 \div 9.7$　　**8** $77 \div 38.5$　　**9** 9.3×3　　**10** 9.68×2.2

Common Factors and GCF

Every move in a Hawaiian hula dance tells a story. In the hula, men and women dance in rows. Suppose there are 24 men and 36 women dancers. You want all women or all men in each row. How can you make rows of dancers with the greatest equal number in each row?

You can solve this problem by finding the **greatest common factor (GCF)** of both 24 and 36.

First, list all the factors of 24 and 36.

Factors of 24: 1, 2, 3, 4, 6, 8, 12, 24
Factors of 36: 1, 2, 3, 4, 6, 9, 12, 18, 36

The **common factors** of 24 and 36 are 1, 2, 3, 4, 6, and 12. The dancers may be arranged in equal rows of 1, 2, 3, 4, 6, or 12. The greatest common factor is 12.

There should be 12 dancers in each row.

You can also use prime factorization to find the GCF.

> **Check Out the Glossary**
> common factor
> greatest common factor
> See page 643.

Step 1	Step 2	Step 3
Write the prime factorization of each number.	Find the prime factors common to both numbers.	Multiply to find the greatest common factor.
$24 = 2 \times 2 \times 2 \times 3$ $36 = 2 \times 2 \times 3 \times 3$	$24 = 2 \times 2 \times 2 \times 3$ $36 = 2 \times 2 \times 3 \times 3$	$2 \times 2 \times 3 = 12$

The GCF of 24 and 36 is 12.

Check for Understanding

Find the greatest common factor (GCF) of the numbers.

1 8 and 12   **2** 18 and 24   **3** 13 and 39   **4** 28 and 42   **5** 36 and 90

Critical Thinking: Generalize   Explain your reasoning.

6 Can the GCF of two composite numbers ever be 1? Give an example to support your reasoning.

Practice

List all the common factors.

1 18 and 36   **2** 9 and 64   **3** 20 and 40   **4** 36 and 60

5 48 and 56   **6** 54 and 72   **7** 25 and 75   **8** 24 and 96

Find the GCF. Explain your method.

9 6 and 24   **10** 9 and 12   **11** 16 and 30   **12** 7 and 16

13 12 and 36   **14** 25 and 15   **15** 18 and 27   **16** 28 and 49

17 44 and 55   **18** 15 and 45   **19** 34 and 51   **20** 36 and 90

21 13 and 40   **22** 52 and 56   **23** 72 and 88   **24** 63 and 75

Solve.

25 The GCF of two numbers is 3. The greater number is 9. What is the other number?

26 The GCF of two numbers is 4. The greater number is 16. What is the other number?

MIXED APPLICATIONS
Problem Solving

27 Suppose you want to make a hula costume. You have 48-inch and 64-inch strips of ribbon. What is the longest length you can cut ribbons and have strips all the same length?

28 There are 125 seventh graders and 100 sixth graders. The principal wants an equal number of children in each class. What is the greatest number she can put in each class?

29 **Make a decision** Use the ads at right. If you had to rent the sound system for each performance of a school play, which store would you choose? The play lasts for 3 days, and is 1.5 hours long.

30 **Write a problem** using information from the ads. Solve it and have others solve it.

Rent-A-Center

Rent a Sound system for $30 per hour. Each delivery and pickup costs $25.

YOUR ELECTRONIC WORLD

Sound system for rent! $100 per day. Free delivery and pickup.

mixed review • test preparation

Estimate.

1 54.5 − 13.4   **2** 47.9 + 58.13   **3** 7 × $3.45   **4** 658 ÷ 93

5 35.6 + 380.08   **6** 501.3 − 96.4   **7** 72.3 × 45.67   **8** 2,898 ÷ 48

Common Multiples and LCM

At the entrance of a nature park, a local shuttle bus leaves every 6 minutes, and an express shuttle bus leaves every 15 minutes. Suppose the two buses leave at the same time when the park opens in the morning. How many minutes later will they leave at the same time again?

You can solve this problem by finding the **least common multiple (LCM)** of both 6 and 15.

First, list some multiples of 6 and 15 to represent the shuttle times.

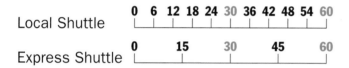

The **common multiples** of 6 and 15 are 30 and 60. Both are divisible by 6 and 15. Since 30 < 60, the LCM is 30.

The buses will leave at the same time again in 30 minutes.

> **Check Out the Glossary**
> common multiple
> least common multiple
> See page 643.

You can also use prime factorization to find the LCM.

Find the greatest number of times a factor appears in either number and multiply.

$$6 = 2 \times 3$$
$$15 = 3 \times 5$$
$$\downarrow \quad \downarrow \quad \downarrow$$
$$LCM = 2 \times 3 \times 5 = 30$$

Check for Understanding

Find the least common multiple (LCM) of the numbers.

1 4 and 6   **2** 3 and 5   **3** 8 and 16   **4** 9 and 12   **5** 15 and 35

Critical Thinking: Generalize   **Explain your reasoning.**

6 Is the LCM of any two numbers divisible by the GCF of these two numbers? Give an example.

7 What is the LCM of two prime numbers? Give an example.

8 Is the product of two numbers always the LCM of both numbers?

Practice

Find the LCM of the numbers.

1 2 and 5   **2** 8 and 6   **3** 4 and 10   **4** 9 and 7

5 12 and 18   **6** 10 and 15   **7** 10 and 12   **8** 12 and 8

9 3 and 18   **10** 15 and 20   **11** 16 and 64   **12** 15 and 45

13 14 and 28   **14** 18 and 45   **15** 26 and 39   **16** 33 and 44

17 35 and 40   **18** 22 and 28   **19** 30 and 40   **20** 48 and 56

MIXED APPLICATIONS
Problem Solving

Pencil & Paper   Calculator   Mental Math

21 The pet show starts every other hour. The snake show starts every third hour. Both start at 10 A.M. When will both shows start together again?

22 Kale spent twice as much for lunch as Betty at the theme park. Together, they spent a total of $10.50. How much did each person spend?

23 A family of 2 adults and 3 children went to a theme park. An adult ticket is $24.75. A child ticket is $12.50. The family used coupons for $2.00 off each adult ticket and $1.50 off each child ticket. What did they pay?

24 At the grand opening of a movie theater, every sixth person in line got free popcorn and every fourteenth person in line got a free ticket. Which person in line will be the first person to get both free gifts?

Cultural Connection The Sieve of Eratosthenes

Eratosthenes was a mathematician who studied in Egypt in the third century B.C. He is well known for his measurement of Earth's circumference and his method of finding prime numbers.

Ancient Egypt

Use the "Sieve of Eratosthenes" described below to find the prime numbers from 1 to 100.

- List all of the numbers from 1 to 100. You will circle each prime number and cross out all its multiples.
- Start by crossing out 1. Next, circle the number 2 and then cross out all multiples of 2. Then, circle 3 and cross out all multiples of 3.
- Continue to circle the next prime number and cross out all its multiples until only prime numbers are left.

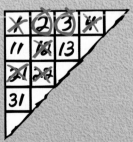

Problem-Solving Strategy

Read
Plan
Solve
Look Back

Make an Organized List

LEARN

Read Your guidebook to Busch Gardens, Florida, says Kumba, Montu, and Tidal Wave have long lines. You decide to ride the closest one first, but you will move on and come back if the line is too long. In how many different orders can you go on the rides?

Plan You need an organized list to find all the possible orders to go on all three rides.

Solve Use letters to stand for each ride. Make an organized list of all of the different orders.

Order of Rides		
1st	**2nd**	**3rd**

	1st	2nd	3rd
Kumba first	K	M	T
	K	T	M
Montu first	M	K	T
	M	T	K
Tidal Wave first	T	M	K
	T	K	M

The list shows that there are 6 different orders to go on the rides.

Look Back How does an organized list help you solve the problem?

CHECK

Check for Understanding

1 **What if** you also don't want to miss Congo River Rapids. In how many different orders could you go on all four of your favorite rides? Explain.

Critical Thinking: Summarize

2 Use problem 1 as an example. Explain how you would organize the data in a meaningful way to get all possible answers.

MIXED APPLICATIONS
Problem Solving

Hot Items		Cold Items		Drinks		Ice Cream Cones	
Hot Dog	$2.50	Ham and Cheese	$2.75	Coke	$2.25	Vanilla	$1.25
Hamburger	$4.50	Submarine	$3.85	Juice	$1.50	Chocolate	$1.25
Cheeseburger	$4.75	Tuna	$2.25	Water	$1.00	Strawberry	$1.25
		Chicken Salad	$4.39				

Use the table to solve problems 1–5.

1 For lunch at an amusement park, you decide to have a hot item and a drink. How many different lunches could you buy? What are the options?

2 **What if** you decide to have a cold item, a drink, and an ice cream. How many different lunches could you buy? What are the options?

3 Each of the 12 members of a tourist group buys a hot item, a drink, and an ice cream cone. About how much will the group's lunch cost?

4 You want to buy a drink and either a hot or a cold item for lunch. You have $6 to spend. How many different lunch combinations could you buy?

5 **Write a problem** using information from the table. Solve the problem and then give it to others to solve.

6 It takes about 30 seconds to serve each person at the park's cafeteria. About how many minutes would it take to serve 180 people?

7 Sabrina wants to fill her album which holds 144 pictures. She prefers film rolls with 36 shots, but the store has only 2. How many more 24 shot rolls should she buy to fill her album?

8 Jacob is making a flag with four stripes. The stripes are either red, green, yellow, or brown. How many different flags can he make if each stripe is a different color?

9 At a school carnival, you set up a Space Explorer fun house. In each group of 6 visitors, 3 get to be pilots, 2 are scientists, and 1 is a reporter. If 42 visitors come to the fun house, how many pilots, scientists, and reporters will there be?

10 It takes Ashley 35 min to jog around the path of a park. It takes Kevin 14 min to bike around the path. What if they both start from the same point of the path and keep jogging and biking. How many minutes later will they meet at the same point?

11 **Spatial reasoning** Identify all the triangles you see in the figure to the right.

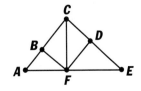

Number Theory and Fraction Concepts **183**

Tell whether the number is divisible by 2, 3, 5, 6, 9, or 10.

1 78   **2** 86   **3** 121   **4** 288   **5** 350

6 760   **7** 825   **8** 964   **9** 342   **10** 875

11 1,455   **12** 4,515   **13** 6,930   **14** 27,412   **15** 31,860

Make a factor tree, and write the prime factorization.
Is the number prime or composite?

16 17   **17** 23   **18** 39   **19** 61   **20** 121

21 15   **22** 28   **23** 48   **24** 60   **25** 72

26 81   **27** 84   **28** 108   **29** 120   **30** 360

Find the GCF and the LCM of the numbers.

31 8 and 10   **32** 10 and 20   **33** 12 and 18   **34** 25 and 50   **35** 30 and 40

36 4 and 12   **37** 7 and 6   **38** 8 and 18   **39** 15 and 12   **40** 18 and 15

41 6 and 12   **42** 5 and 8   **43** 8 and 15   **44** 9 and 7   **45** 12 and 20

Solve.

46 Forty trumpeters and 50 drummers are in a parade. The band leader wants the same number of people in each row, and the trumpeters and the drummers in separate rows. What is the greatest number of people that can be in each row?

47 The world's largest drum was built by the Supreme Drum Company of the United Kingdom. It is 3.96 m wide. Derrick has a drum that is 33 cm wide. How many times greater is the width of the world's largest drum than Derrick's? (Hint: 1 m = 100 cm)

48 Suppose you plan to put together two rectangles like the one below to make a square. Will it work? If not, what is the fewest number of rectangles you need to make a square?

3 cm

2 cm

49 Sixty comic books and 43 coloring books were given to the children at the hospital. Each child received the same number of comic books and coloring books. There are four comic books and one coloring book left. What is the greatest number of children that could be in the hospital? Explain your reasoning.

50 Write a paragraph describing how to find the GCF and the LCM of two numbers. Use examples to illustrate.

Another Way to Find the LCM

You know a lot about multiplication. Use what you know to see relationships among products, factors, and multiples. Think about this: the product of any pair of numbers is equal to the GCF × LCM. Test it out for yourself.

Find the prime factorization of 24 and 30 to find their GCF and LCM.

$24 = 2 \times 2 \times 2 \times 3$
$30 = 2 \times 3 \times 5$

$GCF = 2 \times 3$
$LCM = 2 \times 2 \times 2 \times 3 \times 5$

Now, find the product of the GFC and LCM.

$$\begin{aligned} GCF \times LCM &= (2 \times 3) \times (2 \times 2 \times 2 \times 3 \times 5) \\ &= (2 \times 3 \times 5) \times (2 \times 2 \times 2 \times 3) \quad \leftarrow \textbf{Reorder the factors.} \\ &= \quad 30 \quad \times \quad 24 \end{aligned}$$

Since $24 \times 30 = 720$, the product is equal to GCF × LCM.

> The product of any pair of numbers, a and b, equals the product of the GCF and LCM of the two numbers.
>
> $$a \times b = \textbf{GCF} \times \textbf{LCM}$$

Once you know the GCF, you can find the LCM; and if you know the LCM, you can find the GCF.

The GCF of 12 and 30 is 6. Find the LCM.

$$\begin{aligned} a \times b &= GCF \times LCM \\ 12 \times 30 &= 6 \times n \\ 360 &= 6 \times n \\ 360 \div 6 &= n \\ n &= 60 \\ LCM &= 60 \end{aligned}$$

The LCM of 16 and 24 is 48. Find the GCF.

$$\begin{aligned} a \times b &= GCF \times LCM \\ 16 \times 24 &= n \times 48 \\ 384 &= n \times 48 \\ 384 \div 48 &= n \\ n &= 8 \\ GCF &= 8 \end{aligned}$$

Use the rule to find the LCM or GCF for each pair of numbers.

1 14, 35
GCF = 7

2 23, 41
GCF = 1

3 36, 72
GCF = 36

4 72, 152
GCF = 8

5 105, 120
LCM = 840

6 98, 168
LCM = 1,176

7 102, 136
LCM = 408

8 144, 168
LCM = 1,008

DESIGN A STAGE SET

Work Together

Work with a partner to design some stairs for a stage set.

You will need
- *ruler or yardstick*

▶ Measure some real stairs.

▶ Decide on the width of the tread and the height of the riser for your stairs. A wider tread is easier to dance on.

▶ Choose a reasonable height for the whole staircase.

▶ Make sure the height of your staircase is divisible by the height of each step. If not, make an adjustment to either change the height of the staircase or the height of the riser.

▶ Make a diagram of the staircase you design. Make sure it will fit on a real stage with real dancers.

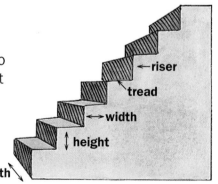

Design the Staircase

1 How did you use the divisibility rules when you designed a staircase?

2 Did you use a trial-and-error method? What adjustments did you need to make?

3 What factors did you consider as you designed the stairs?

4 What would you change if you were designing front steps for a library? a toddlers' gym?

Report Your Findings

5 Prepare a report on what you did. Include the following:

▶ Describe what you think is important to know before designing a staircase for a dance scene.

▶ Describe how you can use divisibility and mathematics to plan your design.

6 Describe how to make adjustments to your plan and your calculations. What might you add or change to make the staircase more dazzling?

▶ Look at each other's designs. Can they be improved? Explain.

Revise your work.
▶ Did you check all your calculations?
▶ Is your explanation of your process clear and easy to understand?
▶ Did you edit your work and proofread the final copy?

MORE TO INVESTIGATE

PREDICT what would happen if you decided to make the treads a different shape, such as those on a spiral staircase. What would happen to your height measurements? number of steps?

EXPLORE the stairs in your school. Are the risers all the same height? Are the treads all the same width?

FIND out how set designers use math. Read interviews in magazines or talk to someone at a local theater.

Understanding Fractions

Rock bands typically have guitars, drums, and keyboards. If there are 4 people in the band, and 3 play guitars, what fraction of the band are guitarists?

You can use a **fraction** to name part of a set or part of a region.

In the band, 3 out of 4, or $\frac{3}{4}$, of the band members are guitarists.

$\frac{3}{4}$ ← **numerator**
$\phantom{\frac{3}{4}}$ ← **denominator**

Read: three fourths

Note: $\frac{3}{4}$ means $3 \div 4$

> **Check Out the Glossary**
> For vocabulary words,
> see page 643.

Here are some different ways to model $\frac{3}{4}$.

Check for Understanding

1 Which of the following shows $\frac{2}{3}$? Explain.

a.   **b.**   **c.**   **d.**

Critical Thinking: Analyze   **Explain your reasoning.**

2 Is $\frac{5}{8}$ of the circle at the right shaded? Why or why not?

3 Draw four squares. Find four different ways to shade $\frac{1}{2}$ of each square. Explain how you know $\frac{1}{2}$ of each is shaded.

Practice

Name the fraction shown.

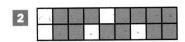

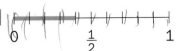

Make a drawing showing the fraction.

7 $\frac{1}{4}$ **8** $\frac{2}{5}$ **9** $\frac{3}{6}$ **10** $\frac{1}{8}$ **11** $\frac{3}{10}$ **12** $\frac{1}{3}$ **13** $\frac{3}{8}$

Each figure represents $\frac{1}{4}$ of the whole drawing. Draw the completed figure.

 14    **15**   **16**

MIXED APPLICATIONS
Problem Solving
Pencil & Paper   *Calculator*   *Mental Math*

17 In a music club, 3 of the members play piano, 4 play violin, 2 play flute, and 1 plays cello. Use fractions to represent the fraction of the members who play each kind of instrument.

18 Vernon folded a sheet of paper in half. Then, he folded it in half two more times and colored one square red before unfolding it. What fraction of the paper is colored red?

19 A Rolling Stones concert had 5,980 more people attending this year than last year. Last year 10,921 people attended. How many people attended this year?

20 Mrs. Martin bought 5 children's tickets for $5.75 each and 2 adult tickets for $19.50 each. She gave the clerk a $100 bill. How much change should she get back?

21 **Spatial reasoning** How can you cut the figure at the right into 8 equal pieces using only three cuts?

---

mixed review • test preparation

Divide. Round to the nearest hundredth if necessary.

1 $322 \div 14$ **2** $11 \div 33$ **3** $18.3 \div 5$ **4** $20.5 \div 0.6$

Find the range, mean, median, and mode for the data.

5 31, 24, 42, 18, 24, 27, 35, 22, 37, 29   **6** 6.7, 5.9, 7.7, 7.8, 7.7, 7.8, 8.0, 7.2, 7.8

Equivalent Fractions

At a dance theater, students can dance in many traditions, from ballet to Bimbe. Four girls and four boys enroll in an advanced class. What fraction of the dancers are boys?

You can use $\frac{4}{8}$ or $\frac{1}{2}$ to represent the fraction of boys in the group. In this situation, $\frac{4}{8}$ and $\frac{1}{2}$ both name the same number. They are **equivalent fractions.**

> **equivalent fractions**
> Fractions that name the same number.

Work Together

Work with a partner. Use models to find equivalent fractions for $\frac{1}{2}, \frac{1}{3}, \frac{2}{3}, \frac{1}{4}, \frac{3}{4}, \frac{1}{5}$.

▶ First, use fraction strips to model the fraction.

▶ Then, find equivalent fractions by placing other fraction strips below the fraction you modeled. Compare the length of the two fraction strips.

IN THE WORKPLACE

Ana Marie Forsythe
Dance Instructor, New York, NY

You will need
- *fraction strips*

$\frac{1}{2} = \frac{2}{4}$ $\frac{1}{2} \neq \frac{3}{5}$ **Note:** $\neq$ means "is not equal to."

▶ Record all the equivalent fractions that you can find in a table.

▶ Compare your equivalent fractions with those of other groups.

Talk It Over

▶ What are all the equivalent fractions you can find for $\frac{1}{2}$?

▶ Look at each of the equivalent fractions for $\frac{1}{2}$. How are the numerators and denominators related?

▶ Without using fraction strips, would you know if $\frac{7}{14}$ is an equivalent fraction for $\frac{1}{2}$? Why or why not?

Make Connections

You can find equivalent fractions by multiplying the numerator and the denominator by the same nonzero number.

$\frac{1}{2}$	$\frac{1}{2}$
$\frac{1}{4}$ $\frac{1}{4}$	$\frac{1 \times 2}{2 \times 2} = \frac{2}{4}$
$\frac{1}{6}$ $\frac{1}{6}$ $\frac{1}{6}$	$\frac{1 \times 3}{2 \times 3} = \frac{3}{6}$

Note: $\frac{2}{2}, \frac{3}{3}, \frac{4}{4}$ are all names for 1.

You can also find equivalent fractions by dividing the numerator and the denominator by a common factor.

$\frac{1}{12}\frac{1}{12}\frac{1}{12}\frac{1}{12}\frac{1}{12}\frac{1}{12}\frac{1}{12}\frac{1}{12}$	$\frac{8}{12}$
$\frac{1}{6}$ $\frac{1}{6}$ $\frac{1}{6}$ $\frac{1}{6}$	$\frac{8 \div 2}{12 \div 2} = \frac{4}{6}$
$\frac{1}{3}$ $\frac{1}{3}$	$\frac{8 \div 4}{12 \div 4} = \frac{2}{3}$

▶ Would you divide the numerator and denominator of $\frac{8}{12}$ by 3 to find an equivalent fraction? Explain.

You can also use what you know about equivalent fractions to find a missing numerator or denominator.

$\frac{2}{5} = \frac{n}{10}$ **Think:** $5 \times 2 = 10$ $\frac{2}{5} = \frac{2 \times 2}{5 \times 2} = \frac{4}{10}$

$\frac{3}{4} = \frac{9}{n}$ **Think:** $3 \times 3 = 9$ $\frac{3}{4} = \frac{3 \times 3}{4 \times 3} = \frac{9}{12}$

Check for Understanding
Tell whether the pair of fractions is equivalent. If not, write an equivalent fraction for the first fraction.

1 $\frac{3}{6}$ and $\frac{1}{2}$

2 $\frac{2}{5}$ and $\frac{4}{6}$

3 $\frac{3}{4}$ and $\frac{9}{12}$

4 $\frac{10}{12}$ and $\frac{4}{6}$

5 $\frac{1}{4}$ and $\frac{1}{8}$

6 $\frac{2}{5}$ and $\frac{5}{12}$

7 $\frac{3}{6}$ and $\frac{2}{3}$

8 $\frac{5}{10}$ and $\frac{2}{4}$

Critical Thinking: Generalize   Explain your reasoning.

9 Malik says, "No matter how many equivalent fractions you name for $\frac{2}{5}$, I can always name another one." Do you agree or disagree?

10 **What if** $\frac{\blacksquare}{15}$ is an equivalent fraction for $\frac{2}{5}$. How would you find the missing numerator?

Turn the page for Practice. ➡

Practice

Complete. Shade the second figure to show an equivalent fraction.

1 $\frac{2}{4} = \frac{n}{16}$

2 $\frac{2}{3} = \frac{c}{6}$

3 $\frac{6}{16} = \frac{d}{8}$

4 $\frac{4}{6} = \frac{a}{12}$

 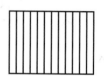

Are the fractions equivalent? Write *yes* or *no*.

5 $\frac{7}{8}, \frac{14}{16}$ **6** $\frac{3}{5}, \frac{5}{3}$ **7** $\frac{4}{7}, \frac{8}{14}$ **8** $\frac{2}{9}, \frac{4}{9}$ **9** $\frac{5}{7}, \frac{5}{14}$

10 $\frac{12}{15}, \frac{4}{5}$ **11** $\frac{20}{40}, \frac{2}{4}$ **12** $\frac{24}{32}, \frac{3}{8}$ **13** $\frac{16}{40}, \frac{2}{5}$ **14** $\frac{17}{18}, \frac{7}{8}$

Write three fractions equivalent to the fraction.

15 $\frac{4}{5}$ **16** $\frac{2}{3}$ **17** $\frac{12}{20}$ **18** $\frac{5}{6}$ **19** $\frac{1}{2}$ **20** $\frac{3}{8}$

Use mental math to complete.

21 $\frac{4}{5} = \frac{n}{10}$ **22** $\frac{1}{2} = \frac{6}{n}$ **23** $\frac{5}{12} = \frac{15}{a}$ **24** $\frac{4}{6} = \frac{8}{b}$

25 $\frac{3}{20} = \frac{c}{40}$ **26** $\frac{1}{4} = \frac{5}{a}$ **27** $\frac{6}{8} = \frac{n}{56}$ **28** $\frac{12}{16} = \frac{s}{4}$

29 $\frac{9}{12} = \frac{b}{4}$ **30** $\frac{20}{30} = \frac{s}{3}$ **31** $\frac{10}{25} = \frac{2}{c}$ **32** $\frac{12}{20} = \frac{6}{n}$

Write *true* or *false*. Give an example to support your answer.

33 If you add the same nonzero number to the numerator and denominator of a fraction, you get an equivalent fraction.

34 If you multiply the numerator and denominator of a fraction by the same nonzero number, you get an equivalent fraction.

Use the table to write the fraction of students wearing each color of sneaker. Then write two equivalent fractions for each.

35 white

36 black

37 red

38 lime-green

Color of Sneakers Students Wear	
Color	**Number of Students**
White	16
Black	8
Red	6
Lime-green	2

Problem Solving

39 One fourth of the performers of an Irish step dance are boys. There are 20 performers. How many performers are boys?

Use the table for problems 41–43.

41 What fraction of all the servings were the tacos? Write this fraction using 100 as the denominator.

42 **Make a decision** as to what type of graph would best show the data in the table. Explain your choice, and make the graph.

43 **Write a problem** that can be solved using the data in the table. Solve the problem and ask others to solve it.

45 How many triangles and rectangles would you add to the diagram below so that it would have $\frac{1}{3}$ squares, $\frac{1}{3}$ triangles, and $\frac{1}{3}$ rectangles?

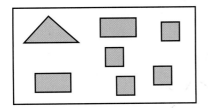

46 About what fraction of the countries in the world are located in Africa?
SEE INFOBIT.

a. $\frac{1}{2}$ **b.** $\frac{1}{4}$ **c.** $\frac{1}{10}$ **d.** $\frac{2}{3}$

40 Raul rents 4 videos for $3 per movie. Tonight is "Rent One Get One Free Night." How much change should he get from a $20 bill?

Foods at World Day Festival

Food	Country	Servings Sold
Spring roll	China	50
Taco	Mexico	60
Italian sausage	Italy	50
Sushi	Japan	15
Gyro	Greece	25

44 One fifth of the students in a class speak Spanish. How many of the 25 students is that?

AFRICA

INFOBIT
On a 1996 political map of the world, there are 192 countries. Among them, 52 countries are located in Africa.

---

mixed review • test preparation

List in order from least to greatest.

1 13.9, 139, 0.139, 1.39 **2** 0.230, 1.032, 0.023 **3** 0.0076, 0.052, 0.3, 0.009

Write in standard form.

4 6^5 **5** 138^2 **6** 10^7 **7** $(4.5)^3$

Simplest Form

Have you ever heard your favorite song so much you got tired of it? A radio station lists its top songs on the Internet. Of its top 18 songs, 6 have been on the countdown as long as 15 weeks! What fraction of these songs have been listed for this long?

To solve this problem, write the fraction $\frac{6}{18}$ in simplest form.

A fraction is in **simplest form** when the only common factor of the numerator and denominator is 1.

Use the divisibility rules and what you learned about equivalent fractions to write fractions in simplest form.

Step 1

Divide the numerator and the denominator by a common factor.

$\frac{6}{18} = \frac{6 \div 2}{18 \div 2} = \frac{3}{9}$ ← **not in simplest form**

Step 2

Divide again until the fraction is in simplest form.

$\frac{3}{9} = \frac{3 \div 3}{9 \div 3} = \frac{1}{3}$ ← **simplest form**

Of the top ten songs, $\frac{1}{3}$ have been listed for 15 weeks.

You can also write a fraction in simplest form by dividing the numerator and the denominator by the GCF.

Find the simplest form of $\frac{18}{27}$.

Think: The GFC of 18 and 27 is 9.　$\frac{18}{27} = \frac{18 \div 9}{27 \div 9} = \frac{2}{3}$

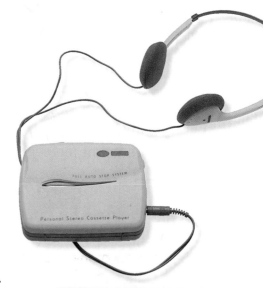

> **Check Out the Glossary**
> simplest form
> See page 643.

Check for Understanding

Write the fraction in simplest form.

1 $\frac{8}{12}$　　**2** $\frac{9}{15}$　　**3** $\frac{2}{4}$　　**4** $\frac{5}{7}$　　**5** $\frac{6}{24}$　　**6** $\frac{8}{20}$

Critical Thinking: Summarize　Explain your reasoning.

7 Write a paragraph summarizing how you simplify a fraction. Give examples to illustrate.

Practice

Tell whether the fraction is in simplest form. Write *yes* or *no*.

1 $\frac{4}{8}$ **2** $\frac{1}{3}$ **3** $\frac{2}{5}$ **4** $\frac{7}{8}$ **5** $\frac{6}{12}$ **6** $\frac{4}{6}$

7 $\frac{5}{12}$ **8** $\frac{3}{5}$ **9** $\frac{2}{6}$ **10** $\frac{5}{20}$ **11** $\frac{4}{16}$ **12** $\frac{3}{24}$

Write the fraction in simplest form. Do as many as you can mentally.

13 $\frac{4}{12}$ **14** $\frac{3}{6}$ **15** $\frac{4}{4}$ **16** $\frac{15}{18}$ **17** $\frac{16}{40}$ **18** $\frac{27}{36}$

19 $\frac{36}{72}$ **20** $\frac{27}{81}$ **21** $\frac{18}{48}$ **22** $\frac{24}{88}$ **23** $\frac{13}{52}$ **24** $\frac{56}{64}$

25 $\frac{17}{51}$ **26** $\frac{21}{49}$ **27** $\frac{25}{75}$ **28** $\frac{18}{63}$ **29** $\frac{13}{26}$ **30** $\frac{40}{120}$

31 $\frac{62}{68}$ **32** $\frac{11}{77}$ **33** $\frac{25}{125}$ **34** $\frac{10}{150}$ **35** $\frac{32}{128}$ **36** $\frac{28}{126}$

MIXED APPLICATIONS
Problem Solving

37 At a dance, the DJ has 96 requests from the crowd. She only has time to play 32 songs. What part of the requests will she be able to play? Write your answer in simplest form.

38 According to *The Guinness Book of Records,* Eldon Wigton is the world's fastest magician. He performed 225 different tricks in 2 min. About how many tricks is that per second?

39 A party host is preparing 60 slips of paper for a drawing for prizes. She makes $\frac{1}{2}$ of the slips win no prize, $\frac{1}{3}$ win a movie ticket, and $\frac{1}{6}$ win a T-shirt. How many of each slip did she need to write?

40 On a nationwide tour, an ice-skating show had ticket sales of $12,417,550 the first month and $10,456,705 the second month. About how much more were the ticket sales in the first month than in the second month?

Simplify Fractions Using a Calculator

You can use a fraction calculator to simplify fractions.
Find the simplest form of $\frac{25}{50}$.

Note: This means the fraction can still be simplified.

25 [b/c] 50 [SIMP] $^{Simp}\frac{5}{10}$ [SIMP] $\frac{1}{2}$

Use a fraction calculator to simplify the fraction.

1 $\frac{20}{24}$ **2** $\frac{18}{45}$ **3** $\frac{34}{98}$ **4** $\frac{48}{64}$ **5** $\frac{125}{200}$ **6** $\frac{212}{240}$

Compare and Order Fractions

L
E
A
R
N

Do you like the elephants or the flying trapeze acts at a circus? Modern circuses have both animal and aerial acts. What if $\frac{2}{5}$ of the circus acts have animal acts and $\frac{1}{2}$ are aerial acts. Are there more animal acts or aerial acts?

Compare $\frac{2}{5}$ and $\frac{1}{2}$.

You can compare fractions with unlike denominators by finding equivalent fractions with a **common denominator.**

Step 1	Step 2
Write equivalent fractions with common denominators.	**Compare the numerators.**
$\frac{2}{5} = \frac{2 \times 2}{5 \times 2} = \frac{4}{10}$ **Think:** The LCM of 2 and 5 is 10.	$4 < 5$ So, $\frac{4}{10} < \frac{5}{10}$.
$\frac{1}{2} = \frac{1 \times 5}{2 \times 5} = \frac{5}{10}$	

> **Cultural Note**
> Circuses can be traced back to the Roman civilization. A common event in these circuses was the chariot race.

Since $\frac{4}{10} < \frac{5}{10}$, then $\frac{2}{5} < \frac{1}{2}$. There are more aerial than animal acts.

> **Check Out the Glossary**
> common denominator
> See page 643.

You can also order fractions using equivalent fractions. Order $\frac{5}{6}$, $\frac{1}{4}$, and $\frac{1}{3}$ from least to greatest, and greatest to least.

Step 1	Step 2	Step 3
Write equivalent fractions with common denominators.	**Compare the numerators.**	**Order the fractions.**
$\frac{5}{6} = \frac{5 \times 2}{6 \times 2} = \frac{10}{12}$	$\frac{5}{6} = \frac{10}{12}$ $10 > 4$	Least to greatest: $\frac{1}{4}, \frac{1}{3}, \frac{5}{6}$
$\frac{1}{4} = \frac{1 \times 3}{4 \times 3} = \frac{3}{12}$	$\frac{1}{4} = \frac{3}{12}$ $4 > 3$	Greatest to least: $\frac{5}{6}, \frac{1}{3}, \frac{1}{4}$
$\frac{1}{3} = \frac{1 \times 4}{3 \times 4} = \frac{4}{12}$	$\frac{1}{3} = \frac{4}{12}$	

C
H
E
C
K

Check for Understanding

Order the fractions from least to greatest.

1 $\frac{3}{4}, \frac{2}{3}, \frac{1}{2}$ **2** $\frac{1}{3}, \frac{4}{5}, \frac{5}{6}$ **3** $\frac{2}{5}, \frac{3}{10}, \frac{2}{3}$ **4** $\frac{4}{5}, \frac{7}{10}, \frac{3}{5}$ **5** $\frac{5}{6}, \frac{1}{3}, \frac{4}{9}$

Critical Thinking: Analyze   Give examples to support your reasoning.

6 Suppose two fractions have the same numerator and different denominators. How can you decide which is greater?

Practice

Compare. Write >, <, or =.

1 $\frac{4}{5} \bullet \frac{3}{5}$　　**2** $\frac{3}{8} \bullet \frac{3}{6}$　　**3** $\frac{7}{8} \bullet \frac{7}{10}$　　**4** $\frac{4}{6} \bullet \frac{3}{6}$　　**5** $\frac{2}{5} \bullet \frac{2}{5}$

6 $\frac{4}{5} \bullet \frac{3}{4}$　　**7** $\frac{4}{20} \bullet \frac{1}{2}$　　**8** $\frac{4}{6} \bullet \frac{7}{8}$　　**9** $\frac{1}{6} \bullet \frac{2}{12}$　　**10** $\frac{2}{8} \bullet \frac{1}{10}$

11 $\frac{6}{12} \bullet \frac{3}{6}$　　**12** $\frac{7}{8} \bullet \frac{3}{4}$　　**13** $\frac{2}{3} \bullet \frac{2}{5}$　　**14** $\frac{1}{12} \bullet \frac{1}{5}$　　**15** $\frac{14}{28} \bullet \frac{1}{2}$

16 $\frac{2}{8} \bullet \frac{3}{8}$　　**17** $\frac{1}{4} \bullet \frac{2}{8}$　　**18** $\frac{5}{12} \bullet \frac{5}{6}$　　**19** $\frac{4}{10} \bullet \frac{1}{5}$　　**20** $\frac{11}{15} \bullet \frac{3}{5}$

Order from least to greatest.

21 $\frac{1}{2}, \frac{1}{4}, \frac{1}{3}$　　**22** $\frac{3}{5}, \frac{3}{6}, \frac{3}{4}$　　**23** $\frac{2}{8}, \frac{5}{8}, \frac{3}{8}$　　**24** $\frac{4}{8}, \frac{4}{6}, \frac{4}{10}$

25 $\frac{3}{4}, \frac{2}{3}, \frac{1}{2}$　　**26** $\frac{2}{8}, \frac{4}{5}, \frac{3}{10}$　　**27** $\frac{7}{8}, \frac{5}{6}, \frac{3}{4}$　　**28** $\frac{1}{4}, \frac{2}{3}, \frac{9}{12}$

29 Sort the fractions in the box. Identify each as greater than $\frac{1}{2}$, or less than $\frac{1}{2}$. Use mental math.

$\frac{13}{25}$	$\frac{47}{90}$	$\frac{15}{31}$	$\frac{123}{256}$	$\frac{17}{32}$
$\frac{72}{115}$	$\frac{27}{50}$	$\frac{17}{36}$	$\frac{19}{42}$	$\frac{137}{300}$

MIXED APPLICATIONS
Problem Solving

Use the table for problems 30–31.

30 Is this statement true: about $\frac{2}{3}$ of the sixth graders, and about $\frac{1}{2}$ of the seventh graders prefer the circus? Explain.

31 What type of graph would best display the data? Create the graph.

Votes for Field Trip			
Grade	Water Park	Circus	Video Arcade
6	8	42	10
7	15	47	18
8	15	27	18

mixed review • test preparation

Use the line plot to answer the questions.

1 How many students watch TV at least 3 hours per day?

2 What conclusions can you draw from the line plot?

3 For the students surveyed, what is the mean number of hours spent watching TV per day?

Hours Spent Watching TV Per Day

```
                      x
                      x
              x       x
              x       x   x
              x       x   x
      x       x       x   x
      x       x       x   x   x   x
    ─────────────────────────────────
      0       1       2   3   4   5
```

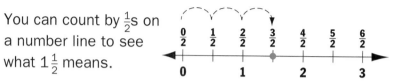

Understanding Mixed Numbers

To make the original movie *King Kong*, a model of King Kong was used that was only $1\frac{1}{2}$-feet tall.

You can count by $\frac{1}{2}$s on a number line to see what $1\frac{1}{2}$ means.

$$\frac{0}{2} \quad \frac{1}{2} \quad \frac{2}{2} \quad \frac{3}{2} \quad \frac{4}{2} \quad \frac{5}{2} \quad \frac{6}{2}$$

$$0 \qquad 1 \qquad 2 \qquad 3$$

You can see that $1\frac{1}{2}$ is three $\frac{1}{2}$s or $\frac{3}{2}$.

A **mixed number** has a whole number part and a fraction part. The number $1\frac{1}{2}$ is a mixed number. $1\frac{1}{2}$ means $1 + \frac{1}{2}$.

Any fraction, such as $\frac{3}{2}$, that has a numerator greater than the denominator is an **improper fraction.**

Sometimes you need to **rename** an improper fraction, such as $\frac{7}{4}$, to a mixed number. Divide the numerator (7) by the denominator (4).

$\frac{7}{4}$ means $7 \div 4$.

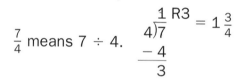

$$\begin{array}{r} 1 \text{ R}3 \\ 4\overline{)7} \\ -4 \\ \hline 3 \end{array} = 1\frac{3}{4}$$

To rename a mixed number to an improper fraction, first multiply the whole number by the denominator, and then add the numerator. Try it for $5\frac{3}{4}$.

$$5\frac{3}{4} \quad (5 \times 4) + 3 = \frac{23}{4}$$

When comparing mixed numbers, compare the whole numbers first. Then compare the fractions, if necessary.

Which is greater: $3\frac{5}{8}$ or $3\frac{7}{16}$? Since $\frac{5}{8} > \frac{7}{16}$, $3\frac{5}{8} > 3\frac{7}{16}$.

> **Check Out the Glossary**
> mixed number
> improper fraction
> See page 643.

Check for Understanding

Write as a whole number or a mixed number in simplest form.

1 $\frac{8}{4}$ **2** $\frac{15}{4}$ **3** $\frac{9}{5}$ **4** $\frac{18}{6}$ **5** $\frac{31}{3}$ **6** $\frac{23}{8}$

Write as an improper fraction.

7 $2\frac{3}{5}$ **8** $9\frac{1}{2}$ **9** $4\frac{3}{8}$ **10** $1\frac{5}{12}$ **11** $10\frac{1}{6}$ **12** $8\frac{2}{3}$

Critical Thinking: Analyze   **Explain your reasoning.**

13 How would you write the number 3 as an improper fraction? Is there more than one improper fraction that you can write?

Practice

Write as a whole number or a mixed number in simplest form.

1 $\frac{15}{7}$ **2** $\frac{12}{3}$ **3** $\frac{38}{4}$ **4** $\frac{40}{8}$ **5** $\frac{67}{8}$ **6** $\frac{27}{5}$

7 $\frac{15}{6}$ **8** $\frac{24}{8}$ **9** $\frac{27}{10}$ **10** $\frac{57}{8}$ **11** $\frac{92}{4}$ **12** $\frac{47}{6}$

Write as an improper fraction.

13 $4\frac{3}{8}$ **14** $9\frac{1}{2}$ **15** $2\frac{3}{4}$ **16** $11\frac{5}{6}$ **17** $10\frac{5}{8}$ **18** $12\frac{1}{3}$

19 $5\frac{1}{4}$ **20** $13\frac{3}{10}$ **21** $2\frac{4}{5}$ **22** $6\frac{5}{12}$ **23** $20\frac{3}{8}$ **24** $120\frac{2}{3}$

Compare. Write >, <, or =.

25 $2\frac{3}{4}$ ● $3\frac{3}{4}$ **26** $4\frac{4}{5}$ ● $5\frac{2}{5}$ **27** $6\frac{2}{3}$ ● $6\frac{2}{5}$ **28** $8\frac{1}{10}$ ● $8\frac{3}{20}$ **29** $10\frac{2}{3}$ ● $10\frac{5}{16}$

30 $\frac{25}{4}$ ● $6\frac{1}{4}$ **31** $4\frac{2}{5}$ ● $\frac{40}{8}$ **32** $5\frac{1}{4}$ ● $5\frac{3}{8}$ **33** $\frac{21}{8}$ ● $2\frac{5}{8}$ **34** $7\frac{5}{8}$ ● $\frac{160}{16}$

Write the greatest number.

35 $5, 3\frac{4}{5}, \frac{12}{3}$ **36** $4, 5\frac{5}{6}, \frac{26}{9}$ **37** $2, \frac{3}{5}, \frac{16}{4}$ **38** $1\frac{2}{3}, 1\frac{3}{4}, \frac{7}{6}$

39 $7, 6\frac{3}{5}, \frac{22}{3}$ **40** $\frac{63}{8}, \frac{29}{4}, 6\frac{7}{8}$ **41** $8\frac{3}{8}, 8\frac{4}{5}, \frac{16}{2}$ **42** $\frac{44}{5}, 7\frac{7}{8}, \frac{20}{3}$

MIXED APPLICATIONS
Problem Solving

43 Percy is 5 feet $3\frac{3}{4}$ inches tall. His friend Ashley is 5 feet $3\frac{5}{8}$ inches tall. Who is taller?

44 **Logical reasoning** The GCF of two numbers is 12, and the LCM is 120. What are the numbers?

45 Shelly has rented the movie *King Kong* six times. At $1.75 per rental, how much has she spent renting *King Kong*?

46 Mark said he is $10\frac{3}{4}$ years old. Rachel said she is 10 years 8 months old. Who is older?

mixed review • test preparation

Estimate.

1 354×27 **2** $697 \div 13$ **3** $315 - 148$ **4** $8,215 + 3,556$

5 $1,055 \times 293$ **6** $734 + 16 + 108$ **7** $43 - 26.95 **8** $4,771 \div 236$

Complete.

9 $300 \text{ cm} = \blacksquare \text{ m}$ **10** $3.7 \text{ L} = \blacksquare \text{ mL}$ **11** $570 \text{ g} = \blacksquare \text{ kg}$ **12** $17.2 \text{ km} = \blacksquare \text{ m}$

Connect Fractions, Mixed Numbers, and Decimals

Has your favorite TV show ever disappeared from the air because no one watched it? Hit shows like *Home Improvement* have a high Nielsen rating. At its peak, *Home Improvement* had about 0.25 of the audience watching each week. What fraction of the TV sets were tuned to *Home Improvement*?

Nielsen Rating Chart	
TV Show	**Share***
NFL Monday Night Football	0.33
World Series Game 1	0.25
Home Improvement	0.25
Cosby	0.20

*Share is the fraction of the television sets in use, tuned to a specific program.

Rename 0.25 as a fraction.

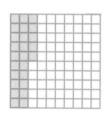

Think: 0.25 is 25 hundredths, or $\frac{25}{100}$.

Simplify.

$$\frac{\overset{1}{\cancel{25}}}{\underset{4}{\cancel{100}}} = \frac{1}{4}$$

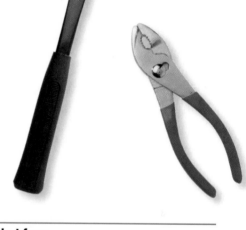

Home Improvement had 0.25, or $\frac{1}{4}$, of the sets tuned in.

You can also write a decimal that is greater than 1 as a mixed number.

Rename 60.2 as a mixed number.

Step 1	Step 2
Write the decimal as a mixed number.	**Write in simplest form.**
$60.2 = 60\frac{2}{10}$ **Think:** 0.2 means two tenths.	$\frac{2}{10} = \frac{2 \div 2}{10 \div 2} = \frac{1}{5}$ **Think:** The GCF of 2 and 10 is 2.
So, $60.2 = 60\frac{1}{5}$	

Talk It Over

▶ How would you use place value to write 0.5, 0.05, and 0.005 as fractions? What pattern do you see?

▶ How would you decide if a decimal is less than or greater than $\frac{1}{2}$? less than or greater than $\frac{1}{4}$?

In the first part of the lesson, you learned how to change a decimal to a fraction or a mixed number. To rename fractions as decimals, divide the numerator by the denominator.

Write $5\frac{3}{4}$ as a decimal.

Think: $\frac{3}{4}$ means $3 \div 4$.

$$\begin{array}{r} 0.75 \\ 4\overline{)3.00} \\ -28\downarrow \\ \hline 20 \\ -20 \\ \hline 0 \end{array}$$

$\frac{3}{4} = 0.75$

So, $5\frac{3}{4} = 5.75$.

If the digits in the quotient start repeating, write a bar on top of the digit that repeats, or round it to a given place.

Rename $5\frac{1}{3}$ as a decimal.

means the digit repeats

 $\frac{1}{3} = 1 \div 3 =$ **0.3333333** or $0.\overline{3}$ So, $5\frac{1}{3} = 5.\overline{3}$.

Sometimes the numbers you have to compare are in different forms. Change them all to the same form and compare.

Which is greatest: 3.45, $3\frac{1}{5}$, or $\frac{17}{5}$?

Rename each as a decimal.

$3.45 = 3.45$

 $3\frac{1}{5} = 3 \boxed{a} 1 \boxed{b/c} 5 \boxed{F \leftrightarrow D} =$ **3.2**

 $\frac{17}{5} = 17 \boxed{b/c} 5 \boxed{F \leftrightarrow D} =$ **3.4**   3.45 is greatest.

Check for Understanding

Write as a fraction or mixed number in simplest form.

1 0.7   **2** 0.48   **3** 2.5   **4** 3.01   **5** 81.202

Write as a decimal. Round the decimal to the nearest hundredth if necessary.

6 $\frac{3}{5}$ **7** $\frac{7}{8}$ **8** $\frac{5}{6}$ **9** $2\frac{1}{4}$ **10** $6\frac{1}{5}$

Critical Thinking: Generalize

11 List some fractions that can be written as nonrepeating decimals and some that can be written as repeating decimals.

12 Can you always write an improper fraction as a decimal greater than 1? Give examples and explain your reasoning.

Turn the page for Practice.

CHECK

Practice

Write as a fraction or mixed number in simplest form.

1 0.4 **2** 0.8 **3** 0.5 **4** 0.65 **5** 2.6 **6** 0.04

7 3.7 **8** 2.1 **9** 12.675 **10** 0.003 **11** 8.64 **12** 2.8

13 12.37 **14** 3.5 **15** 161.9 **16** 1.75 **17** 9.125 **18** 0.025

Write as a decimal. Round the decimal to the nearest hundredth if necessary.

19 $\frac{4}{5}$ **20** $\frac{5}{6}$ **21** $\frac{2}{3}$ **22** $\frac{3}{10}$ **23** $\frac{1}{8}$ **24** $\frac{9}{10}$

25 $2\frac{3}{4}$ **26** $5\frac{3}{8}$ **27** $6\frac{2}{4}$ **28** $12\frac{3}{5}$ **29** $9\frac{1}{4}$ **30** $10\frac{4}{5}$

31 $12\frac{3}{25}$ **32** $6\frac{8}{16}$ **33** $2\frac{11}{20}$ **34** $16\frac{8}{50}$ **35** $3\frac{2}{3}$ **36** $5\frac{5}{6}$

Use the information at the right about a contest on TV. Categorize each player's time.

	Prize Categories	Players
37	More than 15 sec	
38	More than $14\frac{3}{4}$ sec and less than 15 sec	
39	More than $14\frac{1}{2}$ sec and less than $14\frac{3}{4}$ sec	
40	More than 14 sec and less than $14\frac{1}{2}$ sec	
41	More than $13\frac{1}{2}$ sec and less than 14 sec	

Players' Time			
Player	Time (sec)	Player	Time (sec)
1	14.36	8	14.92
2	14.19	9	14.67
3	15.08	10	14.88
4	14.17	11	14.12
5	14.38	12	16.25
6	13.98	13	14.55
7	14.81	14	14.79

Which is the greatest?

42 $\frac{5}{4}$, $\frac{3}{4}$, 1.450   **43** $\frac{19}{8}$, 2.6, $2\frac{4}{5}$ **44** $\frac{18}{3}$, $6\frac{1}{3}$, 6.3   **45** 2.5, $\frac{25}{4}$, $2\frac{1}{3}$

46 $5\frac{7}{20}$, 5.3, $4\frac{7}{8}$ **47** $1\frac{1}{3}$, $\frac{4}{5}$, 1.3   **48** $1\frac{7}{8}$, $\frac{14}{8}$, 1.8   **49** 4.62, $4\frac{3}{5}$, $\frac{29}{6}$

· · · · · · · · · · · · · · · **Make It Right** · · · · · · · · · · · · · · ·

50 Gloria changed $\frac{5}{8}$ to a decimal this way. Tell what the error is and correct it.

$$5\overline{)8}^{\;1.6}$$

Problem Solving

51 The time that Karen had in the contest is less than 13 seconds but more than $12\frac{1}{2}$ seconds. What might be the time to the nearest hundredth second?

52 Sid had a bank balance of $478.91. He wrote a check for $23.90 and deposited a check for $144.00. What was his new balance?

53 The new stadium has 32 sections. Each section has 24 rows. Every row has 40 seats. How many seats does the new stadium have?

54 Vanna White of *Wheel of Fortune* claps an average of 720 times during each of the 5 shows per week. How many times per year is that?

55 On Monday, the weather report said it rained 1.32 in. Was there more or less than $1\frac{1}{4}$ in. of rain? Explain.

56 At the box office, *The Lion King* had ticket sales of $312,844,232. Write the word name for this number.

57 **Data Point** Use the Databank on page 635. Find out if more than $\frac{1}{2}$ of the people in a typical orchestra play string instruments.

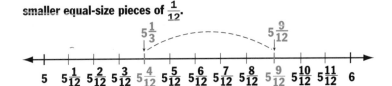

more to explore

Density Property

The Density Property you used for decimals also works for fractions.

Find a number between $5\frac{1}{3}$ and $5\frac{3}{4}$.

Step 1	Step 2
Write equivalent fractions with a common denominator. $$5\frac{1}{3} = 5\frac{4}{12} \qquad 5\frac{3}{4} = 5\frac{9}{12}$$	**Draw a number line. Divide the distance between 5 and 6 into smaller equal-size pieces of $\frac{1}{12}$.**

$5\frac{5}{12}$, $5\frac{6}{12}$, $5\frac{7}{12}$, $5\frac{8}{12}$ are all between $5\frac{1}{3}$ and $5\frac{3}{4}$.

1 Find ten mixed numbers between 3 and 4. List them from least to greatest.

Problem Solvers at Work

PART 1 Expressing Quotients

Suppose the cost of 4 tickets to a school play is $13. If each ticket costs the same amount, how much does each ticket cost?

Work Together
Solve. Be prepared to explain your methods.

1 Jean used her calculator to solve the problem. She divided 13 by 4 and got 3.25 as an answer. Mary used pencil and paper and got $3\frac{1}{4}$ as an answer. Which answer is the most useful? Why?

2 How much does each ticket cost?

3 How is $\frac{1}{4}$, the fraction part of Mary's answer, related to 0.25, the decimal part of Jean's answer?

4 **What if** the cost of the 4 tickets is $14. How much does each ticket cost?

5 What answer do you think Jean would get for problem 4 using her calculator? What answer do you think Mary would get using pencil and paper? How are the two answers related?

6 **Draw Conclusions.** There are 16 seats in each row in the school auditorium. The 68 students in sixth grade are going to sit together. What conclusion can you draw about the number of rows they will fill completely? About how many students will be sitting in an unfilled row?

7 Suppose a microphone costs $125. Drama Club students sell books of 50 raffle tickets for $1 per ticket. How many books must they sell to buy one microphone?

$$3\frac{1}{4}$$
$$4\overline{)13}$$
$$-12$$
$$\overline{1}$$

Srean used the data in the table to write this problem.

Class	Number of Students
Ms. Perry's class	25
Mr. Jacob's class	28
Ms. Walker's class	27
Number of seats in a row: 15	

8 Solve Srean's problem.

9 **Write a problem** of your own in which the quotient will be better expressed as a whole number. Solve your problem.

10 **Write a problem** of your own in which the quotient will be better expressed as a decimal or as a mixed number. Solve your problem.

11 Trade problems. Solve at least one set of three problems written by other students.

12 What was the most interesting problem you solved? Why?

Ms. Perry's class, Mr. Jacob's class, and Ms. Walker's class are planning a field trip to a play. How many rows of seats do they need if there are 15 seats in each row?

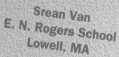

Srean Van
E. N. Rogers School
Lowell, MA

Turn the page for Practice Strategies.

Menu

Choose five problems and solve them. Explain your methods.

1 Bobbie is choosing an outfit to wear to Hershey Park. She has an orange shirt, a gray shirt, a white shirt, striped shorts, and plaid shorts. How many different outfits can she make?

2 Kimi raised giant vegetables. Her 12-pound zucchini won a blue ribbon at the County Fair. She sliced it into 16 pieces for her friends and family. How much did each slice weigh, if they all weighed the same amount?

3 The Carter family is planning a vacation. They want to drive 2,850 mi over a 15-day period. About how many miles should they drive each day?

4 You need to rent a car for 13 days. The local car rental agency has two different rates. You can pay $34.75 per day or $225 a week. Which rate is better for you?

5 Every 6th person in line entering the amusement park got a coupon for one free game of a water-squirting race. Every 9th person in line got a coupon for one free game of breaking balloons with darts. Which person in line got both coupons first?

GOOD FOR FREE GAME

6 The Skaters Club wants to raise $475 for a charity. They made $125 at a car wash, $75 through donations, and $134.50 doing odd jobs. Do they have the amount they want to raise? If not, how much more do they need to raise?

7 Ramona and Rebecca went bowling. The average of their first games was 155. Rebecca scored 14 points more than Ramona scored. What were their scores?

8 Dena went shopping for school clothes. She bought 6 shirts for $12.45 each, 4 pairs of pants for $32.75 each, and a pair of shoes for $46.87. How much did she spend?

BACK TO SCHOOL SALE

Choose two problems and solve them. Explain your methods.

9 A medium pizza without toppings costs $6.45 and feeds 2 people. A large pizza without toppings costs $8.50 and feeds 4 people. Use the chart to help you order enough pizza to feed at least 10 people. Each pizza should have 3 or more toppings. What is the total cost of the pizza?

Pizza Topping	Medium	Large
Olives	$1.25	$2.25
Mushrooms	$1.45	$2.50
Tomatoes	$1.75	$3.00
Onions	$0.75	$1.00
Green peppers	$1.25	$2.00
Pepperoni	$2.50	$4.50
Sausage	$3.25	$6.25

10 **Logical reasoning** In a magic square, the sum of the numbers in each row, column, or diagonal is the same. Use the rest of the numbers 1 through 9 to complete the magic square.

11 Draw a bar graph without a number scale to represent the data from the circle graph.

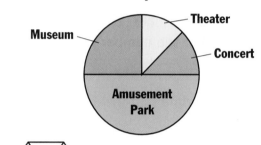

Field Trip Votes

12 **At the Computer** Use a drawing program to copy the figure on the right. Color the shape in as many ways as you can to represent $\frac{1}{2}, \frac{1}{4}, \frac{1}{8},$ and $\frac{1}{16}$. Record the shapes that you created in a table like the one below. Exchange your results with other students. How are they the same? different?

Fractions	Shapes That Represent the Fraction
$\frac{1}{2}$	
$\frac{1}{4}$	
$\frac{1}{8}$	
$\frac{1}{16}$	

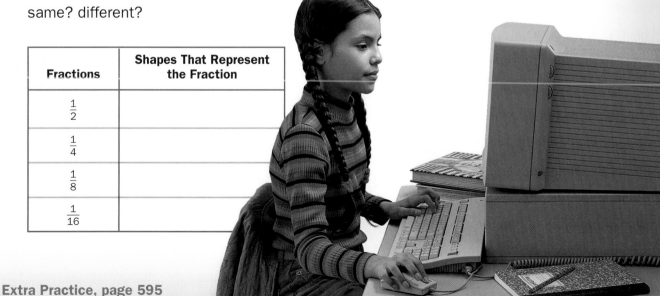

Extra Practice, page 595

Language and Mathematics

Complete the sentence. Use a word in the chart. (pages 172–203)

1 The number 2 is a ■ of 6.

2 A whole number that has more than two factors is called a ■ number.

3 In the fraction $\frac{5}{7}$, the 5 is the ■.

4 The least number greater than 0 that is a common multiple of two numbers is the ■ of the two numbers.

5 The numbers 3, 6, 9, 12, and 15 are all ■ of the number 3.

> **Vocabulary**
> numerator
> denominator
> factor
> prime
> multiples
> composite
> GCF
> LCM

Concepts and Skills

Tell whether the number is divisible by 2, 3, 5, 6, 9, or 10. (page 172)

6 28,740

7 11,555

8 32,001

Write the prime factorization. (page 174)

9 50

10 24

11 144

Find the GCF and LCM. (pages 178, 180)

12 12 and 18

13 3 and 7

14 15 and 25

15 24 and 48

Write the fraction in simplest form. (page 194)

16 $\frac{8}{12}$

17 $\frac{18}{24}$

18 $\frac{25}{30}$

19 $\frac{30}{100}$

Write as a mixed number or a whole number. (page 198)

20 $\frac{7}{5}$

21 $\frac{14}{8}$

22 $\frac{9}{3}$

23 $\frac{26}{4}$

Write as an improper fraction. (page 198)

24 $4\frac{1}{2}$

25 $2\frac{3}{8}$

26 $1\frac{7}{12}$

27 $5\frac{5}{6}$

Compare. Write <, > or =. (pages 196, 198, 200)

28 $\frac{5}{6}$ ● $\frac{4}{5}$

29 $\frac{1}{19}$ ● $\frac{1}{15}$

30 $\frac{6}{12}$ ● $\frac{3}{6}$

31 $2\frac{1}{3}$ ● $3\frac{1}{3}$

32 $5\frac{1}{4}$ ● $5\frac{1}{8}$

33 $\frac{3}{4}$ ● 0.7

34 0.85 ● $\frac{5}{8}$

35 2.1 ● $2\frac{1}{10}$

Write the mixed number as a decimal. Round the decimal to the nearest hundredth if necessary. (page 200)

36 $5\frac{1}{4}$ **37** $5\frac{3}{5}$ **38** $4\frac{5}{8}$ **39** $6\frac{2}{3}$

Write the decimal as a fraction or mixed number in simplest form. (page 200)

40 0.8   **41** 0.125   **42** 2.75   **43** 5.36

Think critically. (page 200)

44 Generalize. Find a pattern for the repeating decimals for fractions with a denominator of 9. Explain how you know the decimal for any fraction with a denominator of 9.

MIXED APPLICATIONS
Problem Solving
Pencil & Paper   Calculator   Mental Math   (pages 182, 204)

45 A bakery donated 150 cookies to be divided equally among 100 students going on a field trip. How many cookies should each student get?

46 There will be 75 fifth graders and 100 sixth graders previewing a video. The students are to sit in rows by grade with the same number in each row. How many chairs should be set up in each row? How many rows will there be?

47 The average rainfall in Honolulu in June is $\frac{1}{2}$ in. The average rainfall in July is 0.59 in. Which month has the greater rainfall?

48 How many different 3-digit numbers can you make using the numbers 1, 2, and 3 only once in each number? What are the numbers?

Use the graph for problems 49–50.

49 Crystal drew a line graph to show the change in value of a stock her grandparents bought for her as an educational fund. How would you write the value of the stock for each day in dollars and cents?

50 What conclusions can you draw from the line graph?

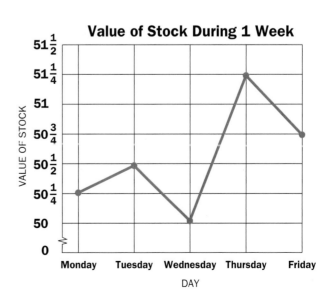

Value of Stock During 1 Week

Write the prime factorization of the number.

1 20

2 540

Find the GCF and LCM of the numbers.

3 12 and 16

4 15, 20, and 40

Write as a fraction in simplest form.

5 $\frac{16}{24}$

6 $\frac{60}{100}$

7 0.8

8 0.25

Compare. Write >, <, or =.

9 $\frac{9}{27}$ ● $\frac{2}{6}$

10 $5\frac{1}{8}$ ● $5\frac{1}{6}$

Order from least to greatest.

11 $\frac{5}{9}, \frac{2}{3}, \frac{9}{18}$

12 $\frac{21}{8}, 2\frac{3}{5}, 2\frac{1}{2}$

Write as a mixed number in simplest form.

13 $\frac{8}{5}$

14 $7\frac{9}{12}$

15 $\frac{22}{6}$

16 8.75

Find two numbers that are greater than the number given. Write the letters.

17 1.4   **a.** $1\frac{7}{10}$ **b.** $\frac{5}{4}$ **c.** $\frac{15}{10}$ **d.** 1.3

18 $3\frac{1}{2}$ **a.** $\frac{7}{2}$ **b.** $\frac{9}{2}$ **c.** 3.6   **d.** $3\frac{3}{8}$

19 $6\frac{7}{8}$ **a.** $\frac{56}{8}$ **b.** $6\frac{1}{2}$ **c.** $6\frac{9}{16}$ **d.** 6.95

20 $\frac{22}{3}$ **a.** 7   **b.** $\frac{13}{2}$ **c.** $7\frac{2}{3}$ **d.** 7.4

21 $\frac{3}{4}$ **a.** $\frac{5}{8}$ **b.** $\frac{7}{8}$ **c.** 0.8   **d.** $\frac{3}{7}$

Solve. Show your work.

22 Tracy has 4 things to do on Saturday: homework, play soccer, clean his room, and watch a video he rented. What are all the possible orders in which he could do the activities?

23 Caro went to a movie that lasted $2\frac{1}{2}$ hours. Jon went to one that lasted 2 h 10 minutes. Whose movie lasted longer?

24 Alex weighs 15 mice in a box on a scale. The mice and box weigh 38.5 ounces. If the box weighs 4 ounces, what is the average weight of the mice?

25 Giorgio ordered 45 pizzas for a party. 120 people came to the party. If each person got the same amount of pizza, what fraction of a pizza did each person get?

What Did You Learn?

Amanda and her friends play Guess the Length. Each tries to cut a piece of string closest to the target length without using a ruler. They then measure the strings and record the measurements.

Target Length	Amanda	Imani	Cindy	José	Joshua	Kayla
$3\frac{1}{2}$ in.	$2\frac{3}{4}$ in.	$4\frac{1}{2}$ in.	$3\frac{7}{16}$ in.	$3\frac{5}{8}$ in.	$2\frac{15}{16}$ in.	$4\frac{1}{4}$ in.

▶ Order the measurements from least to greatest on a number line.

> **You will need**
> * *inch ruler*

▶ Which three measurements are closest to the target? Who wins the contest?

▶ Choose a different target length. Draw three line segments on a piece of paper without a ruler. Then, measure the lengths of the line segments. Record your measurements. What was your closest measurement to the target length?

> • • • • • • • • • • • • • • • • • **A Good Answer** • • • • • • • • • • • • • • • • • •
> * includes an organized, completed number line.
> * accurately places all string lengths on the number line.
> * includes a written explanation about how the closest measurements were chosen.

 You may want to place your work in your portfolio.

What Do You Think

1 Do you feel comfortable solving problems that involve the Greatest Common Factor or the Least Common Multiple? If not, what difficulties do you have?

2 How do you compare numbers in a group that includes a fraction, a mixed number, and a decimal?
* Use an estimate.
* Use paper and pencil.
* Use models.
* Use a fraction calculator.
* Other. Explain.

Explore Pitch and Scale

All sounds are caused by vibrations. Whenever something vibrates, it sets up sound waves in the air. If they are loud enough, they make your eardrum vibrate, and you hear sound.

When a clarinet reed, a guitar string, or the lips of a tuba player vibrate, they make the air in the instrument vibrate. This makes sound.

The highness or lowness of the sound we hear is called *pitch*. The faster that sound waves vibrate, the higher the pitch we hear. The slower the vibration, the lower the pitch.

In this activity, you are going to explore how to change the pitch of a sound.

Cultural Note

Musical instruments are known to have existed at least 6,000 years ago. Among the first instruments were probably hollow bones used as whistles.

Gently tap an empty glass bottle with a pencil. Listen to the sound it makes.

Pour a little water into the bottle and tap it again. Listen to how the sound has changed. Repeat this several times.

▶ What happened to the pitch of the sound as you filled the bottle with water?

▶ What do you think is vibrating when you tap the bottle?

▶ **What if** you gently blow across the top of the bottle rather than tapping it. What happens to the sound as you add water? Why do you think this happens?

How Are Pitches Different?

Do, re, mi, fa, so, la, ti, do—these pitch syllables identify the pitches in a major scale. Each pitch is produced by a specific number of vibrations per second. This number of vibrations per second is called the *frequency* of the pitch.

C-Major Scale		
Pitch Syllable	Pitch Name	Frequency (in cycles per second)
do	C	528
ti	B	495
la	A	440
so	G	396
fa	F	352
mi	E	330
re	D	297
do	C	264

1 What relationship do you notice between the frequencies of the two Cs in the table above?

2 The same relationship exists between each pitch in the first octave (the eight pitches in the table above) and the pitch with the same letter in the next higher octave. What are the frequencies of the pitches in the next higher octave?

3 The improper fraction you can write using two frequencies in order is called their *frequency ratio*. For example, the frequency ratio for D and C is $\frac{297}{264}$, which is equal to $\frac{9}{8}$. Find the frequency ratios for each pair of pitches that are next to each other in the table above.

At the Computer

C-Major Scale		
Pitch Name	Frequency of original pitches (in cycles per second)	Frequency of octave below (in cycles per second)
C	528	264
B	495	247.5
A	440	220

4 Use a spreadsheet program to find the frequencies of the pitches in the octave below the one shown in the table on the left.

5 Do research to find out some of the factors that affect the frequencies that an instrument produces.

ADD AND SUBTRACT FRACTIONS AND MIXED NUMBERS

THEME Leisure Time

In-line skating, soccer, bike racing, and crafts are all activities that sixth graders enjoy. In this chapter you'll see how addition and subtraction of fractions and mixed numbers are used in leisure activities.

What Do You Know ?

1 How far is it to skate east from Table Rock to Sailboat Pond?

2 From the playground, how much farther is it to Table Rock than to Sailboat Pond?

3   Choose a distance from the playground that falls between the playground and Table Rock. A rain shelter will be placed there. Tell how far the shelter is from three points on the map. Explain your methods.

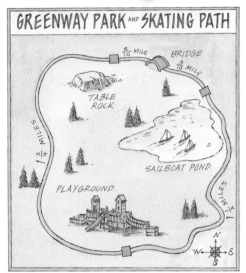

GREENWAY PARK AND SKATING PATH

$\frac{2}{10}$ MILE

BRIDGE

$\frac{3}{10}$ MILE

TABLE ROCK

$1\frac{3}{4}$ MILES

SAILBOAT POND

$1\frac{1}{4}$ MILES

PLAYGROUND

N W E S

Summarize You need 1 pound of chocolate chips and $\frac{3}{4}$ cup of milk to make cookies and $1\frac{1}{2}$ cups of milk to make a cake. Will a pint of milk be enough?

Summarizing a problem can help you see if you understand it.

1 What information in the problem is not needed in order for you to solve the problem?

2 Summarize the problem in your own words.

Vocabulary

least common denominator, p. 222

Estimate Sums and Differences

Many kites are made of fabric, with seams that are sewn rather than glued. A typical seam is $\frac{5}{8}$ in. wide.

You can see on a number line that $\frac{5}{8}$ is closer to $\frac{1}{2}$ than it is to 1. The seam is about $\frac{1}{2}$ inch wide.

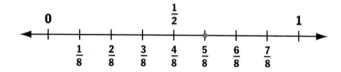

To round fractions, compare the numerator and the denominator.

Round to zero when the numerator is much smaller than the denominator.

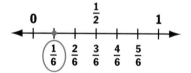

$\frac{1}{6}$ is closer to 0 than to $\frac{1}{2}$.

Round to $\frac{1}{2}$ when the denominator is about two times the numerator.

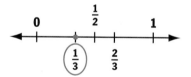

$\frac{1}{3}$ is closer to $\frac{1}{2}$ than to 0.

Round to 1 when the numerator and denominator are about the same.

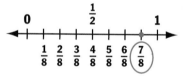

$\frac{7}{8}$ is closer to 1 than to $\frac{1}{2}$.

Talk It Over

▶ Describe how you would compare the numerator and denominator when rounding $\frac{9}{10}$, $\frac{1}{12}$, and $\frac{3}{8}$.

▶ Name a fraction that rounds to 0, another that rounds to $\frac{1}{2}$, and another that rounds to 1. Explain your reasoning for each.

▶ What fraction is as close to 0 as it is to $\frac{1}{2}$? What fraction is as close to $\frac{1}{2}$ as it is to 1?

Suppose a kite has a red stripe $3\frac{9}{16}$ in. wide next to a blue stripe $4\frac{3}{8}$ in. wide. About how much is the width of the two stripes together?

Estimate the width of the two stripes.

You can estimate sums and differences of mixed numbers by rounding to the nearest half.

Estimate: $3\frac{9}{16} + 4\frac{3}{8}$

Think: $3\frac{1}{2} + 4\frac{1}{2}$

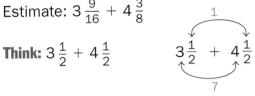

$3\frac{1}{2} + 4\frac{1}{2}$

Think: $7 + 1 = 8$

$3\frac{9}{16} + 4\frac{3}{8}$ is about 8.

The two stripes are about 8 in. wide altogether.

More Examples

A Estimate: $\frac{11}{12} - \frac{3}{8}$ **Think:** Round to the nearest half. $1 - \frac{1}{2} = \frac{1}{2}$

B Estimate: $6\frac{1}{10} - 2\frac{5}{8}$ **Think:** Round to the nearest half. $6 - 2\frac{1}{2}$
$6 - 2 = 4$ and $4 - \frac{1}{2} = 3\frac{1}{2}$

C Estimate: $4\frac{2}{3} + 8\frac{3}{4} + \frac{11}{12}$ **Think:** Round to the nearest whole number. $5 + 9 + 1 = 15$

Check for Understanding

Round each fraction to 0, $\frac{1}{2}$, or 1. Explain your reasoning.

1 $\frac{1}{8}$ **2** $\frac{7}{12}$ **3** $\frac{17}{20}$ **4** $\frac{2}{3}$ **5** $\frac{3}{20}$ **6** $\frac{15}{16}$

Round to the nearest half.

7 $2\frac{4}{5}$ **8** $11\frac{1}{10}$ **9** $4\frac{3}{5}$ **10** $5\frac{1}{20}$ **11** $6\frac{5}{12}$ **12** $13\frac{2}{10}$

Estimate each sum or difference.

13 $\frac{3}{8} + \frac{4}{5}$ **14** $\frac{9}{10} - \frac{3}{5}$ **15** $3\frac{15}{16} - \frac{7}{8}$ **16** $1\frac{5}{12} + 1\frac{5}{6}$ **17** $8 - 2\frac{4}{10}$

Critical Thinking: Analyze   **Explain your reasoning.**

18 In Example C, why do you think the numbers were rounded to the nearest whole number instead of the nearest half?

19 Give an example of estimating the sum of two mixed numbers that you might round to the nearest hundred.

Add and Subtract Fractions and Mixed Numbers **217**

CHECK

Practice

Round each fraction to 0, $\frac{1}{2}$, or 1.

1 $\frac{1}{20}$ **2** $\frac{5}{12}$ **3** $\frac{9}{16}$ **4** $\frac{11}{12}$ **5** $\frac{17}{20}$ **6** $\frac{3}{16}$

7 $\frac{7}{8}$ **8** $\frac{2}{15}$ **9** $\frac{9}{10}$ **10** $\frac{7}{15}$ **11** $\frac{4}{5}$ **12** $\frac{11}{20}$

Round to the nearest half.

13 $3\frac{5}{6}$ **14** $12\frac{1}{8}$ **15** $7\frac{9}{20}$ **16** $6\frac{1}{10}$ **17** $5\frac{3}{8}$ **18** $14\frac{15}{16}$

19 $7\frac{5}{16}$ **20** $33\frac{1}{3}$ **21** $99\frac{3}{4}$ **22** $99\frac{3}{8}$ **23** $17\frac{9}{16}$ **24** $4\frac{11}{12}$

Estimate each sum or difference.

25 $\frac{7}{8} + \frac{5}{6}$ **26** $5\frac{7}{16} + 4\frac{5}{8}$ **27** $1\frac{9}{10} + \frac{9}{16}$ **28** $\frac{7}{8} + 1\frac{1}{6} + 3\frac{5}{12}$

29 $\frac{11}{12} - \frac{2}{5}$ **30** $3\frac{19}{20} - \frac{10}{12}$ **31** $3\frac{7}{8} - 1\frac{1}{2}$ **32** $68\frac{2}{3} - 29\frac{1}{6}$

33 $3\frac{1}{4} + 2\frac{5}{6}$ **34** $6\frac{5}{8} - 4\frac{1}{2}$ **35** $9\frac{3}{5} + 2\frac{1}{4}$ **36** $\frac{3}{5} + 2\frac{7}{8} + 4$

37 $6\frac{5}{6} - 2\frac{3}{5}$ **38** $8\frac{3}{20} - 2\frac{9}{10}$ **39** $\frac{1}{3} + \frac{1}{8} + \frac{5}{12}$ **40** $8\frac{7}{8} - 3\frac{3}{4}$

41 $6 + 4\frac{1}{2} + 3\frac{2}{3}$ **42** $4\frac{3}{8} + 3\frac{7}{12} + 2$ **43** $5\frac{1}{2} + 7\frac{1}{6} + 4\frac{7}{8}$ **44** $6\frac{3}{4} + 3\frac{4}{5} + 2\frac{11}{12}$

Find at least two pairs of numbers in each set that have a sum of about 8; a difference of about 3.

45

$3\frac{5}{6}$	$3\frac{4}{5}$	$6\frac{7}{8}$
	$5\frac{1}{6}$	$5\frac{5}{8}$
$8\frac{1}{12}$	$2\frac{5}{12}$	$3\frac{11}{12}$

46

$4\frac{5}{6}$	$6\frac{3}{8}$	$1\frac{11}{20}$
	$2\frac{7}{8}$	$\frac{1}{10}$
$3\frac{5}{8}$	$7\frac{19}{20}$	$\frac{5}{12}$

47

$3\frac{3}{8}$	$6\frac{9}{10}$	$4\frac{3}{20}$
	$1\frac{2}{20}$	$4\frac{7}{16}$
$9\frac{4}{5}$	$4\frac{1}{12}$	$\frac{15}{16}$

Write *true* or *false*. Use the survey results in the table to solve problems 48–50. Explain your choice.

48 About half the students fly kites and nearly all collect something.

49 About half the students build models or fly kites.

50 Very few build models and about half collect something.

51 **Summarize** Summarize the information in the table.

Sixth-Grader Hobbies	
Hobby	**Students Who Have Hobby**
Fly kites	$\frac{3}{7}$
Build models	$\frac{1}{6}$
Collect baseball cards, stamps, and so on	$\frac{9}{10}$

Problem Solving

52 Suppose kites are shipped in boxes of 48. A store orders 1,728 kites. How many boxes should they receive?

53 About how many days did the Edmonds Community College team keep their kite in the air when they set their record? SEE INFOBIT.

54 Juan said $\frac{1}{8}$ of his class had gone to the kite festival over the weekend. Did very few, about half, or almost all the students go? Explain.

55 Lily has a strip of cloth $72\frac{5}{8}$ in. long to use to make kite tails. She is going to use $33\frac{3}{4}$ in. for one kite tail. Estimate to decide if she will have enough left for another kite tail of about the same length. Explain your reasoning.

56 **Write a problem** that involves estimating a sum or difference of mixed numbers. Solve the problem and then give it to others to solve.

INFOBIT
According to *The Guinness Book of Records*, the longest kite flight was 180 h 17 min set by the Edmonds Community College team at Lynwood, WA, in 1982.

Use the table to answer problems 57–58.

57 Find the mean number of books read per month by the Summer Library Club.
  a. 4,188   **b.** 1,386
  c. 1,396   **d.** 848

58 **Data Point** Make a bar graph to show the data in the table.

Summer Library Club	
Month	**Number of Books Read**
June	1,386
July	1,825
August	977

more to explore

Estimating

You can also estimate sums and differences of mixed numbers by rounding to the nearest whole number.

Estimate: $6\frac{5}{6} + 4\frac{3}{8} + 1\frac{1}{6}$ **Think:** $7 + 4 + 1 = 12$

Estimate by rounding to the nearest whole number.

1 $5\frac{3}{5} + 9\frac{1}{6}$ **2** $7\frac{3}{8} + 6\frac{2}{3} + 1\frac{5}{7}$ **3** $12\frac{3}{8} - 3\frac{2}{3}$ **4** $8\frac{7}{8} + 3\frac{1}{5} + 2\frac{5}{8}$

Add and Subtract Like Fractions

Bicycle racers, like Tinker Juarez, need to train for events. One racer trains for sprints by sprinting for $\frac{3}{10}$ mi at top speed followed by a $\frac{1}{10}$ mi cool-down. How far did he ride altogether?

Add: $\frac{3}{10} + \frac{1}{10}$

You can add or subtract mentally when fractions have common denominators.

Step 1	Step 2
Add the numerators. **Use the common denominator.**	**Write the sum in simplest form.**

$$\frac{3}{10} + \frac{1}{10}$$

$$\frac{3}{10} + \frac{1}{10} = \frac{4}{10}$$

$$\frac{4}{10} = \frac{2}{5}$$

The racer rode $\frac{2}{5}$ mi altogether.

Subtract mentally: $\frac{7}{8} - \frac{3}{8}$

Step 1	Step 2
Subtract the numerators. **Use the common denominator.**	**Write the difference in simplest form.**

$$\frac{7}{8} - \frac{3}{8} = \frac{4}{8}$$

$$\frac{4}{8} = \frac{1}{2}$$

More Examples

A $\frac{5}{6} + \frac{1}{6} = \frac{6}{6} = 1$

B $\frac{13}{16} - \frac{3}{16} = \frac{10}{16} = \frac{5}{8}$

C $\frac{1}{12} + \frac{5}{12} + \frac{7}{12} = \frac{13}{12} = 1\frac{1}{12}$

Check for Understanding

Add or subtract. Write the answer in simplest form.

1 $\frac{3}{5} - \frac{2}{5}$

2 $\frac{1}{12} + \frac{5}{12}$

3 $\frac{2}{3} + \frac{2}{3}$

4 $\frac{3}{8} - \frac{1}{8}$

5 $\frac{3}{10} - \frac{1}{10}$

6 $\frac{3}{4} + \frac{1}{4}$

7 $\frac{5}{8} - \frac{1}{8}$

8 $\frac{7}{10} + \frac{3}{10} + \frac{1}{10}$

Critical Thinking: Analyze Explain your reasoning.

9 Write a paragraph explaining how to add and subtract fractions with like denominators. Use pictures to illustrate.

Practice

Add or subtract. Write the answer in simplest form.

1 $\frac{2}{5} + \frac{2}{5}$

2 $\frac{3}{8} + \frac{1}{8}$

3 $\frac{9}{10} + \frac{7}{10}$

4 $\frac{4}{5} + \frac{4}{5}$

5 $\frac{5}{6} - \frac{1}{6}$

6 $\frac{3}{4} - \frac{1}{4}$

7 $\frac{7}{12} - \frac{5}{12}$

8 $\frac{13}{20} - \frac{1}{20}$

9 $\frac{3}{16} + \frac{1}{16} + \frac{5}{16}$

10 $\frac{5}{8} - \frac{3}{8}$

11 $\frac{1}{6} + \frac{5}{6} + \frac{5}{6}$

12 $\frac{7}{16} - \frac{1}{16}$

13 $\frac{1}{5} + \frac{3}{5}$

14 $\frac{5}{6} + \frac{3}{6}$

15 $\frac{7}{8} - \frac{7}{8}$

16 $\frac{11}{20} - \frac{3}{20}$

17 $\frac{3}{4} + \frac{3}{4}$

18 $\frac{11}{12} - \frac{5}{12}$

19 $\frac{3}{8} + \frac{5}{8} + \frac{1}{8}$

20 $\frac{7}{10} - \frac{3}{10}$

21 $\frac{3}{5} + \frac{1}{5} + \frac{3}{5}$

22 $\frac{15}{16} - \frac{7}{16}$

23 $\frac{3}{10} + \frac{1}{10} + \frac{9}{10}$

24 $\frac{3}{8} + \frac{7}{8} + \frac{3}{8}$

ALGEBRA Find the missing number. Use mental math.

25 $\frac{9}{10} - \frac{3}{10} = \frac{n}{10}$

26 $\frac{1}{5} + \frac{n}{5} = \frac{3}{5}$

27 $\frac{7}{8} - \frac{1}{8} = \frac{n}{8}$

28 $\frac{n}{12} + \frac{1}{12} = \frac{2}{12}$

29 $\frac{7}{20} - \frac{3}{20} = \frac{n}{20}$

30 $\frac{n}{16} + \frac{3}{16} = \frac{8}{16}$

31 $\frac{7}{8} + \frac{5}{8} = \frac{n}{8}$

32 $\frac{n}{8} - \frac{3}{8} = \frac{4}{8}$

MIXED APPLICATIONS
Problem Solving

33 A biker rode $\frac{1}{10}$ mi Monday, $\frac{2}{10}$ mi Tuesday, and $\frac{3}{10}$ mi Wednesday. How far did he ride in all?

34 You have a board $\frac{7}{8}$ in. thick. You want it to be $\frac{5}{8}$ in. thick. How much do you need to cut off?

35 Suppose you buy a pair of in-line skates for $59.95. The tax is $4.20. You give the clerk $80. How much change should you get?

36 There were 24,650 people at the first Rangers game. The stadium holds 56,000. About what fraction of the stadium was full?

37 You are going to separate 36 students equally into teams with at least 2 players each. What are all the possible numbers of players that could be on a team?

38 **Write a problem** that you could solve by adding or subtracting like fractions. Solve the problem and then give it to others to solve.

mixed review • test preparation

1 $4.6 + 2.7$

2 $10 - 3.7$

3 $5.45 + 6.9$

4 $\$21.73 + \$32.69$

5 5.46×100

6 $234.57 \div 10$

7 $76.8 \times 1,000$

8 $3.79 \div 100$

Add Unlike Fractions

This circle graph represents the students in Ms. Sanchez's class. What fraction of the class likes either rock 'n' roll or country most?

Add: $\frac{1}{3} + \frac{1}{6}$

The **least common denominator (LCD)** of two or more fractions is the least common multiple of their denominators.

Favorite Kind of Music

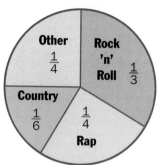

Step 1	Step 2
Write equivalent fractions using the LCD.	**Add. Write the sum in simplest form, if necessary.**

Step 1:

$$\frac{1}{3} = \frac{2}{6}$$
$$+\frac{1}{6} = \frac{1}{6}$$

Think: The LCD of $\frac{1}{3}$ and $\frac{1}{6}$ is 6.

Step 2:

$$\frac{1}{3} = \frac{2}{6}$$
$$+\frac{1}{6} = \frac{1}{6}$$
$$\frac{3}{6} = \frac{1}{2}$$

Half the class likes rock 'n' roll or country most.

You can also use a fraction calculator to add fractions.

 1 [b/c] 3 + 1 [b/c] 6 = Simp $\frac{3}{6}$ [SIMP] $\frac{1}{2}$

Check Out the Glossary
least common denominator
See page 643.

More Examples

A $\frac{3}{4} + \frac{1}{3}$

$$\frac{3}{4} = \frac{9}{12}$$
$$+\frac{1}{3} = \frac{4}{12}$$
$$\frac{13}{12} = 1\frac{1}{12}$$

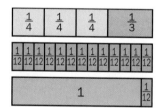

Think: The LCD is 12.

B $\frac{5}{12} + \frac{1}{6} + \frac{3}{8}$

$$\frac{5}{12} = \frac{10}{24}$$
$$\frac{1}{6} = \frac{4}{24}$$
$$+\frac{3}{8} = \frac{9}{24}$$
$$\frac{23}{24}$$

Think: The LCD is 24.

Check for Understanding

Add. You may use models. Write the answer in simplest form.

1 $\frac{5}{8} + \frac{1}{4}$ **2** $\frac{2}{3} + \frac{5}{6}$ **3** $\frac{1}{2} + \frac{1}{3}$ **4** $\frac{7}{10} + \frac{3}{8}$

Critical Thinking: Analyze Explain your reasoning.

5 **What if** you did Example B by first using the denominator 48 instead of the LCD 24. Do you get the same answer?

Practice

Add. Remember to estimate. Write the answer in simplest form.

1 $\frac{5}{6}$
$+ \frac{1}{3}$

2 $\frac{1}{2}$
$+ \frac{2}{3}$

3 $\frac{5}{12}$
$+ \frac{2}{3}$

4 $\frac{7}{12}$
$+ \frac{5}{6}$

5 $\frac{3}{8}$
$+ \frac{1}{8}$

6 $\frac{2}{3}$
$+ \frac{3}{4}$

7 $\frac{1}{6}$
$+ \frac{1}{4}$

8 $\frac{3}{10}$
$+ \frac{5}{6}$

9 $\frac{5}{6}$
$+ \frac{5}{6}$

10 $\frac{5}{6}$
$+ \frac{3}{4}$

11 $\frac{7}{10}$
$+ \frac{5}{12}$

12 $\frac{11}{12}$
$+ \frac{5}{8}$

13 $\frac{3}{4} + \frac{5}{6}$

14 $\frac{7}{8} + \frac{1}{8}$

15 $\frac{3}{4} + \frac{5}{8}$

16 $\frac{1}{2} + \frac{11}{12}$

17 $\frac{5}{8} + \frac{5}{12}$

18 $\frac{3}{8} + \frac{1}{2}$

19 $\frac{7}{16} + \frac{5}{16}$

20 $\frac{3}{5} + \frac{2}{3}$

21 $\frac{3}{5} + \frac{7}{10} + \frac{2}{5}$

22 $\frac{2}{3} + \frac{3}{4} + \frac{1}{2}$

23 $\frac{1}{4} + \frac{1}{2} + \frac{1}{8}$

24 $\frac{7}{12} + \frac{5}{8} + \frac{1}{3}$

MIXED APPLICATIONS
Problem Solving

Use the circle graph on page 222 for problems 25–26.

25 What fraction of Ms. Sanchez's class chose either rock 'n' roll or rap as their favorite?

26 Express as a decimal the fraction of Ms. Sanchez's class that likes rap the most.

27 José and Alex sold lemonade for $0.15 a cup. José sold 22 cups and Alex sold 18 cups. How much money should they have received?

28 If you nail $\frac{1}{2}$-inch-thick and $\frac{1}{4}$-inch-thick pieces of plywood together, what would the combined thickness be?

29 Carlos practices his recital piece for $\frac{1}{2}$ hour. He also practices other pieces for x hours. The expression $x + \frac{1}{2}$ describes how long he practices. Find how long he practices for each value of x.
a. $\frac{1}{2}$ **b.** $\frac{1}{3}$ **c.** $\frac{2}{3}$ **d.** $\frac{5}{6}$

mixed review • test preparation

Compare. Use >, <, or =.

1 $\frac{3}{4} \bullet \frac{3}{8}$

2 $4\frac{3}{4} \bullet 4\frac{5}{6}$

3 $\frac{3}{5} \bullet 0.6$

4 $2.3 \bullet 2\frac{1}{3}$

 ALGEBRA Simplify using order of operations.

5 $24 - 8 \times 2 - 6$

6 $5.8 + (7 + 2)^3$

7 $34 - (5 \times 7.3 - 4 \times 6)$

Subtract Unlike Fractions

LEARN

One figure in a model train set is a person. This figure is $\frac{7}{8}$ in. tall. The height of a flat-bed car is $\frac{1}{2}$ in. How much taller is the person?

Subtract: $\frac{7}{8} - \frac{1}{2}$

Step 1	**Step 2**
Write equivalent fractions using the LCD.	Subtract. Write the difference in simplest form, if necessary.

Step 1

$$\frac{7}{8} = \frac{7}{8}$$
$$-\frac{1}{2} = \frac{4}{8}$$

Think: The LCD of $\frac{7}{8}$ and $\frac{1}{2}$ is 8.

Step 2

$$\frac{7}{8} = \frac{7}{8}$$
$$-\frac{1}{2} = \frac{4}{8}$$
$$\frac{3}{8}$$

The person is $\frac{3}{8}$ in. taller than the flat-bed car.

You can also use a fraction calculator to subtract fractions.

 7 **b/c** 8 − 1 **b/c** 2 = $\frac{3}{8}$

More Examples

A $\frac{1}{2} - \frac{1}{6}$ **Think:** The LCD is 6.

$$\frac{1}{2} = \frac{3}{6}$$
$$-\frac{1}{6} = \frac{1}{6}$$
$$\frac{2}{6} = \frac{1}{3}$$

B $\frac{11}{12} - \frac{3}{4}$ **Think:** The LCD is 12.

$$\frac{11}{12} = \frac{11}{12}$$
$$-\frac{3}{4} = \frac{9}{12}$$
$$\frac{2}{12} = \frac{1}{6}$$

CHECK

Check for Understanding

Subtract. You may use models. Write the answer in simplest form.

1 $\frac{4}{6} - \frac{1}{2}$ **2** $\frac{2}{3} - \frac{1}{4}$ **3** $\frac{5}{8} - \frac{1}{4}$ **4** $\frac{11}{12} - \frac{2}{3}$

Critical Thinking: Analyze   **Explain your reasoning.**

5 **What if** you did Example B by first writing equivalent fractions with a denominator of 48, instead of the LCD 12. Do you get the same answer?

Practice

Subtract. Write the answer in simplest form. Remember to estimate.

1 $\frac{3}{8} - \frac{1}{4}$ **2** $\frac{5}{6} - \frac{2}{3}$ **3** $\frac{3}{4} - \frac{3}{8}$ **4** $\frac{11}{12} - \frac{3}{4}$ **5** $\frac{7}{12} - \frac{1}{3}$

6 $\frac{2}{3} - \frac{1}{2}$ **7** $\frac{11}{12} - \frac{2}{3}$ **8** $\frac{7}{8} - \frac{3}{4}$ **9** $\frac{9}{10} - \frac{2}{3}$ **10** $\frac{1}{2} - \frac{1}{8}$

11 $\frac{5}{6} - \frac{3}{4}$ **12** $\frac{3}{10} - \frac{1}{5}$ **13** $\frac{7}{10} - \frac{1}{2}$ **14** $\frac{5}{12} - \frac{1}{6}$ **15** $\frac{1}{5} - \frac{1}{10}$

 ALGEBRA Simplify using order of operations rules.

16 $\frac{2}{3} - \frac{1}{5} - \frac{2}{15}$ **17** $\frac{3}{4} - \frac{2}{6} + \frac{1}{3}$ **18** $\frac{1}{2} + \frac{2}{3} - \frac{1}{4}$ **19** $\frac{3}{8} + \frac{1}{2} - \frac{3}{4}$

MIXED APPLICATIONS
Problem Solving

20 Kyle ran his model trains $\frac{1}{2}$ hour on Saturday and $\frac{3}{4}$ hour on Sunday. How long did he run them altogether on the weekend?

21 **Write a problem** that can be solved by adding or subtracting fractions. Solve your problem and give it to other students to solve.

22 Complete the magic square so the sum in each row, column, and diagonal is 1.

$\frac{5}{9}$	■	$\frac{7}{18}$
■	$\frac{1}{3}$	■
$\frac{5}{18}$	■	■

23 **Logical reasoning** Alberto ate 3 pieces of cake, Amy ate 2, and Pat ate 1. If $\frac{1}{2}$ the cake is left, into how many pieces was the cake cut?

Cultural Connection Egyptian Fractions

A unit fraction is a fraction with a numerator that is 1, such as $\frac{1}{4}$. Ancient Egyptians wrote unit fractions using the symbol for *mouth* ◯ placed above the denominator. The symbol for *mouth* meant "part". In the denominator a straight line ❙ represented 1 and the symbol ∩ represented 10.

Egyptians wrote fractions that were not unit fractions as a sum of unit fractions. To write a fraction such as $\frac{3}{4}$, they wrote the fractions for $\frac{1}{2}$ and $\frac{1}{4}$ together, because $\frac{1}{2} + \frac{1}{4} = \frac{3}{4}$.

Represent the following fractions in the Egyptian system.

1 $\frac{1}{5}$ **2** $\frac{1}{8}$ **3** $\frac{5}{6}$ **4** $\frac{3}{8}$ **5** $\frac{7}{12}$ **6** $\frac{3}{16}$

Add Mixed Numbers

Anita's family limits the amount of time each week she spends playing games on the computer. Here is Anita's log of her playing time for one week.

Computer Games	Hours Played
Sim City 2000	$1\frac{1}{4}$ hours
Tetris	$1\frac{1}{4}$ hours
MYST	$1\frac{3}{4}$ hours
Chess	$1\frac{1}{2}$ hours

Work Together

Work with a partner. Use models to answer these questions. Use pictures and numbers to record your work.

> **You will need**
> • *fraction strips*

▶ How long did Anita play Sim City 2000 and Tetris altogether?

▶ How long did Anita play Sim City 2000 and chess altogether?

▶ How long did Anita play Sim City 2000 and MYST altogether?

▶ How long did Anita play MYST and chess altogether?

▶ How did you use models to answer the questions?

Make Connections

Here is how one student found $1\frac{3}{4} + 1\frac{1}{2}$ using fraction strips.

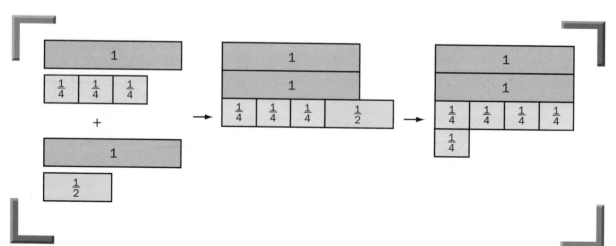

Here is how the student recorded what he did with fraction strips.

$$1\frac{3}{4} = 1\frac{3}{4}$$
$$+ 1\frac{1}{2} = 1\frac{2}{4}$$
$$\overline{\phantom{+1\frac{1}{2} =} 2\frac{5}{4}}$$

$$\frac{5}{4} = 1 + \frac{1}{4}$$
So, $2\frac{5}{4} = 3\frac{1}{4}$

▶ Describe how the student found $1\frac{3}{4} + 1\frac{1}{2}$ using fraction strips and how he recorded what he did.

Check for Understanding
Add. Write the answer in simplest form. You may use fraction strips.

1 $1\frac{1}{2} + 1\frac{1}{6}$ **2** $1\frac{2}{3} + 2\frac{2}{3}$ **3** $2\frac{1}{6} + \frac{2}{3}$ **4** $1\frac{1}{3} + 2\frac{1}{4}$

5 $3\frac{3}{10} + 1\frac{1}{2}$ **6** $2\frac{1}{2} + 3\frac{5}{8}$ **7** $5 + 4\frac{3}{4}$ **8** $6\frac{7}{8} + 1\frac{3}{4}$

Critical Thinking: Analyze

9 How could you add $4\frac{2}{5}$ and $2\frac{3}{5}$ mentally?

Practice
Add, using any method. Write the answer in simplest form.

1 $\begin{array}{r} 1\frac{1}{5} \\ + 2\frac{3}{5} \\ \hline \end{array}$ **2** $\begin{array}{r} 3\frac{5}{6} \\ + 2\frac{1}{6} \\ \hline \end{array}$ **3** $\begin{array}{r} 5\frac{3}{4} \\ + 2\frac{3}{4} \\ \hline \end{array}$ **4** $\begin{array}{r} 4\frac{3}{8} \\ + \frac{7}{8} \\ \hline \end{array}$ **5** $\begin{array}{r} 6\frac{2}{3} \\ + 3\frac{1}{2} \\ \hline \end{array}$ **6** $\begin{array}{r} 3\frac{5}{12} \\ + 4\frac{11}{12} \\ \hline \end{array}$

7 $\begin{array}{r} 7\frac{3}{4} \\ + 5\frac{1}{8} \\ \hline \end{array}$ **8** $\begin{array}{r} 1\frac{1}{4} \\ + 5\frac{1}{2} \\ \hline \end{array}$ **9** $\begin{array}{r} 5\frac{5}{12} \\ + \frac{5}{6} \\ \hline \end{array}$ **10** $\begin{array}{r} 1\frac{7}{8} \\ + 3\frac{3}{4} \\ \hline \end{array}$ **11** $\begin{array}{r} 2\frac{2}{3} \\ + 3\frac{5}{6} \\ \hline \end{array}$ **12** $\begin{array}{r} 4\frac{1}{2} \\ + 3\frac{1}{6} \\ \hline \end{array}$

13 $3 + 5\frac{5}{8}$ **14** $2\frac{3}{4} + 4\frac{5}{6}$ **15** $\frac{11}{12} + 5\frac{1}{4}$ **16** $4\frac{5}{6} + 2\frac{1}{3}$

17 $3\frac{5}{12} + 2\frac{1}{4}$ **18** $4\frac{1}{2} + 1\frac{4}{5}$ **19** $4\frac{5}{8} + 3\frac{2}{3}$ **20** $3\frac{3}{4} + 4\frac{1}{6}$

MIXED APPLICATIONS
Problem Solving

21 If you spend $1\frac{1}{2}$ hours at the library, $1\frac{1}{2}$ hours writing on the computer, and $\frac{3}{4}$ hour revising your report, how much time did you put into your report?

22 Sasha spent $29.99 on a new computer game. He gave the clerk two $20 bills. How much change should he get back?

Add Mixed Numbers

To weave this friendship bracelet takes $2\frac{1}{2}$ yd yellow string and $1\frac{2}{3}$ yd blue string. How much string is needed altogether?

Add: $2\frac{1}{2} + 1\frac{2}{3}$

Estimate the sum.   **Think:** $2\frac{1}{2} + 1\frac{1}{2} = 4$

In the previous lesson you used models to add mixed numbers. You can also use pencil and paper or a calculator to add.

Step 1	**Step 2**	**Step 3**
Write equivalent fractions using the LCD.	Add the fractions. Add the whole numbers.	Write the sum in simplest form.
$2\frac{1}{2} = 2\frac{3}{6}$ **Think:** The LCD $+1\frac{2}{3} = 1\frac{4}{6}$ of the two fractions is 6.	$2\frac{1}{2} = 2\frac{3}{6}$ $+1\frac{2}{3} = 1\frac{4}{6}$ $3\frac{7}{6}$	$2\frac{1}{2} = 2\frac{3}{6}$ $+1\frac{2}{3} = 1\frac{4}{6}$ $3\frac{7}{6} = 4\frac{1}{6}$

 2 1 2 + 1 2 3 = $3\frac{7}{6}$ $\frac{25}{6}$ $4\frac{1}{6}$

You will need $4\frac{1}{6}$ yd of string altogether.

More Examples

A
$4\frac{1}{8}$
$+3\frac{3}{8}$
$7\frac{4}{8} = 7\frac{1}{2}$

B
$2\frac{3}{10}$
$+1\frac{7}{10}$
$3\frac{10}{10} = 4$

C
$2\frac{4}{5}$
$+\ \ \frac{3}{5}$
$2\frac{7}{5} = 3\frac{2}{5}$

D
$3\frac{1}{8} = 3\frac{3}{24}$
$4\frac{1}{6} = 4\frac{4}{24}$
$+2\frac{1}{3} = 2\frac{8}{24}$
$9\frac{15}{24} = 9\frac{5}{8}$

Check for Understanding

Add. Write the answer in simplest form. Remember to estimate.

1 $3\frac{1}{2} + 3\frac{1}{4}$

2 $3\frac{7}{10} + 4\frac{5}{10}$

3 $3\frac{1}{3} + 5\frac{2}{3}$

4 $6\frac{7}{8} + 3\frac{1}{2} + \frac{2}{5}$

Critical Thinking: Analyze   Explain your reasoning.

5 The LCD of $\frac{1}{4}$ and $\frac{1}{3}$ is 12, the product of 4 and 3. When is the LCD of any two fractions the product of their denominators?

Practice

Add. Write the answer in simplest form. Remember to estimate.

1 $\begin{array}{r} 5\frac{3}{4} \\ + 2\frac{1}{4} \\ \hline \end{array}$ **2** $\begin{array}{r} 1\frac{3}{8} \\ + 7\frac{7}{8} \\ \hline \end{array}$ **3** $\begin{array}{r} 5\frac{2}{3} \\ + 3\frac{1}{3} \\ \hline \end{array}$ **4** $\begin{array}{r} 4\frac{1}{6} \\ + 7\frac{1}{6} \\ \hline \end{array}$ **5** $\begin{array}{r} 16 \\ + 8\frac{2}{3} \\ \hline \end{array}$ **6** $\begin{array}{r} 3\frac{1}{2} \\ + 5\frac{1}{2} \\ \hline \end{array}$

7 $3\frac{7}{12} + 1\frac{5}{6}$ **8** $2\frac{3}{4} + \frac{3}{8}$ **9** $2\frac{3}{4} + 8$ **10** $2\frac{8}{15} + 3\frac{2}{3}$

11 $6\frac{3}{4} + 2\frac{1}{3}$ **12** $5\frac{1}{10} + \frac{7}{8}$ **13** $3\frac{2}{3} + 1\frac{1}{2}$ **14** $7\frac{3}{5} + 3\frac{1}{4}$

15 $5\frac{1}{3} + 6\frac{3}{4} + 2\frac{1}{12}$ **16** $7\frac{5}{6} + 4\frac{1}{8} + 3\frac{2}{3}$ **17** $5\frac{2}{3} + 7 + \frac{5}{6}$

★ ALGEBRA Evaluate each expression.

18 $x + \frac{5}{6}$ for $x = 3\frac{1}{2}$ **19** $y + 6\frac{3}{4}$ for $y = 4\frac{3}{8}$ **20** $2\frac{1}{6} + a$ for $a = 3\frac{5}{6}$

21 $x + 1\frac{1}{2}$ for $x = \frac{1}{12}$ **22** $n + 4\frac{2}{3}$ for $n = 1\frac{5}{6}$ **23** $3\frac{1}{2} + y$ for $y = \frac{3}{10}$

MIXED APPLICATIONS
Problem Solving

24 The 8-looper friendship bracelet uses $1\frac{1}{3}$ yd of one color string and two $\frac{1}{3}$-yd pieces of another color. How much string is used altogether?

25 **Write a problem** involving the perimeter of a triangular-shaped object and mixed numbers. Solve your problem and give it to another student to solve.

26 Which has greater mass—a book with a mass of 1,250 grams or a boot with a mass of 1.2 kilograms?

27 Knitting a sweater requires 7 balls of yarn. If each ball costs $3.95, about how much will the yarn cost?

more to explore

Properties of Addition
Recall the Commutative Property and Associative Property for addition and the Identity Property.

Try out these properties with mixed numbers.
Give examples to support your answers.

1 Is the Commutative Property of addition true for all mixed numbers?

2 Is the Associative Property of addition true for all mixed numbers?

3 Is the Identity Property true for all mixed numbers?

Estimate each sum or difference.

1 $\frac{5}{8} + \frac{5}{12}$

2 $\frac{15}{16} - \frac{2}{5}$

3 $2\frac{3}{16} + 3\frac{7}{8}$

4 $4\frac{3}{8} - 1\frac{9}{10}$

5 $5\frac{5}{8} + 3\frac{7}{16}$

6 $7\frac{5}{6} - 4\frac{3}{8}$

7 $6\frac{7}{12} + 4\frac{1}{6} + 3$

8 $2\frac{1}{10} + 5\frac{7}{8} + 4\frac{3}{16}$

Add or subtract. Write the answer in simplest form.
Remember to estimate.

9 $\begin{array}{r} \frac{3}{5} \\ + \frac{1}{5} \\ \hline \end{array}$

10 $\begin{array}{r} 4\frac{3}{10} \\ + 2\frac{1}{10} \\ \hline \end{array}$

11 $\begin{array}{r} \frac{2}{5} \\ + \frac{1}{4} \\ \hline \end{array}$

12 $\begin{array}{r} 5\frac{1}{2} \\ + \frac{3}{8} \\ \hline \end{array}$

13 $\begin{array}{r} 5\frac{1}{2} \\ 8\frac{5}{8} \\ + 2\frac{3}{4} \\ \hline \end{array}$

14 $\begin{array}{r} 7\frac{1}{3} \\ 2\frac{5}{6} \\ + 4\frac{1}{2} \\ \hline \end{array}$

15 $\begin{array}{r} 6\frac{1}{4} \\ - 2\frac{1}{4} \\ \hline \end{array}$

16 $\begin{array}{r} \frac{7}{10} \\ - \frac{3}{10} \\ \hline \end{array}$

17 $\begin{array}{r} 5\frac{2}{3} \\ - 3\frac{1}{6} \\ \hline \end{array}$

18 $\begin{array}{r} \frac{3}{10} \\ - \frac{1}{6} \\ \hline \end{array}$

19 $\begin{array}{r} \frac{2}{3} \\ - \frac{1}{4} \\ \hline \end{array}$

20 $\begin{array}{r} \frac{7}{8} \\ - \frac{2}{3} \\ \hline \end{array}$

21 $1\frac{5}{8} + 2\frac{1}{3}$

22 $6\frac{2}{3} + 1\frac{1}{8}$

23 $4\frac{4}{5} + 2\frac{3}{10}$

24 $7\frac{7}{12} + 1\frac{5}{6}$

25 $\frac{5}{6} - \frac{1}{6}$

26 $\frac{1}{2} - \frac{3}{8}$

27 $\frac{2}{5} - \frac{1}{4}$

28 $\frac{7}{10} - \frac{1}{2}$

29 $\frac{2}{3} - \frac{4}{7}$

30 $15\frac{1}{2} + 9\frac{7}{10}$

31 $8\frac{5}{8} + 5\frac{3}{8}$

32 $16 + 18\frac{3}{4} + 2\frac{1}{2}$

33 $2\frac{1}{2} + 3\frac{1}{4}$

34 $7\frac{3}{8} + 2\frac{3}{8} + \frac{3}{4}$

35 $1\frac{4}{5} + 2\frac{1}{10} + 6$

Solve. Use mental math when you can.

36 The diameter of a 1793 one-cent coin is $\frac{15}{16}$ inch. The diameter of a modern penny is $\frac{3}{4}$ inch. How much wider is the 1793 coin?

37 Charles ran $2\frac{3}{4}$ miles in the morning and $4\frac{1}{4}$ miles in the afternoon. How many miles did he run altogether?

38 Diana bought several pieces of poster board. Each piece of poster board cost $0.39. If Diana spent $2.73 on the pieces, how many did she buy?

39 Suppose your math book is $1\frac{1}{16}$ in. thick and your social studies book is $1\frac{3}{8}$ in. thick. If you stack the two books on top of each other, about how thick is the stack?

40 Journal — Can you add two fractions such as $\frac{1}{2}$ and $\frac{2}{3}$ by adding the numerators and adding the denominators? Draw pictures of models to support your reasoning.

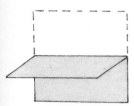
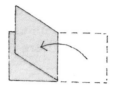

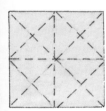
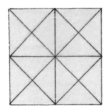

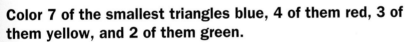

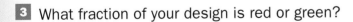

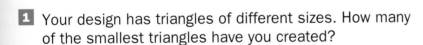

developing spatial sense

MATH CONNECTION

Spatial Visualization

You can fold a square piece of paper and color it to make a design. Start with a square piece of paper.

Fold in half.

Fold in half the other way.

Fold diagonally.

Fold diagonally the other way.

Open up the paper.

Draw lines on the fold lines.

1 Your design has triangles of different sizes. How many of the smallest triangles have you created?

Color 7 of the smallest triangles blue, 4 of them red, 3 of them yellow, and 2 of them green.

2 What fraction of your design is blue? red? yellow? green?

3 What fraction of your design is red or green?

4 What fraction of your design is blue or red?

5 Fold another square piece of paper in the same way and open it up. Using at most 4 colors, color each of the smallest triangles to make a new design. Write a description of your design using fractions.

Crane

Snake

Giraffe

Hikers' Guide

Work with your team to create a hiking guide that helps all hikers at Crooked Mountain State Park. Plan each hike so that it is a round-trip hike: it must begin and end at Northgate Entrance. Keep in mind that not all hikers are alike. Some hikers want a tough workout. Others just want to take a relaxing walk in the woods.

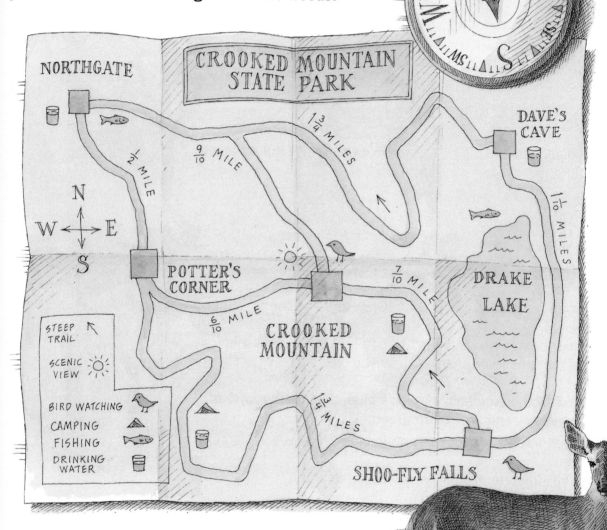

You can classify the hikes you plan in three categories:

Beginning Hikes: less than $3\frac{1}{2}$ miles

Intermediate Hikes: between $3\frac{1}{2}$ and $4\frac{1}{2}$ miles

Advanced Hikes: over $4\frac{1}{2}$ miles

Make a Hikers' Guide

1 Look at the map on the left. Then decide which hikes each member of your team will describe.

2 Give each hike a number. Tell whether the hike is a Beginning Hike, an Intermediate Hike, or an Advanced Hike.

3 Give information about the total distance and the route of each hike you describe.

4 Assemble your team's information into a Hikers' Guide.

Report Your Findings

5 Prepare a report on what your team did. Do the following:

▶ Describe how you decided what hikes to include in your guide.

▶ Tell what the longest and shortest hikes are in your guide. Which hiking category had the greatest number of hikes?

6 Present your Hikers' Guide to the class.

Revise your work.

▶ Are your distance calculations and hiking categories correct?
▶ Did you organize your information so it was easy to find?
▶ Did you edit your work and proofread the final copy?

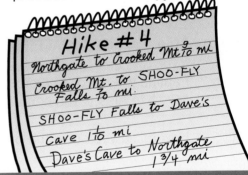

Hike #4
Northgate to Crooked Mt. $\frac{9}{10}$ mi
Crooked Mt. to SHOO-FLY Falls $\frac{7}{10}$ mi
SHOO-FLY Falls to Dave's Cave $1\frac{1}{10}$ mi
Dave's Cave to Northgate $1\frac{3}{4}$ mi

MORE TO INVESTIGATE

PREDICT which of your hikes your classmates would prefer to make. Survey your classmates to test your prediction.

EXPLORE what would happen if a new entrance was built at Shoo-Fly Falls. How would this change your Hikers' Guide? Explain.

FIND out the length of the Appalachian Trail, the longest hiking trail in the United States.

Find a Pattern

LEARN

Read

Pauline is planning a mosaic of green and white tiles. If she follows the pattern below, how many green tiles will she need when there are 12 white tiles in the center?

Plan

Find a pattern for how many more green tiles are needed every time 2 white tiles are added.

Solve

Step 1 Making a table can help you find a pattern.

Number of white tiles	2	4	6	8	10	12
Number of green tiles	10	14	18	22	26	30

+4   +4   +4

 Step 2 ALGEBRA: PATTERNS Use the pattern to complete the table.

Pauline will need 30 green tiles when there are 12 white tiles in the center.

Look Back

How could you solve the problem in a different way?

CHECK

Check for Understanding

1 What if Pauline puts two rows of white tiles in the center instead of one row. How many green tiles would she need when there are 24 white tiles in the center? 28 white tiles? 34 white tiles? Explain.

Critical Thinking: Analyze   **Explain your reasoning.**

2 Suppose that you get $1 on January 1, $2 on January 2, $4 on January 3, $8 on January 4. If the amount you get doubles every day, how much would you get on January 10?

Problem Solving

1 **ALGEBRA: PATTERNS** Describe the mosaic pattern at right. If there are 50 tiles across the top and the pattern continues, what color tile is in the upper right-hand corner?

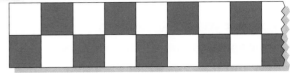

2 Sue left home at 12 noon. She rode her bike until 2:30 P.M. If she rode 10 mi per hour, how far did she ride?

3 **ALGEBRA: PATTERNS** Write the eighth fraction in the series $\frac{1}{2}, \frac{3}{4}, \frac{5}{6}, \frac{7}{8} \cdots$, and describe the pattern you used.

4 In Todd's collection of nickels and quarters, there are 4 more nickels than quarters. He has $2.30. How many quarters does he have?

5 Katrina can buy 10 daffodil bulbs for $2.99 and 10 tulip bulbs for $1.99. If she buys the same number of each, how many can she buy for $20?

6 In a stadium with the ticket prices below, $\frac{2}{8}$ of the seating is in the red area, $\frac{1}{8}$ is in the orange area, and $\frac{3}{8}$ is in the yellow area. What fraction of the seats are $6 seats?

7 **ALGEBRA: PATTERNS** The first four triangular numbers are the numbers of dots in the triangular patterns shown below. What is the seventh triangular number?

Stadium Concert Ticket Prices	
Orange area	$50
Red area	$35
Yellow area	$20
Green area	$ 6

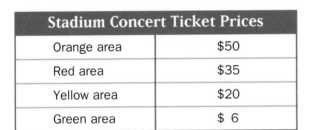

8 **ALGEBRA: PATTERNS** In a display of CDs, each row has two more CDs than the one before it. The first row has one CD. How many CDs in 9 rows?

9 About how far could a clipper ship sail in a day? **SEE INFOBIT.**

10 About how much longer is a $41\frac{7}{8}$-in. model of the *Great Republic* clipper ship than a model of the *Flying Cloud* clipper ship that is $29\frac{3}{8}$ in. long?

INFOBIT
Clipper ships were sailing ships built in the middle 1800s. They had slender hulls and many sails. They could sail up to 20 knots, which is about 23 miles per hour.

Add and Subtract Fractions and Mixed Numbers **235**

Subtract Mixed Numbers

Whatever you are looking for—
from peace and quiet to a thrilling
ride—you can get while canoeing.
If you start $2\frac{1}{4}$ mi downstream of
South Wallingford and stop at
Wallingford, how far did you canoe?

If a friend puts her canoe in at
$1\frac{1}{2}$ mi, how far is she from
Wallingford? How far apart are
the two of you at the start?

Otter Creek, Vermont		
Miles (to this point)	Break Points	Watch Out For
0	South Wallingford	
$5\frac{3}{4}$	Wallingford	
$21\frac{1}{4}$	Rutland	2 dams
$22\frac{1}{2}$	Center Rutland	1 dam
$29\frac{1}{2}$	Proctor	1 dam
$67\frac{1}{2}$	Middlebury	4 dams
$79\frac{3}{4}$	Lemon Fair	

Work Together

Work with a partner.
Use models to help
you subtract these
numbers. Use pictures
and numbers to record
your work.

You will need
• *fraction strips*

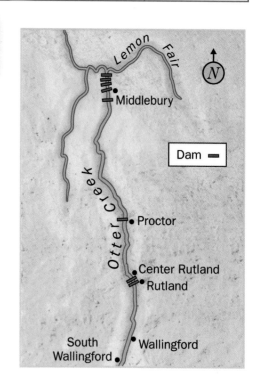

$5\frac{3}{4} - 2\frac{1}{4}$ $5\frac{3}{4} - 1\frac{1}{2}$ $2\frac{1}{4} - 1\frac{1}{2}$

How did you subtract the numbers? Could you
have done it another way?

▶ If someone stops to take pictures at mile $3\frac{5}{8}$,
how far did they canoe if they put the boat in
at mile $1\frac{3}{8}$? at mile $1\frac{1}{2}$? at mile $1\frac{7}{8}$?

▶ How could you use models to find $2\frac{1}{2} - \frac{5}{6}$?

Making Connections

Here is how one student found $2\frac{1}{4} - 1\frac{1}{2}$ using fraction strips.

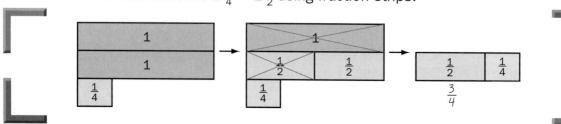

Here is how the student recorded what she did with the fraction strips.

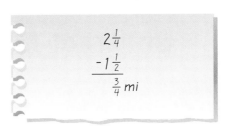

▶ Describe how the student found $2\frac{1}{4} - 1\frac{1}{2}$ using the fraction strips and how she recorded what she did.

▶ How is finding $5\frac{3}{4} - 2\frac{1}{4}$ different from finding $2\frac{1}{4} - 1\frac{1}{2}$?

Check for Understanding
**Subtract. Write the answer in simplest form.
You may use fraction strips.**

1 $5\frac{2}{3} - 1\frac{1}{3}$ **2** $8\frac{5}{8} - 1\frac{1}{4}$ **3** $4 - 2\frac{3}{4}$ **4** $1\frac{1}{4} - \frac{3}{4}$

5 $7\frac{1}{2} - 3\frac{5}{8}$ **6** $5 - 1\frac{2}{3}$ **7** $15\frac{1}{6} - 8\frac{5}{12}$ **8** $3 - 2\frac{1}{5}$

Critical Thinking: Analyze   **Explain your reasoning.**

9 How is subtracting mixed numbers like subtracting whole numbers? Give examples.

Practice
Subtract, using any method. Write the answer in simplest form.

1 $\begin{array}{r} 2\frac{5}{8} \\ -1\frac{3}{8} \\ \hline \end{array}$ **2** $\begin{array}{r} 3\frac{2}{3} \\ -2\frac{1}{6} \\ \hline \end{array}$ **3** $\begin{array}{r} 3\frac{7}{12} \\ -1\frac{11}{12} \\ \hline \end{array}$ **4** $\begin{array}{r} 7 \\ -3\frac{7}{12} \\ \hline \end{array}$ **5** $\begin{array}{r} 4\frac{1}{3} \\ -2\frac{1}{2} \\ \hline \end{array}$ **6** $\begin{array}{r} 6\frac{1}{4} \\ -4\frac{3}{4} \\ \hline \end{array}$

7 $3 - 1\frac{1}{2}$ **8** $4\frac{1}{2} - 2\frac{3}{8}$ **9** $7\frac{1}{2} - 5\frac{2}{3}$ **10** $12 - 4\frac{3}{8}$

11 $7\frac{1}{10} - \frac{9}{10}$ **12** $13 - 4\frac{4}{5}$ **13** $7\frac{5}{6} - 3\frac{1}{4}$ **14** $12\frac{1}{10} - 4\frac{3}{10}$

15 $11\frac{3}{8} - 6\frac{3}{4}$ **16** $14\frac{3}{5} - 6\frac{7}{10}$ **17** $15\frac{7}{8} - 9\frac{1}{3}$ **18** $17\frac{4}{5} - 8\frac{3}{4}$

MIXED APPLICATIONS
Problem Solving

19 If you spent $2\frac{1}{4}$ hours canoeing before lunch and $1\frac{3}{4}$ hours after lunch, how much more time did you canoe before lunch?

20 ALGEBRA: PATTERNS Write the next 3 numbers in the pattern.
15, $13\frac{2}{3}$, $12\frac{1}{3}$, 11, ▪, ▪, ▪

Subtract Mixed Numbers

When you go hiking, you'll enjoy beautiful sights while getting terrific exercise. On this trail, how much farther is Panther Mountain than Round Lake?

Subtract: $6\frac{1}{2} - 2\frac{3}{10}$

Estimate the difference.

Think: $6\frac{1}{2} - 2\frac{1}{2} = 4$

In the previous lesson you used models to subtract mixed numbers. Here is another method.

Step 1	**Step 2**	**Step 3**
Write equivalent fractions using the LCD.	**Subtract the fractions.** **Subtract the whole numbers.**	**Write the difference in simplest form.**
$6\frac{1}{2} = 6\frac{5}{10}$ $-2\frac{3}{10} = 2\frac{3}{10}$ **Think:** The LCD of the two fractions is 10.	$6\frac{1}{2} = 6\frac{5}{10}$ $-2\frac{3}{10} = 2\frac{3}{10}$ $\overline{4\frac{2}{10}}$	$6\frac{1}{2} = 6\frac{5}{10}$ $-2\frac{3}{10} = 2\frac{3}{10}$ $\overline{4\frac{2}{10} = 4\frac{1}{5}}$

Panther Mountain is $4\frac{1}{5}$ miles farther than Round Lake.

Here is how to find the difference using a fraction calculator.

 6 1 2 − 2 3 10 =

Talk It Over

▶ How can you decide if an answer is reasonable?

▶ **What if** in Step 1 you write equivalent fractions with a denominator of 20 instead of the LCD 10. Do you get the same answer?

▶ How would you find $8 - 3\frac{5}{6}$?

You are at Lookout Point, which is on the trail to Panther Mountain. How much farther is it to the top of Panther Mountain?

Subtract: $6\frac{1}{2} - 4\frac{3}{4}$

Estimate the difference.   **Think:** $6\frac{1}{2} - 5 = 1\frac{1}{2}$

Step 1	Step 2	Step 3
Write equivalent fractions using the LCD.	**Rename to subtract the fractions.**	**Subtract. Write the answer in simplest form.**
$6\frac{1}{2} = 6\frac{2}{4}$ **Think:** The LCD is 4. $-4\frac{3}{4} = 4\frac{3}{4}$	$6\frac{1}{2} = 6\frac{2}{4} = 5\frac{6}{4}$ $-4\frac{3}{4} = 4\frac{3}{4} = 4\frac{3}{4}$	$6\frac{1}{2} = 6\frac{2}{4} = 5\frac{6}{4}$ $-4\frac{3}{4} = 4\frac{3}{4} = 4\frac{3}{4}$ $1\frac{3}{4}$

It is $1\frac{3}{4}$ miles farther to Panther Mountain.

Here is how to find the difference using a fraction calculator.

 6 [a] 1 [b/c] 2 − 4 [a] 3 [b/c] 4 = $1\frac{3}{4}$

More Examples

A
$15\frac{3}{5}$
$-\ 8\frac{1}{5}$
—————
$7\frac{2}{5}$

B
$6 = 5\frac{3}{3}$
$-3\frac{2}{3} = 3\frac{2}{3}$
—————
$2\frac{1}{3}$

C
$8\frac{5}{12} = 8\frac{5}{12} = 7\frac{17}{12}$
$-\ 4\frac{2}{3} = 4\frac{8}{12} = 4\frac{8}{12}$
—————
$3\frac{9}{12} = 3\frac{3}{4}$

Check for Understanding

Subtract. Write the answer in simplest form. Remember to estimate.

1 $8\frac{4}{5} - 5\frac{1}{10}$ **2** $6\frac{5}{6} - 3\frac{1}{4}$ **3** $16\frac{1}{2} - 8\frac{2}{3}$ **4** $15 - 7\frac{5}{6}$

5 $4\frac{5}{8} - 3\frac{3}{4}$ **6** $1\frac{2}{8} - \frac{7}{8}$ **7** $9 - 3\frac{2}{5}$ **8** $4\frac{1}{8} - 3\frac{7}{8}$

Critical Thinking: Analyze   Explain your reasoning.

9 When you estimate $6\frac{1}{2} - 4\frac{3}{4}$, you can round $4\frac{3}{4}$ to 5 or to $4\frac{1}{2}$. Does one of those methods give you an estimate that is closer to the exact answer than the other?

10 Describe how to subtract mixed numbers. Give examples.

Turn the page for Practice.

Practice

Subtract. Write the answer in simplest form. Remember to estimate.

1 $3\frac{5}{6}$
$-1\frac{1}{6}$

2 $8\frac{3}{4}$
$-5\frac{2}{3}$

3 $11\frac{7}{8}$
$-4\frac{1}{6}$

4 $5\frac{1}{6}$
$-3\frac{1}{10}$

5 $12\frac{5}{6}$
$-4\frac{1}{5}$

6 $12\frac{2}{3}$
$-8\frac{1}{4}$

7 6
$-4\frac{2}{5}$

8 $4\frac{1}{8}$
$-2\frac{3}{8}$

9 $9\frac{5}{8}$
$-2\frac{3}{4}$

10 $7\frac{1}{4}$
$-\frac{3}{8}$

11 $6\frac{1}{3}$
$-\frac{3}{8}$

12 $15\frac{1}{6}$
$-13\frac{1}{2}$

13 $6\frac{2}{3} - 2\frac{2}{5}$

14 $19 - 7\frac{3}{4}$

15 $13\frac{2}{3} - 10$

16 $19\frac{1}{6} - 16\frac{4}{15}$

17 $5 - \frac{3}{8}$

18 $16\frac{1}{10} - 7\frac{3}{10}$

19 $9\frac{5}{6} - 4\frac{1}{6}$

20 $49\frac{1}{4} - 21\frac{2}{3}$

Add or subtract mentally. Explain your methods.

21 $5 + 3\frac{1}{4}$

22 $11\frac{1}{6} - 4$

23 $1\frac{1}{2} + 7\frac{1}{2}$

24 $8 - 2\frac{1}{2}$

25 $9\frac{3}{5} - 2\frac{1}{5}$

26 $2\frac{1}{2} + 3\frac{1}{4}$

27 $10\frac{1}{2} - 4\frac{1}{4}$

28 $3\frac{1}{2} + 4\frac{1}{2} + 6\frac{1}{2}$

· · · · · · · · · · · · · · · · **Make It Right** · · · · · · · · · · · · · · ·

29 Al subtracted $4\frac{1}{4} - 2\frac{3}{8}$ this way. What did he do wrong? How can he make it right?

$$4\frac{1}{4} = 4\frac{6}{24}$$
$$-2\frac{3}{8} = 2\frac{3}{24}$$
$$2\frac{3}{24} = 2\frac{1}{8}$$

MIXED APPLICATIONS
Problem Solving

30 Miko hiked for $3\frac{1}{2}$ hours Saturday and $2\frac{3}{4}$ hours Sunday. How many hours did she hike altogether?

31 Louise spent $3.95 on each of six craft kits, $14.95 on a model, and $6.99 on a game. What was her total?

32 If $\frac{2}{5}$ of the students in a class are girls, what fraction of the students in the class are boys?

33 Suppose a Brazilian real is worth $1.06. How much are 40 Brazilian reals worth?

34 The distance from the start of the trail to Giant Ledge is $7\frac{1}{4}$ miles. If you have walked $5\frac{1}{2}$ miles of that distance, how much farther do you have to walk?

35 **Data Point** How much longer is the women's outdoor triple jump record than the indoor record for that event? In general, how do indoor and outdoor records compare? Use the Databank on page 636.

The Less Is More Game!

Number of players: 2 or more

Each player makes a copy of the game board as shown.

Play the Game

▶ Each player starts with 30 points.

▶ Set a 10-minute time limit for the game. All players are to begin at the same time.

▶ Trace a path (moving up or to the right but not diagonally) from the $1\frac{1}{2}$ space in the lower left-hand corner to the $1\frac{1}{2}$ space in the upper right-hand corner. You will subtract the first number ($1\frac{1}{2}$) from 30, and then each number along the path from the previous difference, and so on along the path.

▶ Each path should go through seven mixed numbers, including the two $1\frac{1}{2}$s. The player with the path that yields the lowest score wins.

▶ Estimate before you try a path. Then use a calculator to do the computations.

▶ Try as many paths as you have time for.

mixed review • test preparation

Express the number as a product of prime numbers.

1 24 **2** 81 **3** 84 **4** 210

⭐ **ALGEBRA Evaluate each expression.**

5 $x + 4.8$ for $x = 3.57$ **6** $5y$ for $y = 6.2$ **7** $\frac{t}{4}$ for $t = 18$

8 $3n - 7.54$ for $n = 9.3$ **9** $\frac{3}{y}$ for $y = 8$ **10** $6.4m + 2.8$ for $m = 5.35$

Add and Subtract Fractions and Mixed Numbers **241**

Problem Solvers at Work

Read

Plan

Solve

Look Back

PART 1   Missing or Extra Information

Have you ever tried to figure out how much "program" you actually get to see when you watch a TV show? Suppose you watched three $\frac{1}{2}$-hour shows on Monday and counted about 14 commercials during each one. You realize two thirds of the commercials were about toys and snacks. How much program did you actually see if you don't count commercials?

Work Together

Solve. Be prepared to explain your methods.

1. **Summarize** Summarize the information in the problem.

2. What information do you need in order to solve the problem? What extra information does the problem contain?

3. Estimate the missing information. How much program did you actually see?

4. **What if** you watched a $2\frac{1}{2}$-hour movie and timed the commercials. If the commercials took $\frac{3}{4}$ hour, how long was the actual movie?

5. What information is missing from the following problem? Suppose a local cable company has a weekly program during which it airs taped presentations of school activities. How many $\frac{1}{4}$-hour presentations can fit on one videotape?

6. How could you find the missing information in problem 5?

Darrin used the information in this TV schedule to write this problem.

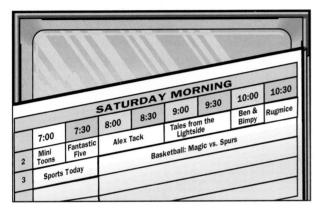

Alex watched Mini Toons. Then, he rode his bike. Then, he watched Ben & Bimpy. How long did he watch TV?

7 Does Darrin's problem have any information you do not need in order to solve the problem? If yes, identify the extra information and rewrite the problem without it.

8 Solve Darrin's problem.

9 **Write a problem** of your own with extra information. Solve your problem.

10 Suppose you plan to tape each of your favorite TV shows during the school week and watch them all during the weekend. How many 6-hour videotapes do you need? Estimate the missing information and solve the problem. Explain your reasoning.

11 **Write a problem** of your own with missing information. Solve it. Be prepared to explain your solution.

12 Trade problems. Solve at least two problems written by other students.

13 What was the most interesting problem that you solved? Why?

Darrin Perry
Snowden Elementary School
Memphis, TN

Turn the page for Practice Strategies.

Menu

Choose five problems and solve them. If there is not enough information, identify the information you need and estimate it. Explain your methods.

1 Maxwell Montes is a mountain found on Venus. It is 6,336 feet higher than Mt. Everest. Mt. Everest is 29,108 ft high and Mt. McKinley is 20,320 ft high. How high is Maxwell Montes?

2 Curt's class sold 150 adult tickets and 216 children's tickets. Adult tickets cost $1.80 and children's tickets cost $0.75. How much did the class make on ticket sales?

3 A recipe for a snack mix requires $\frac{1}{2}$ pound of shelled peanuts, $\frac{1}{3}$ pound of raisins, and $\frac{1}{8}$ pound of chocolate chips. If you follow the recipe, how much will the mixture weigh altogether?

4 A class of 24 students is going on a trip with their teacher. She and some parents are going to drive cars to take students. Estimate how many cars they will need altogether.

5 Albert has $3.25 in quarters and dimes. He has 16 coins altogether. How many coins of each kind does he have?

6 Sally Ann and Maria went on a 5-day camping trip. They walked $8\frac{1}{2}$ miles the first day, $7\frac{3}{4}$ miles the second day, and $6\frac{3}{4}$ miles the third day. How far did they walk in all?

7 Betty, Patrick, and Abdul are posing for pictures in pairs. How many different pictures are possible?

8 Lillian is making muffins for her 7 friends. Her recipe makes 3 dozen. She plans to give 5 muffins to each friend. How many will she have left?

Choose two problems and solve them. Explain your methods.

9 Kenesha eats at the cafeteria every day. She likes to choose something from each type of food, but she doesn't want to spend more than $3 for any meal. Plan five different lunches for her.

TODAY'S MENU

— SANDWICHES —
TURKEY $1.25
CHICKEN 1.10
SWISS CHEESE 0.80

— DRINKS —
JUICE $0.60
SODA 0.50
MILK 0.40

— SALADS —
GARDEN $0.85
POTATO 0.50
MACARONI 0.75

— EXTRAS —
MUFFIN $0.60
PRETZELS 0.55
GRANOLA BAR 0.35

10 Look at the diagrams below. How many points of intersection are possible with seven lines?

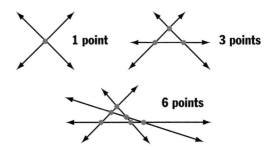

11 Write a title for this line graph. Make three statements about the graph.

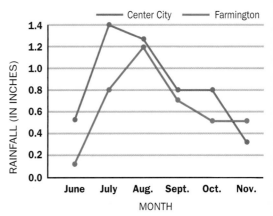

12 **At the Computer** Use a drawing program to draw at least eight different geometric figures. The sides of each figure should be $1\frac{1}{2}$ in. long. List the number of sides of each figure and find its perimeter. Name as many figures as you can.

Number of Sides	Perimeter (in inches)	Name
3	$1\frac{1}{2} + 1\frac{1}{2} + 1\frac{1}{2} = 4\frac{1}{2}$	equilateral triangle

What relationships do you see between the number of sides of a figure and its perimeter when the number of sides is odd? When it is even? Why is that?

Language and Mathematics

Complete the sentence. Use a word in the chart. (pages 216–241)

1 If you round $4\frac{5}{8}$ to the nearest ■, you get $4\frac{1}{2}$.

2 The ■ of $\frac{3}{4}$ and $\frac{1}{6}$ is 12.

3 If two fractions have the same denominator, they have ■.

4 The fractions $\frac{3}{4}$ and $\frac{6}{8}$ are ■.

5 In the fraction $\frac{3}{4}$, the number 4 is the ■.

6 A number that has a whole number and a fraction is a ■.

> **Vocabulary**
> common denominators
> least common denominators
> whole number
> denominator
> half
> mixed number
> equivalent fractions

Concepts and Skills

Estimate each sum or difference. (page 216)

7 $\frac{7}{12} + \frac{9}{10}$

8 $\frac{7}{8} - \frac{3}{5}$

9 $6\frac{5}{12} - 3\frac{1}{8}$

10 $2\frac{3}{8} + 4\frac{9}{16}$

11 $6 - 3\frac{1}{2}$

12 $7\frac{1}{8} - 1\frac{5}{8}$

13 $4\frac{3}{4} - 2$

14 $1\frac{1}{3} + \frac{7}{8}$

Add or subtract. Write the answer in simplest form. (pages 220–229, 236–241)

15 $\frac{3}{8} + \frac{1}{8}$

16 $\frac{1}{2} - \frac{1}{3}$

17 $\frac{7}{10} + \frac{2}{5}$

18 $\frac{3}{4} - \frac{2}{3}$

19 $4\frac{2}{5} + 2\frac{1}{5}$

20 $20\frac{3}{8} - 2\frac{1}{8}$

21 $5\frac{3}{5} + 8\frac{2}{3}$

22 $9 - 3\frac{2}{3}$

23 $11\frac{1}{2} - 8\frac{5}{6}$

24 $4\frac{5}{12} + \frac{3}{8}$

25 $3\frac{1}{2} + 4\frac{3}{4} + 2\frac{1}{6}$

26 $2\frac{5}{6} + 3\frac{5}{6} + 1\frac{1}{2}$

27 $\frac{2}{3} + \frac{2}{3}$

28 $1\frac{2}{5} + 6\frac{1}{3}$

29 $7 - 3\frac{4}{5}$

30 $4\frac{1}{6} - 2\frac{1}{2}$

31 $\frac{3}{8} + \frac{5}{8}$

32 $\frac{7}{10} - \frac{1}{2}$

33 $16 - 5\frac{2}{3}$

34 $5\frac{3}{4} + 9\frac{2}{3}$

35 $1\frac{5}{12} - \frac{3}{8}$

36 $2\frac{3}{4} + 4 + 3\frac{5}{8}$

37 $7\frac{1}{8} - 4\frac{3}{4}$

38 $4\frac{4}{5} + 10\frac{3}{10} + 3\frac{1}{2}$

Think critically. (pages 236, 238)

39 Analyze. Explain the error and correct it.

$$40 = 40\frac{8}{8}$$
$$-16\frac{5}{8} = 16\frac{5}{8}$$
$$24\frac{3}{8}$$

MIXED APPLICATIONS
Problem Solving

Pencil & Paper · Calculator · Mental Math

(pages 234, 242)

40 Helena bought $12\frac{3}{8}$ yards of material. She used $8\frac{7}{8}$ yards to make pillows. How much material is left?

42 ALGEBRA: PATTERNS Kareem is weaving a blanket. His design has a red stripe in the first row, fourth row, seventh row, and so on. Of the first 30 rows, how many are red?

44 James won his first chess game in $1\frac{1}{2}$ hours. The second game took longer, $1\frac{3}{4}$ hours. How long did the two games take in all?

41 Anna weighs 82 lb. A walrus weighs 3,200 lb. About how many times as heavy as Anna is a walrus?

43 Gene worked on his math homework for $\frac{1}{2}$ hour, his social studies homework for $\frac{3}{4}$ hour. He worked on his science homework for $\frac{3}{4}$ hour. How long did he work on his homework?

45 In Marissa's baseball card collection, $\frac{1}{3}$ of the cards are Seattle Mariners cards. What fraction of the cards are from other teams?

Use the table for questions 46–50.

46 About how much time does Joe spend on reading and free time?

47 What fraction of the day does Joe spend eating meals?

48 How much more time does Joe spend sleeping than at school?

49 How much more time does Joe spend on homework and chores than on free time?

50 How many hours is Joe not sleeping?

Joe's Weekday Activities

Activity	Hours
Sleep	$8\frac{1}{2}$
School	$6\frac{1}{2}$
Homework	$2\frac{1}{4}$
Meals	2
Reading	$1\frac{3}{4}$
Chores	$\frac{1}{2}$
Free time	$2\frac{1}{2}$

Estimate the sum or difference.

1 $\frac{6}{7} - \frac{1}{3}$ **2** $\frac{8}{15} + \frac{9}{10}$ **3** $7\frac{1}{3} - 4\frac{2}{3}$ **4** $6\frac{3}{5} + 8\frac{1}{7}$

Add or subtract. Write the answer in simplest form.

5 $\begin{array}{r} \frac{5}{6} \\ -\frac{1}{6} \\ \hline \end{array}$ **6** $\begin{array}{r} \frac{5}{8} \\ +\frac{1}{8} \\ \hline \end{array}$ **7** $\begin{array}{r} \frac{5}{6} \\ +\frac{2}{3} \\ \hline \end{array}$ **8** $\begin{array}{r} \frac{3}{8} \\ -\frac{1}{3} \\ \hline \end{array}$

9 $\begin{array}{r} 18\frac{7}{8} \\ -\ 9 \\ \hline \end{array}$ **10** $\begin{array}{r} 20\frac{5}{8} \\ +\ 6\frac{1}{6} \\ \hline \end{array}$ **11** $\begin{array}{r} 15\frac{2}{3} \\ -\ 7\frac{1}{2} \\ \hline \end{array}$ **12** $\begin{array}{r} 4\frac{1}{4} \\ -3\frac{7}{8} \\ \hline \end{array}$

13 $\frac{3}{5} + \frac{2}{5}$ **14** $14 - 2\frac{2}{3}$ **15** $6\frac{3}{5} + 8\frac{1}{2}$ **16** $16\frac{1}{2} - 3\frac{5}{8}$

17 $\frac{3}{4} + \frac{7}{8} + \frac{1}{2}$ **18** $2\frac{3}{4} + 7\frac{1}{8} + 9\frac{3}{5}$ **19** $\frac{5}{8} + 7\frac{4}{5} + 3\frac{1}{2}$ **20** $2\frac{1}{10} + 6\frac{1}{4} + 3\frac{1}{2}$

Solve.

21 Carrie makes a skirt in size 8 that uses $2\frac{3}{8}$ yards of fabric. She makes a matching skirt for her sister in size 12 that uses $2\frac{1}{2}$ yards. How much material is left if she had 5 yards to begin with?

22 Tim is making a bead pattern of red and blue beads:

R B R R B R R B . . .

How many red beads will there be altogether before the tenth blue bead?

The stock market table shows prices in dollars and fractions of a dollar. Use the table for problems 23–25.

23 Which company had the greatest variation between its 12-month high and its 12-month low?

24 The low for Bender Electronics occurred on December 31. By June 10 of the next year, the stock had risen $3\frac{1}{2}$ points. Find the stock price for June 10.

25 How much profit would you make on each share of Shane Toys that you bought at the low price and sold at the high price?

12-Month Stock Prices		
High	**Low**	**Company**
$18\frac{3}{4}$	$7\frac{7}{8}$	Ryder Co.
16	$12\frac{3}{8}$	Bender Electronics
$28\frac{1}{2}$	$19\frac{3}{4}$	Shane Toys
$116\frac{1}{8}$	$98\frac{1}{4}$	Kelvin Furniture

What Did You Learn?

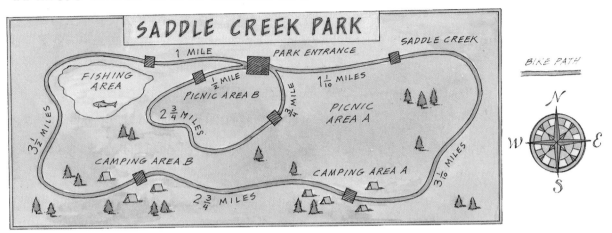

▶ Choose a bike path that passes at least four points on the map. How far would you ride if you followed your path?

▶ **What if** your goal was to ride for $15\frac{1}{2}$ miles. Did you meet your goal? If not, estimate how many more miles you need to ride.

```
•••••••••••••••••• A Good Answer ••••••••••••••••••
• includes an explanation of how you used addition and
  subtraction of mixed numbers and fractions to find
  the exact answer.
• shows your work.
```

 You may want to place your work in your portfolio.

What Do You Think

1 Do you find it easier to add or to subtract mixed numbers? Explain why.

2 What mistakes have you made when you added or subtracted fractions?
  • Renamed mixed numbers incorrectly.
  • Forgot to rename the denominators.
  • Other. Explain.

BAKING

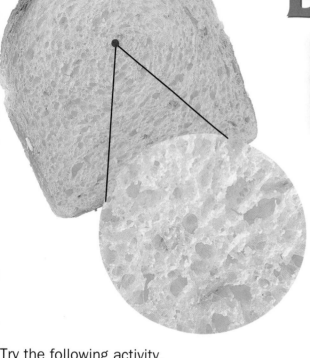

Cultural Note

It is believed that the first bread was made in Egypt about 5,500 years ago. The Egyptians put their bread in the sun to rise.

Have you ever looked closely at a piece of bread or cake? Those tiny bubbles you see are created when carbon dioxide gas bubbles form in the bread. It is these bubbles that make the dough rise (expand).

Try the following activity.

Put about half a teaspoon of baking soda into a cup.

Add a few drops of vinegar.

Record your observations.

Vinegar is a weak form of acetic acid. When baking soda is mixed with any acid, a chemical reaction occurs in which carbon dioxide gas is produced. In cooking most cakes and cookies, a reaction like this is used to make the dough rise while it bakes.

Look at the ingredients listed on a can of baking powder.

▶ What ingredients do you think might cause a chemical reaction when they get wet?

▶ Why do you think that bubbles are an important part of bread and cakes?

You will need
- *teaspoon*
- *cup*
- *baking soda*
- *vinegar*

Nutrition Facts
Serving Size 1/4 tsp (1g)
Servings Per Container about 227

Amount Per Serving
Calories 0

	% Daily Value*
Total Fat 0g	0%
Sodium 95mg	4%
Total Carbohydrate 0g	0%
Protein 0g	

Calcium 2%

* Percent Daily Values are based on a 2,000 calorie diet.

INGREDIENTS: CORNSTARCH, SODIUM BICARBONATE, CALCIUM PHOSPHATE, SODIUM ALUMINUM SULPHATE.

How Do You Make Cupcakes Rise?

The recipe below uses baking powder to make cupcakes rise.

Vanilla Cupcakes

$1\frac{3}{4}$ cups all purpose flour
$1\frac{1}{4}$ cups sugar
2 teaspoons baking powder
1 teaspoon salt
5 tablespoons softened butter
1 cup milk
1 egg
1 teaspoon vanilla

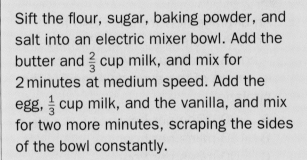

Sift the flour, sugar, baking powder, and salt into an electric mixer bowl. Add the butter and $\frac{2}{3}$ cup milk, and mix for 2 minutes at medium speed. Add the egg, $\frac{1}{3}$ cup milk, and the vanilla, and mix for two more minutes, scraping the sides of the bowl constantly.

Pour into individual paper cups in a cupcake tin, and bake for 20 to 25 minutes in an oven preheated to 375°. Makes about 24 three-inch cupcakes.

1 Suppose you want to make 48 three-inch cupcakes. How much of each ingredient should you use?

2 Suppose you want to make 72 three-inch cupcakes. How much of each ingredient should you use?

At the Computer

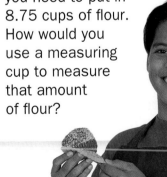

Factor: 5 times recipe amount			
Ingredient	Amount in Original Recipe	New Amount	Unit
Flour	1.75	8.75	cups
Sugar	1.25		cups
Baking Powder	2.00		tsp

3 Use a spreadsheet program to multiply the amounts of the ingredients in the cupcake recipe by any factor. Change the amounts to decimals. Set it up so that you can put in any factor, such as 5, and the spreadsheet will show the amount of each ingredient to mix.

4 Put in the number 5. The spreadsheet should show that you need to put in 8.75 cups of flour. How would you use a measuring cup to measure that amount of flour?

251

T
E
S
T

P
R
E
P
A
R
A
T
I
O
N

Choose the letter of the best answer.

1 Lincoln Middle School has 1,027 students. Washington Middle School has 858 students. How many more students are at Lincoln Middle School?

A 169 students
B 231 students
C 269 students
D 1,885 students
E Not Here

2 Which of these is equal to 24?

F $2 \times 2 \times 8$
G $2 \times 2 \times 2 \times 3$
H $2 \times 2 \times 3 \times 3$
J $2 \times 2 \times 3 \times 5$

3 You are going to enter a race that is 5 kilometers long. How many meters is that?

A 0.005 meter
B 0.05 meter
C 500 meters
D 5,000 meters

4 On Wednesday, Erin spent $2\frac{1}{2}$ hours doing homework before dinner and $1\frac{3}{4}$ hours after dinner. How long did she spend doing homework on Wednesday?

F $3\frac{5}{8}$ hours
G $3\frac{2}{3}$ hours
H $4\frac{1}{4}$ hours
J $4\frac{1}{2}$ hours
K Not Here

5 What number comes next?
1, 4, 9, 16, ■

A 19
B 21
C 23
D 25

6 Find the LCM of 8 and 12.

F 4
G 24
H 48
J 96

7 An airplane flew from El Paso to Boston, a distance of 2,072 miles, in 4 hours 7 minutes. What is the best estimate of the average speed of the airplane?

A 300 miles per hour
B 400 miles per hour
C 500 miles per hour
D 600 miles per hour
E 700 miles per hour

8 Which letter best represents $2\frac{3}{4}$ on the number line?

F R
G S
H T
J U

9 Write $5 \times 5 \times 5 \times 5$ using an exponent.

A 625
B 4^5
C 5^4
D 5^5

10 You need 58 large balloons for a party. They come in packages of 4. How many packages should you buy?

F 2 packages
G 14 packages
H 15 packages
J 16 packages
K Not Here

11 Which question *cannot* be answered based on the table below?

World's Busiest Airports in 1995	
Airport	**Total Passengers**
Chicago-O'Hare	67.3 million
Atlanta	57.7 million
Dallas-Fort Worth	56.5 million

SOURCE: AIRPORT COUNCIL INTERNATIONAL

A How many passengers did Atlanta have in 1995?
B How many people flew on airlines in 1995?
C Which airport had the most passengers in 1995?
D How many more passengers did Chicago-O'Hare have than Dallas-Fort Worth?

12 Write $\frac{10}{8}$ as a mixed number in simplest form.

F $1\frac{1}{4}$

G $1\frac{2}{8}$

H $\frac{4}{5}$

J 1.25

13 On her last four math tests, Danielle scored 85, 77, 90, and 46. What does she need to get on her next test to get an average of at least a 75 on the five tests.

A 71
B 74
C 75
D 77
E Not Here

14 If you are 12 years old, what is a reasonable estimate for the number of days you have been alive?

F Less than 3,000
G Between 3,000 and 3,600
H Between 3,600 and 4,380
J Between 4,380 and 4,750
K More than 4,750

15 Which would you use to measure the length of a pencil?

A grams
B kilometers
C centimeters
D liters

16 What is the greatest common factor of 12 and 18?

F 2
G 3
H 6
J 36

17 Find the missing digit.

$$\begin{array}{r} 4.7\blacksquare \\ \times \quad 5 \\ \hline 23.75 \end{array}$$

A 1
B 3
C 5
D 6

MULTIPLY AND DIVIDE FRACTIONS AND MIXED NUMBERS

THEME Getting It Built

What do homes, rock concert stages, and filming rigs have in common? Getting each built used mathematics. As you'll see in this chapter, builders multiply and divide fractions to get the job done.

What Do You Know ?

1. To make the vertical posts using wooden boards, how many feet of wood are needed for 2 posts? 5 posts?

$4\frac{1}{2}$ ft

2. You need 24 pieces of pipe $\frac{1}{2}$-ft long for a sculpture. How many 4-foot pipes do you need to buy?

All boards: $7\frac{1}{4}$ in. wide.

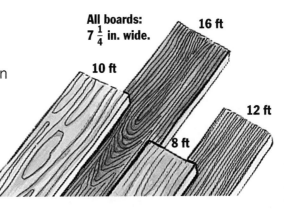

16 ft

10 ft

12 ft

8 ft

3. Estimate the number of wooden boards you will need to build the floor for a deck that is 20 ft by 12 ft. Which size board would you buy? How many pieces? Include a drawing to explain.

Write: How to There are 30 people working at a construction site. Half of them leave. Then six more of them leave. How many are left?

When you write how to do something, it is important to explain the steps clearly.

1. Explain how you could use counters to solve the problem.

Vocabulary

reciprocal, p. 278

Find a Fraction of a Whole Number

L E A R N

To learn a building trade, you could go to a vocational school. When 80 students at a vocational school were surveyed, $\frac{1}{4}$ of them said they plan to be carpenters. How many students plan to be carpenters?

Multiply: $\frac{1}{4} \times 80$

Remember your work with whole numbers. Just as 2×80 means 2 groups of 80, $\frac{1}{4} \times 80$ means $\frac{1}{4}$ of a group of 80.

Think: $80 \div 4 = 20$ $\quad \frac{1}{4}$ of $80 = 20$ $\qquad$ Twenty students plan to be carpenters.

Three fourths of the students surveyed are taking courses in metalworking. How many of the students is that?

Multiply: $\frac{3}{4} \times 80$ $\qquad$ **Think:** $\frac{1}{4} \times 80 = 20$

$\frac{2}{4} \times 80 = 2 \times 20 = 40$

$\frac{3}{4} \times 80 = 3 \times 20 = 60$

Sixty of the students are taking metalworking courses.

More Examples

A $\frac{1}{5} \times 20 = 4$

Think: $20 \div 5 = 4$

B $\frac{1}{3} \times 600 = 200$

Think: $600 \div 3 = 200$

C $\frac{5}{8} \times 48 = 30$

Think: $48 \div 8 = 6$

$5 \times 6 = 30$

C H E C K

Check for Understanding
Multiply mentally.

1 $\frac{1}{4}$ of 8 $\qquad$ **2** $\frac{3}{4}$ of 8 $\qquad$ **3** $\frac{1}{6} \times 18$ $\qquad$ **4** $\frac{5}{6} \times 18$ $\qquad$ **5** $\frac{5}{9} \times 540$

Critical Thinking: Summarize

6 Explain how you can tell mentally that $\frac{1}{2}$ of 16 is less than $\frac{1}{2}$ of 20.

Practice

Multiply mentally.

1 $\frac{1}{5}$ of 20 **2** $\frac{3}{5}$ of 20 **3** $\frac{1}{2}$ of 14 **4** $\frac{5}{7}$ of 14

5 $\frac{1}{4} \times 28$ **6** $\frac{3}{4} \times 28$ **7** $\frac{1}{3} \times 15$ **8** $\frac{2}{3} \times 15$

9 $\frac{1}{8} \times 56$ **10** $\frac{1}{4} \times 40$ **11** $\frac{2}{5} \times 10$ **12** $\frac{3}{7} \times 21$

13 $\frac{1}{6} \times 42$ **14** $\frac{1}{10} \times 30$ **15** $\frac{1}{3} \times 27$ **16** $\frac{1}{5} \times 25$

17 $\frac{1}{8} \times 240$ **18** $\frac{2}{7} \times 280$ **19** $\frac{1}{11} \times 22$ **20** $\frac{1}{2} \times 160$

21 $\frac{2}{3} \times 900$ **22** $\frac{3}{5} \times 500$ **23** $\frac{1}{9} \times 720$ **24** $\frac{1}{6} \times 300$

25 $\frac{1}{2}$ of a dozen = ■ **26** $\frac{1}{2}$ of a foot = ■ inches **27** $\frac{1}{4}$ of an hour = ■ minutes

ALGEBRA Find the missing number.

28 $\frac{1}{2} \times n = 8$ **29** $\frac{1}{5} \times b = 2$ **30** $\frac{1}{4} \times a = 6$ **31** $\frac{1}{3} \times c = 10$

32 $c \times 18 = 6$ **33** $s \times 18 = 9$ **34** $t \times 12 = 3$ **35** $n \times 8 = 2$

MIXED APPLICATIONS
Problem Solving

36 In a survey of 24 students at a vocational high school, one fourth of them said they switched from carpentry to plumbing. How many students was that?

37 Suppose you drive 60 miles and it is only $\frac{2}{3}$ the distance of your entire journey. What is the total distance of your journey?

38 To find the total cost of repainting a day-care center, add the cost of materials and labor. Find the total cost if the materials cost $792.18 and the labor was 17 hours at $38 an hour.

39 When four whole numbers are ordered from greatest to least, each number is half as much as the number before it. The sum of the numbers is 45. What are the four numbers?

mixed review • test preparation

1 $4\frac{3}{4} + 2\frac{1}{8}$ **2** $7\frac{5}{6} - 3\frac{2}{3}$ **3** $8\frac{3}{4} + \frac{7}{12}$ **4** $9\frac{3}{4} - 5\frac{4}{5}$

5 $\frac{2}{3} + 1\frac{5}{6}$ **6** $7\frac{7}{8} - 3\frac{5}{12}$ **7** $2\frac{3}{4} + 4\frac{5}{12}$ **8** $9 - 3\frac{5}{6}$

Multiply and Divide Fractions and Mixed Numbers **257**

Multiply Fractions

A carpenter sawed a board in half. Then he took one fourth of one of the halves. What fraction of the length of the original board is the new piece?

The carpenter took one fourth of one half. $\frac{1}{4} \times \frac{1}{2}$ means $\frac{1}{4}$ of $\frac{1}{2}$.

You can use models to find $\frac{1}{4} \times \frac{1}{2}$.

Represent $\frac{1}{2}$ with a $\frac{1}{2}$ strip.

Exchange the $\frac{1}{2}$ strip for four strips equivalent to $\frac{1}{2}$. One of these four strips is $\frac{1}{4}$ of $\frac{1}{2}$.

So $\frac{1}{4} \times \frac{1}{2} = \frac{1}{8}$.

Work Together

You will need
• *fraction strips*

Work with a partner. Use fraction strips to find these products.

$\frac{1}{2} \times \frac{2}{3}$ $\qquad$ $\frac{2}{3} \times \frac{1}{2}$ $\qquad$ $\frac{1}{2} \times \frac{1}{2}$

$\frac{3}{4} \times \frac{1}{2}$ $\qquad$ $\frac{1}{2} \times \frac{3}{4}$ $\qquad$ $\frac{1}{2} \times \frac{1}{3}$

Talk It Over

▶ What relationships do you see between the factors and their products in the second row?

▶ For which multiplications did you get the same answers? Explain why that happened.

Make Connections

Here is how Miko modeled and recorded $\frac{2}{3} \times \frac{1}{2}$ using fraction strips.

First I looked for 3 fraction strips equal to $\frac{1}{2}$ so I could find $\frac{1}{3}$ of $\frac{1}{2}$.

Then I looked at two of those strips to find $\frac{2}{3}$ of $\frac{1}{2}$. I saw that $\frac{2}{3} \times \frac{1}{2} = \frac{2}{6}$.

Then I found an equivalent fraction for $\frac{2}{6}$.

So, $\frac{2}{3} \times \frac{1}{2} = \frac{1}{3}$.

▶ Which factor did Miko model first? Why?

▶ Why did Miko need to find three fraction strips equal to $\frac{1}{2}$?

Check for Understanding

Write the product in simplest form. You may use fraction strips.

1 $\frac{1}{2} \times \frac{2}{5}$ **2** $\frac{1}{4} \times \frac{4}{5}$ **3** $\frac{1}{3} \times \frac{3}{8}$ **4** $\frac{1}{5} \times \frac{5}{6}$ **5** $\frac{1}{2} \times \frac{1}{5}$

6 $\frac{1}{2} \times \frac{1}{4}$ **7** $\frac{1}{2} \times \frac{1}{3}$ **8** $\frac{2}{3} \times \frac{1}{2}$ **9** $\frac{3}{4} \times \frac{1}{3}$ **10** $\frac{2}{5} \times \frac{5}{12}$

Critical Thinking: Summarize

11 Write a paragraph describing how to find the product of two fractions with and without using a model. Use examples to illustrate.

Turn the page for Practice. ➡

Practice

Use the diagram to help you multiply. Write the product in simplest form.

1 $\frac{1}{3} \times \frac{3}{12}$

2 $\frac{1}{5} \times \frac{5}{10}$

3 $\frac{1}{2} \times \frac{4}{6}$

4 $\frac{3}{5} \times \frac{1}{2}$

5 $\frac{2}{3} \times \frac{1}{4}$

6 $\frac{1}{2} \times \frac{3}{4}$

Multiply using any method. Write the answer in simplest form.

7 $\frac{1}{4} \times \frac{4}{5}$

8 $\frac{1}{3} \times \frac{3}{5}$

9 $\frac{1}{5} \times \frac{5}{12}$

10 $\frac{1}{4} \times \frac{8}{10}$

11 $\frac{1}{4} \times \frac{8}{12}$

12 $\frac{1}{2} \times \frac{8}{12}$

13 $\frac{1}{2} \times \frac{1}{6}$

14 $\frac{1}{3} \times \frac{1}{4}$

15 $\frac{1}{5} \times \frac{1}{2}$

16 $\frac{1}{2} \times \frac{3}{5}$

17 $\frac{1}{4} \times \frac{1}{3}$

18 $\frac{1}{5} \times \frac{5}{8}$

19 $\frac{3}{4} \times \frac{2}{3}$

20 $\frac{4}{5} \times \frac{1}{2}$

21 $\frac{2}{5} \times \frac{5}{8}$

22 $\frac{3}{4} \times \frac{1}{2}$

23 $\frac{3}{4} \times \frac{4}{5}$

24 $\frac{2}{3} \times \frac{9}{10}$

25 $\frac{3}{5} \times \frac{5}{12}$

26 $\frac{2}{3} \times \frac{3}{8}$

27 $\frac{2}{3} \times \frac{3}{10}$

28 $\frac{4}{5} \times \frac{5}{8}$

29 $\frac{3}{4} \times \frac{4}{8}$

30 $\frac{3}{5} \times \frac{5}{10}$

MIXED APPLICATIONS
Problem Solving

31 Half of the metalworkers in the city are welders. Two thirds of the welders are also electricians. What fraction of the metalworkers are electricians?

32 A plumber spent $546.17 on pipe for a job. He paid an assistant $15 an hour for 32 hours. How much did he pay altogether for the pipe and for his assistant?

33 **Spatial reasoning** Find at least three different ways to divide the 4 × 4 grid in half using the lines of the grid.

34 About how many times as much did the average house cost in 1995 compared to 1965? SEE INFOBIT.

INFOBIT
The average price of a house in 1965 was $21,500, and in 1995, it was $154,500.

Greatest Product Game!

You will need
- *12 index cards*

Number of players: 2 or more

On a sheet of paper, make a game sheet like the one below for each player.

Sample Game Sheet

Round: 1   Round: 2

$\frac{\blacksquare}{\blacksquare} \times \frac{\blacksquare}{\blacksquare} =$ $\frac{\blacksquare}{\blacksquare} \times \frac{\blacksquare}{\blacksquare} =$

Score:

Sample Round for
Two Players

Write one of the numbers 1, 2, 3, 4, 5, or 6 on each of the twelve cards so that each number is only on two cards.

Play the Game

▶ The players take turns. When it is your turn, take four cards from the top of the pile and write the numbers on your game card.

▶ Use the four numbers to make two fractions less than 1 with the greatest possible product. Record the fractions and their product on your game sheet.

▶ After every player has taken a turn, the players compare their products. The player with the greatest product gets 1 point.

▶ Continue playing until one player gets 5 points.

What strategies can you use to make the greatest possible product?

Allie

2 4 5 6

$\frac{2}{4} \times \frac{5}{6} = \frac{10}{24} = \frac{5}{12}$

George

1 2 3 4

$\frac{1}{2} \times \frac{3}{6} = \frac{3}{12} = \frac{1}{4}$

Since $\frac{5}{12} > \frac{1}{4}$,
Allie scores 1 point.

---

mixed review • test preparation

1 45.67 × 10   **2** 79.2 ÷ 100   **3** 6.05 × 1,000   **4** 5,677 ÷ 100

Write the mixed number as an improper fraction and as a decimal.

5 $3\frac{2}{5}$ **6** $8\frac{1}{2}$ **7** $4\frac{3}{4}$ **8** $6\frac{3}{10}$ **9** $1\frac{1}{5}$ **10** $2\frac{3}{8}$

Multiply by Fractions

A carpenter needs to cut a piece of plywood from a full sheet of plywood. She needs a piece that is $\frac{3}{4}$ of the width and $\frac{2}{3}$ of the length. First she cuts $\frac{3}{4}$ of the width. Then she cuts $\frac{2}{3}$ of the length. What fraction of the original full sheet is she using?

Multiply: $\frac{2}{3} \times \frac{3}{4}$

In the last lesson, you used fraction strips to find products of fractions. Here is another way to find $\frac{2}{3} \times \frac{3}{4}$.

Where the shading overlaps is $\frac{2}{3}$ of $\frac{3}{4}$.
Six out of 12 squares are shaded twice.

$$\frac{2}{3} \times \frac{3}{4} = \frac{6}{12} = \frac{1}{2}$$

She is using $\frac{1}{2}$ of the full sheet of plywood.

You can also multiply fractions using pencil and paper or a calculator.

Step 1	Step 2	Step 3
Multiply the numerators.	**Multiply the denominators.**	**Write the answer in simplest form.**
$\frac{2}{3} \times \frac{3}{4} = \frac{2 \times 3}{\underline{}} = \frac{6}{\underline{}}$	$\frac{2}{3} \times \frac{3}{4} = \frac{2 \times 3}{3 \times 4} = \frac{6}{12}$	$\frac{6}{12} = \frac{6 \div 6}{12 \div 6} = \frac{1}{2}$

 2 `b/c` 3 x 3 `b/c` 4 = ^{Simp} $\frac{6}{12}$ `SIMP` ^{Simp} $\frac{3}{6}$ `SIMP` $\frac{1}{2}$

Talk It Over

▶ How could you represent this problem using fraction strips?

▶ Compare multiplying fractions to multiplying whole numbers.
   a. When is the product always greater than both of the factors?

   b. When is the product always less than both of the factors?

A utility company's year-end records show that $\frac{1}{6}$ of its customers installed new water heaters. If $\frac{4}{5}$ of the new heaters are electric, what fraction of the customers installed electric water heaters?

Multiply: $\frac{1}{6} \times \frac{4}{5}$

$$\frac{1}{6} \times \frac{4}{5} = \frac{1 \times 4}{6 \times 5} = \frac{4}{30}$$

$$\frac{4}{30} = \frac{4 \div 2}{30 \div 2} = \frac{2}{15}$$

Sometimes, it is easier to divide before you multiply.

$$\frac{1}{\overset{}{\underset{3}{6}}} \times \frac{\overset{2}{4}}{5}$$ **Think:** The GCF of 6 and 4 is 2.
Divide both the numerator and the denominator by 2.

$$\frac{1}{3} \times \frac{2}{5} = \frac{1 \times 2}{3 \times 5} = \frac{2}{15}$$

So $\frac{2}{15}$ of the customers installed electric water heaters.

More Examples

A $\frac{3}{5} \times 7$ **Think:** $7 = \frac{7}{1}$

$$\frac{3}{5} \times \frac{7}{1} = \frac{21}{5} = 4\frac{1}{5}$$

B $\frac{3}{4} \times \frac{2}{9}$

$$\frac{\overset{1}{\underset{2}{3}}}{\overset{}{\underset{2}{4}}} \times \frac{\overset{1}{2}}{\overset{}{\underset{3}{9}}} = \frac{1 \times 1}{2 \times 3} = \frac{1}{6}$$

Think: The GCF of 3 and 9 is 3.
The GCF of 2 and 4 is 2.

Check for Understanding

Multiply. Write the product in simplest form.

1 $\frac{1}{2} \times \frac{3}{5}$ **2** $\frac{4}{5} \times \frac{3}{8}$ **3** $\frac{3}{4} \times 2$ **4** $\frac{3}{8} \times \frac{2}{3}$

5 $16 \times \frac{3}{8}$ **6** $\frac{7}{12} \times \frac{6}{7}$ **7** $\frac{5}{6} \times \frac{1}{2}$ **8** $\frac{3}{4} \times \frac{8}{9}$

Critical Thinking: Generalize

9 When you multiply whole numbers, the order of the factors does not change the product. Is that true for fractions? Give examples to support your conclusion.

10 When you multiply a whole number and a fraction, does the order of the factors ever change the product? Give examples to support your conclusion.

11 How is multiplying $\frac{1}{3} \times 12$ different from multiplying $\frac{1}{3} \times 5$?

Turn the page for Practice. ➡

Practice

Write the product in simplest form. Do as many as you can mentally.

1 $\frac{1}{2} \times \frac{1}{3}$ **2** $\frac{1}{2} \times \frac{1}{7}$ **3** $\frac{2}{3} \times \frac{3}{10}$ **4** $\frac{3}{4} \times \frac{5}{6}$ **5** $\frac{1}{3} \times \frac{5}{8}$

6 $\frac{2}{3} \times \frac{2}{3}$ **7** $\frac{7}{10} \times \frac{6}{7}$ **8** $\frac{2}{3} \times \frac{27}{100}$ **9** $\frac{3}{5} \times \frac{15}{24}$ **10** $\frac{3}{4} \times \frac{3}{4}$

11 $\frac{1}{5} \times 10$ **12** $\frac{2}{3} \times 12$ **13** $4 \times \frac{1}{5}$ **14** $7 \times \frac{5}{6}$ **15** $14 \times \frac{3}{10}$

16 $\frac{3}{4} \times 6$ **17** $4 \times \frac{1}{4}$ **18** $\frac{3}{8} \times 10$ **19** $\frac{3}{8} \times 2$ **20** $\frac{5}{12} \times 10$

21 $\frac{3}{5} \times \frac{5}{9}$ **22** $15 \times \frac{2}{3}$ **23** $\frac{4}{5} \times \frac{1}{2}$ **24** $\frac{5}{12} \times \frac{11}{15}$ **25** $\frac{7}{8} \times 5$

26 $\frac{5}{12} \times 12$ **27** $\frac{12}{25} \times \frac{5}{16}$ **28** $\frac{9}{10} \times \frac{5}{12}$ **29** $\frac{1}{5} \times \frac{4}{5}$ **30** $8 \times \frac{3}{8}$

31 $\frac{2}{3} \times \frac{3}{5}$ **32** $\frac{9}{10} \times \frac{5}{8}$ **33** $\frac{2}{3} \times \frac{5}{6}$ **34** $\frac{4}{5} \times \frac{15}{16}$ **35** $\frac{11}{16} \times \frac{4}{5}$

ALGEBRA Evaluate the expression.

36 $\frac{5}{6}n$ for $n = \frac{3}{10}$ **37** $\frac{5}{8}x$ for $x = \frac{8}{25}$ **38** $\frac{3}{5}s + 1\frac{1}{2}$ for $s = 5$

39 $\frac{3}{8}y$ for $y = \frac{2}{3}$ **40** $16z$ for $z = \frac{3}{4}$ **41** $\frac{12}{25}t$ for $t = \frac{5}{6}$

42 $\frac{1}{10}z$ for $z = 150$ **43** $\frac{7}{8}b - \frac{1}{8}$ for $b = \frac{1}{4}$ **44** $12x$ for $x = \frac{4}{5}$

ALGEBRA Simplify using the order of operation rules.

45 $\frac{3}{8} \times \frac{1}{2} - \frac{1}{8}$ **46** $2\frac{3}{4} + \frac{1}{2} \times \frac{3}{4}$ **47** $2 - \frac{3}{4} \times \frac{1}{9}$

48 $\frac{1}{3} \times \left(\frac{1}{4} + \frac{1}{2}\right)$ **49** $\frac{3}{4} \times 4 + 2\frac{1}{8}$ **50** $3\frac{1}{3} + \frac{2}{3} \times \frac{3}{4} - \frac{1}{2}$

Compare. Write >, <, or

51 $\frac{1}{2} \times \frac{1}{4}$ $\frac{1}{4}$ **52** $\frac{2}{3} \times \frac{7}{8} \bullet \frac{7}{8} \times \frac{2}{3}$ **53** $\frac{3}{5} \times \frac{1}{2} \bullet \frac{3}{5} \times \frac{1}{4}$

54 $\frac{3}{4} \times 8 \bullet \frac{1}{2} \times 12$ **55** $\frac{7}{8} \times \frac{1}{2} \bullet \frac{3}{8} \times \frac{1}{2}$ **56** $\frac{3}{10} \times \frac{1}{5} \bullet \frac{4}{5} \times \frac{1}{10}$

57 $\frac{1}{2} \times 4 \bullet \frac{1}{4} \times 4$ **58** $\frac{3}{8} \times 12 \bullet \frac{3}{4} \times 16$ **59** $\frac{9}{10} \times 60 \bullet \frac{5}{8} \times 72$

· · · · · · · · · · · · · · · · · · Make It Right · · · · · · · · · · · · · · · · · ·

60 Here is how Sean found $\frac{2}{3} \times \frac{8}{15}$.

$$\frac{\cancel{2}}{\cancel{3}} \times \frac{\cancel{8}}{\cancel{15}} = \frac{4}{5}$$

Tell what the error is and correct it.

Problem Solving

61 Two thirds of all the materials bought by Moira's building company are paints. What fraction of total materials is each type of paint?
  a. ceiling paint
  b. trim enamel
  c. wall paint

Type	Fraction of Paint	Fraction of All Materials
Deck paint	$\frac{1}{12}$	$\frac{1}{18}$
Ceiling paint	$\frac{5}{12}$	n
Trim enamel	$\frac{1}{6}$	n
Wall paint	$\frac{1}{3}$	n

62 A roofer has $\frac{3}{5}$ of a 5-gallon can of tile glue left over from his last job. How much does he have left?

63 **Write a problem** that involves finding the product of two fractions. Solve your problem. Ask others to solve it.

64 The state of Florida has an area of approximately 65,800 square miles. In 1994, its population was about 14,000,000. Find, to the nearest whole number, the average number of people per square mile at that time.

65 **Spatial reasoning** Look at the pattern. What is the next number?

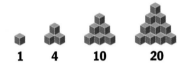

  1   4   10   20

66 **Data Point** Use the Databank on page 637 to describe how patterns of home ownership changed from 1982 to 1992.

Cultural Connection Cubits, Palms, and Digits

A cubit is a unit of length used by early peoples including Babylonians, Egyptians, and Romans.

The cubit of the ancient Egyptians was about 21 inches. It was divided into palms and digits.

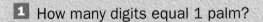

1 How many digits equal 1 palm?

2 If a desk is 12 palms long, how many cubits is that?

3 Which is greater, 10 palms or 8 hands? Explain.

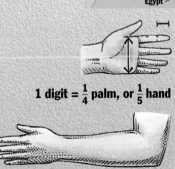

1 digit = $\frac{1}{4}$ palm, or $\frac{1}{5}$ hand

1 palm = $\frac{1}{6}$ cubit

Estimate Products

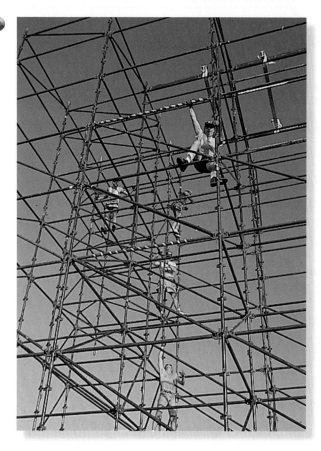

Would you like to work with a rock star? If you're a construction worker, you could be building the stage and lighting scaffolding for rock concerts. Almost $\frac{7}{8}$ of the pipe used for scaffolding a concert stage is reused. If the concert used 15 truckloads of pipe, about how much is reused?

Estimate to find the amount of pipe reused. Use compatible numbers so you can find the product mentally.

Estimate: $\frac{7}{8} \times 15$

Think: $\frac{7}{8} \times 16$

$\frac{1}{8} \times 16 = 2$

$\frac{7}{8} \times 16 = 7 \times 2 = 14$

About 14 truckloads of pipe are reused.

More Examples

A Estimate: $\frac{3}{7} \times 58\frac{1}{2}$

Think: $\frac{3}{7} \times 56$

$\frac{1}{7} \times 56 = 8$

$\frac{3}{7} \times 56 = 3 \times 8 = 24$

B Estimate: $\frac{9}{10} \times 21\frac{7}{8}$

Think: $1 \times 22 = 22$

C Estimate: $\frac{1}{6} \times 174$

Think: $\frac{1}{6} \times 180 = 30$

Check for Understanding

Estimate the product.

1 $\frac{1}{6} \times 47$

2 $\frac{3}{4} \times 25$

3 $17 \times \frac{2}{3}$

4 $\frac{7}{8} \times 21\frac{3}{5}$

5 $208 \times \frac{2}{5}$

6 $\frac{11}{12} \times 18\frac{1}{4}$

7 $15\frac{1}{2} \times \frac{5}{8}$

8 $8\frac{4}{5} \times \frac{5}{6}$

Critical Thinking: Compare

9 Some people estimate products by rounding each fraction to 0, $\frac{1}{2}$, or 1 and each mixed number to the nearest whole number. Try that for ex. 5–8. Which method do you prefer? Explain why.

Practice

Estimate the product.

1 $\frac{1}{7} \times 34$ **2** $\frac{3}{5} \times 9$ **3** $31 \times \frac{15}{16}$ **4** $\frac{2}{3} \times 25$ **5** $34 \times \frac{3}{8}$

6 $\frac{1}{3} \times 17\frac{2}{3}$ **7** $11\frac{1}{2} \times \frac{2}{3}$ **8** $\frac{7}{8} \times 4\frac{1}{4}$ **9** $18\frac{2}{3} \times \frac{1}{6}$ **10** $\frac{2}{5} \times 8\frac{2}{7}$

11 $\frac{3}{10} \times 64$ **12** $36 \times \frac{3}{4}$ **13** $\frac{1}{5} \times 44$ **14** $\frac{9}{10} \times 112$ **15** $47\frac{1}{4} \times \frac{1}{2}$

16 $\frac{4}{9} \times 71$ **17** $\frac{1}{7} \times 19\frac{2}{3}$ **18** $13 \times \frac{5}{6}$ **19** $\frac{1}{4} \times 230$ **20** $27\frac{2}{5} \times \frac{2}{3}$

21 $31 \times \frac{19}{20}$ **22** $\frac{3}{8} \times 15\frac{1}{2}$ **23** $135 \times \frac{3}{7}$ **24** $\frac{5}{8} \times 24$ **25** $\frac{5}{16} \times 141$

Tell whether the estimate is reasonable. Write yes or no. Explain.

26 $\frac{7}{8} \times 39;\ 20$ **27** $\frac{2}{3} \times 5\frac{3}{8};\ 4$ **28** $\frac{9}{10} \times 41;\ 41$ **29** $\frac{3}{5} \times 17;\ 18$

MIXED APPLICATIONS
Problem Solving

30 ALGEBRA: PATTERNS A crew has a phone tree in case of rain. The crew leader calls 2 workers. These workers each call 2 more, and so on. How many workers can be called on the fifth level of the tree?

31 Adam was paid $10,000 for repainting cars. He paid $\frac{3}{4}$ of that amount to the people working for him and $\frac{1}{10}$ for supplies. What is left is his profit. How much is his profit?

32 A gallon of off-white latex wall paint will cover about 400 square feet. Todd has four cans with about $\frac{3}{4}$ gallon of paint in each. About how many square feet can he cover?

33 Corey estimates he spends $\frac{1}{8}$ of his time moving the ladder when building a stage set. Of the 12 hours on his latest set, about how much time was spent moving the ladder?

34 Kim is painting a picture that is $46\frac{1}{2}$ in. long. To have a pleasing shape, she wants the width of the picture to be $\frac{3}{5}$ of its length. About how wide should she make the picture?

35 Data Point Conduct a survey of other students to find the most popular color to paint the corridors of the school. Make a frequency table and a bar graph of the data.

mixed review • test preparation

1 $8 - 3.56$ **2** $4.89 + 5.3$ **3** 5.34×3.2 **4** $\$700.00 - \$4.98$

Estimate.

5 $1\frac{1}{3} + 2\frac{1}{8}$ **6** $5\frac{3}{4} - 4\frac{1}{8}$ **7** $6\frac{5}{6} - 4\frac{11}{12}$ **8** $4\frac{1}{4} + 1\frac{7}{8}$

Multiply Mixed Numbers

A plumber earns about $26 per hour for a 40-hour week and is paid $1\frac{1}{2}$ times this rate for overtime. What is her overtime pay per hour?

Multiply: $1\frac{1}{2} \times 26$

Estimate the product.

Note: Overtime is the amount of time a person works that is over his or her regular number of hours.

Think: $2 \times 30 = 60$

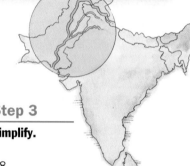

You can use paper and pencil or a calculator to find the exact product.

Step 1	Step 2	Step 3
Write all the mixed numbers as fractions.	Multiply.	Simplify.
$1\frac{1}{2} \times 26 = \frac{3}{2} \times \frac{26}{1}$	$\frac{3}{2} \times \frac{26}{1} = \frac{3 \times 26}{2 \times 1} = \frac{78}{2}$	$\frac{78}{2} = 39$

 1 [a] 1 [b/c] 2 × 26 = **39.**

Her overtime pay per hour is $39.

More Examples

A $\frac{2}{3} \times 20\frac{1}{2}$

$\frac{\overset{1}{\cancel{2}}}{3} \times \frac{41}{\underset{1}{\cancel{2}}} = \frac{41}{3} = 13\frac{2}{3}$

B $3\frac{3}{4} \times 4\frac{2}{5}$

$\frac{15}{4} \times \frac{22}{5} = \frac{330}{20} = \frac{33}{2} = 16\frac{1}{2}$ or

$\frac{\overset{3}{\cancel{15}}}{\underset{2}{\cancel{4}}} \times \frac{\overset{11}{\cancel{22}}}{\underset{1}{\cancel{5}}} = \frac{33}{2} = 16\frac{1}{2}$

Check for Understanding

Write the product in simplest form. Remember to estimate.

1 $10 \times 1\frac{1}{5}$ **2** $1\frac{1}{2} \times 1\frac{1}{4}$ **3** $1\frac{1}{3} \times \frac{1}{8}$ **4** $1\frac{1}{4} \times 7$ **5** $2\frac{2}{3} \times 3\frac{3}{4} \times \frac{1}{2}$

Critical Thinking: Generalize

6 In example B, the product was found in two different ways. Which method do you prefer? Explain why.

Practice

Write the product in simplest form. Remember to estimate.

1 $3 \times 1\frac{1}{9}$ **2** $4\frac{2}{3} \times 18$ **3** $3\frac{1}{4} \times 14$ **4** $16 \times 2\frac{3}{4}$ **5** $6\frac{4}{5} \times 9$

6 $1\frac{1}{5} \times 1\frac{7}{8}$ **7** $2\frac{1}{2} \times 3\frac{1}{2}$ **8** $3\frac{3}{5} \times 2\frac{1}{9}$ **9** $5\frac{2}{3} \times 6\frac{1}{4}$ **10** $1\frac{1}{2} \times 1\frac{1}{2}$

11 $\frac{1}{6} \times 1\frac{1}{3}$ **12** $4\frac{1}{2} \times \frac{2}{3}$ **13** $\frac{5}{6} \times 2\frac{8}{11}$ **14** $1\frac{3}{4} \times \frac{5}{8}$ **15** $\frac{7}{8} \times 4\frac{2}{3}$

16 $1\frac{5}{16} \times 8$ **17** $\frac{1}{2} \times 13$ **18** $1\frac{2}{5} \times \frac{2}{3}$ **19** $2\frac{5}{8} \times 1\frac{3}{7}$ **20** $3\frac{1}{4} \times 2\frac{2}{3}$

21 $24 \times \frac{3}{4}$ **22** $6\frac{1}{8} \times 1\frac{1}{7}$ **23** $\frac{3}{4} \times 4\frac{5}{6}$ **24** $2\frac{7}{9} \times \frac{3}{5}$ **25** $4 \times 5\frac{7}{8}$

26 $\frac{1}{2} \times 1\frac{1}{2} \times 1\frac{1}{3}$ **27** $1\frac{1}{8} \times 2\frac{4}{5} \times 1\frac{3}{7}$ **28** $6\frac{2}{3} \times 4\frac{1}{8} \times 1\frac{8}{11}$ **29** $3\frac{5}{8} \times 2 \times 1\frac{1}{3}$

ALGEBRA Evaluate the expression.

30 $3\frac{1}{2} x$ for $x = 12$ **31** $4n$ for $n = 2\frac{3}{4}$ **32** $\frac{2}{7} a$ for $a = 4\frac{2}{3}$

33 $\frac{3}{5} b$ for $b = \frac{5}{8}$ **34** $\frac{3}{4} t$ for $t = 100$ **35** $1\frac{3}{5} y$ for $y = 3\frac{3}{4}$

MIXED APPLICATIONS
Problem Solving

36 A plumbing contractor drove $\frac{3}{4}$ of an hour to pick up a load of iron pipe. At 40 mi. per hour, how far did she drive?

37 Mr. Rodriguez makes $26 an hour as a plumber. How much does he make during a $33\frac{1}{2}$-hour week?

38 To cover a wall 90 feet long and $4\frac{1}{2}$ feet high with bricks, Kendra needs 2,430 bricks. She allows $\frac{1}{25}$ of that number for breakage. About how many bricks does Kendra need?

39 **Make a decision** To rent a wallpaper stripper costs $29.95 per day. The cost of buying one is $974.95. If you plan to use a wallpaper stripper for 8 days, should you rent or buy? Explain.

more to explore

Multiplying by Changing Fractions to Decimals
Sometimes, it is easier to change fractions to decimals before multiplying.

$2\frac{3}{4} \times 7$ **Think:** $2\frac{3}{4} = 2.75$ $2.75 \times 7 = 19.25$

Find the product by using decimals.

1 $1\frac{1}{4} \times 9$ **2** $1\frac{1}{2} \times 1\frac{1}{2}$ **3** $\frac{7}{10} \times \frac{4}{5}$ **4** $\frac{2}{5} \times 3\frac{3}{4}$

5 $2,765 \times \frac{1}{2}$ **6** $47\frac{1}{4} \times 82\frac{1}{2}$ **7** $73\frac{3}{5} \times \frac{1}{2}$ **8** $528 \times 4\frac{3}{4}$

Choose the multiplication sentence that matches the diagram.

1

a. $\frac{1}{3} \times \frac{2}{3} = \frac{2}{9}$

b. $\frac{1}{6} \times \frac{1}{2} = \frac{1}{12}$

c. $\frac{1}{2} \times \frac{2}{3} = \frac{1}{3}$

d. $\frac{1}{2} \times \frac{1}{3} = \frac{1}{6}$

2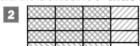

a. $\frac{1}{4} \times \frac{1}{4} = \frac{1}{16}$

b. $\frac{3}{4} \times \frac{3}{4} = \frac{9}{16}$

c. $\frac{1}{3} \times \frac{1}{4} = \frac{1}{12}$

d. $\frac{3}{4} \times \frac{1}{12} = \frac{1}{16}$

3

a. $\frac{1}{3} \times \frac{1}{3} = \frac{1}{9}$

b. $\frac{2}{3} \times \frac{1}{8} = \frac{1}{12}$

c. $\frac{1}{3} \times \frac{2}{3} = \frac{2}{9}$

d. $\frac{1}{7} \times \frac{1}{3} = \frac{1}{21}$

4

a. $\frac{2}{3} \times \frac{2}{3} = \frac{4}{9}$

b. $\frac{2}{3} \times \frac{1}{3} = \frac{2}{9}$

c. $\frac{1}{2} \times \frac{1}{2} = \frac{1}{4}$

d. $\frac{4}{9} \times \frac{5}{9} = \frac{20}{81}$

Multiply mentally.

5 $\frac{1}{2} \times 8$

6 $\frac{1}{4} \times 416$

7 $\frac{3}{8} \times 24$

8 $\frac{1}{9} \times 270$

9 $\frac{2}{5} \times 50$

10 $\frac{2}{7} \times 140$

11 $\frac{3}{11} \times 110$

12 $\frac{4}{9} \times 3,600$

Estimate the product.

13 $\frac{3}{10} \times 324$

14 $23\frac{3}{4} \times \frac{1}{5}$

15 $8\frac{2}{7} \times 378$

16 $23\frac{3}{5} \times 38\frac{1}{2}$

17 $41\frac{6}{7} \times 39\frac{4}{9}$

18 $52\frac{1}{2} \times 59\frac{9}{11}$

19 $11\frac{7}{12} \times 97\frac{1}{3}$

20 $9\frac{2}{3} \times 302$

Multiply. Write the answer in simplest form. Remember to estimate.

21 $\frac{2}{3} \times \frac{3}{8}$

22 $10 \times \frac{2}{3}$

23 $6\frac{3}{4} \times 1\frac{1}{3}$

24 $3\frac{1}{2} \times \frac{3}{10}$

25 $\frac{3}{4} \times \frac{5}{6}$

26 $\frac{1}{3} \times 10\frac{1}{2}$

27 $9 \times 2\frac{1}{3}$

28 $\frac{2}{3} \times \frac{2}{3}$

29 $1\frac{2}{3} \times 1\frac{3}{4}$

30 $3\frac{1}{3} \times 15$

31 $\frac{5}{8} \times \frac{4}{15}$

32 $9 \times \frac{2}{3}$

33 $\frac{4}{7} \times 49$

34 $2\frac{1}{2} \times 3\frac{1}{3}$

35 $1\frac{1}{4} \times 1\frac{1}{15}$

36 $1\frac{1}{2} \times 18$

Solve. Use mental math if you can.

37 A plumber used 363 feet of pipe in a project. He used $\frac{1}{3}$ of the pipe outdoors. How many feet of pipe did he use outdoors?

38 A painter spent $1\frac{1}{2}$ hours priming a wall, $2\frac{3}{4}$ hours painting the wall, and $\frac{1}{4}$ hour cleaning up. How much time did he spend in all?

39 Hair grows about $\frac{1}{2}$ inch per month. If you don't get a haircut for 3 months, about how much longer is it?

40 *Journal* Write a paragraph describing how to find the product of two mixed numbers.

Properties of Addition and Multiplication

You can state the properties of operations for whole numbers, fractions, and mixed numbers in words or using variables.

	In Words	Using Variables	Examples
Commutative Property of Addition	The order of the addends does not change the sum.	$a + b = b + a$	$2 + 7 = 7 + 2$ $\frac{5}{6} + 2\frac{3}{4} = 2\frac{3}{4} + \frac{5}{6}$
Associative Property of Addition	The way the addends are grouped does not change the sum.	$(a + b) + c = a + (b + c)$	$(3 + 4) + 6 = 3 + (4 + 6)$ $(\frac{1}{2} + 4) + 1\frac{1}{3} = \frac{1}{2} + (4 + 1\frac{1}{3})$
Identity Property of Addition	The sum of any number and 0 is that number.	$a + 0 = a$	$\frac{7}{8} + 0 = \frac{7}{8}$ $5\frac{1}{2} + 0 = 5\frac{1}{2}$
Distributive Property for Multiplication over Addition	To multiply a sum by a number, you can multiply each addend by the number, and add the products.	$a \times (b + c) = (a \times b) + (a \times c)$	$5 \times (6 + 9) = (5 \times 6) + (5 \times 9)$ $\frac{3}{4} \times (4\frac{1}{2} + \frac{6}{7}) = (\frac{3}{4} \times 4\frac{1}{2}) + (\frac{3}{4} \times \frac{6}{7})$

Using multiplication properties can help you find some products mentally.

Commutative Property: $a \times b = b \times a$ $\qquad\qquad \frac{1}{4} \times \frac{1}{2} = \frac{1}{2} \times \frac{1}{4}$

Associative Property: $\quad a \times (b \times c) = (a \times b) \times c \qquad \frac{1}{3} \times (\frac{1}{2} \times \frac{3}{4}) = (\frac{1}{3} \times \frac{1}{2}) \times \frac{3}{4}$

Identity Property: $\qquad\quad a \times 1 = a \qquad\qquad\qquad \frac{4}{5} \times 1 = \frac{4}{5}$

Zero Property: $\qquad\qquad a \times 0 = 0 \qquad\qquad\qquad \frac{7}{8} \times 0 = 0$

Distributive Property

Multiply: $6 \times 2\frac{1}{3}$ **Think:** $2\frac{1}{3} = 2 + \frac{1}{3}$

$6 \times (2 + \frac{1}{3}) = (6 \times 2) + (6 \times \frac{1}{3})$

$\qquad = 12 + 2$

$\qquad = 14$

Associative Property

Multiply: $\frac{2}{3} \times (1\frac{1}{2} \times \frac{5}{8})$

$= \frac{2}{3} \times (\frac{3}{2} \times \frac{5}{8})$

$= (\frac{2}{3} \times \frac{3}{2}) \times \frac{5}{8}$

$= 1 \times \frac{5}{8} = \frac{5}{8}$

Multiply mentally.

1 $4 \times 1\frac{1}{2}$ **2** $6 \times 3\frac{1}{3}$ **3** $4 \times 2\frac{3}{4}$ **4** $10 \times 4\frac{1}{2}$ **5** $8 \times 3\frac{1}{4}$

6 $5 \times 1\frac{2}{5}$ **7** $9 \times 2\frac{1}{3}$ **8** $12 \times 1\frac{2}{3}$ **9** $20 \times 2\frac{1}{5}$ **10** $27 \times 1\frac{2}{3}$

Blueprints

When industrial-design students create a new product to enter in a design competition, they must draw plans, often called *blueprints*. The actual dimensions of the product are scaled down to a size that will fit on paper. In this activity, your team will make a blueprint of one of the chairs or desks in your classroom.

You will need
- *tape measure*

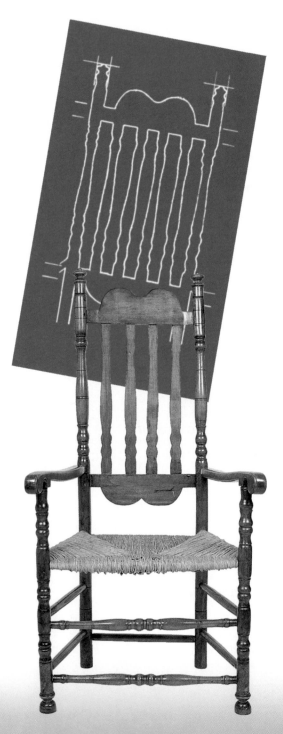

The blueprint dimensions of this chair were scaled down by multiplying by the unit fraction $\frac{1}{12}$. So the scale has each inch in the real object equal to $\frac{1}{12}$ inch on the drawing. You can use a different fraction when you make your blueprint.

The actual length of a front chair leg is $16\frac{1}{2}$ in. Here is how you can find how long to draw the leg on the blueprint.

$$\frac{1}{12} \times 16\frac{1}{2} = \frac{1}{12} \times \frac{33}{2} = \frac{33}{24} = 1\frac{3}{8}$$

Rounded to the nearest half inch, the blueprint measurement for the length of the front chair leg is $1\frac{1}{2}$ inches.

Make a Blueprint

1 Measure the lengths of the parts of your desk or chair to the nearest inch. Multiply each of your measurements by the same unit fraction. Round your answers to the nearest half inch to get the blueprint measurements.

2 Make a rough sketch of your desk and chair using the blueprint measurements. Does it fit well on your paper? If not, try multiplying by a different fraction. Continue until you find a fraction that works well.

3 Using the blueprint measurements, make a blueprint of your desk or chair, showing the lengths of the pieces and their locations in relation to each other.

Report Your Findings

4 Portfolio Prepare a report on how you made your blueprints. Include the following:

▶ A table of all your data, including the original desk or chair measurements and the blueprint measurements.

▶ A description of how you scaled down the measurements for your drawing. Name the fraction you used.

▶ Your blueprint.

5 Compare your blueprints with the blueprints made by other teams.

Revise your work.
▶ Are the measurements in your blueprint reasonable?
▶ Does the shape of your blueprint closely resemble the shape of the actual desk or chair?
▶ Is your blueprint clear? Could a furniture builder use it as a guide to make a desk or chair like yours?

MORE TO INVESTIGATE

PREDICT what fraction you would multiply by if you were going to make a blueprint of the desk or chair on a larger sheet of paper. You want the blueprint to fill most of the paper.

EXPLORE how designers use computers to make blueprints.

FIND a set of blueprints that was used to manufacture a real product.

Work Backward

Read Scene shops in film studios build sets. Suppose you start a job buying the scene shop's supplies. In the paint cabinet are 3 cans of black paint. The painters say they used $\frac{1}{2}$ of the black paint last week. They took 6 more cans this morning. How many cans of black paint did they start with?

Plan You can work backward to find the original number of cans.

Solve The scene shop has 3 cans left. The painters just took 6 cans. So before the painters left this morning, they had 6 more than 3 cans, which is 9 cans.

Last week, they went through $\frac{1}{2}$ of the black paint, leaving 9 cans. So they must have had twice as many as 9 at the beginning of last week.

Since $9 \times 2 = 18$, they started with 18 cans of paint.

Look Back Does the answer make sense? Check by working forward: $\frac{1}{2} \times 18 = 9$ cans left after using up last week's paint; $9 - 6 = 3$ cans left after taking paint out today.

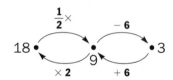

Check for Understanding

1 What if the painters used 8 cans of black paint instead of 6 today. If there are still 3 cans of paint left, how many did they start with?

Critical Thinking: Compare

2 Use the diagrams above to explain how working backward works and why it works.

Problem Solving

1 Suppose at the beginning of building a set, the plywood rack is half full. The manager buys plywood sheets to refill the rack. Then the carpenters take 8 sheets. If 40 sheets are left, how many sheets of plywood did the manager buy?

2 **ALGEBRA: PATTERNS** Each year since it has been in business, Light-Year Pictures has made double the number of films it made the year before. If it made 1 film the first year, how many films has it made in the 5 years the company has been in business?

3 It takes $3\frac{1}{2}$ sheets of foam board for one skyscraper prop, and at least $4\frac{1}{2}$ sheets for another. How many sheets of foam board do you need to be sure you have enough for both?

4 **Write a problem** that can be solved by working backward. Solve your problem and ask others to solve it.

5 On May 7, you deposited $16.73 in your bank account. Later that day, you withdrew $25. You then had a balance of $105.12 in the account. What was your balance at the beginning of the day?

6 Joe has to be at work at 8:15 A.M. It will take him 30 minutes to drive to work and 10 minutes to park his car and walk to the construction site. He plans to allow 25 minutes for breakfast and 15 minutes to get dressed. What time should he get up?

7 Suppose an airbrush holds 12 ounces of paint. An entire sky backdrop takes 40 ounces of blue paint to cover it. If the airbrush is filled every time it runs out, how many ounces of blue will be left in the airbrush holder when the sky is done?

8 **ALGEBRA: PATTERNS** A radioactive form of iodine has a half-life of 8 days. That means that half of it turns into something else every 8 days. Suppose you have 400 grams to start with. After 8 days, there are 200 grams, after 16 days, 100 grams, and so on. How many grams are there after 48 days?

9 **Spatial Reasoning** The perimeter of each T-shaped tile is 10 in. The longest side is 3 in. long. All of the other sides are equal. What is the length of a wall that has 20 T-shaped tiles in the pattern shown? Explain your reasoning.

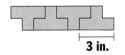

3 in.

Divide Fractions

Models made whole number division easy to understand. They also can help you understand how to divide by a fraction.

Just as $8 \div 2$ means "How many groups of 2 can be made from 8 items?" $3 \div \frac{1}{2}$ means "How many halves are in 3?"

Divide: $3 \div \frac{1}{2}$

1

| $\frac{1}{2}$ | $\frac{1}{2}$ |

1

| $\frac{1}{2}$ | $\frac{1}{2}$ |

1

| $\frac{1}{2}$ | $\frac{1}{2}$ |

$3 \div \frac{1}{2} = 6$

Divide: $\frac{2}{3} \div \frac{1}{6}$

| $\frac{1}{3}$ | $\frac{1}{3}$ |

| $\frac{1}{6}$ | $\frac{1}{6}$ | $\frac{1}{6}$ | $\frac{1}{6}$ |

$\frac{2}{3} \div \frac{1}{6} = 4$

Work Together

Work with a partner to discover relationships between these pairs of exercises. Use models to help you.

You will need
- *fraction strips*

a. $1 \div \frac{1}{5}$ 1×5

b. $2 \div \frac{1}{4}$ 2×4

c. $\frac{5}{6} \div \frac{1}{6}$ $\frac{5}{6} \times 6$

d. $\frac{3}{4} \div \frac{1}{8}$ $\frac{3}{4} \times 8$

▶ What relationships did you find between dividing by a unit fraction and multiplying by a whole number that is the same as the denominator of the fraction?

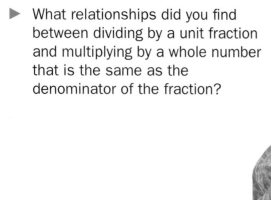

Make Connections

Fraction strips can help you see why you can multiply to divide.

Divide: $2 \div \frac{1}{4}$

1

$\frac{1}{4}$	$\frac{1}{4}$	$\frac{1}{4}$	$\frac{1}{4}$

1

$\frac{1}{4}$	$\frac{1}{4}$	$\frac{1}{4}$	$\frac{1}{4}$

Think: To divide a number by a unit fraction, a fraction with a numerator of 1, you can multiply the number by the denominator of the fraction.

$$2 \div \frac{1}{4} = 2 \times 4 = 8$$

▶ Describe how you could find $3 \div \frac{1}{6}$ without using models.

▶ Describe how you could find $\frac{4}{5} \div \frac{1}{10}$ without using models.

Check for Understanding

Divide using any method. Write the answer in simplest form.

1 $2 \div \frac{1}{3}$

2 $\frac{5}{8} \div \frac{1}{8}$

3 $3 \div \frac{1}{5}$

4 $\frac{7}{12} \div \frac{1}{12}$

5 $2 \div \frac{1}{2}$

6 $\frac{3}{10} \div \frac{1}{10}$

7 $\frac{2}{3} \div \frac{1}{12}$

8 $3 \div \frac{1}{4}$

Critical Thinking: Generalize   Explain your reasoning.

9 Why does dividing a whole number by $\frac{1}{3}$ give the same answer as multiplying the whole number by 3? Give examples.

Practice

Divide using any method. Write the answer in simplest form.

1 $1 \div \frac{1}{2}$

2 $2 \div \frac{1}{5}$

3 $3 \div \frac{1}{3}$

4 $1 \div \frac{1}{10}$

5 $\frac{3}{8} \div \frac{1}{8}$

6 $\frac{2}{3} \div \frac{1}{3}$

7 $\frac{3}{5} \div \frac{1}{5}$

8 $\frac{7}{10} \div \frac{1}{10}$

9 $\frac{1}{2} \div \frac{1}{4}$

10 $\frac{2}{3} \div \frac{1}{6}$

11 $\frac{1}{5} \div \frac{1}{10}$

12 $\frac{5}{6} \div \frac{1}{12}$

13 $\frac{3}{4} \div \frac{1}{4}$

14 $6 \div \frac{1}{4}$

15 $2 \div \frac{1}{6}$

16 $\frac{3}{5} \div \frac{1}{10}$

17 $3 \div \frac{1}{4}$

18 $7 \div \frac{1}{8}$

19 $\frac{4}{5} \div \frac{1}{5}$

20 $5 \div \frac{1}{8}$

Compare. Write >, <, or =.

21 $4 \div \frac{1}{2}$ ● 4×2

22 $\frac{2}{3} \div \frac{1}{3}$ ● $\frac{2}{3} \div \frac{1}{6}$

23 $\frac{3}{5} \div \frac{1}{10}$ ● $\frac{3}{5} \div \frac{1}{5}$

24 $6 \div \frac{1}{3}$ ● 6×3

25 $5 \div \frac{1}{2}$ ● $5 \div \frac{1}{4}$

26 $\frac{3}{4} \times 4$ ● $\frac{3}{4} \div \frac{1}{4}$

27 $7 \div \frac{1}{9}$ ● $9 \div \frac{1}{10}$

28 $4 \div \frac{1}{5}$ ● $3 \div \frac{1}{4}$

29 $\frac{1}{2} \div \frac{1}{8}$ ● $8 \div 2$

Divide with Fractions

IN THE WORKPLACE
Rusty Moore, Shoemaker or "cordwainer," Plymouth, MA

In the living museum Plimoth Plantation, it is always 1622. To imitate colonial times, the shoemakers use wooden pegs. If a shoemaker cuts $\frac{3}{4}$-inch pegs from a 15-inch stick, how many pegs can he cut?

Divide: $15 \div \frac{3}{4}$

Estimate: $15 \div \frac{3}{4}$ **Think:** $15 \div 1 = 15$

Two numbers are **reciprocals** of each other if their product is 1. The number $\frac{4}{3}$ is the reciprocal of $\frac{3}{4}$ because $\frac{4}{3} \times \frac{3}{4} = 1$.

Step 1

Rewrite as a multiplication using the reciprocal of the divisor.

$15 \div \frac{3}{4} = \frac{15}{1} \times \frac{4}{3}$

Step 2

Multiply. Write the answer in simplest form.

$\overset{5}{\underset{1}{\frac{15}{1}}} \times \underset{1}{\frac{4}{3}} = \frac{5 \times 4}{1 \times 1} = \frac{20}{1} = 20$

Calculator $15 \div 3$ [b/c] $4 =$ **20.**

He can cut 20 pegs.

Check Out the Glossary
reciprocal
See page 643.

More Examples

A $\frac{5}{8} \div 3$ **Think:** $3 = \frac{3}{1}$.

$\frac{5}{8} \div \frac{3}{1} = \frac{5}{8} \times \frac{1}{3} = \frac{5}{24}$

B $\frac{8}{21} \div \frac{4}{7}$

$\frac{8}{21} \div \frac{4}{7} = \overset{2}{\underset{3}{\frac{8}{21}}} \times \overset{1}{\underset{1}{\frac{7}{4}}} = \frac{2}{3}$

Check for Understanding
Divide. Write the answer in simplest form.

1 $\frac{1}{2} \div \frac{2}{5}$ **2** $4 \div \frac{3}{8}$ **3** $\frac{11}{12} \div \frac{2}{3}$ **4** $\frac{3}{4} \div 2$ **5** $\frac{1}{2} \div \frac{1}{2}$ **6** $8 \div \frac{3}{4}$

Critical Thinking: Summarize

7 **Write: How to** How can you find the reciprocal of a fraction? a whole number?

8 When is the quotient of two fractions a fraction? Give examples.

Practice

Divide. Write the answer in simplest form.

1 $\frac{1}{2} \div \frac{1}{4}$ **2** $\frac{1}{4} \div \frac{1}{2}$ **3** $\frac{3}{4} \div \frac{1}{4}$ **4** $\frac{1}{4} \div \frac{3}{4}$ **5** $\frac{5}{8} \div \frac{1}{2}$

6 $\frac{1}{2} \div \frac{5}{8}$ **7** $\frac{5}{12} \div \frac{5}{6}$ **8** $\frac{5}{6} \div \frac{5}{12}$ **9** $\frac{7}{8} \div \frac{1}{4}$ **10** $\frac{1}{4} \div \frac{7}{8}$

11 $4 \div \frac{1}{2}$ **12** $7 \div \frac{3}{4}$ **13** $8 \div \frac{2}{3}$ **14** $5 \div \frac{1}{4}$ **15** $6 \div \frac{4}{5}$

16 $\frac{1}{2} \div 4$ **17** $\frac{2}{3} \div 8$ **18** $\frac{3}{4} \div 6$ **19** $\frac{1}{4} \div 5$ **20** $\frac{4}{5} \div 6$

21 $3 \div \frac{2}{5}$ **22** $\frac{1}{2} \div \frac{2}{3}$ **23** $\frac{2}{5} \div 3$ **24** $\frac{5}{6} \div \frac{3}{4}$ **25** $6 \div \frac{7}{8}$

26 $\frac{1}{5} \div 3$ **27** $\frac{3}{10} \div \frac{3}{4}$ **28** $8 \div \frac{3}{8}$ **29** $\frac{7}{12} \div 7$ **30** $\frac{4}{5} \div \frac{2}{5}$

ALGEBRA Simplify using the order of operation rules.

31 $\left(\frac{1}{4} + \frac{3}{4}\right) \div \frac{2}{3}$ **32** $\frac{1}{4} + \frac{3}{4} \div \frac{2}{3}$ **33** $\left(\frac{5}{6} + \frac{1}{3}\right) \div 4$

34 $\frac{5}{6} + \frac{1}{3} \div 4$ **35** $\frac{1}{4} \times \frac{2}{3} \div \frac{3}{4}$ **36** $\frac{5}{8} \div \frac{3}{4} + \frac{1}{2} \div \frac{3}{4}$

MIXED APPLICATIONS
Problem Solving

37 A cabinetmaker, called a "joiner" in colonial times, used wooden pegs about $\frac{1}{4}$-foot long. How many pegs can be cut from a 5-foot stick?

38 At the plantation, the cabinetmaker also builds musical instruments. How many $\frac{7}{8}$-inch-long pegs can he cut from a 21-inch-long piece of stick?

39 Two students spent $3\frac{1}{4}$ hours playing Monopoly and $1\frac{1}{2}$ hours playing Scrabble. How much more time did they spend playing Monopoly?

40 **Write a problem** that can be solved by dividing a whole number by a fraction. Solve your problem and ask others to solve it.

more to explore

Another Way to Divide Fractions
Sometimes you can use the method shown below to divide.

$$\frac{6}{25} \div \frac{2}{5} = \frac{6 \div 2}{25 \div 5} = \frac{3}{5}$$

Check: $\frac{2}{5} \times \frac{3}{5} = \frac{6}{25}$

Divide. Solve each problem in two ways.

1 $\frac{12}{25} \div \frac{4}{5}$ **2** $\frac{2}{5} \div \frac{1}{5}$ **3** $\frac{15}{16} \div \frac{3}{4}$ **4** $\frac{3}{8} \div \frac{3}{4}$ **5** $\frac{49}{50} \div \frac{7}{10}$

6 When doesn't this method work well?

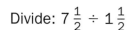

Divide with Mixed Numbers

The rigger for a film company is cutting a $7\frac{1}{2}$-ft pipe into pieces $1\frac{1}{2}$-ft long to make a frame to mount a movie camera on a boat. How many pieces will she get?

Divide: $7\frac{1}{2} \div 1\frac{1}{2}$

Estimate: $7\frac{1}{2} \div 1\frac{1}{2}$ **Think:** $8 \div 2 = 4$

You can use pencil and paper or a calculator to find the exact quotient.

Step 1	Step 2
Rename the mixed numbers as fractions.	**Multiply the dividend by the reciprocal of the divisor. Write the answer in simplest form.**
$7\frac{1}{2} \div 1\frac{1}{2} = \frac{15}{2} \div \frac{3}{2}$	$\frac{\overset{5}{\cancel{15}}}{\underset{1}{\cancel{2}}} \times \frac{\overset{1}{\cancel{2}}}{\underset{1}{\cancel{3}}} = \frac{5}{1} = 5$
Think: $1\frac{1}{2} = \frac{3}{2}$	

 Calculator 7 $\boxed{a}$ 1 $\boxed{b/c}$ 2 $\div$ 1 $\boxed{a}$ 1 $\boxed{b/c}$ 2 = **5.**

She will get 5 pieces.

More Examples

A $3\frac{1}{3} \div 4$

$\frac{10}{3} \div \frac{4}{1} =$

$\frac{\overset{5}{\cancel{10}}}{3} \times \frac{1}{\underset{2}{\cancel{4}}} = \frac{5}{6}$

B $2\frac{3}{4} \div \frac{2}{3}$

$\frac{11}{4} \div \frac{2}{3} = \frac{11}{4} \times \frac{3}{2} = \frac{33}{8} = 4\frac{1}{8}$

C $\frac{3}{5} \div 4\frac{1}{2}$

$\frac{3}{5} \div \frac{9}{2} =$

$\frac{\overset{1}{\cancel{3}}}{5} \times \frac{2}{\underset{3}{\cancel{9}}} = \frac{2}{15}$

Check for Understanding

Divide. Write the answer in simplest form. Remember to estimate.

1 $2\frac{2}{3} \div \frac{2}{3}$

2 $1\frac{5}{8} \div 2$

3 $1\frac{7}{10} \div 3\frac{2}{5}$

4 $5 \div 6\frac{1}{4}$

Critical Thinking: Analyze

5 Division of whole numbers is not commutative. For example, $6 \div 2$ is not equal to $2 \div 6$. Is division of fractions commutative? Give examples.

Practice

Divide. Write the answer in simplest form. Remember to estimate.

1 $3\frac{2}{3} \div \frac{2}{3}$ 2 $4\frac{1}{2} \div \frac{3}{4}$ 3 $2\frac{1}{8} \div \frac{3}{16}$ 4 $3\frac{1}{2} \div \frac{5}{8}$ 5 $5\frac{3}{4} \div \frac{1}{2}$

6 $6\frac{3}{8} \div 3$ 7 $4\frac{1}{2} \div 5$ 8 $1\frac{2}{3} \div 4$ 9 $5\frac{3}{4} \div 2$ 10 $3\frac{1}{4} \div 6$

11 $3\frac{5}{6} \div 1\frac{2}{3}$ 12 $4\frac{2}{3} \div 1\frac{7}{9}$ 13 $6\frac{2}{3} \div 1\frac{1}{4}$ 14 $1\frac{1}{4} \div 1\frac{1}{2}$ 15 $2\frac{3}{4} \div 1\frac{1}{8}$

16 $6 \div 1\frac{1}{5}$ 17 $8 \div 2\frac{1}{2}$ 18 $5 \div 6\frac{1}{8}$ 19 $7 \div 2\frac{4}{5}$ 20 $3 \div 2\frac{1}{3}$

21 $\frac{2}{8} \div 4\frac{3}{8}$ 22 $\frac{5}{8} \div 1\frac{1}{2}$ 23 $\frac{3}{4} \div 2\frac{1}{4}$ 24 $\frac{2}{5} \div 4\frac{4}{5}$ 25 $\frac{3}{10} \div 3\frac{1}{2}$

26 $2\frac{4}{5} \div 2\frac{1}{3}$ 27 $5 \div 1\frac{5}{8}$ 28 $6\frac{1}{4} \div 6$ 29 $4\frac{2}{3} \div \frac{2}{3}$ 30 $\frac{7}{8} \div 6\frac{5}{12}$

a **ALGEBRA Complete.**

31 $2\frac{1}{2} \div n = 4$ 32 $a \div 2 = 3\frac{3}{8}$ 33 $x \div 1\frac{1}{2} = 2$ 34 $5 \div d = 2$

MIXED APPLICATIONS
Problem Solving

35 Nilo is building a special-effects model. He has to connect $1\frac{1}{2}$-in.-long pieces of hose to a total length of $19\frac{1}{2}$ in. How many pieces of hose will be used?

36 Sonia has $1\frac{1}{3}$ yards of linen. She uses $\frac{2}{3}$ yard of the linen to replace the shade of an antique lamp. How much linen does Sonia have left?

37 About how many times higher is the Gateway Arch than the Statue of Liberty? SEE INFOBIT.

INFOBIT
The St. Louis Gateway Arch is 630 feet high. The Statue of Liberty is 305 feet high.

mixed review • test preparation

Find the quotient to the nearest hundredth.

1 $56\overline{)2,398}$ 2 $16\overline{)734}$ 3 $25\overline{)21,784}$ 4 $68\overline{)112,000}$

Find the least common multiple of the numbers.

5 3 and 5   6 4 and 8   7 10 and 12   8 8 and 6

Apply Fractions: Customary Units of Length

Whether you're a welder, electrician, carpenter, or plumber, you need to use fractions and customary measurements when you estimate your materials and costs.

Welders frequently need to measure to a fraction of an inch.

The iron bar is:

- **3 in.** to the nearest inch.
- $2\frac{1}{2}$ **in.** to the nearest quarter inch.
- $2\frac{5}{8}$ **in.** to the nearest eighth of an inch.

0   1   2   3

You can use relationships between customary units of length to solve problems.

A welder made an $8\frac{1}{2}$-foot length of iron into a hanger for a museum's sign. How many inches long is the iron? How many yards long?

Customary Units of Length		
1 foot (ft)	=	12 inches (in.)
1 yard (yd)	=	3 ft
1 mile (mi)	=	5,280 ft or 1,760 yd

To change to a smaller unit, multiply.

Think: 1 ft = 12 in. $8\frac{1}{2} \times 12 = 102$

The piece of iron is 102 inches long.

To change to a larger unit, divide.

Think: 1 yd = 3 ft $8\frac{1}{2} \div 3 = 2\frac{5}{6}$

The piece of iron is $2\frac{5}{6}$ yards long.

Check for Understanding

Choose an appropriate unit for measuring the length. Write *in., ft, yd,* or *mi.* Explain.

1 thickness of a door

2 distance to the moon

3 height of a building

Complete.

4 4 ft = ▇ in.

5 13,200 ft = ▇ mi

6 $3\frac{1}{2}$ yd = ▇ ft

Critical Thinking: Summarize

7 Write a paragraph about measuring length that compares using the metric system with using the customary system. Do you prefer one of the systems? If so, why?

Practice

Choose an appropriate unit for measuring the length.
Write *in., ft, yd,* or *mi.* Explain.

1 diameter of a quarter

2 length of a classroom

3 length of a brick

4 distance from your house to school

5 length of a football field

6 distance from Boston to Chicago

Estimate. Then use a ruler or a tape measure to measure.

7 height of a door

8 length of your shoe

9 thickness of this book

Complete.

10 5 yd = ■ ft

11 6 ft = ■ in.

12 2 mi = ■ ft

13 2 ft 5 in. = ■ in.

14 3 yd 2 ft = ■ ft

15 28 in. = ■ ft ■ in.

16 $\frac{1}{10}$ mi = ■ ft

17 45 in. = ■ ft ■ in.

18 4 ft = ■ yd

19 $8\frac{3}{4}$ ft = ■ in.

20 102 in. = ■ ft

21 $3\frac{1}{2}$ mi = ■ yd

MIXED APPLICATIONS
Problem Solving

22 A welder measures a garden to find out how many metal bars she needs to make a fence. The bars are 72 in. long and $\frac{3}{4}$ in. wide. Should she estimate to the nearest foot, or measure to the nearest inch? Explain your choice.

23 **Make a decision** Your class plans to make a set of bookshelves. Estimate the height of the three largest books in your class. Then decide what tool to use to measure them. Work with a partner to determine the height of the books to the nearest half inch and quarter inch.

24 Distances at sea are measured in nautical miles (1 nautical mile ≈ 6,076 feet). To the nearest tenth of a mile, how many customary miles equal $4\frac{1}{2}$ nautical miles?

25 **Write a problem** that can be solved by changing a smaller unit to a larger unit. Solve your problem and have others solve it.

mixed review • test preparation

1 $\frac{3}{5} + \frac{2}{5}$

2 $\frac{3}{4} + \frac{2}{3}$

3 $\frac{7}{8} - \frac{1}{8}$

4 $2\frac{3}{8} + 4\frac{1}{8}$

5 $5\frac{3}{4} - 3\frac{1}{8}$

6 $9\frac{4}{5} + 2\frac{7}{12}$

7 $12 - \frac{3}{10}$

8 $\frac{3}{4} + \frac{2}{3} + 3\frac{5}{8}$

Apply Fractions:
Customary Units of Capacity and Weight

Hardware stores are amazing. One large store stocks over 1 million different items. People who work or shop in hardware stores need to understand measurements—from gallons of paint to pounds of nails.

You can use the relationships between units to solve problems.

Customary Measurement		
Capacity		
1 cup (c)	= 8 fluid ounces (fl oz)	
1 pint (pt)	= 2 c or 16 fl oz	
1 quart (qt)	= 2 pt or 4 c or 32 fl oz	
1 gallon (gal)	= 4 qt	
Weight		
1 pound (lb)	= 16 ounces (oz)	
1 ton (T)	= 2,000 lb	

How many quarts is $\frac{3}{4}$ of a gallon?

To change to a smaller unit, multiply.

$\frac{3}{4} \times 4 = $ ■   **Think:** 1 gal = 4 qt

$\frac{3}{4} \times 4 = \frac{3}{4} \times \frac{4}{1} = \frac{3}{1} = 3$

$\frac{3}{4}$ gal = 3 qt

How many pounds is 24 ounces?

To change to a larger unit, divide.

$24 \div 16 = $ ■   **Think:** 1 lb = 16 oz

$$\begin{array}{r} 1\frac{8}{16} = 1\frac{1}{2} \\ 16)\overline{24} \\ -16 \\ \hline 8 \end{array}$$

24 oz = $1\frac{1}{2}$ lb

More Examples.

A 40 oz = ■ lb ■ oz

40 ÷ 16 = 2 R8

40 oz = 2 lb 8 oz

B 17 qt = ■ gal ■ qt

17 ÷ 4 = 4 R1

17 qt = 4 gal 1 qt

C $2\frac{1}{2}$ qt = ■ fl oz

$2\frac{1}{2} \times 32 = 80$

$2\frac{1}{2}$ qt = 80 fl oz

Check for Understanding

Complete.

1 32 fl oz = ■ c

2 3 T = ■ lb

3 5 c = ■ pt ■ c

4 1 qt = ■ c

5 18 qt = ■ gal ■ qt

6 40 fl oz = ■ pt

Critical Thinking: Analyze

7 What is the difference between an ounce and a fluid ounce?

Practice

Choose an appropriate unit for measuring. Explain.

1 capacity of a paint can

2 weight of a large truck

3 weight of a paintbrush

4 capacity of a pitcher

5 capacity of a spoon

6 weight of a table

Estimate.

7 capacity of a water glass

8 weight of your shoe

9 weight of five of your books

10 capacity of a bowl

11 capacity of a sink

12 weight of a calculator

Complete.

13 3 qt = ■ c

14 5 gal = ■ qt

15 48 oz = ■ lb

16 4,800 lb = ■ T ■ lb

17 7 c = ■ pt ■ c

18 12 fl oz = ■ c ■ fl oz

19 17 qt = ■ gal ■ qt

20 10 pt = ■ qt

21 54 oz = ■ lb ■ oz

22 $\frac{3}{8}$ lb = ■ oz

23 60 oz = ■ lb

24 21 fl oz = ■ c

25 $3\frac{1}{2}$ qt = ■ pt

26 7 cups = ■ pt

27 3 qt = ■ gal

28 17 oz = ■ c ■ oz

29 10 gal = ■ pt

30 2 qt 1 pt = ■ c

MIXED APPLICATIONS
Problem Solving

31 A fluid ounce of water weighs about 1 oz. Estimate the weight of a plastic container holding a gallon of water.

32 **Logical reasoning** Nails are often sold by the pound. Should nails be weighed to the nearest pound or nearest ounce?

33 Hardware stores sell cement patch in 5-qt tubs. If 1 qt of the patch weighs $1\frac{1}{2}$ lb, how many pounds does the 5-qt tub weigh?

34 **Write a problem** using the facts that the Wright brothers' airplane weighed 750 lb and a Boeing 747 jumbo jet weighs 775 T. Solve your problem and have others solve it.

mixed review • test preparation

1 6.8 + 4.7

2 2.7 × 3.9

3 18.1 − 5.02

4 $12 − $6.73

5 11.32 + 15.7

6 1.4 × $6.15

7 11.3 − 9.66

8 100 − 20.46

Problem Solvers at Work

Read

Plan

Solve

Look Back

PART 1   Choose Whether to Use Fractions or Decimals

Many people in the construction trades are paid by the hour. Suppose you earn $21.50 per hour and work $31\frac{1}{2}$ hours one week. How much money do you earn for the week?

Work Together

Solve. Be prepared to explain your methods.

1 How can you find how much you earn that week using decimals?

2 How can you find how much you earn that week using fractions?

3 How much do you make that week?

4 Which method do you prefer? Explain.

5 **What if** you work $35\frac{3}{4}$ hours in a week. How much do you earn that week?

6 You are paid $1\frac{1}{2}$ times as much for any time over 40 hours that you work in a week. How much do you earn in a week if you work 42 hours?

Crystal used the data in the table to write this problem.

Construction Crew Payroll Earnings Week of January 12		
	Hourly Rate	**Hours**
Marco	$18.25	$39\frac{1}{2}$
Tom	$15.70	$24\frac{1}{4}$
Mary	$23.60	$30\frac{3}{4}$
Ana	$17.50	$35\frac{1}{2}$

Mary worked an extra 4 hours not shown on the table. She earned $2.75 per hour more than her usual pay. How much did she earn during the week of January 12?

7 Solve Crystal's problem.

8 **Write a problem** Write another problem that can be solved using data in the table.

9 Solve the new problem.

10 **Write: How To** Ana worked 36 hours the week of January 19. How much more did she earn that week than the week of January 12? Explain in words how to solve the problem two different ways. Solve the problem at least one of the ways you described.

11 Trade problems. Solve at least three problems written by other students.

12 Which problems were the most interesting? Why?

Crystal Stribling
Madison Middle School
Marshall, NC

Menu

Choose five problems and solve them.
Explain your methods.

1 A carpenter bought $3\frac{1}{2}$ pounds of "20-penny" nails for $0.66 a pound. How much did she pay?

2 One year, 15,309,338 people visited Golden Gate National Park in San Francisco. That year, 3,140,510 people visited Independence National Historic Park in Philadelphia. About how many times as many people visited Golden Gate National Park as visited Independence National Historic Park?

3 An electrician is earning $34.85 per hour. He works $39\frac{1}{4}$ hours one week. How much does he earn that week?

4 A plumber drove 11 miles in $\frac{1}{4}$ hour to get to a house to fix a clogged drain. What was his average speed?

5 A woman translates articles into Spanish. She is paid by the hour. For one article, it took 3 hours 35 minutes one day and 3 hours 45 minutes another day. How long did it take altogether?

6 In a college football stadium, $\frac{1}{4}$ of the seats are reserved for alumni, and $\frac{1}{3}$ are reserved for students. What fraction of the seats are not reserved for alumni or students?

7 A man bought 100 shares of stock in a computer company for $16\frac{3}{4}$ per share. He sold them later for $20\frac{1}{4}$. How much profit did he make?

8 New York City subway tokens cost $1.50. How many can you buy for $20? How much change should you get?

Choose two problems and solve them. Explain your methods.

9 Estimate the number of minutes that you have been alive. Show how you made your estimate.

10 **Spatial Reasoning** The figure below was a cube 4 blocks high, 4 blocks wide, and 4 blocks long before some blocks were removed. The outside of the figure was painted blue. How many blocks are missing? Of those, how many would be blue on one side?

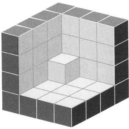

11 Suppose a million sixth graders could form a tower by standing on each other's shoulders, one on top of the other. Estimate the number of miles high the tower would end up to be. Explain.

12 **At the Computer** Use the yellow pages of your phone book to find the number of carpenters, plumbers, painting contractors, and electricians in your area. Make a bar graph to show the number in each category. Write three statements about your graph.

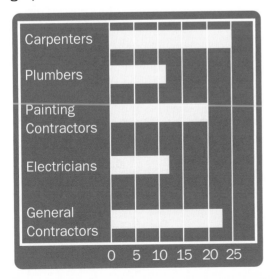

chapter review

Language and Mathematics

Complete the sentence. Use a word in the chart.
(pages 256–285)

(pages 256–285)

1 The ■ of $\frac{1}{2}$ is $\frac{2}{1}$.

2 $3\frac{1}{2}$ is a ■.

3 The ■ is a customary unit of capacity.

4 The ■ is a customary unit of weight.

Vocabulary

fluid ounce
inch
foot
ounce
reciprocal
mixed number
whole number

Concepts and Skills

Estimate the product. (page 266)

5 $\frac{3}{4} \times 25$

6 $\frac{1}{3} \times 40$

Multiply. Write the answer in simplest form. (pages 258, 262, 268)

7 $\frac{1}{8} \times 16$

8 $\frac{2}{3} \times 24$

9 $\frac{1}{2} \times \frac{1}{3}$

10 $\frac{1}{5} \times \frac{5}{8}$

11 $\frac{6}{7} \times \frac{11}{12}$

12 $\frac{5}{6} \times \frac{4}{5}$

13 $8 \times 5\frac{1}{4}$

14 $5\frac{7}{8} \times 6$

15 $6\frac{3}{4} \times \frac{2}{3}$

16 $5\frac{1}{3} \times 4\frac{1}{2}$

17 $\frac{8}{15} \times 3\frac{3}{8}$

18 $2\frac{5}{8} \times 1\frac{5}{7}$

Divide. Write the answer in simplest form. (pages 276, 278, 280)

19 $8 \div \frac{1}{2}$

20 $5 \div \frac{15}{16}$

21 $\frac{1}{3} \div \frac{3}{4}$

22 $\frac{3}{4} \div \frac{3}{8}$

23 $\frac{3}{4} \div 3$

24 $2\frac{5}{8} \div \frac{3}{5}$

25 $\frac{3}{4} \div 1\frac{3}{5}$

26 $2\frac{1}{4} \div 3\frac{3}{8}$

27 $11\frac{1}{3} \div 2\frac{5}{6}$

28 $3 \div 2\frac{1}{8}$

29 $4\frac{1}{5} \div 3$

30 $1\frac{7}{16} \div \frac{2}{3}$

Complete. (page 278)

31 $\frac{4}{5} \times n = 1$

32 $12 \times n = 1$

33 $n \times 100 = 1$

34 $2\frac{1}{2} \times n = 1$

Write the letter of the best estimate. (page 282)

35 width of a textbook
   a. 8 in.   **b.** 28 in.   **c.** 3 ft

36 length of a baseball bat
   a. 3 in.   **b.** 1 ft   **c.** 1 yd

Complete. (pages 282, 284)

37 6 yd = ■ ft

38 30 in. = ■ ft ■ in.

39 $4\frac{3}{4}$ ft = ■ in.

40 4 qt = ■ c

41 4 gal = ■ qt

42 $\frac{5}{8}$ lb = ■ oz

Think critically. (pages 258–265, 276–281)

43 Analyze. Explain what the error is in this student's work. Then correct it.

$$\frac{2}{3} \div \frac{3}{5} = \frac{3}{2} \times \frac{3}{5} = \frac{9}{10}$$

44 Generalize. Write *greater than* or *less than*. Give examples to support your answer.
   a. The product of two fractions less than 1 is ■ either factor.
   b. The quotient of a number divided by a fraction less than 1 is ■ the dividend.
   c. The quotient of a number divided by a mixed number is ■ the dividend.

MIXED APPLICATIONS
Problem Solving
Pencil & Paper Calculator Mental Math

(pages 274, 286)

45 Half of the T-shirts that Felix has designed are rock-group shirts. These are divided equally among concert shirts, CD shirts, and commemorative shirts. What fraction of the shirts he has designed are concert shirts?

46 A cookie recipe uses $1\frac{1}{3}$ cups of flour and a bread recipe uses $5\frac{3}{4}$ cups. About how many cups of flour are needed for both recipes?

47 When you multiply $5\frac{2}{5}$ by this number and double the result, you get 18. What is the number?

48 The city's electrician wants to divide her 23 repair technicians into teams with as many teams of 4 technicians as possible. How many teams of 4 can she make? How many technicians will be on the team with less than 4?

Use the table for problems 49–50.

49 Jarek's company clears and prepares construction sites. To clear an average site, Jarek uses 4 hours of excavator work and 2 hours of bulldozer work. What is the average charge?

Jarek Preconstruction, Inc. Labor Rates	
Backhoe	$60.00 per hour
Bulldozer	$75.50 per hour
Excavator	$85.00 per hour

50 When he was building a new house, Hans rented a backhoe from Jarek for $7\frac{1}{2}$ hours to dig trenches for pipes and wires. How much did it cost?

Estimate the product.

1 $\frac{1}{6} \times 37$ **2** $\frac{3}{4} \times 49$ **3** $14 \times \frac{2}{5}$ **4** $\frac{6}{7} \times 32\frac{1}{4}$

Multiply. Write the answer in simplest form.

5 $\frac{3}{4} \times 12$ **6** $\frac{1}{2} \times \frac{1}{4}$ **7** $\frac{3}{5} \times \frac{2}{3}$

8 $6 \times 2\frac{1}{3}$ **9** $2\frac{1}{2} \times \frac{3}{4}$ **10** $3\frac{1}{3} \times 1\frac{2}{5}$

Divide. Write the answer in simplest form.

11 $3 \div \frac{3}{4}$ **12** $\frac{4}{9} \div \frac{1}{2}$ **13** $\frac{1}{4} \div \frac{3}{8}$

14 $\frac{5}{8} \div 2$ **15** $4\frac{1}{2} \div \frac{3}{4}$ **16** $3\frac{1}{6} \div 1\frac{2}{3}$

Write the letter of the best estimate.

17 length of a pen **a.** 6 in. **b.** 20 in. **c.** 2 ft

18 length of a classroom **a.** 40 in. **b.** 50 ft **c.** 2 mi

Complete.

19 18 yd = ▪ ft **20** 17 in. = ▪ ft ▪ in. **21** $\frac{3}{4}$ lb = ▪ oz

Solve. Show your work.

22 A plumber has $18\frac{1}{2}$ ft of tubing in her truck. She needs 9 in. of tubing to remodel each sink in an apartment building. How many sinks can she remodel with the tubing in the truck?

23 A set of 4 screwdrivers costs $20. If you buy each screwdriver individually, it will cost $1\frac{1}{4}$ times as much. How much will you save by buying the set?

24 At a paint store, a customer bought 5 paintbrushes from a bin. Then another customer bought $\frac{1}{2}$ of the remaining brushes in the bin. There were 12 brushes left in the bin. How many brushes were in the bin at the start?

25 A lumberyard truck has 3 deliveries to make this morning. Each will take about $\frac{3}{4}$ of an hour. The truck needs to be back at noon. What is the latest time the truck can start to make deliveries?

What Did You Learn?

Do you agree with what Daniel says?

$9 \times \frac{1}{3}$ is greater than $9 \div \frac{1}{3}$ because multiplication makes a number bigger and division makes a number smaller.

$$9 \times \frac{1}{3} = ?$$
$$9 \div \frac{1}{3} = ?$$

You will need
- *fraction strips*
- *paper and markers*

▶ Use models or drawings to show $9 \times \frac{1}{3}$ and $9 \div \frac{1}{3}$. Include a written explanation of how the models or drawings illustrate the problem.

▶ Write a letter to Daniel explaining why you agree or disagree with his statement.

· A Good Answer ·
- includes a clear illustration of $9 \times \frac{1}{3}$ and $9 \div \frac{1}{3}$ using either drawings or models.
- shows a comprehensive explanation of why Daniel's thinking is correct or incorrect.
- includes word problems that can be solved by using $9 \times \frac{1}{3}$ and $9 \div \frac{1}{3}$ as well as solutions that shows accurate steps and calculations.

 You may want to place your work in your portfolio.

What Do You Think

1 Which is easier for you—dividing decimals or dividing fractions? Explain why.

2 When you solve a problem that involves multiplying and dividing fractions, do you use:
- an estimate?
- pencil and paper?
- models?
- a fraction calculator?

math science technology
CONNECTION

SNOW LOADS

You have probably seen houses (like the one at the right) and other buildings being built. Notice the framing, the wood that will be inside the walls. The walls and roof are attached to this framing.

How do builders know how strong the framing must be? Rules known as building codes have been established so that houses are built to be safe and strong. The codes can vary around the country due to climate in different areas.

If high winds are common, roofs must be designed so they do not blow off.

In earthquake zones, walls must be reinforced to withstand the violent shaking that can occur.

In areas where there is snow in the winter, roofs must be built to withstand the heavy weight of snow.

Cultural Note
Archaeologists have uncovered houses from about 9000 B.C. near the border of Turkey and Iran. These round, grass and mud houses had stone bases.

▶ What other examples of extreme weather or other conditions do you think should be taken into account when building codes are being written?

▶ How can the shape of a roof help lessen the load of snow on it?

How Heavy Is That Snow?

A cubic foot of snow weighs about 5 pounds. The weight can vary depending on how much water is in the snow.

1 cubic foot

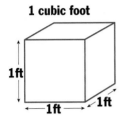

1 ft
1 ft
1 ft

Use the diagram below for problems 1–3. Explain your methods.

1 What is the total area of the roof in square feet?

2 What will the total weight of the snow on this roof be if it is covered with:
   a. 1 foot of snow?
   b. 2 feet of snow?
   c. $2\frac{1}{2}$ feet of snow?

3 **What if** the snow weighed $7\frac{1}{2}$ pounds per cubic foot. What would the total weight of the snow on the roof be after a $1\frac{1}{2}$-ft snowfall?

At the Computer

In different parts of the country, builders construct roofs to withstand different amounts of snow.

Snow Loads for Five Areas	
City	Snow Load[1]
Atlanta, GA	3.5
Buffalo, NY	28
Detroit, MI	14
Duluth, MN	42
Presque Isle, ME	70

[1] Load is given in pounds per square foot.

Use the table for problems 4–5.

4 Assume that a cubic foot of snow weighs 5 pounds. Using a spreadsheet program, add a column to the table above to show the depth of snow that roofs in these cities are built to withstand.

5 Which of these cities do you think gets the most snow? Explain why you think so.

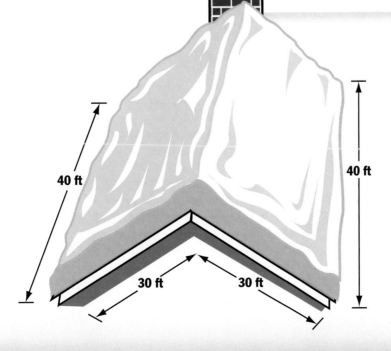

40 ft
40 ft
30 ft
30 ft

CHAPTER 8 GEOMETRY

THEME: Art and Design

Geometry gives shape to everything around us. In this chapter you'll experience the expected—the geometry of buildings—and even the unexpected—the geometry of cartoons.

What Do You Know ?

This stained-glass window was created by Frank Lloyd Wright. He used geometric shapes in his plans for buildings and furniture.

1 What different types of angles do you see in the window? How are they different?

2 What different types of quadrilaterals do you see in this window? What makes each type of quadrilateral different?

3 Create a stained-glass window design using different geometric shapes. Write a description of the arrangement using geometric terms.

Use Diagrams John F. Kennedy International Airport in New York is one of the busiest airports in the United States. It has long runways laid out in different directions. Use geometric terms to describe the runways.

Diagrams are used to show designs and layouts.

1 Write a paragraph to describe the runways. Compare your paragraph with the diagram. Which is clearer? Why?

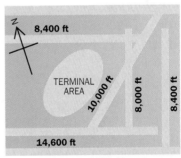

Runways of JFK Airport

Vocabulary*   * partial list

closed figure, p. 298	**intersecting lines,**	**congruent angles,**	**central angle,** p. 322
polygon, p. 298	p. 304	p. 306	**translation,** p. 324
regular polygon,	**parallel lines,**	**parallelogram,**	**rotation,** p. 324
p. 299	p. 304	p. 307	**congruent figures,**
ray, p. 300	**perpendicular**	**trapezoid,** p. 307	p. 324
angle, p. 300	**lines,** p. 304	**rhombus,** p. 307	**reflection,** p. 326
vertex, p. 300		**kite,** p. 307	**symmetric,** p. 326

Classify 2-Dimensional Shapes

Artists and fashion designers often use geometric shapes in their works. Vasily Kandinsky (1866–1944) used the combinations of lines, angles, polygons, and circles in his designs.

This is a detail from Kandinsky's larger work titled *Swinging*.

Work Together

▶ Work with a partner. Create at least three different shapes using three, four, five, six, eight, and ten straws. At least one end of each straw should connect with the end of another straw.

▶ Draw each shape you create and write down any characteristics that you notice about the shapes.

▶ Find a way to sort the shapes into groups, other than using the number of sides.

▶ Exchange the drawings of your shapes with another group. Discuss how each group classified its shapes.

You will need
• *straws*

Check Out the Glossary
For vocabulary words, see page 643.

Make Connections

A **line** is a straight path that goes in two directions without end. A **line segment** is a part of a line that has two endpoints.

The figures that started and stopped at the same point are called **closed figures.**

A **polygon** is a closed figure with sides that are line segments. The sides do not cross each other.

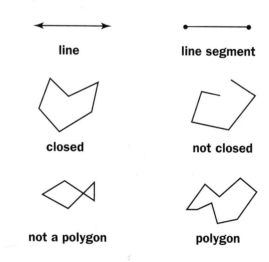

line   line segment

closed   not closed

not a polygon   polygon

Polygons can be classified by the number of sides or angles. All the sides of a **regular polygon** are the same length, and all the angles are the same measure.

Polygons

| Triangle | Quadrilateral | Pentagon | Hexagon | Octagon | Decagon |

▶ Which figures above are not regular polygons? How do you know?

▶ Draw at least two more examples of each type of polygon. Explain how they are the same or different.

Check for Understanding

Name each polygon.
If the figure is not a polygon, explain why.

1   **2**   **3**   **4**

Critical Thinking: Generalize

5 Why isn't a circle a polygon?

6 Find examples of polygons in your surroundings. Sketch and name each shape and identify its characteristics.

Practice

Tell if the figure is a polygon. If it is a polygon, name it.
If the figure is not a polygon, explain why.

1   **2**   **3**   **4**

Name each shaded figure.

5   **6**   **7**   **8**

9   **10**   **11**   **12**

Extra Practice, page 604

Angles

IN THE WORKPLACE
Donald Stull,
Architect, Cambridge, MA

Architects, such as Donald Stull, use angles to create interesting effects in the buildings they design. They use the angles of roof lines and staircases as well as the angles of windows and sunlight to make their creations beautiful and functional.

A **ray** is a part of a line that has one endpoint and continues without end in one direction. Putting two rays together with the same endpoint makes an **angle.**

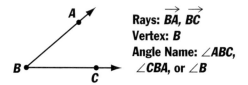

Rays: $\overrightarrow{BA}$, $\overrightarrow{BC}$
Vertex: **B**
Angle Name: $\angle ABC$,
$\angle CBA$, or $\angle B$

As you can see in the diagram, the endpoint, or **vertex**, of the angle is labeled B. Angles are measured in **degrees** (°) and are named by their vertex or rays.

Note: When angles are named by their rays, the vertex is always listed in the middle.

Work Together
Work with a partner. Follow the steps on how to measure angles.

Step 1	Place the center of the protractor on the vertex of the angle.
Step 2	Line up the zero of the scale with one side of the angle.
Step 3	Read the measure of the angle by counting from zero until you get to the other side of the angle.

You will need
• *a protractor*
• *a straightedge*

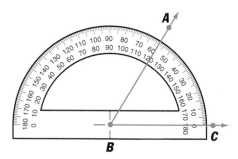

The measure of $\angle B$ is 58°.

Note: You may need to extend the rays to read the protractor.

▶ Draw several angles. Estimate and then measure each angle.

Talk It Over
▶ Does the measure of an angle change depending on the side of the angle you use to line up with the 0° mark? Explain.

Check Out the Glossary
For vocabulary words,
see page 643.

Make Connections

You can classify an angle by the number of degrees it contains.

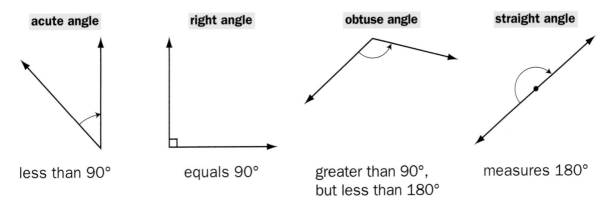

acute angle

less than 90°

right angle

equals 90°

obtuse angle

greater than 90°, but less than 180°

straight angle

measures 180°

▶ How can you use the corner of a sheet of paper to help you classify angles?

You can also use a protractor to draw angles. Draw a 65° angle.

Step 1	Step 2	Step 3
Draw one ray of an angle. Mark and label the ray.	**Place the center of the protractor on the vertex and line up the 0° mark with the ray.**	**Find 65° on the scale. Mark a point at 65°and label it C. Draw a line to connect the point with the vertex.**

Check for Understanding

Name, measure, and classify each angle.

1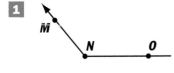

2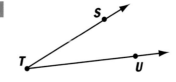

3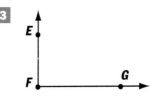

Critical Thinking: Generalize

4 Sketch or describe an example of an acute, a right, and an obtuse angle that you see in daily life.

5 When you are measuring an angle with a protractor, when do you use the numbers on the inner scale?

Turn the page for Practice. ➡

Practice

Name, measure, and classify each angle.

1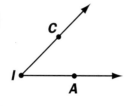

2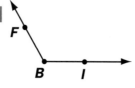

3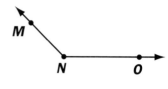

4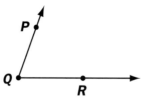

5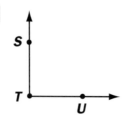

6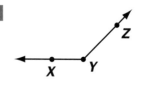

Estimate the measure of each angle and then measure it to see how close your estimate is.

7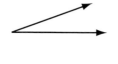

8

9

10

Find the measure of each angle.

11 ∠A

12 ∠B

13 ∠C

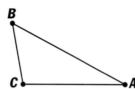

14 ∠D

15 ∠E

16 ∠F

Draw angles with the indicated measure.

17 60°   **18** 120°   **19** 90°   **20** 55°   **21** 145°

Write *true* or *false*. Explain your reasoning.

22 If you combine two acute angles, you always form an angle that is more than 90°.

23 If you combine a right angle and an acute angle, you always form an obtuse angle.

.... **Make It Right** ....

24 Eric used a protractor to measure angle *A* and found the measure to be 143°. Explain what the error is and correct it.

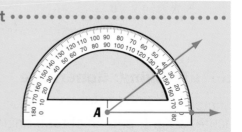

Problem Solving

25 Ernesto works for an architectural firm. His annual salary is $37,500. About how much money does he get paid each month?

26 A double-pane window costs $45.60 more than a regular one. The double-pane window costs $156.80. What is the cost of a regular window?

27 The window below has 3 equal sections. What would the measure of each angle be if there were 6 equal sections?

28 A spinner for a game was designed to favor some numbers more than others. Measure the angles for each section of the spinner, and list them from greatest to least.

29 **Spatial reasoning** If you squeeze the vertex of each of the figures below, which figure will change its shape?

a. **b.** **c.**

30 A painter puts 2 gal of paint into half-gallon containers. How many half-gallon containers does she need?

31 A roofer leans a ladder against a two-story house. What range of angle measures would be best for climbing up to the roof?

32 What type of angle is formed between an escalator and the ground? What do you think might happen if the angle were less than 30°? greater than 30°? SEE INFOBIT.

INFOBIT
Architects often make the angle between the escalator and the floor 30 degrees.

───── **more to explore** ─────

Complementary and Supplementary Angles

Two angles are *complementary* if the sum of their measures is 90°.

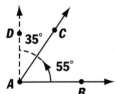

The measure of ∠CAB is 55°. ∠DAC is a complement of ∠CAB because 55° + 35° = 90°.

Two angles are *supplementary* if the sum of their measures is 180°.

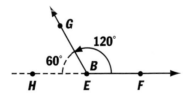

The measure of ∠GEF is 120°. ∠HEG is a supplement of ∠GEF because 120° + 60° = 180°.

Find the measure of the complement and supplement of each angle.

1 a 30° angle   **2** a 45° angle   **3** a 68° angle   **4** a 75° angle

Lines

So what do you know about lines? They are everywhere you look, and people from dress designers to engineers need to understand their relationships.

Intersecting lines are lines that cross each other. The opposite angles in intersecting lines have equal measure.

Check Out the Glossary
For vocabulary words, see page 643.

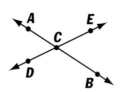

Write: $\overleftrightarrow{AB}$ intersects $\overleftrightarrow{DE}$.

Read: Line *AB* intersects line *DE*.

Note: *C* is the point of intersection.

Two lines are **perpendicular** if they intersect and form right angles.

Two lines that never cross are called **parallel** lines. The distance between parallel lines is always the same.

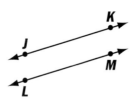

This symbol means the angle measures 90°

Write: $\overleftrightarrow{FG} \perp \overleftrightarrow{HI}$

Read: Line *FG* is perpendicular to line *HI*.

Write: $\overleftrightarrow{JK} \parallel \overleftrightarrow{LM}$

Read: Line *JK* is parallel to line *LM*.

Check for Understanding

Use the diagram. Name pairs of lines or angles.

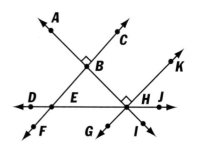

1 intersecting lines

2 parallel lines

3 perpendicular lines

4 angles with equal measure

Critical Thinking: Predict

5 If you have two parallel lines and draw a line perpendicular to one, is the new line perpendicular to the other parallel line?

6 When a pair of parallel lines is intersected by another pair of parallel lines that are perpendicular to the first pair, what shape is formed by the line segments?

Practice

Use the diagram. Name two pairs of lines or angles for each.

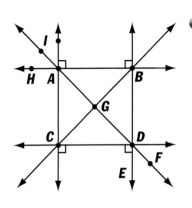

1 parallel lines

2 perpendicular lines

3 intersecting lines

4 angles of equal measure

Tell if the lines are intersecting, perpendicular, or parallel.

5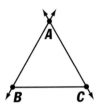

6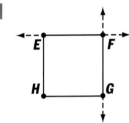

7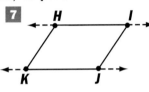

8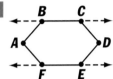

MIXED APPLICATIONS

Problem Solving

9 Piet Mondrian (1872–1944) used many perpendicular lines in his paintings. How many right angles are in his painting *Red, Yellow and Blue Composition*?

10 Nobuko has saved $\frac{3}{4}$ of the cost of an $86.00 bicycle. How much more money does she need to save?

11 **Write a problem** using these scores for a basketball team: 98, 115, 90, 124, and 102. Solve your problem and have others solve it.

---

more to explore

Skew Lines

In a 3-dimensional object, you can find lines that never meet but are not parallel. They are *skew* lines.

1 Name two more pairs of skew lines in the diagram to the right.

2 Identify skew lines in your classroom.

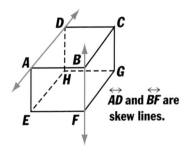

$\overleftrightarrow{AD}$ and $\overleftrightarrow{BF}$ are skew lines.

Triangles and Quadrilaterals

I. M. Pei is an architect famous for creative use of light, shadow, and geometric shapes in the buildings he designs. His designs are often created using triangles.

Two line segments are **congruent** if they have the same length. Two angles are **congruent** if they have the same measure.

Triangles are classified by the lengths of their sides.

scalene triangle	isosceles triangle	equilateral triangle
No sides are congruent.	At least two sides are congruent.	Three sides are congruent.

Triangles are also classified by the measure of their angles.

acute triangle	obtuse triangle	right triangle
All angles are acute.	One angle is obtuse	One angle is a right angle.

You can describe a triangle in more than one way.

Think: This is an obtuse scalene triangle. It has no congruent sides and no congruent angles.

Think: This is a right isosceles triangle. It has two congruent sides and two congruent angles.

Check Out the Glossary
For vocabulary words, see page 643.

Talk It Over

▶ Are all equilateral triangles isosceles triangles? Explain.

▶ Can a triangle have more than one obtuse angle? Explain.

▶ Is a scalene triangle always an obtuse triangle? Explain.

Quadrilaterals are classified by their sides and their angles.

parallelogram

Opposite sides are parallel and congruent. Opposite angles are congruent.

rectangle

Opposite sides are congruent and parallel. It also has 4 right angles.

square

Opposite sides are parallel, and all sides are congruent. It also has 4 right angles.

trapezoid

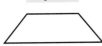

Only one pair of sides is parallel.

rhombus

Opposite sides are parallel, and opposite angles are congruent. All sides are congruent.

kite

Both pairs of adjacent sides are congruent.

▶ Which shapes above are also parallelograms? Explain.

▶ A **diagonal** of a polygon is a line segment other than a side connecting two of the vertices of the polygon. Will you always form two triangles when you draw a diagonal in a quadrilateral? Give examples.

Check for Understanding

Give all the possible ways to classify each polygon.

1 4 cm, 4 cm, 4 cm, 4 cm

2 2 cm, 2 cm, 2 cm, 2 cm

3 3 cm, 5 cm, 4 cm

Name the new shapes that are formed by the diagonal.

4

5

6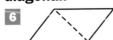

7

Critical Thinking: Analyze

8 Make a design from many kinds of triangles and quadrilaterals, and name the types of each you used.

Turn the page for Practice. ➡

Practice

Give all the possible ways to classify each polygon.

1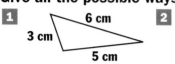
3 cm, 6 cm, 5 cm

2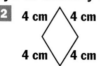
4 cm, 4 cm, 4 cm, 4 cm

3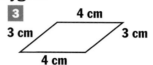
4 cm, 3 cm, 3 cm, 4 cm

4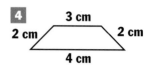
3 cm, 2 cm, 2 cm, 4 cm

5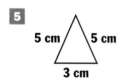
5 cm, 5 cm, 3 cm

6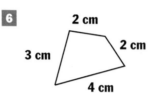
2 cm, 2 cm, 3 cm, 4 cm

7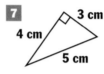
3 cm, 4 cm, 5 cm

8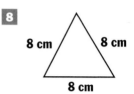
8 cm, 8 cm, 8 cm

Sketch and classify the triangles.

9 all angles less than 90°, no congruent sides

10 only one right angle, two sides congruent

11 all sides congruent and all angles equal

Name all the quadrilaterals for which the statement is true.

12 All the sides are equal.

13 All the angles are equal.

14 The opposite sides are parallel and congruent.

15 Only one pair of opposite sides is parallel.

Write *true* or *false*. Give examples to support your reasoning.

16 All scalene triangles are acute.

17 All parallelograms are rhombuses.

18 A trapezoid may have two right angles.

19 A parallelogram may have two obtuse and two acute angles.

Find the length of the missing sides. Explain.

20 equilateral triangle

a, 12 cm, *b*

21 parallelogram
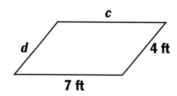
c, *d*, 4 ft, 7 ft

22 isosceles triangle
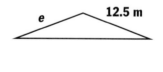
e, 12.5 m

· · · · · · · · · · · · · · · Make It Right · · · · · · · · · · · · · · · ·

23 Jeff made these two statements about quadrilaterals.

• All rectangles are squares.

• All quadrilaterals are rectangles

Help Jeff understand what is wrong with these statements.

Make Connections

The fanlight you created out of the triangle formed a straight line along the bottom. This means that *the sum of the measures of the angles of the triangle is 180°*. This is true for all triangles.

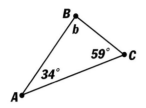

Find *b*, the measure of ∠B, in △ABC.

Think: $b + 34° + 59° = 180°$
$34° + 59° = 93°$
So $b = 180° - 93° = 87°$

▶ If all of the angles of a triangle are equal, what is the measure of each angle?

When you repeated the process using a quadrilateral, the pieces formed a circle. Since there are 360° in a circle, this means that *the sum of the measures of the angles of the quadrilateral is 360°*. This is true for all quadrilaterals.

▶ How can you find the measure of angle *E* without measuring? What is its measure?

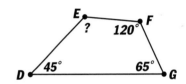

Check for Understanding
Find the measure of the missing angles.

 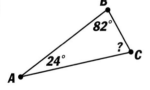

2
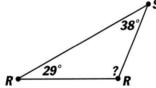

3
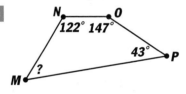

Critical Thinking: Generalize

4 Emily said, "The sum of the measures of the angles of a quadrilateral is 360° because the quadrilateral can be divided into two triangles and the sum of the measures of each triangle is 180˚." Do you agree? Give examples.

Practice
Find the measure of the missing angles.

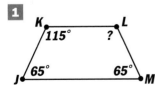 **2** 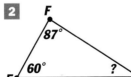 **3** 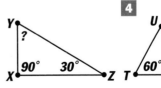 **4**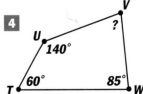

Find the missing angle measure for each quadrilateral.

5 90°, 45°, 90°, *n*   **6** 100°, 120°, 60°, *n*   **7** 68°, 32°, 40°, *n*

Problem-Solving Strategy

Read
Plan
Solve
Look Back

Make a Model

Read Kid's CAD is a computer program you can use when designing. Suppose you have an idea for a new bicycle and you want to try out different lengths of the triangular frame. Will sides that measure 18 cm, 9 cm, and 6 cm on the screen make a triangle?

Plan To solve the problem, you need to answer these questions.

▶ Can you make a triangle from any three line segments?

▶ How do you find out if 18 cm, 9 cm, and 6 cm can be the sides of a triangle?

Solve You can make a model to solve this problem.

▶ Cut three straws that measure 18 cm, 9 cm, and 6 cm.

▶ The model shows that it is not possible to make a triangle using the three straws.

No, 18 cm, 9 cm, and 6 cm cannot make a triangle.

Look Back How can you check if your answer is correct?

Check for Understanding

1 **What if** the lengths of the straws are the following. Which lengths make a triangle?

   a. 12 cm, 4 cm, and 6 cm   **b.** 15 cm, 9 cm, and 12 cm

   c. 18 cm, 11 cm, and 7 cm   **d.** 15 cm, 7 cm, and 6 cm

Critical Thinking: Generalize

2 *The length of any side of a triangle is always less than the sum of the lengths of the other two sides.* Give some examples of triangles you see in daily life to show that the statement is true.

MIXED APPLICATIONS

Problem Solving

1 Emily and seven of her friends were sitting around a circular table. Going clockwise around the table, there was Emily, Rita, Flora, Cam, Lani, Nina, Sue, and Lily. They played a game to see who would be the last to get up. Starting with Emily, they counted off from 1 to 3 in a clockwise direction. Whoever said 3 had to stand up. Who was the last one sitting? Explain.

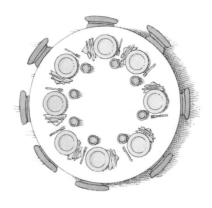

2 Nick has 35 books in his library. He has 2 more adventure books than mystery books, and 6 more mystery books than joke books. How many mystery books does he have?

3 According to the *Guinness Book of Records,* Takayuki Koike of Japan rode a unicycle for 100 mi in about 7 hours. To the nearest whole number, what was Takayuki's average speed?

4 Maria uses beads of different colors to make a necklace. For every 4 white beads, she uses 2 green beads and 1 red bead. She uses a total of 84 beads. How many of each color does she use?

5 In a bicycle club, the mean age of the 7 members is 14 years old. The range of the ages is 5. Four of the members are 12 years old, and they are the youngest of the club. What are the ages of the members?

6 Which of the four groups of line segments below can make the same type of quadrilateral? Name the quadrilateral.
  a. 12 cm, 15 cm, 7 cm, and 9 cm
  b. 16 cm, 8 cm, 5 cm, and 10 cm
  c. 12 cm, 14 cm, 12 cm, and 14 cm
  d. 15 cm, 9 cm, 12 cm, and 15 cm

7 There were new cans of paint in Matthew's art studio on Monday. Matthew used $\frac{3}{4}$ of the cans on Tuesday and $\frac{2}{3}$ of the remaining cans on Wednesday. He had 2 cans left on Thursday. How many cans of paint were there on Monday?

8 **ALGEBRA: PATTERNS** If the pattern continues, how many blocks are needed for the sixth triangle? What is the perimeter of the sixth triangle?

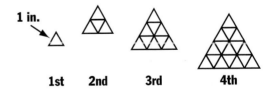

1 in.

1st   2nd   3rd   4th

9 There are five equally-spaced parallel lines labeled *a, b, c, d, e.* The distance between the first (*a*) and last (*e*) lines is 2.8 cm. What is the distance between lines *b* and *d* ?

10 **Write a problem** about angles in an object in your classroom. Solve it and have others solve it.

Name the shapes. Classify the angles in each shape as *acute*, *right*, or *obtuse* angles.

1

2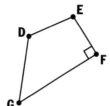

3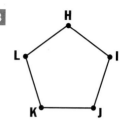

Use the map at the right for ex. 4–6. Write *true* or *false*.

4 Thomson Ave. is parallel to Fairfield Ave.

5 49th Street is perpendicular to Thomson Ave. and Warren Blvd.

6 Warren Blvd. intersects 48th St. and 49th St. only.

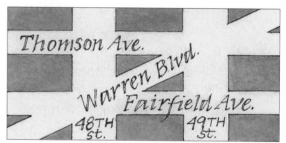

Name, measure, and classify each angle.

7

8

9

Draw angles with the indicated measure.

10 30°

11 90°

12 35°

13 150°

Find the missing angle.

14

15

16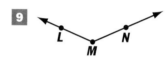

17

Solve.

18 Each side of the Pentagon building is 276.3 m long. Matthew said that the walk around the Pentagon is about 1.5 km. Do you agree? Explain.

19 For the first round in an architectural competition, $\frac{2}{3}$ of the designs were not selected. For the second round, only $\frac{1}{4}$ were selected. For the last round, only $\frac{1}{3}$ were selected. If 7 designs received awards, how many designs were submitted?

20 Describe how to use a protractor to measure and draw angles. Give examples.

Möbius Strips

The figure in the Brazilian stamp at the right is a Möbius strip. The Möbius strip is a very special geometric figure which has only one side.

 Use Diagrams Follow these steps to make your own Möbius strip.

You will need
- *2-in. strip of paper*
- *tape*

Cultural Note
The Möbius strip was created by the German mathematician August Möbius (1790–1868).

▶ Mark the ends of the strip *A* and *B*.

▶ Bring the two ends together to form a loop.

▶ Twist the end of *B* to make *B* face the inside of the loop. Then tape the two ends together.

▶ You can now draw a line from *A* down the middle of the loop until it meets itself without lifting your pencil.

Use your Möbius strip to answer the following questions.

1 What do you think would happen if you cut along the line that you drew? What does happen?

2 Make another Möbius strip. What would happen if you cut down the center of the Möbius strip twice? Try it.

3 Make another strip with ends *A* and *B*. **What if** you twist the end of *B* twice and then tape the two ends together. How is the loop different from the original Möbius strip you made?

4 Cut the loop you made in problem 3 down the middle line. What happens?

REFLECTION OF LIGHT

Interior designers often use light to create some special effects when decorating a room. In this activity, your team will investigate one of the properties of light used by designers.

Work Together
Work in a small group to investigate how light reflects from a flat mirror.

You will need
- *mirror*
- *cardboard*
- *flashlight*

▶ Cut a tiny hole in the middle of a piece of paper. Cover the front of the flashlight with the piece of paper so the hole is in the middle of the front of the flashlight.

▶ Place the mirror flat on the table.

▶ Turn off the lights of your classroom. Make sure to close all the curtains.

▶ Have one group member shine the flashlight at the center of the mirror from one side of the mirror.

▶ Have another group member hold a piece of cardboard perpendicular to the table on the other side of the mirror so that the reflection of the light hits the cardboard.

Reflection of Light

1 Use a protractor to measure the angle that the light makes with the mirror as it strikes the mirror and the angle that the light makes with the mirror as it leaves the mirror. Are they about the same?

2 Repeat Step 1 with the flashlight beam striking the mirror at other angles. Record the two angles that the beam makes each time.

Report Your Findings

3 **Portfolio** Prepare a report on your investigation on the reflection of light. Do the following in your report:

▶ Describe how your team conducted the experiment and gathered the data. How did you use the protractor to measure the angles?

▶ Record your data in a table.

▶ Compare your conclusion with other teams. What can you conclude about how light bounces off the surface of a mirror?

Revise your work.
▶ Did you include any diagrams in your report to explain how the experiment worked?
▶ Is your report clear and organized?

PREDICT what the angle of light bouncing off the mirror will be if the angle of the light striking the mirror is 20°, 30°, or 90°.

EXPLORE how artists and architects use light waves to enhance their designs.

FIND some other properties of light in an encyclopedia or science reference book.

Constructions

Geometric tools are very important to architects and engineers. They help them construct geometric shapes accurately. Some geometric tools, such as the compass and T-square, have been used for centuries.

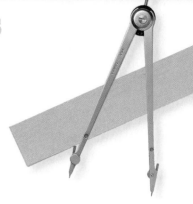

You can use a **compass** and a **straightedge** as shown at right to construct congruent line segments.

Step 1

Draw a ray with endpoint *C*.

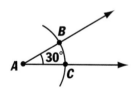

Step 2

Open the compass the length of line segment $\overline{AB}$. Mark off point *D* on the ray so that $\overline{AB}$ is congruent to $\overline{CD}$.

$\overline{AB} \cong \overline{CD}$ Note: $\cong$ means "is congruent to."

You can also use a compass and straightedge to construct an angle congruent to $\angle A$.

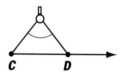

Step 1

Draw an arc that intersects both sides of $\angle A$. Label these points *B* and *C*.

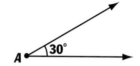

Step 2

Draw $\overline{DE}$.

Step 3

Using the same compass opening, place the compass point on *D*. Draw an arc that intersects $\overline{DE}$ at point *F*.

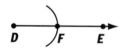

Step 4

Open the compass to the distance between points *B* and *C*. Then place the compass point on *F* and draw an intersecting arc. Label this point *G*. Draw $\overrightarrow{DG}$.

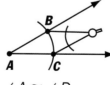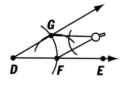

$\angle A \cong \angle D$

Talk It Over

▶ How could you check to see that $\overline{AC} \cong \overline{DF}$? that $\angle A \cong \angle D$?

Bisecting means cutting something in half. You can use a compass and a straightedge to bisect line segments.

A •———————• B

Step 1	Step 2	Step 3
Use a compass radius more than half the length of $\overline{AB}$.	Draw intersecting arcs with the same radius with centers *A* and *B*. Label intersections *P* and *Q*.	Connect *P* and *Q* to form the bisector.
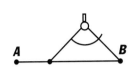	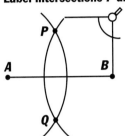	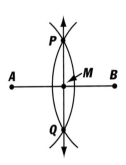

Line $\overleftrightarrow{PQ}$ bisects line segment $\overline{AB}$ at *M*, so $\overline{AM} \cong \overline{MB}$.

Point *M* is the **midpoint** of line segment $\overline{AB}$.

Line $\overleftrightarrow{PQ}$ is perpendicular to line segment $\overline{AB}$.

You can also use a compass and straightedge to bisect angles.

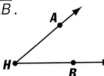

> **Check Out the Glossary**
> For vocabulary words, see page 643.

Step 1	Step 2	Step 3
Draw an arc with center at *H*. Label points *A* and *B*.	Using the same compass opening, draw an arc with center at *A* and an arc with center at *B*. Label the intersection *J*.	Draw $\overrightarrow{HJ}$.
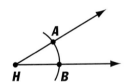	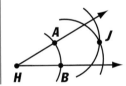	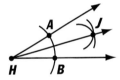
		$\overrightarrow{HJ}$ bisects $\angle AHB$
		$\angle AHJ \cong \angle JHB$

Check for Understanding

Draw each figure. Use a compass and straightedge to construct congruent line segments or angles.

1 $\overline{AB}$ is 3 cm long. **2** $\overline{CD}$ is 1.5 cm long. **3** $\angle G = 45°$ **4** $\angle H = 110°$

Use a compass and straightedge to construct the following.

5 Bisect a 5.5-cm line segment. **6** Bisect a 105° angle.

Critical Thinking: Generalize

7 Draw three different triangles. Bisect all the angles. What do you notice about the bisectors? What conclusion can you draw?

8 Do the two diagonals of a quadrilateral always bisect the angles of the quadrilateral? Give examples to support your reasoning.

Turn the page for Practice. ➡

Practice

Trace each figure. Use a compass and straightedge to construct congruent line segments or angles.

1

2

3

4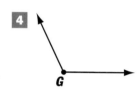

5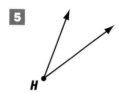

6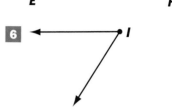

Draw each figure. Then use a compass and straightedge to construct congruent line segments or angles.

7 $\overline{AB}$ is 5 cm long.

8 $\overline{KL}$ is 12 cm long.

9 $\overline{MN}$ is 8 cm long.

10 a 60° angle

11 a 90° angle

12 a 120° angle

Use a compass and a straightedge to bisect the following.

13 a 7.7-cm line segment

14 an 83° angle

15 a 117° angle

16 ∠G

17 ∠F

18 $\overline{IH}$

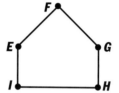

Find the measure of each angle. $\overline{CD}$ is the angle bisector of ∠C.

19 ∠CDB

20 ∠DCA

21 ∠CDA

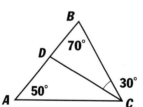

Solve. W is the midpoint of $\overline{XV}$.

22 Find the length of $\overline{VW}$.

23 Find the perimeter of trapezoid TUVX.

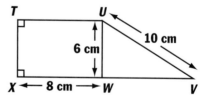

Write always, sometimes, or never. Give examples.

24 When you draw an angle bisector from any angle of a rhombus, you form two isosceles triangles.

25 When you connect the midpoints of each side of a square, you form another square.

26 When you bisect an obtuse angle, you form acute angles.

27 When you bisect the longer side of a rectangle, you form two squares.

Problem Solving

28 Look at the art design at the right. Explain how the design was created. Copy the frame of the parallelogram and create and color a similar design.

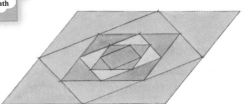

29 The largest angle of a triangle is twice the smallest one. If the third angle is 60°, what is the measure of the other two angles?

30 A $12\frac{3}{4}$-inch silk cord was cut at its midpoint. How long is each half of the cord?

31 **What if** the original price of the portfolio case at the right was $45. How much would you save if you buy two of them at the sale price?

32 Ray has $10.45 left after buying 2 boxes of tracing paper, 1 box of stencil paper, 1 T-square, 1 palette, and 1 sketchbook at the sale. How much did he start with?

Art Supplies on Sale	
Compass	$4.99
Tracing paper (box)	$7.69
T-square	$6.53
Stencil paper (box)	$21.76
Palette	$12.33
Drawing board	$15.78
Sketchbook	$15.55
Portfolio case	$35.99

Cultural Connection
Geometric Patterns in Native American Art

The art of Native Americans, both past and present, show rich geometric patterns.

Here are some patterns found on pots made by the Mound Builders over 1,200 years ago.

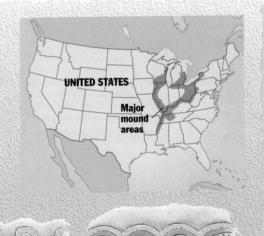

1 Copy and continue the patterns above.

2 Create your own pattern. Describe your pattern.

Extra Practice, page 606

Circles

Circles are one of the shapes that you see most often in nature and daily life. You can find them in arts and crafts, furniture, and buildings.

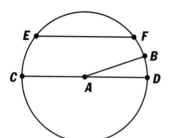

Center: **A**
Chord: $\overline{EF}$
Radius: $\overline{AB}$
Diameter: $\overline{CD}$

Cultural Note
The Huichol (WEE-chohl) Indians of Mexico make bowls from dried half-gourds decorated with symbolic pictures.

All the points of a **circle** are the same distance from its **center.** A circle can be named by its center. The circle above can be called circle **A.**

A **radius** is a line segment from the center to a point on the circle.

A **chord** is a line segment that connects two points on the circle.

A **diameter** is a chord that passes through the center of the circle.

A **central angle** is an angle formed between two radii. In circle *F*, $\angle CFA$, $\angle AFD$, $\angle DFB$, and $\angle BFC$ are all central angles. The sum of the measures of these four central angles is 360°.

Check Out the Glossary
For vocabulary words, see page 643.

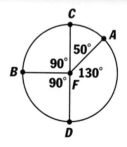

Check for Understanding
Identify the parts of circle *G*.

1 Name a diameter.

2 Name four radii.

3 Name a chord shown.

4 Identify three central angles shown.

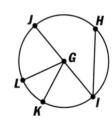

Critical Thinking: Generalize

5 What is the relationship between a diameter and a radius? How many of each can you find in a circle?

6 *Journal* Use a compass to draw a circle. List all the properties you know about a circle.

Practice

Use circle _P_ for ex. 1–8.

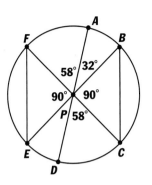

1 Name the radii.

2 Name the diameters.

3 Name the chords.

4 What is the measure of ∠*DPE*?

5 What kind of triangle is △*EPF*?

6 What kind of triangle is △*BPC*?

7 If $\overline{FC}$ is 4 cm, how long is $\overline{PB}$?

8 What is the measure of ∠*APC*?

MIXED APPLICATIONS

Problem Solving

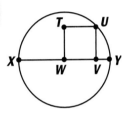

9 In circle _W_, _TUVW_ is a square. The length of diameter $\overline{XY}$ is 13 cm. What is the length of diagonal $\overline{WU}$?

10 **Number sense** Joe ate one fourth of a round pizza for lunch and half of the rest for dinner. Which diagram below represents the amount of pizza left?

a.

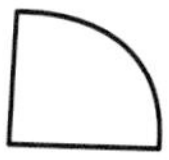

b.

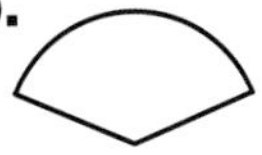

c.

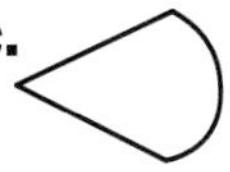

d.

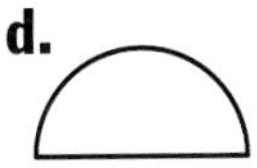

11 Summer Middle School held a survey to decide on a new mascot. The results were shown as below. Order the popularity of the mascots from greatest to least.

12 A circular table has a diameter of 150 cm. Judy wants to make a tablecloth that hangs 15 cm below the edge of the table. What is the diameter of the tablecloth that Judy should make?

13 **Make a decision** At the bakery, a round cheesecake costs $24. The cake is cut into 12 equal pieces, each costing $2.45. To serve 10 people, would you rather buy the whole cake or the pieces? Explain.

---

mixed review • test preparation

1 $2\frac{1}{3} + 3$

2 $4\frac{1}{8} + 1\frac{3}{4}$

3 $1\frac{5}{6} + 1\frac{3}{8}$

4 $7\frac{1}{2} + 9\frac{5}{8}$

5 $6 - 2\frac{2}{8}$

6 $9\frac{5}{6} - 4\frac{2}{3}$

7 $11 - 3\frac{3}{4}$

8 $2\frac{1}{3} - 1\frac{5}{6}$

Extra Practice, page 606

Translations and Rotations

As you know, motion-picture cartoons are made by a technique called animation. You can create an animation from a series of pictures by translating and rotating the figures in a picture.

In a **translation**, the original object can be moved horizontally, vertically, or diagonally.

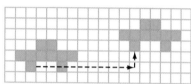

Think: Slide the car 10 squares to the right and 2 squares up.

In a **rotation**, the original object is rotated around a point.

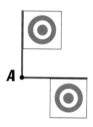

A•

Think: The flag is rotated 90° clockwise around point A.

Check Out the Glossary
For vocabulary words, see page 643.

Two figures are **congruent** if they have the same size and shape. In both cases above, the original object and its image are congruent.

Check for Understanding

Tell whether figure **B** is a translation, rotation, or neither of figure **A**. Is figure **B** congruent to figure **A**?

1

2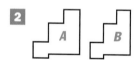

3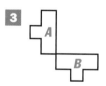

4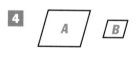

Copy the figure on graph paper. Then draw the figure after the described translation or rotation.

5  4 squares right

6 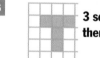 3 squares left, then 2 squares up

7 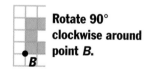 Rotate 90° clockwise around point **B**.

Critical Thinking: Generalize

8 How does a translation differ from a rotation?

9 What motions do you see in daily life that remind you of translations or rotations?

Practice

Tell whether figure *B* is a translation, rotation, or neither of figure *A*. Is figure *B* congruent to figure *A*?

1

2

3

4

5

6

7

8

Copy the figure on graph paper. Then draw the new figure after the described translation or rotation.

9

5 squares left

10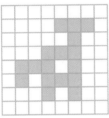

4 squares right, then 3 squares down

11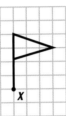

Rotate around point *X* 90° counterclockwise.

12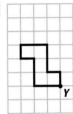

Rotate around point *Y* 180° clockwise.

MIXED APPLICATIONS
Problem Solving

13 Sketch a car at the top of a hill. What if you want to make an animation showing the car sliding down the hill. Sketch the series of pictures that you would draw. Are your drawings an example of a translation or rotation?

14 About how many still drawings are needed for a 2-hour animated movie?
SEE INFOBIT.

INFOBIT
An animated movie is made from thousands of still drawings. It takes 24 still drawings to create a one-second motion.

mixed review • test preparation

1 $\frac{2}{3} \times 3\frac{1}{5}$

2 $6\frac{3}{4} \div \frac{1}{2}$

3 $8\frac{2}{5} \div 5\frac{1}{4}$

4 $2\frac{2}{3} \times 4\frac{1}{4}$

5 $4.25 - 2.654$

6 $3,543 - 885$

7 $\$2.19 - \$1.65$

8 $3.8 + 0.743 + 12$

Reflections and Line Symmetry

LEARN

Mirrors create optical illusions because they reflect images. Sometimes, interior designers use mirrors to create a spacious feeling.

If you put a mirror along the edge of an object, you will see the **reflection** of the object in the mirror.

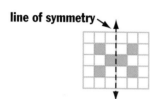

A figure is **symmetric** if it can be folded along a line so that the two halves match exactly. The line is a **line of symmetry.**

You may find symmetric figures and reflections in art, architecture, and nature.

Taj Mahal in India

Check Out the Glossary
For vocabulary words, see page 643.

CHECK

Check for Understanding

Trace each figure. Tell whether the figure is symmetric. Draw all lines of symmetry in the symmetric figures.

1 **2** **3** **4**

Copy the figure and the line on graph paper. Draw the reflection.

5 **6** **7**

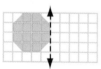

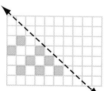

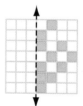

Critical Thinking: Generalize

8 How is a reflection different from a translation?

9 Which shape has an unlimited number of lines of symmetry?

Practice

Tell whether the figure is symmetric. Is the dashed line a line of symmetry? Write yes or no.

1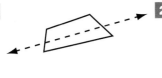

2

3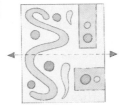

4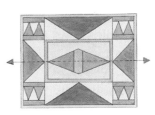

Copy the figure and the line on graph paper. Draw the reflection. Is the reflection congruent to the original figure?

5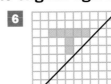

6

7

Tell how the figure at the left arrived at the position on the right. Identify what motions might have occurred.

8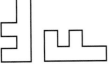

9

10

MIXED APPLICATIONS
Problem Solving

11 The figure at the right shows a paper that was folded along the dashed line. The shaded parts show holes that were cut out of the folded paper. What will the paper look like when it is unfolded?

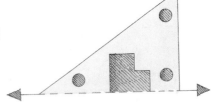

12 A quadrilateral has a 50° angle and an 80° angle. What are the measures of the other two angles if the angles are congruent?

13 **Data Point** Find at least two examples of symmetric figures in art, nature, or architecture. You may use magazines or reference books.

---

mixed review • test preparation

Estimate. Then find the exact answer.

1 36.2 + 45.08

2 156.8 − 67.08

3 3.2 × 0.4

4 60.3 ÷ 0.9

Find the greatest common factor.

5 6 and 21

6 8 and 20

7 15 and 32

8 33 and 77

Extra Practice, page 607

Geometry **327**

Tessellations

Tessellations are used in the design of wallpaper, floor tiles, and fabrics. Look at these examples of tessellations.

A **tessellation** of an area is an arrangement of shapes covering the entire area without any overlaps or gaps. A shape **tessellates** if copies of the shape fit together to make a tessellation.

Work Together

▶ Work in a small group. Make a square 3 centimeters on a side.

▶ Trace and cut out 20 copies of each shape in Group A.

You will need
• *scissors*

Group A

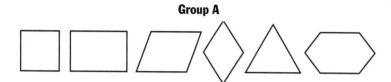

Group B

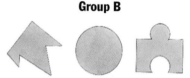

▶ Use the shapes from Group A and B. Test the shapes, one at a time. Which ones can form a tessellation that will cover the square you made? Draw a picture to show each tessellation.

Check Out the Glossary
For vocabulary words,
see page 643.

Make Connections

The tessellations formed by regular polygons are called **regular tessellations**.

One way to check whether a regular polygon can tessellate or not is by positioning the corners of copies of the polygon around a common point. If the sum of the angle measures is 360° without any gaps or overlappings, then the regular polygon will tessellate.

These regular polygons tessellate.

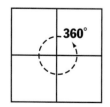 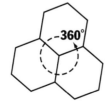

Some regular pentagons do not tessellate.

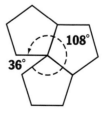

You can create a tessellation by translating part of a shape which tessellates to the opposite side. Start with a piece of paper that is a square. Then follow the steps to create a tessellation.

Step 1	Step 2	Step 3	Step 4
Cut out the part along the dotted line.	**Translate the part to the opposite side. Tape the two pieces.**	**Cut out the part along the dotted line.**	**Translate the part to the opposite side. Tape the two pieces.**

▶ Create a tessellation with the pattern above.

Identify the shapes that will tessellate. Explain why or why not.

1  **2**   **3**   **4**

Critical Thinking: Analyze

5 Can you make a pentagon that will tessellate? If so, show a tessellation?

6 Does a circle tessellate? Give an illustration to explain.

Practice

Tell whether each of the following is an example of a tessellation.

1 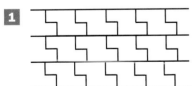 **2**  **3**

Identify the shapes that will tessellate. Tell how you know.

4   **5**  **6**  **7**

Problem Solvers at Work

Read
Plan
Solve
Look Back

PART 1   Find a Pattern

L
E
A
R
N

Computer-aided design (CAD) programs are used by engineers around the world. You can tell the program how to make any shape you want. What would you need to know to tell the program how to make a regular hexagon?

Work Together
You need to know the measure of each angle. Use what you know about the sums of the measures of the angles of a triangle to find that sum for other regular polygons.

A diagonal divides a square into two triangles.
Note: Any polygon can be divided into triangles by diagonals drawn between vertices.

1 Make a table like the table below to record your findings.

Polygon	Equilateral Triangle	Square	Regular Pentagon	Regular Hexagon
Number of sides	3			
Number of triangles	1			
Sum of angle measures	180°			
Measure of each angle	60°			

a **2** **ALGEBRA: PATTERNS** What relationships do you see in the table you made?

3 What is the measure of each angle of a regular hexagon?

The diagram below shows how people can be seated around tables. Naomi used this information to write this problem.

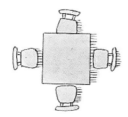

One table

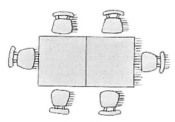

Two tables

Naomi Malette
John Yeates Middle School
Suffolk, VA

Two more tables are added to the two tables shown. If the tables are in a row, how many people can sit at the tables?

4 Solve Naomi's problem.

5 **Use Diagrams** Explain how you solved Naomi's problem. Include any charts or diagrams you may have used.

6 Change Naomi's problem so it is more difficult to solve. Solve it and have others solve it.

7 **Write a problem** Create a pattern. Write problems about the pattern you created.

8 Trade problems. Solve at least three problems written by other students.

Menu

**Choose five problems and solve them.
Explain your methods.**

1 ALGEBRA: PATTERNS If the pattern continues, what will be the perimeter for the next staircase? the sixth? the seventh?

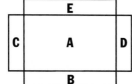

1 cm

1st   2nd   3rd   4th

3 Spatial reasoning What figure on the right results if you follow the steps below?

Fold flap B over A. Next, fold over flaps C and D. Then, fold over flap E.

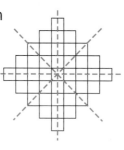

E

C   A   D

B

4 Use different pattern blocks to create a symmetric design. Sketch the outline, including all the lines of symmetry.

2 Fill in the missing numbers. Explain your reasoning.

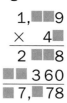

$$
\begin{array}{r}
1,\blacksquare\blacksquare9 \\
\times\ \ 4\blacksquare \\
\hline
2\ \blacksquare\blacksquare8 \\
\blacksquare\blacksquare\ 360 \\
\hline
\blacksquare7,\blacksquare78
\end{array}
$$

a. 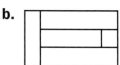   b.

c.   d.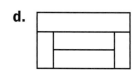

5 How do you think the figure below was drawn? Use your compass to try out your ideas.

6 The Olympic Stadium in Atlanta covers 55,300 square meters. The Colosseum in Italy covers 23,225 square meters. Is the area of the Colosseum about $\frac{1}{2}$ the area of the Olympic Stadium in Atlanta? Explain how you would use estimation to support your answer.

8 The Leaning Tower of Pisa in Italy forms angles with the ground. Which angle is obtuse? acute?

A   B

7 Data Point Use the Data Bank on page 638. Use tangram pieces shown to make the shapes shown. Then create your own designs. Trace the shape of your designs. Exchange shapes with other students. Try to create each other's shapes with tangram pieces.

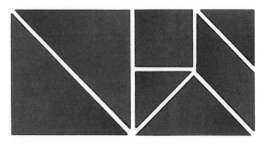

Choose two problems and solve them. Explain your methods.

9 Every polygon has two types of angles. The angles inside are called *interior angles.* The angles on the outside are called *exterior angles.* If you extend the side of a polygon, the angle that is formed is the exterior angle. Measure the exterior angles for various regular polygons. What conclusion can you make about the sum of the measures of exterior angles of regular polygons?

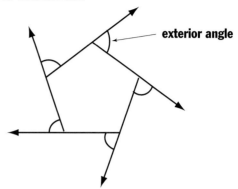

exterior angle

10 Spatial reasoning Each toothpick in the diagram at the right is the same length. Show how you can change the position of 3 toothpicks to form only 3 squares.

11 Use the map at the right. Name the streets that are parallel to each other and the streets that are perpendicular to each other. Identify at least 5 different routes you can choose if you travel from City Hall to Lila's Restaurant.

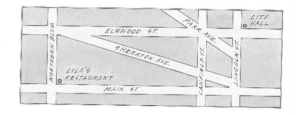

12 An architect wants to cover a floor with a tessellation. She wants to use two types of tiles. One type is shaped like a regular hexagon. The other type is shaped like an equilateral triangle. The length of a side of each tile measures 0.5 m. If she needs to, she can cut either type of tile in half. Draw a diagram showing the tessellation and list how many of each type of tile is used.

13 At the Computer Use a drawing program to create tessellations. Add designs to the tessellations that you created.

Language and Mathematics

Complete the sentence. Use a word in the chart. (pages 298–329)

1 The ▮ of a circle passes through the center and both ends are on the circle.

2 A polygon with three sides of unequal length is called a ▮ triangle.

3 Two polygons are ▮ if they have the same shape and size.

4 A ▮ has its vertex at the center of a circle.

5 Two lines are ▮ if they maintain the same distance between them.

> **Vocabulary**
> congruent
> parallel
> perpendicular
> central angle
> radius
> diameter
> scalene

Concepts and Skills

Name each figure below. Give all possible classifications. (pages 298, 306)

6   **7**   **8**   **9** 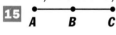 **10**

Draw each figure. (pages 300, 304)

11 parallel lines **12** perpendicular lines **13** an obtuse angle **14** an acute angle

Name, measure, and classify each angle. (page 300)

15 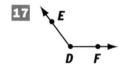 **16**  **17**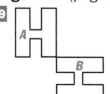

Tell whether figure B is a translation, rotation, reflection or none of these of figure A. Is figure B congruent to figure A? (pages 324, 326)

18 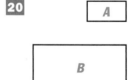 **19** 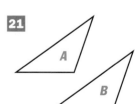 **20** **21**

Find the length of the missing side or angle. (pages 306, 310)

22 kite

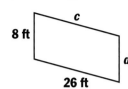

4 cm   8 cm   *a*   *b*

23 parallelogram

8 ft   *c*   *d*   26 ft

24 isosceles triangle

?   45°

Think critically. (pages 306, 326)

25 Analyze. Juan is asked to complete the shape he began in Figure *A* so that the dashed line will be a line of symmetry. Figure *B* shows Juan's work. Explain the error and correct it.

Figure A   **Figure B**

26 Compare. How are isosceles and equilateral triangles alike? different?

27 Compare and contrast parallelogram, rhombus, square, and rectangle.

MIXED APPLICATIONS
Problem Solving   Pencil & Paper   Calculator   Mental Math   (pages 312, 330)

28 Show how you can use three of the regular hexagons below to make a shape that has a perimeter of 12 inches. Sketch your shape.

1 in.

29 Point *A* and point *B* are the centers for the two circles below. What is the relationship between the length of $\overline{CA}$ and the length of $\overline{BD}$?

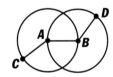

D   *A*   *B*   *C*

   a. $\overline{CA} > \overline{BD}$
   b. $\overline{CA} < \overline{BD}$
   c. $\overline{CA} = \overline{BD}$

30 Graph the data in the table at the right. Explain why you chose that graph and write a conclusion about the data.

Shadow Length at the Same Time Each Day					
Month	Aug.	Sept.	Oct.	Nov.	Dec.
Meters	3.5	4.5	5.5	6.5	7.5

31 What is the greatest whole number you can multiply by 66 to get a product between 1,200 and 1,500? Explain.

32 A tile has four congruent sides, but it is not a square. What shape is the tile? Sketch how the tile will tessellate.

33 **ALGEBRA: PATTERNS** If the pattern continues, what is the next number? $\frac{5}{3}, \frac{4}{6}, \frac{3}{9}, \frac{2}{12}, \blacksquare$?

Name the polygon. Give all possible classifications.

1    **2**    **3**   **4**

5 Draw two perpendicular lines.   **6** Draw two parallel lines.

For ex. 7–8, measure and classify the angle.

7   **8**

9 Tell whether the figure is symmetric. If it is, tell how many lines of symmetry it has.

Tell whether figure *B* is a translation, rotation, reflection or none of these of figure *A*. Is figure *B* congruent to figure *A*?

10   **11**   **12**   **13**

Find the missing measures. Explain.

14   **15** 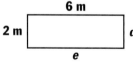   **16**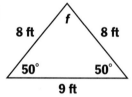

Solve. Show your work.

17 This is a number with both digits the same. The sum of the digits is less than 10. If you add 16 or subtract 16 from the number, the result is a multiple of 4. What is the number?

18 You enter a city park on the north side of the park. A path takes you 4 blocks south, 3 blocks east, 2 blocks south, and 8 blocks west. How many blocks south and west are you from the entrance?

19 If the pattern continues, what is the next number? 1, 2, 6, 24, 120, ■

20 A designer is using four trapezoids rotating around a point as the design logo for a new energy company. Draw a possible sketch for this new logo.

What Did You Learn?

A figure or a pattern that can be perceived in several ways is called an **optical illusion.** Some optical illusions are very easy to create. Here are some examples.

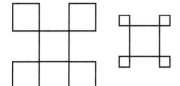

Which inner square is larger?

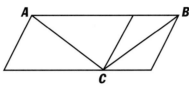

Is $\overline{AC}$ longer than $\overline{BC}$?

Is the dot in the center of the line?

▶ Answer all three questions relying only on your eye. Then, use measuring tools to check. What do you find?

▶ Use some geometric tools to help you draw each of the pictures. Explain your method.

•••••••••••••••• **A Good Answer** ••••••••••••••••
- compares visual estimates with actual measurements.
- shows a clear description of each picture, using geometric terms.
- includes a step-by-step explanation of how the picture was created.

Portfolio You may want to place your work in your portfolio.

What Do You Think

1 Are you able to use geometric terms to describe objects in your surroundings? If not, what difficulties do you have?

2 When you measure or construct an angle congruent to another angle, do you use:
- a compass?
- a protractor?
- a straightedge?
- other? Explain.

Comfortable Chairs

What is it about chairs that make some of them comfortable and others not? The table below is a guide that is used by designers of wooden chairs so that the chairs are comfortable for the greatest possible number of people.

Chair Dimensions	
Seat height from floor	17 to 18 inches
Seat pitch (angle)	3° to 5° sloping to the back
Arms	7 to 9 inches above seat
Back pitch (angle)	5° to 15° sloping back
Distance between arms	at least 18 inches
Back height	30 to 36 inches

Cultural Note

The Egyptians may have been the first to build chairs. The chair shown belonged to King Tutankhamen (too-tahng-KAH-muhn). The common people had only one piece of furniture, a three-legged stool.

▶ Why do you think it is important for the seat to slope slightly to the back?

▶ Why do you think it is important for the back of the chair to slope backward rather than being perpendicular to the floor?

How Does Your Chair Measure Up?

1 Use a tape measure or yardstick to find the height of your chair from the floor, the height of its arms above the seat, the distance between the arms, and the height of its back.

2 Use a protractor to measure the seat pitch and the back pitch of your chair.

3 Compare your measurements with those given in the table on page 338. Are your measurements reasonable?

4 Do you feel that your chair is comfortable or uncomfortable? Explain why.

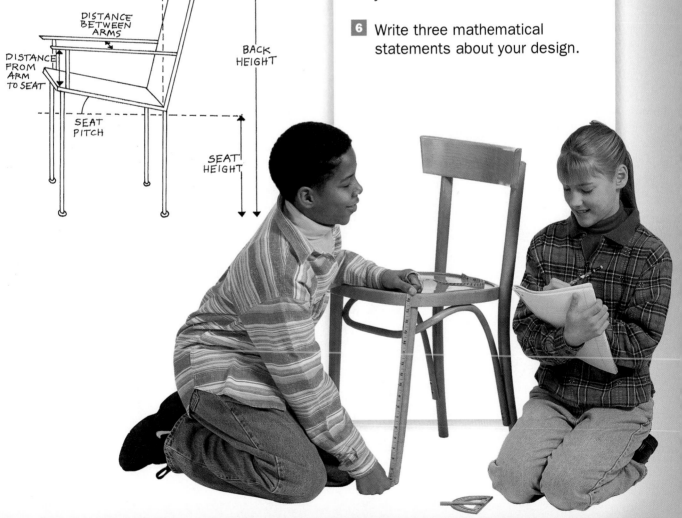

BACK PITCH

DISTANCE BETWEEN ARMS

DISTANCE FROM ARM TO SEAT

BACK HEIGHT

SEAT PITCH

SEAT HEIGHT

At the Computer

5 Use drawing software to design your own chair.

6 Write three mathematical statements about your design.

INTRODUCTION TO ALGEBRA

THEME

Science and the World Around Us

Figuring out the weight of a kitten, determining weights of objects on planets, and plotting a baboon's travels are just some of the ways you'll use algebra in this chapter.

What Do You Know

The extent to which a spring will stretch depends on the amount of force or weight applied to it. This relationship is known as Hooke's Law. Look at the illustration to answer the following questions.

1 How long is the coil when a 10-pound weight is applied to it?

2 What weight was applied to the coil if the coil stretched 6 in.? 8 in.?

3 Make a table that shows the relationship between the weight and the length of the coil. Describe any patterns that you see.

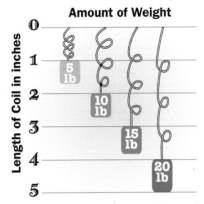

Amount of Weight

Length of Coil in inches

HOOKE'S LAW

Sequence of Events **A student did a science project on plant growth rates. She made these cards to put on her display board. She needs to arrange them so they are in the proper order.**

A sequence of events is the order in which the events happened.

1 Arrange the cards in the correct order. Explain how you did it.

Feb. 3	The mean height of the plants is 3 cm.
Feb. 10	The mean height of the plants is 6 cm.
Feb. 17	I planted the seeds.
Feb. 24	The mean height of the plants is 1 cm.

Vocabulary

function, p. 342
equation, p. 342
axes, p. 344

origin, p. 344
ordered pair, p. 344
coordinate, p. 344

formula, p. 350
solution, p. 361
inverse operations,
    p. 364

Functions

You can grow some kinds of crystals in your classroom. Crystals grow at a controlled rate that depends on the size and shape of the seed crystal. Here is a chart of one crystal's growth.

1 day old

2 days old

3 days old

4 days old

You can make a function table to show the relationship between the age of a crystal and the number of cubes it has.

Age (in days)	1	2	3	4
Number of Cubes	4	7	10	13

One way to describe the relationship is to find the number of cubes in the crystal, multiply its age by 3, and add 1.

Work Together

1 Create at least three different growing crystals that have cube parts. There should be a relationship between the age and the number of cubes for each. Use graph paper to show what each crystal looks like each day for at least a week.

2 Make a function table for each crystal that shows the relationship between its age and the number of cubes it has, from day 1 to day 8.

3 Use words to describe the relationship shown in each table.

You will need
• *graph paper*

Check Out the Glossary
For vocabulary words, see page 643.

Make Connections

The relationship between the age of the crystal and its number of cubes is a function. A **function** is a relationship in which one quantity depends on another quantity.

A function can be represented by an **equation.** An equation is a mathematical statement with an equal sign in it.

▶ Show that the equation $n = 3d + 1$ represents the function in the table by substituting 1, 2, 3, and 4 for d and finding n. Compare your results with the table.

▶ Write an equation to represent one of the function tables you created.

$$n = 3d + 1$$

number ⎯⎯ ⎯⎯ **age**

Check for Understanding

Copy and complete the table for the toothpick function.

1

Number of Triangles	1	2	3	4	5
Number of Toothpicks	3	5	■	■	■

2

Rhombuses	1	2	3	4	5
Tacks	4	6	■	■	■

3 Describe the function in ex. 1 in words and with an equation. Tell what each variable in the equation represents.

Critical Thinking: Analyze

4 Create a crystal so that the relationship between its age and the number of cubes it has can be represented by $n = 4d - 1$.

Practice

Copy and complete the table. Describe the function in words and with an equation. Tell what each variable represents.

1

Pattern Number	1	2	3	4	5
Picture					
Number of Dots	4	6	8	■	■

2

Pattern Number	1	2	3	4	5
Picture					
Number of Dots	1	4	9	■	■

Write an equation for the function described in words. Tell what each variable in the equation represents.

3 The weight in ounces of a crystal is always 2 times the number of days it has been growing.

4 The cost of using a laboratory's supercomputer is $100 plus $57 per hour.

5 Distance traveled is the product of your speed and the time you were traveling.

6 The cost of using a computer club's software is a $10 membership plus $2 per rental.

7 The length of a certain rectangle is twice its width.

8 The perimeter of a rectangle is twice its length plus twice its width.

9 The number of students on a field trip is 6 times the number of chaperones.

10 The total cost of a catalog item is the cost of the item plus $4.95 for shipping.

Graph Functions

Ever wonder how a baboon spends his day? A wildlife biologist observes the movements of a baboon who is wearing a collar with a tiny radio transmitter. To mark the location of the baboon, the biologist uses a grid over a map.

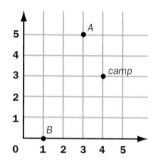

The two darker lines are called **axes.** The point where the axes intersect is the **origin.**

The biologist attaches a special collar to the baboon at the origin and releases it. The baboon travels to a point 3 units to the right and 5 units up before stopping for the first time. The biologist labels this as point with the letter *A* on the map.

You can write the location of point *A* using the **ordered pair** (3, 5). The numbers 3 and 5 are the **coordinates** of the point.

(3, 5)

first coordinate   second coordinate
(distance to the right of 0)   (distance above 0)

The origin is represented by the ordered pair (0, 0).

To graph (4, 3), start at the origin. Count 4 units to the right and 3 units up. The ordered pair (4, 3) on the biologist's map is the location of the biologist's camp.

Talk It Over

▶ What are the coordinates of point *B,* the location of the baboon's nest?

▶ **What if** point *C* were at (1.5, 3). Where would it be on the graph?

▶ Does the order in which you give the coordinates make a difference? Explain.

The biologist walks from his camp at a rate of 2 miles per hour. How can you show the relationship between the distance he has walked and the time he has walked?

Check Out the Glossary
For vocabulary words, see page 643.

The relationship between the distance and the time is a function. You can represent a function using an equation, a table, or a graph.

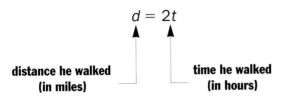

$$d = 2t$$

distance he walked (in miles)   time he walked (in hours)

d = 2t		
t	**d**	**Ordered Pairs**
0	0	(0, 0)
1	2	(1, 2)
2	4	(2, 4)
3	6	(3, 6)

Biologist's Walk

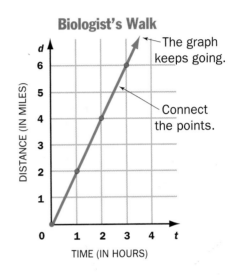

The graph keeps going.

Connect the points.

DISTANCE (IN MILES)

TIME (IN HOURS)

Check for Understanding

Give the coordinates of the point.

1 A   **2** D   **3** E

Name the point for the ordered pair.

4 (1, 4)   **5** $(3, 2\frac{1}{2})$ **6** (0, 5)

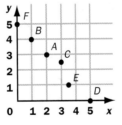

7 Copy and complete the table for the function represented by the equation $y = 2x + 1$.
Then graph the function.

y = 2x + 1				
x	0	1	2	3
y	1	3	■	■

Critical Thinking: Analyze

8 How are the equation, the table, and the graph of the biologist's walking related?

9 Copy the graph titled Biologist's Walk and choose at least two new values for *t*. Graph the points for the times. Are those points on the line? Can you generalize? Explain?

Practice

Name the coordinates of the point.

1 A   **2** C   **3** D

4 F   **5** H   **6** J

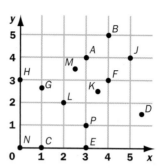

Name the point for the ordered pair.

7 (3, 0)   **8** (4, 5)   **9** $(1, 2\frac{2}{3})$

10 (2, 2)   **11** (3.5, 2.5)   **12** (0, 0)

Copy and complete the table for the function represented by the equation. Then graph the function.

13

d = 4t				
t	0	1	2	3
d	■	■	■	■

14

a = b + 4				
b	0	1	2	3
a	■	■	■	■

15

y = 3x − 2				
x	1	2	3	4
y	■	■	■	■

16

y = 2x + 3				
x	0	1	2	3.5
y	■	■	■	■

17

ℓ = 5w				
w	0	1	2	$2\frac{1}{2}$
ℓ	■	■	■	■

18

y = 4x − 2				
x	1	2	3	4
y	■	■	■	■

19

w = 2ℓ − 1				
ℓ	1	2	4	8
w	■	■	■	■

20

c = 2x + 3				
x	0	2	4	6
c	■	■	■	■

21

p = 4ℓ				
ℓ	3	5	7	9
p	■	■	■	■

MIXED APPLICATIONS

Problem Solving

22 Suppose the equation $d = 14t$ gives the distance d (in meters) that an animal sprints in t seconds. How far does the animal sprint in 10 seconds?

23 Alan bought 4 wildlife books for $10.99 each and 2 posters for $6.25 each. How much change should he get from three $20 bills?

24 Complete the table. Then, write an equation to tell how many squares there are for any age. Tell what the variables in your equation represent.

Age (in days)	1	2	3	4	5
Number of Squares	2	6	10	■	■

25 **Data Point** Count the number of breaths you take in 1, 2, and 3 minutes. Record your results in a table and a graph.

Four in a Row Game!

Draw a coordinate grid like the one at the right.

Form two teams.

You will need
- *graph paper*
- *colored pencils or pens*

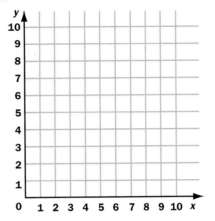

Play the Game

▶ Each team chooses a color. The two teams take turns naming ordered pairs and then circling the point with their color.

▶ The first team to graph four ordered pairs in a row horizontally, vertically, or diagonally wins. (It does not count if you have skipped a point.)

What strategies did you use for choosing ordered pairs to name?

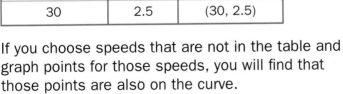

more to explore

Curved Graphs

Not all graphs are straight lines. Let r represent the speed of a jeep in miles per hour and t represent the time in hours that it would take to drive 75 miles at that speed. The graph of the equation $t = \frac{75}{r}$ is not a straight line.

Speed (in mi per hour)	Time (in hours)	Ordered Pairs
10	7.5	(10, 7.5)
15	5	(15, 5)
25	3	(25, 3)
30	2.5	(30, 2.5)

75-Mile Trip

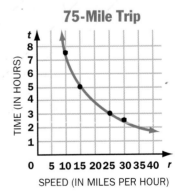

If you choose speeds that are not in the table and graph points for those speeds, you will find that those points are also on the curve.

Make a table and a graph for the equation.

1 $y = 2x^2$ **2** $y = x^2 + 1$ **3** $y = 2x^2 + 1$ **4** $y = 10/x$

Extra Practice, page 608

Describe Change

Even if there are no numbers on the axes, you can tell a story about what a graph shows. This sketch of a graph shows how the height of one of the corn plants in a science experiment depends on its age.

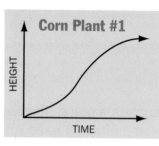

Here is one story about this graph.

Corn Plant #1 grew steadily until just before it reached its greatest height. Then, it started growing more and more slowly until it stopped growing altogether.

More Examples

A The graph shows the amount of water that flows into a tub per minute.

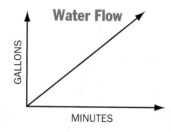

B Sketch a graph to show how your height depends on your age.

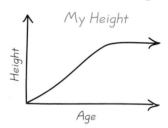

Check for Understanding
Tell a story about what the graph shows.

1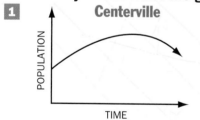

2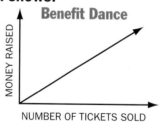

3

4 Sketch a graph showing how a dog's weight might depend on its age. Put the age of the dog on the horizontal axis.

Critical Thinking: Analyze

5 **Journal** What if you sketched a graph to show how yesterday's temperature depended on the time of day. Describe how the graph would look. Would it be a straight line? Why or why not?

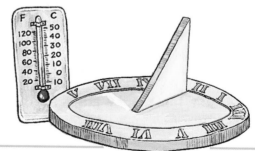

Practice

Tell a story about what the graph shows.

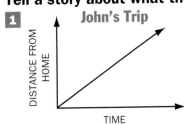

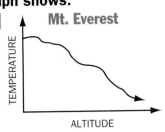

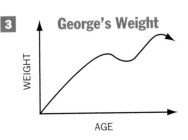

Sketch a graph showing how the quantity on the vertical axis might depend on the quantity on the horizontal axis.

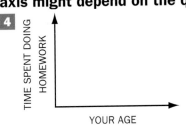

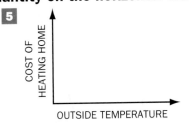

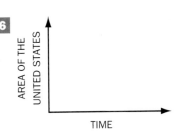

MIXED APPLICATIONS
Problem Solving

7 Suppose two thirds of the area of a garden is treated with fertilizer and one third is not. Of the area treated with fertilizer, you treat half with fertilizer A and half with fertilizer B. What fraction of the total area of the garden is treated with fertilizer A?

8 A mudflow traveled to a bridge 15 miles downstream from Mount St. Helens by 11:30 A.M. What time should it get to a logging camp $27\frac{1}{2}$ miles from the volcano?
SEE INFOBIT.

INFOBIT
Mudflows from the Mount St. Helens eruption traveled at 7 feet per second, or about 5 miles per hour, tearing apart bridges and destroying everything in their path.

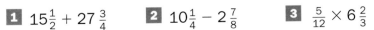

mixed review • test preparation

1 $15\frac{1}{2} + 27\frac{3}{4}$ **2** $10\frac{1}{4} - 2\frac{7}{8}$ **3** $\frac{5}{12} \times 6\frac{2}{3}$ **4** $8\frac{2}{5} \div 1\frac{1}{2}$

Find the range, mean, median, and mode of the data. Round to the nearest tenth if necessary.

5 0, 0, 1, 1, 2, 2, 2, 3, 3, 4, 4   **6** 9.7, 9.8, 9.2, 9.9, 8.9, 8.7, 8.8

Use Graphs to Solve Problems

Scientists usually measure temperature in degrees Celsius. To understand what a Celsius temperature means, you can use the following formula.

$$F = (1.8 \times C) + 32$$

In this formula, F is the Fahrenheit temperature and C is the Celsius temperature. For example, 0 degrees Celsius (written 0°C) is equivalent to 32 degrees Fahrenheit (written 32°F).

A **formula** is an equation with at least two variables. A formula shows how one variable depends on one or more other variables.

You can make a graph of the relationship between Celsius temperatures and Fahrenheit temperatures. First make a table and then graph the results.

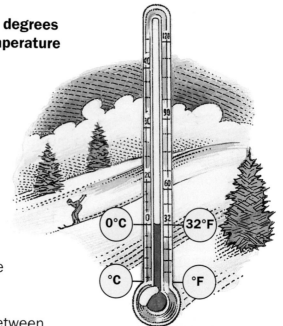

Check Out the Glossary
formula
See page 643.

$F = (1.8 \times C) + 32$	
C	**F**
20	68
30	86
40	104

Now, you can use the graph as well as the formula to find the Fahrenheit temperature for a given Celsius temperature.

What if the temperature outside is 6°C. Start at 6°C on the horizontal axis and move up to the graphed line. Then, move across to the vertical axis. The temperature outside is about 42°F or 43°F.

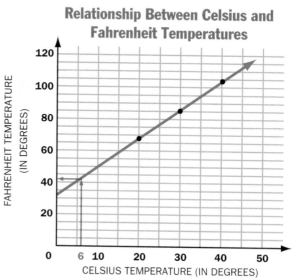

Relationship Between Celsius and Fahrenheit Temperatures

Talk It Over

▶ Describe the graph of the function relating Fahrenheit and Celsius temperatures.

▶ **What if** the temperature outside is 14°C. How could you use the graph to find the Fahrenheit temperature?

What is the Celsius temperature when the temperature outside is 63°F?

You can also use the graph of the formula $F = (1.8 \times C) + 32$ to find the Celsius temperature when you know the Fahrenheit temperature.

Find 63°F on the vertical axis and move across to the graphed line. Then, move down to find the value on the horizontal axis. It is about 17°C or 18°C.

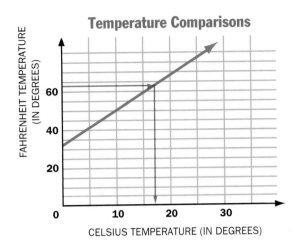

Temperature Comparisons

More Examples

A Find the time traveled when you've gone 100 mi at 40 mi per hour.

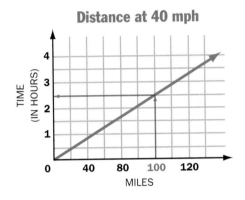

Distance at 40 mph

You traveled $2\frac{1}{2}$ hours.

B Suppose you are paid $8.50 an hour. Find about how many hours you would have to work to earn $35.

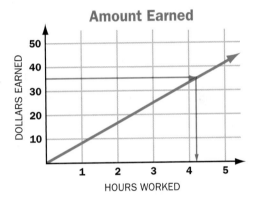

Amount Earned

You have to work about 4 hours.

Check for Understanding

A plane's Mach (mahk) number is the ratio of the speed of the plane to the speed of sound at the plane's altitude. Use the graph for ex. 1–2.

1 What is the Mach number for a plane flying at 1,300 miles per hour?

2 What is the approximate speed of a plane flying at Mach number 2.5?

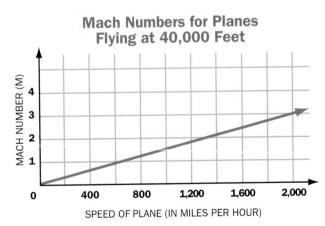

Mach Numbers for Planes Flying at 40,000 Feet

Critical Thinking: Analyze

3 Given the Celsius temperature, what is an advantage of finding the Fahrenheit temperature on the graph at the top of this page rather than using the formula? What is a disadvantage?

Turn the page for Practice.

Practice

A scientist is planning a new rectangular work space. She has 100 m of movable walls that she can arrange for her space. The graph shows how the various possible lengths and widths of her space are related.

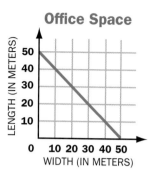

Office Space

Use the graph above to find the length for each width.

1 10 m   **2** 20 m   **3** 25 m   **4** 15 m   **5** 22 m

Use the graph above to find the width for each length.

6 30 m   **7** 35 m   **8** 45 m   **9** 5 m   **10** 19 m

Use the graph at the right for ex. 11–18.
Find the sales tax for each given price.

11 $1.50   **12** $2.50

13 $3.25   **14** $3.75

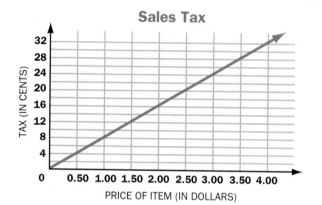

Sales Tax

Find the price for each given tax.

15 16 cents   **16** 28 cents

17 30 cents   **18** 14 cents

Scientists measured water pressure at different depths below sea level. Use their table to solve problems 19–21.

19 Graph the relationship between depth and water pressure.

20 Find the pressure at a depth of 20 ft.

21 At what depth is the pressure 5 lb per square inch?

Depth (in feet below sea level)	Water Pressure (in pounds per square inch)
5	2.25
10	4.5
15	6.75

22 Suppose you plan to use movable walls to build a rectangular lab 7 m wide. If F is the total length of the walls available and L is the length of the lab, then $F = 2L + 14$. Make a table and a graph for this relationship.

Use the graph you made for problem 22 to find the length of the office when the total length of the walls available is:

23 30 m.   **24** 36 m.   **25** 40 m.   **26** 48 m.

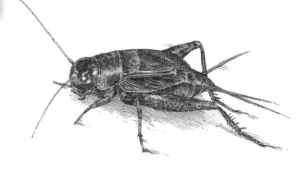

27 The number of times a cricket chirps per minute depends on the air temperature. If C is the Celsius temperature and N is the number of chirps per minute, then N is approximately $7C - 30$. Make a graph of the equation $N = 7C - 30$, with C on the horizontal axis and N on the vertical axis, for temperatures between 10°C and 30°C.

28 Use your graph from problem 27 to find the number of chirps per minute when the temperature is:
a. 15°C   **b.** 20°C   **c.** 25°C

29 Use your graph from problem 27 to estimate the temperature when there is this number of chirps per minute:
a. 90   **b.** 130   **c.** 150

30 Do you think you can use the equation in problem 27 to estimate the number of chirps when the temperature is 300°C? Explain.

31 **Logical reasoning** A clock strikes 6 times in 5 seconds. How many times will it strike in 10 seconds? Explain.

32 A rectangular science lab in a middle school is 10.8 meters wide and 16.5 meters long. What is the perimeter of the lab?

33 **Spatial reasoning** How many triangles are in the figure?

34 **Data Point** Use the Databank on page 639 to make a graph about computer use. Write at least two statements based on your graph.

35 **Write a problem** about a situation that could be described using the equation $y = 3x + 2$. Graph the equation and ask another student to use your graph to solve your problem.

mixed review • test preparation

1 $438{,}297 \div 1{,}000$ **2** $29{,}366 \times 100$ **3** $50.273 \times 10{,}000$ **4** $0.0638 \div 100$

Classify each polygon in as many ways as you can.

5   **6**    **7**   **8**

Solve Simpler Problems

LEARN

Read Suppose 8 scientists meet at a conference and each scientist shakes hands with every other scientist. How many handshakes will there be?

Plan One way to solve this problem is to solve simpler problems. Decide how many handshakes there are when there are fewer scientists and then generalize.

Solve Draw pictures to represent the problem for 2, 3, 4, and 5 scientists. Make a table to organize the results.

Number of Scientists	2	3	4	5
Number of Handshakes	1	3	6	10

+2 +3 +4

2 scientists
1 handshake

3 scientists
3 handshakes

The number of handshakes increases by 1 more each time. Extend the table using this rule.

Scientists	2	3	4	5	6	7	8
Handshakes	1	3	6	10	15	21	28

+2 +3 +4 +5 +6 +7

4 scientists
6 handshakes

5 scientists
10 handshakes

Look Back How could you solve this problem in a different way?

CHECK

Check for Understanding

1 **What if** there were 9 scientists. How many handshakes would there be if each of the scientists shook hands with each other?

Critical Thinking: Analyze

2 How is the second table above related to the sums 1 + 2, 1 + 2 + 3, 1 + 2 + 3 + 4, and so on?

MIXED APPLICATIONS

Problem Solving

1 How many diagonals does a decagon have? (Hint: Try solving a simpler problem.)

2 Find the ones digit of 9^{47}. (Hint: Find the ones digit of 9^1, 9^2, 9^3, 9^4 and look for a pattern.)

3 On the Richter scale, an earthquake of magnitude 7 is ten times as strong as one with magnitude 6. One of magnitude 6.4 is 10 times as strong as one of magnitude 5.4, and so on. About how many times as strong was the earthquake in Mexico City than the one in Whittier, California?

Magnitude of Some Major Earthquakes on the Richter Scale		
1964	Anchorage, AK	8.6
1971	San Fernando Valley, CA	6.5
1981	Samoa Islands	7.0
1985	Mexico City, Mexico	8.1
1987	Whittier, CA	6.1
1994	Northridge, CA	6.8
1995	Kobe, Japan	7.2

4 The freezing point of water is 0°C. Use $F = (1.8 \times C) + 32$ to find the freezing point of water in degrees Fahrenheit.

5 The lighting arrangement in the Science Museum has 10 rows of lights. There is 1 light in the first row, and there are 3 lights in the second row. Each row has two more lights than the row before it. How many lights are there in all 10 rows?

6 **READING ARITHMETIC WRITING** **Sequence of Events** There are 30 people in a bus. One third get off at the Inverness Museum. Half that number get on. At the next stop, $\frac{2}{5}$ of the people on the bus get off. List the sequence of events. What fraction of the original number is left on the bus?

7 The state using the most water per resident in a recent year was Idaho. The people in Idaho used a total of 19,700,000,000 gallons per day. The population of Idaho is about 1 million. About how many gallons per day per resident was that?
a. 20   **b.** 200
c. 20,000   **d.** 20,000,000

8 **Write a problem** that can be solved by first solving a simpler problem. Solve it. Then give it to another student to solve.

9 About how much soil will be washed from the surface of the United States from now until you graduate from the eighth grade? SEE INFOBIT.

INFOBIT
Much soil erosion in the United States results from clearing of land and excessive grazing by farm animals. Three billion metric tons of soil are washed away each year.

1 The table below shows the number of toothpicks it takes to make these arrangements.

Complete the table. Then describe the relationship shown in the table in words.

Number of Squares	1	2	3	4	5	6
Number of Toothpicks	4	7	10	■	■	■

2 For problem 1, let s represent the number of squares. Let n represent the number of toothpicks. Write an equation that shows the relationship between s and n.

3 The function $d = 5t$ gives the distance in miles that something traveling 5 miles per hour will go in t hours. Complete the function table and then graph the function.

$d = 5t$		
Input: t		Output: $d = 5t$
2		■
3		■
5		■

The graph at the right shows the cost of renting a video camera when there is a basic charge of \$10 and an additional hourly fee of \$2.

4 What is the cost of renting a video camera for 3 hours? for 4 hours?

5 How long can the video camera be rented for \$20? for \$26?

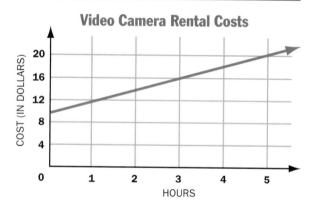

Video Camera Rental Costs

Tell a story about what the graph shows.

6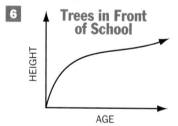

Trees in Front of School

7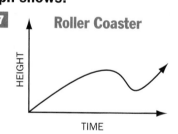

Roller Coaster

8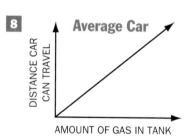

Average Car

9 Find the ones digit of 4^{31}. (Hint: Find the ones digits of 4^1, 4^2, 4^3, 4^4, and 4^5, and look for a pattern.)

10 *Journal* Describe how you would make the graph of the function $A = 12.95n$, where n is the number of pairs of T-shirts you are buying for \$12.95 each and A is the cost. Make the graph.

developing technology sense

MATH CONNECTION

Use Graphs to Make Predictions

Weather balloons gather data about the upper atmosphere as they rise at a rate of about 3 miles per hour. If one balloon is released at sea level and another at 2 miles above sea level, how high will they be after 3 hours? 5 hours?

You can link a table and a graph on a computer to see both numerical and visual representations of data. This makes it easier to make predictions and solve problems.

Use the table tool to complete the spreadsheet below. Link the spreadsheet to a line graph to display the data.

Rate of Rise*	Number of Hours	Altitude**	
		Balloon 1	Balloon 2
3	0	0	2
3	1	3	5
3	2	6	8
3	3	9	11
3	4	12	14
3	5	15	17
3	6	18	20

*In miles per hour   **In miles

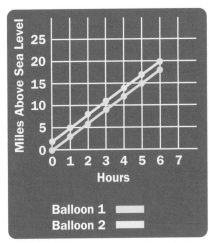

▶ What formula can you use to find the altitude of balloon 1? balloon 2?

▶ Complete the spreadsheet and graph your results.

1 Suppose both balloons are designed to burst when they reach a height of 17 miles. Use the graph to find how long they will rise before bursting.

2 **What if** the balloons were redesigned to rise at a slower rate of 2 miles per hour. Enter this data in the spreadsheet. How did the spreadsheet and graph change?

Critical Thinking: Generalize   **Explain your reasoning.**

3 How does using a computer help you make predictions? What other kinds of predictions could computers be used for?

Introduction to Algebra   **357**

Bouncing Balls

When you drop a ball, such as a tennis ball, how high does it bounce? In this activity, you will work in teams to answer that question.

Prepare ▶ Tape pieces of paper to a wall from the floor to about 2 meters high. Then, tape a tape measure over the paper with the 0 mark touching the floor and the tape measure extending to 2 meters high.

Drop Ball ▶ Hold a ball at the 50-centimeter mark on the paper. Drop it—do not throw it.

Mark Heights ▶ Have a second person mark on the paper the highest point the ball reaches after the first bounce.

▶ Have a third person mark on the paper the highest point the ball reaches after the second bounce.

▶ Take turns dropping the ball from the 50-centimeter mark and marking the heights after the first bounce and after the second bounce. Continue until you have dropped the ball a total of five times.

Measure ▶ Measure the heights of all the marks.

Organize Data ▶ Find the mean height that the ball bounces after the first bounce. Then, find the mean height after the second bounce.

DECISION MAKING

Drop the Ball

1 Predict how high the ball would bounce if dropped from 100, 150, and 200 cm. Test your predictions. Repeat the experiment, but drop the ball five times each from 100, 150, and 200 cm.

2 Make two tables like the ones below to record your mean heights.

First Bounce		Second Bounce	
Drop Height	**Mean Height**	**Drop Height**	**Mean Height**
50 cm		50 cm	
100 cm		100 cm	
150 cm		150 cm	
200 cm		200 cm	

3 Make a double-line graph to show your mean bouncing heights for the first two bounces. Make the horizontal axis the ball drop heights.

4 Use the graph to predict how high the ball would bounce on the first bounce and second bounce if it were dropped from 300 cm and 400 cm.

Report Your Findings

5 Prepare a report on what you learned. Do the following:

▶ Make tables showing the mean heights after the ball bounces.

▶ Graph your results and write a paragraph comparing the results.

▶ Predict, based on your graph, ball bouncing heights from drop heights of 300 and 400 cm.

6 Compare your report with the reports of other teams.

▶ How do your bounce heights compare?

Revise your work.
▶ Did you include all the data you needed and check all your calculations?
▶ Did you give reasons to support your predictions?
▶ Did you proofread and edit your report carefully?

MORE TO INVESTIGATE

PREDICT how high the ball would bounce on the third bounce and the fourth bounce from various heights, based on your data. Experiment to test your predictions.

EXPLORE how high other balls, such as a golf ball or a basketball, would bounce.

FIND how high a basketball is supposed to bounce if it is to be used in a professional game.

Solve Equations

Even though most people don't realize it, they solve for unknowns in equations every day.

Look at this equation: $m + 7 = 23$

You can use models to solve the equation.

Note: The equal sign in an equation means that both sides must balance, or be equal.

 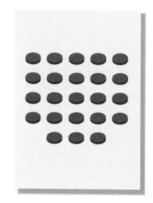

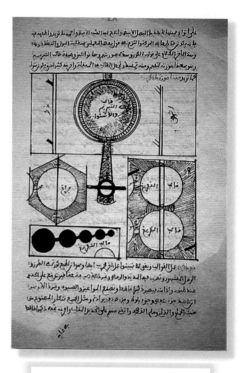

Think: How many counters need to be in cup m so that both sides of the equation represent the same number?

Work Together

Work with a partner. Decide how you can use cups and counters to solve each equation and record your work.

Cultural Note

In Arabic countries in the tenth century, solving equations was known as the "science of restoration and balancing." The Arabic word for restoration is *al-jabr*, from which the word *algebra* is derived.

You will need
- *cups*
- *counters*

Addition equations: $n + 8 = 22$ $P + 4 = 17$ $24 = x + 5$

Multiplication equations: $2d = 24$ $3s = 21$ $34 = 2L$

Talk It Over

▶ Explain your methods for solving the addition equations.

▶ Explain how you can use cups and counters to solve multiplication equations.

Make Connections

Here is how one group recorded what they did to find **solutions** for the two equations: $n + 8 = 22$ and $2d = 24$.

  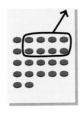  

$$n + 8 = 22 \qquad\qquad n + 8 - 8 = n \qquad\qquad 22 - 8 = 14 \qquad n = 14$$

 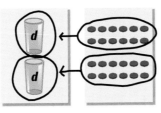 

$$2d = 24 \qquad\qquad 2d \div 2 = d \qquad\qquad 24 \div 2 = 12 \qquad d = 12$$

▶ Why is $n + 8 - 8 = n$ no matter what number n is?

▶ Why is $2d \div 2 = d$ no matter what number d is?

> **Check Out the Glossary**
> solution
> See page 643.

Check for Understanding

Solve the equation using models.

1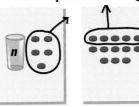

$$n + 5 = 13$$

2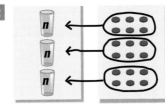

$$3n = 18$$

3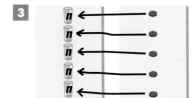

$$5n = 5$$

4 $x + 3 = 22$ **5** $2n = 28$ **6** $25 = d + 4$ **7** $27 = 3y$

8 $21 = n + 6$ **9** $4a = 24$ **10** $y + 13 = 17$ **11** $22 = 2b$

Critical Thinking: Analyze

12 Some equations have more than one solution. Give at least three solutions of the equation $0x = 0$.

13 Give an example of an equation with no solution.

Turn the page for Practice.

Practice

Write the equation for the picture and solve it.

1

2

3

4

5

6

Solve the equation. Use any method.

7 $n + 4 = 12$ **8** $21 = x + 8$ **9** $a + 5 = 21$ **10** $23 = y + 5$

11 $2m = 26$ **12** $30 = 3c$ **13** $4x = 28$ **14** $42 = 3a$

15 $b + 6 = 17$ **16** $3t = 51$ **17** $52 = 4r$ **18** $34 = n + 9$

19 $x + 20 = 30$ **20** $63 = 7t$ **21** $5s = 150$ **22** $240 = 6y$

23 $4x = 160$ **24** $9s = 900$ **25** $m + 8 = 52$ **26** $100 = 5D$

27 $39 = 3n$ **28** $f + 32 = 64$ **29** $73 = g + 55$ **30** $2n = 50$

Use mental math to solve the equation. Explain your methods.

31 $x + 3 = 7$ **32** $2y = 16$ **33** $14 = c + 9$ **34** $45 = 5a$

35 $41 = n + 31$ **36** $3y = 60$ **37** $z + 29 = 32$ **38** $20m = 800$

Choose the equation for which the value of *n* is a solution.

39 $n = 3$ **a.** $4n = 7$ **b.** $3n = 9$ **c.** $3n = 12$

40 $n = 12$ **a.** $2n = 12$ **b.** $n - 2 = 10$ **c.** $6n = 18$

41 $n = 10$ **a.** $2n + 1 = 21$ **b.** $2n + 1 = 20$ **c.** $2n = 18$

42 $n = 100$ **a.** $6n + n = 70$ **b.** $6n + n = 700$ **c.** $6n + n = 600$

43 $n = 3$ **a.** $n^2 = 9$ **b.** $2n = 9$ **c.** $n + n = 9$

44 A plane uses fuel at a rate of $8\frac{1}{2}$ gal per hour. There are 17 gal left. How long will the fuel last?

45 Suppose you bought a book for $7.37, including tax. If the tax was $0.42, how much did the book cost?

46 **Write a problem** that can be solved using the equation $12d = 24$.

47 The average adult has about 5 quarts of blood. How many gallons is that?

48 **Make a decision** Suppose a family is planning a trip and they think they will drive about 1,200 miles. If the gas they use will cost about $1.30 per gallon and their car gets about 30 miles to the gallon, how much money should they take for gas?

49 **Spatial visualization** Which circle has a greater diameter? Measure to make sure.

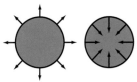

50 The area A of a rectangle is given by the formula $A = \ell w$, in which ℓ is its length and w is its width. Suppose the area of a rectangle is 144 sq in. and its width is 9 in. Find its length.

51 Mark agrees to paint part of the garage floor each day. He always paints $\frac{1}{2}$ of what is left, or at least 1 square foot, whichever is greater. How long will it take him to paint the 25-by-20-ft garage?

more to explore

Here is how you can solve the equation $2m + 3 = 15$ using models.

$2m + 3 = 15$

$2m + 3 - 3 = 15 - 3$

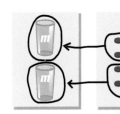

$2m = 12 \qquad m = 6$

Solve the equation using any method.

1 $2x + 5 = 25$ **2** $3b + 8 = 23$ **3** $17 = 2b + 3$ **4** $4y + 5 = 21$

5 $3a + 6 = 24$ **6** $19 = 3z + 7$ **7** $4s + 10 = 18$ **8** $23 = 2n + 5$

9 $4n + 12 = 28$ **10** $28 + 9n = 100$ **11** $64 = 8n + 8$ **12** $25 = 3n + 4$

Solve Addition and Subtraction Equations

How do you get a pet to stand on a scale to be weighed? When a veterinarian needs to weigh a small kitten, she first weighs a cardboard box. The box weighs 6 ounces when empty and 25 ounces with the kitten inside. What does the kitten weigh?

Date	Weight in Ounces of Kitten and Box	Weight in Ounces of Kitten
Jan. 13	25	
Feb. 13	28.25	

IN THE WORKPLACE

Sherilyn Brannon,
Veterinarian, Boston, MA

You can use an addition equation to solve the problem. On January 13:

$$k + 6 = 25$$

weight of the kitten ⬈   ⬈ weight of the kitten and the box

Check Out the Glossary
inverse operations
See page 643.

In the last lesson you used models to help you solve equations. Here is another method you can use.

$$k + 6 = 25$$

$$k + 6 - 6 = 25 - 6$$ **Subtracting 6 from *both sides* of the equation keeps the equation balanced.**

$$k = 19$$ **Note:** Adding and subtracting the same number are **inverse operations:** they undo each other.

The kitten weighed 19 ounces on January 13.

Check your answer by substituting 19 for *k:*
$$k + 6 = 25$$
$$19 + 6 = 25$$
$$25 = 25 \checkmark$$

Talk It Over

▶ Why does subtracting 6 from *both sides* of the equal sign keep the equation balanced?

▶ Why can $k + 6 - 6 = 25 - 6$ be simplified to $k = 19$?

A veterinarian weighs a red panda cub and reports any change in the cub's weight to the biologist. The veterinarian reports that the cub has lost 2.75 kg since the last checkup. If the cub weighs 32 kg now, how much did it weigh the last time?

You can use a subtraction equation to solve the problem. Let y represent the cub's weight at the last checkup.

$$y - 2.75 = 32$$

To find the value of y, undo the subtraction.

$$y - 2.75 = 32$$

$$y - 2.75 + 2.75 = 32 + 2.75$$ **Adding 2.75 to both sides of the equation keeps the equation balanced.**

$$y = 34.75$$

Check your answer by substituting 34.75 for y:

$$y - 2.75 = 32$$
$$34.75 - 2.75 = 32$$
$$32 = 32 \checkmark$$

The cub weighed 34.75 kg last time.

More Examples

A Solve: $24.8 = m - 15.2$

$$24.8 + 15.2 = m - 15.2 + 15.2$$

$$40 = m$$

Check: $24.8 = m - 15.2$
$$24.8 = 40 - 15.2$$
$$24.8 = 24.8 \checkmark$$

B Solve: $t + \frac{3}{4} = 6$

$$t + \frac{3}{4} - \frac{3}{4} = 6 - \frac{3}{4}$$

$$t = 5\frac{1}{4}$$

Check: $t + \frac{3}{4} = 6$
$$5\frac{1}{4} + \frac{3}{4} = 6$$
$$6 = 6 \checkmark$$

Check for Understanding
Solve the equation. Check your solution.

1 $x + 5 = 21$

2 $t - 3 = 11$

3 $m + 1.6 = 22.5$

4 $w - 8.2 = 29.04$

5 $z - 4\frac{2}{3} = 6\frac{1}{2}$

6 $x + 1\frac{1}{2} = 16$

Critical Thinking: Analyze

7 Journal How are solving addition equations and subtraction equations alike? How are they different?

Turn the page for Practice.
Introduction to Algebra **365**

Practice

Solve the equation. Check your solution.

1 $n + 7 = 32$ **2** $r + 89 = 101$ **3** $n - 6.2 = 10.1$ **4** $t + 4.9 = 12$

5 $t - 8 = 13$ **6** $m - 12 = 71$ **7** $n - 2.7 = 12.8$ **8** $v + 18 = 37$

9 $r + 17 = 45$ **10** $t - 35 = 16$ **11** $w + 21.5 = 32.6$ **12** $y - 50 = 30$

13 $h + 200 = 470$ **14** $s - \frac{1}{2} = 16$ **15** $w = 25 + 32$ **16** $43 = n + 16$

17 $x + 26.7 = 102.4$ **18** $45 - 17 = t$ **19** $147 = x - 238$ **20** $21 = h - \frac{3}{5}$

Without solving the equation, tell whether the solution is greater than 57, less than 57, or equal to 57.

21 $x + 5 = 57$ **22** $n - 12 = 57$ **23** $57 = y + 28$

24 $57 = t - 25$ **25** $v - 57 = 0$ **26** $b - 57 = 57$

Solve. For ex. 27–34 use mental math.

27 $n + 7 = 12$ **28** $t - 8 = 13$ **29** $h + 200 = 470$ **30** $y - 50 = 30$

31 $n - 12 = 71$ **32** $r + 89 = 101$ **33** $w - 65 = 208$ **34** $v + 18 = 37$

35 If x is 4, what is $x + 10$?   **36** If $y - 3$ is 4, what is y?

37 If $p + 5$ is 20, what is p?   **38** If n is 18, what is $n - 9$?

Copy and complete the table.

Rule: $y = x - 5$	
x	**y**
9	4
39 7.75	■
40 88	■
41 5,053	■

Rule: $y = x + 21.5$	
x	**y**
7	28.5
42 10.5	■
43 25	■
44 83.6	■

⋯⋯⋯⋯⋯⋯⋯⋯⋯⋯ **Make It Right** ⋯⋯⋯⋯⋯⋯⋯⋯⋯⋯

45 Here is how Donna solved $x + 236 = 281$. Explain what the error is and correct it.

$$x + 236 = 281$$
$$x + 236 - 236 = 281 + 236$$

Problem Solving

46 Kara placed her two hamsters, Rocky and Millie, on a balance scale as shown at the right. She discovered that if she added $\frac{5}{8}$ oz to Millie's side, the scale balanced. If Rocky weighs $4\frac{1}{4}$ oz, find Millie's weight.

47 On a science field trip, Trina discovered that her 1-qt collecting pail could hold 67 small rock samples. About how many rock samples can she put in the new 5-gal storage bucket she keeps at home?

48 In a triangle, the sum of the measures of two angles is 123°. Find the measure of the third angle. Write an equation to solve.

49 **Write a problem** that can be solved by writing and solving an equation. Solve your problem and give it to others to solve.

50 **Data Point** Survey at least ten students. Ask them to name as many careers that require an understanding of science as they can. Show your data in a graph.

Cultural Connection Pascal's Triangle

Pascal's Triangle, shown below, was named after the French mathematician Blaise Pascal (1623–1662). However, more than 300 years earlier it appeared in the work of the Chinese scholar Chu Shih-chieh (jü-shi(ə)r-jē-e).

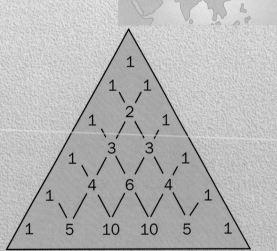

1 What patterns do you see in Pascal's triangle?

2 Except for the 1's, each number in the triangle is the sum of the two numbers above it. Using this data, find the next two rows of Pascal's triangle.

3 Find the sum of the numbers in each of the first 6 rows across. What patterns do you see? Predict the sum of the numbers in the next 3 rows.

Solve Multiplication and Division Equations

The Mars Pathfinder *Sojourner* was able to move at about 25 meters per hour. How can you represent how far the *Sojourner* could go in *t* hours? How long would it take the *Sojourner* to travel 225 meters?

Mars Pathfinder *Sojourner*

You can use a multiplication equation to represent the relationship between the distance *Sojourner* travels and the time.

Let *d* represent the distance, in meters, the *Sojourner* could go in *t* hours. Then

$$d = 25t$$

When $d = 225$, the equation becomes

$$225 = 25t$$

> ### Cultural Note
> The planet Mars was named after Mars, the ancient Roman god of war, because it appears to be slightly reddish in the night sky.

In the last lesson, you used inverse operations to help you solve addition and subtraction equations. You can also use inverse operations to help you solve multiplication and division equations.

$$225 = 25t$$

$$225 \div 25 = 25t \div 25$$ **Dividing both sides of the equation by 25 keeps**
$$9 = t$$ **the equation balanced.**

It would take *Sojourner* 9 hours to travel 225 meters.

Check your answer by substituting 9 for *t*:
$$225 = 25t$$
$$225 = 25 \times 9$$
$$225 = 225 \checkmark$$

Talk It Over

▶ Why does dividing *both* sides of the equation by 25 keep the equation balanced?

▶ How long would it take *Sojourner* to go 60 meters? Use the equation $d = 25t$ to write an equation to find out. Solve the equation and answer the question.

You can find the approximate weight of an object on the moon by dividing its weight on Earth by 6. How can you represent this relationship? How much would an object that weighs 570 pounds on the moon weigh on Earth?

Many thousands of pounds of scientific equipment have been left on the moon.

You can use a division equation to solve the problem. Let m represent the weight of an object on the moon in pounds and e represent its weight on Earth in pounds.

Then $e \div 6 = m$

When $m = 570$, the equation becomes

$$e \div 6 = 570$$

To find the weight of an object on Earth, find the value of e.

$$e \div 6 = 570$$
$$e \div 6 \times 6 = 570 \times 6$$
$$e = 3,240$$

Multiplying both sides of the equation by 6 keeps the equation balanced.

The object weighs about 3,420 pounds.

To check your answer, substitute 3,420 for e:

$$e \div 6 = 570$$
$$3,420 \div 6 = 570$$
$$570 = 570 \checkmark$$

More Examples

A **Solve:** $4.2y = 23.1$
$$4.2y \div 4.2 = 23.1 \div 4.2$$
$$y = 5.5$$

B **Solve:** $\frac{x}{5} = \frac{2}{3}$
$$\frac{x}{5} \times 5 = \frac{2}{3} \times 5$$
$$x = \frac{2}{3} \times 5$$
$$x = \frac{10}{3} = 3\frac{1}{3}$$

Check for Understanding

Solve the equation. Check your solution.

1 $4y = 48$ **2** $n \times 7 = 63$ **3** $n \div 5 = 9$ **4** $6y = 6$

5 $\frac{a}{6} = 2.5$ **6** $11.7 = 1.3n$ **7** $x \div 1.5 = 3.45$ **8** $\frac{x}{250} = 5$

Critical Thinking: Analyze

9 Compare solving addition and subtraction equations to solving multiplication and division equations. How are they alike? different?

Turn the page for Practice. ➡

Introduction to Algebra   **369**

Practice

Solve the equation. Check your solution.

1 $5x = 60$ **2** $6z = 78$ **3** $45 = 5a$ **4** $7b = 63$

5 $t \div 12 = 5$ **6** $7 = \frac{n}{3}$ **7** $w \div 4 = 9$ **8** $\frac{n}{2} = 4$

9 $t \div \frac{1}{2} = 36$ **10** $1\frac{1}{2}b = 18$ **11** $13 = 3w$ **12** $2z = \frac{1}{2}$

13 $5.4q = 10.8$ **14** $\frac{s}{4.5} = 8.6$ **15** $6y = 44.4$ **16** $f \div 0.2 = 100$

Solve the equation. Tell whether you used mental math, pencil and paper, or a calculator.

17 $3x = 24$ **18** $12a = 210$ **19** $w \div 7 = 3$ **20** $\frac{b}{4} = 2$

21 $345a = 2,760$ **22** $72 \div y = 12$ **23** $45 = 1.5n$ **24** $4.6 = h \div 0.426$

25 If x is 7, what is $7x$? **26** If $5p$ is 20, what is p? **27** If $s \div 6$ is 4, what is s?

Use the table for ex. 28–30. Write and solve an equation to find each amount.

28 the price of a package of beakers

29 the cost of a package of test tubes

30 the price of a petri dish

Science Lab Supplies		
Item	Number	Total Cost
Beakers	4 packages of 6	$55.80
Test tubes	8 packages of 24	$82.00
Petri dishes	8 packages of 30	$48.00

Copy and complete the table.

Rule: $y = 8.3\,x$	
Input x	Output y
31 4	▦
32 2.3	▦
33 ▦	41.5
34 60	▦

Rule: $y = \frac{x}{3}$	
Input x	Output y
35 4.2	▦
36 $2\frac{2}{5}$	▦
37 ▦	11
38 93.6	▦

•••••••••••••••••••••••••••• **Make It Right** ••••••••••••••••••••••••••••

39 Here is how Calvin solved $4x = 28$.
Explain what the error is and correct it.

$4x = 28$
$4x \div 4 = 28$
$x = 28$

40 Luis read in his science book that he could divide the weight of an object on Earth by 6 to determine its weight on the moon. He wrote in his science report that his lunch would weigh $\frac{1}{2}$ lb on the moon. How much does his lunch weigh on Earth?

41 Make a decision Suppose your class is making a terrarium. You need to buy special plant food. At the store a package of nine 8.45-fl oz food packs costs $5.99. A 64-fl oz bottle of the same food costs $5.29. Which would you buy? Explain.

42 Ships use an echo sounder to find ocean depths. The echo sounder measures the time for a sound wave to travel from a ship to the ocean bottom and back. In the equation $d = 750t$, d is the ocean depth in meters and t is a sound wave's time in seconds. If a sound wave travels to the ocean bottom and back in 2.5 seconds, how deep is the ocean beneath the ship?

43 Logical reasoning Sandy had to meet her friend in 3 hours. She biked for 30 minutes, read for 90 minutes, and talked to another friend for 33 minutes. It took her 10 minutes to shower and dress and 15 minutes to get to her friend's house. Which statement is correct?

a. 10 min late   **b.** 10 min early
c. 2 min early   **d.** on time

44 Write a problem called What's My Number?—for example: "I'm thinking of a number. When it is multiplied by 1.6, the product is 4.8. What is my number?" Solve your problem and give it to others to solve.

--- more to explore ---

Solving Two-Step Equations

You can solve the equations like $3x - 5 = 22$ by undoing one operation at a time.

$$3x - 5 = 22$$
$$3x - 5 + 5 = 22 + 5 \quad \text{Adding 5 to \textit{both sides} of the equation keeps the}$$
$$3x = 27 \quad \text{equation balanced.}$$
$$3x \div 3 = 27 \div 3 \quad \text{Dividing \textit{both sides} of the equation by 3 keeps the}$$
$$x = 9 \quad \text{equation balanced.}$$

Solve the equation. Check your solution.

1 $3y + 6 = 78$ **2** $4a + 5 = 73$ **3** $172 = 5b - 13$ **4** $6b + 9 = 147$

5 $4x - 27 = 145$ **6** $426 = 7c + 20$ **7** $6t + 32 = 230$ **8** $109 = 13d + 5$

Problem Solvers at Work

Read
Plan
Solve
Look Back

PART 1 Work Backward

●●

**At a virtual-reality center, you are exploring
the ocean in a submarine. At 2:00 P.M., you
are 600 ft below the surface. Ten minutes
before, you were 500 ft deeper. Ten minutes
before that, you were half as deep as you
were at 1:50 P.M.**

Work Together

Solve. Be prepared to explain your methods.

1 **Sequence of Events** List the times
and the positions of the submarine
described in the problem above in reverse
order, starting at 2:00 P.M.

2 To find how deep you were at 1:40 P.M., what do you
need to find first? How deep were you at 1:40 P.M.?

3 Using your answer for problem 2, at what time were
you at your deepest depth?

4 **What if** you were 800 ft below the surface at
2:00 P.M. How deep were you at 1:50 P.M.?

5 Suppose you visit a virtual-reality center that has three
games. The first game costs $1.75 for 2 minutes. The
second costs $2.00 for 4 minutes. The third costs
$5.00 for 5 minutes. The center also offers a package
for $10.00 that allows you to experience all three
games and spend 15 minutes on the Internet.
Which would you choose? Explain.

Corrine made up this problem.

6 Solve Corrine's problem.

7 **Write a problem** that you can solve by working backward.

8 Solve your problem. Then, trade problems with at least three other students.

9 Did you work backward to solve any of the problems written by other students?

10 What was the most interesting problem you solved? Why?

I bought some candy bars at the store for $0.95 each. I paid $7.12 including a tax of $0.47. How many candy bars did I buy?

Corrine Hamilton
Webster Middle School
St. Louis, MO

Turn the page for Practice Strategies. ➡️

Menu

Choose five problems and solve them. Explain your methods.

1 A solar car uses 150 watt-hours of energy to start and 60 watt-hours of energy for each mile it travels. How many watt-hours of energy will it use to start and then drive 100 miles?

2 You have saved $80. You want to purchase a video for $12, two $16.95 CDs, and a book for $5.80. Should you overestimate or underestimate to see if you have enough money? Why? Do you have enough?

3 The rectangle below has a perimeter of 10 cm and is made up of squares that are 1 cm by 1 cm. Which square or squares could you remove that would change the perimeter to 12 cm?

4 Terry used 9 rolls of film to take pictures at a science exhibit. Some rolls had 12 pictures and some had 36. He took 180 pictures altogether. How many rolls of each type did Terry use?

5 A person loses $\frac{1}{300}$ of his or her weight at 6.6 miles above sea level. How many ounces less would a 90-pound person weigh in an airplane 6.6 mi above sea level?

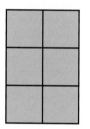

6 Suppose the cost of repairing your TV is $50 plus $35 per hour for labor. If the bill is $155, how many hours are you being charged for?

7  Bamboo can grow as much as 35.4 inches in one day. At that rate, how much could it grow in July?

8 Suppose you bought packs of baseball cards for $3.95 each. If the total, including tax, was $25.12 and the total tax was $1.42, how many packs did you buy?

Choose two problems and solve them. Explain your methods.

9 **Make a decision** Mu Lan wants to plan an exercise program for herself. She wants a variety of activities so she won't get bored. She hopes to exercise between 20 and 30 minutes each day, 5 days a week, and would like to burn between 1,000 and 2,000 calories a week. Plan an exercise program for her.

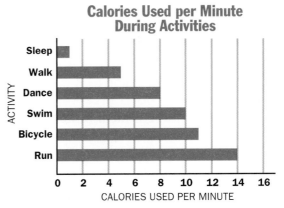

Calories Used per Minute During Activities

10 Put 12 dots in the following figure so that 4 dots do not appear in any vertical, horizontal, or diagonal row. Only 1 dot can be in a box.

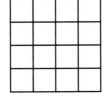

11 Find the number of diagonals in an octagon. (Hint: solve a simpler problem first.)

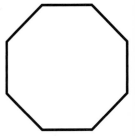

12 **At the Computer** Conduct an experiment. Ask ten people in your class to predict how many times their heart beats in a minute. Then, have each person determine the actual number of beats per minute.

Make a spreadsheet to show each person's estimated and actual data. Then, make a double-bar graph that shows the estimated and actual values for each person. Use your spreadsheet to calculate the average estimate and average number of actual heartbeats per minute. Are they close in value?

Heartbeats per minute		
Name	Predicted Number	Actual Number

chapter review

Language and Mathematics

Complete the sentence. Use a word in the chart. (pages 342–371)

1 A ▇ is a relationship in which one quantity depends on another quantity. It can be represented by a graph, an equation, or a table.

2 An ▇ is a mathematical statement with an equal sign in it.

3 A ▇ is an equation with at least two variables.

4 Adding and subtracting the same numbers are ▇.

5 In (4, 1), the numbers 4 and 1 are the ▇ of the point.

> **Vocabulary**
>
> coordinates
> equation
> formula
> function
> inverse operations
> ordered pair

Concepts and Skills

6 Describe the function in words and with an equation. Tell what each variable in the equation represents. (page 342)

Pattern Number	1	2	3
Picture	• • • • •	• • • • • • • • •	• • • • • • • • • • •
Number of Dots	5	7	9

Tell a story about what the graph shows. (page 348)

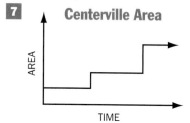

7 Centerville Area (AREA vs. TIME)

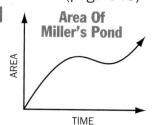

8 Area Of Miller's Pond (AREA vs. TIME)

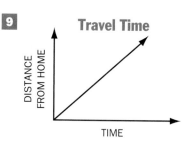

9 Travel Time (DISTANCE FROM HOME vs. TIME)

Solve the equation. Check your solution. (pages 360, 364, 368)

10 $x + 17 = 52$

11 $y - 7 = 3$

12 $5m = 40$

13 $s \div 7 = 3$

14 $68 = 4n$

15 $53 = a + 17$

16 $21 = \frac{L}{4}$

17 $25 = s - 9$

18 $w - 6.3 = 7$

19 $z + 1.6 = 4.2$

20 $2.5b = 10.25$

21 $x + \frac{1}{2} = 13$

22 $2.5n = 75$

23 $104 = x - 38$

24 $\frac{1}{2}b = 4$

25 $b + 2\frac{2}{3} = 8$

26 $4m + 6 = 16$

27 $3p = 6\frac{3}{4}$

28 $9.5 - x = 7.66$

29 $\frac{n}{3} = 24$

376 Chapter 9 Review

Think critically. (page 368)

30 Analyze. Explain what the error is and correct it.

$$2x = 4$$
$$x = 8$$

Generalize. Tell whether the statement is *true* or *false*. Support your answer with an example or explanation. (pages 360, 364, 368)

31 You can solve a multiplication equation by dividing both sides of the equation by the same number.

32 You can solve an addition equation by multiplying both sides of the equation by the same number.

MIXED APPLICATIONS
Problem Solving Pencil & Paper · Calculator · Mental Math

(pages 354, 372)

33 Suppose *t* represents the number of hours your microwave is used, *E* represents the amount of energy in kilowatt-hours that is used in that time, and $E = 1.5t$. Copy and complete the table represented by the equation. Graph the function.

t	0	1	2	3	4
E	0	1.5	■	■	■

34 Ken wants to purchase some scientific equipment from a company in Japan. He knows he can multiply the cost in U.S. dollars by 101 to determine the cost in yen. If the equipment costs 5,656 yen, write an equation to find the cost in U.S. dollars and solve it.

35 Your dog won't stand on the scales, so you weigh yourself with your dog. If you weigh 87 pounds, and together you weigh 103 pounds, how much does your dog weigh?

36 Find the ones digit of 3^{40}. (Hint: Find the ones digit of 3^1, 3^2, 3^3, 3^4, 3^5, 3^6, 3^7, 3^8, and 3^9, and look for a pattern.)

Use this information to solve problems 37–38.
A bottle dropped in a gulf stream current traveled 16 km in 2 hours and 24 km in 3 hours.

37 Make a function table to show the relationship between the distance, *d* (in km), and the time, *t* (in hours), the bottle traveled. Graph the function.

38 **What if** the bottle continued traveling at the same rate. How far would it have traveled in $4\frac{1}{2}$ hours?

39 A bottle holds 56 fl oz. Write the amount using quarts, pints, and cups.

40 You dropped a bottle in the ocean on June 24. Someone found the bottle September 25. How many days elapsed before it was found?

Describe the function in words and with an equation. Tell what each variable in the equation represents.

1

Pattern Number	1	2	3
Number of Dots	2	5	8

2

length	4	8	12	16
width	8	16	24	32

Tell a story about what the graph shows.

3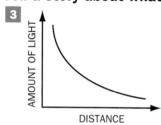

4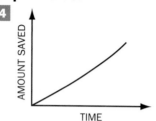

5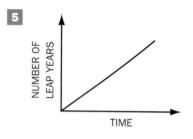

Solve the equation. Check your solution.

6 $g + 23 = 48$ **7** $z - 5 = 19$ **8** $8y = 72$ **9** $t \div 5 = 12$

10 $56 = 7b$ **11** $85 = n - 12$ **12** $13 = \frac{r}{7}$ **13** $36 = q + 11$

14 $c + 2.8 = 15$ **15** $x - 4.5 = 7.6$ **16** $3.2w = 16.64$ **17** $d + \frac{3}{8} = 16$

Solve.

18 A water pump can fill a swimming pool at a rate of 4.5 gal per second. You can write the equation $W = 4.5t$ to represent the total amount of water in the pool, so that W is the total number of gallons and t is the number of seconds the pump is on. Copy and complete the table represented by the equation. Then graph the function.

t	w
1	4.5
2	9
3	▪
4	▪
5	▪

19 A U.S. scientist wants to order some new satellite equipment from an Italian company. She knows she can divide the cost in lire by 1,600 to determine the cost in U.S. dollars. If the equipment costs 640,000 lire, write an equation and solve it to find the cost in U.S. dollars for the equipment.

20 Scientists discovered a city that had been buried for 500 years. The city had 21 streets that went north and south and 17 streets that went east and west. How many intersections were there in this ancient city?

What Did You Learn?

▶ In A, what is the unknown mass? Write an equation for this problem and solve it.

▶ In B, the four unknown masses are the same. What is the unknown mass? Write an equation for this problem and solve it.

▶ Use cups and counters or drawings to show different solution strategies. Include a written explanation.

You will need
- *cups*
- *counters*

•••••••••••••••••• **A Good Answer** ••••••••••••••••••
- includes an algebraic equation for each diagram above with solution.
- includes a written explanation of the use of manipulatives or drawings.

 You may want to place your work in your portfolio.

What Do You Think ?

1 Do you like using a graph to solve a problem? Why or why not?

2 To represent number patterns, do you use:
- models?
- a graph?
- a table?
- other? Explain.

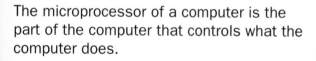

Computers and Binary Numbers

Charles Babbage, an English mathematician, designed the first mechanical computer in 1822. He was not able to build a working model of his design because no one at that time could construct the complicated gears needed.

Babbage's computer was designed to represent numbers the way people ordinarily do, in the base-ten number system.

Even today's computers use transistors that can act as tiny electric switches to represent numbers in the base-two, or *binary,* number system. When a switch is on, it represents 1. When the switch is off, it represents 0. These are the only digits used to represent all numbers in the binary system.

Charles Babbage

The microprocessor of a computer is the part of the computer that controls what the computer does.

▶ What is the advantage of using electric circuits rather than mechanical gears?

▶ Intel's first microprocessor had 2,300 transistors on it. Intel's Pentium microprocessor has over 3.2 million transistors on it. What is the advantage of having more and more transistors on a microprocessor?

Cultural Note

In ancient times, when people ran out of fingers for counting, they used pebbles. In fact, the Latin word for pebble is *calculus,* which means "to calculate." Our word *calculator* comes from this Latin word.

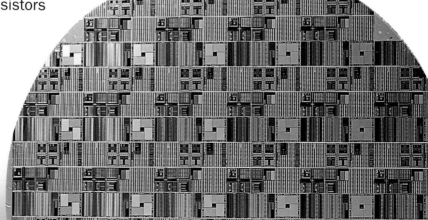

Computer Chip

Count 0, 1, 2, as 0, 1, 10

Notice that in the base-two place value system, only the digits 0 and 1 are used to represent all numbers.

Think: $4 = 1 \times 2^2$
$5 = (1 \times 2^2) + 1$

Look at the patterns in the base-two representations:

Base-10 Name	Base-2 Place Value			
	2^3	2^2	2^1	1
0				0
1				1
2			1	0
3			1	1
4		1	0	0
5		1	0	1
6		1	1	0
7		1	1	1
8	1	0	0	0

1 Write the base-ten number 9 as a base-two number.

2 What is the base-ten name for the base-two number 1100?

3 What is the greatest base-two number you can write with four places? Expand the table above to that number.

At the Computer

Base ten	Base two			
	Eights	Fours	Twos	Ones
13	1	1	0	1

4 Set up a spreadsheet to convert binary numbers with less than five places to decimal numbers.

5 How could you change your spreadsheet to change base-two numbers with less than six places to base-ten numbers?

381

RATIO AND PROPORTION

THEME
Travel and Vacations

Have you ever helped your family plan a trip or a vacation? In this chapter you will see how ratios and proportions help in planning travel time and gas consumption, reading maps, and making best buys.

What Do You Know❓

A park is having a sale on its entrance tickets. If you buy
3 tickets, you can buy a fourth ticket at half price.

1 A family of 8 purchased 8 tickets altogether. What is the ratio
of the discounted tickets to the regular-priced tickets?

2 A tourist guide purchased 20 tickets altogether for his
group members. What is the ratio of the discounted tickets
to the regular-priced tickets? Compare the answer for problem 1
to the answer for problem 2. Are the ratios equal? Why or why not?

3 You can also find ratios in your classroom. What is the ratio
of boys to girls in your class? What other ratios can you write
about the students in your class? Explain what each ratio means.

Write an Advertisement

READING
ARITHMETIC
WRITING

**Advertisements give information about
products or services that you can buy.
They often include descriptions, photos
or illustrations, and prices.**

Beach Family Vacation

3 days 2 nights for
$240

7 days 7 nights for
$490

Meals included.
Whale watching,
windsurfing, or
sailing classes are
$20 per person!

1 Write an advertisement for a vacation you
would like to take. Include all the information
you would want to know.

Vocabulary

ratio, p. 384
equal ratios, p. 388
rate, p. 390
unit rate, p. 391
unit price, p. 394

proportion, p. 400
cross product, p. 400
similar, p. 404
**corresponding
angles,** p. 405

corresponding sides,
p. 405
scale drawing, p. 408
scale, p. 408

Understanding Ratios

Overnight camping trips are a wonderful way for a class to get to know one another. Suppose 12 boys, 15 girls, and 3 adults go on a camping trip to Acadia National Park in Maine. What is the ratio of adults to students?

A **ratio** is a comparison of two numbers.

To find the ratio of adults to students, you need to know the number of adults and the number of students.

Adults = 3
Students = 12 + 15 = 27

Once you know the two numbers, you can write the ratio.

Adults to Students
　3　 to 　27

This means that for every 3 adults there are 27 students.

Other ratios that you can write from the problem are:

Girls to Boys	Adults to Boys	Girls to Students
15 to 12	3 to 12	15 to 27

Work Together

▶ Work in a group to create as many meaningful ratios as you can, using people or objects. Represent each of the ratios with actual objects.

▶ Record the ratios using words and using numbers.

▶ Exchange your ratios with another group. Check each other's ratios.

> **Check Out the Glossary**
> ratio
> 　See page 643.

Talk It Over

▶ What are some ratios you created? How did you write them?

▶ Paul says that the ratio of girls to boys can be written as either 15 to 12 or as 12 to 15. Is he correct? Explain your thinking.

Make Connections

Here are three different ways to express ratios.

campers to tents: $\frac{10}{5}$

girls to all students in class: 14 out of 29

granola bars to campers: 30:15

▶ Express one of the ratios you created in at least three different ways.

Check for Understanding

Use the picture at the right. Write the ratio in three different ways.

1 circles to triangles

2 red figures to blue figures

3 triangles to circles

4 circles to total figures

5 total figures to blue figures

6 red triangles to total red figures

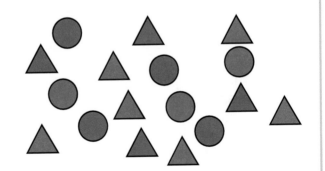

Critical Thinking: Analyze

7 **What if** one of the blue circles changed to a red circle. Which of the ratios in ex. 1–6 would change? How would the ratios change?

8 Suppose the ratio of girls to boys in a group is $\frac{5}{3}$. Would it make sense to write this as a mixed number? Explain.

Turn the page for Practice. ▶

Practice

Write a ratio comparing the shaded region to the unshaded region.
Then write a ratio comparing the shaded region to the whole figure.

1

2

3

4

5

6

Use the survey results to write the ratio in three different ways.

Kind of Hiking Boot	Dexter	L. L. Bean	Rockport	Timberland	Other
Preferred Brand	6	10	8	4	3

7 Other to Dexter

8 L. L. Bean to Rockport

9 Timberland to Dexter

10 L. L. Bean to the total

Draw a picture to show each ratio.

11 The ratio of black squares to red squares on a 10-by-10 grid is 3 to 4.

12 The ratio of green colored pencils to red colored pencils is 5:4.

13 The ratio of chairs to desks is 6 to 5.

14 The ratio of tents to campers is $\frac{1}{2}$.

15 The ratio of apples to oranges is two to seven.

16 The ratio of bottled drinks to canned drinks is three to five.

Write the cost. Use the price list for ex. 17–21.

17 2 thermoses

18 1 T-shirt

19 10 pairs of socks

20 1 pair of shorts

21 How many T-shirts can you buy at Green's for $50?

Green's Outdoor Store

Special Sale

Thermos 1 for $4.99
Socks 5 pairs for $3.50
Shorts 2 pairs for $25.00
T-shirts 3 for $24.00

• **Make It Right** •

22 Phil created the ratio for spoons to forks using the picture. Explain what the error is and correct it.

9 to 7

Problem Solving

Pencil & Paper   Calculator   Mental Math

23 There are 245 sixth graders and 25 adults going on the camping trip. Only 40 people can fit on a bus. How many buses are needed?

24 In the school, there were 562 boys and 578 girls. What is the ratio of girls to total students?

25 A carpenter at the camp is repairing one of the cabins. She needs three boards. Each board is supposed to be $2\frac{1}{2}$ ft long. If she has a board that is 8 ft long, how much extra board will she have?

26 **Make a decision** Sue wants to make lemon bars for her and her 5 friends to share equally during the trip. The recipe can make 30 or 40 bars. If she wants to distribute the bars equally, which quantity should she make so that there are no leftovers?

27 The cost for the camping trip is $30 for students and $60 for adults. If there are 204 students and 37 adults, estimate how much money is needed to pay for the trip.

28 **Write a problem** that has as its answer one of these three ratios: 27:53 or 17:25 or 23:47. Check that the answer is correct. Then give the problem to others to solve.

29 Leta's recycling club collected cans and brought them to a recycling center for a year to benefit a local homeless shelter. She made a table of the amount of money they earned and then donated to the shelter each month. What was the total amount they donated for the year? What was their average monthly donation?

Month	Amount	Month	Amount
Jan.	$14.30	July	$35.70
Feb.	$15.65	Aug.	$38.85
March	$21.10	Sept.	$20.05
April	$9.65	Oct.	$8.00
May	$15.50	Nov.	$11.35
June	$27.85	Dec.	$6.40

more to explore

Combining Ratios

1 What is the ratio of triangles to circles in each picture? Write the ratios in fractional form.

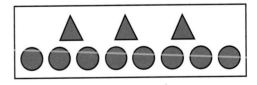

2 What would the ratio of triangles to circles be if you combined the two pictures together?

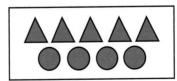

3 How does combining ratios compare to adding fractions?

Equal Ratios

L
E
A
R
N

If you want to go rafting on the Dolores River in Utah, an outfitter will rent you a large raft that can hold your guide, tour leader, and 7 passengers. How many rafts would you need if there were 35 passengers in your tour group?

One way to find the number of needed rafts is to make **equal ratios.** Two ratios are equal if fractions that represent them are equivalent. To find equal ratios, you can multiply or divide the numerator and denominator by the same number.

$$\begin{array}{l}\text{Rafts} \rightarrow \\ \text{Passengers} \rightarrow\end{array} \quad \frac{1}{7} \qquad \frac{1 \times 2}{7 \times 2} = \frac{2}{14} \qquad \frac{1 \times 3}{7 \times 3} = \frac{3}{21} \qquad \frac{1 \times 4}{7 \times 4} = \frac{4}{28} \qquad \frac{1 \times 5}{7 \times 5} = \frac{5}{35}$$

Your tour group will need 5 rafts.

More Examples

Find the missing number to make the ratios equal.

> **Check Out the Glossary**
> **equal ratios**
> See page 643.

A $\frac{3}{4} = \frac{n}{24}$

Think: $\frac{3 \times 6}{4 \times 6} = \frac{18}{24}$

$n = 18$

B $\frac{5}{7} = \frac{40}{b}$

Think: $\frac{5 \times 8}{7 \times 8} = \frac{40}{56}$

$b = 56$

C $\frac{36}{100} = \frac{a}{25}$

Think: $\frac{36 \div 4}{100 \div 4} = \frac{9}{25}$

$a = 9$

C
H
E
C
K

Check for Understanding

Tell whether the ratios are equal. Explain your reasoning.

1 $\frac{4}{5}$ and $\frac{24}{30}$

2 12 to 5 and 24 to 30

3 40:60 and 2:3

4 $\frac{8}{9}$ and $\frac{65}{81}$

a **ALGEBRA** **Find the missing number to make the ratios equal.**

5 $\frac{4}{8} = \frac{n}{36}$

6 $\frac{50}{10} = \frac{b}{1}$

7 $\frac{6}{7} = \frac{48}{c}$

8 $\frac{12}{10} = \frac{6}{y}$

Critical Thinking: Summarize

9 In your own words, explain how to tell whether two ratios are equal.

Practice

Are the ratios equal? Write *yes* or *no*.

1 $\dfrac{4}{5}, \dfrac{12}{15}$

2 $\dfrac{3}{2}, \dfrac{6}{4}$

3 $\dfrac{34}{20}, \dfrac{17}{10}$

4 $\dfrac{50}{100}, \dfrac{5}{10}$

5 $\dfrac{3}{6}, \dfrac{27}{48}$

6 $\dfrac{7}{8}, \dfrac{42}{48}$

7 $\dfrac{9}{3}, \dfrac{15}{9}$

8 $\dfrac{16}{44}, \dfrac{12}{40}$

9 $\dfrac{23}{1}, \dfrac{90}{45}$

10 $\dfrac{5}{7}, \dfrac{35}{56}$

a **ALGEBRA Find the missing number to make equal ratios.**

11 $\dfrac{2}{3} = \dfrac{n}{18}$

12 $\dfrac{n}{4} = \dfrac{45}{36}$

13 $\dfrac{2}{11} = \dfrac{20}{n}$

14 $\dfrac{42}{n} = \dfrac{7}{2}$

15 $\dfrac{5}{8} = \dfrac{a}{72}$

16 $\dfrac{b}{9} = \dfrac{63}{81}$

17 $\dfrac{1}{15} = \dfrac{7}{y}$

18 $\dfrac{24}{d} = \dfrac{3}{8}$

19 $\dfrac{c}{4} = \dfrac{16}{32}$

20 $\dfrac{n}{8} = \dfrac{7}{56}$

21 $\dfrac{5}{f} = \dfrac{100}{120}$

22 $\dfrac{225}{y} = \dfrac{45}{20}$

Copy and complete the table.

23

Pieces of Candy	24	48	72
Number of Boxes	3	n	n

24

Earnings	$192.00	$96.00	$38.40
Weeks	10	n	n

MIXED APPLICATIONS
Problem Solving

25 A small raft has room for 12 duffel bags of passengers' gear. If the raft holds 4 passengers, may each passenger bring 3 or 4 bags?

26 Laura took 72 good pictures on the trip. She had 2 good pictures for every 3 bad pictures. How many pictures did she take in all?

Use the graph for problems 27–28.

27 What is the ratio of students who own cats to the total number of students surveyed?

28 What statement can you make comparing the number of dog owners to the number of fish owners?

Animal Owners

(Bar graph titled "Animal Owners." Vertical axis: NUMBER OF STUDENTS, from 0 to 20. Horizontal axis: ANIMALS — Dogs ≈ 15, Cats ≈ 18, Birds ≈ 5, Fish ≈ 5, Other ≈ 10.)

mixed review · test preparation

Compare. Write >, < or =.

1 $\dfrac{3}{4} \bullet \dfrac{1}{2}$

2 $\dfrac{8}{3} \bullet \dfrac{8}{5}$

3 $\dfrac{12}{4} \bullet \dfrac{15}{5}$

4 $2.78 \bullet 2.59$

5 $0.08 \bullet 0.87$

a **ALGEBRA Evaluate each expression.**

6 $3x + 7$ for $x = 9$

7 $6x + 8$ for $x = 0$

8 $5x - 2$ for $x = 12$

Rates

On to Oregon! How would you like to follow a trail traveled by settlers during the 1800s?

On your summer vacation, you could travel by car along part of the Oregon Trail. In the first 3 hours you might travel 150 miles. If you kept up that rate, how far would you travel in 6 hours?

A **rate** is a ratio that compares measurements or amounts.

Here are examples of rates.   **Note:** *Per* means "for each."

Scales on a Map
1 inch to 30 miles

Money Exchange Rates
115 yen to 1 dollar

Gas Mileage
25 miles per gallon

Sales Tax Rates
$6 for every $100

Speed
55 miles per hour (mph)

Pay Rate
$6.75 per hour

> ### Cultural Note
> The Oregon Trail was used in the westward expansion of the United States. The movement of the settlers into the West spread European customs to other parts of the New World.

You can use equal ratios or division and multiplication to solve the problem above.

Equal Ratios

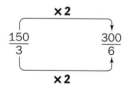

Division and Multiplication

$$\frac{150}{3} = 50$$

$$6 \times 50 = 300$$

At a rate of 150 miles in 3 hours, you would travel 300 miles in 6 hours.

Talk It Over

▶ What other method can you use to find how far you would travel in 6 hours?

▶ How would you find the distance you would travel in 2 hours?

▶ Name some other ratios that are rates.

If you spend $70.05 on food for the first three days of your Oregon Trail journey, and you continue to spend at this rate, how much will you spend on food in 7 days?

You can solve this problem by first finding the *unit rate*. A **unit rate** is a rate in which the second measurement is 1 unit.

Examples of unit rates are: 45 miles per hour (mph)
                                24 miles per gallon (mpg)

To find the unit rate, divide. $\frac{\$70.05}{3 \text{ days}} = \$23.35$ per day

Then multiply to find the dollar amount for 7 days.

$\$23.35$ per day $\times$ 7 days $= \$163.45$

You will spend $163.45 on food in 7 days.

> **Check Out the Glossary**
> For vocabulary words,
> see page 643.

More Examples

A If a motorcycle travels 550 mi on 10 gal of gas, how far can it travel on 30 gal?

$$\frac{550 \text{ mi}}{10 \text{ gal}} = \frac{550 \times 3}{10 \times 3} = \frac{1,650 \text{ mi}}{30 \text{ gal}}$$

It can travel 1,650 mi.

B If 4 tires cost $185.95, how much does 1 tire cost?

$$\frac{\$185.95}{4 \text{ tires}} = \frac{\$185.95 \div 4}{4 \div 4} \approx \frac{\$46.49}{1 \text{ tire}}$$

One tire costs $46.49.

Check for Understanding

Solve. Explain your methods.

1 If you can buy 5 bottles of juice for $3.75, how much would 7 of these bottles cost?

2 If you travel 450 mi on 15 gallons of gas, how far can you go with 25 gal traveling at the same rate?

3 If your car can go 432 mi on a tank of gas, and your gas tank holds 18 gal, what is your mpg?

4 If you travel at a rate of 65 mph for 3 hours, how many miles can you travel?

Critical Thinking: Analyze

5 What are some examples of unit rates?

6 What is the advantage of knowing a unit rate?

7 How can you change any rate to a unit rate?

C
H
E
C
K

Turn the page for Practice. ➡

Practice

Find the unit rate.

1 560 mi on 20 gal = ■ mi per 1 gal

2 640 mi to 4 in. = ■ mi to 1 in.

3 45 mi in 4 h = ■ mi in 1 h

4 $29.50 for 10 maps = ■ for 1 map

5 $2,456 per 4 weeks = ■ per week

6 $5.76 for 16 oz = ■ for 1 oz

7 648 pictures in 18 rolls of film = ■ pictures in 1 roll

8 560 people to 28 square miles = ■ people per square mile

★ ALGEBRA Use the rate of 380 miles in 5 hours to find the missing number for the rate. Round to the nearest tenth, if necessary.

9 ■ mi in 15 h

10 190 mi in ■ h

11 1,330 mi in ■ h

12 ■ mi in 45 h

13 ■ mi in 3 h

14 548 mi in ■ h

15 760 mi in ■ h

16 ■ mi in 0.5 h

17 76 mi in ■ h

Use the table and mental math for ex. 18–30.

18 10 marks = ■ dollars

19 10 pounds = ■ dollars

20 100 pesos = ■ dollars

21 1,000 yen = ■ dollars

22 10 kroner = ■ dollars

23 10 pesos = ■ dollars

24 1,000 pounds = ■ dollars

25 100 marks = ■ dollars

26 100 yen = ■ dollars

27 100 kroner = ■ dollars

28 1,000 pesos = ■ dollars

29 100 pounds = ■ dollars

30 1,000 marks = ■ dollars

Foreign Exchange November 3, 1997		
Country	**Currency**	**U.S. Value**
Germany	1 mark	$0.576
Britain	1 pound	$1.677
Mexico	1 peso	$0.122
Japan	1 yen	$0.008
Norway	1 krone	$0.142

· **Make It Right** ·

31 Tina calculates the number of gallons of gas it would take to travel 3,450 mi. She knows that her car can go 358 miles on 12 gallons. Tell what the error is and correct it.

358 miles ÷ 12 gallons = 29.8 miles per gallon
3,450 × 29.8 gallons = 102,810 gallons

Pencil & Paper   Calculator   Mental Math

32 The Oregon Trail from Independence, Missouri, to Portland, Oregon, is about 2,170 mi long. In the 1850s, it would take about 6 months to complete the trail. About how many miles per day was this?

33 In 1990, the Census Bureau found the population of Oregon to be 2,842,321. In 1800, the population of Oregon was about $\frac{1}{7}$ of the 1990 population. What was the population of Oregon in 1800?

34 A farmer in Oregon has 258 cattle, 67 chickens, 28 pigs, and 6 horses. What is the ratio of horses to total number of animals?

35 **Write a problem** about a family driving on vacation. Solve the problem. Give your problem to another student to solve.

36 **Data Point** Use the Databank on page 639. Determine which city has the greatest number of people per square mile.

37 Chet wanted to make punch for 20 people. The recipe calls for 3 cups of water for every 2 cups of punch mix. He has 15 cups of punch mix. How much water should he add?

38 Use the gift prices at the right. What is the cost of 2 mugs and a pencil?

39 **Make a decision** If you have $25 to spend on souvenirs listed at the right, what would you buy?

T-Shirt $12.99
Oregon Travel Map $4.95
Pencil $1.25
Mug $6.95
Covered Wagon $16.99

---

more to explore

Changing Rates

What if you are in a car that is traveling 45 miles per hour. How many feet per minute are you traveling?

Since 1 h = 60 min, multiplying by $\frac{1\ h}{60\ min}$ is the same as multiplying by 1.

Since 5,280 ft = 1 mi, multiplying by $\frac{5,280\ ft}{1\ mi}$ is the same as multiplying by 1.

$$\frac{45\ mi}{1\ h} \times \frac{5,280\ ft}{1\ mi} \times \frac{1\ h}{60\ min} = \frac{237,600\ ft}{60\ min} = \frac{3,960\ ft}{1\ min}$$

1 If you are traveling at a speed of 38 miles per hour, how many feet per minute is that?

2 If you are traveling at a rate of 1,500 feet per minute, about how many miles per hour is that?

Better Buys

**L
E
A
R
N**

Think about taking a trip to a seaside boardwalk where you will see food vendors, clothing vendors, games, and rides.

Look at the ticket-booth sign at the right. Which ticket package is the better buy?

TICKETS
$1.50 for 5 tickets
$6.00 for 25 tickets

To find the better buy, make each ratio a unit ratio of price per ticket. A unit ratio showing a price is called a **unit price.**

Price: $1.50 for 5 tickets

$$\frac{\$1.50}{5} = \frac{1.50 \div 5}{5 \div 5} = \frac{\$0.30}{1}$$

The cost is $0.30 per ticket.

Price: $6.00 for 25 tickets

$$\frac{\$6.00}{25} = \frac{6.00 \div 25}{25 \div 25} = \frac{\$0.24}{1}$$

The cost is $0.24 per ticket.

Since $0.24 < $0.30, the better buy is 25 tickets for $6.00.

Sometimes you may need to round to the nearest tenth of a cent. Find the better buy between the two containers of lemonade.

BEST
LEMONADE
$0.75
9 oz
$2.85
32 oz

$$\frac{2.85}{32 \text{ oz}} = \frac{2.85 \div 32}{32 \div 32} = \frac{0.0890625}{1}$$ The price is about $0.089 per ounce.

$$\frac{0.75}{9 \text{ oz}} = \frac{0.75 \div 9}{9 \div 9} \approx \frac{0.0833333}{1}$$ The price is about $0.083 per ounce.

> **Check Out the Glossary**
> **unit price**
> See page 643.

Since $0.083 < $0.089, the 9-oz container for $0.75 is the better buy.

**C
H
E
C
K**

Check for Understanding

Tell which is the better buy. Explain the reasoning.

1 T-shirts: 3 for $19.99, or 2 for $13.99

2 Sun lotion: 16 oz for $7, or 6 oz for $2.59

3 Pairs of socks: 6 pair for $8.99, or 8 pair for $12.99

4 Chocolate milk: 1 gal for $3.29, or 1 qt for $0.95

Critical Thinking: Generalize **Explain your reasoning.**

5 Is the larger product in a store always the better buy?

6 Should you always purchase the better buy?

Practice

Find the unit price. Round to the nearest cent if necessary.

1 12 lb for $16.20   **2** 4 L for $9.36   **3** 8 ft for $7.49   **4** 2 pt for $0.79

5 6.75 oz for $3.87   **6** 275 g for $1.69   **7** 9.5 lb for $26.41   **8** 3 for $1

Tell which of the two items is the better buy. Explain your reasoning.

9

10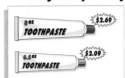

11

Solve.

12 Which vacation package for whitewater rafting is the best deal?
   a. 12 days for $390.00
   b. 4 days for $142.80
   c. 10 days for $311.70

13 Which vacation package for a cruise is the best deal?
   a. 3 days for $855
   b. 4 days for $1,160
   c. 5 days for $1,660

MIXED APPLICATIONS
Problem Solving

Pencil & Paper   Calculator   Mental Math

14 READING ARITHMETIC WRITING **Write an Advertisement** A painting contractor needs to seal 3,000 square feet of boardwalk with a wood preservative. A 5-gallon can that covers 1,000 square feet sells for $56.49. A 1-gallon can that covers 300 square feet sells for $18.19. Which is the better buy? Write an advertisement for the better buy.

15 While camping, John made several S'mores, a graham cracker sandwich with melted marshmallow and chocolate. Amber ate $\frac{1}{4}$ of them, Irene ate $\frac{1}{3}$, and Ted ate $\frac{1}{6}$. What fraction of the original S'mores is left?

16 **Make a decision** From which of these two stores at the left would you rent a windsailing surfboard? Explain your reasoning.

mixed review • test preparation

Solve.

1 $\frac{5}{8} + \frac{3}{8}$ **2** $2\frac{1}{5} - \frac{3}{5}$ **3** $1\frac{2}{3} \times \frac{3}{8}$ **4** $6\frac{3}{7} \div 1\frac{2}{7}$

a **ALGEBRA Solve the equation. Check your solution.**

5 $t + 4 = 17$ **6** $w - 5 = 9$ **7** $0.2p = 5$ **8** $n \div 3 = 8$

Find the ratio.

1 rock bass to yellow perch

2 brook trout to catfish

3 bluegill to white perch

4 catfish to total

Type of Fish	Number Stocked in Lake
Rock bass	340
Catfish	250
White perch	600
Yellow perch	480
Brook trout	555
Bluegill	900

Write the ratio in two other ways.

5 7:8   **6** 9 to 5   **7** $\frac{15}{5}$ **8** $\frac{13}{4}$ **9** 28 to 47   **10** 85:3

⭐ **ALGEBRA Find the missing number to make equal ratios.**

11 $\frac{5}{8} = \frac{a}{72}$ **12** $\frac{n}{2} = \frac{16}{8}$ **13** $\frac{9}{10} = \frac{63}{c}$ **14** $\frac{25}{n} = \frac{75}{27}$

15 $\frac{56}{20} = \frac{y}{60}$ **16** $\frac{b}{1} = \frac{42}{6}$ **17** $\frac{17}{11} = \frac{34}{d}$ **18** $\frac{150}{a} = \frac{10}{30}$

19 $\frac{n}{24} = \frac{5}{3}$ **20** $\frac{x}{104} = \frac{11}{52}$ **21** $\frac{9}{16} = \frac{n}{64}$ **22** $\frac{12}{y} = \frac{72}{6}$

Find the unit rate. Round to the nearest tenth if necessary.

23 740 miles on 37 gallons = ▇ miles per 1 gallon

24 586 miles on 29.5 gallons = ▇ miles per 1 gallon

25 200 miles to 3 inches = ▇ miles to 1 inch

26 620 miles in 14 hours = ▇ miles per hour

27 100 miles in 1.5 hours = ▇ miles per hour

Solve.

28 Noah drove 842.4 miles on 36 gallons of gas. About how much will he use on a trip of 329 miles?

29 Which is the better buy: 18.75 lb of fish for $60.75 or 6.2 lb of fish for $17.02?

30 Molly saved $345 for a vacation. If she spends $23 per day, how long will the money last?

31 Portfolio Illustrate the ratio 3:5 using a picture or a graph. Describe how you could use your illustration to find ratios equal to 3:5.

32 Joseph filled his 16 gallon tank with gas three times for his 1,500 mi trip. How many miles per gallon does his car get?

33 Ruby was practicing for a basketball tournament. She made 48 free throws out of 100 attempts. What is the ratio of shots made to misses?

Bottle Functions

At summer fairs, you often see artists selling bottles filled with layers of colored sand. To make a design, you need to know how much sand it takes to fill up a bottle.

Cultural Note

Colored sands and clays have been used by Native American artists for many thousands of years to paint designs on walls and create "sand paintings" on the floor.

Suppose you graph the amount of sand and the height of the sand in a bottle. What would the graph look like?

To create a graph of volume and height, follow these steps.

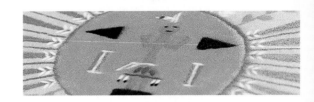

Step 1	Step 2	Step 3
Measure an amount of sand and add it to the bottle. Measure the height of the sand in the bottle.	Repeat Step 1 several times and record your data in a table.	Plot data points on a coordinate graph and connect the dots.

Amount of Sand	Heights of Sand
100 mL	2 cm
200 mL	4 cm
300 mL	8 cm
400 mL	12 cm

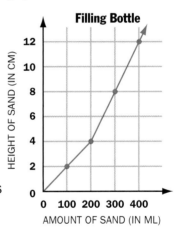

Notice that after the sand fills the bottom part, the sand gets higher at a faster rate. The graph shows the wider section of the bottle with a flatter line segment.

▶ Match the bottle to the graph. Explain your reasoning.

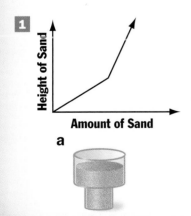

a

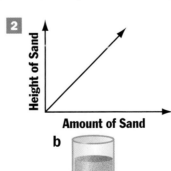

b

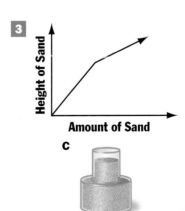

c

A Wave Around Your School Gymnasium

Have you ever gone to a ball game when you were on vacation? While you were there, you might have done the "wave." How long would it take for a wave to go all the way around your gymnasium?

You can experiment with short lines of students to try to answer this question.

Work Together

▶ Form a line of chairs for at least ten students. Students should sit as close together as possible and still have some room to move.

▶ Measure the length of the line of chairs.

▶ Signal to the first person in line to begin the wave by standing up straight and sitting down. The second person begins standing as the first person begins sitting. The third person stands as the second sits, and so on. The last person in line calls out when he or she has sat back down.

▶ A timer records the start and finish times of the wave.

▶ Repeat the experiment several times. Find the average time for a wave.

DECISION MAKING

Wave Around Your Gym

1 Pace off the distance around your school gymnasium.

2 Measure the number of feet in ten paces. Convert the number of paces around the gym into feet.

3 From the data you collected by experimenting with the wave, give the ratios of:
- ▶ the number of students to length of line.
- ▶ the number of students to time of wave.

4 Using equal ratios or unit ratios, find out how many students are needed for a wave around your gymnasium.

5 Use the enrollment in each class to decide if there are enough students in your school to do the wave around your gym.

6 Using equal ratios or unit rates, find out how long the wave will take.

Report Your Findings

7 **Portfolio** Prepare a letter to other classes about your prediction of the number of students needed for a wave around the gym. Include the following in your letter:

- ▶ a paragraph describing the wave around the gym

- ▶ the distance around the gym and an explanation of how you figured it out

- ▶ your classroom experiment and an explanation of how you made the measurements

- ▶ the steps you used to predict the number of students needed for a wave around the gym and the length of time it would take

- ▶ the things you will need to take into account for the wave to take place, such as teacher approval and safety precautions.

Revise your work.
- ▶ Are your calculations correct?
- ▶ Is your report clear and organized?
- ▶ Did you proofread your work?

MORE TO INVESTIGATE

PREDICT how long it would take and how many people would be needed to do the wave around a stadium near you.

EXPLORE methods of raising money through a local "Wave-a-Thon." Describe the event and where it would be held.

FIND things that effect the speed of waves traveling across lakes and oceans.

Proportions

Biking can cause quite a thirst. One bike's water bottle holds 5 cups of water and another's holds 4 cups. If 7 tablespoons of Kool Aid mix goes in with the 5 cups of water, and 6 tablespoons goes in with the 4 cups, are the two mixtures the same?

Work Together
Work with a partner.

▶ Write a ratio for number of cups of water to number of tablespoons of Kool Aid mix for each mixture.

▶ Make a list of equal ratios for each ratio.

▶ Find two ratios, one from each list, that have the same number of tablespoons.

▶ Are the ratios equal? Explain your reasoning.

▶ Using what you know about ratios, how can you tell if the two mixtures described above taste the same?

Make Connections
Two ratios that are equal form a **proportion**. To determine whether two ratios form a proportion, you can use equivalent fractions or cross products.

Compare a mixture of 12 tablespoons of Kool Aid mix in 8 cups of water with a mixture of 9 tablespoons of Kool Aid mix in 6 cups of water.

> **Check Out the Glossary**
> proportion
> cross products
> See page 643.

Equal Ratios

$$\frac{12}{8} = \frac{n}{24} \qquad \frac{12}{8} = \frac{12 \times 3}{8 \times 3} = \frac{36}{24}$$

$$\frac{9}{6} = \frac{n}{24} \qquad \frac{9}{6} = \frac{9 \times 4}{6 \times 4} = \frac{36}{24}$$

Think: LCD = 24

Both ratios are equal to $\frac{36}{24}$, so $\frac{12}{8} = \frac{9}{6}$.

Cross Products

12 × 6 and **8 × 9** are called **cross products.**

Both cross products equal 72, so $\frac{12}{8} = \frac{9}{6}$.

Using either method $\frac{12}{8}$ and $\frac{9}{6}$ are equal ratios, so they form a proportion. The two mixtures are the same.

Tell whether the two ratios $\frac{4}{10}$ and $\frac{6}{15}$ form a proportion.
Use both methods.

Equal Ratios

$$\frac{4}{10} = \frac{n}{30} \qquad \frac{4}{10} = \frac{4 \times 3}{10 \times 3} = \frac{12}{30}$$

$$\frac{6}{15} = \frac{n}{30} \qquad \frac{6}{15} = \frac{6 \times 2}{15 \times 2} = \frac{12}{30}$$

Think: LCD = 30

Both ratios equal $\frac{12}{30}$, so $\frac{4}{10} = \frac{6}{15}$.
They form a proportion.

Cross Products

4 × 15 and **10 × 6** are
the two cross products.

Both cross products equal 60.
So they form a proportion.

▶ Is it easier to test whether two ratios form a proportion using
equivalent ratios or cross products? Explain.

Check for Understanding

 ALGEBRA Solve.

1 $\frac{6}{7} = \frac{n}{14}$

2 $\frac{6}{12} = \frac{9}{n}$

3 $\frac{5}{2} = \frac{15}{n}$

4 $\frac{8}{4} = \frac{n}{3}$

5 $\frac{4}{5} = \frac{y}{30}$

6 $\frac{7}{3} = \frac{g}{30}$

7 $\frac{17}{4} = \frac{34}{b}$

8 $\frac{2}{c} = \frac{16}{24}$

Critical Thinking: Generalize

9 If two ratios are unequal, what can you say about
their cross products?

Practice

Do the ratios form a proportion? Write *yes* or *no*.

1 $\frac{5}{9}$ and $\frac{4}{11}$

2 $\frac{1}{7}$ and $\frac{5}{35}$

3 $\frac{10}{12}$ and $\frac{5}{6}$

4 $\frac{12}{8}$ and $\frac{21}{14}$

5 $\frac{6}{9}$ and $\frac{8}{16}$

6 $\frac{4}{1.2}$ and $\frac{3}{0.9}$

7 $\frac{55}{11}$ and $\frac{2}{0.4}$

8 $\frac{2.1}{11}$ and $\frac{8}{44}$

 ALGEBRA Solve.

9 $\frac{3}{4} = \frac{n}{8}$

10 $\frac{2}{8} = \frac{x}{32}$

11 $\frac{8}{5} = \frac{16}{w}$

12 $\frac{9}{7} = \frac{27}{y}$

13 $\frac{6}{2} = \frac{a}{10}$

14 $\frac{b}{3} = \frac{16}{24}$

15 $\frac{9}{c} = \frac{99}{22}$

16 $\frac{6}{3} = \frac{15}{d}$

17 $\frac{f}{4} = \frac{9}{12}$

18 $\frac{42}{c} = \frac{6}{8}$

19 $\frac{12}{20} = \frac{60}{n}$

20 $\frac{11}{8} = \frac{x}{48}$

Write an Equation

L
E
A
R
N

Read In Seattle, Washington, it rains about 2 out of every 9 days in the summer. If you were to plan a 60-day summer vacation in Seattle, about how many days should you expect rain?

Plan To solve the problem, you need to answer these questions:

▶ How many days are there in the summer vacation?

▶ What is the ratio of rainy days to total days?

Solve Decide on the ratio.   rainy days to total days

Write a proportion. $\dfrac{\text{rainy days} \rightarrow}{\text{total days} \rightarrow} \dfrac{2}{9} = \dfrac{r}{60}$

a **ALGEBRA** Find the cross products. $2 \times 60 = 9 \times r$

$$120 = 9r$$

Divide both sides of the equation by 9. $\dfrac{120}{9} = \dfrac{\overset{1}{\cancel{9}}r}{\underset{1}{\cancel{9}}} = \dfrac{120}{9} \approx 13$

Plan on about 13 rainy days. $r \approx 13$

Look Back Does the answer make sense?

C
H
E
C
K

Check for Understanding

1 **What if** 3 out of 9 days in Mobile, Alabama, are rainy. How many rainy days would you expect to have there during a 4-week vacation?

Critical Thinking: Analyze

2 Silver Lake, Colorado, received 76 inches of snow in 1 day, the greatest snowfall in North America in a 24-hour period. Explain how you would estimate how much snow the city received in the first 6 hours of the storm.

Problem Solving

Use the table to solve ex 1–5.

1 Estimate the average number of inches of rain for a 3-month period in Miami, Florida.

2 Which two cities have the same ratio of rainy days to 365 days of the year?

3 Find and compare the unit rate of rainfall per rainy day for Juneau, Alaska, and Honolulu, Hawaii.

City	Average Monthly Temperature				Average Yearly Rain	
	Jan.	April	July	Oct.	Inches	Days
Baton Rouge, LA	50.8	68.4	82.1	68.2	55.77	108
Fargo, ND	4.3	42.1	70.6	46.3	19.59	100
Honolulu, HI	72.6	75.7	80.1	79.5	23.47	100
Juneau, AK	21.8	39.1	55.7	41.8	53.15	220
Miami, FL	67.1	75.3	82.5	77.9	57.55	129
New York, NY	31.8	51.9	76.4	57.5	42.82	119
San Francisco, CA	48.5	54.8	62.2	60.6	19.71	63

4 **Make a decision** Of the cities in the chart, where would you like to take a vacation and when? Why?

5 **Write a problem** using information from the table. Solve it and give it to others to solve.

6 **Data Point** Conduct a survey of the students in your class about a place they would like to visit on vacation. Write three or more ratios using your collected data.

7 You have to decide on what to wear to school. You have three pairs of jeans and four shirts to choose from. How many different outfits can you choose from?

8 **Spatial reasoning** In the picture at the right, the top blocks are in a ratio of 2 to 3. If the ratio for the bottom blocks is equal to the ratio for the top, how many blocks does the question mark represent?

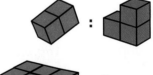

9 **Logical reasoning** Sally, Mary, Beth, and Sue wear 4 different-colored dresses. Their shoes are the same 4 colors, but no one wears the same color dress as her shoes. Mary and Sally each wear something blue. Beth and Mary each wear something green. Sue wears a white dress, and Beth wears a red dress. What is each person wearing?

10 In your class, there are 30 students. You want to buy cupcakes for everyone. If cupcakes cost $0.75 each, how much money do you need?

Similar Figures

Many people take snapshots to remember their vacations. These photos show the Rock and Roll Hall of Fame and Museum in Cleveland, Ohio. One photo is an enlargement of the other. Do the outlined figures keep the same shape from one photo to the other?

Geometric figures are **similar** if they are the same shape. They may or may not be the same size.

Work Together

Work with a partner. Draw each pair of figures shown at the right on centimeter dot paper.

▶ Which pairs of figures are similar?

▶ Measure the angles of each figure using a protractor. Then measure the lengths of all the sides using a centimeter ruler. Record the measurements on your drawings.

▶ Record patterns you see among the similar figures.

▶ On dot paper, draw two figures similar to figure *A* and to figure *E*.

You will need
- *centimeter dot paper*
- *centimeter ruler*
- *protractor*

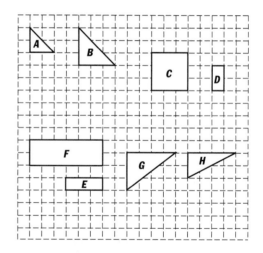

Talk It Over

▶ What patterns do you see in the angles of similar figures?

▶ What patterns do you see among the sides of similar figures?

▶ Write ratios using the matching sides of similar figures. What do you notice?

▶ How can you use these patterns to test whether the figures you have drawn are similar to figure *A* and to figure *E* ?

Make Connections

Trapezoid *ABCD* is similar to trapezoid *WXYZ*.
You can write this as *ABCD* ~ *WXYZ*.

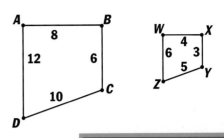

Corresponding angles	**Corresponding sides**
∠*A* corresponds to ∠*W*.	$\overline{AB}$ corresponds to $\overline{WX}$.
∠*B* corresponds to ∠*X*.	$\overline{CD}$ corresponds to $\overline{YZ}$

In similar figures, corresponding angles are congruent, and the ratios of corresponding sides are equal.

Check Out the Glossary
For vocabulary words, see page 643.

$$\frac{AB}{WX} = \frac{8}{4} \qquad \frac{BC}{XY} = \frac{6}{3} \qquad \angle DCB \cong \angle ZYX \qquad \angle ADC \cong \angle WZY$$

▶ What proportions can you write for the similar trapezoids above?

You can use proportions to find the missing side lengths of similar figures.

For the similar parallelograms at the right, you can write the proportion $\frac{6}{2} = \frac{9}{n}$.
Then solve for *n*.

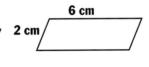
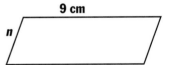

You can use cross products to solve the proportion.

$$6 \times n = 2 \times 9$$
$$6n = 18$$
$$n = 18 \div 6$$
$$n = 3 \qquad \text{The length of side } n \text{ is 3 cm.}$$

▶ What other method can you use to solve the proportion?

Check for Understanding

ALGEBRA Find the missing length for the pair of similar figures.

1

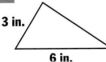
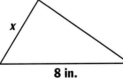

2

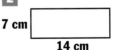
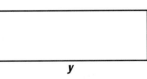

Critical Thinking: Analyze

3 Can two geometric shapes have the same angle measures and not be similar? Explain.

4 If the side lengths of two parallelograms form proportions, are the parallelograms always similar? Give examples.

Turn the page for Practice. ➡

Practice

In the picture at the right, _RSTUV_ ~ _JKLMN_. Find the corresponding side.

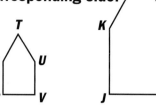

1 RS   **2** TU   **3** MN

Find the corresponding angle.

4 ∠S   **5** ∠V   **6** ∠J

Complete the statement.

7 $\dfrac{RS}{JK} = \dfrac{ST}{\blacksquare}$

8 If ∠R = 90°, then ∠J = ▨

9 If ∠T = 60°, then ∠L = ▨

10 $\dfrac{TU}{LM} = \dfrac{RV}{\blacksquare}$

α **ALGEBRA The figures in each pair are similar. Solve for the variable.**

11
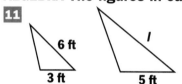

12
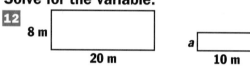

13
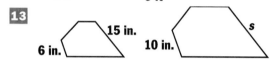

14
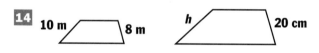

15
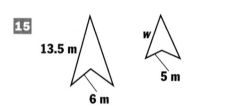

16
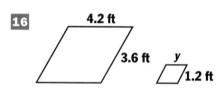

17
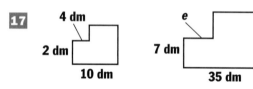

18
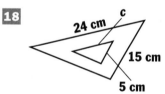

On dot paper, sketch a pair of geometric shapes for each.

19 similar rectangles   **20** similar rhombi   **21** not similar triangles

22 similar triangles   **23** not similar rectangles   **24** not similar trapezoids

• **Make It Right** •

25 Paula solved for the missing side by writing the proportion at the right and solving it. Explain her error and correct it. What is length _y_?

60 cm

28 cm ▢   7 cm ▢ _y_

$\dfrac{28}{y} = \dfrac{60}{7}$

$28 \times 7 = 60 \times y$

$196 = 60y$

$3.3 = y$

a **26** **ALGEBRA: PATTERNS** In casting shadows, the sun forms two similar triangles as shown at the right. Use the diagram at the right and proportions to find the height of the birch tree.

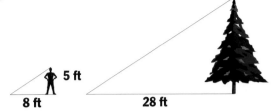

5 ft

8 ft   28 ft

27 **What if** a rock star earns 1.8 million dollars for concert appearances in one year. If there were 8 concert appearances, how much does she average per concert?

28 About how much did two top-grossing concert tours earn each night of their tour? Explain. SEE INFOBIT.

29 James needs $45 for a concert ticket. He earns $5 per week baby-sitting while a neighbor grocery shops. He has $24.50 in his bank. How many weeks does he need to baby-sit to have enough money for the ticket?

30 Tara listens to about 8 hours of jazz music a week. About how many hours of jazz music does she listen to in February? in a year?

INFOBIT
In 1992, Genesis made $6,515,992 in three days, and Bruce Springsteen made $6,295,707 in eleven days.

Cultural Connection
Golden Ratios and Golden Rectangles

Since the fifth century B.C., Greeks have often used the **golden ratio** in their art and architecture, because this ratio is pleasing to the eye. Verify by measuring that the ratio of the length to width of the rectangle outlining the Parthenon at the right is about 1.6:1.

Ancient Greece

Construct your own **golden rectangles** by finding other lengths and widths that are in the ratio 1.6 to 1.

Conduct a survey. Draw several rectangles with different proportions, including a golden rectangle, and ask others to pick their favorite rectangle. What conclusions can you draw from the data?

Scale Drawings

Duck your head and swim! Pat Kambesis often had to swim through tight passageways when she helped to map Lechuguilla Cave. Below is a scale drawing of the cave. How long is the cave from east to west?

IN THE WORKPLACE

Pat Kambesis, Speleologist, Atlanta, GA

A **scale drawing** is a reduced or enlarged version of an actual object. The drawings and actual objects are similar because they have the same shape.

The **scale** of the drawing is the ratio of a length in the drawing to an actual length. In the scale drawing at the right, the scale is 1 cm = 500 m.

Check Out the Glossary
scale drawing
scale
See page 643.

In this drawing, the length of the cave is 6 cm. You can verify this with a ruler. You can find the actual length in meters using the scale and proportions.

length in drawing (m) → $\dfrac{1}{500} = \dfrac{6}{n}$
actual length (m)

$1 \times n = 500 \times 6$
$n = 3{,}000$

The actual length is about 3,000 m.

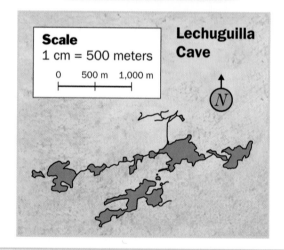

Scale
1 cm = 500 meters

0   500 m   1,000 m

Lechuguilla Cave

N

Check for Understanding
Use the scale 1 inch = 20 miles to find the actual distances.

1 4 in.   **2** 10 in.   **3** 7 in.   **4** 5.25 in.

5 2.5 in.   **6** 3.25 in.   **7** 1.8 in.   **8** 0.5 in.

Critical Thinking: Analyze
9 How can the same floor plan have several different-sized scale drawings?

Practice

The scale on a drawing is 1 in. = 5 ft. Find the actual distances for the scale distances below.

1 2 in.

2 $4\frac{1}{2}$ in.

3 $6\frac{1}{4}$ in.

4 $10\frac{1}{8}$ in.

5 $18\frac{3}{4}$ in.

The scale on a map is 5 cm = 36 km. Find the actual distances for the scale distances below.

6 3 cm

7 1.4 cm

8 3.9 cm

9 27.4 cm

10 0.6 cm

Use the map for ex. 11–13. The map scale is 0.5 in. = 50 mi.

11 What is the actual distance between the Lechuguilla Cave and Las Cruces?

12 What is the actual distance between Columbus and Las Cruces?

13 If the city of Albuquerque is 225 mi northwest of Lechuguilla Cave, what should be the distance between them on the map?

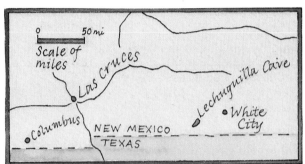

MIXED APPLICATIONS
Problem Solving

Pencil & Paper   Calculator   Mental Math

14 Lechuguilla Cave is the deepest cave in the U.S. If a detailed map uses a scale of 1 in. = 200 ft, and the cave measures 8 in. deep on the map, how deep is the actual cave?

15 Did the group that set the depth record for cave exploration descend to a depth of greater or less than a mile? How close to a mile deep were they? SEE INFOBIT.

INFOBIT
The world depth record of 5,256 ft for cave exploration was set in the Gouffre Jean Bernard Cave in France. No one has ever been to the bottom of this cave.

mixed review • test preparation

Solve. Round to the nearest hundredth or the nearest cent.

1 $54.94 + $128.47

2 382 − 287.394

3 22 × 0.593

4 3.291 ÷ 0.21

Find the missing angle for a triangle given the two angles.

5 ∠1 = 23°, ∠2 = 67°

6 ∠1 = 54°, ∠2 = 38°

7 ∠1 = 78°, ∠2 = 51°

Problem Solvers at Work

Read
Plan
Solve
Look Back

PART 1   Solve Multistep Problems

What a deal! You can often save money on both a room and a rental car because many hotels and car rental companies offer joint discount plans. Here are two competing plans.

Plan	Hotel Rates (per day)		Car Rental Rates* (per day)	
	Regular	Discount	Regular	Discount
Plan A	$88	$76	$45	$36
Plan B	$91	$72	$42	$38

*Unlimited free miles

Work Together

Solve. Be prepared to explain your methods.

1 **Write an Advertisement** How much do you save each day using Plan A rather than paying the regular rates? using Plan B? Write an advertisement for Plan A or Plan B that shows the savings.

2 Which plan is a better buy? How much more do you save each day using this plan?

3 **Make a decision** Plan A offers a weekly rate of $510 for a room and $240 for the rental car. Which plan would you use if you were staying 7 days?

4 **What if** another car rental company offered a rate of $19 per day and $0.12 per mile. How far do you have to drive in a day for Plan A to be a better buy?

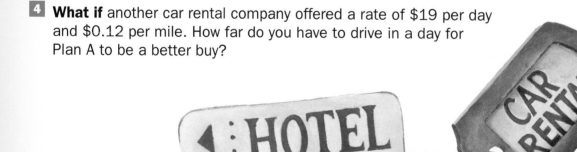

Tim used the information below to write a problem.

Airport Travel Services	
Bus	$14 per person
Car Service	Flat rate—$54
Taxi	$1.50 for first mile $0.38 for each $\frac{1}{4}$ mile

5 Solve Tim's problem.

6 Change Tim's problem so that a different travel service is the best buy.

7 Solve the new problem and explain why it is easier or harder to solve than Tim's problem.

8 **Write a problem** that requires more than two steps to solve.

9 Trade problems. Solve at least three problems written by your classmates.

10 What was the most interesting problem that you solved? Why?

Suppose you take a bus from the airport with 4 other people. Returning from the airport, all of you take 1 taxi for $5\frac{1}{2}$ miles. If you share the cost equally, how much does each person pay?

Tim Asher
Highlander Way Middle School
Howell, MI

Turn the page for Practice Strategies.

PRACTICE

Menu

**Choose five problems and solve them.
Explain your methods.**

1 The plane from Dallas to Miami travels at an average rate of 540 mi per hour. About how long will it take the plane to travel 1,111 mi?

2 Jenna earned $26.75 by selling recyclables, $43.50 by cat-sitting, and $75 by dog-walking. Does she have enough money to pay for a ski trip that costs $125?

3 You can buy 10 lb of mixed candy for $44.58 or 5 lb for $34.58. Which is the better buy?

4 ALGEBRA: PATTERNS
What are the next two numbers in the pattern below? 73, 53, 106, 86, 172, ...

24 135

5 In 1990, the total population of the United States was 248,709,873. The population of children under five years of age in the United States was 18,901,950. About what fraction of the total U.S. population was children under five years of age?

6 At a recent rally, the speaker couldn't hold the people's attention. After ten minutes, $\frac{1}{2}$ of the people left. Five minutes later, 20 people left. When the speaker paused, $\frac{2}{3}$ of the remaining group left, leaving only 100 people in the audience. How many people were there at the beginning?

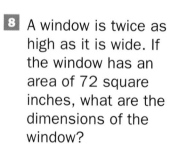

7 A farmer wants to sell 2.4 acres of land. He can get $1.23 per square foot. If an acre has 43,560 square feet, how much will the farmer get?

8 A window is twice as high as it is wide. If the window has an area of 72 square inches, what are the dimensions of the window?

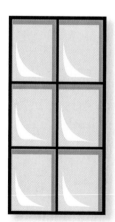

Choose two problems and solve them. Explain your methods.

9 A famous mathemagician claims she can predict the future. She says, "Pick a number—any number! Follow the steps at the right. Your result will be a 5!"

Repeat these steps for several numbers. What are your results? Why do you think the mathemagician claims the result is 5?

Double your number.

Increase the new amount by 5.

Triple that amount.

Subtract 3.

Divide your new number by 6.

Subtract your original number.

Add 3.

10 **Spatial reasoning** Suppose the hexagonal piece at the right stands for 1 unit. What fractional part of the whole would the other pieces be?

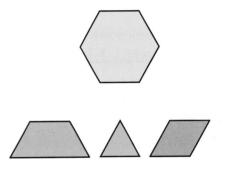

11 Suppose a restaurant chain claims to have sold over 1 billion hamburgers. Would a stack of all the hamburgers sold reach all the way to the moon? (The moon is about 384,000 km away.) Show your estimate.

12 **At the Computer** To build a scale model for a house requires converting many measurements from actual dimensions to scale dimensions. Use a spreadsheet program to create a table of scale dimensions for actual dimensions. The table should show actual dimensions from 1 foot to 60 feet in $\frac{1}{2}$-foot increments. Use the scale 1 in. = 4 ft.

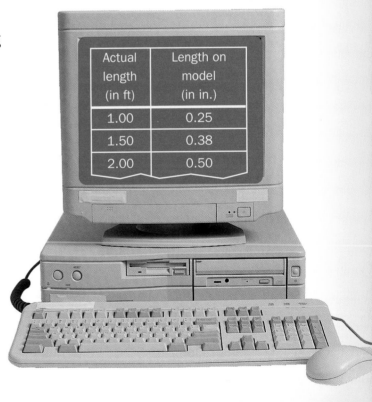

Actual length (in ft)	Length on model (in in.)
1.00	0.25
1.50	0.38
2.00	0.50

Language and Mathematics

Complete the sentence. Use a word in the chart. (pages 384–409)

Vocabulary

ratio
proportion
scale
actual
congruent
similar
rate
unit rate

1 If two geometric figures have the same shape but are not the same size, they are ■.

2 Two equal ratios form a ■.

3 If two shapes are similar, their corresponding angles are ■.

4 In a scale drawing, the ■ is the ratio between the scale length and the actual distance.

Concepts and Skills

Use the picture on the right to write the ratio in three forms. (page 384)

5 blue tiles to white tiles

6 gray tiles to all tiles

7 gray tiles to blue tiles

8 all tiles to white tiles

9 white tiles to gray tiles

10 shaded tiles to white tiles

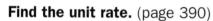

Find the unit rate. (page 390)

11 780 miles on 35 gallons = ■ miles per gallon

12 $19.40 for 8.5 lb = ■ for 1 lb

13 250 kilometers to 3 centimeters = ■ kilometers per centimeter

14 1,250 people to 40 square miles = ■ people to 1 square mile

Use the chart of unit rates for ex. 15–17. (page 390)

15 100 cords = ■ cubic feet

16 10 nautical miles = ■ miles

17 20 kilograms = ■ pounds

1 mile	5,280 feet
1 nautical mile	1.151 miles
1 cord	128 cubic feet
1 kilogram	2.205 pounds

Decide which is the better buy. (page 394)

18 6 oranges for $1.00 or 10 oranges for $1.50

19 100 pencils for $12.50 or 10 pencils for $1.00

20 8.4 lb for $25.78 or 6.1 lb for $19.70

21 $\frac{4}{5} = \frac{n}{15}$ **22** $\frac{3}{2} = \frac{27}{n}$ **23** $\frac{5}{40} = \frac{y}{32}$ **24** $\frac{6}{n} = \frac{24}{36}$

25 $\frac{3}{8} = \frac{n}{72}$ **26** $\frac{3}{15} = \frac{8}{c}$ **27** $\frac{n}{3} = \frac{49}{21}$ **28** $\frac{6}{n} = \frac{12}{14}$

 ALGEBRA **The figures in each pair are similar. Solve for the variable.** (page 404)

29

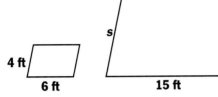

4 ft

6 ft

s

15 ft

30

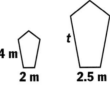

4 m

2 m

t

2.5 m

 ALGEBRA **Solve for *n*.** (page 408)

31 scale: 1 in. = 6 ft; scale distance: 4.5 in.; actual distance: *n*

32 scale: 1 cm = 15 km; map distance: *n*; actual distance: 180 km

33 scale: 1 cm = *n*; map distance: 6 cm; actual distance: 45 km

Think critically. (page 404)

34 Generalize. Are all congruent figures similar? Explain.

MIXED APPLICATIONS
Problem Solving

(pages 402, 410)

35 On a trip you drove 275 miles in 5 hours. About how many miles did you drive each hour? At that rate, how long will it take you to drive another 140 miles?

36 Suppose you drive 323 miles on 12 gallons of gas. At that rate, how far could you drive on 17 gallons of gas? Round your answer to the nearest 10 miles.

37 You are decorating the house for a birthday party. You will need $22\frac{1}{2}$ ft of streamers for the stairs, $13\frac{3}{4}$ ft for the table, and $17\frac{3}{4}$ ft for the patio. Is a 45-ft roll of streamers enough? Explain.

38 There are more than 1,980 people attending a party you are catering. If you estimate that every person at the party will drink about 3 cans of soda, about how many cans should you buy?

39 ALGEBRA How many $2\frac{3}{4}$-inch-long pieces of pipe can be cut from a 22-inch-long piece of pipe? Write an equation, solve it, and show your solution for the problem.

40 It costs $9.78 for a bag of fertilizer that covers 3,000 square feet. If your lawn is 13,568 square feet, how much will it cost to fertilize it?

Write the ratio in three different ways.

1 circles to triangles

2 circles to total figures

3 red triangles to total red figures

Find the missing number to make equal ratios.

4 $\frac{2}{5} = \frac{n}{15}$ **5** $\frac{n}{2} = \frac{12}{24}$ **6** $\frac{2}{7} = \frac{18}{n}$ **7** $\frac{48}{n} = \frac{6}{2}$

Find the unit rate.

8 125 miles to 2 inches = ■ miles to 1 inch

9 $29.90 for 9.2 lb = ■ for 1 lb

Decide which is the better buy.

10 12 peaches for $1.30 or 8 peaches for $0.79

11 10 disks for $9.95 or 20 disks for $18.95

Do the ratios form a proportion? Write *yes* or *no*.

12 $\frac{2}{3}$ and $\frac{10}{15}$ **13** $\frac{5}{4}$ and $\frac{25}{20}$ **14** $\frac{6}{4}$ and $\frac{1}{2}$ **15** $\frac{27}{24}$ and $\frac{38}{16}$

a **ALGEBRA Solve.**

16 $\frac{3}{5} = \frac{n}{15}$ **17** $\frac{2}{10} = \frac{x}{30}$ **18** $\frac{27}{24} = \frac{18}{w}$

a **ALGEBRA The figures in the pair are similar. Solve for the variable.**

19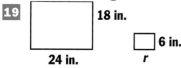

18 in.

6 in.

24 in.   *r*

20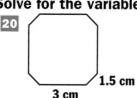

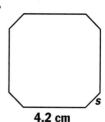

1.5 cm

3 cm

4.2 cm   *s*

a **ALGEBRA Solve for *n*.**

21 Scale: 1 cm = 8 m
Scale distance: 4.5 cm
Actual distance: *n*

22 Scale: 1 in. = 30 mi
Map distance: *n*
Actual distance: 120 mi

23 Scale: 1 cm = *n*
Map distance: 8 cm
Actual distance: 44 km

Solve.

24 On a trip you drove 360 miles in 8 hours. How many miles did you average per hour? At that rate, how long will it take you to drive another 135 miles?

a **25** **ALGEBRA** While on a vacation, you stopped to get gas and some snacks. The total was $21.50. If the gas cost $18.45, how much did the snacks cost? Write an equation, solve it, and show your solution for the problem.

What Did You Learn?

Do you know how to read a road map? When people travel from one place to another, they use a road map to help them estimate the distance between places.

You will need
• *inch ruler*

▶ Choose two places. Use string and a ruler, or some other way, to estimate the actual distance between the two places. Explain how you can use ratios to solve.

▶ Suppose you are a salesperson who has to travel to all four places on the map in one day. Estimate the actual distance that you have to travel. Explain how you can use ratios to solve.

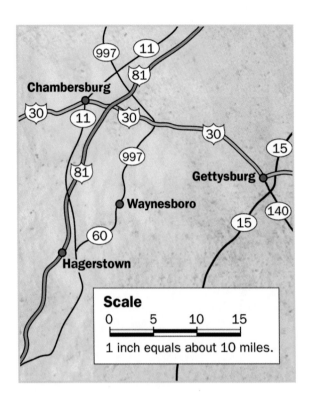

Scale

0   5   10   15

1 inch equals about 10 miles.

•••••••••••••••••• **A Good Answer** ••••••••••••••••••
• includes a written explanation of the method you used to estimate the map distances.
• explains how knowing ratios helps you read maps and find actual distances.

 You may want to place your work in your portfolio.

What Do You Think

1 What is easy and what is difficult about solving problems that involve ratios and proportions?

2 Which method would you tell someone to try when using ratios to compare numbers?
• Use counters.   • Write a proportion.
• Use a diagram.   • Other? Explain.

THE PLANETS

Earth is one of the nine planets that revolve around the sun in our solar system. What would you find if you could take a trip to the different planets in the solar system?

The four planets that are closest to the sun are Mercury, Venus, Earth, and Mars. They are called the *inner planets*. The inner planets are rocky and have few if any moons. Compared with Jupiter and Saturn, they are small.

The *outer planets* are Jupiter, Saturn, Uranus, Neptune, and Pluto. Except for Pluto, the outer planets are large and made up totally or almost totally of gases. Again except for Pluto, they also have more moons than the inner planets.

Cultural Note

It was probably the ancient Greeks who first noticed that from night to night the planets move in relation to the stars. For this reason they called them *planetae*, meaning "wanderers."

▶ What are some differences between the inner and outer planets?

▶ How do you think the temperatures of the outer planets compare to the temperatures of the inner planets? Why?

How Much Would You Weigh on Other Planets?

You have weight because of the force of gravity between you and Earth. If you were standing on a planet that had a different mass, your weight would be different. Look at the table below. A person who weighs 100 pounds on Earth would weigh 38 pounds on Mars.

Weight on Various Planets	
Planet	**Weight**
Mercury	38 lb
Venus	91 lb
Earth	100 lb
Mars	38 lb
Jupiter	287 lb
Saturn	132 lb
Uranus	92 lb
Neptune	124 lb
Pluto	3 lb

You can use the ratio of 38 to 100 to figure out how much a person weighing 115 pounds on Earth would weigh on Mars.

$$\frac{38}{100} = 0.38$$

On Mars, a person weighs 0.38 of his or her weight on Earth.

0.38×115 pounds = 43.7 pounds

A person who weighs 115 pounds on Earth would weigh 44 pounds on Mars, to the nearest pound.

1 How much would an astronaut who weighs 150 pounds on Earth weigh on each of the other planets?

At the Computer

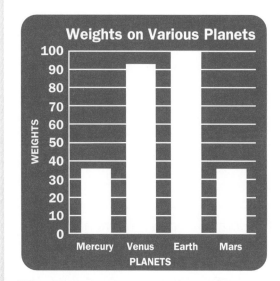

2 Use the table at the left and graphing software to show how much a person who weighs 100 pounds on Earth would weigh on each of the planets.

3 Write two statements based on your graph.

Choose the letter of the best answer.

1 Which group of ratios are all equivalent to $\frac{2}{3}$?

  A $\frac{4}{6}, \frac{8}{12}, \frac{10}{15}$

  B $\frac{4}{6}, \frac{8}{12}, \frac{5}{15}$

  C $\frac{2}{6}, \frac{8}{12}, \frac{5}{10}$

  D $\frac{3}{6}, \frac{4}{12}, \frac{10}{15}$

2 A library is open 8 hours a day, except for Sunday, when it is closed. Using this information, a librarian writes this equation. What does H represent?

$$H = 6 \times 8$$

  F   the number of hours the library is open each day

  G   the number of days the library is open each week

  H   the total number of hours the library is open each week

  J   the number of hours the librarian works each day

3 Which statement about parallelogram STUV is not true?

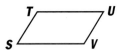

  A   Side ST is parallel to side UV.

  B   Side TU and side SV are congruent.

  C   Angle T and Angle V are congruent.

  D   The sum of the measurements of angle S, T, U, and V is 180°.

4 Anthony is 5 feet 3 inches tall. How many inches tall is Anthony?

  F   35 in.

  G   53 in.

  H   63 in.

  J   83 in.

5 The driver of a car slowed to a stop at a constant rate. Use the graph to determine when the car was traveling at 30 miles per hour.

Time for Car to Slow to a Stop

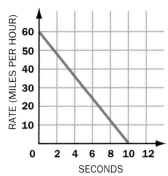

  A   after 30 seconds

  B   after 20 seconds

  C   after 10 seconds

  D   after 5 seconds

6 Which expression is equivalent to $\frac{1}{4} \times (4 - 2)$?

  F $\frac{1}{4} \times 4 - 2$

  G $4 \times \frac{1}{4} - 2$

  H $\frac{1}{4} \times 4 - \frac{1}{4} \times 2$

  J $\frac{1}{4} \times 4 \times 2$

7 If $Y + 8 = 8$, then $Y = ?$

  A   14

  B   7

  C   1

  D   0

8 Which ordered pair is inside both the square and the triangle?

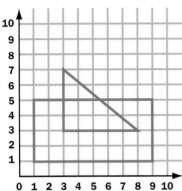

- **F** (2, 4)
- **G** (4, 4)
- **H** (4, 7)
- **J** (9, 4)

9 Which picture shows a reflection (flip) of the letter?

A   C

B   D

10 The two ski slopes at Bearsville measure $1\frac{5}{8}$ miles and $\frac{3}{4}$ mile. Sam went on each slop twice. What is the total distance that Sam skied?

- **F** $2\frac{3}{8}$ mi
- **G** $2\frac{2}{3}$ mi
- **H** $4\frac{1}{2}$ mi
- **J** $4\frac{5}{8}$ mi
- **K** Not Here

11 Which statement is **not** true?

- **A** $\angle ACB = \angle ACD$
- **B** $\angle ACD = 40°$
- **C** $\angle BCE = 40°$
- **D** $\angle ACB = \angle DCE$

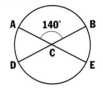

12 Which pair of figures are congruent?

F   H

G   J

13 A tower cast a shadow 180 feet long. At the same time, a tree that is 12 feet tall casts a shadow 20 feet long. What is the height of the tower?

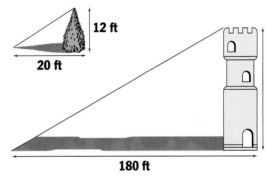

- **A** 108 ft
- **B** 172 ft
- **C** 300 ft
- **D** 356 ft
- **E** Not Here

14 The greatest common factor of 12, 18, and 30 is

- **F** 6.
- **G** 12.
- **H** 180.
- **J** 6,480.

PERCENT

THEME Buying and Selling

Are you a smart shopper? When you see items that are on sale, do you know how much you really save? In this chapter, you will learn what discount means and learn how percents are used in buying and selling.

What Do You Know ?

1 Find the percents in the ads. Write as many as you can as fractions.

2 If a Discman costs $100 at both stores before the sale, would you buy it on sale at J & P's or Wilson's? Explain.

3 Create your own ads that show sales with percents. Use graph paper to explain how you can write each percent as a decimal.

Use Graphs Shannon Wheeler owns a car lot called More Than Wheels. She uses a circle graph to display data on monthly sales figures.

You can use graphs to display data visually.

1 Which two types of vehicles did More Than Wheels sell the most of in May?

2 Write a paragraph describing More Than Wheels's sales during May.

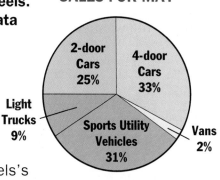

MORE THAN WHEELS
SALES FOR MAY

Vocabulary

percent, p. 424   **sale price,** p. 442   **circle graph,** p.446
discount, p. 442

Percent

So much data is thrown at you every day that if you don't understand percents, you'll miss out on a lot. The clothing label at the right tells you that 85% of the cloth is made out of cotton.

RN 40052
85% Cotton
15% Rayon

Machine wash cold. Tumble dry.
Do not bleach.
Made in U.S.A.

The word **percent** means "per hundred." The symbol for percent is %.

You can use a 10-by-10 grid to show percent. Each of the 100 small squares on the grid represents 1%.

85 squares out of 100 are shaded, or 85% of the grid.

Work Together

Work in a group. Use graph paper to make nine 10-by-10 grids.

> **You will need**
> • graph paper

Shade a grid to show each fraction, ratio, or decimal. Tell what percent is shaded.

$\frac{75}{100}$	$\frac{20}{100}$	6:100
$\frac{3}{4}$	$\frac{1}{2}$	1:4
0.75	0.32	0.4

▶ Is $\frac{1}{2}$ the same as 50%? Explain.

▶ How many small squares on a 10-by-10 grid would you shade to show 100%?

▶ **What if** a label says 100% cotton. What does it mean?

Cultural Note

Alexander the Great called cotton "vegetable wool." He is credited with bringing it to Europe from India in the fourth century B.C.

Make Connections

Look at the model below. It can be used to represent a fraction, a decimal, a ratio, and a percent.

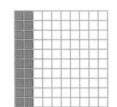

$\frac{1}{5}$ One fifth of the squares are shaded.
0.20   Twenty hundredths are shaded.
20:100   20 out of 100 squares are shaded.
20%   20% of the squares are shaded.

> **percent** The ratio of a given number to 100.

$$\frac{1}{5} = \frac{20}{100} = 0.20 = 20:100 = 20\%$$

▶ Describe how to represent 80% with a 10-by-10 grid, as a ratio of a number to 100, as a decimal, and as a fraction.

Check for Understanding

Write a fraction, a decimal, and a percent to show what part is shaded in each color.

1 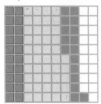 **2** 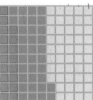 **3**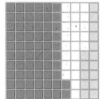

Write the fraction, ratio, or decimal as a percent. You may use a model to help you.

4 $\frac{70}{100}$ **5** 23:100 **6** 0.45 **7** $\frac{5}{10}$ **8** 0.9 **9** 0.1

Critical Thinking: Analyze

10 Look at ex. 2. Explain two ways to find, without counting, the percent of the grid that is not shaded red.

Practice

Write the fraction, ratio, or decimal as a percent. You may use a model to help you.

1 $\frac{15}{100}$ **2** 9:10 **3** 0.37 **4** $\frac{3}{5}$ **5** 0.7 **6** $\frac{4}{5}$

7 $\frac{3}{10}$ **8** 64:100 **9** $\frac{7}{100}$ **10** 0.1 **11** $\frac{2}{5}$ **12** $\frac{1}{4}$

Solve.

13 **What if** a clothing label says that the cloth is 75% cotton. What fraction of the cloth is made out of cotton?

14 There are 100 stores at a mall. Of them, 12 sell sporting goods. What percent sell sporting goods?

Percent, Fractions, and Decimals

Do you look for brand names when you shop? In a survey of sixth-grade boys, 25% said brand names are important when they shop for clothes. What fraction of the boys think brand names are important?

Write 25% as a fraction.

In the previous lesson you learned that a percent can be written as a fraction.

Step 1	Step 2
Write the percent as a fraction with a denominator of 100.	Simplify the fraction.
$25\% = \frac{25}{100}$	$\frac{25}{100} = \frac{25 \div 25}{100 \div 25} = \frac{1}{4}$

Brand names are important to $\frac{1}{4}$ of the boys surveyed.

In the previous lesson you also learned that a percent can be written as a decimal.

Write 30% as a decimal.

Step 1	Step 2
Write the percent as a fraction with a denominator of 100.	Then write an equivalent decimal.
$30\% = \frac{30}{100}$	$30\% = \frac{30}{100} = 0.30$, or 0.3

Talk It Over

▶ How would you write 80% as a fraction in simplest form?

a ▶ **ALGEBRA: PATTERNS** Look at the table at the right. What pattern do you see when you write a percent as a decimal?

Percent	Decimal
75%	0.75
63%	0.63
50%	0.5
25%	0.25
8%	0.08

In a survey of sixth-grade girls, $\frac{2}{5}$ of the girls said that brand names are important to them when they shop for clothes. What percent of the girls consider brand names important?

Write $\frac{2}{5}$ as a percent.

Step 1	Step 2
Write an equivalent fraction with a denominator of 100.	**Then write as a percent.**
$\frac{2}{5} = \frac{2 \times 20}{5 \times 20} = \frac{40}{100}$	$\frac{40}{100} = 40\%$

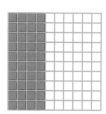

Brand names are important to 40% of the girls.

You can also write a decimal as a percent.

Write 0.6 as a percent.

Step 1	Step 2
First, write an equivalent decimal in hundredths.	**Then, write a fraction with a denominator of 100 and a percent.**
$0.6 = 0.60$	$\frac{60}{100} = 60\%$

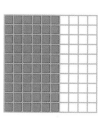

More Examples

A Write 6% as a fraction in simplest form.

$6\% = \frac{6}{100} = \frac{3}{50}$

B Write 5% as a decimal.

$5\% = \frac{5}{100} = 0.05$

C Write 0.02 as a percent.

$0.02 = \frac{2}{100} = 2\%$

Check for Understanding

Write the percent as a decimal and as a fraction in simplest form.

1 4%   **2** 8%   **3** 16%   **4** 35%   **5** 75%   **6** 95%

Write the fraction or decimal as a percent.

7 $\frac{2}{5}$ **8** 0.26   **9** 0.8   **10** $\frac{9}{10}$ **11** 0.03   **12** $\frac{1}{5}$

Critical Thinking: Analyze

 13 **ALGEBRA: PATTERNS** What pattern do you see when you write a decimal as a percent? Give examples.

Turn the page for Practice.

Practice

Write the percent as a fraction in simplest form.

1 3% **2** 5% **3** 8% **4** 10% **5** 15% **6** 17%

7 36% **8** 40% **9** 55% **10** 65% **11** 82% **12** 94%

Use mental math to write the percent as a decimal.

13 1% **14** 6% **15** 8% **16** 10% **17** 21% **18** 33%

19 43% **20** 50% **21** 56% **22** 61% **23** 78% **24** 99%

Write the fraction as a percent.

25 $\frac{11}{100}$ **26** $\frac{25}{100}$ **27** $\frac{1}{100}$ **28** $\frac{45}{50}$ **29** $\frac{26}{50}$ **30** $\frac{1}{5}$

31 $\frac{3}{4}$ **32** $\frac{3}{5}$ **33** $\frac{3}{10}$ **34** $\frac{9}{20}$ **35** $\frac{11}{20}$ **36** $\frac{20}{25}$

Use mental math to write the decimal as a percent.

37 0.25 **38** 0.36 **39** 0.11 **40** 0.43 **41** 0.85 **42** 0.97

43 0.07 **44** 0.03 **45** 0.09 **46** 0.4 **47** 0.5 **48** 0.7

Write as a percent, a fraction in simplest form, and a decimal.

49 65 people out of 100 people

50 8 days out of 10 days

51 5 stores out of 25 stores

·············· Make It Right ··············

52 Hana wrote 0.1 as a percent this way. Tell what the error is and correct it. Use a diagram to support your reasoning.

$0.1 = 1\%$

MIXED APPLICATIONS
Problem Solving

53 Did more than $\frac{1}{2}$ of the adults like L.A. Gear the most? Explain.

54 Jasmine said, "One out of every 4 adults surveyed liked Nike the most." Do you agree or disagree? Explain.

55 **Write a problem** using information from the survey. Solve it and have others solve it.

Brand Name Survey of 100 Adults	
Brand Name of Sneakers	**Shoppers' First Choice**
L.A. Gear	51%
Nike	25%
All Stars	15%
Reebok	6%
Others	3%

Reach 100 Percent Game!

Play this game with a partner. Your goal is to get as close as possible to 100% without going over.

You will need
* *index cards*

Play the Game

▶ Write each fraction, decimal, or percent at the right on an index card.

▶ Mix up the cards. Place the stack facedown.

▶ Take turns picking a card from the stack. If you pick a fraction or decimal, rename it as a percent. Keep track of your total.

▶ You can stop when you think you are as close to 100% as you can get without going over.

▶ After both players have stopped, compare the totals. The player closest to 100% without going over is the winner.

$\frac{1}{2}$	$\frac{1}{4}$	$\frac{3}{4}$	$\frac{1}{5}$	$\frac{2}{5}$	$\frac{4}{5}$	$\frac{1}{8}$	$\frac{1}{10}$	$\frac{1}{20}$	$\frac{1}{100}$

0.01 0.05 0.1 0.2 0.25 0.4
0.5 0.6 0.75 0.8

1% 5% 10% 20% 40% 50%
60% 75% 80%

Example:

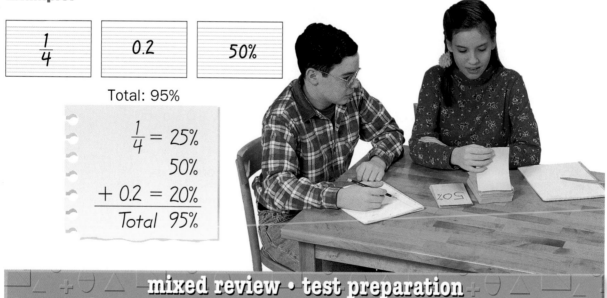

$\frac{1}{4}$ 0.2   50%

Total: 95%

$$\frac{1}{4} = 25\%$$
$$50\%$$
$$+ 0.2 = 20\%$$
$$\overline{Total\ 95\%}$$

---

mixed review • test preparation

Estimate. Then find the exact answer.

1 5,487 + 1,934   **2** 8,529 − 4,276   **3** 368 × 27   **4** 672 ÷ 84

5 49,210 + 63,859   **6** 55,386 − 24,562   **7** 829 × 769   **8** 5,642 ÷ 62

Percent of a Number

Would you believe that 50% of fourth graders surveyed go to video arcades each week? If 80 fourth graders were surveyed, how many go to the arcade each week?

Work Together

Work in a group. Use graph paper to model a percent of a number.

> **You will need**
> • *graph paper*

Look at the grid. What percent of the 80 small squares are shaded red?

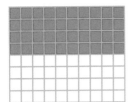

Think: $\frac{1}{2}$ of the squares are shaded red.

$\frac{1}{2} = 50\%$

Fifty percent of the small squares are shaded red.

▶ What is 50% of 80? How do you know?

▶ Use graph paper to model and find the following:
   a. 50% of 30   **b.** 25% of 40   **c.** 20% of 50   **d.** 10% of 60

▶ Explain how you use graph paper to model and find a percent of a number. Be prepared to present your work to the class.

Make Connections

Here is how Emily found 25% of 24.

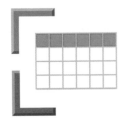

Rename 25% as $\frac{1}{4}$.
$\frac{1}{4}$ of 24 is 6.
25% of 24 is 6.

▶ How would you model 25% of 32? What is 25% of 32?

▶ Which is the greater number: 20% of 15 or 25% of 12? Use models to support your answer.

Check for Understanding

Tell how many small squares should be shaded to show the percent.

1 25%

2 20%

3 50%

Find the percent of the number. Use a model to support your answer.

4 10% of 50

5 20% of 20

6 25% of 40

7 50% of 30

8 25% of 8

9 20% of 25

10 25% of 28

11 50% of 32

Critical Thinking: Analyze

12 What is 100% of a number?

13 Five is 50% of what number? Draw a model to support your reasoning.

14 Write a paragraph to describe how to find 10%, 20%, 25%, or 50% of a number. Give examples and include models to support your reasoning.

Practice

Find the percent of the number. You may use a model to help.

1 50% of 16

2 20% of 30

3 25% of 36

4 50% of 48

5 10% of 90

6 25% of 16

7 20% of 55

8 50% of 120

9 10% of 120

10 25% of 200

11 20% of 150

12 50% of 240

13 25% of 64

14 50% of 300

15 20% of 20

16 30% of 90

17 20% of 200

18 10% of 300

19 25% of 32

20 25% of 60

Solve.

21 What is 20 percent of 45?

22 What is 25 percent of 32?

23 Fifty percent of the students in a class said they go to a mall at least once per week. There are 28 students in the class. How many of them go to a mall at least once per week?

24 In a test, a student answered 10% of the questions incorrectly. The test had 20 questions. How many questions did the student answer correctly?

Percent of a Number

During the celebration of Kwanza, candles are lit every night. You can buy a candleholder from a mail-order catalog. The price of the candleholder is $29.95. There is a shipping and handling charge of 20%. How much is the shipping and handling charge?

In the previous lesson you used models to find the percent of a number. You can find the percent of a number by renaming the percent as a fraction or as a decimal.

Find 20% of $29.95.

Step 1

Write the percent as a fraction.

$$20\% = \frac{20}{100} = \frac{1}{5}$$

Cultural Note

Kwanza is a week-long African American celebration, beginning on December 26. It was originally an African harvest festival.

Step 2

Multiply.

$$\frac{1}{5} \times \$29.95 = \$5.99$$

The shipping and handling charge is $5.99.

Benchmarks are common fractions and percents that are easy to work with. You can use benchmarks and mental math to help you find the percent of a number.

Find 25% of $20.00.

$$\frac{1}{4} \times \$20 = \$5$$

Benchmarks for Percent	
$10\% = \frac{1}{10}$	$33\frac{1}{3}\% = \frac{1}{3}$
$20\% = \frac{1}{5}$	$50\% = \frac{1}{2}$
$25\% = \frac{1}{4}$	$75\% = \frac{3}{4}$

Talk It Over

▶ What happens to the percent of a number when the percent increases? decreases? Give an example to support your reasoning.

▶ Is $2 both 20% of $10 and 40% of $5? Explain.

Have you ever been surprised at the cash register to find you had to pay a sales tax? If the tax is 6% and your purchases cost $5.95, how much tax must you pay? What is your total bill?

You can also find the percent of a number by renaming the percent as a decimal.

Step 1	Step 2	Step 3
Write the percent as a decimal.	Multiply to find the sales tax and round to the nearest cent.	Add the tax to the total purchases.
6% = 0.06	$5.95 × 0.06 $0.3570→ $0.36	$5.95 + 0.36 $6.31

The sales tax is $0.36, and the total bill is $6.31.

You can also find the sales tax and the total bill on a calculator.

 5.95 × 6 [%] = **0.357** Round to 0.36.

5.95 + 0.36 = **6.31**

More Examples

A Find 75% of 12.
$\frac{3}{4} \times 12 = 9$

B Find 30% of 50.
0.3 × 50 = 15

C Purchase price: $40   Sales tax: 5%

40 × 5% = **2.** $2 + $40 = **42.**
↑   ↑
Sales tax   Total purchase price

Check for Understanding

Find the percent of the number. Round to the nearest hundredth or nearest cent if necessary. Explain your methods.

1 75% of 16   **2** 9% of $20   **3** 20% of $5.50   **4** 3% of $7.50

Critical Thinking: Analyze

5 For ex. 1 and 2, is it easier to use a fraction or a decimal to solve? Why?

6 Sarah used a calculator to find 5% of $16 and said the answer is $0.08. How could she have checked this mentally?

Turn the page for Practice. ➡

Practice

Write the letter of the correct answer.

1 40% of 50   **a.** 50   **b.** 40   **c.** 20

2 60% of 15   **a.** 60   **b.** 15   **c.** 9

3 30% of 90   **a.** 30   **b.** 27   **c.** 24

4 100% of 57   **a.** 5.7   **b.** 57   **c.** 570

Find the percent of the number. Round to the nearest hundredth or nearest cent if necessary.

5 25% of 36

6 50% of 82

7 10% of 70

8 75% of 40

9 1% of 20

10 20% of 50

11 55% of 80

12 80% of 80

13 45% of 20

14 25% of $4.60

15 3% of $42

16 4% of 60

17 98% of 300

18 50% of $28.95

19 6% of $19.95

20 8% of $3.49

21 10% of $4.99

22 12% of $25.49

23 20% of $89.50

24 5% of 120

Use mental math to compare. Write >, <, or =.

25 25% of 10 ● 25% of 12

26 40% of $18 ● 30% of $18

27 50% of $10 ● 10% of $50

28 20% of 40 ● 25% of 36

29 50% of 20 ● 30% of 30

30 60% of $40 ● 40% of $60

☆ ALGEBRA Complete the table.

31

n	8	■	■	■	■
25% of n	2	4	8	32	64

32

n	■	100	■	■
1% of n	5	1	0.5	0.1

Find the total cost of each item, including a 5% tax.

33 cap

34 jeans

35 jacket and shoes

Item	Shoes	Cap	Jacket	Jeans
Price	$24.99	$9.99	$49.95	$29.99

•••••••••••••••••• **Make It Right** ••••••••••••••••••
36 Marla found 5% of $50 this way: $50 ÷ 5 = $10
Tell what the error is and correct it.

Problem Solving

37 Sales tax is 6% in Kentucky and 4% in Alabama. How much more does a $15 item cost in Kentucky than in Alabama?

38 Justin bought a CD for $15 and 2 cassette tapes for $7 each. Find the total cost of his purchases if he pays a 6% sales tax on the items.

39 A desk normally selling for $35.99 is on sale for 25% off. About how much can you save buying it on sale?

40 **Write a problem** that can be solved by finding a percent of a number. Solve it and have others solve it.

41 Amber sold handmade items at a craft fair. She sold $\frac{1}{3}$ as many quilts as napkin holders, 3 times as many picture frames as napkin holders, 6 more aprons than picture frames. If she sold 24 aprons, how many quilts did she sell?

42 Paul can order a shirt from a catalog for $19.95 plus $4.95 for shipping and handling. He can get the same shirt at a local store for $21 plus 7% sales tax. Which is cheaper? How much cheaper?

43 **Spatial reasoning** How many pairs of congruent triangles are in the figure to the right?

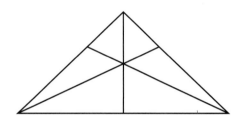

---

more to explore

Estimating a Tip

When you eat in a restaurant, it is common to leave a tip of 15% of the total bill. Here is a method to find the amount of the tip mentally.

Find 15% of a $60 bill.   **Think:** 5% is half of 10%.

First, find 10% of $60.	$6
Then, find 5% by dividing $6 by 2.	+ 3
Add to find 15% of 60.	$9

Estimate a 15% tip for the amount given.

1 $20

2 $40

3 $50

4 $18

5 $42.25

6 $78.50

7 $58.75

8 $32.95

Percent One Number Is of Another

Teens have buying power. Yvonne Campos, like other market researchers, surveys teens to find out what will sell. Of 300 teens in this survey, what percent chose pizza as their favorite food?

Favorite Foods of Teenagers	
Favorite Food	**Number**
Pizza	132
Chicken nuggets	100
Hot dogs	52
Hamburgers	16

IN THE WORKPLACE

Yvonne Campos, Market Researcher, Pittsburgh, PA

Find what percent of 300 is 132.

You can use a model to think about the problem.

From the model, you can write and solve a proportion.

$$\frac{132}{300} = \frac{n}{100}$$

$300 \times n = 132 \times 100$

$300n = 13{,}200$

$n = 44$

	Part **132**	Whole **300**
0		
0	*n*	100%

So 44% of the teens surveyed chose pizza.

You can also solve this problem by renaming the fraction as a percent.

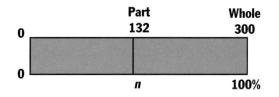 $\frac{132}{300} = 132 \div 300 = \boxed{0.44} = 44\%$

Another Example

What percent is $\frac{32}{300}$? $32 \div 300 = \boxed{0.106667}$ $\frac{32}{300} \approx 11\%$

Check for Understanding

Find the percent. Round to the nearest hundredth if necessary.

1 What percent of 32 is 8?

2 2 is what percent of 50?

3 15 is what percent of 45?

4 What percent of 8 is 1?

Critical Thinking: Analyze   Explain your reasoning.

5 **What if** the number of teens surveyed increases and the number who choose pizza stays the same. Will the percent increase or decrease?

Practice

Find the percent. Round to the nearest hundredth if necessary.

1 26 out of 50

2 36 out of 48

3 1 out of 25

4 10 out of 50

5 49 out of 70

6 8 out of 40

7 10 out of 200

8 4 out of 200

9 60 out of 80

10 18 out of 40

11 8 out of 300

12 15 out of 60

13 $33 is what percent of $220?

14 20 points is what percent of 30 points?

15 What percent of 60 kg is 21 kg?

16 What percent of 120 m is 8 m?

MIXED APPLICATIONS
Problem Solving

17 Of the 200 people surveyed, 98 said they have ordered merchandise from a Home Shopping TV network. What percent is this?

18 Of the 3,382 people who went to the mall cinemas on the weekend, 9% went to the 2:00 P.M. shows. About how many people was that?

19 A rectangular room in a scale model measures 4 in. by 5 in. The scale is $\frac{1}{2}$ in. = 1 ft. What are the dimensions of the actual room?

20 **Data Point** Make a bar graph to show the data in the table on page 436. Use percents on the vertical axis.

more to explore

Percents and Banking

When people borrow money, they must repay the loan and pay a percent of the loan, called *interest*.

Use this formula to find the interest and total cost of $2,000 borrowed for 2 years at a rate of 11% per year.

amount borrowed × *interest rate* × *time* = *total interest*

$2,000 × 11% × 2 = $440

Total amount owed = $2,000 + $440 = 2,440

Find the interest and the total amount owed.

1 Borrow: $3,000
Interest rate: 12%
Time: 3 years

2 Borrow: $4,000
Interest rate: 11%
Time: 4 years

3 Borrow: $5,000
Interest rate: 9%
Time: 5 years

Write a percent, a ratio, a fraction, and a decimal to show what part is shaded.

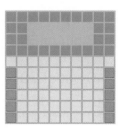

1 red

2 blue

3 green

4 yellow

5 green and blue

6 yellow and red

Rename the fraction or decimal as a percent.

7 $\frac{78}{100}$

8 $\frac{7}{10}$

9 $\frac{3}{5}$

10 $\frac{3}{4}$

11 0.64

12 0.35

13 0.06

14 0.7

Find the percent of the number. Round to the nearest hundredth or nearest cent if necessary.

15 25% of 60

16 50% of 48

17 75% of 80

18 10% of 90

19 35% of 600

20 5% of $4.99

21 16% of 80

22 15% of $12.99

Find the percent.

23 What percent of 32 is 4?   **24** What percent of 80 is 20?   **25** 36 is what percent of 50?

Find the percent of the total spent on the category. Round to the nearest whole number percent if necessary.

26 supplies

27 clothes

28 backpack

Sasha's Back-To-School Spending	
Clothes	$212
Supplies	$18
Miscellaneous	$22
Backpack	$48

Solve. Use mental math when you can.

29 James bought a coat for $70 and jeans for $35. He had to pay 8% sales tax on his purchases. How much sales tax did he pay? What was his total bill?

30 In a taste test, 1 out of 2 students surveyed liked soft drink A, 38% liked soft drink B, and $\frac{1}{8}$ liked soft drink C. Which soft drink was the most popular? the least popular?

31 When Top Mall opened, 36 of its 50 shops were rented. What percent of the shops was not rented when the mall opened?

32 Courtney bought a fishing pole for $18. Together with the tax, she paid $18.90. What percent of the total cost was the tax?

33 Journal Explain how you would find the percent of a number using a fraction and a decimal. Give examples.

Estimate with Percents

A sixth-grade class sells breakfast bagels for 50¢ each. The class pays 23¢ for each bagel that they buy, so their profit on each bagel is 27¢. About what percent of the selling price is the profit?

Use number sense to estimate what percent 27 is of 50.

Teresa says 27 out of 50 is about $\frac{25}{50}$, which is $\frac{1}{2}$, or 50%.

Jasmine says 27 out of 50 is about $\frac{30}{50}$, which is $\frac{3}{5}$, or 60%.

Otis says $\frac{27}{50}$ is $\frac{54}{100}$, which is 54%.

All of these are reasonable estimates for the problem.

You can also estimate to find the percent of a number.

Estimate 34% of 17.

Think: 34% is about $\frac{1}{3}$.

$\frac{1}{3} \times 18 = 6$

So 34% of 17 is about 6.

Estimate the percent.

1 108 out of 299

2 $729 out of $1,624

3 388 out of 1,563

4 $115 out of $1,159

5 234 out of 458

6 40 out of 77

Estimate the number.

7 31% of 23

8 19% of $243

9 74% of 402

10 The sixth graders are selling candy to raise money. The profit on a box of candy that sells for $4.99 is $1.99. About what percent of the selling price is the profit?

11 A computer game producer gives 58% off the selling price of its games to stores that sell the games. About how much will a store get off for a game that sells for $19.95?

Buying a Car

Have you dreamed of owning your own car? Choose a car to buy. Plan to make a 10% down payment and pay the rest in equal monthly payments over a period of 4 years. In this activity, you will work in groups to estimate what the cost would be each year over the 4 years to pay for and operate the car.

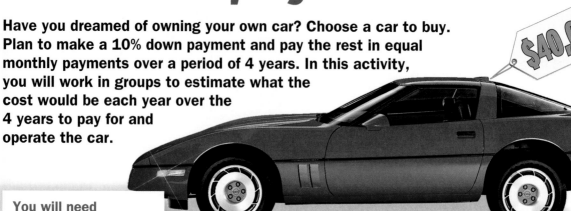

$40,000

You will need
- car advertisements

 Use the price for the car shown above or other prices you find. Many states have sales tax, so add 5% tax to the price.

 Find 10% of the price of the car including tax. Subtract that from the cost of the car including tax. The difference is the amount you have left to pay after the down payment.

 Find the amount of the monthly car payment (not including interest). Divide the amount left to pay by 48, the number of monthly payments you will make.

 Brainstorm the other types of expenses you will have for operating the car.

 Now, do some research to estimate the yearly costs for each type of expense. Record each item and the yearly estimated cost in a table like the one below. Find the total yearly cost and then fill in the column for the percent each item is of the total yearly cost of the car.

Yearly Car Expenses	Estimate	Percent of Total Yearly Cost
Car payments		
Insurance		

Compare Data Displays

1 Make a bar graph showing the estimated yearly dollars spent in each category of your budget. Color each bar a different color.

2 Make a circle graph to show the percent of the budget you spent in each category. Use the same colors as before.

3 **READING ARITHMETIC WRITING** **Use Graphs** Tell what information is easiest to find in the bar graph, what is easiest to find in the circle graph, and what, if anything, is easiest to find in the original table.

Report Your Findings

4 **Portfolio** Prepare a report on your car purchase. Include the following:

► Show your graphs, questions, and table.

► Describe in a paragraph how your team reached agreement on what to buy and what your costs would be.

► Describe anything you did or could have done to spend less money.

5 Compare your report with the reports of other teams.

Revise your work.
► Are your calculations correct?
► Is your report clear and organized?
► Did you proofread your work?

PREDICT what would happen if gas prices rose by 30%.

EXPLORE how much the car payments would be if you made monthly payments for 3 years.

FIND the current interest rates for financing the purchase of new and used cars.

Discounts

L
E
A
R
N

Do you watch for sales? Suppose that at one store Clue usually costs $9.95, but it is on sale for 20% off. How much is the discount, and what is the sale price?

The **discount** is the amount that you save. The **sale price** is the price you pay after the discount is subtracted.

> **Check Out the Glossary**
> discount
> sale price
> See page 643.

Estimate: 20% × $9.95

Think: $\frac{1}{5}$ × $10 = $2 ← discount

$10 − $2 = $8 ← sale price

You can use paper and pencil or a calculator to find the exact amount.

Step 1	Step 2
Find the discount.	**Subtract the discount from the original price.**
$9.95 × 0.20 **Think:** 20% = 0.20 $1.9900	$9.95 − 1.99 $7.96

 9.95 × 20 **%** = **1.99**   9.95 − 1.99 = **7.96**

The discount, or savings, is $1.99. Clue costs $7.96 on sale.

Another Example

Find the amount of the discount and the sale price.

Regular price: $4.99   0.1 × $4.99 = $0.4999
Discount: 10% off   Round to the nearest cent: $0.50
                  $4.99 − $0.50 = $4.49

Amount of the Discount ⎯⎯⏋   ⎩⎯ Sale price

C
H
E
C
K

Check for Understanding

Find the discount and the sale price to the nearest cent.

1 Regular price: $200
Discount: 15% off

2 Regular price: $80
Discount: 10% off

3 Regular price: $110
Discount: 2% off

Critical Thinking: Analyze

4 **What if** you have a rebate coupon for an additional 10% off Clue. What is the final price?

Practice

Find the discount and sale price to the nearest cent.

	Regular Price	Discount
1	$6	10%
2	$8	25%
3	$12	15%
4	$15	30%
5	$54	30%
6	$32	15%

	Regular Price	Discount
7	$62.00	5%
8	$3.99	50%
9	$5.25	25%
10	$8.69	20%
11	$9.99	5%
12	$86.99	60%

Estimate the cost of the item on sale.

13 winter jacket originally priced at $56

14 teens' jeans originally priced at $28

15 basketball shoes originally priced at $62.99

LANDER'S
Fine clothes
SAVE
this weekend!
Teens' Clothes—20% off
All winter jackets—30% off
Shoes—25% off

MIXED APPLICATIONS
Problem Solving

16 Latoya bought the Deluxe Edition of Monopoly for 25% off the original price of $21.99. She also paid a 6% sales tax. How much did she pay altogether for the game?

17 Of the 900 students surveyed, 484 were girls. About how many of the students liked sports-related games best? SEE INFOBIT.

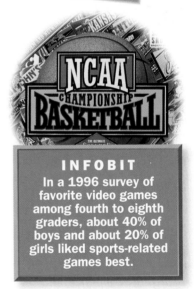

INFOBIT
In a 1996 survey of favorite video games among fourth to eighth graders, about 40% of boys and about 20% of girls liked sports-related games best.

mixed review • test preparation

a **ALGEBRA** **Write an equation for the function. Tell what the variables mean.**

1
Length of side	1	2	3	4
Perimeter of triangle	3	6	9	12

2
Width of rectangle	1	2	3	4
Length of rectangle	1	4	7	10

Find the better buy.

3 5 pt of cheese for $3 or 6 pt for $4

4 3 glue sticks for $1 or 8 for $2.75

Problem-Solving Strategy

Use Alternate Methods

Read You can eat smarter when you make choices at a fast-food restaurant. Say you want a burger at Burger King. A look at the nutrition information shows how many of the calories in each burger are fat calories and how many are not. Find the nonfat calories for a Burger King hamburger.

Plan You can find the number of nonfat calories in two ways.

Method 1: You can find 40% of 275 and subtract the result from 275.

Method 2: You can subtract 40% from 100%, and then multiply the result by 275.

Nutrition		
Burger	Calories	% of Calories from Fat
Hamburger	275	40
Whopper Jr.	322	48

Solve **Method 1**

$40\% = 0.4$ $0.4 \times 275 = 110$

$275 - 110 = 165$

Method 2

$100\% - 40\% = 60\%$

$60\% = 0.6$ $0.6 \times 275 = 165$

A Burger King hamburger has 165 nonfat calories.

Look Back Which method do you prefer? Explain.

Check for Understanding

1 **What if** you want to see if there is any difference in nonfat calories between the hamburger and the Whopper Jr. How would you find out? What is the difference?

Critical Thinking: Analyze

2 Write a paragraph describing why the two methods shown on this page give the same answer.

MIXED APPLICATIONS
Problem Solving

Use the menu for problems 1–3.

1 The restaurant offers a discount of 10% off when you order two entrees. How much will two entrees cost? Show two ways to solve the problem.

2 **Make a decision** You have $8 to spend for dinner. You want to buy an entree, rice, and a side dish. What are all the possible choices? Show your work in an organized way.

3 **Write a problem** using information from the Wok on Wheels menu. Solve the problem and then give your problem to others to solve.

WOK ON WHEELS

Rice
Steamed
Fried $1.00
                         $1.25

Entrees
Sweet & Sour
  Shrimp $5.95
Lemon Chicken $4.75
Broccoli Beef $4.50
Almond Chicken $3.98

Side Dishes
Garlic green
  beans $2.00
Egg roll
Dumplings $2.10
                $2.50

4 **Logical reasoning** The total price of Marty's purchases at the Neon Shop is $62. The shop gives a discount of 5% on any purchase over $50. There is a sales tax of 5% that has to be added to the price after the discount. Will Marty pay more than, less than, or exactly $62? Explain how you solved the problem without computing.

5 In a survey, Elizabeth found the number of people who preferred rice was $\frac{1}{2}$ the number who preferred potatoes. The number who preferred potatoes was $\frac{1}{4}$ the number who preferred pasta. If 48 people preferred pasta, how many preferred rice?

6 Maureen received a 20% discount on a summer shirt she bought in July. If the shirt's price was $25 before the discount, how much did she save? Show two ways to solve the problem.

7 Is getting a 15% discount on a $20 shirt a better buy than getting it on sale for $18.99? Explain.

Use the INFOBIT for problems 8–9.

8 Of the 2,506 children in the survey, how many had been to a fast-food restaurant or drive-in?

9 About how many times as many children ages 6–14 have been to fast-food restaurants as have not been to fast-food restaurants?

INFOBIT
According to a recent survey, 94% of children ages 6–14 in the United States have eaten at a fast-food restaurant or drive-in.

SOURCE: CHILDREN'S MARKET RESEARCH, INC.

Interpret and Make Circle Graphs

Have you ever heard the saying "A picture is worth a thousand words"? Graphs, because they are so visual, can sometimes be more effective for displaying data than a table. Graphs help you make comparisons quickly.

Circle graphs make it easy to compare parts of a whole and to compare parts to each other.

By just looking at the circle graph, you can tell that hanging around with friends is the most popular activity for this group of sixth graders.

Favorite After-School Activities

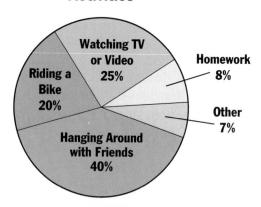

Suppose 160 students were surveyed. You can find how many prefer riding a bike by finding 20% of 160.

$$20\% \text{ of } 160 = 0.2 \times 160 = 32$$

Of the students surveyed, 32 prefer to ride bikes after school.

> **circle graph** A graph in which data are represented by parts of a circle.

Talk It Over

▶ Which activity was half as popular as hanging around with friends?

▶ If 200 students were surveyed, how many rode bikes, watched TV, and did homework?

Suppose you are one of the students who rides a bike after school, and you have an assignment to do research on your favorite activity. How could you create a circle graph to show your research results?

What Kind of Bikes Do People Buy From Bike Dealers	
Kind of Bike	**% of Bikes Sold**
Cross or hybrid bike	10%
Traditional road bike (27-in. wheel)	1%
Mountain bike (26-in. wheel)	63%
Children's bike (20-in. wheel)	20%
Other bikes	6%

SOURCE: NATIONAL BICYCLE DEALERS ASSOCIATION 1994–1995 STATPAK

To make a circle graph find the measures of the central angles for each section of the graph. Then draw the angles on a circle.

Step 1

Multiply 360° by each percent. Round to the nearest degree, if necessary.

$$0.1 \times 360° = \quad 36°$$
$$0.01 \times 360° \approx \quad 4°$$
$$0.63 \times 360° \approx \quad 227°$$
$$0.2 \times 360° = \quad 72°$$
$$0.06 \times 360° \approx + \; 21°$$
$$\overline{\quad\quad\quad\quad\quad 360°}$$

Note: The sum of the measures of the central angles in a circle is 360°.

Step 2

Draw a circle. Draw each angle with the vertex at the center. Label each section. Write a title for the graph.

Bikes People Buy

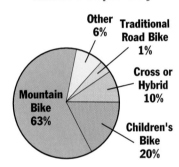

Check for Understanding
Use the circle graph for ex. 1–2.

1 About what fraction of the class has mountain bikes?

2 If there are 35 students in the class, how many do not own a bike?

3 Make a circle graph to show that 55% of adults and 45% of children surveyed own bikes.

Critical Thinking: Compare

4 Compare circle graphs with bar graphs. How are they different?

5 When would you use a circle graph? Give two examples.

Bikes in Ms. Lee's Class

Turn the page for Practice.

Practice

Use the circle graph for ex. 1–5.

1 Which of the following can you tell from the graph?
   a. Of all sixth graders in the U.S., 35% prefer biking.
   b. About $\frac{1}{5}$ of the sixth graders surveyed prefer in-line skating.
   c. Most students who prefer walking don't own bikes.
   d. Mountain bikes are the most popular kind of bike.

**Kennedy Middle School
Sixth Grade Choices
for Getting Around**

2 Do more Kennedy sixth graders prefer in-line skating or skateboarding?

3 What fraction of the students prefer skateboarding?

4 If 521 students were surveyed, about how many preferred walking?

5 Which activities were preferred by half the students?

6 The National Bicycle Dealers Association collects data on bicycle use in the United States. Make a circle graph to display the data from the table at the right.

Where Do You Buy a Bike?	
Type of Store	**Percent**
Department/toy/discount	75%
Family bike shop	18%
Pro shop	7%

SOURCE: NATIONAL BICYCLE DEALERS ASSOCIATION 1994–1995 STATPAK

7 How many degrees did you make the part of the circle to show department/toy/discount stores?

8 One thousand people were surveyed to find out what they used their bikes for. Make a circle graph to show the results of the survey at the right.

9 About how many degrees difference is there between the sections for Transportation and for Bike events?

What Do You Use Your Bike For?	
Purpose	**Number**
Transportation	110
Racing	30
Mountain biking	710
Touring	50
Bike events	100

SOURCE: NATIONAL BICYCLE DEALERS ASSOCIATION 1994–1995 STATPAK

Problem Solving

Pencil & Paper | Calculator | Mental Math

Use the circle graph for problems 10–11.

10 About half the people eat out because:
  a. they enjoy the atmosphere.
  b. they don't want to cook.
  c. they haven't time to fix meals.
  d. none of these

11 About how many times as many people eat out because they don't want to cook as because they don't know how to cook?

12 Write a problem using information from one of the circle graphs in this lesson. Solve the problem and then give it to others to solve.

13 Of all the theaters in the Portland area, 8 movie theaters have 3 or fewer screens, 11 theaters have 4 to 6 screens, and 6 theaters have more than 6 screens. Make a circle graph to show this data.

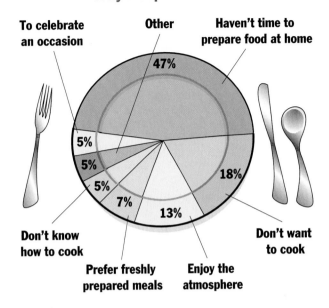

Why People Dine Out

To celebrate an occasion — Other — Haven't time to prepare food at home — 47% — 5% — 5% — 5% — 7% — 13% — 18% — Don't know how to cook — Prefer freshly prepared meals — Enjoy the atmosphere — Don't want to cook

14 Data Point Use the Databank on page 640. Find the average consumption of vegetables, flour and cereal products, and poultry per person, per day in 1993. Round to the nearest tenth.

Cultural Connection Census

According to the 1990 census, about 31.8 million people— 14% of the U.S. population age 5 and over—do not speak English in the home. Spanish is the most common non-English language spoken. The graph shows the states in which most non-English-speaking people live.

Alaska | United States | Hawaii

1 What percent of non-English speakers live in states other than California, New York, or Florida?

2 About how many non-English speakers live in California?

3 What conclusions can you draw from the graph?

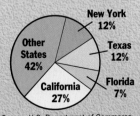

Where Non-English Speakers Live in the United States

New York 12% — Other States 42% — Texas 12% — California 27% — Florida 7%

Source: U.S. Department of Commerce, Bureau of Census

Problem Solvers at Work

Read
Plan
Solve
Look Back

PART 1 Interpret Data

Do you ever find misleading ads in newspapers, magazines, or on television? Look at the ads and the graph put out by Smile Brite. Do you think they are misleading? Why or why not?

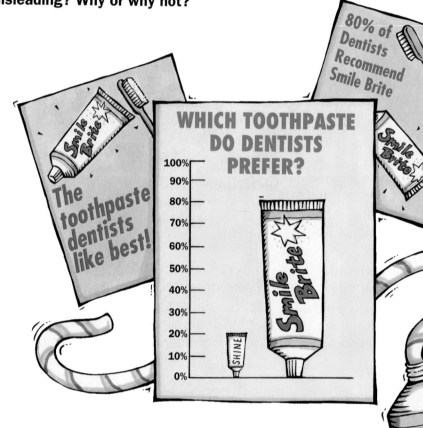

Work Together

Solve. Be prepared to explain your methods.

1 Does the ad give the number of dentists surveyed? Why do you think you need to know that?

2 How many brand names were given as choices for the dentists who were surveyed? As a customer, would you want to know whether the dentists recommended other brand names? Why?

3 **Use Graphs** What does the graph tell you? Is there anything about the visual display that is misleading?

4 **Make a decision** How would you take a survey to give a true picture of dentists' recommendations of toothpaste?

Kandie used the data in this table to write this ad.

What Toothpaste Do You Use?			
Toothpaste Used	Number of People	They Like the Taste	People with Cavities at Last Checkup
Smile Brite	20	18	2
White Plus	300	200	100
Fresh Breath	400	200	300
Minto	180	20	90
Other	100	80	40

5 Is the ad Kandie wrote misleading? Explain why or why not.

6 Write an ad of your own or draw a graph to sell one of the toothpastes listed in the table.

7 Trade ads or graphs. Read at least three ads or graphs. Decide if they are misleading. Explain why or why not.

8 Which ad or graph that you read was most convincing? Tell why.

9 **Write a problem** using information from either the table or your ad. Solve it and have others solve it.

10 Trade problems. Solve at least three problems written by other students.

STUDENT TO STUDENT

Use Fresh Breath Toothpaste! More people use Fresh Breath, and only 75% of the people had cavities at their last checkup.

Kandie Bennett
Madison Middle School
Marshall, NC

CHECK

Menu

Choose five problems and solve them. Explain your methods.

1 Matt and Li-chin earn $5.20 per hour each, and Erin earns $18.40 per hour. Erin says the average wage for all of them is $9.60 per hour, and Matt and Li-chin say it is $5.20. Who is right? Explain.

2 Is the ad below correct? Explain.

SALE — TOTAL DISCOUNT OF 40%

Get a discount of 30% off the original price and an additional 10% off the sale price if you pay with cash.

3 At an amusement park, the Madisons bought some $2.50 tickets for rides and some $1.00 tickets. There were 5 more $1.00 tickets than $2.50 tickets. How many of each kind did they buy if they spent $40?

4 Robin wants to cook a 10-pound pork roast. The roast needs to be cooked 20 minutes per pound and then stand for 15 minutes before slicing. If Robin wants to serve dinner at 6 P.M., at what time should he start the roast?

5 Use the example in the ad to find out if you would really save 65%–75%.

SAVE 65%–75%
On sportswear, dresses, and suits when you take an extra 30%–50% off merchandise already reduced 50%–70%

✓ ORIGINALLY.................................$188.00
✓ SALE, 50% OFF..........................$94.00
✓ AFTER EXTRA 30% OFF................$65.80
✓ FOR A TOTAL SAVINGS OF........ $122.20

6 Everett wants to purchase 6 CDs. They are $9.95 each, and he will get a 5% discount. How much money will he have left? What information is missing in order to solve the problem?

7 In 1994, the members of the Eastern Division of the AFC had the following win-loss records. Make a double-bar graph to show their records.

Team	Wins	Losses
Miami	10	6
New England	10	6
Indianapolis	8	8
Buffalo	7	9
New York	6	10

8 Students will be chosen to contribute one piece of art for a display. There will be art from 1 first grader, 2 second graders, 3 third graders, and so on, through twelfth grade. How many art pieces will there be?

Choose two problems and solve them. Explain your methods.

9 About 40 different elements are found in our bodies. The table shows the elements that make up a large part of our body weight. Show the data on two kinds of graphs. Which graph do you think shows the data better? Explain.

Elements in the Human Body	
Element	**Percent of Body Weight**
Oxygen	65
Carbon	18
Hydrogen	10
Nitrogen	3
Other	4

10 **Write a problem** Look for a circle graph in newspapers and magazines. Write two problems based on information from the graph you find. Solve it and have others solve it.

11 **Spatial reasoning** Draw a line segment that will divide the figure below into two similar figures.

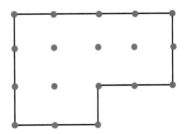

12 **At the Computer** Use a graphing program to make two circle graphs for the data in the table below, one for full-size/intermediate cars and one for compact/sports cars. How do you think car manufacturers and advertisers might use this information?

Most Popular Car Colors		
Color	**Full-Size/ Intermediate**	**Compact/ Sports**
Green	25%	23%
White	18%	15%
Tan	12%	5%
Red	18%	22%
Blue	7%	11%
Black	6%	10%
Purple	3%	6%
Other	11%	8%

SOURCE: AMERICAN AUTOMOBILE MANUFACTURERS ASSOCIATION

chapter review

Language and Mathematics

Complete the sentence. Use a word in the chart. (pages 424–449)

1 A good way to display parts of a whole is with a ■.

2 The word ■ means "per hundred."

3 The percent to be subtracted when an item is on sale is called the ■.

4 The original price minus the discount is called the ■.

Concepts and Skills

Write the percent as a decimal and as a fraction in simplest form. (page 426)

5 10%   **6** 30%   **7** 50%   **8** 75%   **9** 16%

Write the decimal or fraction as a percent. Round to the nearest whole number percent if necessary. (page 426)

10 0.24   **11** 0.56   **12** 0.08   **13** 1   **14** 0.6

15 $\frac{79}{100}$ **16** $\frac{36}{50}$ **17** $\frac{4}{10}$ **18** $\frac{1}{4}$ **19** $\frac{1}{3}$

Find the percent of the number. (page 430)

20 20% of 80   **21** 10% of 250   **22** 30% of $9   **23** 50% of 38

24 25% of 24   **25** 75% of $20   **26** 15% of 28   **27** 30% of 75

Find the percent. Round to the nearest whole number percent if necessary. (page 436)

28 11 is what percent of 110?   **29** What percent of 25 is 5?

30 16 is what percent of 64?   **31** What percent of 90 is 72?

32 31 is what percent of 93?   **33** What percent of 28 is 12?

Find the discount and sale price. Round to the nearest cent if necessary. (page 442)

34 Regular price: $12
Discount: 20% off

35 Regular price: $22
Discount: 10% off

36 Regular price: $28.95
Discount: 5% off

37 Regular price: $34
Discount: 15% off

38 Regular price: $74.85
Discount: 20% off

39 Regular price: $199.99,
Discount: 25% off

Think critically. (pages 426, 430, 432)

40 Analyze. Explain what the error is and then correct it.

Find 5% of 80.
0.5 × 80 = 40
5% of 80 is 40.

41 Generalize. Complete this sentence: To change a decimal to a percent, move the decimal point ■ and add a percent sign.

MIXED APPLICATIONS
Problem Solving

Pencil & Paper   Calculator   Mental Math

(pages 444, 450)

42 How much does it cost to buy 4 folding chairs with a 5% sales tax?

$16.99

43 Suppose you are a U.S. tourist at the Edmonton Mall in Canada. The all-day pass for the rides is 20 Canadian dollars. The ticket to the World Waterpark is 15 Canadian dollars. On that day, one Canadian dollar is equivalent to $0.72 in U.S. dollars. How much will you have to spend for both tickets if you use U.S. dollars?

44 An ad claims that you can save more than 100% of your energy costs if you purchase a new type of light bulb. Do you believe the ad? Explain.

45 Of the 48 stores in a mall, 36 agreed to stay open on Saturday until 9 P.M. What percent of the stores did not agree to stay open?

Use the graph at the right for problems 46–49.

46 During which part of the year are most students more bored?

47 About what fraction of the students are bored in the summer?

48 From the graph, 42% of students are more bored during the school year. If 500 students were surveyed, how many of them said they are more bored during the school year?

49 Marcia said, "One in five students said they were equally bored both during the summer and during the school year." Do you agree? Explain.

50 Make a circle graph for the data in the table at the right.

When Are You More Bored?

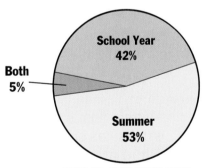

School Year 42%

Both 5%

Summer 53%

SOURCE: SEGA GAME GEAR

Where Athletic Shoes Are Made	
China	35%
South Korea	26%
Indonesia	16%
Taiwan	9%
Other	14%

SOURCE: SPORTING GOODS ASSOCIATION

Write as a decimal and as a fraction in simplest form.

1 20%   **2** 40%   **3** 56%   **4** 84%

Write as a percent.

5 0.19   **6** 0.07   **7** $\frac{37}{100}$ **8** $\frac{3}{4}$

Find the percent of the number.

9 40% of 50   **10** 75% of 80   **11** 25% of $36   **12** 15% of 44

Find the percent.

13 25 is what percent of 125?

14 What percent of 20 is 15?

15 30 is what percent of 60?

Find the discount and sale price to the nearest cent.

16 Regular price: $16
Discount: 25% off

17 Regular price: $18
Discount: 20% off

18 Regular price: $239.59
Discount: 15% off

Use the graph at the right for problems 19–21.

19 On which form of advertising was the most money spent?

20 About how much money was spent on store signs?

21 What fraction of the money was spent on television ads?

**Expenses for Advertising
Total: $150,000**

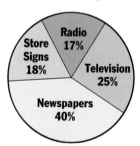

Solve.

22 A store has a total floor space of 1,550 ft². If the sales counters take up a total of 350 ft², what percent of the floor space do the sales counters occupy? Round your answer to the nearest whole number percent.

23 A clothing store is having a clearance sale. Each item in the store is marked at a 40% discount. How much would a $25 pair of jeans cost at the sale before sales tax? Show two different ways to solve the problem.

24 Suppose you bought the discounted jeans in problem 23. If the sales tax was $2.10, how much change would you get from a $20 bill?

25 A music store has three new CDs for customers to preview. Using A, B, C, list all the ways the three CDs can be arranged in the preview display.

What Did You Learn?

STOREWIDE SALE

ON SALE

All **overalls 40% off** regular price

All **pants 30% off** regular price

All **shirts 20% off** regular price

Use this coupon for an

EXTRA 10% OFF
the sale price of any one item.

REGULAR PRICES

$11.99
T-shirts

$14.99
Polo shirts

$40
Overalls

$35
Jeans

$33.95
Cotton Pants

▶ Spend from $130 to $150. Make a list of the items you would buy. Buy at least 3 items and don't forget to use the coupon for one item. You can buy more than one of an item.

•••••••••••••••••• **A Good Answer** ••••••••••••••••••
- shows the number of each item you are buying
- shows your calculations and shows that the total is at least $130 and at most $150

 You may want to place your work in your portfolio.

What Do You Think

1 Do you understand how ratios and percents are alike? different? If not, what are you least sure of?

2 When you change a percent to a fraction or a decimal, do you use:
- an estimate?
- mental math?
- models?
- pencil and paper?
- a calculator?
- another method? Explain.

GOLD

Aztec Necklace

Gold has many uses besides jewelry and pieces of art. It is used for many industrial purposes since it is a very good conductor of electricity. Shields made of gold protected spacecraft from the intense rays of the sun during manned missions to the moon. Gold is also used for fillings and other kinds of dental work.

Other metals are often combined with gold. This is done to make the gold stronger.

Adding other metals also reduces the cost of gold. Pure gold is rather soft. A mixture of two or more metals is called an *alloy.*

One way to measure the purity of gold is in terms of karats. Pure gold is said to be 24 karat. Gold that is 12 karat is $\frac{12}{24}$, or 50% pure gold and 50% other metals. In the United States, in order for an object to be legally called "gold," it must be at least 10 karat, or 10 k.

Gold bars

Gold Mask Lima, Peru

Spacecraft

► What would be the disadvantages of making a necklace out of pure gold?

► Copper also is a very good conductor of electricity. Why do you think copper is more commonly used for electrical wiring than gold?

> **Cultural Note**
> It is not known when people started making things out of gold. Gold cups and jewelry were made in the city of Ur in Mesopotamia, in what is now Iraq, as early as 3500 B.C.

The Value of Gold

1 Complete the table below. Round to the nearest whole number percent.

Percent of Gold	
Karats	**Percent Gold**
8	33
9	38
10	
18	
20	
22	

The price of gold changes daily as it is traded. You can find the value of the gold in a bracelet or other piece of jewelry by using this formula:

Gold value = price × gold content × weight

For example, if the price of gold is $385.70 per ounce and you have a 12-k gold bracelet that weighs 1.5 oz, the value of the gold is:

$385.70 × 50% × 1.5 = $289.28.

2 If the price of gold is $382.50, how much would the gold in a bracelet weighing 2 ounces be worth if it were 10 k? 18 k?

3 If the price of gold is $384.10, how much would the gold in a bracelet weighing 1.75 ounces be worth if it were 20 k? 22 k?

First century gold torc

At the Computer

Percent of Gold		
Karats	**Percent of Gold**	**Fineness**
8	33	333
9	38	
10	42	
18	75	
20	83	

4 In some parts of the world, the purity of gold is measured in fineness, or parts per thousand. Use spreadsheet software and add a column to the table you made for problem 1 that includes fineness. For example, 8 k would be $\frac{8}{24} \approx 0.333$, or a fineness of 333 parts per thousand.

5 Explain how you could use the numbers in the fineness column to solve problems 2 and 3.

Thracian gold mug, 380–350 B.C.

THEME

Games and Sports

Do you tend to be a winner when you play a game? In this chapter, you will use probabilities to find the chance of winning a game, to tell if a game is fair or unfair, and even to create your own game!

What Do You Know

Use the Stick Game to solve the problems.

1 If you toss one stick, what is the probability of getting red?

2 If you toss one stick, what is the probability of getting:
a. green
b. red or blue

3 Taylor tossed two sticks on each turn and scored 30 points. How many turns could he have played? How might he have scored in each turn?

SCORE

2 red	10 points
1 red, 1 blue	3 points
2 blue	5 points

READING ARITHMETIC WRITING

Steps in a Process **It may be difficult to play a new game without the rules. How do rules show the process of playing a game?**

Writing about the steps in a process can help you understand the process and help you organize what you know.

1 Think about your favorite game. Write the steps involved in playing it.

Vocabulary

outcome, p. 462
equally likely, p. 463
event, p. 463
probability, p. 463
favorable outcome,
   p. 463

possible outcome,
   p. 463
more likely, p. 466
less likely, p. 466
certain, p. 466

impossible, p. 466
simulation, p. 468
tree diagram, p. 476
counting principle,
   p. 476

Probability

What are some board games you have played using number cubes? Have you ever hoped for a specific number to turn up?

In this activity, you will conduct a probability experiment using a 1–6 number cube to see how likely it is to get your number.

The **outcomes** of a probability experiment are the possible results. A sample space is a list of all possible outcomes for the experiment. The outcomes for this experiment are tossing 1, 2, 3, 4, 5, and 6.

You will need
• *a 1–6 number cube*

Cultural Note

Since its creation in 1935, Monopoly has been translated into over 25 languages and is sold in over 70 countries, including Russia, Croatia, Malaysia, South Africa, and Colombia.

Work Together

1 Work with a partner. Toss a 1–6 number cube 60 times. Record the numbers that come up with tallies in a frequency table like the one at the right.

2 Fill in the third column of the frequency table with the number of times each outcome occurred.

3 Fill in the fourth column with the fraction of the times each outcome occurred out of the total of 60 tosses.

Results of 60 Tosses

Outcome	Tallies	Number of Times	Fraction of the Total
1	卌 IIII	9	$\frac{9}{60}$
2	卌 卌 III	13	$\frac{13}{60}$
3	卌 卌	10	$\frac{10}{60}$
4	卌 II	7	$\frac{7}{60}$
5	卌 卌 II	12	$\frac{12}{60}$
6	卌 IIII	9	$\frac{9}{60}$

Talk It Over

▶ Compare your fractions with those of other groups. What conclusions can you draw?

▶ Do you think that the chance of getting each outcome is the same when you toss the number cube? Explain.

Make Connections

When you tossed the number cube, you had the same chance of getting each outcome, so the outcomes are **equally likely**.

An **event** is a collection of one or more outcomes.

If all the possible outcomes are equally likely, the **probability** of an event is given by the following formula:

Probability of event $= P(\text{event}) = \dfrac{\text{number of } \textbf{favorable outcomes}}{\text{number of } \textbf{possible outcomes}}$

Find the probability of tossing a 4.

$P(4) = \dfrac{1}{6}$ ← **1 favorable outcome**
        ← **6 possible outcomes**

Finding the probability of tossing an even number.

$P(\text{even}) = \dfrac{3}{6}$ ← **3 favorable outcomes (2, 4, or 6)**
            ← **6 possible outcomes**

Note: A probability can be written as a fraction, a decimal, or a percent.

The probablity is $\frac{3}{6}$, or $\frac{1}{2}$, or 0.5, or 50%.

▶ How would you find the probability of tossing a number that is not 2? What is the probability?

▶ What is $P(3 \text{ or } 5)$?

> **Check Out the Glossary**
> For vocabulary words, see page 643.

Check for Understanding

**Suppose you select one card from a hat without looking.
Find the probability.**

| 1 | 2 | 3 | 4 | 5 | 6 | 7 | 8 | 9 | 10 |

1 $P(4)$ **2** $P(6 \text{ or } 8)$ **3** $P(\text{odd number})$ **4** $P(\text{number greater than 4})$

Critical Thinking: Analyze   **Explain your reasoning.**

5 If two outcomes are equally likely, do they have the same probability? Explain.

6 📓 Suppose you toss a 1–6 number cube and get a 2 four times in a row. What is the probability of getting a 2 on the next toss of the number cube?

Practice

Suppose you spin the spinner. Find the probability. Write each probability as a fraction, a decimal, and a percent.

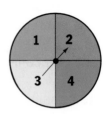

1 P(2)

2 P(odd number)

3 P(1 or 2)

4 P(number greater than 1)

Suppose you select a marble from the bag without looking. Find the probability.

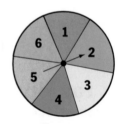

5 P(red)

6 P(blue)

7 P(green)

8 P(red or green)

9 P(red or blue)

10 P(not red)

11 P(green or blue)

12 P(not blue)

Suppose that after mixing the cards, you choose one without looking, record the outcome, and put it back. Find the probability.

13 P(A)

14 P(C)

15 P(D or E)

16 P(vowel)

17 P(consonant)

Suppose you spin the spinner. Find the probability.

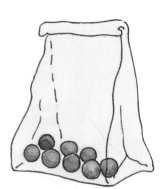

18 P(3)

19 P(even number)

20 P(number greater than 2)

21 P(2 or 6)

22 P(1, 3, or 4)

23 P(not 5)

Suppose that after mixing the cards, you select one without looking. Find the probability.

24 P(red)

25 P(square)

26 P(green)

27 P(triangle)

.... **Make It Right** ....

28 The experiment is spinning the spinner. Explain what Joan's error is and help her correct it.

P(B) = 1/3 because there are 3 possible outcomes and there is one way to get B.

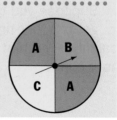

29 Do the experiment described for ex. 13–17 fifty times and record the outcomes in a frequency table. What conclusions can you draw?

30 The distance between two towns on a map is 3.2 cm. If 1 cm represents 57 km, how far apart are the two towns, to the nearest kilometer?

31 **Spatial reasoning** Trace and cut out the pieces, or arrange them mentally. You may need to rotate, flip, or translate some of the pieces. What capital letters of the English alphabet can you form?

32 About how old is the game of Go? **SEE INFOBIT.**

INFOBIT
The game of Go originated either in India or China as early as 2356 B.C.

Cultural Connection Igba-Ego

In Nigeria, the Igbo people play a game called *Igba-ego* (IH-bah-E-goh) using coins. It used to be played with cowrie shells. Here is a simplified version of the game.

AFRICA

Nigeria

Each player has a pile of shells. One player, the challenger, picks up four of his or her shells to toss, while the others drop one shell on a pile in the center. The challenger tosses the four shells and notices how they land. If the openings are all up, all down, or two up and two down, he or she wins all the shells in the center. Otherwise, the challenger adds the four shells to the pile in the center, and the next player becomes the challenger.

1 Use coins instead of shells. Heads can represent openings up; and tails openings down. Toss four coins 100 times and make a frequency table of the outcomes: 4 heads, 3 heads and 1 tail, 2 heads and 2 tails, 1 head and 3 tails, 4 tails.

2 Based on your experiment, which outcome or outcomes are most likely? least likely? Why?

Probability

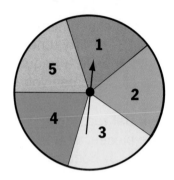

A game uses the spinner at the right. If you spin an odd number, you get 1 point. If you spin an even number, you get 0 points. Is it equally likely that you will spin an odd or even number?

Getting any one of the outcomes—1, 2, 3, 4, 5—is equally likely. However, the spinner has three odd numbers and two even numbers.

$P(\text{odd}) = \dfrac{3}{5}$ ← **favorable outcomes (1, 3, 5)**
← **possible outcomes (1, 2, 3, 4, 5)**

$P(\text{even}) = \dfrac{2}{5}$ ← **favorable outcomes (2, 4)**
← **possible outcomes (1, 2, 3, 4, 5)**

Spinning an odd number and spinning an even number are not equally likely. Spinning an odd number is **more likely**. Spinning an even number is **less likely**.

Check Out the Glossary
For vocabulary words, see page 643.

When the probability of an event is 1, the event is said to be **certain.**

When the probability of an event is 0, the event is said to be **impossible.**

$P(\text{odd or even}) = \dfrac{5}{5} = 1$

$P(6) = \dfrac{0}{5} = 0$

Check for Understanding

For the experiment, tell whether the outcomes listed are equally likely. If they are not equally likely, tell which is the most likely.

1 Experiment: Select a marble from the bag without looking.
Outcomes: red, blue

2 Experiment: Pick a student's name from a hat without looking.
Outcomes: left-handed, right-handed

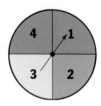

3 Experiment: Spin the spinner.
Outcomes: 1, 2, 3, 4

Critical Thinking: Analyze   **Explain your reasoning.**

4 Give an example of an event that is certain. Give an example of an event that is impossible.

5 Can the probability of an event ever be less than 0 or greater than 1? Explain.

Practice

Are the outcomes listed equally likely? If they are not equally likely, tell which is the most likely.

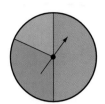

1 Experiment: Flip a coin.
Outcomes: heads, tails

2 Experiment: Toss a 1–6 number cube.
Outcomes: 6, number less than 6

3 Experiment: Spin the spinner above.
Outcomes: red, green, blue

4 Experiment: Toss a 1–6 number cube.
Outcomes: even, odd

Suppose you choose a cube from the bag without looking. Find the probability.

5 P(green)   **6** P(blue)   **7** P(red)   **8** P(white)

9 P(not yellow)   **10** P(red or blue)   **11** P(red, blue, or green)

Suppose you spin the spinner at the right. Find the probability.

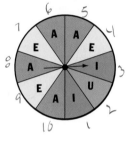

12 P(U)   **13** P(E)   **14** P(A)   **15** P(A or E)

16 P(I or U)   **17** P(vowel)   **18** P(B)   **19** P(not M)

MIXED APPLICATIONS
Problem Solving

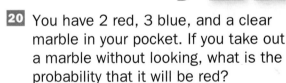

20 You have 2 red, 3 blue, and a clear marble in your pocket. If you take out a marble without looking, what is the probability that it will be red?

21 **Write a problem** about a spinner with 3 outcomes that are not all equally likely. Solve it and then give it to others to solve.

--- more to explore ---

Events and Their Complements

The *complement* of an event is the set of possible outcomes that are not in the event. The sum of the probabilities of an event and its complement is 1.

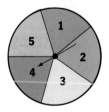

$P(\text{even}) = \frac{2}{5}$ $P(\text{odd}) = \frac{3}{5}$ $\frac{2}{5} + \frac{3}{5} = 1$

Use the spinner. Is the sum of the two probabilities equal to 1? Are the two events complements? Explain.

1 P(yellow) and P(blue)

2 P(odd) and P(a number divisible by 2)

3 P(1) and P(2, 3, 4, or 5)

4 P(even) and P(a number > 3)

Use a Simulation

L E A R N

Read You're a Detroit Tigers fan. Find your chance of winning the cap. If $\frac{1}{6}$ of the packs given out have *T*s, $\frac{1}{6}$ have *I*s, and so on, what is the average number of packs you would have to get in order to get all 6 letters?

TIGERS
★ Collect all 6 Special Detroit Tigers cards and win a baseball cap!
★ Only 1 pack of cards per person at the game.

Plan Use a **simulation**, an experiment that is similar to the problem, to find the average number. Using a simulation is a way of acting out the problem. Assign a letter to each of the six numbers on a number cube. Toss the cube and record the outcome. Repeat until you get an outcome for each of the 6 letters.

Solve Repeat the simulation at least 25 times. Find the average number of times it took to get all 6 numbers. Here is one student's data.

> **Check Out the Glossary**
> simulation
> See page 643.

	Outcomes						Total Number of Tosses
Experiment	T 1	I 2	G 3	E 4	R 5	S 6	
1	///	//	‖‖	///	//	//	17
2	/	///	/	////	/	//	12

> Total number of tosses for each of the 25 experiments:
> 17, 12, 11, 16, 16, 16, 14, 6, 17, 12, 21, 9, 9, 21, 19, 8, 22, 9, 17, 7, 15, 43, 18, 10, 18
>
> Sum: 383   Average: 383 ÷ 25 = 15.32

Based on this student's simulation, you will have to get about 15 packs to get all 6 letters.

Look Back What is another way to do the simulation?

C H E C K

Check for Understanding

1 **READING ARITHMETIC WRITING** **Steps in a Process** How could you use a coin to estimate the probability that one of two evenly matched teams would win the World Series in 4 games? List all the steps in the process.

Critical Thinking: Predict

2 Do you think you would get about the same estimate for the number of packs in the trading card problem if you tried the simulation yourself? Explain.

1 Suppose the Indianapolis Colts football team is giving away packs of football cards with one letter—*C, O, L, T,* or *S*—in each pack. Assume that $\frac{1}{5}$ of the packs have *C*s; $\frac{1}{5}$, *O*s; and so on. Use a simulation to find the average number of packs you would need to get all 5 letters. Explain how you set up your simulation.

2 **Spatial reasoning** A grocer stacked his oranges in the shape of a square pyramid. The base was 4 oranges by 4 oranges square. The next layer was 3 oranges by 3 oranges. The next layer was 2 oranges by 2 oranges, and the last layer was only 1 orange. If he wanted to double the height, how many oranges would he need in all?

3 Use a simulation to find the probability that a family with 3 children will have exactly 2 girls. Assume that it is equally likely that a baby will be a boy or a girl. Explain how you set up your simulation.

4 On a recent trip you and your family traveled for five days in a car. The distance traveled each day was 289 mi, 292 mi, 339 mi, 320 mi, and 298 mi. Estimate the average number of miles your family traveled each day. Explain your strategy.

5 A snail is at the bottom of a well that is 12 ft deep. The snail crawls up 3 ft each day, but it slips back 2 ft each night. How many days will it take the snail to reach the top of the well and get out?

6 For a Health Day project, everyone in a team of ten students takes the pulse of every other team member. How many pulse takings are there altogether?

7 **Data Point** Use the Databank on page 641. Make scale drawings of the playing areas of various sports. Compare the areas of the playing fields you drew.

8 A quiz has 5 true-false questions on it. Suppose you guess on all of the questions. Use a simulation to find the probability of answering at least 3 questions correctly. Explain how you set up your simulation.

9 About what percent of the Super Bowls were won by the San Francisco 49ers between 1967 and 1996?
SEE INFOBIT.

INFOBIT
The first Super Bowl was played in 1967 at the Memorial Coliseum in Los Angeles. Between 1967 and 1996 the San Francisco 49ers and Dallas Cowboys won the Super Bowl five times each.

Are the outcomes listed equally likely? If they are not equally likely, tell which is more likely.

1 Experiment: Spin the spinner.
Outcomes: 1, 2, 3

2 Experiment: Select a marble from the bag without looking. Outcomes: red, green

3 Experiment: Toss a 1–6 number cube.
Outcomes: 1, 2, 3, 4, 5, 6

4 Experiment: Toss a 1–6 number cube.
Outcomes: less than 3, more than 2

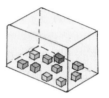

Suppose you select a cube from the box without looking. Find the probability.

5 $P(\text{red})$ **6** $P(\text{yellow})$

7 $P(\text{blue})$ **8** $P(\text{green})$

Suppose you toss a 1–6 number cube. Find the probability.

9 $P(4)$ **10** $P(3 \text{ or } 5)$ **11** $P(\text{even})$ **12** $P(8)$

13 $P(\text{less than 5})$ **14** $P(\text{odd or even})$ **15** $P(\text{less than 6})$ **16** $P(\text{not 2})$

Solve.

17 You are in a class of 25 students. With a friend, you write each student's name on a separate piece of paper, put the pieces in a bag, and shake the bag. The teacher selects a name from the bag without looking. What is the probability that the name she selects will be yours or your friend's?

18 A quiz has multiple choice questions on it. Suppose you guess on a question. How would you set up a simulation to find the probability of answering the question correctly?

19 You buy a game for $7.95. The tax is 8%. You give the clerk a $20 bill. How much change should you get?

20 Journal Suppose you flipped a coin 10 times and got 8 heads. Does that mean that the probability of heads for that coin is greater than $\frac{1}{2}$? Explain.

developing technology sense

MATH CONNECTION

Create a Simulation

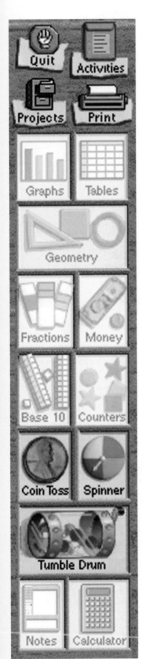

You can use a computer to simulate a game. A spreadsheet linked to a probability tool can help you record and analyze your results.

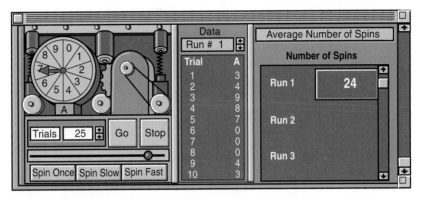

What if a game had 10 different game pieces. The first person to select one of each kind of piece from the surprise box wins. How many times would you expect to have to select a piece to get all 10 if you must replace the piece after each selection?

▶ Use the 0–9 spinner. Let each digit, 0 through 9, stand for one of the game pieces. Spin the spinner, and the table will record your results. Continue spinning until all 10 digits have been spun. Count and record in a spreadsheet the number of spins it took to get all 10 digits.

▶ Repeat the experiment at least 20 times. Use the spreadsheet to calculate the average number of selections it would take to get each of the 10 pieces. Compare your results with those of other students.

1 **What if** 3 of the game pieces were the same. Conduct an experiment to determine how many times you would have to select a piece to get one of each type.

2 Use the probability tools to design your own game. Conduct an experiment to determine if your game is fair.

Critical Thinking: Generalize   Explain your reasoning.

3 Many people use simulations to predict real-world events such as weather. What are the advantages of using a simulation? What are the disadvantages?

Do More and More Trials

Have you ever found the probability for an event, say for heads or tails in a coin flip, and when you've tried it a few times, found that the results didn't match the probability you predicted?

To test why that happens, create a spinner that has 2 outcomes, such as red and blue.

You will need:
- *paper clip*
- *markers or color pencils*

1. Estimate the probability of each outcome on your spinner.

2. Spin the spinner 10 times and record the results in a table like the one below. In this table, the number of trials is the number of times you have done the experiment. Keep spinning and recording the results for 100 trials.

Total Number of Trials	Total Number of Red Outcomes	Total Number of Blue Outcomes	Percent of Red Outcomes	Percent of Blue Outcomes
10	3	7	$\frac{3}{10} = 30\%$	$\frac{7}{10} = 70\%$
20	6 + 3 = 9	4 + 7 = 11	$\frac{9}{20} = 45\%$	$\frac{11}{20} = 55\%$
30	3 + 9 = 12	7 + 11 = 18	$\frac{12}{30} = 40\%$	$\frac{18}{30} = 60\%$

DECISION MAKING

Test Your Spinner

1 Spin your spinner 10 more times and record the results.

2 Combine these results with the results from your previous 10 spins. Record the results for these 20 spins in the table. For example, 3 reds in the first 10 trials plus 6 reds in the second 10 trials is 9 reds in 20 trials.

3 Repeat steps 1 and 2 until you have a total of 100 trials.

4 Compare your percents with the probabilities you estimated for each outcome. What happens to the percent as the number of trials increases?

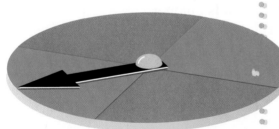

Report Your Findings

5 Prepare a report describing your experiment. Include the following in your report:

► A description of how the percents changed as the number of trials increased.

► A conclusion about why the percents would change as the number of trials increase. Justify your conclusion.

6 Compare your report with the reports of other groups.

Revise Your Work.
► Did you check your calculations?
► Is your report clear and organized?
► Did you proofread your work?

MORE TO INVESTIGATE

PREDICT what the outcomes of the trials and the percents would be for 1,000 trials and for 10,000 trials.

EXPLORE by doing a similar experiment for a spinner with 3 outcomes. Estimate the probabilities for each outcome. Spin and record 10 trials at a time. Find the percents for each outcome for all the trials and compare them with your estimates.

FIND spinners for three games. Compare and contrast the spinners, including how the spinners add fun to the games.

Make Predictions

L
E
A
R
N

At a middle school of 480 students, a random sample of 80 students was asked, "Do you prefer soccer or softball as an after-school sport?" Use the survey results to predict the number of students in the school who would choose soccer.

Survey Results

Soccer	52
Softball	28

In the sample, $\frac{52}{80}$ of the students chose soccer.

Express $\frac{52}{80}$ as a decimal.

 $52 \div 80 =$ **0.65**

Since 0.65 of the sample chose soccer, you can predict that about 0.65 of the whole school would choose soccer.

 $0.65 \times 480 =$ **312.**

About 312 students in the school would choose soccer.

Cultural Note
Soccer is the world's most popular sport.
A worldwide television audience of about 1 billion people watched the World Cup final on July 17, 1994.

Suppose for a simulation you are going to spin this spinner 300 times. Predict how many times you will get green.
Multiply the probability of green by the number of trials.

$P \text{(green)} = \frac{2}{3}$ $\frac{2}{3} \times 300 = 200$

Prediction: about 200 times

Check for Understanding

C
H
E
C
K

1 Use the survey results at the top of the page. Predict the number of students in the school who would prefer softball.

2 Suppose you were going to spin the spinner at the right 100 times. Predict how many times you would get yellow.

Critical Thinking: Analyze

3 If you actually surveyed all 480 students, why might the survey results not match the prediction?

Practice

Predict the number of times you would get each color if you do this experiment 200 times.

Experiment: Take a marble from the bag without looking, write down its color, and then put it back.

1 green   **2** blue   **3** red   **4** yellow

Predict the number who would give the answer if you surveyed each student.

Survey: A random sample of students of a school with 500 students

5 very satisfied

6 somewhat satisfied

7 somewhat dissatisfied

8 very dissatisfied

Are You Satisfied with School Lunches?	
Rating	**Students**
Very satisfied	24
Somewhat satisfied	55
Somewhat dissatisfied	14
Very dissatisfied	7
Total surveyed: 100 students	

Predict to the nearest whole number the number of times the letter will occur in a written sample of 246 letters.

9 E **10** T

11 O **12** N

Average Occurrence of Letters in Written English			
E	13%	N	7%
T	9%	O	8%

MIXED APPLICATIONS
Problem Solving

Pencil & Paper   Calculator   Mental Math

13 In a random sample of students in the district, 32% want softball as a school sport. Out of 5,000 students in the district, predict how many will want softball.

14 **Data Point** Predict the number of left-handed students in your school. Choose a random sample of students to survey for your predictions.

mixed review • test preparation

Round to the nearest hundredth or the nearest cent.

1 12% of 56   **2** 27% of $400   **3** 64% of $32.95   **4** 5% of 97.7

5 Draw a cube and label the vertices. Give a pair of parallel line segments and a pair of perpendicular line segments.

Tree Diagrams and the Counting Principle

IN THE WORKPLACE

Sterling Monroe, Computer Programmer, Seattle, WA

Whether you are creating games or computer programs, you need to understand all the possible outcomes that can happen. Sterling Monroe develops computer programs for football play books. He uses probability in his work.

In this game, you spin two spinners. How many possible outcomes are there?

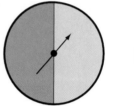

Outcomes: Red, Blue   Outcomes: 1, 2, 3

You can list all possible outcomes for the experiment by making a **tree diagram**.

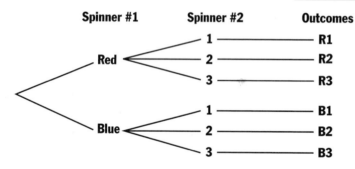

Note: R1 means (Red, 1). The outcomes in the tree are the possible outcomes in this experiment.

There are 6 possible outcomes.

You can also find the number of possible outcomes by using the **counting principle**.

The number of outcomes for an experiment with two or more stages is the product of the number of outcomes at each stage.

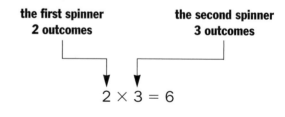

the first spinner
2 outcomes

the second spinner
3 outcomes

$2 \times 3 = 6$

Talk It Over

▶ Why does the tree above start with 2 branches? Why does each of these branches split into 3 branches?

▶ You are going to flip a coin and toss a number cube. How many possible outcomes are there? Make a tree diagram and list the possible outcomes.

Look back at the spinners on page 476. You know there are 6 possible outcomes when spinning both spinners. What is the probability of spinning a red on the first spinner and a 2 on the second spinner?

Check Out the Glossary
tree diagram
counting principle
See page 643.

Find P (red, 2).

1 favorable outcome (red, 2) → $\frac{1}{6}$
6 possible outcomes →

Suppose you take one marble from each pocket. What is the probability of getting a red marble from the left pocket and either a green marble or an orange marble from the right pocket?

left pocket   *right pocket*

Find P(red, green or orange).

You can use the counting principle to find the number of all possible outcomes. Then you can determine the probability.

Step 1	Step 2	Step 3
First, find the number of possible outcomes.	**Find the number of favorable outcomes.**	**Find the probability.**
$3 \times 4 = 12$	$1 \times 2 = 2$	Total favorable outcomes → $\frac{2}{12} = \frac{1}{6}$ Total possible outcomes →
Think: 3 marbles in left pocket 4 marbles in right pocket	**Think:** red in left pocket green and orange in right pocket	P(red, green or orange) is $\frac{1}{6}$.

Check for Understanding

1 Draw a tree diagram to show all of the different outcomes for flipping 2 coins.

2 What is the probability of flipping 2 coins and getting 2 heads?

3 When you roll 2 number cubes, how many outcomes are possible? How did you find the number?

Critical Thinking: Analyze

4 What is different about the information you get from a tree diagram and from the counting principle?

Practice

For ex. 1–3, draw a tree diagram of the possible outcomes. Write the number of possible outcomes.

1 Spinning each spinner once

2 Tossing a number cube and spinning the spinner

3 Selecting a pair of pants from a choice of blue, black, grey, or tan, and a shirt from a choice of blue, green, red, orange, or yellow

Find the total number of possible outcomes. Explain your methods.

4 Selecting a quarterback and center from 5 quarterbacks and 3 centers

5 Ordering a pizza by choosing 1 of 3 kinds of crusts and 1 of 12 toppings

6 Picking a new car from 6 models and 5 colors

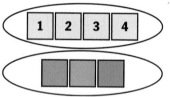

You are going to turn over the cards at the right, mix the cards in each group separately, and select one card from each group. Find the probability of selecting:

7 a 1 and the red card.

8 a 2 and the blue or green card.

9 the blue card and a 2 or 3.

10 a 2 and the red or blue card.

Find the probability for spinning the spinner and tossing the number cube and getting:

11 the letter A and a 3.

12 the letter B and a 2 or 5.

13 the letter C and any number.

•••••••••••••••••••••••••••• **Make It Right** •••••••••••••••••••••••••••

14 Vince drew this diagram to show all the meal and drink combinations of hamburger, hot dog, or pizza with juice, milk, or soda. Help him see his error and fix it.

Hamburger ---------- *Juice*
Hot dog ------------ *Milk*
Pizza -------------- *Soda*
There are only 3 different ways to order.

15 What is the probability of tossing two 1–6 number cubes and getting a sum of 12?

16 A new game sells for $18.75. The tax will be 6%. How much will it cost altogether to buy 3 of the games?

17 Suppose a $\frac{1}{2}$ minute of advertising on TV during a Super Bowl costs $500,000. If the broadcasting company sells $37\frac{1}{2}$ minutes, how much money can they expect to get?

18 What is the probability of tossing a nickel and a penny and getting only 1 head? (Hint: Consider heads on the nickel and tails on the penny and tails on the nickel and heads on the penny as different outcomes.)

19 **Write a problem** that can be solved by making a tree diagram like the one below. Solve your problem. Then give it to others to solve.

more to explore

Permutations

How many different ways can you arrange the letters *A, B*, and *C*?

Make a tree diagram or find the number of ways, using the counting principle. There are 3 choices for the first letter, 2 choices for the second letter, and only 1 choice for the third letter.

Arranging objects in this way is called a *permutation*. Notice that the number of choices decreases by 1 each time.
$3 \times 2 \times 1 = 6$

There are 6 ways to arrange the letters.

First Letter	Second Letter	Third Letter	Outcomes
A	B	C	ABC
A	C	B	ACB
B	A	C	BAC
B	C	A	BCA
C	A	B	CAB
C	B	A	CBA

1 How many ways can you arrange the letters *A, B, C*, and *D*?

2 How many ways can 5 people stand in a row?

3 How many ways can 6 people stand in a row?

4 How many ways can you arrange the letters *A, B, C, D, E, F*, and *G*?

PART 1 Make a Table

You are going to toss two number cubes in a game. If you get a sum of 7, you get an extra move. How often would you expect to get a sum of 7?

Think: The sum of 2 on red and 5 on blue is 7.

Work Together
Solve. Be prepared to explain your methods.

1. Copy and complete the table to show the sums you get when you toss both number cubes.

2. How many different ways are there to get a sum of 7 when you toss two number cubes?

3. What is the probability of getting a sum of 7?

4. What is the probability of getting a sum of 6?

5. **What if** both number cubes are the same color. Will the probability of getting a 7 be the same? Explain.

6. Make a table to find all the different outcomes for spinning these two spinners. Then find the probability of getting a sum of 4 on the spinners.

7. **Make a decision** You are making up rules for a game that uses these spinners. Which sum would you use to give a player an extra move? Explain.

Red	Blue					
	1	2	3	4	5	6
1	2	3	4	5	6	7
2	3	4	5	6	7	8
3						
4						
5						
6						

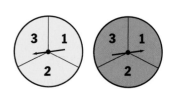

Ryan wrote this problem about the spinners shown below.

8 **Steps in a Process**
Solve Ryan's problem. Explain the steps you used to solve it.

9 **What if** you were going to spin both spinners 100 times? Predict the number of times the sum would be 5.

10 Make up another problem about spinning both spinners.

11 Solve your problem.

12 Trade problems. Solve at least three problems written by other students.

13 Which of the problems written by other students was the easiest? the hardest? Explain why.

What is the probability of spinning the sum 8?

Ryan Marshall
John Yeates Middle School
Suffolk, VA

Turn the page for Practice Strategies. ➡️

Menu

Choose five problems and solve them. Explain your methods.

1 For lunch, you have a choice of 4 salads and 6 sandwiches. In how many ways can you have lunch that includes a salad and a sandwich?

2 In a restaurant a family ordered 5 meals for the same price, which included drinks and desserts. The tax was $2.60, and the total bill was $45.85. How much did each meal cost?

TAX $ 2.60
TOTAL $45.85
Thank you

3 Practicing for an upcoming race, Len has been averaging 20 mph on his bicycle. If the race course is 42 miles long, how long will it take him to complete the race, to the nearest minute?

4 In a new board game, you have to select a card and roll a 1–6 number cube. There are 10 cards numbered 1–10. How many possible outcomes are there? What is the probability of drawing a card numbered 5 and rolling a 5?

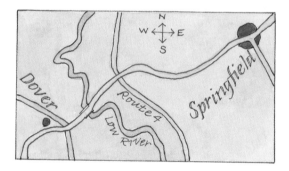

5 The sum of Iris's and Kale's ages is 20 less than their mother's age. If their mother is 40 years old, how old could they be?

6 On a map 3 in. represents 100 mi. If two cities are 7 in. apart on the map, how far apart are they?

7 If you flip 2 coins, what is the probability that you will get 2 tails?

8 If you toss 2 number cubes, what is the probability of getting a sum of 5?

Choose two problems and solve them. Explain your methods.

9 **Make a decision** You are building a bookcase and must decide how many shelves to make and how high each shelf should be. Use the information at the right and, on paper, sketch what your bookcase looks like. Include all of the dimensions.

10 **Spatial reasoning** You want to walk from your home to the park. How many routes can you take by which you are always going north or east?

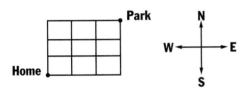

11 Flip a coin 100 times. Find the percent of times you get heads. Flip the coin 100 more times. Of the total 200 flips, what is the percent of times that you got heads? Which percent is closer to 50%?

12 **At the Computer** Use a computer program to simulate flipping a coin 100 times, 200 times, and so on, up to 1,000 times. Find the percent of times you got heads after 100 times, 200 times, and so on. Make a line graph to show how the percents change as the number of times you do the experiment increases. What conclusions can you draw?

Number of Flips	Number of Heads	Percent of Heads
100	54	54%
200	96	48%

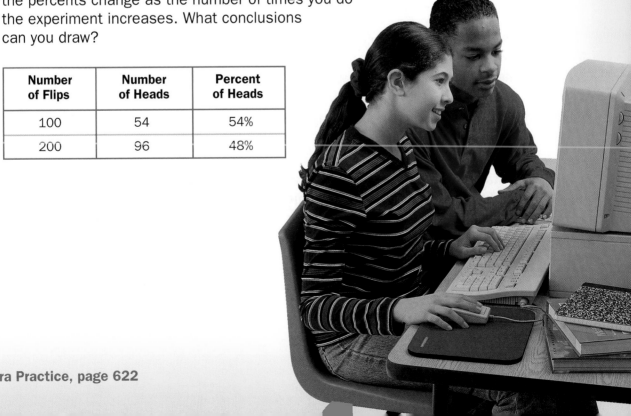

Language and Mathematics

Complete the sentence. Use a word in the chart.
(pages 462–479)

1 If two outcomes are ■, they have the same probability.

2 A ■ is a good way to show all of the outcomes for spinning a spinner twice.

3 The ■ of flipping a coin and getting heads is $\frac{1}{2}$.

4 When the probability of an event is 1, the event is ■.

Concepts and Skills

Suppose you spin the spinner. Find the probability. (pages 462, 466)

5 P(3)

6 P(3 or 5)

7 P(even)

8 P(less than 9)

9 P(1, 2, or 3)

10 P(10)

11 P(less than 6)

12 P(divisible by 3)

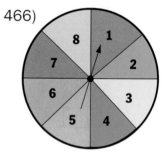

Suppose you select one of the cards from a hat without looking. Find the probability.
(pages 462, 466)

13 P(red)

14 P(green)

15 P(red or green)

16 P(red or blue)

17 P(green or blue)

18 P(white)

19 P(not purple)

20 P(blue)

Predict the number of times you would get the letter if you do this experiment 600 times. (page 474)

Experiment: Select a card from the bag without looking.

21 A

22 B

23 C

Find the total number of possible outcomes. Use a tree diagram to list all the outcomes. (page 476)

24 tossing 2 coins

25 selecting an outfit from 5 shirts and 4 pairs of pants

26 tossing 2 number cubes

Think critically. (pages 462, 466)

27 Analyze. Explain what the error is, then correct it.

I flipped a coin and got 5 heads in a row. Therefore, the probability of tails is 1 for the next throw.

MIXED APPLICATIONS
Problem Solving

(pages 468, 480)

28 In a school of 450 students, a random sample of students was asked about basketball. Use the survey results at the right to predict the number in the school who like basketball.

Survey Results	
Do you like basketball?	
Yes	60%
No	40%

Total surveyed: 100 students

29 Use the table of the lengths of completed passes for this football player. Find his average length of passes completed.

Completed Passes This Year					
Game	1	2	3	4	5
Length	35 yd	21 yd	14 yd	13 yd	28 yd

30 Suppose you spin both spinners. What is the probability of getting a 1 and an *A*?

31 What is the probability of spinning both spinners and getting a total of 6?

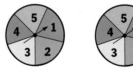

32 Suppose you bought this board game on sale. If the tax was 8%, how much did you pay altogether?

33 Suppose the probability of your making a free throw is $\frac{1}{2}$. How would you set up a simulation to find the probability that you will make at least 5 out of 6 throws?

Suppose you spin the spinner. Find the probability.

1 $P(4)$

2 $P(2 \text{ or } 6)$

3 $P(\text{odd})$

4 $P(\text{less than } 7)$

5 $P(\text{multiple of } 2)$

6 $P(\text{prime number})$

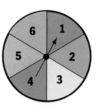

Suppose you choose a cube from the bag without looking. Find the probability.

7 $P(\text{red or green})$

8 $P(\text{not yellow})$

9 $P(\text{red or blue})$

10 $P(\text{red, blue, or green})$

Predict the number of times you will get the colored card if you select a card from the bag 600 times without looking.

11 green

12 red

13 blue

14 orange

Find the total number of possible outcomes. Use a tree diagram to list all the outcomes.

15 selecting an outfit from 4 shirts and 3 pairs of pants

16 making a ham or cheese sandwich on sesame or wheat bread

Solve. Show your work.

17 Suppose you spin the spinner at the right 40 times. Predict the number of times you would expect to spin an A.

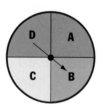

18 You have a Rangers, a Marlins, and a Cubs hat. You choose a hat from your closet each day without looking. How would you set up a simulation to find the average number of times you would wear the Cubs hat during a school week?

19 A dozen golf balls cost $15.95. But during a special sale, you get 15 golf balls for the same price. What is the savings to the nearest cent per golf ball?

20 What is the probability of tossing two number cubes labeled 1–6 and getting a total of 8?

What Did You Learn?

Using a spinner face like the one shown, make a spinner by coloring at least one section red and at least one section green. You are going to spin the spinner 50 times.

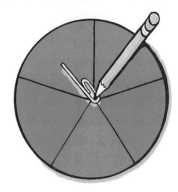

▶ Predict the number of times you will get red. Use a paper clip and pencil for a spinner pointer.

▶ Spin 50 times and record the outcomes. Make a frequency table to show the results.

Number of reds	
Number of greens	

You will need
- *spinners*
- *markers*
- *paper clip*

▶ Compare the results to your prediction. If they are different, explain why you think they are different. If they are the same explain why you think that is.

•••••••••••••••••• **A Good Answer** ••••••••••••••••••
- includes a prediction of the number of reds.
- includes a record of 50 spins and a frequency table.
- includes a comparison of the results to your prediction.

 You may want to place your work in your portfolio.

What Do You Think ?

1 How do you think probability might be helpful to you as you grow older?

2 What are some devices that you have used to solve problems that include probability?
- Number cubes
- Coins
- Spinners
- Other? Explain.

Sports Injuries

No matter what your favorite sport, game, or activity is, there is a chance of being injured while taking part. The most common sports injuries are shown in the table at the right.

The most common injury is a bruise, which is rarely serious. A bruise is an injury to tissue that does not break the skin but causes small blood vessels to rupture and bleed underneath the skin. The bleeding is what causes the discoloration of the skin associated with bruises.

A sprain or strain is an injury to a joint that is caused when the joint is bent or twisted beyond its normal range of motion. When a joint is sprained, the ligaments that connect the bones together are stretched and sometimes torn. The common first aid for sprains is known as RICE—rest, ice, compression, and elevation. Serious sprains should be examined by a doctor.

The three muscles in the back of the thigh are known as the hamstring muscles. These are often pulled or torn by athletes involved in strenuous running. A pulled hamstring is really another type of muscle strain. The RICE technique is helpful first aid for nonserious hamstring pulls.

The Five Most Common Sports Injuries	
1	Bruise
2	Sprained ankle
3	Sprained knee
4	Low-back strain
5	Hamstring tear

SOURCE: *THE TOP TEN OF EVERYTHING, 1996,* BY RUSSELL ASH

Sprained Knee

Low-back strain

Hamstring tear

Bruise

Sprained ankle

▶ How are sprains, strains, and hamstring tears alike?

▶ What are some ways to prevent injuries in sports and physical activities?

Cultural Note
According to the National Sporting Goods Association, the top ten sports/activities in the United States are walking, swimming, bicycle riding, fishing, exercising (with equipment), camping, bowling, billiards/pool, basketball, and motorboating.

What Are the Chances?

The table below shows the number of people who participated in various sports and activities during a recent year. It also lists the total number of injuries for each sport that were treated in hospital emergency rooms. Use the table to answer the questions below.

Sports Participants and Injuries		
Sport	**Participants**	**Injuries**
Baseball/Softball	34,300,000	477,400
Basketball	28,200,000	752,800
Bicycling	54,600,000	649,500
Bowling	42,500,000	24,400
Fishing	47,600,000	82,400
Football	13,500,000	447,300
Golf	24,000,000	37,600
Horseback Riding	8,500,000	73,500
Ice Hockey	1,600,000	59,500
Ice Skating	6,700,000	41,300
Roller Skating	26,500,000	136,400
Soccer	10,600,000	160,300
Swimming	63,100,000	122,700
Table Tennis	9,500,000	1,455
Tennis	17,300,000	31,000
Volleyball	22,100,000	137,700
Water Skiing	7,900,000	17,300

SOURCE: NATIONAL SAFETY COUNCIL

1 For each sport or activity, express as a decimal the probability of a participant's being injured.

2 Explain for two of the sports what the decimal probabilities mean about the chances of getting hurt.

3 Make a table that lists these activities from the lowest to the highest probability.

At the Computer

Favorite Sport

4 Conduct a survey in your school. Ask students what sport they like to participate in the most. Use graphing software to make a bar graph of the results.

5 Write two statements based on your graph.

CHAPTER 13

PERIMETER, AREA, AND VOLUME

THEME Interesting Buildings

Modern buildings are amazing—and so are the structures built hundreds or even thousands of years ago. In this chapter, you will learn how builders and architects use perimeter, area, and volume in their work.

What Do You Know?

Have you ever built 3-dimensional puzzles? You can build a house or make a car that looks real using only puzzle pieces.

1 What are the perimeter and area of the first floor of the building at the right? Explain how you found your answers.

2 What is the volume of the building? Explain how you found your answer.

3 Sketch another building. Show the length and width of your building, as well as any other measurements you may need. Find the volume of the building. Explain your methods.

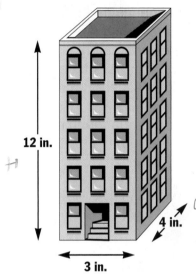

12 in.

4 in.

3 in.

READING ARITHMETIC WRITING

Visualize
Mari enjoys drawing patterns for 3-dimensional shapes. She cuts out the patterns and then folds them into shapes.

Visualizing means imagining what things look like.

1 Visualize what 3-dimensional figure you would get if you traced and cut out the pattern at the right and folded along the dashed lines.

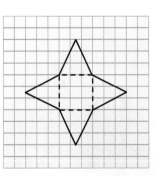

Vocabulary*
*partial list

area, p. 492	**compound figure**, p. 506	**rectangular prism**, p. 514	**square pyramid**, p. 514
square units, p. 492	**2-dimensional**, p. 514	**cube**, p. 514	**cone**, p. 514
base, p. 496, 514	**plane**, p. 514	**triangular prism**, p. 514	**cylinder**, p. 514
height of a triangle, p. 497	**3-dimensional**, p. 514	**triangular pyramid**, p. 514	**sphere**, p. 514
circumference, p. 500	**edge**, p. 514		**surface area**, p. 518
	vertex, p. 514		**volume**, p. 522
	face, p. 514		**cubic units**, p. 522

Perimeter and Area

**L
E
A
R
N**

There are ruins of buildings worldwide. To reconstruct a building, an archaeologist might find the perimeter and the area of the original building.

The **area** of a figure is the measure of the region inside the figure. Area is measured in **square units,** such as square centimeters (cm²) and square inches (in.²). A square centimeter is the area of a square, 1 cm on each side.

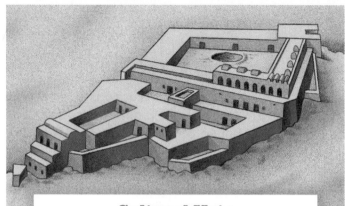

Cultural Note
Tanzania is located in East Africa. In the fourteenth century, the Husuni Kubwa Palace was the largest building in this region.

You can use a formula to find the perimeter or area of a rectangle.

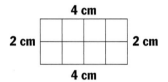

4 cm

2 cm   **2 cm**

4 cm

Check Out the Glossary
For vocabulary words, see page 643.

To find the perimeter *(P)* of a rectangle, add twice the length *(ℓ)* and twice the width *(w)*; $P = (2 \times \ell) + (2 \times w)$

To find the area *(A)* of a rectangle, multiply the length *(ℓ)* times the width *(w)*; $A = \ell \times w$

$P = (2 \times 4) + (2 \times 2) = 8 + 4 = 12$

The perimeter is 12 cm.

$A = 4 \times 2 = 8$

The area is 8 cm².

**C
H
E
C
K**

Check for Understanding
Find the perimeter and area of each rectangle.

1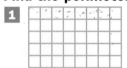

2

3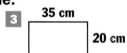
35 cm
20 cm

4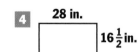
28 in.
16½ in.

Critical Thinking: Generalize

5 How would you write formulas to find the perimeter and area of a square?

6 Explain how perimeter and area are different.

Practice

Find the perimeter and the area for the rectangle.

1

2

3

4

5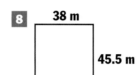

6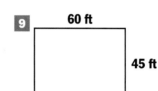

7

32 cm

25 cm

8 38 m

45.5 m

9 60 ft

45 ft

10 $16\frac{3}{4}$ in.

$8\frac{1}{2}$ in.

For the given perimeter of a rectangle, find the length and width that will give the greatest area.

11 20 ft   **12** 16 in.   **13** 24 cm   **14** 32 m   **15** 40 m

---

MIXED APPLICATIONS
Problem Solving

Pencil & Paper   *Calculator*   *Mental Math*

16 A large rectangular lawn measuring 250 m by 120 m needs to be fertilized. Each bag of fertilizer covers 2,000 m^2 and costs $18.79. Find the cost of the fertilizer needed.

17 **What if** you roll a 1–6 number cube four times and get 2, 2, 2, 2. What is the probability of getting a 2 again on your next roll?

Use the floor plan for problems 18–19.

18 How does the sum of the perimeters of each room compare to the perimeter of the apartment? Explain.

19 How does the sum of the areas of each room compare to the area of the apartment? Explain.

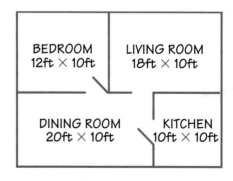

BEDROOM
12ft × 10ft

LIVING ROOM
18ft × 10ft

DINING ROOM
20ft × 10ft

KITCHEN
10ft × 10ft

---

mixed review • test preparation

ALGEBRA Evaluate each expression.

1 $4x + 6$ for $x = 3.5$ **2** $\frac{y}{3} - 7.2$ for $y = 27$ **3** $5.7t + 8$ for $t = 6.3$ **4** $y^2 - 3$ for $y = 4$

ALGEBRA Solve.

5 $\frac{6}{20} = \frac{n}{100}$ **6** $\frac{20}{15} = \frac{16}{x}$ **7** $\frac{50}{60} = \frac{y}{24}$ **8** $\frac{4}{32} = \frac{6}{t}$

Enlarging Rectangles

Steve Crockett, like other engineers, needs to be able to understand how changing dimensions can change area. Suppose a client wants to double the size of a building that is 20 m long and 10 m wide. If you double its length and width to make a new plan, how will the building's area change?

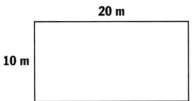

IN THE WORKPLACE

Steve Crockett, Structural Engineer, Needham, MA

Work Together

Work with a partner. Find how the perimeter and area of a rectangle change when its length and width are doubled and tripled.

You will need
- *centimeter graph paper*

▶ Draw and label each of the following six rectangles on graph paper.

a. length = 2 cm, width = 3 cm
b. length = 3 cm, width = 4 cm
c. length = 5 cm, width = 2 cm
d. length = 6 cm, width = 3 cm
e. length = 4 cm, width = 5 cm
f. length = 1 cm, width = 1 cm

▶ Then, double the length and width of each rectangle and draw the six new rectangles on graph paper.

▶ Record the perimeter and area for all twelve rectangles in a table.

Original Rectangles			Doubled Rectangles		Perimeter		Area	
Rectangle	Length	Width	Length	Width	Original	Doubled	Original	Doubled
a.	2 cm	3 cm						
b.								

▶ How do the perimeter and the area of a rectangle change when you double the length and the width of the rectangle? Write a formula to represent the relationship between the new perimeter and the original perimeter and between the new area and the original area.

Make Connections

Two students made the following discovery. They gave these examples.

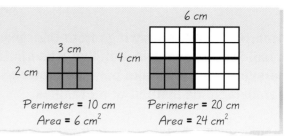

When the length and width of a rectangle are doubled, the perimeter of the rectangle doubles, and the area of the rectangle is 4 times as great.

3 cm
2 cm

Perimeter = 10 cm
Area = 6 cm²

6 cm
4 cm

Perimeter = 20 cm
Area = 24 cm²

▶ Look at the data in your table. Do you agree with the students' finding? Explain.

▶ Look back at the problem at the top of page 494. What is the area of the new building? How many times greater is its area than the original building's area?

✦ ▶ **ALGEBRA: PATTERNS** Make a generalization about perimeter and area when you triple the length and width of a rectangle.

CHECK

Check for Understanding

Double the length and width of the rectangle. Find the perimeter and area of the original and new rectangles. Explain your methods.

1 5 cm / 3 cm

2 6 cm / 2 cm

3 3 in. / 3 in.

4 7 in. / 4 in.

Critical Thinking: Analyze

✦ **5** **ALGEBRA: PATTERNS** How do the perimeters of the new rectangles in ex. 1–4 compare to those of the original rectangles? How do the areas compare? Write ratios to compare.

Practice

PRACTICE

Double the length and width of the rectangle. Find the perimeter and area of the original and new rectangles. Explain your methods.

1 Length: 5 cm
Width: 1 cm

2 Length: 7 in.
Width: 2 in.

3 Length: 8 ft
Width: 3 ft

4 Length: 10 ft
Width: 10 ft

5 Length: 4 cm
Width: 6 cm

6 Length: 7 in.
Width: $2\frac{1}{2}$ in.

7 Length: 15 ft
Width: 5 ft

8 Length: 20 m
Width: 30 m

Solve.

9 **What if** you doubled only the length of a rectangle. How would that affect the perimeter and area? Include drawings to explain your reasoning.

Area of Parallelograms and Triangles

Architects create drawings from their plans to show what a building or room will look like when finished. To create perspective, they make paraline drawings that use parallelograms instead of rectangles.

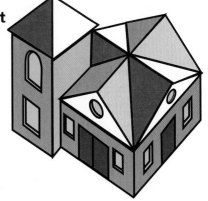

In the previous lesson, you found the areas of rectangles. You can use what you know to find the area of a parallelogram. The diagrams below show how parts of a parallelogram can be rearranged to form a rectangle.

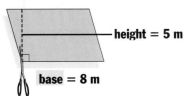

height = 5 m

base = 8 m

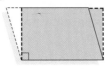

width = 5 m

length = 8 m

Since both shapes are made from the same parts, the area of the parallelogram is the same as the area of the rectangle.

Just as you can use a formula to find the area of a rectangle, you can also use a formula to find the area of a parallelogram.

> To find the area *(A)* of a parallelogram, multiply the base *(b)* times the **height** *(h)*.
>
> $$A = b \times h$$

base A side of a polygon, usually the one at the bottom in a given polygon.

The **height of a parallelogram** is the length of a line segment from a side to the line parallel to that side, perpendicular to both of the sides.

Find the area of the rectangle.

$$A = \ell \times w$$
$$= 8 \times 5$$
$$= 40$$

The area of the rectangle is 40 m².

Find the area of the parallelogram.

$$A = b \times h$$
$$= 8 \times 5$$
$$= 40$$

The area of the parallelogram is 40 m².

The area of the parallelogram equals the area of the rectangle.

Talk It Over

▶ How is finding the area of a parallelogram different from finding the area of a rectangle?

▶ Sketch some parallelograms. Explain how you identify the height and base of the parallelograms.

▶ How would you find the perimeter of a parallelogram?

You can use what you learned about the area of a parallelogram to help you find the area of a triangle. The diagrams below show how a parallelogram can be cut into two congruent triangles.

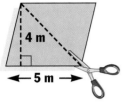

Think: The area of the triangle is $\frac{1}{2}$ the area of the parallelogram.

> The **height of a triangle** is the length of a line segment from a vertex to the side opposite the vertex, perpendicular to that side.

You can use the relationship between the area of a parallelogram and the area of a triangle to write a formula for the area of a triangle.

> To find the area *(A)* of a triangle, multiply the length of a base *(b)* and the **height** *(h)*. Then multiply by $\frac{1}{2}$.
>
> $$A = \frac{1}{2} \times b \times h$$

Find the area of the parallelogram.

$$A = b \times h$$
$$= 5 \times 4$$
$$= 20$$

The area of the parallelogram is 20 m².

Find the area of the triangle.

$$A = \frac{1}{2} \times b \times h$$
$$= \frac{1}{2} \times 4 \times 5$$
$$= 10$$

The area of the triangle is 10 m².

The area of the triangle is $\frac{1}{2}$ the area of the parallelogram.

Check for Understanding

Find the area.

 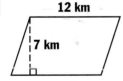
12 km
7 km

 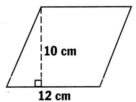
10 cm
12 cm

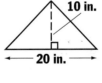
10 in.
20 in.

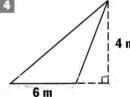
4 m
6 m

Critical Thinking: Summarize

Use a diagram to support your reasoning.

5 **What if** the base and the height of a parallelogram and a triangle are the same. How are the areas related?

6 Describe how you find the area of a parallelogram and a triangle. Give examples.

Turn the page for Practice.

Practice

Find the area of the parallelogram.

1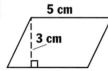
5 cm
3 cm

2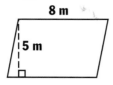
8 m
5 m

3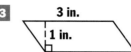
3 in.
1 in.

4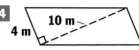
10 m
4 m

5 Base: 12 cm
Height: 8 cm

6 Base: 12 cm
Height: 15.5 cm

7 Base: 16 in.
Height: 9 in.

8 Base: $12\frac{1}{2}$ in.
Height: $5\frac{1}{2}$ in.

Find the area of the triangle.

9
4 ft
2 ft

10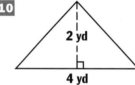
2 yd
4 yd

11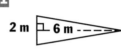
2 m
6 m

12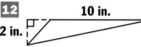
10 in.
2 in.

13 Base: 5 cm
Height: 16 cm

14 Base: 9 cm
Height: 10.5 cm

15 Base: $9\frac{1}{2}$ in.
Height: 5 in.

16 Base: $5\frac{3}{4}$ in.
Height: 8 in.

ⓐ ALGEBRA: Find the height of the parallelogram or triangle with the given base.

17
?
6 m

Area: 30 cm^2

18
?
6.5 m

Area: 16.25 m^2

19
7 ft
?

Area: 17.5 ft^2

20
?
6 in.

Area: $25\frac{1}{2}$ in.^{2}

ⓐ ALGEBRA Use the rule to complete the table.

21

Rule: $A = b \times h$ for $h = 10$				
Input b	2	4	6	8
Output A	▨	▨	▨	▨

22

Rule: $A = \frac{1}{2} \times b \times h$ for $h = 10$				
Input b	2	4	6	8
Output A	▨	▨	▨	▨

·················· **Make It Right** ··························

23 Here's how Amanda found the area of the triangle below. Explain what the error is and correct it.

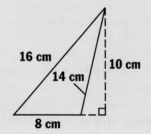
16 cm
14 cm
10 cm
8 cm

$A = \frac{1}{2} \times 8 \text{ cm} \times 14 \text{ cm} = 56 \text{ cm}^2$

Problem Solving

24 The area of a parallelogram is 400 m² and the height is 25 m. What is the measure of the base? What is its new area if the base is doubled? Use a diagram to support your answer.

25 Eight to ten people can live in a Yokut wedge-shaped house. If a village has 100 houses of this type, what is the least and greatest number of people that could be housed?

26 Make a decision Jack wants to enclose the greatest amount of space for a rectangular garden as possible, using all of the 60 ft of fencing he has. Create a design for the garden and find the area.

27 There are 4 marbles in a jar: 1 red and 3 yellow. You shake the jar and choose one without looking. What is the probability of choosing a red marble? Write the answer as a fraction, a decimal, and a percent.

28 The Great Pyramid in Egypt is one of the oldest structures still standing. Its base was a square, 230 m on each side. The four sides were congruent triangles, each with a height of 187 meters. Find the area of the base and the area of each side.

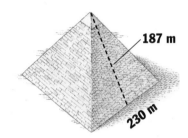

187 m

230 m

---

more to explore

Area of Trapezoids

You can use a formula to find the area of a trapezoid. Two congruent trapezoids can be arranged to form a parallelogram.

> To find the area of a trapezoid, multiply its height and the sum of its bases. Then multiply by $\frac{1}{2}$.
>
> $$A = \frac{1}{2} \times h \times (a + b)$$

Trapezoid base A

Trapezoid B base B

height h

base A'

base B'

base A · base B'

height h · height h

base A' · base B

Think: The area of the trapezoid is $\frac{1}{2}$ the area of the parallelogram.

Find the area.

1
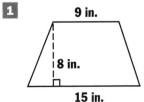
9 in.
8 in.
15 in.

2
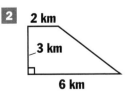
2 km
3 km
6 km

3
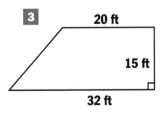
20 ft
15 ft
32 ft

4
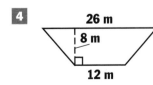
26 m
8 m
12 m

Circumference of a Circle

Early castles were built upon mounds for easier defense. An inside circular wall of stone, called a shell-keep, was added for additional defense. How would you measure the circumference of the outside of a shell-keep?

The **circumference** of a circle is the distance around the circle.

Work Together
Work with a partner to find a relationship between the diameter and the circumference of a circle.

> **You will need**
> - *string*
> - *compass*
> - *round objects*
> - *ruler*

Check Out the Glossary
circumference
See page 643.

▶ Use a compass to draw several circles with different sizes, or trace the circular shapes of round objects from your surroundings.

▶ Lay the string around the outside of the circle and mark the distance around the circle on the string.

▶ Use the ruler to measure the circumference by measuring the string.

▶ Measure the diameter of the circle with the ruler.

▶ Record the results in a chart like the one at the right.

Circumference	Diameter	C ÷ d

▶ What pattern do you find in the third column of your table? What does it tell you?

Make Connections

The ratio of the circumference of any circle to its diameter (C/d) is always the same. This ratio is known as π (pi). For any circle, the ratio π is about 3.14 which is about $3\frac{1}{7}$.

To find the circumference (C) of a circle, multiply π and the diameter (d).

$C = \pi \times d$, or $C \approx 3.14 \times d$

Find the circumference of the circle below.

$$C = \pi \times 2r$$
$$\approx 3.14 \times 2r$$
$$\approx 3.14 \times 2 \times 4$$
$$\approx 25.12$$

A diameter is twice the radius, so $C = \pi \times 2r$.

The circumference of the circle is about 25.12 cm.

▶ **What if** the diameter of a circle increases or decreases. Will the circumference increase or decrease? Give examples.

Check for Understanding

Find the circumference of the circle. Use 3.14 or $3\frac{1}{7}$ for π. Round decimal answers to the nearest tenth.

1 diameter = 12 m **2** diameter = 14 m **3** radius = 2.4 cm **4** radius = $8\frac{1}{2}$ in.

Critical Thinking: Analyze Give examples to support your answer.

5 If the diameter is doubled, how will the circumference change?

Practice

Find the circumference of the circle. Use 3.14 or $3\frac{1}{7}$ for π. Round decimal answers to the nearest tenth.

1 diameter = 21 m **2** diameter = 2.3 cm **3** diameter = $4\frac{1}{2}$ in.

4 radius = 16.4 m **5** radius = 8 in. **6** radius = $2\frac{1}{8}$ in.

Solve.

7 The circumference of a bicycle wheel is about 251.2 cm. Which is the best estimate of the diameter of the wheel?
 a. 60 cm **b.** 80 cm
 c. 100 cm **d.** 120 cm

8 **What if** you roll circle A along a line. About what distance will point P touch the line again?

Area of a Circle

The Great Kiva at Chaco Canyon, New Mexico, is a type of ancient Indian building. Kivas have been used as houses and for ceremonial purposes. How would you find out the area of a circular building like the Great Kiva?

Work Together

Work with a partner to find the area of a circle.

You will need
- *compass*
- *protractor*
- *centimeter graph paper*

Cultural Note
Kivas are often found in Pueblo Indian villages.

Use a compass to draw a circle with a radius of 6 cm.

6 cm

Use a protractor to divide the circle into eight equal sections. Cut out the circle and the sections.

Rearrange the pieces to form a shape like a parallelogram. Find the approximate base and height of the new shape.

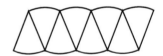

▶ Compare the radius of the circle to the height of the new shape and the circumference of the circle to the base of the new shape.

▶ Find the area of the circle.

Talk It Over

▶ What is the area of the circle? How did you find out?

▶ How does the height of the new shape compare to the radius of the circle?

▶ How does the circumference of the circle compare to the base of the new shape?

Make Connections

The area of the new shape that you made is the same as the area of the circle. You know the formula for the area of a parallelogram. You can use that formula to find the formula for the area of a circle.

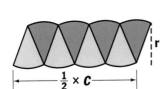

Area of a parallelogram
$A = b \times h$

Think: The base of the new shape is about half the circumference of the circle.

Area of a circle
$$A = (\tfrac{1}{2} \times C) \times r$$
$$= (\tfrac{1}{2} \times 2 \times \pi \times r) \times r$$
$$= (\pi \times r) \times r$$
$$A = \pi \times r^2$$

Think:
$C = 2 \times \pi \times r$

Now you can use the formula to find the area of this circle.

$$A = \pi \times r^2$$
$$\approx 3.14 \times (7)^2$$
$$\approx 3.14 \times 49$$
$$\approx 153.86$$

Think: $\tfrac{1}{2} \times 14 = 7$

To the nearest tenth, the area of a circle with a diameter of 14 cm is 153.9 cm.

▶ Why did you have to divide 14 by 2 before finding the area?

Check for Understanding

Find the area of the circle. Use 3.14 or $3\tfrac{1}{7}$ for π.
Round decimal answers to the nearest tenth.

1 20 m

2 14 cm

3 100 ft

4 6.5 ft

5 $2\tfrac{1}{2}$ in.

6 4 in.

7 18 ft

8 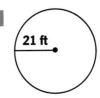 21 ft

Critical Thinking: Generalize

 9 ALGEBRA: PATTERNS What if you double the length of the radius or diameter of a circle. How would the area change? Give an example.

Practice

Find the circumference and area of the circle. Use π = 3.14 or $3\frac{1}{7}$.
Round decimal answers to the nearest tenth.

1

2

3

4

5 diameter = 7 in.

6 diameter = 5 in.

7 diameter = 16 in.

8 radius = 6 ft

9 radius = 700 ft

10 radius = 11.4 cm

✦ **ALGEBRA Fill in the chart. Use π = 3.14 or $3\frac{1}{7}$.**
Round decimals to the nearest tenth.

	Radius	Diameter	Circumference	Area
11	24 cm	▪	▪	▪
12	▪	20 m	▪	▪
13	$3\frac{1}{3}$ yd	▪	▪	▪
14	a	▪	▪	▪

Use mental math to solve. Write the letter of the correct answer.

15 Which have the greatest areas?

a.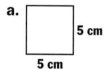
5 cm
5 cm

b.
5 cm
5 cm

c.
5 cm
5 cm

d.
5 cm

16 How many times greater is the area of
circle A than circle B?
a. 2   **b.** 4   **c.** 6   **d.** 8

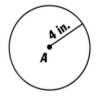

17 How many times greater is the
circumference of circle A than circle B?
a. 2   **b.** 4   **c.** 6   **d.** 8

· **Make It Right** ·

18 Jack computed the area of the circle this way:

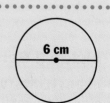
6 cm

$A = 3.14 \times 6 \text{ cm} \times 6 \text{ cm} = 113.04 \text{ cm}^2$

Explain what the error is and correct it.

Problem Solving

19 The round towers on the corners of the castle walls are called barbicans. They were used for defense. Suppose the barbicans had a radius of 6 ft. What is the floor area of each barbican to the nearest ten square feet?

20 For every 3 feet, there would be a 2-foot opening of the barbicans on the outside wall. How many openings did a barbican with a six foot radius have? Explain.

21 Leon forgot what kind of soft drink his mother asked him to buy, so he guessed at one of the 12 kinds they had. What is the probability that he selected the right kind?

22 **Data Point** Use the Databank on page 641 to make three circle graphs. Write a short paragraph to summarize the data.

Cultural Connection Calculating π

Modern mathematicians use computers to generate the value of π. In 1995, two mathematicians in the United States announced they had reached more than 4 billion decimal digits of π.

United States

Many ancient civilizations knew about the relationship between the diameter and the circumference of a circle. They used several methods in their attempts to calculate as accurately as possible the value of π.

The chart shows the value of π used by people in different ancient cultures.

1 Copy the chart. Use a calculator to help you rewrite each value of π in decimal form.

Ancient Culture	Time	Value of π
Babylonians	1800–1600 B.C.	$3\frac{1}{8}$
Egyptians	unknown	$4\left(\frac{8}{9}\right)^3$
Hindus	A.D. 510	$3\frac{177}{1,250}$
Chinese	A.D. 470	$\frac{355}{113}$

2 Which value of π is closest to our present value of 3.1415927?

Area of Compound Figures

Protected from wind and rain, cliff dwellings used every available space by combining different sizes and shapes.

Compound figures are shapes that are made up of two or more shapes. You can find the area of a compound figure by dividing it into smaller regions.

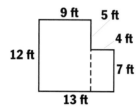

Cultural Note

The most famous cliff dwellings were built by the Anasazi, a group of Native Americans. Most cliff dwellings were built between A.D. 1000 and A.D. 1300.

Divide the shape into two rectangles. Find the area of each rectangle. Then add the areas.

Large Rectangle

$A = 9 \times 12 = 108$

Small Rectangle

$A = 7 \times 4 = 28$

Compound Figure

$A = 108 + 28 = 136$

The area of the compound figure is 136 ft².

To find the area of this compound figure, find the area of the large rectangle and the three small rectangles, then subtract.

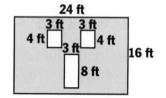

Large Rectangle

$A = 24 \times 16$
$\quad = 384$

Small Rectangles

$A = 3 \times 4 = 12$
$A = 3 \times 4 = 12$
$A = 8 \times 3 = 24$

Compound Figure

$A = 384 - (12 + 12 + 24)$
$\quad = 336$

The shaded area of the compound figure is 336 ft².

Check Out the Glossary
compound figures
See page 643.

Check for Understanding

Find the area of the shaded region. Use 3.14 or $3\frac{1}{7}$ for π.
Round decimal answers to the nearest tenth. Explain your methods.

1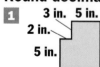

2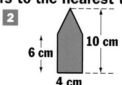

3

4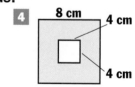

Critical Thinking: Analyze

5 For ex. 1, explain how to solve the problem by using subtraction.

Practice

Find the area of the shaded region. Use 3.14 or $3\frac{1}{7}$ for π. Round decimals to the nearest tenth. Explain your methods.

1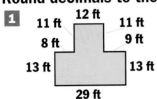

12 ft
11 ft   11 ft
8 ft   9 ft
13 ft   13 ft
29 ft

2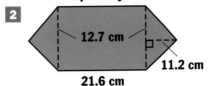

12.7 cm
11.2 cm
21.6 cm

3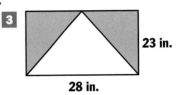

23 in.
28 in.

4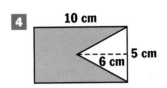

10 cm
5 cm
6 cm

5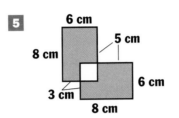

6 cm
5 cm
8 cm
6 cm
3 cm
8 cm

6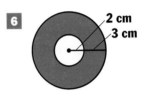

2 cm
3 cm

Draw compound shapes with dimensions that will result in the following areas. Label the dimensions.

7 60 m²   **8** 100 m²   **9** 350 in.²

MIXED APPLICATIONS
Problem Solving

Pencil & Paper   *Calculator*   *Mental Math*

10 Some of the early Americans wove intricate blankets. What is the perimeter and area of a rectangular blanket that is $23\frac{1}{2}$ in. by $34\frac{1}{8}$ in.?

11 A TV can be bought by placing a $50 down payment and paying $15.50 per month for 12 months. This method of payment costs $21 more than the cash price. What is the cash price?

12 **Spatial reasoning** Look at the compound figure below. Find the area of the shaded part.

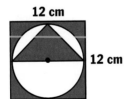

12 cm
12 cm

13 **Logical reasoning** Find the missing lengths in the compound figure. Then compute the perimeter and area.

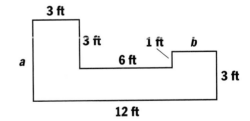

3 ft
3 ft   1 ft   b
a   6 ft
3 ft
12 ft

---

mixed review • test preparation

1 12.3 − 2.66   **2** 43.7 + 1.82   **3** 3.73 × 0.61   **4** 22.62 ÷ 2.6

In a bag, there are 12 red, 4 green, 3 yellow, 6 blue, 5 white, and 6 black marbles. Find the probability of selecting the following.

5 red   **6** green   **7** yellow   **8** blue or white   **9** not yellow

---

Extra Practice, page 625

Perimeter, Area, and Volume **507**

Find the perimeter and area of the shape.

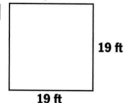
1 19 ft · 19 ft

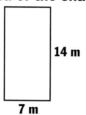
2 14 m · 7 m

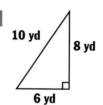
3 10 yd · 8 yd · 6 yd

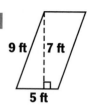
4 9 ft · 7 ft · 5 ft

Find the area of the shaded region.
Round to the nearest tenth.

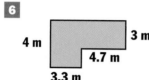
5 5 ft · 3 ft · 5 ft · 3 ft · 2 ft · 3 ft

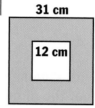
6 4 m · 3 m · 4.7 m · 3.3 m

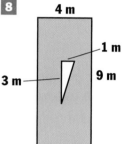
7 31 cm · 12 cm

8 4 m · 1 m · 3 m · 9 m

Find the circumference and area of the circle. Use $\pi = 3.14$ or $3\frac{1}{7}$. Round decimal answers to the nearest tenth.

9 3 m

10 14 ft

11 2.4 cm

12 $2\frac{1}{2}$ in.

13 16 km

14 $\frac{1}{2}$ yd

15 21.2 m

16 $3\frac{1}{4}$ ft

Solve.

17 A unicycle traveled 9.42 feet. This was only $\frac{3}{4}$ of the circumference of the wheel. About how long is the radius of the unicycle's wheel?

18 The largest room in the castle has an area of 704 ft². If the length of the room is 10 ft longer than the width, what are the room's dimensions?

19 **Spatial reasoning** The vertex of each small triangle connects the midpoint of the sides of the triangle it is in. If the area of the smallest triangle is 5 cm², what is the area of the largest triangle?

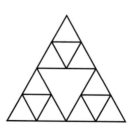

20 *Journal* Explain how you find the circumference and area of a circle. Include diagrams and examples.

developing spatial sense

MATH CONNECTION

Pentominoes

A *pentomino* is made up of five congruent squares connected together. Each square touches at least one other square. When squares touch, their sides match completely.

Pentominoes

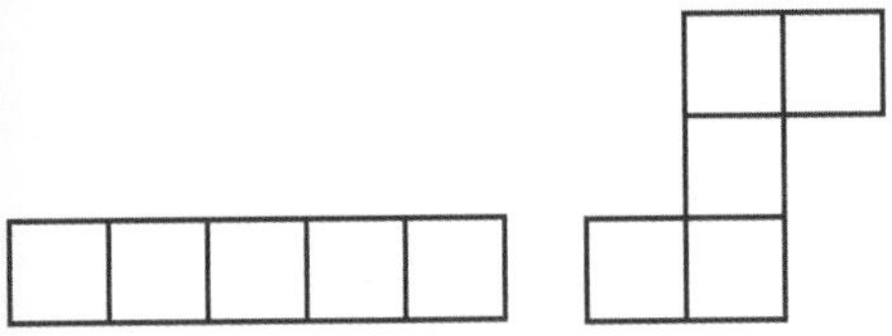

Not Pentominoes

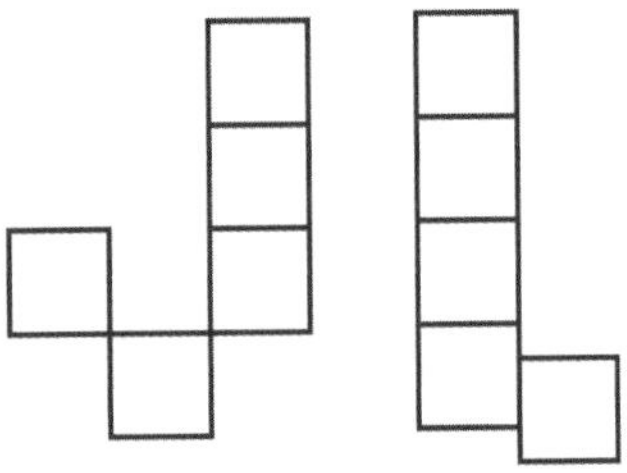

The following figures are congruent so they are the same pentomino.

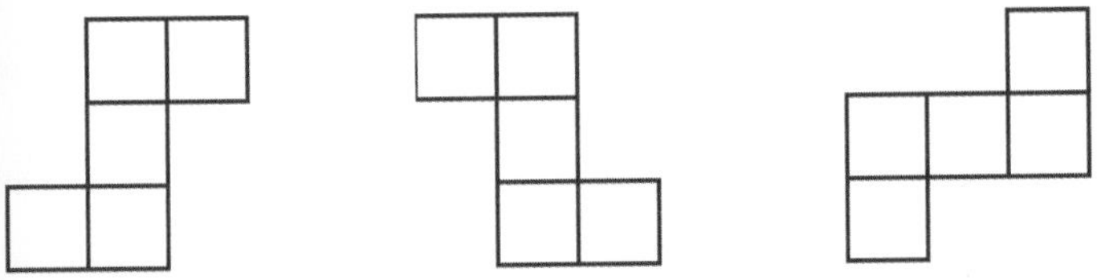

Note: Flips, rotations, and slides do not change the shape of a figure.

There are 12 different pentominoes.

Work Together

- ▶ Work with a partner. Find all 12 different pentominoes.
- ▶ Cut out each pentomino.
- ▶ Use your pentominoes to solve ex. 1–5.

You will need
- *1-inch graph paper*

Solve.

1 Decide which can be folded to form an open box.

2 Do all of the pentominoes have the same area? Why?

3 Do all of the pentominoes have the same perimeter? Give an example to support your answer.

4 Use the pentominoes to make a rectangle that is 2 units by 5 units. Make another rectangle that is 3 units by 5 units.

5 Use the pentominoes to construct a figure that is similar to and bigger than the one at the right. Compare the perimeters and areas of the two figures.

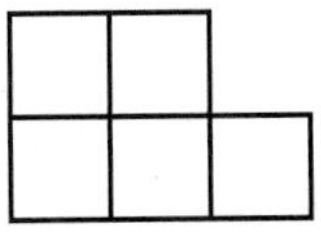

Area Usage

A labyrinth, or maze, is a set of passageways and alleys that are difficult to find your way through. Some castles were built with labyrinths made of stone walls or of shrubs in an outdoor garden. Navigating your way through a maze challenges your problem-solving skills.

In this activity you will work in a small group to plan a maze.

You will need

- graph paper
- rulers
- scissors
- colored markers
- posterboard

▶ The example below is a famous Egyptian labyrinth. What is the area of the maze?

▶ What is the perimeter of the maze?

Cultural Note

Mazes have been popular for centuries. The Cretan labyrinth is shown on this ancient Greek coin. Navigating through mazes became a popular form of entertainment in parts of Europe and Japan by the late nineteenth century.

Length: 1,000 ft

Width: 800 ft

Design the Maze

1 Use $\frac{1}{4}$ inch graph paper to create a blueprint of a maze with an area of 1,000 square feet. Each square should represent 1 foot.

2 Design your maze. Create any geometric shape with an area of 1,000 square feet. Leave 3 feet open for the entrance to the maze. Label the measurements of the perimeter in feet.

3 Carefully design the inside of your maze.

4 Make a poster of your maze or build a three-dimensional model of it, using toothpicks or pebbles.

Report Your Findings

5 *Portfolio* Prepare a report on your labyrinth. Include the following:

▶ A record of your data on the area and perimeter of your labyrinth.

▶ A sketch of the design of your maze.

▶ An explanation of why you selected the shape and how you decided to design the interior of the maze.

6 Compare your sketch to those of other groups.

Revise your work.
▶ Are your measurements accurate?
▶ Did you check your calculations?
▶ Did you proofread your work?

PREDICT how many turns you must make to find your way through another group's maze.

EXPLORE the paths through another group's maze. Is there more than one way through the maze? How well did you predict the number of turns?

FIND information about the maze in the gardens at Hampton Court Palace in England.

Make a Diagram

Read | Castles were often built on the edge of a cliff so that the cliff could be used as part of the castle defense. If a surrounding wall were built out from the ends of a 1,000-m-long cliff, would walls in the shape of a square or a semicircle be longer?

Plan | To solve the problem, make a diagram.

Solve | Make a diagram to represent a square wall and a semicircular wall. Find the length of each wall and compare.

Square Wall

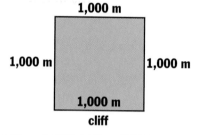

Length = 1,000 × 3 = 3000

Length of 1 side ⟶   ⟵ Length of 3 sides

Semicircular Wall

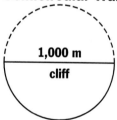

$C = \pi d$
$\approx 3.14 \times 1{,}000 \approx 3{,}140$
$3{,}140 \div 2 = 1{,}570$

Since 3,000 > 1,570 the square wall is longer.

Look Back | Does the answer make sense?

Check for Understanding

1 Would the perimeter of a square with sides of 10 m be longer or shorter than the circumference of a circle with a diameter of 10 m? Explain.

Critical Thinking: Analyze

2 **What if** the side of a square and the diameter of a circle are equal. Will the perimeter of the square always be greater than the circumference of the circle?

Problem Solving

1 **Spatial reasoning** The wall of the castle model is to be made out of bricks like the ones shown at right. If you put two bricks together, what is the least perimeter of the bricks that these two bricks can form?

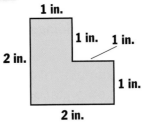

2 In Tina's town, all of the blocks are squares. She lives at the end of a block. She left her house and turned north and went 6 blocks. She turned west and went 4 blocks. She then traveled south for 3 blocks and then east for 8 blocks. Give the directions that would get her home.

3 Bill wants to buy a new guitar. He has been saving his money for two months. Every week he saves $15 from baby-sitting and $22.50 from mowing lawns. The guitar he wants costs $268.90 plus tax. If the sales tax is 9.5%, does he have enough money saved to buy the guitar? Explain your reasoning.

4 **Number sense** The Louisiana Superdome in New Orleans is the world's largest indoor arena. The area of the circular floor of the Superdome is 41,000 square yards. What is your estimate of the diameter of the circular floor?

5 Henry got on the elevator. He went up 10 stories. He then went down 4 stories and back up 7 stories. Finally, he went down 5 stories and got off. If he started on the 3rd floor, on which floor did he get off?

6 **Write a problem** that can be solved using information from the Venn diagram. Solve your problem and have others solve it.

**Sports Participants
of a Sixth-Grade Class**

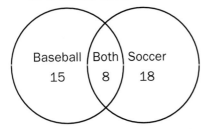

7 Dylan, Mark, Yuki, and Wanda wanted to help out at the local charity drive. Dylan worked only half as long as Yuki. Mark worked 2 hours more than Yuki did. Wanda worked 1 hour longer than Mark. If Yuki worked 5 hours, how long did everyone else work?

8 A balance scale comes with four weights: 5g, 10g, 25g, and 50g. What are all the possible weights that can be measured?

Classify 3-Dimensional Figures

Have you noticed that some buildings have interesting shapes?

Polygons and circles are examples of **2-dimensional** figures. They can be drawn on a **plane,** a flat surface that goes on in all directions without end.
A **3-dimensional** figure, like the one below, is a shape that cannot fit in a plane.

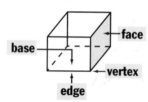

A **prism** is a 3-dimensional figure with 2 faces that are both parallel and congruent and the rest of the faces are rectangles or parallelograms.

Rectangular Prism   **Cube**   **Triangular Prism**

Check Out the Glossary
For vocabulary words,
see page 643.

Here are other examples of 3-dimensional shapes.

Pyramids
Triangular   **Square**   **Cone**   **Cylinder**   **Sphere**

1 base with triangular sides
1 vertex

1 curved surface
1 vertex
1 circular base

1 curved surface
2 circular bases

1 curved surface
No edges, bases,
or vertices

Check for Understanding
Name the figure. Record the number of faces and vertices.

1   **2**   **3**   **4**

Critical Thinking: Analyze

5 How is a cone the same as or different from a pyramid?

Practice

Name the 3-dimensional figure.

1   **2**   **3**   **4**

Name each figure. Write the number of bases, faces, edges, and vertices for each figure.

5   **6**   **7** 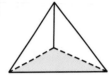 **8**

Predict what shape each net will make when cut and folded.

9 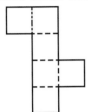 **10** 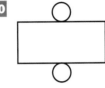 **11**

Problem Solving

Pencil & Paper   Calculator   Mental Math

12 Name all the vertices, faces, and edges of the rectangular prism. What are the 4 edges that are perpendicular to *KO*?

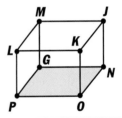

13 **Make a decision** You want to paint a room that has 1,680.5 square feet of wall space. Select a type of paint and calculate the cost. Explain your reason for selecting the type of paint you did.

Paint	Coverage per Gallon	Cost per Gallon	Warranty
Loboys	250 ft²	$23.75	3 year
Cover-Up	300 ft²	$32.40	5 year
Long-Last	150 ft²	$19.80	2 year

mixed review • test preparation

Estimate, then multiply to find the exact answer in simplest form.

1 $\frac{3}{4} \times 5\frac{1}{3}$ **2** $\frac{2}{3} \times 2\frac{1}{2}$ **3** $5\frac{1}{3} \times \frac{1}{2}$ **4** $1\frac{3}{7} \times \frac{7}{10}$

5 Make a circle graph to show the following data for the runners in the 1997 New York City Marathon: ages 18–29: 6,407; ages 30–49: 19,342; age 50 and over: 4,714

Different Views of 3-Dimensional Figures

When architects present their plans to a client, they often make drawings to show how the building will look from different viewpoints.

There are three different views that you can make from a 3-dimensional shape. They are the top view, the front view, and the side view.

A 3-Dimensional Shape

Top View

Front View

Side View

Work Together

Work with a partner to draw different views of a 3-dimensional shape.

You will need
- *graph paper*
- *cubes*

Build three shapes out of cubes. Record the top view, front view, and side view of each shape. Give your drawings to another group and have them build the 3-dimensional shape.

Make Connections

Two students made the following model and drawings of their model.

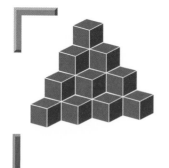

Top View

Front View

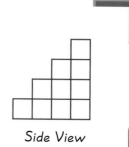

Side View

▶ Do the drawings of the top view, front view, and side view always show every cube in the shape?

▶ Draw the top view, front view, and side view of the 3-dimensional shapes you learned about in the previous lesson.

Check for Understanding

Sketch the top view, front view, and side view of the shape.

1

2

3

Critical Thinking: Analyze   Explain your reasoning.

4 What is the least number of cubes needed to build a figure that has the same top, side, and front views as ex. 1 above?

Practice

Sketch the top view, front view, and side view of the shape.

1

2

3

Decide what is the greatest and least number of cubes needed to build the figure.

4

Top View

Front View   Side View

5

Top View

Front View

Side View

6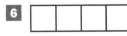

Top View

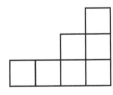

Front View

Side View

Surface Area: Prism

L E A R N

The total **surface area** of a prism is the sum of the areas of all the faces.

The surface area of the cube below is the sum of areas of its 6 faces.

$$1 \text{ in.} \times 1 \text{ in.} = 1 \text{ in.}^2 \quad \leftarrow \textbf{1 face}$$

$$6 \times 1 \text{ in.}^2 = 6 \text{ in.}^2 \quad \leftarrow \textbf{6 faces}$$

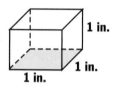

The surface area is 6 in.^{2}.

Work Together
Work with a partner to find the surface area of a 3-dimensional shape.

> **You will need**
> • *ruler*
> • *tape*

▶ Make a net like the one below. Use the measurements shown.

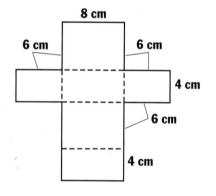

> **Check Out the Glossary**
> surface area
> See page 643.

▶ Use the net to form a rectangular prism. Tape the edges.

▶ Find the area of each face of the rectangular prism.

▶ Find the surface area of the prism.

Talk It Over

▶ What shape is each face of the prism?

▶ Which of the faces are congruent?

▶ What is the surface area of the prism?

Make Connections

You can use what you know about finding the area of triangles and rectangles to find the surface area of a square pyramid.

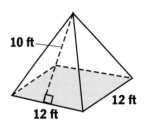

The surface area is the sum of the area of its 5 faces.

Since the base is a square, its area is given by the formula $A = s^2$.

$$s = 12 \text{ ft}$$

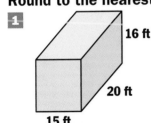

12 ft

12 ft

$$A = 12^2$$
$$= 12 \times 12$$
$$= 144$$

The area of the base is 144 ft².

The 4 sides are congruent triangles. The area of a triangle is given by the formula $A = \frac{1}{2} \times b \times h$.

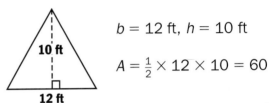

10 ft

12 ft

$b = 12 \text{ ft}, h = 10 \text{ ft}$

$$A = \frac{1}{2} \times 12 \times 10 = 60$$

The area of one triangular side is 60 ft².

The surface area is found by adding the area of the 5 faces together.

Surface area = 144 + 60 + 60 + 60 + 60 = 384.

The surface area of the pyramid above is 384 ft².

Check for Understanding

Find the surface area for the three-dimensional shape. Round to the nearest tenth.

1
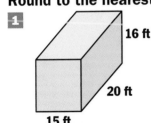
16 ft
20 ft
15 ft

2
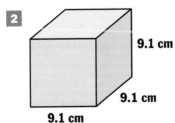
9.1 cm
9.1 cm
9.1 cm

3
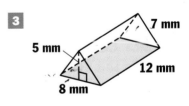
7 mm
5 mm
12 mm
8 mm

Critical Thinking: Summarize   Explain your reasoning.

4 To find the surface area of a rectangular prism, do you have to find the area of all 6 faces?

Turn the page for Practice. ➡

Practice

**Find the surface area for the three-dimensional shape.
Round to the nearest tenth.**

1
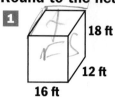
18 ft
12 ft
16 ft

2
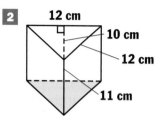
12 cm
10 cm
12 cm
11 cm

3
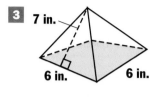
7 in.
6 in.
6 in.

4
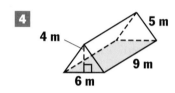
5 m
4 m
9 m
6 m

5
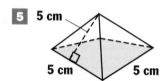
5 cm
5 cm
5 cm

6
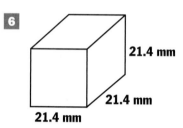
21.4 mm
21.4 mm
21.4 mm

7
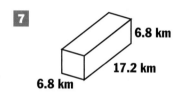
6.8 km
17.2 km
6.8 km

8
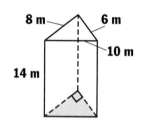
8 m
6 m
10 m
14 m

9
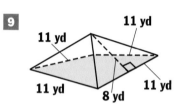
11 yd
11 yd
11 yd
11 yd
8 yd

**Name the 3-dimensional figure the net will make and
find the surface area. Round to the nearest tenth.**

10
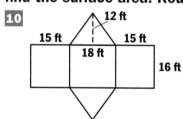
12 ft
15 ft
15 ft
18 ft
16 ft

11
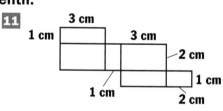
3 cm
1 cm
3 cm
2 cm
1 cm
1 cm
2 cm

⭐ **ALGEBRA Complete the table for the rectangular prism.
Round to the nearest tenth.**

	Length	Width	Height	Surface Area
12	$12\frac{1}{2}$ ft	$21\frac{1}{4}$ ft	$7\frac{1}{8}$ ft	b
13	2.6 cm	1.8 cm	3.7 cm	c
14	4 yd	2 yd	n	76 yd²
15	3 in.	3 in.	a	54 in.²

Problem Solving

16 What is the total surface area of a cardboard box that is 1.2 m long, 0.6 m wide, and 0.3 m high?

17 A rectangular garden is 12 ft by 18 ft. If fencing costs $2.45 per foot, how much will it cost to fence the garden?

18 In a castle, the great room was 34 ft by 42 ft. The walls were 22 ft high. How much wall space was available to hang tapestries?

19 How does the area of the sand castle of Mont Saint Michel compare to the area of your classroom floor? SEE INFOBIT.

20 The tapestry *The Lady with the Unicorn* was created in France in the early sixteenth century. The dimensions are 12 ft $1\frac{3}{4}$ in. by 10 ft 6 in. What is the area of the tapestry?

INFOBIT
The sand castle of Mont-Saint-Michel was about 100 feet in circumference. It took 60 builders, working from dawn to dusk, four days to build it.

21 In Egypt, you can visit some of the most beautiful structures in the world. If you visit 9 pyramids, 1 sphinx, 2 temples, and 3 estates, what percent of the structures that you visited are pyramids?

---

more to explore

Slicing 3-Dimensional Figures

Visualize If you slice a 3-dimensional figure, you get a *cross-sectional* view. The views are different depending on how you slice the figure. Here's how to slice a triangular prism.

Slicing parallel to the triangular base gets a cross section congruent to the base.

Slicing perpendicular to the triangular base gets a rectangular cross section.

Slicing at an angle to the triangular base gets a triangular cross section that is not congruent to the base.

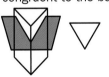

Draw the cross-sectional view of the 3-dimensional figure sliced as shown.

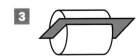

Volume

One of the problems with rooms that have high ceilings is that they are hard to heat and cool. The amount of air in a room determines how much heating or cooling power you need. To find the amount of air in a room, you need to find the volume of the room.

The **volume** of a 3-dimensional shape is the amount of space it encloses. Volume is measured in **cubic units,** such as cubic centimeters (cm^3) and cubic inches (in.^{3}). A cubic centimeter is the volume of a cube with edges 1 centimeter long.

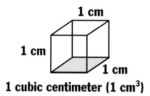

1 cm 1 cm 1 cm

1 cubic centimeter (1 cm^3)

Work Together

Work with a partner to find the volume of a rectangular prism.

You will need
• *cubes*

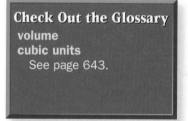

Check Out the Glossary
volume
cubic units
  See page 643.

▶ Build a rectangular prism using between 20 and 30 cubes. The prism should be only 1 cube high.

▶ Record the length, width, height, the area of the base, and number of cubes in a chart.

▶ Add 3 more layers, one at a time. Record the area of the base, dimensions, and number of cubes for each layer.

Rectangular Prism	Length	Width	Height	Area of Base	Number of Cubes
1st layer					
2nd layer					
3rd layer					
4th layer					

Talk It Over

▶ What is the total number of cubes in the rectangular prism with 4 layers? How would you find it without counting each cube?

▶ Repeat the steps of the Work Together for other rectangular prisms. Write a formula to represent the relationship between the base, the height, and the volume of any rectangular prism.

Make Connections

Here is how two students found the volume of a rectangular prism.

First we found the area of the
base. We used the formula
$A = \ell \times w.$
$A = 6 \times 9 = 54 \text{ in.}^2$

To find the volume, we multiplied
the area of the base times the height.
$V = A \times h$
$V = 54 \times 3 = 162$

The volume of the rectangular prism is 162 in.^3.

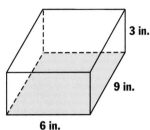

3 in.

9 in.

6 in.

Instead of using two steps, you can also use this formula to find the volume of a rectangular prism.

> To find the volume of a rectangular prism, multiply its length, its width, and its height.
>
> $$V = \ell \times w \times h$$

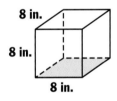

8 in.

8 in.

8 in.

$$
\begin{aligned}
V &= \ell \times w \times h \\
&= 8 \times 8 \times 8 \\
&= 512 \text{ in.}^3
\end{aligned}
$$

Check for Understanding

Find the volume for each rectangular prism. Round to the nearest tenth.

1
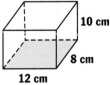
10 cm
8 cm
12 cm

2
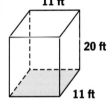
11 ft
20 ft
11 ft

3
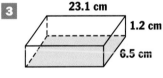
23.1 cm
1.2 cm
6.5 cm

Critical Thinking: Analyze   Explain your reasoning.

4 How many cubes 2 cm by 2 cm by 2 cm could fit into a rectangular prism 6 cm by 6 cm by 6 cm?

5 **Journal** How is the volume of a rectangular prism different from the surface area of a rectangular prism?

Turn the page for Practice. ➡

CHECK

Practice

Find the volume for the rectangular prism.
Round decimals to the nearest tenth.

1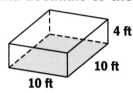
4 ft
10 ft
10 ft

2
9.6 cm
4.1 cm
3.2 cm

3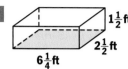
$1\frac{1}{2}$ ft
$2\frac{1}{2}$ ft
$6\frac{1}{4}$ ft

4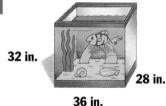
32 in.
28 in.
36 in.

5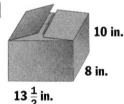
10 in.
8 in.
$13\frac{1}{2}$ in.

6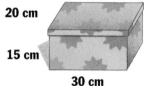
20 cm
15 cm
30 cm

Find the volume of the rectangular prism.
Round decimals to the nearest tenth.

7 ℓ = 4 ft
w = 6 ft
h = 3 ft

8 ℓ = 6 m
w = 10 m
h = 1 m

9 ℓ = 4 m
w = 2 m
h = $\frac{1}{2}$ m

10 ℓ = 1.4 cm
w = 1.4 cm
h = 1.4 cm

11 ℓ = 2.8 m
w = 2.2 m
h = 2.2 m

12 ℓ = $3\frac{1}{2}$ in.
w = $5\frac{1}{8}$ in.
h = 2 in.

✦ **ALGEBRA Complete the table for the rectangular prism. Round decimals to the nearest tenth.**

	Length	Width	Height	Volume
13	$12\frac{1}{2}$ ft	$21\frac{1}{4}$ ft	$7\frac{1}{8}$ ft	n
14	2.6 cm	w	3.7 cm	17.3 cm^3
15	4 yd	2 yd	c	48 yd^3

·················· **Make It Right** ··················
16 Shana found the volume of the cube this way.

$$5 + 5 + 5 = 15 \text{ cm}^3$$

Explain what Shana did wrong and how to
make it right.

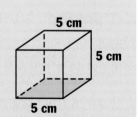
5 cm
5 cm
5 cm

Problem Solving

17 How many of the small cubes will fit into the large rectangular prism?

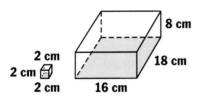

2 cm
2 cm
2 cm
16 cm
18 cm
8 cm

18 **Logical reasoning** The height of a rectangular prism is doubled. Is its volume doubled? Is its surface area doubled? Give an example to support your reasoning.

19 The Empire State Building has 1,860 steps. Dan can average 2 steps every 5 seconds. If he started up at 8:34 A.M. what time would he reach the top?

20 A plastic bottle weighs 9.5 grams. There are 202 cubic centimeters of water in the bottle. What is the total weight of the bottle and water? **SEE INFOBIT.**

21 **Write a problem** that involves the use of a 3-dimensional shape. Solve the problem and have others solve the problem.

22 **Data Point** Collect three items that are in the shape of a rectangular prism. Record the dimensions of the prisms. Identify the ones whose volumes you would want to find out. Explain why.

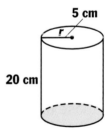

INFOBIT
A cubic centimeter of water weighs 1 gram, measured at 0°C at sea level.

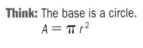

Volume of a Cylinder

A cylinder has 2 congruent circular bases. You can find the volume of a cylinder the same way you find the volume of a prism.

Volume = Area of Base × Height
$= \pi \times r^2 \times h$
$\approx 3.14 \times 5^2 \times 20$
$\approx 1{,}570$

Think: The base is a circle.
$A = \pi r^2$

5 cm
r
20 cm

The volume of the cylinder is 1,570 cm³.

Find the volume of the cylinder. Use 3.14 for π.
Round decimal answers to the nearest tenth.

1 radius = 3 m
height = 7 m

2 radius = 20 cm
height = 50 cm

3 diameter = 1 m
height = 1 m

4 radius = 15 mm
height = 45 mm

Problem Solvers at Work

PART 1   Make a Model

You are building a model of a skyscraper. You decide to double the length, width, and height of the model. How will the surface area and the volume of the model change?

Work Together

Solve. Be prepared to explain your methods.

You will need
<ul><li>cubes</li></ul>

1 Build a small rectangular prism that has a base of 1 cube by 2 cubes and a height of 3 cubes.

2 Record the length, width, height, surface area, and volume on the first row of a table like the one below.

Length	Width	Height	Surface Area	Volume

3 Double the length, width, and height of the rectangular prism. Record the length, width, height, surface area, and volume on the second row of the table.

4 How do the new surface area and volume compare to the old surface area and volume?

5 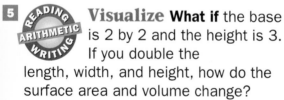 **Visualize What if** the base is 2 by 2 and the height is 3. If you double the length, width, and height, how do the surface area and volume change?

6 **Take a stand** Jim says that if you double the length, width, and height of a rectangular prism, the surface area will be 4 times as great and the volume will be 8 times as great as those of the original rectangular prism. Do you agree? Tell why.

Luciana wrote a problem about a Rubic's cube that she has.

Find the volume of this cube. If you add 2 more layers of little cubes on the top, what would the new volume be?

7 Solve Luciana's problem.

8 Change Luciana's problem. Solve the new problem and explain whether it was easier or harder than Luciana's and why.

9 **Write a problem** that involves surface area or volume.

10 Trade problems. Solve at least three problems written by other students.

11 Which of the problems you solved was the easiest and which was the hardest? Explain your reasons.

Luciana Perelli
St. Theresa Elementary School
Trumbull, CT.

Menu

Choose five problems and solve them. Explain your methods.

1 A farmer bought a new irrigation system that waters the fields in a circular pattern. If the sprinkler can shoot water 35 feet, how many square feet can he water with 10 sprinklers?

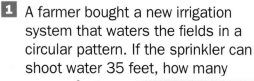

2 Lenno has forgotten the combination of his bike lock. He remembers that the sum of the three numbers is 75. He knows that the middle number is twice the last number and 5 more than the first number. What is the combination?

3 Read the directions on a box of whole-wheat pancake mix. How many cups of milk are needed to make 24 pancakes?

For 16 Pancakes:
2 CUPS FLOUR
1 ½ CUPS MILK

4 Write an equation using the numbers 1 through 5. Use each number exactly once. Use any combination of operations. Below are two ways to get a result of 10. Find one more way to get a result of 10.

$$2 \times (3 + 4) - 5 + 1 = 10$$
$$5 \times 2 \times 1 \times (4 - 3) = 10$$

5 Roland wants to build a shelf all around the living room to display his mother's plate collection. The room is 24 feet by 30 feet. The shelf will be 1 ft wide. How many feet of board does he need?

6 In your closet, you have 4 blue shirts, 2 black shirts, 3 pairs of blue jeans, and 1 pair of black pants. If you had to select an outfit for school without looking at what you were picking, what is the probability that you would pick a blue shirt and blue pants?

7 A traffic light shows red for 55 seconds, yellow for 5 seconds, and green for 60 seconds during rush hour. **What if** the rush hour lasts 2 hours. How much of the time is the light red?

8 A department store has purchased gift boxes that are 10 in. by 4 in. by 11 in. If its shopping bags are $2\frac{1}{2}$ feet by $2\frac{3}{4}$ feet by 1 foot, how many gift boxes can fit into a shopping bag?

Choose two problems and solve them. Explain your methods.

9 The barn below needs painting, and the roof needs new shingles. A gallon of paint costs $23.67 and covers 350 square feet. The shingles for the roof come in packets that cover $33\frac{1}{3}$ square feet and cost $46.75 per packet. The barn has the same number of doors and windows on opposite sides. What will it cost to paint the barn and put on a new roof?

10 A company claims that it has doubled its sales this month over last month. The public relations staff has produced the graph below to show the increase. Explain how the company has misrepresented the increase in sales. Create a graph that more accurately shows what the increase should be.

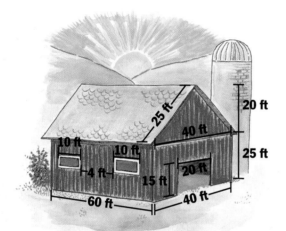

11 **Data Point** Find the letters of the alphabet that are used with the most frequency. Describe your plan for solving this problem. Show your result as a percentage.

12 **At the Computer** A piece of paper is 8 cm by 11 cm. What is the greatest volume that can be created by cutting out square corners and folding it up into an open-top box? Using a spreadsheet program on a computer, design a way of looking at all of the possibilities down to the nearest tenth of a centimeter.

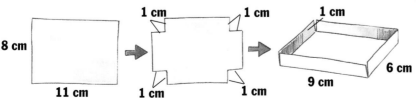

Language and Mathematics

Complete the sentence. Use a word in the chart. (pages 492–525)

1 In measuring the area of a 2-dimensional shape, you use ■ units.

2 The sum of the areas of all the faces of a 3-dimensional figure is called the ■.

3 The ■ of a 2-dimensional figure is the distance around it.

4 The distance around a circle is called the ■.

5 The amount of space enclosed by a 3-dimensional figure is called its ■.

Concepts and Skills

Find the perimeter and area of the shape.
Round decimal answers to the nearest tenth. (pages 492, 496)

6 8.1 cm, 12.7 cm

7 12 ft, 12 ft

8 7 in., 9 in., 10 in.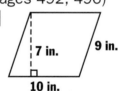

9 13 mm, 14 mm, 16 mm, 16 mm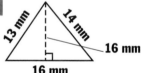

Find the circumference and area of the circle. Use $\pi = 3\frac{1}{7}$ or 3.14.
Round decimal answers to the nearest tenth. (pages 500, 502)

10 7 in.

11 4.1 cm

12 112 km

13 28 in.

Find the perimeter and area of the compound figure.
Round decimal answers to the nearest tenth. (page 506)

14 9 ft, 8 ft, 7 ft, 6 ft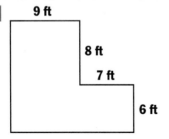

15 4.5 cm, 6 cm, 2 cm, 4 cm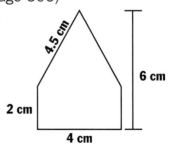

Find the surface area of the prism or pyramid. (page 518)

 16
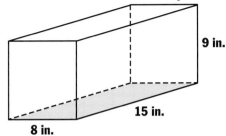
9 in.
15 in.
8 in.

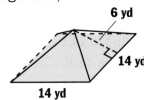 17
6 yd
14 yd
14 yd

Find the volume of the rectangular prism. (page 522)

 18 ℓ = 5 cm
w = 12 cm
h = 2 cm

19 ℓ = 9 in.
w = 9 in.
h = 9 in.

Think critically. (pages 492, 502)

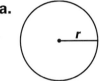 20 **ALGEBRA** Analyze. Which has the greatest area? Explain.

a.

r

Circumference = 100 cm

b.

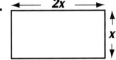
2x
x

Perimeter = 100 cm

c.

y
y

Perimeter = 100 cm

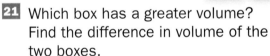 **MIXED APPLICATIONS**
Problem Solving

(pages 512, 526)

 21 Which box has a greater volume?
Find the difference in volume of the
two boxes.

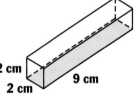
2 cm
6 cm
3 cm
2 cm
2 cm
9 cm

22 To produce the right color of paint,
you need to mix 3 quarts of red with
1 quart of white. How many quarts of
each are needed to make $8\frac{1}{2}$ gallons
of the mix?

23 The walls of a Viking house are 6 ft
thick. The outside walls are 40 ft
long, 20 ft wide, and 10 ft tall. How
many cubic feet of building materials
were used in the four outside walls?

24 A farmer has 120 ft of fence to
enclose a garden. The side of his
house will be used as one of the
longest sides to save fencing. The
width will be half of the length. What
is the greatest possible length and
width for the garden?

25 Of a random sample, 53 out of 67
students surveyed said they enjoyed
studying the Middle Ages. If there are
700 students in the school, about
how many would you predict would
not enjoy studying the Middle Ages?

Find the perimeter or the circumference. Use $3\frac{1}{7}$ or 3.14 for π. Round decimal answers to the nearest tenth.

1 3.2 m, 6.5 m

2 6 in., 10 in., 8 in.

3 5 in.

4 42 mm

Find the area. Use $3\frac{1}{7}$ or 3.14 for π. Round decimal answers to the nearest tenth.

5 12 cm, 6 cm

6 4 cm, 5.5 cm, 7 cm

7 7.5 mm, 6 mm, 5 mm, 3.5 mm

8 21 ft

Find the area of the compound figure. Use $3\frac{1}{7}$ or 3.14 for π. Round decimal answers to the nearest tenth.

9 6 m, 2 m 2 m 2 m, 5 m

10 5 in., 4 in., 5 in., 8 in.

11 5 mm, 5 mm

Find the surface area. Round to the nearest tenth.

12 3 m, 7.2 m, 16.5 m

13 36 cm, 10 cm, 10 cm, 8 cm, 12 cm

Find the volume of the rectangular prisms. Round decimals to the nearest tenth.

14 2.7 km, 5.3 km, 5 km

15 5.8 m, 3.5 m, 2 m

16 6 in., 6 in., 6 in.

Solve.

17 The distance from the center of a castle to its surrounding circular moat is 25 m. What is the circumference of the moat?

18 The rectangular door to the castle has two congruent sides. Each side is 12 ft high and 6 ft wide. What is the area of the whole door?

19 A window in the castle's tower has 3 straight sides and a semicircular top. The bottom of the window is 1 m wide. The 2 straight sides are each 0.5 m long. What is the perimeter of the window?

20 The water trough for the castle's horses is shaped like a rectangular prism. It is 1.5 m long, 0.25 m wide, and 0.8 m high. What is the volume of the trough?

What Did You Learn?

Eduardo used centimeter cubes to build two rectangular prisms.

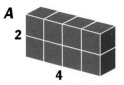

A
2
4

You will need
• *centimeter cubes*

▶ Use the same number of centimeter cubes to make another rectangular prism that has the same volume and a smaller surface area than prism *A*. What is the surface area of the new prism? Draw the rectangular prism you made.

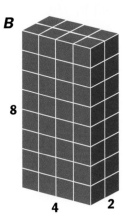

B
8
4   2

▶ Use the same number of centimeter cubes to make another rectangular prism that has the same volume and a greater surface area than prism *B*. What is the surface area of the new prism? Draw the rectangular prism you made.

•••••••••••••••••• **A Good Answer** ••••••••••••••••••
• includes a diagram for each problem.
• shows an accurate calculation of the volume and surface area.

You may want to place your work in your portfolio.

What Do You Think

1 Do you like solving problems that involve perimeter, area, and volume? Why or why not?

2 How would you tell someone the relationship between the area of a triangle and the area of a parallelogram?
• Use models.
• Use a diagram.
• Use an estimate.
• Other. Explain.

SKYSCRAPERS

The Masonic Temple Building in Chicago was built in 1891. It was 20 stories high and was the tallest building in the world at that time. It was built with a steel frame, which was stronger and lighter than bricks or other masonry. The frame supported the entire building, including the walls.

Until that time, buildings were made of bricks or other masonry, and the entire structure was supported by the walls. The tallest masonry building ever was built in Chicago during this time. It is called the Monadnock Building and is 16 stories tall. To support the weight of such a tall masonry building, the walls at the base are 14 ft thick.

Cultural Note

The skyscraper was developed after the Great Fire of Chicago destroyed about a third of that city in 1871. As architects planned for the rebuilding of Chicago, they decided to make buildings taller so that large buildings could be built on relatively small pieces of land.

Try this activity to see why buildings without steel frames need to have very thick walls.

You will need
- *clay*
- *newspapers*

Step 1 Spread newspapers on your desk. Divide the clay you have into thirds. Combine two of the thirds so one lump has twice the volume of the other.

Step 2 Use the smaller lump of clay to build the tallest tower you can that will stand by itself. Measure and record the height.

Step 3 Predict whether you can make a tower twice as tall with twice as much clay. Then use the remaining clay to build the tallest tower you can that will stand by itself. Measure and record the height of the tower.

▶ What conclusions can you draw from this activity?

Why Do Tall Skyscrapers Need Metal Frames?

You were probably not able to build a tower twice as tall when you used twice as much clay. A tower made with twice as much clay weighs twice as much. To support the additional weight, you probably needed to make the base of your second tower quite a bit bigger.

This is the same problem architects have when they try to build a masonry building with self-supporting walls taller than about 20 stories. That is the reason why skyscrapers are now built with steel frames.

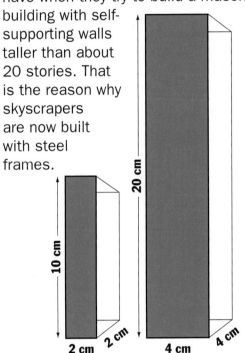

Use the diagram above to answer these questions

1 What is the area of the base of each model?

2 How does the area of the base of the larger model compare to the area of the base of the smaller model?

3 What is the volume of each model?

4 How do the volumes compare? If both models were solid, how would the weights compare?

At the Computer

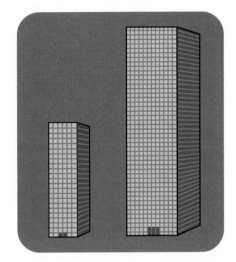

5 Use a drawing program to design a skyscraper. Show the lengths of the different parts of the skyscraper.

6 Calculate the area of the base and total volume of your skyscraper.

Sears Tower in Chicago

CHAPTER

14 INTEGERS

THEME | Earth Science

Did you know that the ocean has a temperature, just like the air, and the air has currents, just like the ocean? In this chapter, you will use integers to explore temperature, ocean tides, and storms.

What Do You Know

Do you ever "have a temperature"? Do you know the temperature in your classroom? As you can see in the table, temperatures can vary quite a lot.

1 What is the coldest temperature given? the hottest?

2 What is the difference in temperatures of the lunar day and lunar night?

3 Arrange the temperatures in order from hottest to coldest or from coldest to hottest. What method did you use to arrange the temperatures?

Temperatures in Different Conditions	
Condition	**Temperature (in °Celsius)**
Water boils	100
Average oven temperature	177
Human body	37
Water freezes	0
Mercury freezes	⁻38.8
Dry ice	⁻80
Lunar day	120
Lunar night	⁻160

READING ARITHMETIC WRITING

Write a Paragraph
The line graph shows the average temperature in Fargo.

Paragraphs should contain a main idea and sentences that support the main idea.

1 Write a paragraph explaining how the temperature in Fargo changes during the year.

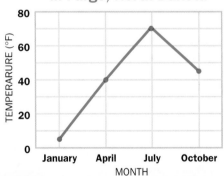

Average Temperature in Fargo, North Dakota

Vocabulary

integer, p. 538
negative integer,
   p. 539

positive integer,
   p. 539
opposite, p. 539

Venn diagram,
   p. 550

Integers

One winter morning a weather forecaster recorded the temperatures shown in the chart.

8 A.M.	9 A.M.	10 A.M.	11 A.M.
⁻6°F	⁻3°F	0°F	⁺5°F

⁻6°F means 6 degrees Fahrenheit below zero.

⁺5°F means 5 degrees Fahrenheit above zero.

Numbers such as ⁻6, ⁻3, 0, and ⁺5 are called **integers**. You can represent integers with two-color counters.

6 degrees below zero

Read: negative 6
Write: ⁻6

5 degrees above zero

Read: positive 5
Write: ⁺5

Note: You can write ⁺5 as 5.

Work Together

Use two-color counters to represent these situations. Draw a diagram and write an integer to label your drawing.

> **You will need**
> • *two-color counters*

- 4°F above zero
- debt of $5
- 6 feet above sea level

- 6°F below zero
- savings of $3
- 9 feet below sea level

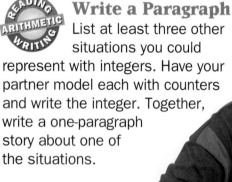

Write a Paragraph
List at least three other situations you could represent with integers. Have your partner model each with counters and write the integer. Together, write a one-paragraph story about one of the situations.

Make Connections

This number line shows some integers. The integers include the positive integers, the negative integers, and zero.

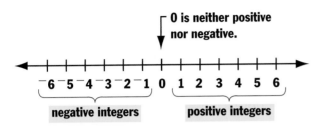

0 is neither positive nor negative.

negative integers   positive integers

Integers are the whole numbers and their opposites.

Positive integers: 1, 2, 3, 4, ...
Negative integers: ⁻1, ⁻2, ⁻3, ⁻4, ...

Each integer has an **opposite.**
The opposite of ⁻4 is 4, and the opposite of 4 is ⁻4.

Zero is its own opposite.

▶ Tell the opposite of each situation in the Work Together. Show the opposites on a number line.

Note: Opposites are the same distance from 0 on a number line, but on opposite sides of it.

Check Out the Glossary
For vocabulary words, see page 643.

Check for Understanding

Write an integer to represent the situation.

1 7 degrees below zero   **2** savings of $40   **3** loss of 6 yd in football

Write the integer.

4 the opposite of 17   **5** the opposite of ⁻8   **6** the opposite of ⁻1

Critical Thinking: Analyze

7 Explain how to find the opposite of an integer. Give examples.

CHECK

Practice

Write an integer to represent the situation.

1 12 ft above sea level   **2** increase of $35   **3** weight loss of 7 lb

4 4-yd loss in football   **5** 20° above zero   **6** 20 ft below ground

Write an integer to represent the situation. Then describe the opposite situation and write an integer to represent it.

7 8° below zero   **8** 3 ft above ground   **9** $12 loss

10 gain of 10 yd in football   **11** profit of $50   **12** bank withdrawal of $20

Describe a situation that can be represented by the integer.

13 ⁻10   **14** ⁺7   **15** ⁻19   **16** ⁺80

PRACTICE

Compare and Order Integers

**L
E
A
R
N**

Do you think that all salt water freezes at exactly the same temperature? The amount of salt in the water affects its freezing point. Arrange the temperatures of these samples of salt water solutions from the coldest to the warmest.

Sample A	⁻3°F
Sample B	⁻5°F
Sample C	2°F

To order integers, you can compare them two at a time.

You can think of a thermometer as a number line. You can use a number line to compare the first two temperatures.

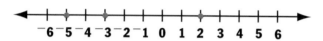

Note: Of any two numbers on a number line, the number to the left is less than the number to the right.

Because ⁻5 is to the left of ⁻3, ⁻5 < ⁻3.

2 is greater than ⁻3 and greater than ⁻5.

The order from least to greatest is ⁻5, ⁻3, 2.

The order of the temperatures from coldest to warmest is ⁻5°F, ⁻3°F, 2°F.

More Examples

A Order from greatest to least:
6, ⁻4, 4, ⁻6, 0

Greatest to least: 6, 4, 0, ⁻4, ⁻6

B Compare: 24 ● ⁻36

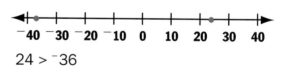

24 > ⁻36

**C
H
E
C
K**

Check for Understanding

1 Which is less, ⁻2 or ⁻5?

2 Which is greater, ⁻15 or 0?

3 Order 0, 6, and ⁻9 from least to greatest.

4 Order ⁻5, 7, and ⁻1 from least to greatest.

Critical Thinking: Generalize **Explain your reasoning.**

5 Is it true or false to say that every positive integer is greater than every negative integer?

6 Is there a greatest negative integer? a greatest positive integer?

Practice

Compare. Write > or <. You may use a number line to help.

1 0 ● 4   **2** 9 ● 6   **3** ⁻5 ● 2   **4** ⁻4 ● 0   **5** ⁻5 ● ⁻7

6 ⁻6 ● 4   **7** ⁻3 ● ⁻20   **8** ⁻90 ● ⁻40   **9** 17 ● 9   **10** ⁻53 ● ⁻62

Write the integers in order from least to greatest.

11 2, ⁻3, 0   **12** ⁻2, 3, ⁻4   **13** ⁻7, ⁻1, 5

14 2, 9, ⁻6   **15** 11, ⁻7, ⁻2   **16** ⁻4, 3, ⁻8, 0

17 ⁻14, 14, ⁻17, 28   **18** ⁻42, 44, ⁻47, 48   **19** ⁻37, 14, ⁻56, ⁻63, 22

Copy and complete the number line.

20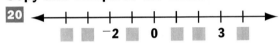

21

MIXED APPLICATIONS
Problem Solving

22 The melting point of radon is ⁻71°C. Is that colder or warmer than the ⁻259°C melting point of hydrogen?

23 If you toss two number cubes, what is the probability of a sum of 2?

24 **Write a problem** that can be solved by comparing two integers. Solve it and ask others to solve it.

25 The coldest temperature ever recorded in Russia was ⁻90°F. Is that higher or lower than the coldest temperature ever recorded in the United States? SEE INFOBIT.

INFOBIT
The coldest temperature ever recorded in the U. S. was ⁻80°F. It occurred in Prospect Creek, AK, on January 23, 1971.

mixed review • test preparation

Find the area and perimeter or circumference of the figure.

1 3 cm / 3 cm   **2** 4 m / 3 m   **3** 3 in.   **4** 3 ft, 5 ft, 4 ft

Solve.

5 A shirt for $18.95 is on sale for 15% off. What is the sale price?

Add Integers

Scientists have discovered that atoms are made up of positively and negatively charged particles. The net charge, or sum, of one positively charged particle and one negatively charged particle is 0.

You can use yellow counters to represent positively charged particles and red counters to represent negatively charged particles.

1 + ⁻1

1 + ⁻2

Net charge: 0
Integer represented: 0
1 + ⁻1 = 0

Net charge: ⁻1
Integer represented: ⁻1
1 + ⁻2 = ⁻1

Note: A pair of positively and negatively charged particles that have a net charge of zero is called a "zero pair".

Bohr's model for atoms.

Work Together

Work with a partner. Use two-color counters to find each sum. Write an equation to record your results.

You will need
• *two-color counters*

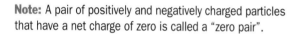

positive + positive: 4 + 6 7 + 8	negative + negative: ⁻3 + ⁻2 ⁻4 + ⁻9
positive + negative: 7 + ⁻4 5 + ⁻9	negative + positive: ⁻6 + 5 ⁻2 + 8
integer + 0: ⁻8 + 0 0 + ⁻5	sum of opposites: 5 + ⁻5 ⁻7 + 7

Talk It Over

▶ How did you find the sums when you worked together?

▶ How could you find the sum of two negative integers without using counters?

Make Connections

The sum of two positive integers is positive.

$3 + 2 = 5$

The sum of two negative integers is negative.

$^-3 + {}^-2 = {}^-5$

The sum of a positive and a negative integer may be positive, negative, or zero.

$^-3 + 5 = 2$

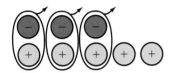

$3 + {}^-5 = {}^-2$

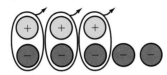

$^-3 + 3 = 0$

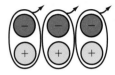

▶ What is the sum of an integer and zero? Give examples.

▶ What is the sum of two integers that are opposites? Give examples.

More Examples

A $^-3 + 3 = 0$

Think: 3 and $^-3$ are opposites

B $^-4 + {}^-4 = {}^-8$

Think: $4 + 4 = 8$

C $6 + {}^-4 = 2$

Think: $6 - 4 = 2$

D $3 + {}^-4 = {}^-1$

Think: $4 - 3 = 1$

Check for Understanding

Complete the number sentence represented by the model.

1

$^-3 + 4 = n$

2

$^-6 + 6 = n$

3

$2 + {}^-4 = y$

Add. You may use counters.

4 $5 + {}^-6 = n$
5 $0 + {}^-4 = n$
6 $^-3 + 7 = n$
7 $^-8 + {}^-2 = n$

8 $5 + 18 = c$
9 $^-7 + 0 = x$
10 $^-2 + 8 = y$
11 $^-16 + 16 = b$

Critical Thinking: Generalize

12 How can you figure out whether the sum of a positive integer and a negative integer is positive, negative, or zero?

Practice

Complete the number sentence represented by the model.

$^-4 + 2 = n$

$^-2 + 3 = n$

$^-2 + ^-6 = n$

Draw pictures of counters to show three different collections of charged particles with a net charge of:

4 $^-1$ **5** $^+1$ **6** $^-2$ **7** $^+3$ **8** $^-4$ **9** 5

Add. You may use counters.

10 $3 + ^-8 = n$ **11** $^-5 + 7 = n$ **12** $5 + 8 = n$ **13** $8 + ^-8 = n$

14 $^-7 + ^-12 = a$ **15** $^-10 + 4 = c$ **16** $^-6 + 6 = d$ **17** $8 + ^-4 = y$

18 $^-3 + ^-10 = x$ **19** $^-7 + 0 = n$ **20** $0 + ^-23 = x$ **21** $^-12 + 12 = c$

22 $7 + 25 + ^-6 = a$ **23** $^-11 + 3 + 2 = n$ **24** $11 + ^-12 + 3 = y$

25 $^-5 + ^-5 = b$ **26** $^-10 + 1 = a$ **27** $8 + ^-3 = x$ **28** $^-1 + ^-1 = s$

Add. Do as many as you can mentally.

29 $2 + ^-3 = b$ **30** $^-4 + ^-2 = x$ **31** $^-7 + 7 + 4 = a$ **32** $10 + ^-6 = x$

33 $^-5 + 3 + ^-3 = y$ **34** $7 + 6 = n$ **35** $^-9 + 3 = d$ **36** $^-6 + ^-8 = y$

37 Explain your methods for doing ex. 33 and 35.

✪ ALGEBRA Complete the function tables.

38

Rule: Add $^-6$.					
Input	$^-6$	0	4	6	8
Output	$^-12$	n	n	n	n

39

Rule:					
Input	$^-8$	$^-2$	0	4	6
Output	$^-10$	$^-4$	$^-2$	2	4

•••••••••••••••••• **Make It Right** ••••••••••••••••••

40 Bradley modeled $^-4 + 7$ as shown and said the answer is 4. Explain the error and correct it.

Problem Solving

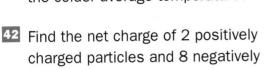

41 The average temperature on Jupiter is ⁻150°C. The average temperature on Saturn is ⁻180°C. Which planet has the colder average temperature?

42 Find the net charge of 2 positively charged particles and 8 negatively charged particles.

43 The length of a rectangular shed is $15\frac{1}{2}$ feet and the area of the shed is $69\frac{3}{4}$ square feet. What is its width?

44 At noon the temperature was 1°F. Between noon and 6 P.M., the temperature went down 4°F and then went up 2°F. What was the temperature at 6 P.M.?

45 At 20 m below sea level, the water temperature is 13.85°C. At the surface of the water it is 1.95°C warmer. Estimate the temperature of the water at the surface.

46 What if you have 3 red counters and 4 yellow counters. List all the different integers you can represent using the counters.

47 **ALGEBRA: PATTERNS** What is the next number in this pattern of numbers: 1, 2, 4, 8, 16? Explain your reasoning.

48 A shirt that usually sells for $18.95 is on sale for 20% off. If the sales tax is 7%, how much will the shirt cost with tax?

49 **Write a problem** about temperature that involves positive and negative integers. Solve your problem and have others solve it.

more to explore

Adding Integers with a Calculator

You can use a calculator to find the sum of two or more integers.
Your calculator must have a $+/-$ key to add integers.

 Note: The $+/-$ key changes positive to negative numbers and negative to positive numbers.

Add: ⁻3 + 6 = n

 3 $+/-$ + 6 = ⬚ **3.**

Add: ⁻6 + ⁻2 = n

 6 $+/-$ + 2 $+/-$ = ⬚ **−8.**

Add using a calculator.

1 ⁻8 + ⁻3 = n

2 15 + ⁻7 = n

3 362 + ⁻410 = y

4 ⁻288 + ⁻119 = x

5 5,827 + ⁻1,436 = t

6 ⁻35 + ⁻44 + 251 = a

Subtract Integers

High and low tides can be described using positive and negative numbers. To find the range of the tides, you need to find the difference between the high and low tides. Let's explore how to subtract integers.

For example, to model $7 - {}^-3$, you could represent 7 like this.

In the last lesson, you saw how to use zero pairs to help you add. You can also use zero pairs to help you subtract integers.

Zero Pair

Note: Adding a zero pair is like adding zero.

$7 - {}^-3 = 10$

Work Together

Work with a group. Use counters to find each difference. Write an equation to record your results.

You will need
- *two-color counters*

$6 - 2 = n$	$2 - 6 = n$	${}^-6 - {}^-2 = n$	${}^-2 - {}^-6 = n$
$6 - {}^-2 = n$	$2 - {}^-6 = n$	${}^-6 - 2 = n$	${}^-2 - 6 = n$
$6 - 0 = n$	$0 - 6 = n$	${}^-6 - 0 = n$	$0 - {}^-6 = n$

Talk It Over

▶ How did you model $6 - 2$ and ${}^-6 - {}^-2$?

▶ How did you model $2 - 6$, ${}^-2 - {}^-6$, $6 - {}^-2$, and ${}^-6 - 2$?

Make Connections

Here are two ways a group found to subtract $^-6 - 2$.

Our first method:
We put down 6 red counters.
We added 2 zero pairs so we could
take away 2 yellow counters.
Then, we had 8 red counters left.

$$^-6 - 2 = ^-8$$

Our second method:
We put down 6 red counters. We
thought that taking away 2 yellow
is like adding 2 red. So we added
two red. We had 8 red counters.

$$^-6 - 2 = ^-6 + ^-2 = ^-8$$

Subtracting an integer is the same as adding its opposite.

▶ Choose three subtraction exercises that you modeled in your group. Rewrite them as addition exercises and find the sum. Compare. Did you get the same answer?

Check for Understanding

Complete the number sentence for the model.

1

$$4 - 3 = n$$

2

$$^-4 - ^-2 = n$$

3

$$^-5 - 1 = a$$

4

$$3 - ^-1 = y$$

Subtract. You may use a model.

5 $2 - 5 = n$ **6** $^-6 - ^-7 = n$ **7** $^-2 - 4 = n$ **8** $8 - ^-5 = n$

9 $5 - 9 = n$ **10** $^-5 - 9 = n$ **11** $^-5 - 5 = n$ **12** $5 - ^-6 = n$

Critical Thinking: Analyze

13 When will the difference of two integers be positive? When will it be negative?

Turn the page for Practice.

Practice

Complete the number sentence represented by the model.

1

$^-5 - ^-3 = n$

2

$5 - ^-1 = c$

3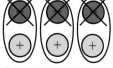

$^-2 - ^-4 = a$

4

$2 - 6 = b$

5

$2 - ^-3 = n$

6

$^-3 - 1 = y$

Subtract. You may use a model.

7 $7 - 4 = n$ **8** $^-8 - ^-2 = d$ **9** $9 - 3 = b$ **10** $^-10 - ^-3 = t$

11 $4 - 9 = a$ **12** $^-16 - ^-3 = b$ **13** $^-10 - ^-7 = x$ **14** $^-6 - 12 = d$

15 $3 - 5 = x$ **16** $^-18 - 5 = n$ **17** $2 - 6 = y$ **18** $3 - ^-12 = c$

19 $^-4 - 10 = y$ **20** $2 - ^-6 = c$ **21** $^-8 - ^-14 = n$ **22** $12 - ^-12 = n$

23 $^-12 - 12 = n$ **24** $^-16 - ^-16 = n$ **25** $4 - ^-6 = a$ **26** $8 - 16 = a$

Copy and complete.

27 $8 - ^-4 = 8 + \blacksquare = \blacksquare$ **28** $^-9 - 5 = ^-9 + \blacksquare = \blacksquare$

29 $^-10 - ^-8 = ^-10 + \blacksquare = \blacksquare$ **30** $^-3 - ^-6 = ^-3 + \blacksquare = \blacksquare$

31 $2 - 7 = 2 + \blacksquare = \blacksquare$ **32** $11 - 3 = 11 + \blacksquare = \blacksquare$

33 $5 - ^-7 = 5 + \blacksquare = \blacksquare$ **34** $^-6 - 8 = ^-6 + \blacksquare = \blacksquare$

35 $4 - 9 = 4 + \blacksquare = \blacksquare$ **36** $^-6 - ^-2 = ^-6 + \blacksquare = \blacksquare$

•••••••••••••••••••••• **Make It Right** •••••••••••••••••••••••••

37 Rob subtracted $^-2$ from 6 as shown. $6 - ^-2 = ^-6 + ^-2 = ^-8$
Explain what the error is and correct it.

Problem Solving

38 A person deposits $1,000 in his savings account each month. He withdraws $450 from the account each month to pay a student loan. He starts the account with $350 in January. In which month will he have more than $3,000 in his account if there are no other deposits and withdrawals?

39 The highest high tide in Galveston one day was 7 ft. The lowest low tide was ⁻6 ft. What was the range in the tides that day?

40 The low temperature of ⁻15°F in Ritter broke the previous record of ⁻12°F. How much lower was the new low than the old one?

41 The temperature was ⁻2°F at 8 A.M. At noon, it was ⁻5°F, and at 6 P.M., it was ⁻1°F. At what time was the temperature the highest? At what time was it the lowest?

42 In a random sample of shirts from a batch at a factory, 2% were defective. Out of 4,000 shirts in the batch, predict how many were defective.

43 **Data Point** Use the Databank on page 642. Find the difference in temperature between the record high and the record low temperatures in the United States for each month.

44 **Write a problem** that can be solved by subtracting integers. Solve your problem. Ask others to solve your problem.

more to explore

Subtracting Integers Using a Calculator

You can use a calculator to find the difference of two integers. Your calculator must have a +/− key to subtract integers.

Subtract: ⁻6 − ⁻2

6 +/− − 2 +/− = −4.

Subtract using a calculator.

1 88 − 97 = n

2 ⁻126 − 324 = x

3 ⁻59 − ⁻17 = y

4 26,384 − 41,215 = d

5 ⁻892 − ⁻710

6 816 − ⁻84 = t

Problem-Solving Strategy

Use Logical Reasoning

LEARN

Read Out of 24 students in a high school science club, 15 are taking chemistry, 8 are taking physics, and 5 are taking both courses. How many are taking neither?

Plan You can draw a **Venn diagram** to solve the problem.

Solve Show the number who are taking both courses.

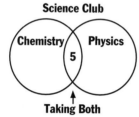

Science Club

Chemistry / Physics

5

Taking Both

Venn diagram A diagram for organizing and showing data by using overlapping circles.

Show the number who are taking only chemistry or only physics.

chemistry		both		chemistry only
15	−	5	=	10

physics		both		physics only
8	−	5	=	3

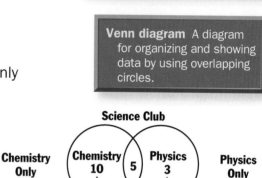

Science Club

Chemistry Only — **Chemistry 10** 5 **Physics 3** — Physics Only

Taking Both

Add to find the number who are taking chemistry or physics or both.

$10 + 5 + 3 = 18$

Subtract from the number in the club to find the number who are taking neither.

$24 - 18 = 6$

Look Back How could you check that your answer is reasonable?

CHECK

Check for Understanding

1 **What if** 9 students in the club are taking chemistry, 11 are taking physics, and 3 are taking both. How many are taking neither?

Critical Thinking: Analyze

2 **What if** 11 students in the club are taking chemistry and 5 are taking physics but not chemistry. How many are taking physics or chemistry or both? Explain your reasoning.

1 In a class of 26 students, 11 are in the computer club, 9 are in the science club, and 6 are in both. How many are in neither?

2 In a class, 12 students like to play volleyball and 10 like to play soccer but not volleyball. How many like to play soccer or volleyball or both?

3 Find the perimeter and the area of a rectangle 4 cm long and 3 cm wide. Find the perimeter and area of a rectangle twice as long and twice as wide. How do the perimeter and area change when the length and the width are doubled?

4 Maureen was planning a 5-day trip to the coast to watch migrating whales. Her hotel room was $89 per night, and she estimated she would spend $23 per day on meals. Estimate how much cash she should take for meals during her vacation.

5 Fresh grapefruit are available in stores all year long. If grapefruit are 3 for a dollar, how much will it cost to buy 12 grapefruit?

6 In a survey, 82 people said they like pizza, 86 said they like tacos, and 73 said they like both. How many like pizza or tacos or both?

7 A scuba diver descended to a depth of 30 ft in 15 seconds on his first dive. After a rest period, he dove 50 ft in 20 seconds on his second dive. How many feet per second did the scuba diver descend on his second dive?

8 Erin uses the Internet to get data on weather conditions around the country. She pays $5.25 for the first 5 hours and $1.50 for each additional hour. If her Internet costs were $27.75 one month, how many hours did she spend on the Internet?

9 **What if** you need to order a telephone pole that sticks out of the ground 42 ft. Use the chart below to decide how tall a pole to order.

10 There are 23 people in a class. Of these, 9 are in band, and 10 are in a special after-school science program. If 4 students are in both, how many students are in neither?

Height Above Ground	Amount Below Ground
20 feet to 25 feet	4 feet
25 feet to 30 feet	$4\frac{1}{2}$ feet
30 feet to 35 feet	5 feet
35 feet to 40 feet	$5\frac{1}{2}$ feet
40 feet to 45 feet	6 feet
45 feet to 50 feet	$6\frac{1}{2}$ feet

Write an integer to express each situation.

1 12° above zero   **2** loss of 6 yd in football   **3** debt of $40

4 Write an integer to describe 40 in. above ground. Describe the opposite situation and write an integer for the opposite situation.

Write > or <.

5 ⁻6 ● ⁻2   **6** 8 ● ⁻1   **7** 0 ● ⁻4   **8** ⁻11 ● ⁻14

9 ⁻5 ● ⁻7   **10** 4 ● ⁻8   **11** ⁻2 ● 4   **12** ⁻5 ● ⁻1

Write the integers in order from least to greatest.

13 ⁻6, 0, 4, ⁻8, ⁻2   **14** ⁻10, 12, 14, ⁻16, 18   **15** 3, ⁻8, 5, ⁻1, ⁻4

Write the integers in order from greatest to least.

16 6, ⁻4, 9, 0, ⁻7   **17** 15, ⁻19, ⁻12, 4, ⁻11   **18** ⁻3, ⁻9, ⁻6, ⁻4, 0

Add or subtract.

19 $5 + {}^-3 = n$ **20** ${}^-6 - {}^-2 = a$ **21** $0 - 5 = x$ **22** ${}^-11 + 0 = d$

23 ${}^-7 + {}^-9 = d$ **24** ${}^-7 - {}^-9 = b$ **25** $4 - {}^-8 = y$ **26** $7 + {}^-2 = c$

Use the table for ex. 27–29.

27 What was the range in the morning tides of December 12?

28 What was the range in the afternoon tides on December 10?

29 Was the afternoon low tide lower on December 11 or December 12?

December Tide Table (in feet)				
	Morning		Afternoon	
Date	High	Low	High	Low
10	8	3	10	⁻1
11	8	3	10	⁻2
12	7	2	9	⁻1
13	8	2	9	0
14	8	3	9	1

30 In a class of 28 students, 12 are in the chorus, 10 are in the band, and 7 are in both. How many are in neither?

31 Find the net charge of 6 positively charged particles and 8 negatively charged particles.

32 The temperature in Racine was ⁻2°F at 8 A.M. and ⁻4°F at noon. By 6 P.M., the temperature had dropped another 11°F. What was the temperature at 6 P.M.?

33 *Journal* Write a paragraph describing how to find the difference of two integers by finding a sum. Give examples to support your reasoning.

Multiplication of Integers

NASA scientists must monitor launch temperatures very closely. Suppose the temperature dropped 2° every hour for 4 hours. By how much did the temperature change in all?

Multiply: $4 \times {}^-2$

You can use what you already know about multiplication to create a pattern to answer this question.

Start with a multiplication fact that you know, such as 4×2. Use a pattern to work through the multiplication facts to find $4 \times {}^-2$. Determine whether the product is positive or negative.

$4 \times 2 = 8$ ⎫ Subtract 4.
$4 \times 1 = 4$ ⎫ Subtract 4.
$4 \times 0 = 0$ ⎫ Subtract 4.
$4 \times {}^-1 = {}^-4$ ⎫ Subtract 4.
$4 \times {}^-2 = {}^-8$

The temperature changed by $^-8°$ in 4 hours.

You can also use patterns to find $^-2 \times 3$ and $^-2 \times {}^-3$.

$2 \times 3 = 6$ ⎫ Subtract 3.
$1 \times 3 = 3$ ⎫ Subtract 3.
$0 \times 3 = 0$ ⎫ Subtract 3.
$^-1 \times 3 = {}^-3$ ⎫ Subtract 3.
$^-2 \times 3 = {}^-6$

$2 \times {}^-3 = {}^-6$ ⎫ Add 3.
$1 \times {}^-3 = {}^-3$ ⎫ Add 3.
$0 \times {}^-3 = 0$ ⎫ Add 3.
$^-1 \times {}^-3 = 3$ ⎫ Add 3.
$^-2 \times {}^-3 = 6$

⭐ **ALGEBRA: PATTERNS** **Find the product. You can use patterns.**

1 $5 \times {}^-2$ **2** $6 \times {}^-2$ **3** $4 \times {}^-3$ **4** $6 \times {}^-4$ **5** $^-6 \times 3$

6 $^-9 \times 5$ **7** $^-2 \times {}^-3$ **8** $^-4 \times {}^-3$ **9** $^-8 \times {}^-7$ **10** $^-4 \times {}^-9$

Effects of Salt on Water & Ice

You will need
- *container (two cup or larger)*
- *salt*
- *water and ice*
- *Celsius thermometer*
- *measuring cup*
- *scale*
- *tablespoon*

How cold is a mixture of water and ice? What happens when you add salt to the mixture? In this activity, you will work with a partner to investigate the effect of salt on the temperature of a mixture of water and ice.

STEP 1 Put a thermometer, 5 ounces of ice (by weight) and $\frac{2}{3}$ cup of water in a container.

STEP 2 Measure the temperature of the ice-water mixture using a Celsius thermometer and record it. Add $\frac{2}{3}$ cup of ice and measure the temperature again.

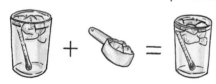

STEP 3 Empty the container and repeat Step 1. Add 1 tablespoon of salt to the water. Stir thoroughly and record the temperature. Stir again and record the lowest temperature the mixture reaches.

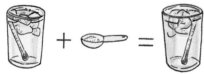

STEP 4 Repeat Steps 1 and 3 at least 5 times. Add 1 more tablespoon of salt each time. For example, the second time you do Step 3, you add 2 tablespoons of salt.

Experiment with Temperature

1 What was the temperature of the water and ice mixture after Step 1? Did it change when you added more ice to the mixture?

2 Take turns adding salt, stirring, and measuring the temperature.

3 Make a table like the one below to show how the temperature of the water-ice-salt mixture changes as the amount of salt changes.

Amount of Salt (in tablespoons)	Temperature (in °C)
0	
1	
2	
3	

4 Make a line graph to represent the data in your table.

5 What happened to the temperature as you added salt?

Report Your Findings

6 **Portfolio** Prepare a report based on what you learned. Include the following:

► Make a copy of the table and the graph you prepared.

► Describe how the temperature of the water-ice-salt mixture changes as the amount of salt changes.

7 Compare your report with those of other teams.

Revise your work.
► Is your graph clearly labeled and accurate?
► Do your conclusions make sense based on your data?
► Have you answered all the questions posed in this investigation?

PREDICT what would happen to the temperature of the mixture if you kept adding salt.

EXPLORE why road crews spread salt on icy roads in the winter and why cooks add salt to water when boiling it.

FIND what happens when lakes freeze. Do they freeze solid? Do bodies of saltwater such as the Great Salt Lake freeze? Share your findings with the class.

Coordinate Graphing in All Four Quadrants

Meteorologists map the position of storms on grids. This grid shows several storms that surround Charlotte, North Carolina, which is located at the point (0, 0) on the grid. Where is the center of storm *A* located on this grid?

IN THE WORKPLACE
Dr. Peter Ray, Florida State University, Tallahassee, FL

Note: The point at which the axes intersect, point (0,0), is called the **origin.**

Point *A* is 3 units to the left and 2 units down from the origin. The ordered pair that represents *A* is (⁻3, ⁻2).

$$(^-3, \ ^-2)$$

first coordinate
distance to the right or the left of 0

second coordinate
distance above or below 0

Talk It Over

▶ Are the points (⁻3, 1) and (1, ⁻3) the same? Explain.

▶ Name the coordinates of points *B, C,* and *D.* How are their coordinates alike? How are they different?

▶ A point has two negative coordinates. In what part of the graph is it located? Explain.

Look at the grid on page 556. What if storm _A_ traveled in a straight line described by the following equation: _y_ = _x_ + 1.

Graph the path of the storm.

Step 1

Make a function table by substituting different values for _x_ in the equation and calculating y each time.

$y = x + 1$		
_x_	_y_	Ordered Pairs
⁻3	⁻2	(⁻3, ⁻2)
⁻1	0	(⁻1, 0)
1	2	(1, 2)
3	4	(3, 4)

Step 2

Graph the function.

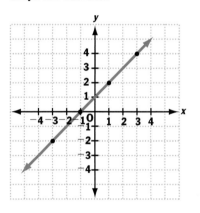

HURRICANE HUGO
8 PM EDT
17 SEPTEMBER 1989
140 MPH   939 MB

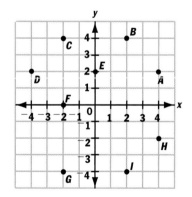

Check for Understanding
Give the coordinates of the point.

1 _A_   **2** _G_   **3** _D_   **4** _E_

Name the point for the ordered pair.

5 (⁻2, 4)   **6** (⁻2, 0)   **7** (2, ⁻4)   **8** (4, ⁻2)

9 Make a function table and graph _y_ = _x_ + 3.

Critical Thinking: Analyze

10 Why can you draw a line connecting the points after you graph the ordered pairs on the grid in Step 2 above for _y_ = _x_ + 1?

11 How are the graphs of _y_ = _x_ + 1 and _y_ = _x_ + 3 alike? different?

Turn the page for Practice. ➡

Practice

Give the coordinates of the point.

1 A **2** B **3** C

4 I **5** J **6** K

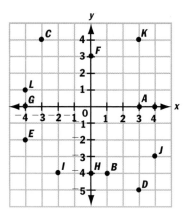

Name the point for the ordered pair.

7 $(3, {}^-5)$ **8** $({}^-4, 0)$ **9** $({}^-4, {}^-2)$

10 $(0, 3)$ **11** $(0, {}^-4)$ **12** $({}^-4, 1)$

Copy and complete the table for the function represented by the equation. Then, graph the function.

13

y = x + 2				
x	⁻4	⁻2	0	2
y	▣	▣	▣	▣

14

y = x − 3				
x	⁻1	0	1	2
y	▣	▣	▣	▣

15

y = 3 − x				
x	⁻2	0	2	4
y	▣	▣	▣	▣

16

y = x − 4				
x	⁻3	⁻1	1	3
y	▣	▣	▣	▣

17

y = x + 4				
x	⁻3	⁻2	0	2
y	▣	▣	▣	▣

18

y = 4 − x				
x	⁻2	0	2	4
y	▣	▣	▣	▣

MIXED APPLICATIONS
Problem Solving

19 A meteorologist discovered that a storm followed a path determined by the equation $y = 2 - x$. Graph the path and decide if the storm passed over the point $(1, 1)$ on the graph, the location of her house.

20 Three coordinates of the vertices of a square are $(0, 4)$, $(4, 0)$, and $(0, {}^-4)$. Find the coordinates of the fourth vertex.

21 **Write a problem** in which you draw a picture on a coordinate grid. Give the coordinates of the vertices of your picture to other students and see if they can draw your picture.

22 Suppose that at 4,500 m, the temperature is 4°C. At what altitude above that point is the temperature ⁻8°C? SEE INFOBIT.

INFOBIT
Up to a height of about 12 km, air tends to get cooler as the altitude increases. For every 1,000-meter increase in altitude, there is an average decrease of 6°C in temperature.

Find the Figure Game!

This is a game for two teams, with two players on each team.

Each team should make two grids like the one shown at the right. Label them *Grid A* and *Grid B*.

Play the Game

▶ In secret, each team draws a rectangle on its Grid A.

▶ The teams take turns making guesses to figure out the location of the other team's rectangle.

▶ When it is your turn, agree on a good point to guess, and record it on your Grid B. The other team marks it on its Grid A and tells you whether the point is "inside," "outside," "on a line," or "on a vertex." Use Grid B for recording what you find out about the location of the other team's rectangle.

▶ Continue playing until one team has discovered what the vertices of the other team's rectangle are.

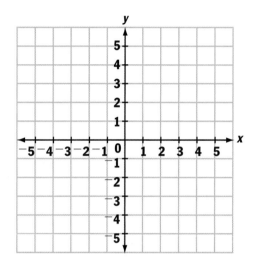

What strategies did you use to select points to guess?

---

mixed review • test preparation

Find the volume of the rectangular prism.

1 $\ell = 12$ cm, $w = 12$ cm
$h = 26$ cm

2 $\ell = 6$ m, $w = 6$ m
$h = 6$ m

3 $\ell = 4$ yd, $w = 6\frac{1}{2}$ yd,
$h = 2\frac{1}{4}$ yd

Find the area of the shaded region.

4
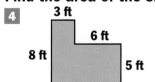

5
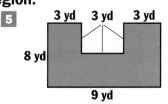

6
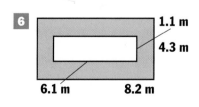

Addition and Subtraction Equations

Did you know you can add to solve a subtraction equation?

Solve: $h - {}^-3 = {}^-6$

Since subtracting an integer is the same as adding its opposite, you can think of $h - {}^-3 = {}^-6$ as $h + 3 = {}^-6$.

Model $h + 3 = {}^-6$ using a cup and counters.	Add 3 red counters to both sides.	Remove zero pairs to get the cup by itself. Record the result.

        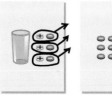

$$h = {}^-9$$

Work Together

Work with a partner to solve these equations. Explain how you got your answers.

You will need
- *cups*
- *two-color counters*

Addition equations:

$5 = x + {}^-3 \qquad y + 7 = {}^-4 \qquad a + {}^-1 = {}^-3$

Subtraction equations:

$9 = b - {}^-2 \qquad n - 3 = {}^-2 \qquad c - {}^-4 = {}^-5$

Talk It Over

▶ How can you check your solutions?

▶ How can you solve an addition equation with integers in it?

▶ Did you always solve by getting the variable alone on one side of the equation? If so, explain why.

Make Connections

You solve addition and subtraction equations that have integers just as you solve equations with whole numbers.

$$a + {}^-1 = {}^-3$$
$$a + {}^-1 - {}^-1 = {}^-3 - {}^-1$$
$$a = {}^-3 + 1$$
$$a = {}^-2$$

$$c - {}^-4 = {}^-5$$
$$c - {}^-4 + {}^-4 = {}^-5 + {}^-4$$
$$c = {}^-9$$

Check: $a + {}^-1 = {}^-3$
$${}^-2 + {}^-1 = {}^-3$$
$${}^-3 = {}^-3 ✓$$

Check: $c - {}^-4 = {}^-5$
$${}^-9 - {}^-4 = {}^-5$$
$${}^-9 + 4 = {}^-5$$
$${}^-5 = {}^-5 ✓$$

▶ How do you undo adding $^-1$ in the first equation?

▶ How do you undo subtracting $^-4$ in the second equation?

Check for Understanding

Solve each equation.

1

$$x + {}^-4 = {}^-3$$

2

$$y + 2 = {}^-5$$

3

$$n - {}^-3 = 6$$

4

$$c - 1 = {}^-3$$

Solve the equation. You may use a model to help. Check the solution.

5 $x + 6 = {}^-2$

6 $n + {}^-4 = 6$

7 $m + {}^-8 = 0$

8 $a + {}^-1 = 1$

9 $y - 3 = {}^-3$

10 $w - {}^-6 = {}^-8$

11 $t - 3 = {}^-2$

12 $x - {}^-2 = 5$

13 $n - {}^-8 = 10$

Critical Thinking: Summarize

14 Write a paragraph describing how to solve addition and subtraction equations with integers in them.

Turn the page for Practice. ➡

Practice

Solve each equation.

    1   **2**   **3**

$x + {}^-2 = 3$ $a + 5 = {}^-6$ $b - 3 = {}^-4$

Solve the equation. You may use any method. Check the solution.

4 $x + 4 = {}^-2$ **5** $w + 4 = {}^-1$ **6** ${}^-8 = x + {}^-3$ **7** $0 = w + {}^-6$

8 $a - {}^-2 = {}^-1$ **9** $n - {}^-2 = 7$ **10** $t - 8 = {}^-10$ **11** $x - 7 = {}^-2$

12 $t + 6 = {}^-8$ **13** $b - {}^-3 = {}^-8$ **14** $m + {}^-6 = 4$ **15** ${}^-5 - 3 = y$

16 ${}^-7 = t + 5$ **17** $x = 11 + {}^-9$ **18** $c - 7 = {}^-8$ **19** ${}^-20 = c + 8$

20 ${}^-3 + n = 12$ **21** $c - {}^-1 = 10$ **22** ${}^-4 + b = {}^-6$ **23** $c - {}^-4 = 5$

The table shows temperatures in Chicago on one day in January.

24 Write an equation to find the range in temperatures on the day shown and solve it.

25 The temperature rose 5° between 8 A.M. and 10 A.M. Write an equation to find the temperature at 10 A.M. and solve it. Tell what any variable in your equation represents.

Chicago Temperatures	
Time	**Temperature**
12 midnight	${}^-20°$F
4 A.M.	${}^-22°$F
8 A.M.	${}^-21°$F
12 noon	${}^-10°$F
4 P.M.	${}^-6°$F
8 P.M.	${}^-10°$F

Write a problem that can be solved by finding the solution to the equation. Then, solve the equation.

26 $m - {}^-6 = 4$ **27** $x + {}^-8 = 16$ **28** $t - 4 = 2$

• • • • • • • • • • • • • • • • • • **Make It Right** • • • • • • • • • • • • • • • • • •

29 Here is how Chan solved $x - {}^-6 = {}^-4$. Tell what the error is and correct it.

$$x - {}^-6 = {}^-4$$
$$x - {}^-6 + 6 = {}^-4 + 6$$
$$x = 2$$

Problem Solving

30 From the daytime high, the temperature dropped 10°F to a low of ⁻2°F at night. What was the daytime high temperature?

31 The path of a storm followed a line determined by $y = x - 3$. Graph the line of the storm and decide if it will pass over a town located at (⁻2, ⁻4).

32 **Data Point** Collect data on the record high and low temperatures in five places, including the place you live. Work with a partner to display the data in a double-bar graph.

33 **Write a problem** that will require addition or subtraction of integers to solve. Solve it and give it to others to solve.

34 The average distance from Earth to the moon is 238,860 mi. About how many times as far away was Comet Hyakutake during March and April of 1996? SEE INFOBIT.

INFOBIT
Comet Hyakutake was clearly visible in the United States during March and April of 1996, partly because it was within 9.3 million miles of Earth.

Cultural Connection Ancient Chinese Rod Numbers

At least as early as 200 B.C., Chinese mathematicians used rod numerals to represent the numbers 1 through 9. They used two kinds of symbols. They alternated symbols of each kind.

First Kind

Second Kind

1	2	3	4	5	6	7	8	9

Sometime between A.D. 800 and A.D. 900, they began to use ○ to represent zero. Also, they used a slanting stroke written through the last sign of a number's representation to indicate the number was negative.

⁻1,305

Write the numeral for the Chinese number.

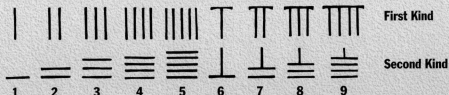

1 **2** **3** **4**

PART 1 Interpret Data

When you go outside on a cold day, you may notice that it seems much colder if the wind is blowing. The combined cooling effect of temperature and wind is called *windchill*.

From the table, you can see that if the air temperature is 10°F and the wind is blowing at 15 miles per hour, it feels as cold as if the temperature is ¯18°F and the air is still.

Air Temperature (in degrees Fahrenheit)	Wind Speed (in miles per hour)								
	0	5	10	15	20	25	30	35	40
30	30	27	16	9	4	1	¯2	¯4	¯5
25	25	22	10	2	¯3	¯7	¯10	¯12	¯13
20	20	16	3	¯5	¯10	¯15	¯18	¯20	¯21
15	15	11	¯3	¯11	¯17	¯22	¯25	¯27	¯29
10	10	6	¯9	¯18	¯24	¯29	¯33	¯35	¯37
5	5	0	¯15	¯25	¯31	¯36	¯41	¯43	¯45
0	0	¯5	¯22	¯31	¯39	¯44	¯49	¯52	¯53
¯5	¯5	¯10	¯27	¯38	¯46	¯51	¯56	¯58	¯60
¯10	¯10	¯15	¯34	¯45	¯53	¯59	¯64	¯67	¯69
¯15	¯15	¯21	¯40	¯51	¯60	¯66	¯71	¯74	¯76

Equivalent Windchill Temperatures

Work Together
Solve. Be prepared to explain your methods.

1 If the temperature outside is 25°F and the wind speed is 20 miles per hour, what is the windchill temperature?

2 If the temperature is 30°F, what happens to the windchill temperatures as the wind speed increases?

3 For each air temperature, how do the windchill temperatures change as the wind speed increases?

4 Compare windchill temperatures for higher wind speeds to windchill temperatures at lower wind speeds.

5 **What if** the temperature where you live is 12°F and the wind speed is 20 mph. About what temperature would the windchill temperature be?

Paul used the graph of ocean temperatures to write this problem.

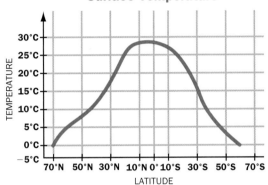

Average Mid-Ocean
Surface Temperature

CHECK

At what latitude is the average mid-ocean surface temperature highest?

6 Solve Paul's problem by explaining the graph.

7 Change Paul's problem so it is easier or harder to solve. Do not change the data in the graph.

8 **Write a Paragraph** Solve the new problem. Write a paragraph explaining why the new problem is easier or harder to solve.

9 **Write a problem** of your own involving temperature.

10 Trade problems. Solve at least three problems written by other students.

11 What methods did you use to solve the other students' problems? Explain.

Paul Richert-Garcia
Russell Sage Junior High School
Forest Hills, NY

Menu

Choose five problems and solve them. Explain your methods.

1 You want to design a screen saver for a computer. Your design will need to fit in a rectangular space 33 cm by 25 cm. If you use a rectangle with a length of 5 cm and a width of 3 cm, how many rectangles will you need to make a tessellation of the screen?

2 One day in April, the hottest spot in the nation was Camarillo, California, with 90°F. The coldest spot was Bismarck, North Dakota, with ⁻1°F. The wettest spot was Abilene, Texas, which had 1.81 in. of rain. What was the temperature range in the United States that day?

3 A survey of teens indicated that 46% of them got their spending money from their parents and from occasional jobs. If the U.S. teen population was 29.1 million at that time, how many got their money from parents and occasional jobs?

4 A circular outdoor thermometer is to be cemented to a square piece of wood so that the circle just touches the four sides of the square. The diameter of the circle is $11\frac{1}{4}$ in. Find the area of the square to the nearest square inch.

5 Raphael bought a poster for $5.50 and a desk lamp for $16.50. Because the store was having a sale, he got a 10% discount on his purchases. Describe two ways to determine the amount he paid. Find the amount.

6 One week, America Online's stock dropped from $53\frac{7}{8}$ to $45\frac{3}{4}$, and Netcom Online Communications' stock dropped from $28\frac{1}{4}$ to $24\frac{1}{2}$. Which stock lost more value?

7 Raymond has $1.45 in his pocket. He has 17 coins in all. He has more dimes than any other coin. How many pennies, nickels, dimes, and quarters does he have?

8 The ratio of boys to girls in a class is 4:5. If there are 27 students in the class, how many are boys? girls?

Choose two problems and solve them. Explain your methods.

9 A department store is having a special 10%-off sale. You have $200 to spend on back-to-school clothes. Use their ad below to decide what clothes you can purchase for your money. Make at least two different lists.

SALE! 10% off

Item	Regular Price	Item	Regular Price
Slacks...	$29	Sweatshirts....	$25
Skirts....	$29	Jackets.........	$98
T-shirts..	$12	Sweaters.......	$40
Shoes....	$65		

10 You are going to toss 3 coins 100 times. Predict the number of times you will get each of the following outcomes: 0 heads, 1 head, 2 heads, and 3 heads. Do the experiment and record your results. Compare the results with your predictions.

11 **Data Point** Find out the average monthly temperatures in your town and make a graph to show the temperatures. Explain why you picked the kind of graph you did. Then make a graph to show what the average temperatures might be if your town were 700 miles farther north. Compare your graphs.

12 **At the Computer** Make tables for $y = x - 3$ and $y = 5 - x$ to find an ordered pair of numbers that is in both tables. Then use a graphing program on a computer to graph both lines on the same coordinate grid. Do they intersect at the ordered pair that is in both tables? Repeat, using $y = x + 2$ and $y = {}^-4 - x$.

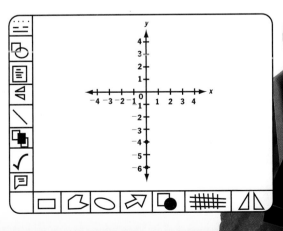

chapter review

Language and Mathematics

Complete the sentence. Use a word in the chart. (pages 538–563)

1 The ■ are made up of the positive integers, the negative integers, and zero.

2 The ■ is the point at which the axes of a grid intersect.

3 The ■ of $^{-}4$ is 4.

4 The integers less than zero are ■.

Vocabulary

integers
negative integers
opposite
origin
positive integers
zero pair

Concepts and Skills

Order the integers from least to greatest. (page 540)

5 $4, {}^{-}8, 0, {}^{-}3$

6 $^{-}5, {}^{-}11, {}^{-}6, {}^{-}4$

7 $^{-}3, 5, 3, {}^{-}6, 1$

8 $^{-}15, {}^{-}34, 0, 2, {}^{-}6$

Order the integers from greatest to least. (page 540)

9 $^{-}4, {}^{-}9, {}^{-}1, 0, {}^{-}8$

10 $^{-}5, {}^{-}7, 3, 8, {}^{-}12$

11 $^{-}14, 12, {}^{-}9, 7, {}^{-}1$

12 $0, 3, {}^{-}3, 1, {}^{-}1$

Write > or <. (page 540)

13 $^{-}12$ ● $^{-}14$

14 $^{-}4$ ● 0

15 $^{-}24$ ● 10

16 $^{-}8$ ● $^{-}6$

Add. (page 542)

17 $3 + {}^{-}2 = n$

18 $^{-}4 + {}^{-}2 = d$

19 $5 + {}^{-}9 = y$

20 $66 + 14 = n$

21 $^{-}8 + {}^{-}23 = a$

22 $16 + {}^{-}12 = x$

23 $^{-}25 + 12 = b$

24 $^{-}6 + 6 = d$

Subtract. (page 546)

25 $4 - {}^{-}2 = n$

26 $^{-}3 - 8 = y$

27 $5 - 11 = x$

28 $23 - 15 = y$

29 $^{-}6 - {}^{-}2 = b$

30 $^{-}9 - {}^{-}15 = c$

31 $^{-}9 - 8 = x$

32 $^{-}4 - {}^{-}9 = n$

Name the point for the ordered pair. (page 556)

33 ($^-$2, 4) **34** (0, $^-$3) **35** (4, 2)

Give the coordinates of the point. (page 556)

36 C **37** F **38** E

39 Graph $y = x + 2$ on a coordinate grid.

Solve the equation. (page 560)

40 $x + 1 = 0$ **41** $a - {}^-4 = 2$ **42** $a + {}^-3 = {}^-6$

Think critically. (pages 542, 546)

43 Analyze. Explain what the error is and correct it.

$$^-6 - 4 = {}^-6 + 4 = {}^-2$$

44 Generalize. Write *always, sometimes,* or *never.* Give examples to support your answer.
   a. The sum of two negative numbers is negative.
   b. The difference of two negative numbers is negative.
   c. The difference of two positive numbers is positive.

MIXED APPLICATIONS
Problem Solving *Pencil & Paper* *Calculator* *Mental Math* (pages 550, 564)

45 The greatest temperature range in a day was recorded at Browning, Montana, in January 1916. The high was 44°F and the low was $^-$56°F. What was the range?

46 The equation $t - {}^-33 = 77$ can be used to find the highest temperature, in degrees Celsius, ever recorded in Alabama. (The record low was $^-$33°C.) Find t, the record high.

47 Three vertices of a rectangle have coordinates (5, 3), ($^-$5, $^-$3), and ($^-$5, 3). What are the coordinates of the fourth vertex?

48 Find the net charge of 4 positively charged particles and 7 negatively charged particles.

49 In a sample of 55 families, 28 had computers in their homes, 34 had microwaves, and 21 had both. How many had neither?

50 Find all the possible outcomes if you spin the spinner at the right twice. Tell how you solved the problem.

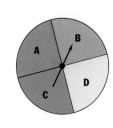

Compare. Write >, <, or = .

1 $^-5$ ● $^-9$

2 $^-18$ ● 14

Order from least to greatest.

3 $^-10$, $^-20$, $^-15$, $^-3$

4 19, $^-19$, $^-1$, $^-9$

Add.

5 $^-3 + 8 = n$

6 $^-1 + ^-9 = x$

7 $^-17 + 17 = y$

8 $^-12 + 5 = t$

Subtract.

9 $6 - ^-4 = n$

10 $^-5 - 10 = y$

11 $3 - 9 = d$

12 $^-15 - ^-11 = a$

Name the point for the ordered pair.

13 $(3, ^-1)$

14 $(^-4, 2)$

Give the coordinates of the point.

15 G

16 D

17 Graph $y = x - 3$ on a coordinate grid.

Solve the equation.

18 $x + 3 = ^-3$

19 $y - ^-4 = ^-4$

20 $z - 8 = 0$

21 $a + ^-5 = ^-2$

Solve. Show your work.

22 Three vertices of a square have coordinates $(0, ^-1)$, $(^-3, ^-1)$, and $(^-3, ^-4)$. What are the coordinates of the fourth vertex?

23 In the first round of a game, you lost 24 points. In the second round, you gained 18 points. What was your score after two rounds?

24 You can use integers to represent scores in golf. A score of 1 below par can be represented as $^-1$. Find the amount below par for a golfer with par scores of $^-2$, 3, $^-4$, and $^-2$ for each of the four rounds of a tournament.

25 The equation $y - \$15 = \$35$ can be used to find the amount of profit a class made washing cars to pay for a class trip. Find y, the amount of money collected at the car wash.

What Did You Learn?

Each expression between the spokes of the wheel at the right is equal to ⁻6, the integer in the center of the wheel.

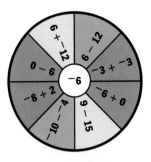

▶ Complete each wheel below with four addition expressions and four subtraction expressions between the spokes. In each wheel, the value of each expression must equal the number in the center.

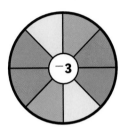
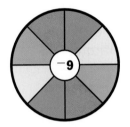
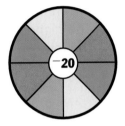
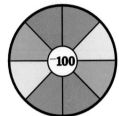

▶ Use one of the expressions you filled in. Verify your answer by drawing a number line or using counters.

You will need
• *ruler*
• *counters*

················A Good Answer····················
• shows accurate expressions that match the number in the center of a wheel.
• includes the evaluation for one of the expressions. from the wheels and shows how to use a number line or counters to add or subtract integers.

 You may want to place your work in your portfolio.

What Do You Think

1 Can you solve equations that have integers? If not, what difficulties do you have?

2 When you add or subtract integers, which do you do?
• Use counters.
• Use a number line.
• Use a calculator.
• Other. Explain.

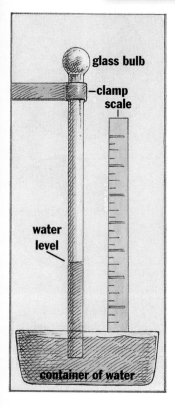

TEMPERATURES

Galileo heated air in a glass tube that was closed at one end and open at the other end. Then, he put the open end of the tube into a container of water. When the air in the tube cooled, it contracted, or got smaller. This caused the water in the container to be drawn up into the tube as shown in the picture. The higher the water level was, the lower the temperature.

In 1714, Gabriel Fahrenheit, a German instrument maker living in Holland, invented a thermometer similar to ones that are used today. It had a column of mercury in a glass tube. As the mercury got warmer, it expanded, causing it to travel up the glass tube. The higher the mercury level was, the higher the temperature.

Fahrenheit also developed a scale for measuring temperature. Fahrenheit chose 32°F as the freezing point of water and 212°F as the boiling point of water.

The Celsius scale was developed a few years later, in 1742, by Anders Celsius, a Swedish astronomer. His scale was also based on the freezing and boiling points of water. Celsius, however, selected 0°C for freezing and 100°C for boiling.

▶ Upon what scientific principle were both Galileo's and Fahrenheit's thermometers based?

▶ How were their thermometers different?

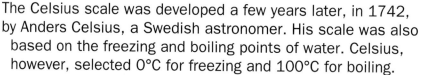

Cultural Note

The first thermometer was invented in 1603 by Galileo, an Italian scientist. Among other things, Galileo suggested the use of pendulums in clocks and developed the astronomical telescope.

**Galileo Galilei,
17th Century Scientist**

How Cold and How Hot?

How cold and how hot does it get where you live? Many weather records have been kept for years. The table below shows the highest and lowest temperatures ever recorded for some states.

State	Lowest Temperature (in °F)	Highest Temperature (in °F)
Alabama	⁻27	112
Alaska	⁻80	100
Arizona	⁻40	127
Florida	⁻2	109
Georgia	⁻17	112
Hawaii	12	100
Iowa	⁻47	118
Louisiana	⁻16	114
Michigan	⁻51	112
Montana	⁻70	117
New York	⁻52	108
Ohio	⁻39	113
Texas	⁻23	120
Virginia	⁻30	110
Wisconsin	⁻54	114

Extreme-Temperature Records for Some States

SOURCE: NATIONAL CLIMATIC DATA CENTER, U.S. DEPARTMENT OF COMMERCE

1 Make another table that lists the states in order from the coldest to the warmest low temperature ever.

2 Which state has the greatest difference between its coldest and warmest recorded temperatures? What is the difference?

3 Which state has the least difference between its coldest and warmest recorded temperatures? What is the difference?

At the Computer

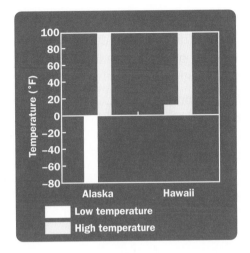

4 Choose five of the states in the table. Use graphing software to make a bar graph of the highest and lowest temperatures for those states.

5 Write two statements based on your graph.

Integers **573**

Choose the letter of the correct answer.

1 Which quadrilateral could have 4 sides of the same length and no right angles?

  A rhombus
  B trapezoid
  C rectangle
  D square

2 What is the probability of spinning the spinner and getting a 1?

  F $\frac{1}{6}$
  G $\frac{1}{5}$
  H $\frac{1}{4}$
  J $\frac{1}{3}$

3 Suppose you buy two CD's for $13.95 and a tape for $11.95. Which number sentence can be used to find t, the total cost of the items, not including tax?

  A $t = 13.95 + \$11.95$
  B $t = 2 \times (13.95 + 11.95)$
  C $t = (2 \times 13.95) + 11.95$
  D $t = 13.95 + (2 \times 11.95)$
  E $t = (3 \times 13.95) + 11.95$

4 Which letter best represents 1.5 on the number line?

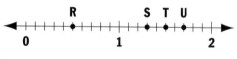

  F R
  G S
  H T
  J U

5 How much fencing material would it take to enclose this garden?

  A 11m
  B 15m
  C 22m
  D 28m

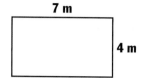

6 In how many different ways can you select one pair of pants and one shirt from 3 pairs of pants and 5 shirts?

  F 3 ways
  G 5 ways
  H 15 ways
  J 30 ways

7 Kevin spent $3.36 for a box of screws and $4.80 for a screwdriver. If there are 24 screws in a box, what is the cost of each screw?

  A $0.14
  B $0.20
  C $0.34
  D $1.44
  E Not Here

8 A magazine sent out 2,000 letters to get people to subscribe to the magazine. From those letters, they got 60 subscriptions. If they send out 8,000 letters, what is the best estimate of the number of subscriptions they would get?

  F 15 subscriptions
  G 120 subscriptions
  H 240 subscriptions
  J 480 subscriptions

9 The wheel of a bicycle has a diameter of 28 inches. If the wheel turns 3 times on the ground, how many inches will the bicycle travel?

A 88 inches
B 264 inches
C 528 inches
D 1,848 inches

10 Molly runs 5.35 kilometers on Monday, 4.75 kilometers on Tuesday, amd 6.7 kilometers on Wednesday. How far did she run altogether in the three days?

F 10.77 km
G 15.8 km
H 16.7 km
J 16.8 km
K Not Here

11 Find the area of the parallellogram.

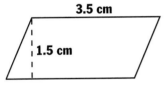

3.5 cm

1.5 cm

A 5 cm^2
B 5.25 cm^2
C 10 cm^2
D 52.5 cm^2

12 Ashley bought a portable stereo for $125. She got a 5% discount but had to pay 5% sales tax on the discounted price. How much did the stereo cost?

F $6.25
G $118.75
H $124.69
J $125
K Not Here

13 Tani has a rectangular garden plot that measures 12 ft by 18 ft. Alana's rectangular plot measures $13\frac{1}{2}$ ft by 16 ft. Which is true about the areas?

A Tani's is greater by 1 ft^2.
B Alana's is greater by 1 ft^2.
C Alana's is less by 8 ft^2.
D They have the same area.

14 The figure shows a square with its two diagonals drawn. Which procedure could you use to find the area of the shaded region?

F Find the area of the square and divide by 4.
G Find the area of the square and divide by 3.
H Find the perimeter of the square and divide by 4.
J Find the perimeter of the square and subtract the perimeter of the shaded region.
K Find the area of the square and divide by 2.

15 There were 135 students at a rally of sixth, seventh, and eighth graders. Four fifths of the students were in the sixth grade. One fifteenth of the students were seventh graders. How many eighth graders were there?

A 9 eighth graders
B 15 eighth graders
C 18 eighth graders
D 108 eighth graders
E Not Here

extra practice

Collect, Organize, and Display Data page 5
Use the pictograph for ex. 1–3.

1 How many students bought fewer than 3 CDs in August?

2 If each 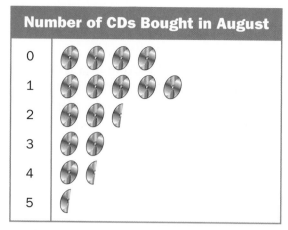 stood for 2 students, how many students bought 5 CDs?

3 How would the pictograph change if 6 more students each bought 5 CDs?

Use the line plot for ex. 4–5.

4 Analyze the line plot. Identify any clusters or gaps in the data. What conclusions can you make?

5 What is the most common length of the students' first names? What is the least common length?

Number of CDs Bought in August

0	💿 💿 💿 💿
1	💿 💿 💿 💿 💿
2	💿 💿 💿
3	💿 💿
4	💿 💿
5	💿

💿 = 4 students

Letters in First Names

```
                    x
        x           x   x
        x   x   x   x
x   x   x   x   x   x           x
2   3   4   5   6   7   8   9
```

Bar Graphs page 9
Make bar graphs for the data in the tables.

1

Favorite Ethnic Foods

Type	Number of Students
Italian	25
Chinese	16
Greek	8
Mexican	32
Thai	5
Moroccan	12

2

Hair Color

	Number of Boys	Number of Girls
Blond	10	11
Brown	15	18
Black	8	5
Red	4	7

Use the bar graph for exercises 3–5.

3 About how many more boys ride the bus to school than bike?

4 About how many more girls than boys walk to school?

5 About how many more students take the bus than ride in a car? than walk?

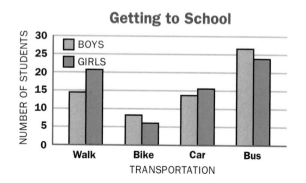

Getting to School

Range, Median, Mode page 11

Find the range, median, and mode for each set of data.

1 2, 9, 6, 4, 9

2 12, 16, 21, 18, 12, 12

3 7, 2, 6, 3, 9, 13, 15

4 41, 43, 37, 39, 41, 37

5 4, 8, 9, 5, 6, 8, 8, 8, 6

6 12, 45, 33, 56, 56, 21

7 3, 6, 7, 1, 0, 3, 5, 0, 2

8 10, 14, 30, 25, 21, 28

9 100, 125, 125, 123

Solve.

10 Tyler's baseball team scored these runs in 6 games: 0, 6, 0, 5, 3, 1. They score 3 runs in the next game. How does this change the range, median, and mode of the data?

Mean page 15

Find the range, mean, median, and mode for the set of data.

1 2, 10, 8, 3, 2

2 0, 8, 7, 1, 5, 0, 7

3 20, 50, 40, 70, 20

4 50, 75, 25, 80, 60, 70

5 2, 7, 8, 6, 2, 6, 7, 2

6 120, 175, 350, 155

Solve.

7 In one week, Ardith calculated that the mean time it took her to get to work was 14 minutes. She recorded times of 10, 20, 15, and 13 minutes. What was her time for the fifth day?

Problem-Solving Strategy: Make a Table page 17

Solve. Explain your methods

1 Roberto conducts a survey about the price of clock radios. Do more clock radios cost between $11 and $20 or between $21 and $30?

Clock Radio Costs Survey			
$12.50	$32.75	$15.80	$35.00
$17.00	$21.80	$19.90	$38.25
$14.25	$26.75	$28.65	$25.00

2 **Logical reasoning** Allison, Calvin, José, and Mandy are in line for lunch. José was directly behind Allison. Mandy sees what José bought and gets the same thing. Allison borrows some of the money Calvin receives as change. In what order were the students standing?

3 Copy and cut out these shapes. Use your cutouts to make a pattern that covers one sheet of paper. Color the design you made.

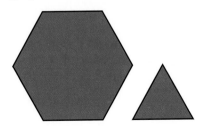

Line Graphs page 25
Use the tables to make line graphs.

1

Dakota's Allowance	
Year	Weekly Allowance
1995	$ 5.00
1996	$ 6.00
1997	$10.00
1998	$11.00
1999	$15.00

2

Students in the After-School Program		
Year	Boys	Girls
1985	22	20
1990	25	25
1995	30	29
2000	32	35

Use the double-line graph for problems 3–5.

3 In which month were chocolate milk sales equal to white milk sales?

4 About how many cartons of chocolate milk were sold in January?

5 About how many more cartons of chocolate milk than white milk were sold in October?

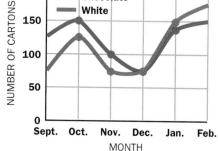

Milk Sales

- - Chocolate
- - White

NUMBER OF CARTONS

MONTH

- -

Stem-and-Leaf Plots page 27
Make a stem-and-leaf plot for the set of data. Draw conclusions based on the plot you made.

1 Number of words on vocabulary list: 25, 10, 15, 17, 9, 11, 25, 17, 18, 15, 15, 15, 14, 20, 21, 28

2 Number of minutes on math homework: 26, 28, 45, 58, 32, 37, 18, 33, 36, 43, 45, 47, 34, 30, 29, 16, 25, 24, 40, 39, 36, 26, 37

Use the stem-and-leaf plot for problems 3–6.

3 At how many school events were songs played?

4 How many school events played 15 or fewer songs?

5 What are the range, median, and mode of the data?

6 What needs to happen for the median to be 24?

7 What needs to happen for the mode to be 15?

Songs per School Event

0	1 1 1 1 4 4 9 9
1	5 5 8 8 9
2	3 3 4 6 7 7 8
3	0 0 1 3 5 5

Key: 3|5 = 35

**Identify the population and sample in the situation.
Tell if you think the sample is representative.**

1 In a school of 248 students, choose 15 sixth graders at random to make up a student council.

2 Survey every tenth person leaving the school cafeteria about his or her satisfaction with lunch.

Solve.

3 I am a three-digit number. My hundreds digit is equal to the sum of the tens and ones digits. The product of my tens and ones digits is 18. My tens digit is greater than my ones digit. What number am I?

4 In one hour, Sandra can address 8 invitations and Mike can address 6 invitations. How long will it take them together to address 126 invitations? How many will Sandra address? How many will Mike address?

5 Enrique bought 3 books for $4 each, 2 bookmarks for $1 each, and one magazine. He received $3 in change from his twenty-dollar bill. How much did the magazine cost?

6 There are 15 students in the school play. Of these, there are twice as many boys as girls. How many boys are in the play? How many girls are in the play?

Problem Solvers at Work page 33
Solve. Explain your methods.

1 Make a graph to show how many students at King School earned free meals by reading.

Grade	Boys	Girls
Third graders	23	21
Fourth graders	22	31
Fifth graders	16	25
Sixth graders	32	28

2 Use the dart board. List 3 different ways can you score 10 points in 3 throws.

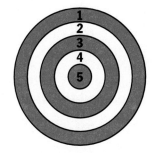

3 **Spatial reasoning** Bessie walked 6 blocks south and 4 blocks east to Anita's house. Together, they walked 8 blocks north to the mall. How far must they walk to Bessie's house?

4 Jeremy had a mean quiz score of 7 points. The range for his 5 quizzes was 5, the mode 6, and the median 6. What were Jeremy's test scores?

5 Paula baby-sits a neighbor's child every third day. She baby-sat on Monday, August 1. What is the date of the next Monday she will baby-sit?

6 Matthew was at the swimming pool from 3:45 P.M. until 5:20 P.M. Was he at the pool more than 1 hour and a half? Explain.

Exponents page 45
Write using an exponent.

1 $3 \times 3 \times 3 \times 3 \times 3$ **2** $25 \times 25 \times 25 \times 25$ **3** $8 \times 8 \times 8 \times 8 \times 8 \times 8$

Write in standard form.

4 9^1 **5** 6^2 **6** 3^3 **7** 2^5 **8** 10^7

a **ALGEBRA: PATTERNS Solve.**

9 Study the pattern. How many dots will be in the sixth square?

1st   2nd   3rd   4th

Place Value: Whole Numbers page 47
Tell the place and the value for the underlined digit.

1 12<u>8</u>,432   **2** <u>6</u>,321,080   **3** $23,4<u>3</u>6,198   **4** 73,402,<u>5</u>81

5 $57,<u>9</u>00,240   **6** 1<u>4</u>,321,111,962   **7** 87,<u>5</u>31,000,000

Write the number in standard form.

8 16 million, 40 thousand, eight

9 $(6 \times 1,000,000) + (4 \times 1,000) + 9$

Solve.

10 An oil spill of about 3,840,000 barrels occurred in 1979. Write this number in at least two different ways.

11 Attendance at the last five swim practices was 11, 6, 7, 11, and 10 swimmers. Find the mean, median, and mode number of swimmers.

Place Value: Decimals page 51
Write the place and the value of the underlined digit.

1 1.<u>9</u>2   **2** 65.34<u>6</u>   **3** 0.0<u>1</u>6   **4** 0.0000<u>2</u>   **5** 0.00<u>1</u>0

6 <u>3</u>0.083   **7** 25.9<u>8</u>73   **8** 7.<u>0</u>001   **9** 84.93<u>2</u>   **10** 96.1221<u>1</u>

Name the equivalent decimals.

11 0.6   0.60   0.06

12 3.6100   3.061   3.0610

Solve.

13 **Spatial reasoning** Make a design on a 10 × 10 grid. Color 0.4 of it blue, 0.23 of it red, and 0.1 of it yellow. Name the part that is not colored.

14 Cassidy spent $16.78 on clothes, $15.09 on CDs, and $19.74 on a gift. Did she need to use more than one fifty-dollar bill? Explain.

Compare and Order Decimals page 53

Write >, <, or =.

1 2.70 ● 2.700   **2** 1.67 ● 16.7   **3** $4.90 ● $4.09   **4** 0.620 ● 0.062

5 7.02 ● 6.98   **6** 4.888 ● 4.889   **7** 20 ● 20.00   **8** 6.293 ● 62.93

Order the numbers from least to greatest.

9 3.2, 3.92, 3.29

10 54.23, 45.32, 54.32, 45.23

11 $23, $230, $23.02, $23.20

12 6.031, 6.310, 6.103, 6.013

Solve.

13 Which numbers have the same digits and places as 3.01, but have a lesser value?

14 A dredge displaces 100 cubic yards of slurry in one minute. How much slurry will it displace in 1 hour?

- -

Mental Math: Estimate Sums and Differences page 55

Estimate the sum or difference by rounding.

1 9.31 + 6.82   **2** 8.58 − 2.15   **3** 16.2 + 42.85   **4** $18.50 − $6.25

5 $\begin{array}{r} 6.05 \\ -\ 0.82 \end{array}$ **6** $\begin{array}{r} 18.9 \\ +\ 4.63 \end{array}$ **7** $\begin{array}{r} 26.15 \\ -\ 9.4829 \end{array}$ **8** $\begin{array}{r} 8.763 \\ +\ 1.042 \end{array}$ **9** $\begin{array}{r} 2.985 \\ -\ 0.981 \end{array}$

Solve.

10 Texas has 16.0 million acres of wetland. Michigan has 11.2 million acres. Florida has 20.3 million acres. Estimate how many more acres of wetland there are in Texas and Michigan than there are in Florida.

- -

Add Decimals page 59

Estimate. Then add.

1 $\begin{array}{r} 6.04 \\ +\ 2.95 \end{array}$ **2** $\begin{array}{r} \$63.75 \\ +\ 12.36 \end{array}$ **3** $\begin{array}{r} 3.694 \\ +\ 8.397 \end{array}$ **4** $\begin{array}{r} 5.75 \\ +\ 0.69 \end{array}$ **5** $\begin{array}{r} 8.91 \\ 229 \\ +\ 78.36 \end{array}$

6 21.68 + 18.14   **7** 0.71 + 0.17   **8** 142.3 + 111.27

9 6.9 + 2.87 + 4   **10** 1.203 + 6.42 + 29.7   **11** $2.45 + $1.36 + $0.60

Solve.

12 Relay teammates have times of 33.8, 36.9, 40.15, and 41.17 seconds. What is the team's total time?

13 Doris has a blue skirt, a black skirt, a blue shirt, and a red shirt. List all the different outfits she can wear.

extra practice

Subtract Decimals page 63
Estimate. Then subtract.

1
```
   3.29
 − 1.73
```
2
```
   3.08
 − 2.90
```
3
```
   0.543
 − 0.03
```
4
```
  $597.50
 −  98.62
```
5
```
   257.391
 − 108.062
```

6 5.24 − 3.5   **7** 17.89 − 5.792   **8** 56 − 41.83   **9** 1,005 − 198.7

Solve.

10 Aquarium admission is $7.50 for adults and $4.95 for children under 12. How much more does an adult ticket cost?

11 Tell how to solve this problem: Louisa plays a fish tape 30 minutes each day for her cat. How many hours does the tape run in 2 weeks?

Problem-Solving Strategy: Guess, Test, and Revise page 69
Solve. Explain your method.

1 The sum of the number of whales and dolphins is 11. The product is 24. There are more dolphins than whales. How many of each are there?

2 A class at the aquarium had this attendance: 6, 8, 7, 9, 5, 8, and 6. What is the average attendance?

3 A human's temperature is normally 98.6°F. A fish's temperature varies and can be 57.2°F. How much greater is the human's temperature?

4 **Spatial reasoning** A table seats 1 person on each side. You need to push 10 tables together to make one large table. What is the greatest number of people you can seat?

5 Monica has 14.5 meters of ribbon. She bought 9.6 more meters. How many meters does she have in all?

6 A bar graph of favorite water sports shows water skiing with the longest bar. What does that mean?

Addition and Subtraction Expressions page 71
α **ALGEBRA Evaluate the expression.**

1 $a - 2$ for $a = 11$ **2** $b + 7$ for $b = 6.5$ **3** $13 - c$ for $c = 8.8$

4 $4.19 + d$ for $d = 5.2$ **5** $e - 7.29$ for $e = 15.2$ **6** $3.72 + f$ for $f = 10.6$

7 $g - 6.3$ for $g = 8.03$ **8** $h - 7$ for $h = 100$ **9** $3.4 + i$ for $i = 4.8$

α **ALGEBRA Solve.**

10 Write an expression representing the distance left to travel, t, during a 25.5-mile cruise. Then, evaluate for $t = 13.75$.

Applying Decimals: Metric Units of Length page 73

Tell whether you would use km, m, cm, or mm to measure.

1 the length of a boat

2 the length of a hammer

3 the distance an ocean liner travels

4 the thickness of a fishing line

Draw lines of the given length.

5 75 mm

6 7.5 cm

7 4.9 cm

8 52 mm

Solve.

9 The basking shark is about 1.7 m long at birth. Is this about the same as the height of a grown-up, a mountain, a house, or a puppy?

Applying Decimals: Metric Units of Capacity and Mass page 75

Name the most sensible unit of capacity or mass. Explain.

1 capacity of a bottle of liquid vitamins

2 mass of a sea horse

3 mass of a large ship

4 capacity of a tanker

Write the letter of the best estimate.

5 mass of a 12-year-old water-skier
   a. 39 mg   **b.** 39 g   **c.** 39 kg

6 capacity of a water glass
   a. 3 L   **b.** 350 mL   **c.** 35 mL

Solve.

7 How many fleets are represented in the stem-and-leaf plot?

8 What is the mode number of tankers?

Tankers in Each Fleet

1	1	7	9	
2	1	3	7	8
3	0	5	6	9	9

Key: 1|1 = 11

Problem Solvers at Work page 79

Solve. Explain your methods.

1 John's car averages 23 miles per gallon. He has about 10 gallons of gas and 225 more miles to drive. Should he overestimate or underestimate how far he can drive until he must fill up his car? Why?

2 **Spatial reasoning** Cathy wants to pack 36 similar shells in one layer of a box. She can pack 6 rows with 6 shells in each row. List the other ways she can pack the shells. You may draw a picture to solve.

3 The catch at three ports in 1989 was 312.2 million pounds, 504.3 million pounds, and 113.5 million pounds, respectively. Estimate the total catch.

4 **ALGEBRA** The expression $30.98 - x$ represents a drop in barometric pressure during a tornado. If the drop is 1.91 inches, what is the barometric pressure?

Patterns and Properties page 91

Multiply mentally.

1 6 × 83

2 20 × 4,000

3 81 × 100

4 (11 × 30) × 5

5 700 × 800

6 4 × 92

7 400 × 1 × 25

8 30 × 30 × 30

9 26 × 0 × 2

10 7 × 49

11 6 × 9 × 5

12 76 × 1,000

Solve.

13 Each tour of the exhibition has 20 people. There are 10 tours daily. How many people can view the exhibit during the entire month of April?

14 Julian has 5 rolls of film from his trip to Zimbabwe. Each roll has 36 pictures. How many pictures did Julian take on his trip?

Estimate Products page 93

Estimate the product.

1 4 × 528

2 $8.42 × 46

3 367 × 611

4 54 × 96

5 2.5 × 74

6 8 × 51.862

7 83 × 25.02

8 351 × 2,143

9 3.245 × 11.842

10 $742.10 × 36

11 8 × 437

12 19.12 × 82.98

Estimate. Write > or <.

13 25.2 × 28.1 ● 925.02

14 63 × 24.19 ● 1,192.27

15 3.8 × 155.67 ● 852.96

16 2.21 × $14 ● $19.68

17 5.3 × 48.9 ● 175.98

18 32.09 × 19.9 ● 890.08

Solve.

19 Each of the 142 passengers on a flight is awarded 352 frequent flier points. Estimate how many points the airline awarded in all.

20 Jennifer has twice as many quarters as dimes and twice as many dimes as nickels. She has $10.00. How many of each coin does she have?

21 **Spatial reasoning** Which shape below does not belong? Why?

22 Jim walks 1.6 kilometers to the store, then 2.2 kilometers to the park. Then he walks the same route home. How far does he walk in all?

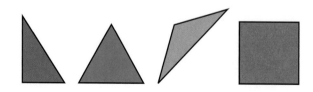

Multiplying Whole Numbers page 95

Multiply. Remember to estimate.

1
$$\begin{array}{r} 408 \\ \times\ \ 6 \\ \hline \end{array}$$

2
$$\begin{array}{r} 43 \\ \times 72 \\ \hline \end{array}$$

3
$$\begin{array}{r} \$396 \\ \times\ \ 28 \\ \hline \end{array}$$

4
$$\begin{array}{r} 264 \\ \times\ \ 53 \\ \hline \end{array}$$

5
$$\begin{array}{r} 1,207 \\ \times\ \ \ \ \ 4 \\ \hline \end{array}$$

6
$$\begin{array}{r} 482 \\ \times\ \ 7 \\ \hline \end{array}$$

7
$$\begin{array}{r} 26 \\ \times 54 \\ \hline \end{array}$$

8
$$\begin{array}{r} \$245 \\ \times\ \ 93 \\ \hline \end{array}$$

9
$$\begin{array}{r} 805 \\ \times\ \ 36 \\ \hline \end{array}$$

10
$$\begin{array}{r} 1,082 \\ \times\ \ \ \ 80 \\ \hline \end{array}$$

11 623×8

12 46×34

13 87×56

14 804×26

15 648×53

16 519×49

17 $1,204 \times 8$

18 $3,124 \times 7$

Solve.

19 Mary saves $15 each week. How much does she save in 2 years?

20 Margarita spends $25.34 for a shirt and $63.19 for shoes. How much change does she get from $100?

21 **Logical reasoning** Lu, Stu, Juan, and Eli gave talks lasting 4, 5, 8, and 10 minutes. Lu's talk was the shortest. Juan's talk was twice as long as Stu's. How long did each person talk?

Multiply Decimals by Whole Numbers page 97

Multiply. Remember to estimate.

1
$$\begin{array}{r} \$2.64 \\ \times\ \ \ \ 4 \\ \hline \end{array}$$

2
$$\begin{array}{r} 4.09 \\ \times\ \ \ 8 \\ \hline \end{array}$$

3
$$\begin{array}{r} 43 \\ \times 0.5 \\ \hline \end{array}$$

4
$$\begin{array}{r} 16.21 \\ \times\ \ \ \ 53 \\ \hline \end{array}$$

5
$$\begin{array}{r} 0.459 \\ \times\ \ \ \ \ 17 \\ \hline \end{array}$$

6 82×0.78

7 5×3.3

8 19×5.27

9 62×16.11

10 35×6.2

11 95×1.3

12 1.345×6

13 67×10.1

ALGEBRA Complete. Find the rule for each function table.

14

Rule: ■				
Input	0.21	3.2	45.9	1.07
Output	2.1	32	459	10.7

15

Rule: ■				
Input	72	6.7	80.1	9.03
Output	0.72	0.067	0.801	0.0903

Solve. Use the line plot.

16 How many students were surveyed?

17 What is the mode allowance?

18 How many students have an allowance less than $7?

Allowances

```
                              x
              x               x
  x     x                     x
  x     x           x         x
  x     x     x     x         x
  x     x     x     x         x
 $5    $6    $7    $8    $9   $10
```

Problem-Solving Strategy: Solve Multistep Problems page 99
Solve. Explain your methods. Use the bar graph for ex. 3–6.

1 Angela has 6 twenty-dollar bills and 5 one-dollar bills. Raymond has 12 ten-dollar bills and 25 quarters. Who has more money? How much more?

2 Nancy bought 3 necklaces for $15.48 each. She gave the store clerk 3 twenty-dollar bills. How much change did she get in return?

3 How much more did the play with the greatest receipts earn than the play with the least receipts?

4 What were the receipts for all plays?

5 What is the mean receipt amount?

6 What is the median receipt amount?

7 What were the receipts for a play that sold 315 tickets for $1.25 each?

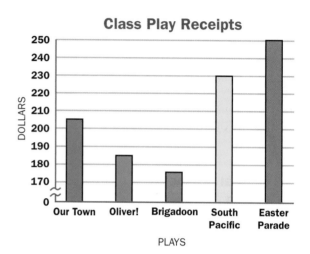

Class Play Receipts

Multiply Decimals by Decimals page 105
Multiply. You may use graph paper to help you.

1 0.2 × 0.3 **2** 0.5 × 0.5 **3** 0.4 × 0.8 **4** 0.9 × 0.3

5 0.6 × 0.7 **6** 0.4 × 0.1 **7** 0.7 × 0.5 **8** 0.5 × 0.8

9 Find the product of 0.9 and 0.4. **10** Find the product of 0.6 and 0.6

11 The factors are 0.5 and 0.4. What is the product? **12** The factors are 0.2 and 0.7. What is the product?

Write >, < or =.

13 0.1 × 0.9 ● 0.3 × 0.3 **14** 0.8 × 0.4 ● 0.6 × 0.5 **15** 0.4 × 0.40 ● 0.2 × 0.8

16 0.5 × 0.2 ● 0.4 × 0.3 **17** 0.7 × 0.8 ● 0.9 × 0.6 **18** 0.7 × 0.3 ● 0.4 × 0.6

19 Suppose a toy costs 1.3 pesos. If 1 peso is worth $0.15 in U.S. money, what is the cost of the toy?

20 **ALGEBRA** Find the value of each symbol. The value is the same for each equation.

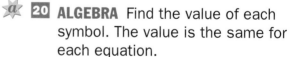

▶ + ▶ = ■
■ − 5 = ●
● + ▶ = 7

Multiply Decimals page 109
Multiply. Remember to estimate.

1   1.53
    × 0.5

2   0.48
    × 0.8

3   2.5
    × 1.6

4   46.71
    × 1.3

5   0.7109
    × 3.6

6   0.02
    × 0.031

7   17.82
    × 6.4

8   9.24
    × 0.16

9   0.23
    × 0.019

10   1.3
    × 7.3

11 0.4×0.7

12 1.4×3.52

13 4.5×0.39

14 4.7×26

15 7.01×0.001

16 6.5×1.8

17 3.04×3.04

18 3.124×7

Solve.

19 Wendell wants to cover a bulletin board that is 1.3 meters long and 0.8 meters wide. How much paper will he need to cover the area?

20 One action movie lasted from 4:00 P.M. until 5:35 P.M. A comedy lasted from 2:15 P.M. until 3:43 P.M.. Which movie lasted longer? How much longer?

Problem Solvers at Work page 113
Solve. Explain your methods.

1 Yvette earns $4.22 per hour after taxes. She works 5 hours one day. Did she earn enough to buy 2 festival tickets that cost $9.95 each? Use over- and under- estimation to explain your answer.

2 **Spatial reasoning** Each side of a square measures 2.3 centimeters. Each side of a triangle measures 3.2 centimeters. Which figure has the greater perimeter? How much greater?

Use the line graph for exercises 3–7.

3 What was the attendance in 1992?

4 How much greater was the attendance in 1993 than in 1990?

5 What trend is shown by the graph?

6 Predict the attendance for 1995.

7 What changes would you see in the graph if the scale increased by 500 instead of 100?

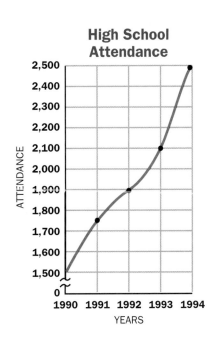

High School Attendance

Estimate Quotients page 127

Divide mentally.

1 480 ÷ 6

2 3,600 ÷ 40

3 63,000 ÷ 90

4 56,000 ÷ 800

Use compatible numbers to estimate the quotient.

5 735 ÷ 8

6 3,962 ÷ 8

7 25,128 ÷ 40

8 37,702 ÷ 521

Solve.

9 All tour groups at a railroad museum are about the same size. If there are 8 guides for 296 visitors, about how many people are on each tour?

10 Elizabeth sells new cars. She sells an average of 175 cars each month. At this rate, how many cars will she sell in two years?

Whole Number Division: 1-Digit Divisors page 129

Divide. Remember to estimate. Do as many as you can mentally.

1 4)98

2 7)329

3 9)1,125

4 5)4,050

5 3)22,115

6 580 ÷ 6

7 775 ÷ 8

8 1,328 ÷ 4

9 3,681 ÷ 2

10 6,066 ÷ 6

11 894 ÷ 8

12 5,800 ÷ 8

13 23,198 ÷ 7

14 28,143/5

15 52,107/4

Solve.

16 Fresh Air Inc. sells air fresheners in packages of three. It has 9,726 air fresheners in stock. How many packages can it make to sell?

17 A model ship costs $16.84, a model train costs $21.34, and a model car costs $18.66. How much will 3 model ships and 2 model cars cost?

Whole Number Division: 2-Digit Divisors page 133

Divide. Remember to estimate.

1 26)735

2 44)411

3 65)5,200

4 84)2,526

5 74)11,544

6 52)3,709

7 38)4,674

8 84)6,468

9 31)17,704

10 90)64,170

11 589 ÷ 28

12 4,362 ÷ 68

13 7,290 ÷ 90

14 48,325 ÷ 28

Solve.

15 Joe Bob has earned $22,410 in wages so far this year. He has worked 18 weeks. If his salary does not change, how much will he earn in one full year?

16 Ms. Ho needs to graph the number of ships that used the port last year. She will organize the data by ship-cargo weight. Which type of graph would best display the data? Why?

Multiplication and Division Expressions page 135

 **ALGEBRA Evaluate the expression.**

1 $3a$ for $a = 11$

2 $\frac{60}{b}$ for $b = 15$

3 $12c$ for $c = 12$

4 $\frac{d}{8}$ for $d = 96$

5 $\frac{16}{e}$ for $e = 8$

6 $5f$ for $f = 50$

7 $3.5g$ for $g = 1.2$

8 $\frac{h}{40}$ for $h = 640$

9 $\frac{81}{x}$ for $x = 3$

ALGEBRA Solve.

10 A student in Texas has a 28-mile round-trip bus ride between home and school. Write an expression to show the number of miles the student travels in t days. Then solve for the number of miles traveled in 24 days.

Order of Operations page 137

Simplify using order of operations rules.

1 $15 + 30 \div 10$

2 $(60 - 18) \div 6$

3 $(4.5 - 3.1) \times 8$

4 $(2 + 2)^3 \div 8$

5 $7 + 5 \times 4 \div 2$

6 $18 - 2 \times 6 + 4$

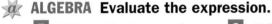 **ALGEBRA Evaluate the expression.**

7 $100 - 6x$ for $x = 9$

8 $(36 + y) \div 2$ for $y = 14$

9 $10z + 3 \times 5$ for $z = 10$

Solve.

10 There are 17 couples, 22 foursomes, and 116 other passengers on a ferry. Write an expression for the number of riders. How many riders in all?

11 Every other year, Damian buys a new car on January 1. He bought his first new car in 1972. As of today, how many new cars has he bought?

Problem-Solving Strategy: Use a Formula page 139

Solve. Explain your methods.

1 Chester's family rode 146 miles before lunch. Then they rode another 253 miles. Their average speed was 57 miles per hour. How long did they ride in the car?

2 Margo saw 536 more sedans than convertibles on her trip. She saw eight times as many trucks as convertibles. She saw 144 trucks. How many sedans did she see?

3 The speedway charges $7.50 for each driver. Cody and 4 friends each want to drive. They have $4.50, $20, $8.09, $1.22, and $3.40. Should he overestimate or underestimate to find if they have enough money? Why?

4 **Logical reasoning** Daphne's flight leaves 46 minutes before Arnold's, which leaves 8 minutes after Rolanda's. Rolanda's flight leaves at 10:22 P.M. What time does Daphne's flight leave?

Divide Decimals by Whole Numbers page 147

Divide. Remember to estimate.

1 $6\overline{)4.8}$ **2** $16\overline{)5.76}$ **3** $42\overline{)\$7.56}$ **4** $34\overline{)0.544}$ **5** $75\overline{)95.85}$

6 $58\overline{)255.78}$ **7** $21\overline{)0.441}$ **8** $68\overline{)703.8}$ **9** $9\overline{)10.9593}$ **10** $45\overline{)0.4185}$

11 $7.92 \div 4$ **12** $56.07 \div 18$ **13** $0.427 \div 7$ **14** $\dfrac{258.856}{26}$

Solve.

15 Harry biked 40.29 kilometers in 3 hours. What was his average speed in kilometers per hour?

16 The Hills started hiking at 3:45 P.M. They hiked 95 minutes. What time did they finish their hike?

Multiplication and Division Patterns page 149

Multiply or divide mentally.

1 286×10 **2** 50.2×100 **3** $1,000 \times 39.46$ **4** 0.15×100

5 $87.5 \div 10$ **6** $5,108 \div 100$ **7** $195.6 \div 1,000$ **8** $17.27 \div 10$

9 10×3.96 **10** $45.17 \times 1,000$ **11** $2,345 \div 1,000$ **12** $0.45 \div 100$

Solve.

13 Citizens made 726 donations of $10 each and 482 donations of $100 each to restore the train depot. What was the total number of dollars received from these donations?

14 Paco bought a pair of in-line skates for $146.95. He spent $37.50 on a helmet and $15.75 for each set of knee pads, wrist guards, and elbow pads. How much did he spend in all?

Divide by Decimals page 153

Divide using the model.

1 $0.45 \div 0.15$

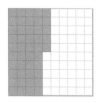

2 $1.28 \div 0.08$

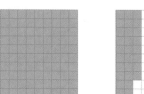

Solve.

3 It takes 0.2 meters of ribbon to make a scrunchie. How many scrunchies are made from one meter of ribbon?

4 Ryan traveled 20 kilometers per hour on his jet ski. How far did he ride in 45 minutes?

Divide by Decimals page 157
Divide. Remember to estimate.

1 $0.9\overline{)162}$ **2** $2.6\overline{)117}$ **3** $4.1\overline{)5.74}$ **4** $0.03\overline{)0.0297}$

5 $8 \div 51.2$ **6** $10.56 \div 4.8$ **7** $372.6 \div 1.8$ **8** $4.23 \div 0.3$

Divide. Round the quotient to the nearest tenth, if necessary.

9 $0.48\overline{)20.2}$ **10** $5.7\overline{)55.72}$ **11** $9 \div 0.4$ **12** $0.057 \div 0.16$

Solve.

13 A club sends 2 mailings to members each month. They have sent 234 mailings. For how many years has the club sent mailings?

Changing Metric Units page 159
Complete.

1 450 cm = ▦ mm **2** 90 g = ▦ kg **3** 0.3 kL = ▦ L

4 8 m = ▦ cm **5** 1,500 mg = ▦ g **6** 75 mL = ▦ L

7 2.7 km = ▦ m **8** 2,580 g = ▦ kg **9** 45 L = ▦ mL

10 6.2 m = ▦ mm **11** 4.82 kL = ▦ L **12** 630 mg = ▦ g

Solve.

13 Kitty wants to make thank-you gifts for the school bus drivers. Each gift uses 15 centimeters of foil paper. She has 3.75 meters of foil paper. How many gifts can she make?

Problem Solvers at Work page 163
Solve. Explain your methods.

1 Flora makes signs for hot-air balloon rides. She has 48 pieces of plywood. It takes 3.5 pieces to make each sign. How many signs can she make?

2 Ty has an average of 6.4 points after 5 quizzes in his math class. What is the total number of points he has scored on the quizzes?

3 A train travels at an average speed of 120 miles per hour. Ivan has been riding the train for 3 hours. He still has another 540 miles until he arrives at his destination. How far will he travel on the train in all? How long will he ride the train?

4 **Logical reasoning** Casey, Tami, Gordon, and Nakuri rode horses named Trigger, Beauty, Silver, and Babe. Neither Gordon nor Casey rode a horse with a six-letter name. Gordon and Tami rode horses whose name starts with the letter *B*. Which horse did each person ride?

extra practice

Divisibility page 173
Use the divisibility rules to tell whether the number is divisible by 2, 3, 5, 6, 9, or 10.

1 24   **2** 90   **3** 46   **4** 113   **5** 230

6 408   **7** 843   **8** 1,026   **9** 6,039   **10** 45,615

Solve.

11 Opal displays 20 dolls with the same number of dolls in each row. What are all the possible numbers of dolls that could stand in each row?

12 Jasper is placing 5 treats in each bag lunch. He has 121 treats. How many bag lunches can he make?

Prime Factorization page 177
Tell whether the number is prime or composite.

1 14   **2** 21   **3** 23   **4** 49   **5** 52

6 61   **7** 77   **8** 89   **9** 95   **10** 107

Write the prime factorization of the number.

11 10   **12** 36   **13** 57   **14** 60   **15** 99

Solve.

16 A number can be found by multiplying the next prime number greater than 13 by three. Find the number?

17 A go-cart traveled 5 mi in 10 minutes. What was its average speed per hour?

Common Factors and GCF page 179
List all the common factors of the two numbers.

1 8 and 12   **2** 15 and 25   **3** 24 and 36   **4** 42 and 54

5 36 and 48   **6** 40 and 60   **7** 18 and 72   **8** 30 and 41

Find the GCF of the numbers. Explain your method.

9 6 and 15   **10** 12 and 18   **11** 45 and 60   **12** 16 and 24

Solve.

13 Ed wants to cut some balloon strings of equal length. He has 48-inch and 72-inch pieces of string. What are the longest equal lengths he can cut?

14 Randy scored 21,405 points in a video game. Louisa scored 21,504 points. How many more points did Louisa score than Randy?

Common Multiples and LCM page 181
Find the LCM of the numbers.

1 3 and 6   **2** 5 and 8   **3** 6 and 9   **4** 4 and 14

5 8 and 12   **6** 15 and 25   **7** 10 and 15   **8** 2 and 11

9 5 and 12   **10** 2, 5 and 9   **11** 3, 4, and 6   **12** 4, 6, and 10

Solve.

13 Every 30 minutes, a short tour of a museum begins. A long tour begins every 45 minutes. Both tours begin at 9:00 A.M. When is the next time that both tours begin at the same time? How many minutes later is that?

- - -

Problem-Solving Strategy: Make an Organized List page 183
Solve. Explain your methods.

1 Alano was baby-sitting and planned to play a board game, kickball, and cards with the children. In how many different orders can they play the three games? What are the orders?

2 Mandy was the high scorer on her bowling team with game scores of 130, 110, and 123. What would she need to score on her fourth game to have a mean score of 126?

3 Reid can make 4 posters each hour to advertise the school fair. Angelica can make 3 posters in one hour. How long will it take them to make 35 posters together? How many will Reid make? How many will Angelica make?

4 **Logical reasoning** Toni, Jim, and Erik hit all 5 home runs in the last four baseball games. Toni hit twice as many home runs as Erik. Erik hit one home run. How many more home runs did Jim hit than Erik?

- - -

Understanding Fractions page 189
Name the fraction shown by the shaded part.

1   **2**   **3**

Make a drawing showing the fraction.

4 $\frac{1}{2}$ **5** $\frac{1}{3}$ **6** $\frac{1}{6}$ **7** $\frac{3}{5}$ **8** $\frac{5}{8}$ **9** $\frac{1}{4}$ **10** $\frac{7}{10}$

Solve.

11 There are 5 aluminum bats and 6 wood bats. Use a fraction to represent the number of wood bats.

12 The two-digit number on Nancy's jersey is a prime number. The sum of the digits is 14. What is the number?

Equivalent Fractions page 193

Are the pairs of fractions equivalent? Write *yes* or *no*.

1 $\frac{3}{5}, \frac{6}{10}$　　**2** $\frac{4}{8}, \frac{2}{4}$　　**3** $\frac{3}{12}, \frac{1}{3}$　　**4** $\frac{14}{24}, \frac{1}{2}$　　**5** $\frac{2}{6}, \frac{1}{3}$

Write three fractions equivalent to the fraction.

6 $\frac{2}{5}$　　**7** $\frac{3}{4}$　　**8** $\frac{2}{12}$　　**9** $\frac{5}{8}$　　**10** $\frac{7}{10}$　　**11** $\frac{3}{9}$

Solve.

12 Gary taped 3 hours of music videos and 2 hours of cartoons. Use a fraction to write how much of his tapes has music videos. Then, write 3 equivalent fractions.

13 Jennifer has 2.4 L of sports beverage to share with her 3 teammates. How many milliliters will each person have to drink?

Simplest Form page 195

Write the fraction in simplest form. Do as many as you can mentally.

1 $\frac{6}{10}$　　**2** $\frac{4}{16}$　　**3** $\frac{9}{27}$　　**4** $\frac{12}{12}$　　**5** $\frac{8}{20}$　　**6** $\frac{12}{48}$

7 $\frac{28}{42}$　　**8** $\frac{15}{75}$　　**9** $\frac{6}{24}$　　**10** $\frac{45}{50}$　　**11** $\frac{18}{54}$　　**12** $\frac{32}{80}$

13 $\frac{25}{150}$　　**14** $\frac{10}{80}$　　**15** $\frac{20}{25}$　　**16** $\frac{54}{63}$　　**17** $\frac{49}{56}$　　**18** $\frac{81}{108}$

Solve.

19 Vicky read 12 mysteries, 6 novels, and 2 nonfiction books. What fraction of the books read were mysteries? Write your answer in simplest form.

20 An art class meets from 10:25 A.M. until 11:10 A.M. three times each week. How long does the class meet each week?

Compare and Order Fractions page 197

Compare. Write >, <, or =.

1 $\frac{1}{2} \bullet \frac{2}{3}$　　**2** $\frac{3}{4} \bullet \frac{1}{4}$　　**3** $\frac{1}{3} \bullet \frac{2}{6}$　　**4** $\frac{5}{6} \bullet \frac{3}{4}$　　**5** $\frac{2}{5} \bullet \frac{2}{10}$

6 $\frac{3}{12} \bullet \frac{1}{4}$　　**7** $\frac{1}{6} \bullet \frac{1}{8}$　　**8** $\frac{4}{8} \bullet \frac{4}{6}$　　**9** $\frac{8}{10} \bullet \frac{6}{8}$　　**10** $\frac{6}{8} \bullet \frac{9}{12}$

Order from least to greatest.

11 $\frac{2}{3}, \frac{2}{5}, \frac{2}{4}$　　**12** $\frac{5}{6}, \frac{1}{6}, \frac{3}{6}$　　**13** $\frac{3}{5}, \frac{1}{3}, \frac{2}{4}$　　**14** $\frac{2}{8}, \frac{3}{4}, \frac{1}{3}$

Solve.

15 Li's trail mix uses $\frac{3}{4}$ pound of nuts, $\frac{5}{8}$ pound of raisins, and $\frac{1}{2}$ pound of seeds. Order the ingredients from least to greatest amount used.

Understanding Mixed Numbers page 199

Write as a whole number or mixed number in simplest form.

1 $\frac{11}{4}$ **2** $\frac{16}{8}$ **3** $\frac{14}{3}$ **4** $\frac{35}{6}$ **5** $\frac{24}{9}$ **6** $\frac{58}{8}$

7 $\frac{15}{2}$ **8** $\frac{25}{5}$ **9** $\frac{42}{5}$ **10** $\frac{35}{8}$ **11** $\frac{26}{6}$ **12** $\frac{46}{10}$

Write as an improper fraction.

13 $5\frac{2}{3}$ **14** $4\frac{3}{5}$ **15** $1\frac{3}{4}$ **16** $3\frac{5}{8}$ **17** $2\frac{1}{6}$ **18** $3\frac{9}{10}$

Solve.

19 The flat three-leg race course is $8\frac{1}{2}$ yards long. The hilly course is $\frac{25}{3}$ yards long. Which is longer—the flat course or the hilly course?

Connect Fractions, Mixed Numbers, and Decimals page 203

Write as a decimal. Round the decimal to the nearest hundredth if necessary.

1 $\frac{1}{6}$ **2** $\frac{3}{4}$ **3** $\frac{5}{8}$ **4** $\frac{1}{2}$ **5** $\frac{2}{5}$ **6** $\frac{1}{3}$

7 $2\frac{3}{8}$ **8** $4\frac{1}{4}$ **9** $3\frac{4}{5}$ **10** $2\frac{4}{10}$ **11** $1\frac{4}{6}$ **12** $3\frac{5}{25}$

Write as a fraction or mixed number in simplest form.

13 0.7 **14** 0.35 **15** 0.56 **16** 1.6 **17** 2.75 **18** 2.125

Solve.

19 Cora was in $\frac{2}{3}$ of the drama shows. Art was in 0.75 of them. Who was in more shows? Explain.

Problem Solvers at Work page 207

Solve. Explain your methods.

1 On the first day, 235 people went to the sixth-grade fun house. Admission was by donation. They collected 475 pennies, 80 nickels, 152 dimes, 432 quarters, and 96 dollars. What was the average donation?

2 **Spatial reasoning** Copy the triangle and divide it into four equal parts.

3 Alice made 2 three-point field goals, 4 two-point field goals, and 5 free throws (1 point each). Use a fraction to represent how many of her total points were made in 3-point goals.

4 Letty, Dolan, Chucha, and Yori want to sit together at the music concert. Yori wants to sit next to Letty. In how many different orders can they sit? What are the orders?

Estimate Sums and Differences page 219
Round each fraction to 0, $\frac{1}{2}$, or 1.

1 $\frac{7}{16}$ **2** $\frac{2}{15}$ **3** $\frac{11}{20}$ **4** $\frac{5}{6}$ **5** $\frac{14}{15}$ **6** $\frac{1}{12}$

Estimate each sum or difference.

7 $\frac{7}{8} + \frac{2}{3}$ **8** $2\frac{1}{4} + 1\frac{8}{9}$ **9** $\frac{15}{16} - \frac{2}{5}$ **10** $1\frac{5}{8} - \frac{3}{7}$

11 $5\frac{3}{8} + 4\frac{1}{2}$ **12** $6\frac{19}{20} - 2\frac{5}{12}$ **13** $2\frac{1}{16} + 5\frac{19}{20} + 3\frac{5}{6}$ **14** $1\frac{1}{2} + 3\frac{9}{20} + 2\frac{7}{16}$

Solve.

15 After school, students fill about $\frac{11}{20}$ of the seats at a restaurant. Do they fill very few, about half, or almost all of the seats? Explain.

16 Ed runs at least 25 miles each week. He has already run $13\frac{3}{4}$ miles this week. If he runs $12\frac{1}{2}$ more miles, will he achieve his goal? Explain.

17 ___ is to ___ as ___ is to: a. ___ b. ___ c. ___

18 **Logical reasoning** Karen is 3 times as old as Janet. In 5 years Karen will be twice as old as Janet. How old is each girl now?

Add and Subtract Like Fractions page 221
Add or subtract. Write the answer in simplest form.

1 $\frac{3}{10} + \frac{3}{10}$ **2** $\frac{3}{5} + \frac{1}{5}$ **3** $\frac{5}{8} + \frac{5}{8}$ **4** $\frac{2}{9} + \frac{7}{9} + \frac{1}{9}$

5 $\frac{8}{15} - \frac{2}{15}$ **6** $\frac{4}{5} - \frac{1}{5}$ **7** $\frac{11}{18} - \frac{1}{18}$ **8** $\frac{9}{20} - \frac{3}{20}$

9 $\frac{1}{3} + \frac{2}{3}$ **10** $\frac{1}{6} + \frac{1}{6}$ **11** $\frac{1}{10} + \frac{7}{10}$ **12** $\frac{7}{16} - \frac{5}{16}$ **13** $\frac{11}{12} - \frac{5}{12}$ **14** $\frac{13}{20} - \frac{7}{20}$

Solve.

15 Marcia sells fabric picture frames. She needs $\frac{3}{4}$ yard of fabric for each of two sides and $\frac{1}{4}$ yard for each of the other two sides. How much fabric does she need in all?

16 Evan makes origami animals from 2-inch squares of paper. He has a piece of paper measuring $11\frac{1}{2}$ inches by 8 inches. How many animals can he make?

17 Carmen bought 2 roses for $1.50 each and 2 daisies for $0.25 each. How much did she spend in all?

18 Summer camp lasts each day from 8:45 A.M. until 3:15 P.M. How long does summer camp last each day?

Add. Write the answer in simplest form. Remember to estimate.

1 $\dfrac{1}{3}$ **2** $\dfrac{3}{8}$ **3** $\dfrac{1}{5}$ **4** $\dfrac{7}{10}$ **5** $\dfrac{4}{5}$ **6** $\dfrac{1}{6}$

   $+\dfrac{7}{12}$ $+\dfrac{3}{4}$ $+\dfrac{3}{10}$ $+\dfrac{4}{5}$ $+\dfrac{2}{3}$ $+\dfrac{5}{12}$

7 $\dfrac{3}{4} + \dfrac{2}{3}$ **8** $\dfrac{3}{4} + \dfrac{1}{8}$ **9** $\dfrac{3}{4} + \dfrac{5}{12}$ **10** $\dfrac{2}{3} + \dfrac{1}{5}$

11 $\dfrac{1}{8} + \dfrac{3}{4} + \dfrac{1}{2}$ **12** $\dfrac{1}{3} + \dfrac{1}{4} + \dfrac{5}{6}$ **13** $\dfrac{1}{2} + \dfrac{2}{3} + \dfrac{1}{6}$ **14** $\dfrac{1}{2} + \dfrac{2}{3} + \dfrac{3}{4}$

Solve.

15 Alice walks $\dfrac{3}{5}$ mile to Anna's house and another $\dfrac{7}{10}$ mile to the mall. How far did she walk in all?

16 Sally studies 2 hours each night. She has studied 23 minutes tonight. How much longer will she study?

17 One school has a 5-minute break between classes. There are 6 classes each day. How many minutes of break are there?

18 Betty swam $\dfrac{1}{4}$ mile Monday, $\dfrac{3}{4}$ mile Wednesday, and $\dfrac{1}{2}$ mile Friday. How far did she swim altogether on those three days?

Subtract. Write the answer in simplest form. Remember to estimate.

1 $\dfrac{2}{3}$ **2** $\dfrac{4}{5}$ **3** $\dfrac{11}{12}$ **4** $\dfrac{3}{8}$ **5** $\dfrac{5}{6}$ **6** $\dfrac{4}{5}$

   $-\dfrac{5}{12}$ $-\dfrac{1}{3}$ $-\dfrac{1}{3}$ $-\dfrac{1}{3}$ $-\dfrac{1}{4}$ $-\dfrac{3}{10}$

7 $\dfrac{7}{10} - \dfrac{1}{5}$ **8** $\dfrac{2}{5} - \dfrac{1}{6}$ **9** $\dfrac{7}{12} - \dfrac{3}{8}$ **10** $\dfrac{2}{3} - \dfrac{2}{5}$

11 $\dfrac{1}{6} - \dfrac{1}{8}$ **12** $\dfrac{7}{10} - \dfrac{1}{4}$ **13** $\dfrac{5}{6} - \dfrac{1}{12}$ **14** $\dfrac{3}{5} - \dfrac{1}{10}$

Solve. Use the line graph to answer questions 16–18.

15 Fran's school is $\dfrac{9}{10}$ miles away from his home. The park is $\dfrac{1}{2}$ mile away. How much farther from home is the school?

16 Explain the change in 1995.

17 What trend is shown by the graph?

18 How could the data be shown another way?

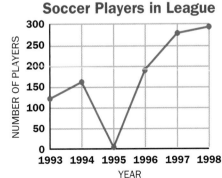

Soccer Players in League

extra practice

Add Mixed Numbers page 227
Add, using any method. Write the answer in simplest form.

1 $2\frac{3}{8}$
$+3\frac{1}{8}$

2 $3\frac{7}{12}$
$+4\frac{7}{12}$

3 $2\frac{4}{5}$
$+1\frac{3}{5}$

4 $3\frac{9}{10}$
$+1\frac{1}{5}$

5 $3\frac{3}{4}$
$+1\frac{5}{8}$

6 3
$+2\frac{1}{6}$

7 $2\frac{1}{3}+1\frac{5}{6}$ **8** $4\frac{3}{10}+1\frac{4}{5}$ **9** $1\frac{5}{8}+1\frac{1}{2}$ **10** $2\frac{2}{3}+1\frac{3}{4}$

Solve.

 11 ALGEBRA: PATTERNS Complete the pattern.
1, 1, 2, 3, 5, 8, 13, 21, ■, ■, ■, ■

12 Juan used $2\frac{1}{2}$ cups of milk and $1\frac{1}{3}$ cups of water to make a cream soup. How much liquid was that altogether?

Add Mixed Numbers page 229
Add. Write the answer in simplest form. Remember to estimate.

1 $1\frac{7}{8}$
$+2\frac{5}{8}$

2 $2\frac{11}{12}$
$+1\frac{5}{12}$

3 $3\frac{3}{5}$
$+1\frac{4}{5}$

4 $2\frac{1}{4}$
$+1\frac{7}{8}$

5 $1\frac{5}{6}$
$+2\frac{7}{12}$

6 $2\frac{7}{8}$
$+3\frac{1}{4}$

7 $2\frac{3}{4}+1\frac{3}{8}$ **8** $1\frac{1}{5}+2\frac{7}{10}$ **9** $3+1\frac{3}{4}+2\frac{1}{2}$ **10** $1\frac{1}{2}+2\frac{3}{5}+5\frac{7}{10}$

Solve.

11 Find the perimeter of a square with sides measuring $3\frac{7}{8}$ feet.

12 A kit costs $16.95. How much will 2 kits cost at a sale price of $2.00 off each?

Problem-Solving Strategy: Find a Pattern page 235
Solve. Explain your methods.

1 An artist uses 3 green tiles for each red tile and 5 blue tiles for each green tile. How many green and blue tiles will she need if she uses 8 red tiles in her design?

2 It costs $0.75 for a juice, $0.50 for milk, $1.50 for pizza, and $1.95 for a hamburger. You want one drink and one food item. What is the least you can spend? What is the most?

3 How many cubes were used to make the shape below?

4 Ann buys $1\frac{1}{2}$ pounds of cashews. Al buys $2\frac{3}{4}$ pounds of pistachios. How many pounds did they buy in all?

Subtract Mixed Numbers page 237

Subtract, using any method. Write the answer in simplest form.

1 $\begin{array}{r} 2\frac{3}{4} \\ -\ 1\frac{1}{4} \\ \hline \end{array}$ **2** $\begin{array}{r} 3\frac{2}{5} \\ -\ 1\frac{3}{5} \\ \hline \end{array}$ **3** $\begin{array}{r} 2\frac{5}{8} \\ -\ 1\frac{3}{4} \\ \hline \end{array}$ **4** $\begin{array}{r} 5\frac{1}{12} \\ -\ 2\frac{1}{2} \\ \hline \end{array}$ **5** $\begin{array}{r} 6 \\ -\ 2\frac{1}{2} \\ \hline \end{array}$ **6** $\begin{array}{r} 3 \\ -\ 1\frac{1}{3} \\ \hline \end{array}$

7 $5\frac{7}{12} - 1\frac{1}{4}$ **8** $5\frac{2}{3} - 3\frac{1}{6}$ **9** $4\frac{1}{5} - 2\frac{9}{10}$ **10** $8\frac{1}{2} - 1\frac{1}{3}$

Solve.

11 A major league baseball bat may not be more than $2\frac{3}{4}$ inches in diameter. A softball bat may not be more than $2\frac{1}{4}$ inches in diameter. How much wider is a baseball bat's diameter?

Subtract Mixed Numbers page 241

Subtract. Write the answer in simplest form. Remember to estimate.

1 $\begin{array}{r} 4\frac{4}{5} \\ -\ 1\frac{2}{5} \\ \hline \end{array}$ **2** $\begin{array}{r} 3\frac{3}{8} \\ -\ 1\frac{5}{8} \\ \hline \end{array}$ **3** $\begin{array}{r} 4 \\ -\ 1\frac{7}{12} \\ \hline \end{array}$ **4** $\begin{array}{r} 3\frac{1}{4} \\ -\ 2\frac{7}{8} \\ \hline \end{array}$ **5** $\begin{array}{r} 6\frac{1}{3} \\ -\ 3\frac{5}{6} \\ \hline \end{array}$ **6** $\begin{array}{r} 4\frac{1}{6} \\ -\ 3\frac{2}{3} \\ \hline \end{array}$

7 $5\frac{3}{10} - 2\frac{3}{5}$ **8** $7\frac{1}{2} - 4\frac{4}{5}$ **9** $7\frac{1}{6} - 3\frac{2}{3}$ **10** $5\frac{5}{12} - 2\frac{1}{2}$

Solve.

11 George has $4\frac{1}{2}$ pounds of clay. He gives $1\frac{3}{4}$ pounds to Lynne. How many pounds does he have left?

12 Hal earned $47.25 last week. He makes $5.25 an hour at his job. How many hours did he work?

13 If every U.S. dollar is worth 3.39 Egyptian pounds, how many Egyptian pounds can you get for $100?

14 Misty practices the piano 45 minutes each day, 7 days a week. How many hours does she practice each week?

Problem Solvers at Work page 245

Solve. If there is not enough information, identify the information you need. Explain your methods.

1 **ALGEBRA: PATTERNS** The top of a display has one item, the second layer has two items, and the third layer has three items. If this pattern continues, how many items are there when there are 5 layers?

2 A season ticket to 12 games costs $12.50. It costs $1.25 to buy one ticket to a game. How much money will you save by buying a season ticket if you attend all the games?

3 Al ran for one hour and then jogged. Estimate the length of his workout.

4 Connie ran $1\frac{3}{4}$ mile. Jill ran $2\frac{1}{2}$ miles. How much farther did Jill run?

extra practice

Find a Fraction of a Whole Number page 257
Multiply Mentally.

1 $\frac{1}{8}$ of 64   **2** $\frac{1}{3}$ of 12   **3** $\frac{1}{5}$ of 35   **4** $\frac{1}{4}$ of 36

5 $\frac{3}{10}$ of 40   **6** $\frac{5}{9}$ of 72   **7** $\frac{4}{7}$ of 63   **8** $\frac{5}{6}$ of 240

Solve.

9 One third of the 240 pieces of lumber used to make a clubhouse are cedar. How many pieces of clubhouse lumber are from other types of wood?

10 Ryan traveled 20 kilometers per hour on his bulldozer. How far did he ride in 45 minutes?

Multiply Fractions page 261
Multiply using any method. Write the answer in simplest form.

1 $\frac{1}{3} \times \frac{3}{4}$ **2** $\frac{3}{8} \times \frac{1}{2}$ **3** $\frac{1}{6} \times \frac{2}{3}$ **4** $\frac{1}{5} \times \frac{5}{10}$

5 $\frac{3}{5} \times \frac{5}{12}$ **6** $\frac{3}{4} \times \frac{4}{5}$ **7** $\frac{2}{4} \times \frac{1}{3}$ **8** $\frac{3}{4} \times \frac{6}{12}$

Solve.

9 Tia bought $\frac{3}{4}$ lb of Rome apples and $1\frac{3}{8}$ lb of Granny Smith apples. How many pounds of apples did she buy?

10 Elvin has 48 CDs. He lent $\frac{1}{4}$ of them to a friend. How many did he lend? How many does he have left?

11 Of the 18 girls in a class, $\frac{1}{3}$ are blonds. Of those girls, half have blue eyes. What fraction of the girls have blond hair and blue eyes?

12 Tim works 4 hours each Saturday. He earns $4.38 per hour. How much money does he earn in 4 weeks?

Multiply by Fractions page 265
Multiply. Write the product in simplest form. Do as many as you can mentally.

1 $\frac{2}{3} \times \frac{1}{4}$ **2** $\frac{3}{4} \times \frac{3}{4}$ **3** $\frac{4}{5} \times \frac{1}{4}$ **4** $\frac{3}{8} \times \frac{3}{6}$ **5** $\frac{2}{8} \times \frac{2}{3}$

6 $\frac{2}{6} \times \frac{3}{4}$ **7** $\frac{4}{10} \times \frac{2}{4}$ **8** $\frac{2}{9} \times \frac{3}{4}$ **9** $\frac{5}{16} \times \frac{3}{5}$ **10** $\frac{1}{3} \times \frac{5}{6}$

Solve.

11 Three fourths of Mindy's marbles are red. Four fifths of the red marbles are solid red; the rest have a pattern. What fraction of Mindy's marbles are red with a pattern?

12 A group of 214 students and 25 teachers are going on a field trip. Each bus holds 48 people. How many buses will they need to charter in order to transport all the teachers and students?

Estimate Products page 267
Estimate the product.

1 $\frac{1}{5} \times 46$ **2** $\frac{3}{8} \times 42$ **3** $\frac{2}{3} \times 10$ **4** $\frac{3}{4} \times 31$

5 $73 \times \frac{3}{8}$ **6** $\frac{5}{10} \times 49\frac{2}{3}$ **7** $\frac{1}{2} \times 18\frac{1}{10}$ **8** $22\frac{4}{5} \times \frac{7}{8}$

9 $\frac{3}{10} \times 51\frac{7}{8}$ **10** $\frac{5}{8} \times 65\frac{1}{2}$ **11** $28\frac{1}{4} \times \frac{1}{3}$ **12** $\frac{2}{5} \times 39$

Solve.

13 A ladder sells for $29. It goes on sale for $\frac{1}{4}$ off the original price. Estimate the sale price in dollars. Tell whether the estimate is more than or less than the actual sale price.

14 Which 3-digit and 1-digit numbers made using the digits 2, 3, 4, and 5 result in the largest product when multiplied together? You can use each digit only once.

Multiply Mixed Numbers page 269
Multiply. Write the answer in simplest form. Estimate to check.

1 $4 \times 2\frac{1}{4}$ **2** $3\frac{1}{2} \times 6$ **3** $2\frac{1}{3} \times 15$ **4** $1\frac{1}{3} \times 8$ **5** $1\frac{2}{5} \times \frac{2}{3}$

6 $1\frac{1}{2} \times 2$ **7** $\frac{2}{5} \times 3\frac{1}{4}$ **8** $2\frac{1}{8} \times 3\frac{1}{5}$ **9** $2\frac{1}{4} \times 1\frac{2}{3}$ **10** $4\frac{3}{8} \times 1\frac{2}{5}$

11 $\frac{1}{3} \times 2\frac{2}{3} \times 1\frac{1}{2}$ **12** $3\frac{1}{5} \times 3 \times 1\frac{2}{3}$ **13** $1\frac{1}{4} \times 2\frac{4}{5} \times 1\frac{1}{2}$ **14** $3\frac{1}{8} \times 1\frac{2}{5} \times 2\frac{2}{3}$

Solve.

15 Miriam walks $2\frac{1}{2}$ miles to work and $2\frac{1}{2}$ miles from work to home each day. Jack's walk to work and back is $1\frac{1}{3}$ as far as Miriam's. How far does Jack walk each day?

Problem-Solving Strategy: Work Backward page 275
Solve. Explain your methods.

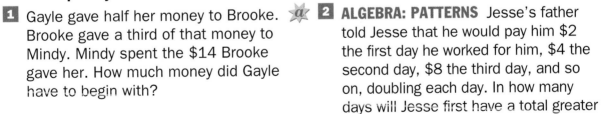

1 Gayle gave half her money to Brooke. Brooke gave a third of that money to Mindy. Mindy spent the $14 Brooke gave her. How much money did Gayle have to begin with?

2 **ALGEBRA: PATTERNS** Jesse's father told Jesse that he would pay him $2 the first day he worked for him, $4 the second day, $8 the third day, and so on, doubling each day. In how many days will Jesse first have a total greater than $500?

3 How many different ways using just bills can you give change from a $100 bill for a $79 purchase if the customer will accept no more than six ones? List the ways.

4 Mr. Ho sold his house for $100,000. This was $10,000 more than twice as much as he paid for it. What was his purchase price?

Divide Fractions page 277
Divide using any method. Write the answer in simplest form.

1 $1 \div \frac{1}{8}$ **2** $5 \div \frac{1}{4}$ **3** $7 \div \frac{1}{3}$ **4** $\frac{3}{10} \div \frac{1}{10}$ **5** $\frac{3}{4} \div \frac{1}{8}$

6 $\frac{2}{3} \div \frac{1}{6}$ **7** $9 \div \frac{1}{2}$ **8** $\frac{5}{6} \div \frac{5}{12}$ **9** $\frac{3}{4} \div \frac{3}{8}$ **10** $6 \div \frac{1}{4}$

Solve.

11 A worker saws 10 sheets of plywood into halves. She then had 4 times as many half-sheets of plywood as Jack. How many did Jack have?

12 Draw a model that would show how to find $\frac{3}{4} \div \frac{1}{8}$.

Divide with Fractions page 279
Divide. Write your answer in simplest form.

1 $7 \div \frac{2}{3}$ **2** $\frac{2}{3} \div \frac{3}{4}$ **3** $\frac{5}{6} \div \frac{2}{3}$ **4** $9 \div \frac{3}{5}$ **5** $\frac{4}{5} \div \frac{3}{5}$

6 $\frac{1}{3} \div 5$ **7** $\frac{7}{10} \div \frac{3}{5}$ **8** $\frac{1}{5} \div \frac{3}{4}$ **9** $\frac{7}{8} \div \frac{3}{4}$ **10** $70 \div \frac{7}{8}$

11 $\frac{7}{8} \div 7$ **12** $21 \div \frac{7}{8}$ **13** $\frac{2}{5} \div \frac{9}{10}$ **14** $\frac{7}{12} \div 7$ **15** $\frac{5}{8} \div 10$

Solve.

16 A wooden rod is 3 feet long. How many half-inch long dowels can be cut from the rod?

17 A 12-oz jar of Big Job hand cleaner sells for $3.98. A 16-oz jar of Hardy Man hand cleaner is on sale for $5.29. Which is the better buy?

Divide with Mixed Numbers page 281
Divide. Write your answer in simplest form. Estimate to check the reasonableness of your answer.

1 $1\frac{1}{2} \div 1\frac{2}{3}$ **2** $1\frac{1}{2} \div 12$ **3** $4\frac{1}{2} \div \frac{3}{5}$ **4** $7\frac{1}{5} \div 1\frac{1}{5}$ **5** $\frac{1}{2} \div 1\frac{2}{3}$

6 $1\frac{2}{3} \div 2\frac{2}{3}$ **7** $\frac{4}{5} \div 1\frac{1}{10}$ **8** $7 \div 1\frac{3}{4}$ **9** $6\frac{1}{2} \div 1\frac{1}{4}$ **10** $2\frac{1}{4} \div \frac{9}{10}$

11 $7\frac{1}{2} \div 8$ **12** $1\frac{2}{5} \div 2\frac{1}{10}$ **13** $4\frac{1}{2} \div 1\frac{1}{2}$ **14** $1\frac{1}{8} \div 3\frac{3}{4}$ **15** $3\frac{3}{10} \div \frac{11}{12}$

Solve.

16 A stack of lumber measures $13\frac{1}{2}$ in. tall. The measure of the side of a piece of lumber is $\frac{3}{4}$ in. How many pieces of lumber are in the stack?

17 There are 6 cars on each bullet train ride. Each car can hold 8 people. How many times must the train run to accommodate 300 riders?

Customary Units of Length page 283
Complete.

1 5 ft = ▇ in.

2 48 in. = ▇ yd

3 11 yd = ▇ ft

4 $\frac{1}{4}$ ft = ▇ in.

5 $1\frac{2}{3}$ yd = ▇ ft

6 75 in. = ▇ yd

7 $\frac{1}{5}$ mi = ▇ ft

8 68 in. = ▇ ft ▇ in.

9 $2\frac{1}{4}$ mile = ▇ ft

Solve.

10 Nancy has $5\frac{3}{4}$ yards of plumber's tape. She uses 12 inches of tape for most repairs. How many 12-inch pieces of tape can she cut? What fraction of a yard will be left over?

11 **Logical reasoning** Carlos has 3 model cars, 4 model trains, and 480 model airplanes. Explain why this data would be hard to display on a pictograph.

Customary Units of Capacity and Weight page 285
Complete.

1 28 fl oz = ▇ c

2 $1\frac{1}{4}$ gal = ▇ qt

3 50 oz = ▇ lb ▇ oz

4 17 pt = ▇ qt

5 9 c = ▇ pt ▇ c

6 $2\frac{1}{2}$ c = ▇ fl oz

7 13 pt = ▇ c

8 $2\frac{1}{2}$ lb = ▇ oz

9 $1\frac{3}{8}$ gal = ▇ pt

Solve.

10 LeRoy has 9 gallons of paint. He uses 12 quarts to paint the den and 10 quarts to paint the dining room. How many gallons of paint does he have left?

11 Keisha runs 2.3 miles each weekday, 3.5 miles on Saturday, and 2 miles on Sunday. Find the mean (rounded to the nearest tenth), median, and mode for a week.

Problem Solvers at Work page 289
Solve. Explain your methods.

1 Al bikes 2.4 miles in $\frac{1}{2}$ hour. His construction site is 3.6 miles away. How long will it take him to bike to the construction site?

2 The 5-gallon gas tank in Zoey's garden tractor is $\frac{1}{4}$ full. How many more gallons can be added to the tank to fill it up?

3 Latisha wants to make three 21-inch necklaces using beads that are $1\frac{3}{4}$ in. long. Each package contains 25 beads. How many packages must she buy?

4 The winner of the Indy 500-mile race in 1911 averaged 74.59 mi per hour. The winning average in 1994 was 160.87 mi per hour. To the nearest tenth, how much longer did the race last in 1911?

Classify 2-Dimensional Shapes page 299
List the name for the shaded figure.

Solve.

5 Kirk pulls a quarter from his pocket and says it is an example of a curved polygon. Is he correct? Explain why?

6 Write the missing number in this pattern: 2, 5, 11, 23, 47, ■, 191, 383. Explain how you know.

Angles page 303
Name, measure, and classify the angle.

 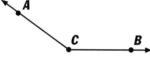 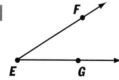

Draw and label the angle.

3 ∠A = 80°   **4** ∠B = 150°   **5** ∠C = 45°   **6** ∠D = 100°   **7** ∠A = 170°

Solve.

8 Draw a 5-sided polygon with 1 acute, 2 right, and 2 obtuse angles.

9 Mike is 5 ft 9 in. tall. Jack is 70 in. tall. Who is taller? By how much?

Lines page 305
Use the diagram at the right for exercises 1–4.

1 Name a pair of perpendicular lines.

2 Name a pair of parallel lines.

3 Name a pair of intersecting lines.

4 Name a pair of equal angles.

Solve.

5 What is the greatest number of points of intersection you can draw using 4 straight lines? Draw a model.

6 Five boys will shake hands with each of the other boys one time. How many handshakes will there be?

Triangles and Quadrilaterals page 309
Give all the possible ways to classify the shape.

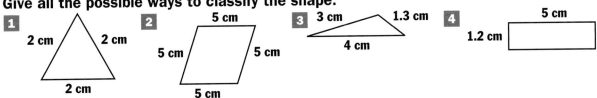

1 2 cm, 2 cm, 2 cm

2 5 cm, 5 cm, 5 cm, 5 cm

3 3 cm, 1.3 cm, 4 cm

4 5 cm, 1.2 cm

Solve. Draw each figure if possible. If not possible, write *can't do*.

5 a quadrilateral with 4 acute angles

6 a triangle with 3 acute angles

7 a quadrilateral with 3 obtuse angles

8 a triangle with 3 obtuse angles

9 a quadrilateral with 4 right angles

10 a triangle with 1 right angle

Sums of Angles page 311
Find the measure of the missing angles.

1 A, 44°, 90°, ?, B, C

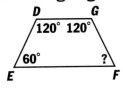

2 D, G, 120°, 120°, 60°, ?, E, F

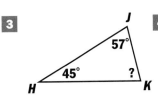

3 J, 57°, 45°, ?, H, K

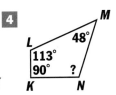

4 M, 48°, L, 113°, 90°, ?, K, N

Solve.

5 Use what you know about the sum of measures of a trapezoid to help you predict the sum of measures of a regular hexagon. Explain.

6 Janine has an average score of 89 for 7 math tests. What score must she get on her next test to raise her average to 90?

Problem Solving Strategy: Make a Model page 313
Solve. Explain your methods.

1 Maria wants to put 6 posts at the side of her yard. She plans to run rope through a hole in the middle of each post. Each post is 6 inches wide (diameter) and is 6 feet from the next post. How many yards of rope does she need to buy?

2 **Spatial reasoning** Which shape does not belong? Explain why.

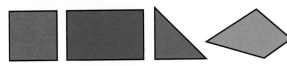

3 Una has a coupon that allows her a $2 discount for every $10 she spends. She buys clothes costing $210. What is her discount? How much will she actually pay?

4 There are 395 calories in Jodie's breakfast. This is $\frac{1}{4}$ of her daily calorie requirement. What is her daily calorie requirement?

Constructions page 321

Use a compass and straightedge to bisect the following.

1 a 45° angle

2 a 125° angle

3 a 9.3-cm line segment

4 a 5.9-cm line segment

Solve.

5 Draw a quadrilateral. Bisect each side and connect the consecutive midpoints. Draw four more different-shaped quadrilaterals and repeat. Describe the pattern you find.

Circles page 323

Use the circle for exercises 1–3.

1 Name the radii.

2 Name the diameters.

3 Name the chords.

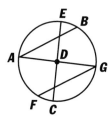

Solve.

4 A knothole in a fence has a $3\frac{1}{2}$ in. diameter. Will a cable with a radius of $1\frac{7}{8}$ in. go through the hole? Explain.

5 A slice of pepper pizza weighs the same as a slice of plain pizza plus 5 oz. Write an equation to represent this relationship. Tell what each variable represents.

Translations and Rotations page 325

Identify the motion as a translation, rotation, or neither.

Solve.

5 Draw any figure on graph paper. Write directions on how to make the moves to draw a translation. Then ask a friend to follow your steps and make the drawing.

6 **Logical reasoning** Jerry spent 60 min on homework. He spent 10 min more on math than on reading, and 10 min more on reading than on science. How long did he spend on each?

Reflections and Line Symmetry page 327

Copy the figure and the line on graph paper. Draw the reflection.

1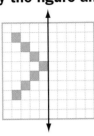

2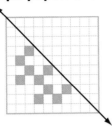

3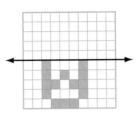

Solve.

4 Predict how many lines of symmetry a figure will have if you fold a piece of paper two times before cutting out a figure. Test your prediction.

5 In the science lab, there are 3-legged stools and 4-legged chairs. Alex counted a total of 21 legs. How many stools and chairs are in the lab?

Tessellations page 329

Tell whether each of the following is an example of a tessellation.

1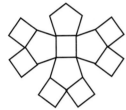

2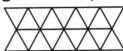

3

Solve.

4 Begin with a square and make at least two cuts to create an irregular tessellation design of your own.

5 **ALGEBRA: PATTERNS** Write the missing numbers in this number pattern: 1; 2; 5; 14; 41; ■; ■; 1,094.

Problem Solvers at Work page 333

Solve. Explain your methods.

1 What is the least number of pins Paco can use to put 24 photos on the bulletin board if he puts a pin in the corner of each photo? Draw a diagram to support your answer.

2 **Logical reasoning** Don, Lee, and Bob each play a different sport. One plays football, one plays baseball, and one plays basketball. Bob doesn't like basketball. Don went to football camp. Who plays each sport?

3 Paul buys a sweater for $64, pays with a $100 bill, and requests at least two $5 bills and no more than six $1 bills in change. List all the ways he can get his change in bills.

4 A 20-oz box of Bix cereal costs $3.19. A 16-oz box of Krackle cereal costs $2.67. A 40-oz box of Yum-Yum cereal costs $6.60. Which is the best buy? Explain.

Functions page 343

Complete the table. Describe the function in words and with an equation. Tell what the variable in the equation represents.

1

Pattern Number	1	2	3	4
Picture	··	·· ··	··· ···	■
Number of Dots	3	5	7	n

2

Pattern Number	1	2	3	4
Picture	□	⊟	⊟	■
Number of Squares	1	3	5	n

Write an equation for the function described in words. Tell what the variable in the equation represents.

3 The number of seats in the science lab at tables seating 6 people.

4 The cost of buying a $3 admission ticket to a science fair and buying some raffle tickets at $2 per ticket.

5 The total cost of a compound microscope for the science lab if the tax rate is 0.07.

6 The average weight of students in a science lab at $2\frac{1}{2}$ pounds for each inch in height.

Graph Functions page 347

Name the coordinates of the point.

1 C **2** E **3** B

Name the point for the ordered pair.

4 $(0, 2)$ **5** $(5\frac{3}{4}, 3)$ **6** $(3, 4)$

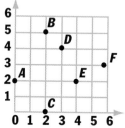

Copy and complete the table for the function represented by the equation. Then graph the function.

7

Rule: $k = m + 4$				
m	0	1	2	3
k	■	■	■	■

8

Rule: $y = x - 1$				
x	1	2	3	$3\frac{2}{3}$
y	■	■	■	■

9

Rule: $a = 4b + 2$				
b	0	1	2	2.5
a	■	■	■	■

Solve.

10 Suppose the equation $C = \$0.14F$ gives the total cost C for making party favors F for the science party. How much will 50 favors cost?

11 Tanisha runs $1\frac{1}{4}$ miles each morning and each afternoon. How far will she run in February (not a leap year) if she runs only on weekdays?

Decribe Change page 349

Tell a story about what the graph shows.

1 Vacation Trip

2 Airplane Altitude

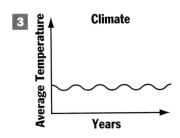

3 Climate

Solve.

4 Sketch a graph that reflects this information. It is calm early in the morning. Winds pick up shortly before lunch and become very strong after lunch. By early evening, hurricane-force winds are blowing. Later, the eye passes over, and then the storm resumes full force once again.

5 Five sixths of Joellyn's crystal collection consists of teddy bears. One third of the teddy bears have a red ribbon around the neck. What fraction of Joellyn's crystal collection has a red ribbon around the neck?

6 Choose the two numbers that will produce a product closest to 800:   12   15   27   31

7 Carrie has $40. Can she purchase a set of beakers for $15.95 and 5 measuring pitchers each priced at $6.95? Explain.

Use Graphs to Solve Problems page 353

Use the graph to find the number of heartbeats for the period of time.

1 30 s   **2** 15 s   **3** 20 s

4 12.5 s   **5** 27.5 s   **6** 17.5 s

Use the graph to find the period of time it takes for the number of heartbeats.

7 20 beats   **8** 10 beats   **9** 30 beats

10 5 beats   **11** 15 beats   **12** 25 beats

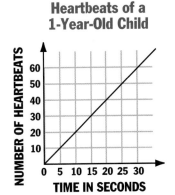

Heartbeats of a 1-Year-Old Child

Solve. Use the graph to help you.

13 A 12-year-old's heart beats $\frac{5}{6}$ as fast as a 1-year-old's heart. How many times will a 12-year-old's heart beat in 30 seconds?

14 An adult's heart beats $\frac{2}{3}$ as fast as a 1-year-old's heart. How many times will an adult's heart beat in 30 seconds?

Problem-Solving Strategy: Solve Simpler Problems page 355

Solve.

1 Ryan wants to know how many straight lines he needs to draw to connect the vertices of a 10-sided figure. He started sketching the figures at the right. What will his answer be?

2   5   9

2 Jack needs $7\frac{1}{2}$ feet of lumber to make a border for a square flower bed. What is the length of each side of the bed?

3 A time line is 25 inches in length and covers a period of 1,000 years. How long would the time line need to be to cover events for 15,000 years?

4 **Logical reasoning** Tim, Juan, Maria, Rosa, and Jane stood in line to get tickets for the science fair. Neither Tim nor Jane was last. Rosa was first. There were at least two people behind Juan. Tim was third in line. In what order were they?

5 Three sixth-grade classes sent 28 representatives to the science fair. There were 6 students from one class and twice as many from another class. How many representatives were from the third class?

- -

Solve Equations page 363

Complete the equation for the picture and solve it.

1

$$3c = 18$$

2

$$13 = c + 8$$

3

$$c + 5 = 21$$

Solve.

4 $a + 3 = 10$ **5** $x + 4 = 21$ **6** $14 = m + 2$ **7** $35 = d + 21$

8 $5r = 35$ **9** $32 = 4t$ **10** $7k = 63$ **11** $132 = 12g$

Solve.

12 The total cost of a meal when dining out is the price of the meal plus the tip, or $C = p + t$. Suppose the price of a meal is $12 with a $1.80 tip. Find the total cost.

13 Solve this mystery number puzzle. The sum of two numbers is 100. If you divide one of them by the other, the quotient is 3. Write the numbers.

Solve Addition and Subtraction Equations page 367
Solve the equation. Check the solution.

1 $h + 23 = 35$ | **2** $14 = j - 3$ | **3** $2 + s = 28$ | **4** $n + 2.5 = 7.9$

5 $w + 4 = 5.2$ | **6** $21 = y + 10$ | **7** $z - 4 = 13$ | **8** $6.2 = b - 3.9$

9 $0.5 + d = 7.5$ | **10** $a - 4.8 = 10.3$ | **11** $h - \frac{1}{3} = 2\frac{1}{6}$ | **12** $3\frac{5}{8} = f + 1\frac{1}{2}$

Solve.

13 Write an equation for the following problem. Then solve. The science students measured $1\frac{3}{4}$ in. of rain on January 2. The total year-to-date rainfall was $3\frac{5}{8}$ in. How much rain fell on January 1?

Solve Multiplication and Division Equations page 371
Solve the equation. Check your solution.

1 $4d = 20$ | **2** $56 = 7c$ | **3** $3b = 36$ | **4** $3.2g = 12.8$

5 $x \div 4 = 2$ | **6** $5 = y \div 3$ | **7** $\frac{a}{2} = 9$ | **8** $\frac{1}{3}k = 12$

9 $1.4d = 9.8$ | **10** $t \div 1.8 = 4.3$ | **11** $3m = \frac{1}{4}$ | **12** $p \div 2\frac{1}{2} = 7$

Solve.

13 Write an equation for this problem. Then solve. Jim spends $1\frac{1}{4}$ hours each week cleaning up the lab after daily science class. What is the average time he spends each day?

Problem Solvers at Work page 375
Solve. Explain your methods.

1 Abdul had many books on weather. He returned 10 books to the library and checked out 4 new ones. Then, he returned 12 books, leaving him with 7. How many books did he have to begin with?

2 There are twice as many beakers as pitchers in the science lab. If 20 beakers are taken away, there will be the same number of both. How many beakers and pitchers are there in all?

3 Suki's backpack weighed $3\frac{3}{8}$ lb when she left for school and $5\frac{1}{8}$ lb when she left school to go home. How much more did it weigh when she left school?

4 Cara brought 5 qt of punch to the Science Club party. Joe brought $2\frac{1}{2}$ gal, and Don brought 4 pt. How many gallons of punch were there?

Understanding Ratios page 387

Write a ratio comparing the shaded to the unshaded region and one comparing the shaded region to the whole figure.

 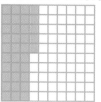 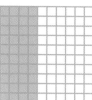

Solve.

4 The hikers have 10 blue canteens and 8 red ones. Seven blue ones have black stripes. Write a ratio of striped canteens to blue ones.

5 The hiking trail is $1\frac{1}{2}$ miles long. Ming hiked $\frac{3}{4}$ mile to the first rest stop and $\frac{3}{8}$ mile to the second. How far does she have yet to hike?

Equal Ratios page 389

Are the ratios equal? Use the symbols = or ≠.

1 $\frac{2}{3}$ ● $\frac{12}{18}$

2 $\frac{1}{2}$ ● $\frac{12}{24}$

3 $\frac{3}{5}$ ● $\frac{14}{20}$

4 $\frac{3}{8}$ ● $\frac{1}{3}$

5 $\frac{3}{6}$ ● $\frac{4}{8}$

6 $\frac{3}{4}$ ● $\frac{10}{12}$

7 $\frac{25}{20}$ ● $\frac{5}{4}$

8 $\frac{3}{1}$ ● $\frac{75}{25}$

9 $\frac{3}{25}$ ● $\frac{1}{8}$

10 $\frac{16}{4}$ ● $\frac{8}{2}$

11 $\frac{3}{15}$ ● $\frac{6}{45}$

12 $\frac{24}{28}$ ● $\frac{3}{4}$

Solve.

13 Two out of 8 sleeping bags are red in Camp A. In Camp B, 8 out of 32 are red. Write the ratios. Are they equal?

14 Caren hiked $\frac{1}{2}$ of the 12-mile trail, then $\frac{1}{3}$ of the remaining distance. How far does she have left to hike?

Rates page 393

Find the unit rate.

1 54 caps for 6 teams = ■ caps per team

2 56 buns in 7 bags = ■ buns in 1 bag

3 $35 for 7 camp shirts = ■ for 1 shirt

4 $5.80 for 5 grams = ■ for 1 gram

5 15 mi in 4 hours = ■ mi per hour

6 314 km in 4 hours = ■ km per hour

Solve.

7 Joe's truck uses 10 gal of gas to travel 125 mi. At this rate, how far will the truck travel on 1 gal of gas?

8 A 58-passenger bus makes 12 trips each week. Estimate the number of passengers it can carry in a year.

Better Buys page 395
Find the unit price. Round to the nearest cent.
 1 14 pounds for $15.60   **2** 25 ounces for $12.49   **3** 3.5 liters for $5.38

Tell which of the two items is the better buy.
4 8 oz of popcorn for $2.19, or 13 oz for $3.69

5 2 cans of soda for $0.72, or 3 cans for $1.00

Solve.
6 While on vacation, Randy's car averaged 16 mi in 15 min and Carol's car averaged 21.5 mi in 20 min. At this rate, which car will cover more miles in an hour?

7 One department store is selling $39.99 sleeping bags at $\frac{1}{3}$ off. Another store is selling $45.00 sleeping bags at $\frac{1}{2}$ off. Which is the better buy?

8 **ALGEBRA: PATTERNS Spatial reasoning**
Draw the next three figures in the pattern at the right. How many squares will be in the tenth figure?

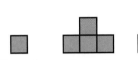
Figure 1   Figure 2   Figure 3

Proportions page 401
Do the ratios form a proportion? Write *yes* or *no*.
1 $\frac{3}{4}$ and $\frac{12}{16}$ **2** $\frac{3}{5}$ and $\frac{4}{15}$ **3** $\frac{2}{9}$ and $\frac{6}{27}$ **4** $\frac{5}{8}$ and $\frac{9}{16}$

5 $\frac{6}{9}$ and $\frac{10}{15}$ **6** $\frac{6}{8}$ and $\frac{12}{16}$ **7** $\frac{6}{1.2}$ and $\frac{4}{0.8}$ **8** $\frac{1}{9}$ and $\frac{3}{18}$

9 $\frac{96}{12}$ and $\frac{1.6}{0.2}$ **10** $\frac{0.9}{10}$ and $\frac{9}{100}$ **11** $\frac{2.1}{42}$ and $\frac{3.15}{64.5}$ **12** $\frac{3.2}{8}$ and $\frac{2.8}{7}$

ALGEBRA: Solve for the variable.
13 $\frac{3}{8} = \frac{n}{24}$ **14** $\frac{5}{6} = \frac{25}{b}$ **15** $\frac{x}{20} = \frac{10}{4}$ **16** $\frac{12}{d} = \frac{3}{4}$

17 $\frac{5}{3} = \frac{10}{m}$ **18** $\frac{y}{4} = \frac{14}{8}$ **19** $\frac{3}{z} = \frac{15}{5}$ **20** $\frac{8}{9} = \frac{16}{t}$

Solve.
21 Six muffins cost $7.14. Fifteen muffins cost $17.85. Write two ratios. Do they form a proportion?

22 Jeremy biked 41.4 miles in 3 hours. What was Jeremy's average speed per hour?

23 Jesse can make 4 name tags each minute. Allison can make 5 name tags each minute. How long will it take them together to make 27 name tags?

24 On the hike, Marian picked $2\frac{1}{2}$ baskets of wild strawberries. Flo picked $2\frac{1}{4}$ times as many baskets. How many baskets did Flo pick?

Problem-Solving Strategy: Write an Equation page 403
Solve.

1 Two out of every 10 campers signed up for the Long Hard Climb trek. Of the 110 campers attending camp, how many signed up for the trek?

2 Cara observed a worm at the side of the trail and clocked its speed. It traveled 21.3 cm in 3 minutes. How far can it travel in 5 minutes?

3 **Logical reasoning** Five campers line up for meals. Jack was somewhere behind Basil, who was in the middle. Nuru was directly behind Paka. Andy was neither first nor last. How did these five campers line up?

4 Milo left camp at 9:15 A.M. and returned to camp at 3:48 P.M. During his hike, he spent 24 minutes eating lunch and took two 15-minute rest periods. How long did he walk?

5 There are 8 campers. Five are wearing blue jeans. Three are wearing bandannas. Two are wearing both. How many of the campers are wearing neither blue jeans nor bandannas?

6 How many triangles can you count?

Similar Figures page 407
The figures at the right are similar.
Find the corresponding side.

1 $\overline{AB}$ **2** $\overline{CD}$ **3** $\overline{AF}$

Find the corresponding angle.

4 $\angle E$ **5** $\angle A$ **6** $\angle W$

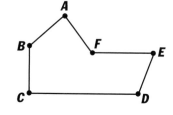
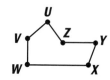

a **ALGEBRA The figures in the pair are similar. Solve for the variable.**

7

7 cm

21 cm

42 cm

x cm

8

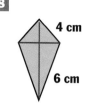
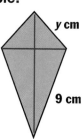

4 cm

6 cm

y cm

9 cm

Solve.

9 Rose took a snapshot at camp that measured 4 in. by 6 in. when it was developed. She asked for an enlargement with a width of 10 in. What will be the length of the other side?

10 Janine has a pair of shorts, a pair of blue jeans, a sleeveless T-shirt, and a shirt with sleeves. How many different outfits can she make using these garments?

Scale Drawing page 409

Use the scale 1 inch = 4 feet to find the actual distance.

1 6 in. **2** $9\frac{1}{2}$ in. **3** 5.75 in. **4** 12 in.

Use the scale $\frac{1}{2}$ inch = 3 feet to find the actual distance.

5 3 in. **6** 8 in. **7** $2\frac{1}{2}$ in. **8** $7\frac{1}{2}$ in.

Solve. Use a centimeter ruler and the map for exercises 9–12.
The map scale is 0.5 cm = 50 m.

9 What is the actual distance from camp to Mossy Stone?

10 What is the actual distance from camp to Forest Hill?

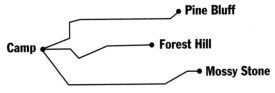

11 How many meters farther is Mossy Stone from camp than Forest Hill?

12 If Swimming Hole is 150 m farther from the campsite than Pine Bluff, what should be the distance of this trail on the map?

- -

Problem Solvers at Work page 413
Solve. Explain your methods.

1 Four campers can sit at one table. If two tables are pushed together, 6 campers can be seated. How many tables must be placed together to seat 10 campers? 20 campers? 30 campers?

2 Carl was given a huge bag of potatoes to peel. He peeled 80 potatoes, then another 53. The cook gave him another 100 potatoes, and he had 160 left to peel. How many did he have to begin with?

3 Rita has a 1-quart canteen. How many times can she fill the canteen from a 4-gal water jug?

4 Anna is half Carly's age. The sum of their ages is 21. How old are Anna and Carly?

5 Exactly 100 students are going on a class trip. Six out of 20 students pack only 1 suitcase each. The others pack more than one. How many will pack more than one suitcase?

6 Ian walked $1\frac{2}{3}$ hours before stopping for lunch. He took 45 minutes for lunch. He then took a $\frac{3}{4}$-hour walk, arriving home at 4:25 P.M. What time did he begin his walk?

7 **ALGEBRA: PATTERNS** Write the missing number in this number pattern: 6, 11, 18, *n*, 38. Explain how you know.

8 Write 5 test scores that will result in a mean of 75, a mode of 72, and a median of 74.

Percent page 425
Write the fraction, ratio, or decimal as a percent.
You may use a model to help you.

1 $\frac{25}{100}$ **2** $\frac{3}{10}$ **3** 0.63   **4** 55:100   **5** 0.4

6 37:100   **7** $\frac{9}{10}$ **8** 14:100   **9** 0.7   **10** $\frac{1}{2}$

Solve.

11 Seven tenths of the neck chains on display at a jewelry store in the mall were gold. What percent of the chains were gold?

Percent, Fractions, and Decimals page 429
Write the percent as a fraction in simplest form.

1 6%   **2** 85%   **3** 24%   **4** 40%   **5** 13%   **6** 50%

Write the fraction or decimal as a percent.

7 $\frac{7}{10}$ **8** 0.6   **9** 0.11   **10** $\frac{3}{5}$ **11** 0.01   **12** $\frac{1}{4}$

Write as a percent, a fraction in simplest form, and a decimal.

13 34 blouses out of 100   **14** 6 pairs of socks out of 20 pairs

Solve.

15 About 40% of the sneakers on sale were sold on an opening sale day. Is this closer to $\frac{1}{4}$ or to $\frac{1}{2}$? Explain.

16 Abram has $115 in five- and ten-dollar bills. He has 15 bills in all. How many of each does he have?

Percent of a Number page 431
Find the percent of a number. You may use a model to help you.

1 10% of 60   **2** 25% of 24   **3** 20% of 50   **4** 25% of 28

5 5% of 64   **6** 20% of 75   **7** 50% of 78   **8** 10% of 50

9 25% of 72   **10** 50% of 56   **11** 20% of 125   **12** 25% of 48

Solve.

13 Twenty-five percent of the 20 shirts on display in a clothing store had button-down collars. How many had button-down collars?

14 The clerk gives Jed $5.25 in change. Show all the different ways to make change if the clerk uses only dollars and/or quarters.

Percent of a Number page 435

Find the number. Round to the nearest hundredth or cent, if necessary.

1 25% of 96

2 80% of 115

3 12% of 76

4 35% of 96

5 7% of 85

6 14% of 58

7 90% of 50

8 75% of 144

9 6% of $5.38

10 8% of $3.75

11 35% of $21.38

12 50% of $125.14

Use mental math to compare. Write >, <, or =.

13 40% of 110 ● 50% of 88

14 10% of $60 ● 20% of $45

15 20% of 60 ● 40% of 20

16 10% of 30 ● 25% of 12

17 25% of $24 ● 30% of $21

18 50% of 20 ● 20% of 50

Solve.

19 Thirty-five percent of the 100 families in Trouble Creek shop at the local grocery. How many families shop at the local grocery? How many do not shop at the local grocery?

Percent One Number Is of Another page 437

Find the percent. Round decimals to the nearest percent, if necessary.

1 38 is what percent of 40?

2 18 is what percent of 72?

3 6 is what percent of 24?

4 35 is what percent of 84?

5 What percent of $80 is $8?

6 What percent of $45 is $9?

7 What percent of 250 is 30?

8 What percent of 300 is 15?

Complete the table. Then use the table to solve problems 9–12.

9 What percent of the 200 buyers did *not* choose red?

10 What fraction of the buyers chose either blue or black binders?

11 Each binder sells for $2.89. How much money did the store receive for the red binders? for the black binders? for the blue binders?

Binders Sold in April		
Color	Number Sold	Percent Sold
Red	50	■
Black	120	■
Blue	30	■

12 In May, 500 binders are sold. The percents remain the same. How many more black binders are sold than red and blue combined?

Discount page 443
Find the discount and sale price.

1 Regular price: $12
Discount: 20% off

2 Regular price: $28
Discount: 15% off

3 Regular price: $34
Discount: 10% off

4 Regular price: $52
Discount: 25% off

5 Regular price: $8
Discount: 30% off

6 Regular price: $110
Discount: 35% off

7 Regular price: $324
Discount: 50% off

8 Regular price: $7.95
Discount: 40% off

9 Regular price: $12.95
Discount: 20% off

Solve.

10 The regular price of a suit was $175. It is on sale for 25% off. How much will 2 suits cost at the sale price?

11 Write an equation that shows the discount if the original price is $6.95 and the percentage off is 40%.

12 Eric pays $0.59 for a pen. Lu pays twice as much, and Bo pays $0.29 less than Lu. How much did Bo pay?

13 There are 120 stores in the mall. Seventy-two of the stores sell clothing. What percent sell clothing?

Problem-Solving Strategy: Use Alternate Methods page 445
Solve.

1 The music store sells compact discs for $10 each. They are on sale 2 for $18. What is the discount if you purchase 2 disks?

2 Kerri spent $40 at the mall, loaned $35 to a friend, found $14 on the floor, and has $25 left. How much money did she have to start with?

3 Four out of every 10 earrings bought by a jewelry store are clip-ons. The store bought 910 earrings. How many are not clip-ons?

4 Tasha met Leon at the mall. She visits the mall every 3 days; Leon visits every 4 days. How many days will it be before they meet again?

5 **ALGEBRA: PATTERNS** Study the figures at the right. Draw the next figure in the pattern. Then tell how many blocks there would be in the fifth figure; in the tenth figure.

Figure 1   Figure 2   Figure 3

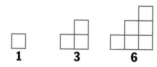

1   3   6

6 To rent a chain saw, the rental store charges $23.15 for each of the first two days and $12.95 for each additional day. How much will it cost to rent the saw for a week?

7 Carolee purchases items priced at $3.98, $19.35, $43.59, and $11.98. Gerald spends $75.98 in all. Who spends more money? How much more?

Interpret and Make Circle Graphs page 449
Use the circle graph for ex. 1–3.

1 Does Joely spend more on food or entertainment?

2 What fraction of her budget does she spend on clothing?

3 If she receives $20 each week, how much of this will she spend on food?

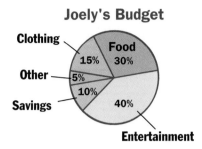

Joely's Budget

Clothing · Food 30% · 15% · Other · 5% · Savings · 10% · 40% · Entertainment

Use the table for ex. 4–7.

4 Jackson surveyed his friends and recorded their favorite activities in the table at the right. Make a circle graph to display the data from the table.

5 Of the 200 students surveyed, how many prefer activities other than the ones listed?

6 How many more students prefer to play sports than listen to music?

7 How many students altogether prefer reading and listening to music?

Favorite Activites	
Activity	**Percent**
Engage in sports activities	35%
Watch TV, movies, video games	25%
Listen to music	10%
Read	25%
Other	5%

Problem Solvers at Work page 453
Solve. Explain your methods.

1 Tell why this graph is misleading.

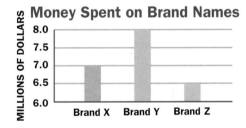

Money Spent on Brand Names

MILLIONS OF DOLLARS: 8.0, 7.5, 7.0, 6.5, 6.0

Brand X   Brand Y   Brand Z

2 In a survey of 600 sixth graders, 80% reported that they have homework every school night; and of those students, 45% said that they spent 1 hour or more on homework each night. How many of the sixth graders surveyed spend 1 hour or more on homework on school nights?

3 A dress is on sale for 25% off the original price of $68. Another dress is on sale for 40% off the original price of $84. Which sale price is lower? How much lower?

4 A computer network charges $3.50 each month plus $0.29 per minute on-line. Andy's monthly bill for August was $16.55. How many minutes was he on-line that month?

5 Hank's gas tank contains 5 gal of gas and is $\frac{1}{4}$ full. How many gal will he need to buy to have a full tank?

6 Jo can use cash to buy a stereo for $367 or pay $48/month for 8 months. What will she save if she pays cash?

Probability page 465

Suppose you select a coin from the box without looking. Find the probability.

1 P(penny)   **2** P(nickel)

3 P(dime)   **4** P(quarter)

5 P(penny or dime)   **6** P(coin worth less than 10¢)

Suppose you toss a 1–6 number cube. Find the probability.

7 P(1)   **8** P(4)   **9** P(1 or 6)

10 P(1, 2, 3, or 5)   **11** P(odd number)   **12** P(number less than 6)

Solve.

13 The letters that spell BASKETBALL are written on cards. What is the probability you will select "L" if you choose one card without looking?

14 Mark made 12 out of 20 free throws during basketball practice. What percentage of free throws did he make?

Probability page 467

For the experiment, tell whether the outcomes listed are equally likely. If they are not equally likely, tell which is the most likely.

1 Draw a card. Outcomes: G, A, M, or E

2 Pick a ball. Outcomes: red or yellow

Suppose you spin the spinner. Find the probability.

3 P(yellow)   **4** P(green)

5 P(orange)   **6** P(red)

Solve.

7 Design a spinner for which the probability of landing on red is $\frac{1}{2}$, on blue $\frac{1}{4}$, on yellow $\frac{1}{8}$, and on green $\frac{1}{8}$. Describe how to change the spinner so that the probability of landing on yellow is $\frac{3}{16}$ and on green is $\frac{1}{16}$.

8 Geoffrey makes $7 per hour at the Gameland Arcade. At the end of the week, he has earned $269.50. How many hours has he worked? After taxes of 20% are deducted, how much money will he actually receive?

Problem-Solving Strategy: Use a Simulation page 469

Solve.

1 Suppose that it is equally likely that a baby will be a boy or a girl. Use a simulation to find the probability that a family of 4 children will have at least 3 girls. Explain how you set up your simulation.

2 **Logical reasoning** Anthony, Nicholas, and George are each an expert at one of these games: chess, checkers, or marbles. George is a spectator at chess and marbles. Nicholas does not like board games. Which student plays each game?

3 Suppose a model train car is 16 in. long and 4 in. wide. If 1 in. on the model represents 3 ft on an actual car, what is the length and width of an actual car?

4 Tiffany spent $23.41 for a sweater, $35.38 for a skirt, and $25.98 for a pair of shoes. She had $21.11 left. How much money did she have before making the purchases?

5 Eleanor played 12 more games of Blast Off! than Seek! on her computer during one month. She played 3 times as many games of Seek! as Win! She played 2 games of Win! How many games of Blast Off! did she play?

6 Maxine's average time playing a computer game is 50 min. She played 6 games. Her times for the first five games were 63 min, 45 min, 39 min, 75 min, and 49 min. What was her time for the other game?

Make Predictions page 475

Predict the number of times you would get a card showing one of the shapes if you do this experiment at right 64 times:

Experiment: Put the cards in a bag and shake. Without looking, choose a card, record the shape, and then put it back.

1 square   **2** triangle   **3** circle

Predict the number out of 600 middle school students who would choose each sport if you surveyed each student.

4 basketball

5 football

6 baseball

Solve. Use the student survey above.

7 Predict how many more students at the middle school will prefer basketball than will prefer baseball.

Random Sample Survey Results	
Favorite Sport	**Number of students**
Basketball	45
Football	34
Baseball	21
Total surveyed	100

Tree Diagrams and the Counting Principle page 479

Use the spinner for ex. 1–6.

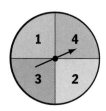

 Make a tree diagram to find the number of possible outcomes if you spin the spinner twice each turn.

2 Find the total number of possible outcomes for tossing a 1–6 number cube and spinning the spinner.

3 Use the counting principle to verify your answer for ex. 2.

4 Find the probability of tossing a 4 and spinning a 4.

5 Find the probability of tossing a 1 and spinning a 2.

6 Find the probability of tossing a 5 and spinning a 6.

Solve.

7 What is the probability of tossing two 1–6 number cubes and getting a product of 4?

8 The distance around a rectangular gameboard is 84 in. One side is 18 in. What are its dimensions?

Problem Solvers at Work page 483

Solve. Explain your methods.

1 After the chess tournament, the photographer asks Jack, Martina, and Charles to line up for a photograph. In how many ways can they line up for the photograph? What is the probability the random order will be Martina, Jack, Charles?

2 A blueprint of the new clubhouse uses this scale: 1 to 5. The actual length of a card room is 15 ft, and the width is 10.5 ft. Find the length and width of the room as it appears on the blueprint.

3 Two stores had the same computer game on sale. Best Computers advertised it at 20% off the regular price of $100. Better Buy advertised it for $\frac{1}{3}$ off its regular price of $120. Which store has the better sale price?

4 The answer to a "Guess the Number" contest is a palindrome with five digits. The last digit is twice as great as the middle digit. The middle digit, an even number, is $\frac{1}{3}$ as great as the second digit. Find the number.

Perimeter and Area page 493
Find the perimeter and area.

1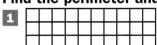

2 17 m, 13.5 m (rectangle)

3 9 $\frac{1}{2}$ in., 4 $\frac{1}{4}$ in. (rectangle)

4 rectangle:
ℓ = 4.5 cm
w = 1.2 cm

5 rectangle
ℓ = 3 $\frac{3}{4}$ in.
w = 4 $\frac{1}{8}$ in.

6 rectangle
ℓ = 8.8 m
w = 3.5 m

7 square
s = 2 $\frac{1}{2}$ ft

Solve.

8 A castle is on a rectangular plot of land with an area of 825 m². If the rectangular castle has walls 18 m by 26 m, what area of land is outside the castle?

9 The drawbridge of the castle is lowered over the moat to get into the castle. Would you describe this motion as a translation, rotation, or reflection?

Enlarging Rectangles page 495
Find the perimeter and area of the rectangle. Double and triple the length and width of the rectangle, and find their perimeters and areas.

1 Length: 4 m
Width: 2 m

2 Length: 6 in.
Width: 3 in.

3 Length: 9 ft
Width: 5 ft

4 Length: 8 cm
Width: 1 $\frac{1}{2}$ cm

Solve.

5 A rectangular castle gate is 4 m long and 3 m wide. What is the perimeter and area of the gate?

6 I am a rectangle. My area is 16 in.² My length is four times my width. Draw me. Label my dimensions with my perimeter and area.

7 Use the data at the right to make a bar graph. Then make up two questions that can be answered using the data represented in the graph.

8 Make a circle graph using the data in the table.

Card Game Scores	
Name	**Score**
Bob	110
May	95
Alex	80
Don	75

Area of Parallelograms and Triangles page 499
Find the area of the parallelogram or triangle.

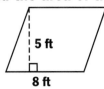

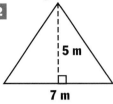

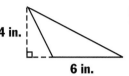

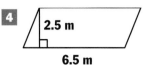

5 parallelogram:
$b = 3\frac{1}{4}$ in.
$h = 2$ in.

6 parallelogram:
$b = 6.3$ cm
$h = 4.8$ cm

7 triangle:
$b = 8$ in.
$h = 3$ in.

8 triangle:
$b = 6\frac{1}{2}$ in.
$h = 1$ in.

Find the height of the parallelogram or triangle.

10 cm
Area: 80 cm²

12 in.
Area: 120 in.²

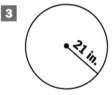

6 m
Area: 9 m²

9.5 ft
Area: 38 ft²

Circumference of a Circle page 501
Find the circumference of the circle. Use 3.14 or $3\frac{1}{7}$ for π.
Round decimal to the nearest tenth.

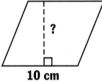

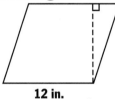

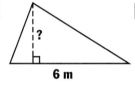

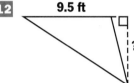

5 diameter: 3 in.

6 diameter: $5\frac{1}{2}$ in.

7 radius: 4 cm

8 radius: 1.8 cm

Solve.

9 A circular fountain in front of a building has a diameter of 12 ft. A circular path around the fountain starts 2 ft from the fountain's edge. What is the circumference of the path?

10 The company ordered 510 bricks to make the path. The path has 350 bricks, but 29 bricks broke during the making of the path. How many bricks are left?

Area of a Circle page 505

Find the circumference and area of the circle. Use π = 3.14 or 3 1/7. Round decimal answers to the nearest tenth.

1
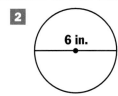
1.5 cm

2
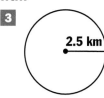
6 in.

3

2.5 km

4

$3\frac{1}{2}$ in.

5 diameter: 3.4 cm   **6** diameter: 35 in.   **7** radius: 0.6 km   **8** radius: 8 m

Solve.

9 David picked apples from his tree. He gave 10 apples to Alberto and $\frac{1}{2}$ of the remaining apples to Maria. He had 14 apples left. How many did he pick?

10 A town park has a circular bicycle path around it. The circumference of the path is 706.5 m. What is the radius of the path?

Area of Compound Figures page 507

Find the area of the shaded regions. Use 3.14 or 3 1/7 for π. Round decimal answers to the nearest tenth. Explain your methods.

1
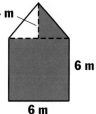
4 m
6 m
6 m

2
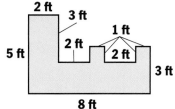
2 ft
3 ft
1 ft
5 ft
2 ft
2 ft
3 ft
8 ft

3

20 cm
10 cm

Solve.

4 Sirens are used to alert people to an approaching tornado. A siren can be heard within a 4,000-ft radius. What area does the siren sound cover?

5 A square castle has walls that are 24 m long. The walls of the castle are 2 m thick. What amount of area is left inside the castle?

Use the data below to complete problems 6–7.

6 Use the data at the right to make a line graph.

7 Extend the graph to find the price of 8 games.

Retail Price of Wacky Words Game		
Number of Games Sold	Price Per Game	Ordered Pairs
1	$2.50	(1, 2.50)
2	$5.00	(2, 5.00)
3	$7.50	(3, 7.50)

Problem-Solving Strategy: Make a Diagram page 513

Solve.

1 A CD has a radius of 6 cm. The radius of the hole and area without recorded information is 2 cm. How much of the area of the CD has recorded information?

2 A door is 6 ft 6 in. high. The doorknob is 32 in. from the bottom of the door. What is the height of the door above the doorknob?

3 **Logical reasoning** Eric, Kristen, Jeff, and Brittany are riding in a tram. If two students are seated opposite the other two students, in how many different ways can the students be arranged?

4 You want to put wall-to-wall carpeting in a 9-ft-by-12-ft room. The carpeting costs $16.95 per sq yd, and installation will cost $125. What is the total cost to carpet the room (not including sales tax)?

Classify 3-Dimensional Figures page 515

For the figure write what type of figure, the number of faces, the number of edges, and the number of vertices.

1 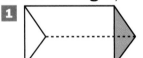 **2** 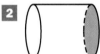 **3**  **4**

Solve.

5 Name all the vertices, faces, and edges of the cube. Which face is parallel to *ABCD*?

6 If you shade 3 of the faces of the cube, what percent of the cube will be shaded?

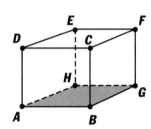

Different Views of 3-Dimensional Figures page 517

Sketch the top view, front view, and side view of the figure.

1  **2**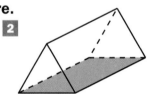

Solve.

3 The top view of a building is an equilateral triangle. What kind of 3-dimensional figure is the building?

4 In a building, the ratio of corner offices to all offices on a floor is 4 to 25. If there are 300 offices in the building, how many are corner offices?

Integers page 539

Write the integer to represent the situation. Then describe the opposite situation and write an integer to represent it.

1 a weight gain of 3 lb   **2** 12° below zero   **3** a price drop of $2

4 up 8 floors   **5** a profit of $100   **6** 15 m below sea level

7 pay $1 for lunch   **8** grow 2 inches   **9** 4 days late

Solve.

10 Divers discovered an ancient treasure ship 2 km below sea level. Use an integer to represent this situation?

11 Scientists determined that the ship had left the Caribbean in 1629. How long ago was that?

12 Divers found 3 coins worth $250,000 each, 5 coins worth $100,000 each, and 10 coins worth a total of $50,000. How much were the coins worth altogether?

13 The water temperature at the depth of the treasure ship was 25° below zero. Use an integer to represent this situation.

Compare and Order Integers page 541

Compare. Write > or <. You may use a number line to help you.

1 ⁻7 ● ⁻8   **2** 0 ● ⁻5   **3** 4 ● 7   **4** ⁻6 ● 6   **5** 0 ● 3

6 12 ● ⁻10   **7** ⁻15 ● ⁻13   **8** ⁻1 ● ⁻17   **9** 21 ● 0   **10** ⁻35 ● ⁻40

Write the integers in order from greatest to least.

11 ⁻2, 0, 5   **12** 6, ⁻3, ⁻6   **13** ⁻8, ⁻4, 1

14 ⁻9, 0, 1, ⁻6   **15** ⁻8, 3, ⁻5, 7   **16** ⁻32, 37, 42, ⁻46, 0

Solve.

17 The element mercury freezes at ⁻39° C. The temperature of dry ice is ⁻78° C. Which of these temperatures is colder?

18 The melting point of copper is 1,083° C. However, its boiling point is 217° greater than that. What is the boiling point of copper?

19 A weather station near the North Pole is 18 ft long. If the area of the rectangular station is 270 ft², what is the width of the weather station?

20 A hurricane caused a river to overflow. The water level was at 4 ft above ground level. What percent of a 20-ft-tall building was above the water level?

Surface Area: Prism page 521

Find the surface area for the 3-dimensional shape. Round to the nearest tenth.

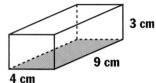

1 3 cm, 9 cm, 4 cm

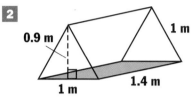

2 1 m, 0.9 m, 1 m, 1.4 m

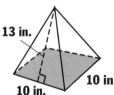

3 13 in., 10 in., 10 in.

Solve.

4 What is the total surface area of a cereal box that is 19 cm wide, 6.5 cm deep, and 29.5 cm high?

5 You spin a 4-part spinner labeled *A*, *B*, *C*, and *D*. What is the probability that you will spin *C*?

Volume page 525

Find the volume for the rectangular prism. Round to the nearest tenth.

1 ℓ = 9 in.
w = 7 in.
h = 5 in.

2 ℓ = 10 m
w = 8.5 m
h = 0.5 m

3 ℓ = 9.5 cm
w = 7.8 cm
h = 4.2 cm

Solve.

4 A swimming pool is 25 m long, 15 m wide, and 3.5 m deep. What is the volume of the pool?

5 There are six swimming lanes in a pool. How many floating lane dividers are used to make the six lanes?

Problem Solvers at Work page 529

Solve.

1 A sprinkler waters the lawn in a circular pattern with a 14-ft radius. What area of the lawn does the sprinkler cover?

2 The Sears Tower, at 1,454 ft high, is about 3 times taller than the Washington Monument and about 5 times taller than the Statue of Liberty. What are the heights of the structures?

Use the menu at the right for problems 3–4.

3 Which meal costs less than $11.00: appetizer, chicken dinner, iced tea, ice cream or appetizer, steak, iced tea, ice cream

4 For each meal in problem 3, calculate a 20% tip. Round your answer to the nearest dime.

C and B Restaurant	
Appetizers	$3.25
Chicken dinner	$4.20
Steak	$7.25
Iced tea	$0.70
Ice cream	$1.25

Add Integers page 545
Add. Use counters or mental math.

1 $2 + {}^-3 = n$ **2** ${}^-8 + 3 = n$ **3** $6 + 9 = n$ **4** $5 + {}^-1 = n$

5 ${}^-7 + {}^-2 = c$ **6** $14 + {}^-6 = y$ **7** $4 + {}^-8 = d$ **8** ${}^-10 + 10 = s$

9 ${}^-9 + 0 = n$ **10** $5 + {}^-7 + {}^-3 = a$ **11** ${}^-9 + 11 + {}^-1 = t$

⭐ **ALGEBRA Complete the function tables.**

12

Rule: Add ⁻4	
Input	**Output**
⁻4	■
0	■
4	■
9	■

13

Rule: ☐	
Input	**Output**
⁻6	⁻9
⁻3	⁻6
0	⁻3
5	2

Solve.

14 Which numbers will make the following statement true?
$19.\blacksquare 6 < 19.49$

15 Find the net charge of 3 negatively charged particles and 5 positively charged particles.

Subtract Integers page 549
Subtract. You may use a model.

1 $7 - 4 = n$ **2** ${}^-3 - {}^-1 = n$ **3** ${}^-9 - {}^-9 = n$ **4** ${}^-5 - 8 = n$

5 ${}^-4 - 6 = b$ **6** $7 - {}^-3 = a$ **7** ${}^-13 - 5 = n$ **8** $12 - {}^-7 = b$

9 ${}^-7 - {}^-6 = d$ **10** ${}^-8 - {}^-3 = n$ **11** $6 - {}^-6 = y$ **12** ${}^-9 - 3 = c$

Copy and complete.

13 ${}^-9 - 5 = {}^-9 + \blacksquare = \blacksquare$ **14** $5 - {}^-4 = 5 + \blacksquare = \blacksquare$ **15** ${}^-8 - {}^-2 = {}^-8 + \blacksquare = \blacksquare$

16 $7 - 8 = 7 + \blacksquare = \blacksquare$ **17** $6 - 10 = 6 + \blacksquare = \blacksquare$ **18** ${}^-11 - {}^-3 = {}^-11 + \blacksquare = \blacksquare$

Solve.

19 Scientists launch two weather satellites. One satellite will send a signal every 3 seconds, while the other will send a signal every 5 seconds. If both satellites are put into operation at the same time, how long will it take before both satellites send a signal at the same time?

20 In some hot places on Earth, temperatures may reach 136°F, while in some cold places, temperatures may be as low as ⁻89°F. What is the difference between these two temperatures?

extra practice

Problem-Solving Strategy: Use Logical Reasoning page 551
Solve.

1 In a class of 24 students, 12 are in the mountain-bike club, 10 are in the photography club, and 6 are in both clubs. How many are in neither club?

2 Each slice of a pizza is $\frac{1}{8}$ of the whole pizza. If $\frac{3}{4}$ of the pizza is left, how many slices are left?

3 An appliance store sells a new refrigerator for $925. During this month it is sold at a 25% discount. What is the discount and final sale price this month?

4 A research submarine was 15 m below sea level. At that depth the ocean temperature was 13° C. The surface ocean temperature was 1.5° warmer. What was the surface temperature?

5 A metal rod was heated and measured to see how much it had expanded. If the metal was 15 cm long and expanded to 15.3 cm, what percent of an increase was that?

6 In a survey, 26 people said they like convertible cars, and 57 people prefer hardtops. Of these people, 19 said they like both. How many people like convertibles, hardtops, or both?

Coordinate Graphing in All Four Quadrants page 559
Give the coordinates of the point.

1 D **2** C **3** B

4 L **5** H **6** I

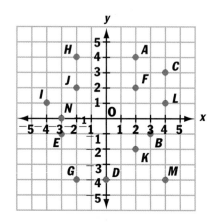

Name the point for the ordered pair.

7 (2, ⁻2) **8** (⁻3, 0) **9** (2, 2)

10 (⁻3, ⁻1) **11** (4, ⁻4) **12** (2, 4)

ⓐ ALGEBRA Copy and complete the table. Then graph the function.

13 $y = x - 1$

Rule: y = x – 1			
x	⁻1	0	1	3
y	■	■	■	■

14 $y = x + 3$

Rule: y = x + 3			
x	⁻3	0	3	4
y	■	■	■	■

15 $y = 1 - x$

Rule: y = 1 – x			
x	⁻1	0	1	3
y	■	■	■	■

Solve.

16 Spatial reasoning A science team has placed 4 motion detectors in a state to warn of earthquakes. The devices form a rectangle on a coordinate grid. Three coordinates of the vertices of the rectangle are (3, 3), (3, ⁻3), and (⁻3, ⁻3). What is the coordinate of the fourth vertex?

Addition and Subtraction Equations page 563

Solve the equation. You may use any method. Check the solution.

1 $x + 2 = {}^-4$

2 $r + 3 = {}^-5$

3 $b + {}^-1 = 0$

4 ${}^-6 = e + {}^-5$

5 $m - 2 = {}^-3$

6 ${}^-10 = g - 7$

7 $y - {}^-7 = 5$

8 $d - 6 = {}^-3$

9 $f - {}^-4 = 7$

10 $x + {}^-9 = 3$

11 ${}^-8 = k - 4$

12 $s + {}^-4 = 9$

13 $u - {}^-3 = 5$

14 ${}^-10 = v + {}^-6$

15 $z - {}^-3 = 0$

16 $x - 6 = {}^-12$

Solve.

17 After a rise of 14° F, the temperature was ${}^-3°$ F. Write an equation and solve it to find the temperature before the rise.

18 A restaurant serves $\frac{1}{4}$-lb hamburgers. How many hamburgers can they make from 30 pounds of meat?

· ·

Problem Solvers at Work page 567

Solve.

1 The current reading on the electric meter for an office building is 19,829 kilowatt hours. Last month, the reading was 8,453 kilowatt hours. If the electric company charges $0.0958 per kilowatt hour, what is the amount of the electric bill for this month for the office building? Round your answer to the nearest cent.

2 The table at the right shows Keisha's growth over the years. Make a line graph to solve the following problems.
   a Estimate Keisha's height at age 8.
   b Estimate Keisha's age when she was 47 in. tall.

Age	Height (in.)
birth	21
5	45
10	56
15	63
20	64

3 Melinda has $3.25 in quarters and dimes. She has 16 coins altogether. How many coins of each kind does she have?

4 Wind makes the air temperature feel colder than it actually is. Suppose the actual termperature is 28°F and the wind is blowing at 25 mi per h. Your body would think it is ${}^-3°$F. What is the difference between the two temperatures?

5 Here are two views of the same cube. Letter *A* is opposite letter *D*. Which letter is opposite letter *C*?

6 A music store has a special sale on boxed sets of CDs. A set that you want is marked $54. During the sale, there is a 20% discount. If you buy the boxed set in the next hour, you receive an additional 10% off. What is the final sale price (before sales tax) if you buy in the next hour?

United States Population by Gender and Age: 1995 to 2000 (in Thousands)

GENDER AND AGE	1995	2000*
Total population	**268,151**	**281,542**
MALE	130,577	137,163
Under 5 years old	10,653	10,508
5–17 years old	26,074	27,842
18–24 years old	12,325	12,811
25–44 years old	42,282	41,581
45–64 years old	25,518	30,074
65 years old and over	13,725	14,277
FEMALE	137,574	144,379
Under 5 years old	10,161	10,022
5–17 years old	24,915	26,592
18–24 years old	11,908	12,445
25–44 years old	42,262	41,398
45–64 years old	27,435	31,953
65 years old and over	20,893	21,969

*The figures for the year 2000 are projections.

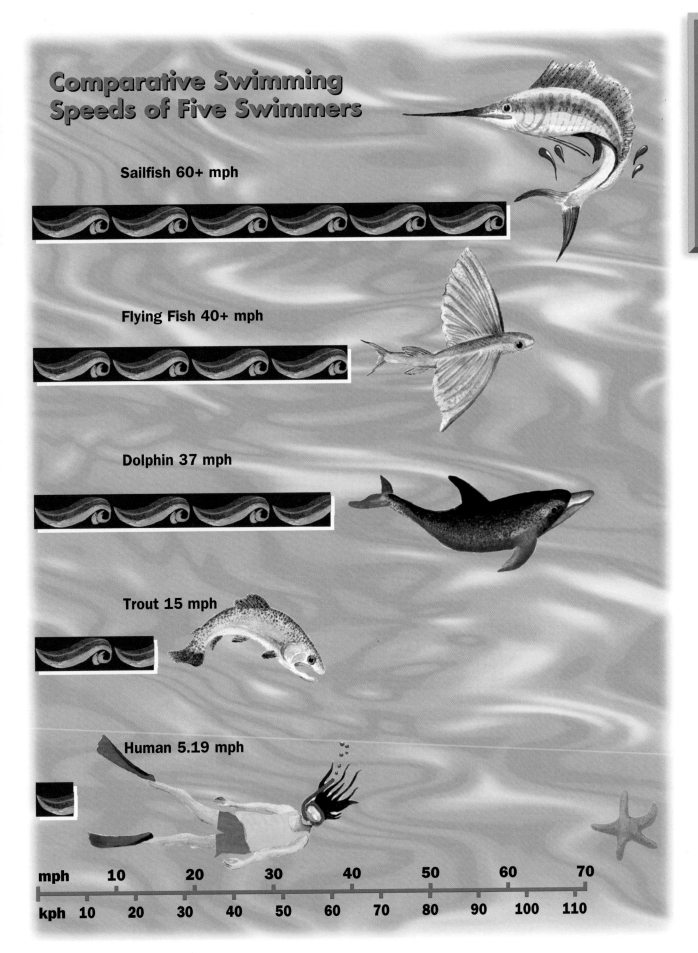

Comparative Swimming Speeds of Five Swimmers

Sailfish 60+ mph

Flying Fish 40+ mph

Dolphin 37 mph

Trout 15 mph

Human 5.19 mph

| mph | 10 | 20 | 30 | 40 | 50 | 60 | 70 |

| kph | 10 | 20 | 30 | 40 | 50 | 60 | 70 | 80 | 90 | 100 | 110 |

Value of 1 U.S. Dollar in Japanese Yen

(rounded to the nearest yen—actual amounts given in parentheses)

Year	Value
1986	158 (158.18)
1987	121 (121.37)
1988	125 (124.93)
1989	144 (143.72)
1990	136 (135.62)
1991	125 (124.93)
1992	125 (124.83)
1993	112 (111.61)
1994	100 (99.77)
1995	103 (103.43)

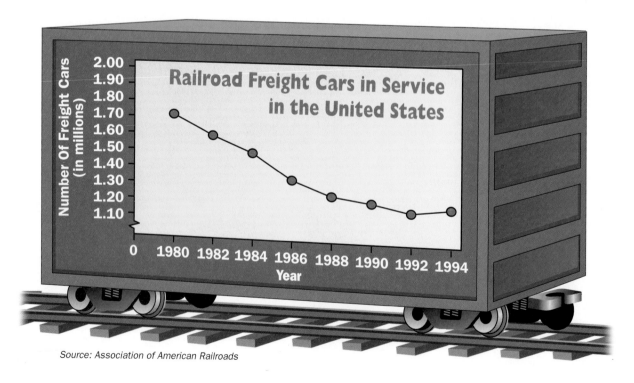

Railroad Freight Cars in Service in the United States

Number Of Freight Cars (in millions) vs. Year (1980–1994)

Source: Association of American Railroads

634

A Typical Orchestra

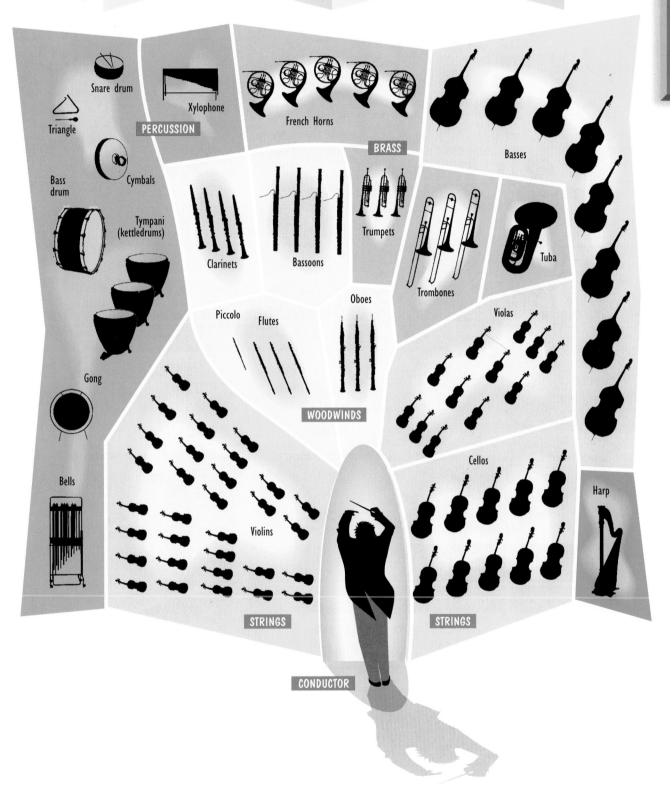

Snare drum

Xylophone

Triangle

PERCUSSION

French Horns

BRASS

Basses

Bass drum

Cymbals

Tympani (kettledrums)

Clarinets

Bassoons

Trumpets

Trombones

Tuba

Oboes

Gong

Piccolo

Flutes

WOODWINDS

Violas

Cellos

Bells

Harp

Violins

STRINGS

STRINGS

CONDUCTOR

635

World Track and Field Records

Women

	Indoor	Outdoor
High Jump	6 ft $9\frac{1}{2}$ in.	6 ft $10\frac{1}{4}$ in.
Long Jump	24 ft $2\frac{1}{4}$ in.	24 ft $8\frac{1}{4}$ in.
Triple Jump	48 ft $10\frac{3}{4}$ in.	50 ft $10\frac{1}{4}$ in.
Shot Put	73 ft 10 in.	74 ft 3 in.

Men

	Indoor	Outdoor
High Jump	7 ft $11\frac{1}{4}$ in.	8 ft $\frac{1}{2}$ in.
Long Jump	28 ft $10\frac{1}{4}$ in.	29 ft $4\frac{1}{2}$ in.
Triple Jump	58 ft $3\frac{3}{4}$ in.	60 ft $1\frac{3}{4}$ in.
Shot Put	74 ft $4\frac{1}{4}$ in.	75 ft $10\frac{1}{4}$ in.

Home Ownership

The portion of homes owned by married couples over the 10-year period from 1982 to 1992.

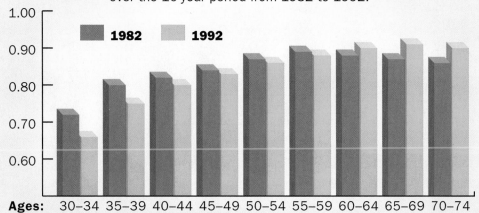

1982 1992

| | 1.00 | 0.90 | 0.80 | 0.70 | 0.60 |
| Ages: | 30–34 | 35–39 | 40–44 | 45–49 | 50–54 | 55–59 | 60–64 | 65–69 | 70–74 |

Source: Bureau of the Census—Dept. of Commerce

The seven-piece tangram puzzle originated in China in ancient times.

Horse

Cat

Telephone

Boat

Pig

Person

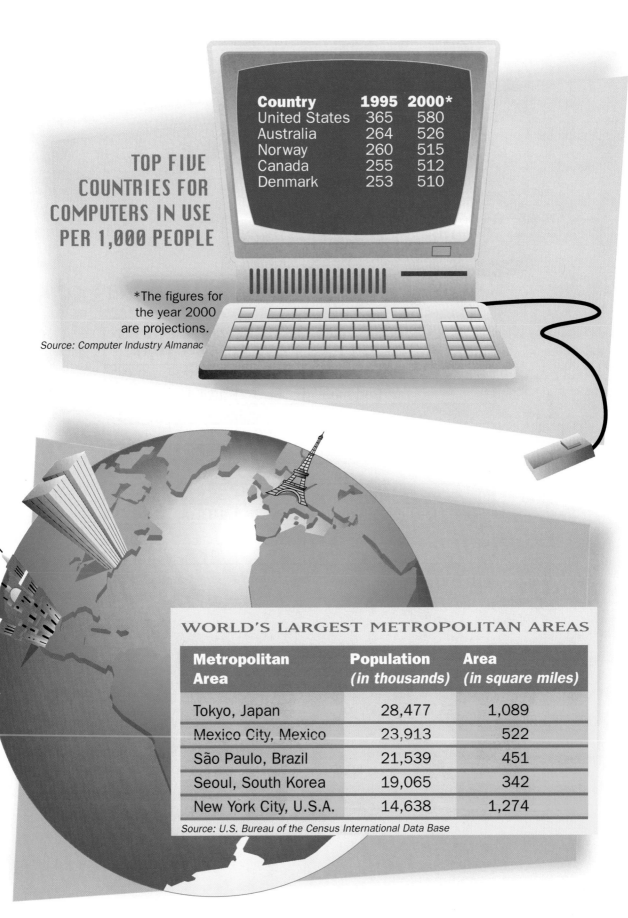

TOP FIVE COUNTRIES FOR COMPUTERS IN USE PER 1,000 PEOPLE

Country	1995	2000*
United States	365	580
Australia	264	526
Norway	260	515
Canada	255	512
Denmark	253	510

*The figures for the year 2000 are projections.

Source: Computer Industry Almanac

WORLD'S LARGEST METROPOLITAN AREAS

Metropolitan Area	Population (in thousands)	Area (in square miles)
Tokyo, Japan	28,477	1,089
Mexico City, Mexico	23,913	522
São Paulo, Brazil	21,539	451
Seoul, South Korea	19,065	342
New York City, U.S.A.	14,638	1,274

Source: U.S. Bureau of the Census International Data Base

U.S. CONSUMPTION OF PRINCIPAL FOODS PER PERSON PER YEAR (IN POUNDS)

Food	1993	1992	1991
Red meat	111.9	114.1	111.9
Poultry	61.1	60.0	58.0
Fish and shellfish	14.9	14.7	14.8
Cheese	26.2	26.0	25.0
Fruits	308.7	291.7	289.5
Vegetables	396.6	391.7	388.5
Flour and cereal products	189.2	187.0	184.4
Sugar	64.2	64.5	63.7
Ice cream	16.1	16.3	16.3

Playing Areas of Various Sports

Sport	Dimensions of Playing Area	Area
Volleyball	18 m x 9 m	162 m²
Softball	18.3 m x 18.3 m (infield diamond)	335 m²
Basketball	26 m x 14 m	364 m²
Baseball	27.4 m x 27.4 m (infield diamond)	751 m²
Ice hockey	61 m x 30.5 m	1,861 m²
U.S. football	109.7 m x 48.8 m	5,353 m²
Soccer	110 m x 75 m	8,250 m²

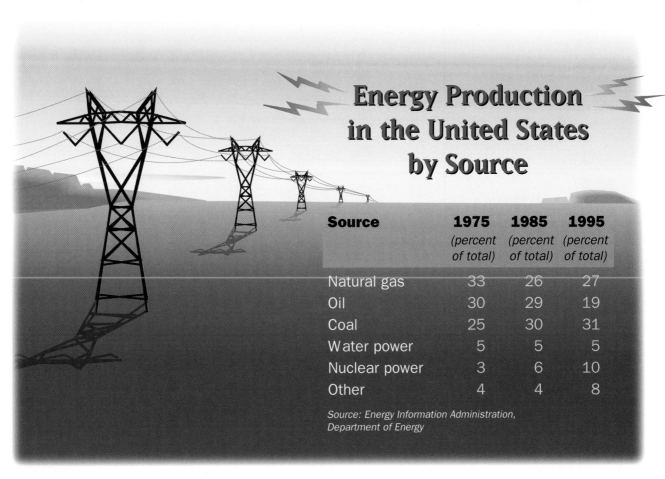

Energy Production in the United States by Source

Source	1975 (percent of total)	1985 (percent of total)	1995 (percent of total)
Natural gas	33	26	27
Oil	30	29	19
Coal	25	30	31
Water power	5	5	5
Nuclear power	3	6	10
Other	4	4	8

Source: Energy Information Administration, Department of Energy

Highest and Lowest Recorded Temperatures In U.S. For Each Month

	HIGHEST	**LOWEST**
January	98°F, Laredo, TX, 1936/1945	⁻70°F, Rogers Pass, MT, 1954
February	105°F, Montezuma, AZ, 1963	⁻66°F, Riverside Ranger Station, MT, 1933
March	108°F, Rio Grande City, TX, 1954	⁻50°F, Snake River, WY, 1906
April	118°F, Volcano Springs, CA, 1898	⁻36°F, Eagle Nest, NM, 1945
May	124°F, Salton, CA, 1896	⁻15°F, White Mountain, CA, 1964
June	129°F, Volcano Springs, CA, 1902	2°F, Tamarack, CA, 1907
July	134°F, Greenland Ranch, CA, 1913	10°F, Painter, WY, 1911
August	127°F, Greenland Ranch, CA, 1933	5°F, Bowen, MT, 1910
September	126°F, Mecca, CA, 1950	⁻70°F, Riverside Ranger Station, MT, 1926
October	116°F, Sentinel, AZ, 1917	⁻33°F, Soda Butte, WY, 1917
November	105°F, Craftonville, CA, 1906	⁻53°F, Lincoln, MT, 1959
December	100°F, La Mesa, CA, 1938	⁻59°F, Riverside Ranger Station, MT, 1924

Glossary

(*Italicized terms* are defined elsewhere in this glossary.)

acute angle An *angle* that has a measure of less than 90°.

acute triangle A triangle with three *acute angles.*

addend A number to be added.

adjacent angles Two angles that have the same *vertex* and a common side and have no common *interior points.*

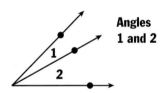

Angles
1 and 2

adjacent sides Two sides of a *polygon* that share a common *vertex.*

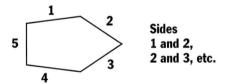

Sides
1 and 2,
2 and 3, etc.

algebraic expression An algebraic expression has one or more *variables.* It usually contains at least one number and one or more operations.

Example: 4 + *n*

angle A figure formed by two *rays* (sides) with the same *endpoint (vertex).* A *right angle* has a measure of 90°. An *acute angle* has a measure of less than 90°. An *obtuse angle* has a measure greater than 90° but less than 180°. A *straight angle* has a measure of 180°.

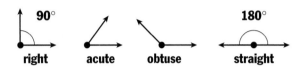

right acute obtuse straight

arc A part of a *circle* or curve between two *points.*

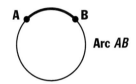

Arc *AB*

area The number of *square units* needed to cover a region or figure.

Associative Property When adding or multiplying, the grouping of *addends* or *factors* does not affect the result.
Examples: 3 + (4 + 5) = (3 + 4) + 5
2 x (4 x 3) = (2 x 4) x 3

average **a.** Another name for *mean.*
b. Average speed is found by dividing distance travelled by the travel time.

axis One of the two reference number lines on a graph.

bar graph A graph that displays *data* using bars.

base **a.** The number that is to be raised to a given power.
Example: In 2^3, the base is 2.

b. A side of a *polygon,* usually the one at the bottom in a given position.

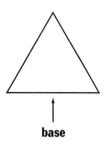

base

c. A *face* of a *3-dimensional figure,* usually the one on which it stands in a given position.

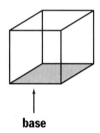

base

biased data Data collected in a survey from a *sample* that does not represent the *population* as a whole. For example, using basketball players as a sample to find the average height of an adult would produce biased data.

binary number system A system for representing numbers using the base two. The value of each place is a power of 2. The only digits used are 0 and 1.

bisect To divide into two *congruent* parts.

blueprints The design plans of a product or structure using actual dimensions that are scaled down or up to a size that is useful.

capacity The amount a container can hold.

cell Each individual box or *square* within the coordinate grid of an electronic *spreadsheet.*

center The *point* that is an equal distance from every point on a *circle.* (*See* circle.)

central angle An angle formed by two *radii* of a *circle.* (*See* circle.)

certain event An *event* that is certain to happen. Its *probability* is 1.

chord A *line segment* that connects two *points* on a *circle.* (*See* circle.)

circle A *2-dimensional figure* having all *points* an equal distance from a given point, called the *center.*

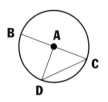

center: *A*

radii: $\overline{AB}, \overline{AC}, \overline{AD}$

diameter: $\overline{BC}$

chords: $\overline{BC}, \overline{DC}$

central angles: $\angle BAD,$ $\angle DAC, \angle BAC$

circle graph A graph in which *data* are represented by parts of a *circle.*

circumference The distance around a *circle.* The circumference is about 3 times the length of the *diameter.*

closed figure A *2-dimensional figure* that starts and ends at the same *point.*

clustering Estimating a *sum* by changing the *addends* that are close in *value* to one common number and then multiplying that number by the number of addends.

Example: 47 + 55 + 59   Estimate: 3 x 50 = 150

common denominator A *denominator* that is a *multiple* of the denominators of two or more *fractions.*

Example: 48 is a common denominator of $\frac{1}{12}$ and $\frac{1}{8}$.

common factor A number that is a *factor* of two or more numbers.

Example: 3 is a common factor of 6 and 15.

common multiple A number that is a *multiple* of two or more numbers.

Commutative Property When adding or multiplying, the order of *addends* or *factors* does not change the result.

Examples: 5 + 8 = 8 + 5   8 x 2 = 2 x 8

compatible numbers Two numbers that are close to the actual numbers and are easy to multiply or divide mentally.

Example:
1,323 ÷ 44 becomes 1,200 ÷ 40 = 30.

complement The set of possible *outcomes* that are not in an *event*. The sum of the *probability* of an event and its complement is 1.

complementary angles Two angles are complementary if the sum of their measures is 90°.

composite number A *whole number* greater than 1 that has *factors* other than itself and 1.
Example: 6 is a composite number. Its factors are 1, 2, 3, and 6.

compound figure A shape that is made up of two or more simpler shapes.

cone A *3-dimensional figure* with one curved surface, one *vertex,* and one circular *base.*

congruent angles *Angles* that have the same measure.

congruent figures Figures that have the same shape and size.

congruent line segments *Line segments* that have the same length.

coordinate One of the numbers in an *ordered pair.*

corresponding parts Matching parts of *congruent figures.*

Counting Principle The number of *outcomes* for an experiment with two or more stages is the product of the number of outcomes at each stage.

cross product In *equal ratios,* the result of multiplying the *numerator* of one fraction by the *denominator* of the other.

cross-sectional view The *2-dimensional figure* produced when you slice through a *3-dimensional figure.*

cube A rectangular *prism* all of whose *faces* are *squares.*

cubic centimeter (cm³) The *volume* of a *cube* with *edges* 1 cm long.

cubic unit A unit for measuring *volume.*
Examples: cubic inch (in.³), cubic centimeter (cm³)

cylinder A *3-dimensional figure* with one curved surface and two circular *bases.*

data Information.

decagon A *polygon* with ten sides and ten *angles.*

decimal A number expressed using a decimal point.
Examples: 3.0, 0.45, and 4.678

decimal places Places to the right of a decimal point.

degree (°) A unit used to measure *angles.*

denominator The number below the bar in a *fraction.*

diagonal A *line segment* other than a side that connects two *vertices* of a *polygon.*

diameter A *chord* that passes through the *center* of a *circle.* (See circle.)

discount The *percent* or amount off the original price of something that is on sale.

Distributive Property To multiply a *sum* by a number, you can multiply each *addend* by the number and add the *products.*
Example: 4 x (30 + 2) = (4 x 30) + (4 x 2)

dividend A number to be divided.

divisibility rule A rule that is used to tell whether one number is *divisible* by another.

divisible by One number is divisible by another if the *remainder* is 0 after dividing.

divisor The number by which a *dividend* is divided.

double-bar graph A graph that displays *data* using two sets of bars to show comparisons.

double-line graph A graph that displays *data* using two lines to show trends and changes over time.

edge A *line segment* where two *faces* of a *3-dimensional figure* meet.

endpoint A point at the end of a *ray* or a *line segment.*

equal ratios Two *ratios* are equal if *fractions* that represent them name the same number.
Example: $\frac{2}{3}$ and $\frac{10}{15}$ are equal ratios.

equally likely *Outcomes* are equally likely when they have the same *probability*.

equation A mathematical statement with an is-equal-to (=) sign in it.

equilateral triangle A triangle with three *congruent* sides.

equivalent decimals Decimals that name the same number.
Example: 1.3 = 1.30

equivalent fractions Fractions that name the same number.
Example: $\frac{1}{4} = \frac{2}{8} = \frac{3}{12}$

estimate To find a number that is close to the exact answer.

evaluate In an *algebraic expression*, to substitute *values* for the *variable* or variables.
Example:
If you evaluate $x + 3$ for $x = 5$, you get 8.

event A collection of one or more *outcomes* of a *probability* experiment.

expanded form A way of writing a number in terms of its digits.
Example:
7,456 = (7 x 1,000) + (4 x 100) + (5 x 10) + (6 x 1)

exponent The number which tells how many times the *base* is used as a *factor*.
Example:
In 2^3, 3 is the exponent. $2^3 = 2 \times 2 \times 2$

expression A combination of numbers and operational signs that may also include *variables*.

face A flat side of a *3-dimensional figure*.

factor A number that is multiplied to give a *product*.

factor form A number shown as the *product* of its *factors*.
Example: 60 = 2 × 2 × 3 × 5

factor tree A diagram used to find the *prime factors* of a number.

favorable outcomes In finding the *probability* of an *event*, the favorable outcomes are the outcomes that are in the event.
Example: If you are finding the probability of getting an even number when you toss a number cube, the favorable outcomes are 2, 4, and 6.

fluid ounce (fl oz) A customary unit of *capacity*. (*See* Table of Measures.)

foot (ft) A customary unit of length. (*See* Table of Measures.)

formula An *equation* with at least two *variables*, showing how one variable depends on one or more other variables.

fraction A number that names part of a whole or a part of a group.
Example: $\frac{2}{3}$ ← numerator
← denominator

frequency table A table for organizing a set of *data*, showing the number of times each item or number appears.

function A relationship in which one quantity depends on another quantity.

gram (g) A metric unit of *mass*. (*See* Table of Measures.)

greatest common factor (GCF) The greatest number that is a *common factor* of two or more numbers.
Example: 5 is the GCF of 15 and 20.

height of a parallelogram The length of a *line segment* from a side to the line *parallel* to that side, *perpendicular* to both of the sides.

height of a triangle The length of a *line segment* from a *vertex* to the side opposite the vertex, *perpendicular* to that side.

hexagon A *polygon* with six sides and six angles.

histogram A *bar graph* that shows the frequency of *data* for various intervals.

Identity Property When 0 is added to a number, the *sum* is the number. When 1 is multiplied by a number, the *product* is the number.

Examples: 0 + 2 = 2   1 x 4 = 4

impossible event An *event* that has no chance of occurring. Its *probability* is 0.

improper fraction A fraction with a *numerator* that is greater than or equal to the *denominator*.

inch (in.) A customary unit of length. (*See* Table of Measures.)

integer A whole number or its opposite.

interest An amount of money paid for the use of money.

intersecting lines Lines that meet or cross at a common *point*.

inverse operations Operations that "undo" each other.

Examples: addition and subtraction
multiplication and division

isosceles triangle A triangle with at least two *congruent* sides.

key The part of a *graph* that tells what the symbols in the graph represent. (*See* pictograph, bar graph, *and* line graph.)

kilogram (kg) A metric unit of *mass*. (*See* Table of Measures.)

kite A *quadrilateral* with two pairs of *adjacent congruent* sides.

least common denominator (LCD) The *least common multiple* of the *denominators* of two or more *fractions*.

Example: The LCD of $\frac{1}{3}$ and $\frac{3}{5}$ is 15 because the LCM of 3 and 5 is 15.

least common multiple (LCM) The least nonzero number that is a multiple of two or more numbers.

Example: multiples of 3: 3, 6, 9, 12, *15*, . . .
multiples of 5: 5, 10, *15*, 20, . . .
The LCM of 3 and 5 is 15.

less likely One *outcome* is less likely than another when the *probability* of the first is less than the probability of the second.

line A straight path that goes in two directions without end.

line graph A graph that uses one or more lines to show changes in *data*.

line of symmetry A line that divides a figure into two halves that match exactly.

line plot A vertical graph that shows *data* by using *x*s above a line.

What is Your Favorite Pet?

	x		
	x		
x	x		
x	x	x	
x	x	x	x
Dog	Cat	Fish	Snake

line segment A part of a line that has two *endpoints*.

liter (L) A metric unit of *capacity*. (*See* Table of Measures.)

mass The amount of matter in an object.

mean The mean of a set of numbers is found by adding the numbers and dividing their *sum* by the number of *addends*.

Example: 85 + 65 + 87 = 237
237 ÷ 3 = 79
79 is the mean.

median The middle number in a set of numbers arranged in order from least to greatest. If there is an even number of numbers, it is the *mean* of the two middle numbers.

Examples: The median of 42, 86, and 92 is 86. The median of 4, 7, 8, and 15 is 7.5.

meter The basic unit of length in the *metric system*. (*See* Table of Measures.)

metric system A *decimal* system of measurement whose basic units include *meter, liter,* and *kilogram.* (*See* Table of Measures.)

midpoint A point that divides a *line segment* into two *congruent* segments.

milliliter (mL) A metric unit of *capacity.* (*See* Table of Measures.)

mixed number A number greater than 1, such as $5\frac{1}{2}$, that has a *whole number* and a *fraction.*

mode The number or numbers that occur most often in a group of numbers.

more likely One *outcome* is more likely than another when the *probability* of the first is greater than the probability of the second.

multiple The *product* of a number and any *whole number.*

Example: The multiples of 3 are 0 (0 x 3), 3 (1 x 3), 6 (2 x 3), 9 (3 x 3), . . .

negative integer An *integer* less than zero.

numerator The number above the bar in a *fraction.*

numerical expression A combination of numbers and operational signs.

Example: 24 x 47

obtuse angle An *angle* that has a measure greater than 90° but less than 180°.

obtuse triangle A triangle with one *obtuse angle.*

octagon A *polygon* with eight sides and eight *angles.*

opposite integers Two integers that are the same distance from 0 on the number line.

Example: +8 and −8

ordered pair A pair of numbers that gives the location of a point on a graph, map, or grid.

Example: (4, 8) is an ordered pair. 4 and 8 are the *coordinates* of the ordered pair.

order of operations The proper sequence of operations: multiply or divide from left to right, then add or subtract from left to right.

origin The *point* in a graph where the vertical *axis* meets the horizontal axis.

ounce (oz) A customary unit of *weight.* (*See* Table of Measures.)

outcome A possible result in a *probability* experiment.

overestimate To find an approximate answer that is greater than the exact answer.

parallel lines Lines in the same plane that never intersect.

parallelogram A *quadrilateral* with opposite sides that are *parallel.* Each pair of opposite sides and *angles* is *congruent.*

pattern A series of numbers or figures that follows a rule.

Examples: 1, 3, 5, 7, 9, 11 . . .

pentagon A *polygon* with five sides and five *angles.*

percent (%) The *ratio* of a given number to 100, expressed with a percent sign.

Example: 7% means 7 out of 100, or $\frac{7}{100}$.

perimeter The distance around a *closed figure.*

permutation An arrangement of objects in a particular order.

Example: There are 6 permutations of the 3 letters A, B, and C: ABC, ACB, BAC, BCA, CAB, CBA.

perpendicular lines *Intersecting lines* that cross each other at *right angles.*

pi (π) The *ratio* of the *circumference* of a *circle* to its *diameter* (about 3.14 or $\frac{22}{7}$).

pictograph A graph that shows *data* by using picture symbols.

place The position of a digit in a number.
Example: In 41.79, the 7 is in the tenths place.

place value The *value* of a digit depends on its *place* in a number.
Example: In 3,248, the 2 is in the hundreds place and has a value of 200.

plane A flat surface that is endless in all directions.

point An exact location in space.

polygon A closed *2-dimensional figure* with sides that are *line segments.* The sides do not cross each other.

Polygon	Number of Sides and Vertices
triangle	3
quadrilateral	4
pentagon	5
hexagon	6
octagon	8
decagon	10

population The entire group about which information is gathered.

positive integer An *integer* greater than zero.

possible outcome Any of the results that could occur in a *probability* experiment.

power of ten A number obtained by raising 10 to an *exponent.*
Examples: $10^2 = 100$, $10^4 = 10,000$

prediction A general statement based on reasoning. A prediction may be based on the results of a survey.

prime factorization A name for a *composite number* that is a product of *prime numbers.*
Example: $12 = 2 \times 2 \times 3$

prime number A *whole number* greater than 1 with only itself and 1 as *factors.*
Example: 11 is a prime number. 2 is the only even number that is prime.

prism A *3-dimensional figure* with two *parallel congruent* bases. The rest of the faces are *rectangles* or *parallelograms.*

rectangular prism   **cube**   **triangular prism**   **hexagonal prism**

probability A number from 0 to 1 that measures the likelihood of an *event* occurring.

product The result of *multiplication.*

proportion A true statement that two *ratios* are equal.
Example: $\frac{2}{5} = \frac{6}{15}$

protractor An instrument used to draw and measure *angles.*

pyramid A *3-dimensional figure* having a *polygon* for its base and *triangles* for the rest of its *faces,* meeting at a point.

triangular pyramid   **square pyramid**   **rectangular pyramid**

quadrilateral A *polygon* with four sides and four *angles.*

quotient The result of *division.*

radius A *line segment* that connects a *point* on a *circle* with the *center.* (*See* circle.)

random sample A *sample* of people or items that are chosen by chance from a *population* to avoid *biased data.*

range The *difference* between the greatest and least numbers in a group of numbers.

rate A *ratio* that compares measurements or amounts.

ratio A comparison of two quantities.
Examples: 5 to 6, 5:6, or $\frac{5}{6}$

ray A part of a *line* that has one *endpoint* and continues without end in one direction.

reciprocals Two numbers whose *product* is 1.

Example: $\frac{1}{6}$ and $\frac{6}{1}$

rectangle A *parallelogram* with four *right angles*.

rectangular prism A *prism,* all of whose *faces* are *rectangles.*

rectangular pyramid A *pyramid* whose *base* is a *rectangle.*

reflection The mirror image of a figure about a *line of symmetry.*

regular polygon A polygon with all sides *congruent* and all angles *congruent.*

regular tessellation A *tessellation* formed by regular *polygons.*

remainder In *division,* the number left after the *quotient* is found.

rename To express a number in a different way—for example, to write $10\frac{1}{2}$ as 10.5 or $\frac{21}{2}$.

repeating decimal A decimal with a pattern of repeating digits that continues indefinitely.

Example: 2.3454545. . .

representative sample A *random sample* large enough or typical enough to be used to make *predictions* about the entire *population.*

rhombus A *parallelogram* with four *congruent* sides.

right angle An *angle* that has a measure of exactly 90°.

right triangle A triangle with one *right angle.*

rotation In a rotation, the original figure is rotated around a *point.*

sale price The amount to be paid for an item after a *discount* has been subtracted.

sample The part of a *population* that is used in a survey to represent the whole population.

scale a. The *axis* of a graph that is divided into units at regularly spaced intervals. **b.** Numbers that tell how distances are represented on a map.

Example: 1 inch = 50 miles

scale drawing A reduced or enlarged drawing of an actual object.

scalene triangle A triangle with no *congruent* sides.

scatter plot A graph comparing two sets of *data* to determine the correlation between the two.

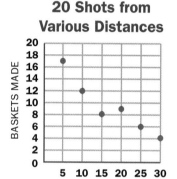

20 Shots from Various Distances

similar figures Figures that have the same shape but not necessarily the same size.

simplest form A *fraction* is in simplest form if the *numerator* and *denominator* have no common *factor* other than 1.

simulation A method of solving a problem by doing an experiment that is similar to the situation in the problem.

skew lines Any lines in space that do not *intersect* and are not *parallel.*

sphere A *3-dimensional figure* that is the set of all points that are an equal distance from a given point.

spreadsheet A computer program that arranges *data* and formulas in a table of *cells.*

square A *rectangle* with four *congruent* sides.

square pyramid A *pyramid* whose *base* is a *square*.

square unit A unit for measuring *area*.
Examples: *square inch (in.²), square foot (ft²), square centimeter (cm²), and square meter (m²).*

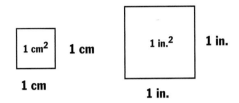

standard form The usual way to write a number.
Example: 23

statistics The science of collecting, organizing, and analyzing *data.*

stem-and-leaf plot The arrangement of *data* with numbers separated, for example, into tens and ones, with tens lined up in a stem formation and ones branching off to the side like leaves.

Stems	Leaves	
2	1 2 4 7	(21, 22, 24, 27)
3	5 6 7	(35, 36, 37)
4	0 5	(40, 45)

straight angle An *angle* that has a measure of exactly 180°.

sum The result of addition.

supplementary angles Two angles are supplementary if the *sum* of their *measures* is 180°.

surface area The total area of the surface of a *3-dimensional figure.*

symmetric A figure is symmetric if it can be folded along a *line* so that the resulting halves match exactly, or are *congruent.*

tessellation An arrangement of repeated shapes that cover an area without any overlaps or gaps.

3-dimensional figure A figure that has length, width, and height. (*See also* prism and pyramid.)

cone   cylinder   sphere

translation In a translation, the original figure is moved horizontally, vertically, or diagonally.

trapezoid A *quadrilateral* with exactly one pair of *parallel* sides.

tree diagram A diagram used to show combinations of things.

triangle A *polygon* with three sides and three *angles.*

triangular prism A *prism* with two parallel, congruent *bases* that are *triangles.*

triangular pyramid A *pyramid* whose *base* is a *triangle.*

2-dimensional figure A figure that has only length and width.

Examples: angles, polygons, circles

underestimate To find an approximate answer that is less than the exact answer.

unit fraction A *fraction* with a *numerator* of 1.
Example: $\frac{1}{5}$

unit price The cost of a single item or the cost per unit of volume or weight.

unit rate A *rate* in which the second measurement is 1 unit.
Examples: 7 meters per second; $6.25 per hour

value The number obtained by substituting a specific number for a *variable* in an *algebraic expression.*

Example: For $x = 2$, the value of $x + 5$ is 7.

variable A symbol used to represent a number or group of numbers.

Venn diagram A way to organize and show *data* by using overlapping *circles*.

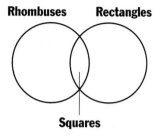

vertex The common *point* of the two *rays* of an *angle*, two sides of a *polygon*, or three or more *edges* of a *3-dimensional figure*.

volume The amount of space enclosed by a *3-dimensional figure*, measured in *cubic units*.

weight The measure of how heavy something is.

whole number Any one of the numbers 0, 1, 2, 3, 4, 5, 6, . . .

zero pair A pair of positive and negative *integers* whose *sum* is zero.

Zero Property When one *factor* is zero, the *product* is zero.

Table of Measures

Metric Units

LENGTH
1 millimeter (mm) = 0.001 meter (m)
1 centimeter (cm) = 0.01 meter
1 decimeter (dm) = 0.1 meter
1 dekameter (dam) = 10 meters
1 hectometer (hm) = 100 meters
1 kilometer (km) = 1,000 meters

MASS/WEIGHT
1 milligram (mg) = 0.001 gram (g)
1 centigram (cg) = 0.01 gram
1 decigram (dg) = 0.1 gram
1 dekagram (dag) = 10 grams
1 hectogram (hg) = 100 grams
1 kilogram (kg) = 1,000 grams
1 metric ton (t) = 1,000 kilograms

CAPACITY
1 milliliter (mL) = 0.001 liter (L)
1 centiliter (cL) = 0.01 liter
1 deciliter (dL) = 0.1 liter
1 dekaliter (daL) = 10 liters
1 hectoliter (hL) = 100 liters
1 kiloliter (kL) = 1,000 liters

AREA
1 square centimeter (cm2) = 100 square millimeters (mm2)
1 square meter (m2) = 10,000 square centimeters
1 hectare (ha) = 10,000 square meters
1 square kilometer (km2) = 1,000,000 square meters

Customary Units

LENGTH
1 foot (ft) = 12 inches (in.)
1 yard (yd) = 36 inches
1 yard = 3 feet
1 mile (mi) = 5,280 feet
1 mile = 1,760 yards

WEIGHT
1 pound (lb) = 16 ounces (oz)
1 ton (T) = 2,000 pounds

CAPACITY
1 cup (c) = 8 fluid ounces (fl oz)
1 pint (pt) = 2 cups
1 quart (qt) = 2 pints
1 quart = 4 cups
1 gallon (gal) = 4 quarts

AREA
1 square foot (ft2) = 144 square inches (in.2)
1 square yard (yd2) = 9 square feet
1 acre = 43,560 square feet
1 square mile (mi2) = 640 acres

TIME
1 minute (min) = 60 seconds (s)
1 hour (h) = 60 minutes
1 day (d) = 24 hours
1 week (wk) = 7 days
1 year (y) = 12 months (mo)
1 year = about 52 weeks
1 year = 365 days
1 century (c) = 100 years

Formulas

$P = 2(\ell + w)$	Perimeter of a rectangle
$P = 4s$	Perimeter of a square
$A = \ell \times w$	Area of a rectangle
$A = s \times s$, or s^2	Area of a square
$A = b \times h$	Area of a parallelogram
$A = \frac{1}{2}(b \times h)$	Area of a triangle

$C = \pi \times d$, or $2 \times \pi \times r$	Circumference of a circle
$A = \pi \times r^2$	Area of a circle
$V = \ell \times w \times h$	Volume of a rectangular prism
$V = B \times h$	Volume of any prism
$V = \pi \times r^2 \times h$	Volume of a cylinder

Symbols

=	is equal to	$1.\overline{3}$	repeating decimal 1.333...	$\triangle ABC$	triangle ABC
≠	is not equal to	%	percent	‖	is parallel to
>	is greater than	π	pi (approximately 3.14)	⊥	is perpendicular to
<	is less than	°	degree	2:5	ratio of 2 to 5
≥	is greater than or equal to	°C	degree Celsius	10^2	ten to the second power
≤	is less than or equal to	°F	degree Fahrenheit	$^+4$	positive 4
≈	is approximately equal to	$\overleftrightarrow{AB}$	line AB	$^-4$	negative 4
≅	is congruent to	$\overline{AB}$	line segment AB	$|^-4|$	absolute value of $^-4$
~	is similar to	$\overrightarrow{AB}$	ray AB	$(^+3, ^-4)$	ordered pair 3, $^-4$
...	continues without end	$\angle ABC$	angle ABC	$P(E)$	probability of event E

Index

A

Acute angles, 300–303, 314
Acute triangles, 306–309, 314
Addition
  applying, 66–67
  associative property of, 56–57, 59, 229, 271
  commutative property of, 56–57, 59, 271
  decimals in, 56–59, 64, 80–81, 95, 129, 149, 221, 285
  equations, 364–366, 376–377, 560–563, 568–569
  estimating sums, 54–55, 64, 76–81, 216–219, 230
  front end, 65
  expressions, 70–71
  fractions
    and mixed numbers, 226–230, 240, 246–247
    like fractions, 220–221, 230, 246–247
    unlike fractions, 222–223, 230, 246–247
  identity property of, 56–57
  in measurement, 310-311, 330-331
  mental math in, 45, 54–55, 59, 216–221, 230
  of integers, 542-545, 552
  of ratios, 387
  whole numbers in, 42–70
  zero property of, 56–57, 229, 271
Addition equations, solving, 364–367, 376–377, 560–563
Addition properties, 56–57, 59, 229, 271
Additions, equal, 56–57
Algebra
  addition and subtraction equations, 364–367, 376–377, 560–563
  addition and subtraction expressions, 70–71
  applying, 358–359, 554–555
  balanced equations, 360-361, 364-371
  bottle functions, 397
  coordinate graphing, 344–352, 556–559
  describing change, 348–349
  equations, 342-343, 360–370, 376–377
  functions, 342–349, 376–377, 397
  graphing functions, 344–349, 376–377, 556–558
  integers, 538–549, 553
  introduction to, 342–381
  inverse operations, 364–367, 376–377
  multiplication and division equations, 368–370, 376–377
  multiplication and division expressions, 134–135
  order of operations, 136–137, 225, 264, 279
  parentheses in, 136–137
  patterns, relations, and functions, 42–45, 58, 71, 88–91, 124–126, 140, 148–150, 152, 234–235, 247, 267, 269, 275, 309, 330–333, 335, 426, 427, 495, 503, 545, 553
  problem solving in, 350–353
  solving equations, 360–367, 376–377
  using graphs in, 344–353

  variables, 70–71, 271, 350–352, 360–370
  writing equations, 342–352, 366–367
Algebra, applying strategies for, 58, 62, 90, 129, 149, 152, 156, 176, 221, 225, 229, 257, 264, 269, 279, 281, 389, 401, 434, 498, 504, 520, 524, 538, 540, 542, 544, 546, 556, 560
Algebra sense, developing
  another way to find the LCM, 185
  bottle functions, 397
  properties of addition and multiplication, 271
Alternate solution methods, using, 444–445. See also Problem-solving skills and strategies.
Angles
  acute, 300–303, 314
  bisecting, 318–321
  central, 322–323
  complementary, 303
  congruent, 318–321
  constructions of, 318–321
  corresponding, 404–405
  degrees in, 300–303, 308, 310-311, 314, 318-321, 330-331, 404-405
  estimating, 300–303, 314
  measuring, 300–303, 308, 310-311, 314, 330-331
  missing, 311, 409
  obtuse, 300–303, 314
  right, 300–303, 304, 314
  straight, 300–303, 314
  sums of, 310–311, 330-331
  supplementary, 303
Arcs, 310–311, 318–321
Area
  of circles, 502–505
  of compound figures, 506–507
  of irregular figures, 506–507
  of parallelograms and triangles, 496–497, 502-503
  of rectangles, 494–495, 506–507
  of trapezoids, 499
  rectangles, 506–507
  relating perimeter and, 492–493, 510–511, 530-531, 541
  square miles and, 84-85
  sum of, 518–521
  surface, 518–521
  using, 510–511
Associative property
  of addition, 56–57, 59, 229, 271
  of multiplication, 88–90, 101, 271
Axes, 6–7, 22, 344–351, 359, 437, 556–558

B

Bar graphs, 6–9, 18, 23, 24, 32–35, 37, 79, 85, 207, 289, 437, 441, 489, 573
Bases (numbers) of exponents, 42–44, 80–81
Bases (sides) of shapes, 496–498, 502-503, 521, 522-525
Base- ten, 380-381
Base-two, 380-381

Benchmarks, 432-435
Biased data, 28–29
Billions, 46–47
Binary numbers, 380-381
Bisecting, 318–321
Bisector, 318–321
Blueprints, 272–273

C

Calculation methods, choosing, 128, 136, 198, 222, 224, 228, 238, 262, 272, 280, 545, 549
Calculators, 11–13, 15, 17, 25, 27, 35, 42, 43, 45, 53, 55–57, 59–61, 63, 69, 71, 73, 75, 81, 91, 93-95, 97, 99, 107–108, 115, 127–129, 133, 135, 136, 137, 139, 145, 147, 149, 152, 155, 157, 159, 165, 172-173, 176, 179, 181, 183–184, 189, 193, 195, 197, 199, 201, 203, 209, 221-223, 224–225, 229, 235, 240, 257, 260, 265, 267–269, 275, 278–281, 283, 285, 291, 303, 305, 309, 313, 321, 323, 325, 327, 335, 341, 346, 349, 355, 363, 367, 371, 377, 387, 389, 393, 395, 403, 407, 409, 415, 428, 435, 437, 443, 445, 449, 455, 465, 467, 469, 475, 479, 485, 493, 499, 507, 513, 515, 521, 525, 531, 541, 545, 549, 551, 563, 569
  adding integers on, 545
  subtracting integers on, 549
  using a fraction calculator, 222, 224, 228, 238–239, 262, 268, 278, 280
  using integer division key, 128
  using to find standard forms of numbers, 43
  using to simplify fractions, 195
Capacity, 74-75, 284–285
Careers,
  architect, 300
  automobile road tester, 154
  cordwainer, 278
  dance academy director, 190
  engineer, 494
  marine biologist, 74
  market researcher, 12
  marketing executive, 436
  meteorologist, 556
  mountain biker, 220
  speleologist, 408
  treasury analyst, 106
  veterinarian, 364
Celsius degrees, 350-351, 540–541, 545, 552-555, 572-573
Center of circles, 322–323
Centimeter (cm), 72–73, 80–81, 158–159, 358-359, 492–495, 522–526, 529, 534-535
Changing rates, 393
Changing units of measurement, 72–75, 158–159
Chapter review, 34–35, 80–81, 114–115, 164–165, 208–209, 246–247, 290–291, 334–335, 376–377, 414–415, 454–455, 484–485,

530–531, 568–569

Chapter test, 36, 82, 116, 166, 210, 248, 292, 336, 378, 416, 456, 486, 532, 570

Choosing the appropriate graph, 30–33

Choosing to use fractions or decimals, 286–289

Chord of circle, 322–323

Circle graphs, 207, 441, 446–448, 453

Circles
  area of, 502–505
  center of, 322–323
  chord of, 322–323
  circumference of, 500–503. 512-513. 541
  diameter of, 322–323
  radius, 322–323, 500–504

Circumference, 500–503, 512–513, 541

Closed figures, 298–299

Common denominators, 216–229, 238–239

Common factors, 178–179, 184, 185, 194–197

Common multiples, 180–181, 185

Commutative property
  of addition, 56–57, 59, 229, 271
  of multiplication, 88–90, 101, 271

Comparing
  decimals, 52–53, 64, 80–81, 93, 159, 223
  fractions and mixed numbers, 196–197, 208–209
  graphs, 19, 33
  integers, 540–541, 552
  measurements, 38-39
  numerators and denominators, 216-218
  sets of data, 6-7, 20-21, 22-23, 38-39

Compass, drawing with, 310–311, 318–323

Compatible numbers, 93, 125–126, 164, 266–267

Complementary angles, 303

Complements of events, 467

Composite numbers, 174–177

Compound figures, area of, 506–507

Computers
  bar graph, 85, 289, 419, 489
  binary numbers, 380-381
  calculating volume on, 529
  circle graphs, 453
  coloring shapes, 207
  copying figures that represent fractions, 207
  creating irregular and regular tessellations, 333
  designing a chair, 339
  double-bar graphs, 79
  drawing programs, using, 207, 245, 333, 339, 535
  finding the patterns of an ordered pair, 567
  geometric figures, 245
  graphing programs, using, 19, 33, 39, 79, 85, 357, 419, 453, 483, 489
  line graphs, 357, 483
  linking tables and graphs, 357
  making tables, 357. 567
  probability simulation, 471, 483
  spreadsheets, 113, 119, 141, 163, 169, 213, 251, 295, 357, 375, 381, 413, 471, 529
  using a probability tool, 471

Concave polygons, 298–299, 301

Conclusions, drawing, 22–27

Conducting a simulation, 468–469, 471, 472-473

Cones, 514–515

Congruence, 306–309, 318–321, 499,

518-521, 525

Congruent angles, 318–321

Congruent figures, 318–321

Congruent line segments, 318–321

Congruent sides, 306-309

Congruent squares, 509

Consumer math, 32, 56–59, 65, 72–77, 87-119,142-143, 183, 204–207, 241-245, 257, 260, 268–269, 286–289, 352, 390–395, 424–459

Constructions, 318–321

Converting customary measures, 282–285

Converting metric measures, 72–75, 158–159

Convex polygons, 298–299, 301

Cooperative learning
  decision making, 15, 21, 25, 45, 55, 67, 71, 75, 76, 91, 95, 99, 103, 108, 133, 143, 179, 187, 193, 233, 269, 273, 283, 317, 323, 359, 363, 371, 375, 387, 393, 395, 399, 403, 410, 441, 445, 450, 473, 480, 483, 499, 511, 515, 555
  sharing problems, 31, 77, 111, 161, 205, 243, 287, 331, 373, 411, 451, 481, 527, 565
  talking it over, 2, 6, 12, 22, 42, 48, 56, 60, 88, 106, 124, 130, 144, 150, 154, 174, 190, 200, 216, 238, 258, 262, 300, 306, 318, 344, 350, 360, 364, 368, 384, 390, 404, 426, 432, 446, 462, 476, 496, 502, 522, 542, 546, 556, 560
  working together, 2, 12, 21, 28, 42, 66–67, 104, 110–111, 150, 153, 174, 190, 204, 226, 236, 242–243, 258, 276, 286, 298, 300, 310, 316, 328, 330, 342, 347, 360, 372, 384, 398, 400, 404, 410, 424, 430, 450, 462, 480, 494, 500, 502, 509, 516, 518, 522, 526, 538, 542, 546, 560, 564 *See also* Problem solvers at work, Math/science/ technology connections, Real-life investigations.

Coordinate graphs, 344–352, 397, 556–559, 567

Coordinate grids, 344–345, 347–349, 556–557, 567

Coordinates of points, 344–347, 556–557

Correlations, positive or negative, 20–21

Corresponding angles, 404–405

Corresponding sides, 404–406

Counting principle, 476–479

Critical thinking
  analyzing, 13, 16, 43, 46, 49, 52, 54, 57, 68, 70, 72, 74, 80, 92, 94, 98, 125, 128, 134, 136, 138, 145, 151, 155, 165, 172, 188, 196, 198, 217, 220, 222, 224, 227–228, 234, 237, 239, 280, 284, 291, 307, 329, 335, 343, 345, 348, 351, 353, 354, 361, 365, 377, 385, 389, 391, 402, 405, 408, 425, 427, 431, 433, 436, 442, 444, 455, 463, 466, 474, 477, 485, 492, 495, 501, 506, 512, 514, 517–518, 523, 531, 539, 547, 550, 557, 569
  comparing, 266, 274,447
  generalizing, 7, 10, 23, 26, 29, 35, 61, 89, 96, 105, 107, 148, 158, 178, 180, 191, 201, 209, 263, 268, 277, 299, 301, 311, 312, 319, 322, 324, 326, 357, 394, 401, 415, 471, 492, 503, 540, 542
  predicting, 304, 468
  summarizing, 175, 182, 194, 256, 259, 278, 282, 388, 497, 519, 561

Cross products, 400–403

Cross sections, 521

Cubes, 514–518

Cubic centimeter, 522–527

Cubic feet, 294-295

Cubic units, 522–527

Cultural connections
  Ancient Chinese rod numerals, 563
  Ancient Egyptian division, 133
  Ancient Egyptian numerals, 47
  Australian coins, 97
  Calculating, 505
  Census, 449
  Cubits, palms, digits, 265
  Egyptian fractions, 225
  Geometric patterns in Native American art, 321
  Golden ratios and golden rectangles, 407
  Igba-Ego, 465
  Pascal's triangle, 367
  Quipu, 5
  Sieve of Eratosthenes, 181

Cultural notes, 2,38, 42, 61, 84, 88, 96, 106, 168, 118, 138, 168, 172, 196, 212, 217, 250, 268, 294, 315, 322, 338, 360, 380, 397, 418, 424, 432, 458, 462, 474, 488, 492, 506, 510, 534, 542

Cumulative review, 120–121, 252–253, 420–421, 574–575

Cup (c), 284–285

Curriculum connections, 38–39, 84–85, 118–119, 168–169, 212–213, 250–251, 294–295, 338–339, 380–381, 418–419, 458–459, 488–489, 534–535, 572–573

Curved graphs, 347

Customary units of measurement
  applying fractions to, 282–285, 419
  capacity and weight, 284–285
  length, 282–283, 338-339, 518-519

Cylinders, 514–515, 525

D

Data, cluster, 2–5, 32

Data collection and analysis, 2–13, 16–35, 66–67,79, 84-85, 102–103, 113, 119, 141-143, 160–161, 163, 168-169, 213, 232-233, 251, 289, 295, 357, 358-359, 372–375, 381, 410–413, 440-441, 446–448, 450–453, 459, 480–483, 489, 510–511, 529, 563, 564–567, 572-573

Data, organizing
  bar graphs, 6–9, 18,23, 24, 32–35, 37, 79, 85, 207, 289, 441
    double-bar graphs, 6–9, 18, 30, 37, 79, 375
  circle graphs, 207, 441, 446–448, 453
  choosing the appropriate graph, 30–33
  coordinate graphs, 344–352, 397, 556–559, 567
  databases, 19
  diagrams, 186, 245, 304-305, 331, 476-479, 497, 512-513 ,538, 550–551
  displaying data, 2–5, 34–35
  frequency tables, 2–5, 9, 462–464
  function tables, 342–347, 498, 544, 556–558
  line graphs, 22–25, 34–35, 209, 357, 483, 555
    double-line graphs, 22–25, 34–35
  line plots, 2–5, 7, 17, 63, 197
  pictographs, 2–5, 7, 51
  scatter plots, 20–21

spreadsheets, 113, 119, 141, 163, 169, 213, 251, 295, 357, 375, 381, 413, 471, 529

stem-and-leaf plots/double stem-and-leaf plots, 26–27, 34–35

tables, 2–5, 9, 16–17, 42, 79, 85, 113, 169, 342–347, 459, 462–465, 480–483, 498, 544, 556–558, 567, 573

Data Point, 5, 17, 25, 45, 63, 75, 95, 99, 108, 139, 147, 176, 203, 219, 265, 267, 309, 327, 346, 367, 393, 403, 437, 449, 475, 525, 529, 549, 563, 567

Databank, 632–642

Decimals

addition of, 56–59, 64, 75, 80–81, 95, 129, 149, 221, 285

applying, 72–75

choosing to use fractions or, 286–289

comparing, 52–53, 80–81

connecting with mixed numbers and fractions, 200–203

density property in, 53

division by, 150–157, 164–165

division by whole numbers, 144–146, 164–165

equivalent, 48–50, 52–53, 56–57, 61

estimating products, 92–93, 96-97, 100

estimating quotients, 128–132

estimating sums and differences of, 54–55, 64, 80–81

fractions and, 200–203, 426–429, 438, 454–455

front-end estimation and, 65

greater than 1, 200–201

in money amounts, 98–99

measurement and, 72–75

mental math, 148–149

mixed numbers and, 200–203

multiplication of, 104–109, 114–115, 285

by decimals, 104–105

multiplication of whole numbers, 96–97, 100, 114–115

ordering, 52–53, 64

patterns, 148–149

percents and, 426–429, 432–434, 438, 454–455

place value and, 48–51

points, 56–58, 60–61, 96–97, 104–107, 144–146, 148–149, 154–155

renaming, 200-203

repeating, 157, 201

rounding, 54–55, 189, 200–203, 349, 434, 436–437, 442–443, 508, 520, 524–525

standard forms of, 48–50

subtraction of, 60–64, 75, 80–81, 221, 285

understanding, 48–50

using money to model, 48–50

words names of, 48–50

writing as fractions or mixed numbers, 48–50

zeros with, 49

Decision making, 15, 21, 25, 45, 55, 67, 71, 75, 76, 91, 95, 99, 103, 108, 133, 143, 179, 187, 193, 233, 269, 273, 283, 317, 323, 359, 363, 371, 375, 387, 393, 395, 399, 403, 410, 441, 445, 450, 473, 480, 483, 499, 511, 515, 555

Degrees, in angles, 300–303, 308, 314

Denominators, 188-202, 216-228, 236-240, 262-265, 276-279, 388-389, 400-401, 426-427

in fractions, 188–201, 208–209, 216–217, 220–223, 256–265, 276–279

division of fractions, 278–279

multiplication of fractions, 256–265

writing percent as fractions, 426-429

Describing change, 348-349

Diagonals, 330-331

Diagrams

interpreting/using, 304–305, 497, 538

tree, 476–479

Venn, 550–551

Diameter, 322–323, 500-501, 512–513

Discounts, 442–443

Differences

estimating by front-end estimation, 65

estimating with decimals, 54–55, 80–81

estimating with fractions, 216–219

of like and unlike fractions, 220–223

Distributive property of multiplication, 89–90, 100–101, 271

Dividends, 124–125, 150–151, 153–155, 280–281

Divisibility, 172–173, 184, 186–187, 194-195

by four, 173

rules for, 172–173

Division

adjusting estimates in, 130–131

applying, 142–143, 186–187

by decimals, 144–146, 150–155, 164–165

by four, 173

by multiples of 10, 124–125, 150–151, 154–155

by one-digit divisors, 128–129, 140, 164–165

by powers of 10, 148–149, 151, 154–155

by two-digit divisors, 130–133, 140, 164–165

by whole numbers, 144–146, 164–165

divisibility rules for, 172–173

equations, 268–271

estimating quotients, 124–132, 144–146, 164–165

expressions, 134–135

fractions, 276–279, 290-291, 309

interpreting quotients and remainders, 160–163

mental math in, 124–126, 140, 148–149

of decimals, 144-147

patterns in, 124–126, 148–149

quotients as whole numbers, 172–173

relating multiplication and, 134–135, 148–149, 158–159, 276, 368–371

remainders of 0, 172–173

to change measurements, 158–159

using models in, 144–146, 150–151, 276–277

whole numbers, 94–97, 128–133, 144–146

with fractions, 278–279, 290–291

with mixed numbers, 280–281, 290–291, 325

zeros in, 135, 140, 145, 154–155, 172-173

Division equations, solving, 368–371

Divisors, 124–125, 128–129, 130–133, 140, 150–151, 164–165, 280–281

Double-bar graphs, 6–9, 18, 30, 37, 79

Double-line graphs, 22–25, 32, 34–35

Double stem-and-leaf plot, 26–27, 34–35

Drawings, using data from, 526–529

Edges of figures, 514–515

Eighth inch, 282–283

Endpoints, 300–303, 318–321

Equal ratios, 388, 396, 400–401, 414-415

Equations

addition and subtraction, 360–362, 364–367, 560–563

balanced, 364–367

inverse operations in, 364–365

multiplication and division, 360–362, 368–371

proportions, 400–401

two-step, 371

understanding, 342–343, 347

with integers, 560–562

writing and solving, 360–370, 402–403

Equilateral triangles, 306–309

Equivalent decimals, 48–50, 52-53, 56–57, 61

Equivalent fractions, 190–193, 196–197, 228–229, 238–239, 426-428

Estimating/estimation,

angles, 300–303, 314, 334–335

a tip, 435

compatible numbers, 124–126, 266–267

decimal products, 92–93, 96–97, 100

differences, 54–55, 216–219

fraction products, 266–267

fraction sums and differences, 216–219, 223

front-end, 65

products, 92–997, 114–115, 118–119, 266–267

quotients, 124–132, 140, 144–146, 154–157, 164–165

rounding and, 54–55, 92–93, 96–97, 100, 114–115, 216–219, 266–267

sums, 54–55, 58, 64, 76–81, 216–219

underestimates and overestimates, 110–113

using for problem solving, 76–79

with percents, 430-435, 439, 442–443

Events

certain, 466–467

complement of, 467

impossible, 466–467

probabilities, 462–467, 474–475

Expanded forms, 46–47, 137

Experiments conducting, 84-85

Explore activities

algebra/adding integers, 542–545

algebra/addition and subtraction equations, 560–563

algebra/functions, 342–343

algebra/integers, 538–539

algebra/solve equations, 360–363

algebra/subtracting integers, 546–549

decimals/dividing by decimals, 150–153

decimals/multiplying decimals by decimals, 104–105

exponents, 42–45

fractions/adding mixed numbers, 226–227

fractions/dividing fractions, 276–277

fractions/equivalent fractions, 190–193

fractions/multiplying fractions, 258–261

fractions/subtracting mixed numbers, 236–237

geometry/classify 3-dimensional figures, 514–515

geometry/classifying 2-dimensional shapes, 298–299

geometry/different views of 3-dimensional shapes, 516–517

geometry/sums of angles, 310–311

geometry/tessellations, 328–329

measurement/area of a circle, 502–505

measurement/circumference of a circle, 500–501

measurement/enlarging rectangles, 494–495
measurement/surface area: prism, 518–521
measurement/volume, 522–525
percent, 424–425
percent/percent of a number, 430–431
prime factorization, 174–177
probability 462–465
proportions, 400–401
proportion/similar figures, 404–407
ratio/understanding ratios, 384–387
statistics/collect, organize, and display data, 2–3
statistics/mean, 12–15
statistics/sampling and predicting, 28–29
Exponents, 42–45, 64, 136-137
Expressing quotients, 204–207
Expressions, 70–71, 134–135
  addition and subtraction, 70–71
  evaluating, 70–71
  multiplication and division, 134–135
Extra practice, 576–631

Faces of figures, 514–515
Factor forms, 42–44
Factor tree, 174–176
Factorization, prime, 174–180, 184–185
Factors
  common, 178–179, 184–185, 194–197
  greatest common, 178–179, 184–185, 194–197
Fahrenheit degrees, 350-351, 538–541, 545, 552–555, 562, 564–567, 572-573
Figures
  areas of compound, 506–507
  closed, 298–299
  concave or convex, 298-299
  congruent, 318–321
  different views of 3-dimensional figures, 516–517
  drawing, 325, 326
  faces and sides of, 514–515
  geometric, 298–333, 514–519
  symmetrical, 326–327
Finding a pattern, 234–235, 330–333. *See also* Patterns, identifying, relations and functions; Problem-solving skills and strategies.
Finding missing or extra information, 242–245
Fluid ounces (fl oz), 284–285
Foot (ft), 282–283. 294–295, 518–519
Formulas, using, 138–139, 350–352, 437, 492–493, 496–497, 500–503, 518–519, 522–523, 525. *See also* Problem-solving skills and strategies.
Fractions
  adding like, 220–221, 230, 246-247
  adding mixed numbers and, 226–230, 240, 246–247
  adding unlike, 222–223, 230, 246–247
  applying, 232–233, 272–273, 282–285
  comparing and ordering, 196–197, 208–209
  compatible numbers and, 266–267
  decimals and, 200–203, 208–209
  density property of, 203
  differences of, 216–221, 224–225, 230
  division of, 276–277, 290–291, 309
  division with, 278–279, 290–291
  division with mixed numbers, 280–281, 290–291

equivalent, 190–193, 196–197, 228–229, 426–428
estimating products, 266–267
estimating sums and differences, 216–219, 230
finding a fraction of a whole number, 256–257
improper, 198–199, 213
measurement and, 282–285
mental math and, 192, 197, 216-219, 256–257, 266–267, 271
mixed numbers and, 198–203, 208–209, 226–230, 240
multiplication by, 262–265, 270, 290–291
multiplication of, 258–261, 270, 272–273, 290–291
multiplication of mixed numbers and, 268–270
naming parts of a set or region, 188–189
number theory and, 188–299
ordering, 196–197, 208–209
percents, 426–428, 432–434
renaming, 430–431, 436–438
rounding, 216–219, 230, 266–267
simplest form of, 194–195, 202, 208–209, 262–263, 268–269, 278–281, 426–428
subtracting like, 220–221, 230
subtracting mixed numbers and, 236–241, 246–247
subtracting unlike, 224–225, 230
understanding, 188–189, 208–209
using models, 188–192, 276–277
zeros in, 216–218
Frequency ratio, 213
Frequency tables, 2–5, 9, 462–464
Front-end estimation, 65
Function tables, 342–347, 376–377, 498, 544, 556–558
Functions, 342–347, 350-351, 376–377, 498, 544, 556–558

Gallon (gal), 284–285
Games
  Decimal concentration, 51
  Finding a path, 153
  Find the figure, 559
  Four in a row, 347
  Greatest product, 261
  Less is more, 241
  Prime or composite, 177
  Reach 100 percent, 429
  Splash relay, 66
  Travel around the world, 109
GCF (greatest common factor), 178–179, 184–185, 194–197
Geometric figures, 298–335, 514–519
Geometry
  angles, 300–303, 310–311, 314, 318-321,330-331, 404-405, 409
  applying, 316–317
  circles, 322–323, 334–335, 500–505, 508
  circumference, 500–503, 512-513, 541
  classifying shapes/figures, 298–299, 514–515
  cones, 514–515
  congruence, 306–309, 318–321, 499, 518-521, 525
  constructions, 318–321
  cubes, 514–518
  cylinders, 514–515, 525

diagonals, 330-331
different views of three-dimensional figures, 516-517
endpoints/midpoints,300-303, 318–321
estimating and measuring,300–303, 308,310-311,314,330-331
figures, 298–333, 514–519
hexagons, 298–299, 330-331
kite, 306-309
line segments, 298–299, 318–321
line symmetry, 326–327, 334–335
lines, 298-299, 304–305, 314, 318–321
making models,312-313, 526–529
Möbius strip, 315
octagons, 298–299
parallelograms, 306–309, 404–405, 496–499, 502–503
pentagons, 298–299, 330-331
pentominoes, 509
planes, 514–515
polygons, 298–299, 306-314
pyramids, 514–515
quadrilaterals, 298–299, 306–311, 314
rays, 300, 318-321
rectangles, 306–309, 492–495, 506–507, 521
rectangular prism, 514–515, 518-519, 522–525, 526–529
reflections, 326–327, 334–335
reflections of light, 316–317
rhombus, 306–309
rotations, 324–325,334–335
sides of figures, 298–299
similar figures, 404–407
slicing three-dimensional figures, 521
spheres, 514–515
square pyramids, 514–515
squares,306–309, 330–331, 509
sums of angles, 310–311
symmetry, 326–327
tessellations,328–329
three-dimensional figures, 514–527
translations, 324–325, 334–335
trapezoidal prism, 514–515
trapezoids, 306–309, 320, 404–405, 514–515
triangles, 306–309, 312–314, 318-321, 496–499, 521
triangular prisms, 514–515, 521
triangular pyramids, 514–515
two-dimensional figures, 298–299,314, 334–335
vertex, 300-303
Glossary, 643–649
Gram (g), 74–75, 158–159
Graphin
  choosing the appropriate graph, 30–33
  coordinate, in all four quadrants, 556–559
  functions, 344–349, 350–352, 556–558
  to describe change, 348-349
  to solve problems, 350–353
  volume and height, 397
Graphs
  bar graphs, 6–9, 18,23, 24, 32–35, 37, 79, 85, 207, 289, 441
    double-bar graphs, 6–9, 18, 30, 37, 375
  circle graphs, 207, 441, 446–448, 453
  choosing the appropriate graph, 30–33
  coordinate graphs,344–352, 397, 556–559, 567
  curved graphs, 347
  functions,344-352, 556-558
  line graphs, 22–25, 34–35, 209, 483, 555
    double-line graphs, 22–25, 34–35, 483

pictographs, 2–5, 7, 51
using to make predictions, 357
Greater numbers, 52–53, 196–197
Greatest common factor (GCF), 178–179, 184–185, 194–197
Grids, coordinate, 344–345, 347, 348–349, 556–557
Guess, test, revise, 68–69. *See also* Problem-solving strategies and skills.

Hexagons, 298–299, 330-331
Histograms, 9
Horizontal axis, 6–7, 348–351, 359

Identifying missing or extra information, 242–245. *See also* Problem-solving skills and strategies.
Identity property, 56–57, 88-90, 101, 271
Improper fractions, 198-199, 213
Inch (in.), 272-273, 282–283, 338-339, 518-519
Independent events, probability of, 462–467
Infobit, 9, 25, 59, 91, 97, 127, 135, 193, 219, 235, 260, 281, 303, 325, 349, 355, 407, 409, 443, 445, 465, 469, 521, 525, 541, 563
Information, missing or extra, 242–245
Integers
addition of, 542–545, 552
applying, 554–555
comparing and ordering, 540–541, 552
coordinate graphing and, 556–559
multiplication of, 553
negative and postive, 538–545, 546–547, 553
opposite, 538–539, 546–547
subtraction of, 546–549, 552
using models, 542–548, 560–562
writing number sentences with, 543–544, 548
zero pairs, 542–543, 546–547, 560–562
Interest, 437
Interpreting data, 450–453, 564-567
Interpreting quotients and remainders, 160–163. *See also* Problem solving skills and strategies.
Intersecting arc, 318–321
Intersecting lines, 304–305, 318–321
Inverse operations, 364–367, 376–377
Irregular tessellations, 328–329
Isosceles triangles, 306–309, 314

Journal writing opportunities, 18, 52, 64, 96, 100, 127, 140, 151, 175, 184, 220, 230, 239, 259, 270, 299, 307, 314, 322, 348, 356, 365, 405, 438, 444, 463, 470, 477, 508, 543, 552

Kilogram (kg), 74–75, 80
Kilometer (km), 72–73, 80, 158–159
Kite, 306–307, 334–335

Least common denominator (LCD), 222–225, 228–229, 238–239

Least common multiple (LCM), 180–181, 185, 222–223
Length
in customary units, 282–283, 338–339, 518-519, 534-535
applying fractions to, 282–283
in metric units, 68-69, 72–73, 80, 158=159, 358-359, 492-495, 522-526, 529, 534-535
applying decimals to, 72–73
Line graphs, 22–25, 34–35, 209, 357, 483, 555
Line plot, 2–5, 7, 17, 63, 197
Line segments, 298–299, 318–323
straight segments, 298–299
Lines
crossing, 298–299
intersecting, 304–305, 318–321
of symmetry, 326–327
parallel, 304–305, 521
perpendicular, 304–305, 318–321, 521
skew lines, 305
List, making an organized, 182–183. *See also* Problem-solving skills and strategies.
Liter (L), 74–75, 80
Logical reasoning, 17, 64, 73, 95, 137, 139, 147, 173, 199, 207, 225, 285, 353, 371, 403, 445, 507, 525, 545, 550–551. *See also* Problem-solving skills and strategies.

Make it right, 8, 44, 58, 62, 90, 108, 126, 132, 156, 202, 264, 302, 308, 366, 370, 386, 392, 406, 428, 434, 464, 478, 498, 504, 544, 548, 562
Making a model, 312–313, 526–529
Making a table, 16–17, 480–483
Mass in metric units, 74–75
Math connection
another way to find the LCM, 185
bottle functions, 397
comparing graphs, 19
create a simulation, 471
front-end estimation, 65
Möbius strips, 315
multiplication of integers, 553
networks, 357
pentominoes, 509
properties of addition and multiplication, 271
spatial visualization, 231
using a spreadsheet, 141
using computers to do simulations, 471
using graphsto make predictions, 357
using properties to multiply mentally, 101
Math, science, technology connection
auto emissions, 168–169
average sixth grader 38–39
bake it, 250–251
coins, 118–119
comfortable chairs, 338-339,380-381
explore pitch and scale, 212-213
gold, 458-459
oceans, 84-85
the planets, 418-419
skyscrapers, 534-535
snow loads, 294-295
sports injuries, 488-489
temperatures, 572-573
Mean, 12–15, 18, 34–35
Measurement
applying decimals in, 72–75
applying fractions in, 282–285
area, 492–493, 496–499, 502–505, 507–508, 510–511

of a circle, 502–504
of compound figures, 506–507
of parallelograms and triangles, 496–499
changing units of, 158–159
circumference of a circle, 500–501, 512-513, 541
classifying 3-dimensional figures, 514–515
customary units
capacity and weight, 284–285, 419
length, 282–283, 338-339, 518-519, 534-535
different views of 3-dimensional figures, 516–517
enlarging rectangles and, 494–495
estimating, 73, 75, 283, 285
metric units
capacity and mass, 74–75
changing units of, 158–159
length, 68-69, 72–73, 80, 158–159, 358-359, 492-495, 522-526, 529, 534-535
relating through multiplication and division, 158–159
of angles,300-303, 308, 310-311, 314, 330-331
of length and distance, 38-39
perimeter, 320, 492–493, 510–511
surface area: prism, 518–521
volume, 522–525
Median, 10–11, 13–15, 34–35, 71
Mental math strategies
divisibility, 172–173
estimating products, 92-93, 266–267
estimating quotients, 124–127
estimating sums and differences, 54–55, 216–219
finding a fraction of a whole number, 256–257
finding a percent of a number, 432-433, 438
multiplication and division patterns, 148–149
patterns and properties, 88–91
Meter (m), 68-69, 72–73, 80, 158–159
Metric ton, 74-75
Metric units of measurement
applying decimals to, 72–75, 80
capacity and mass, 74–75, 80
length, 68-69, 72–73, 80, 158–159, 358-359, 492-495, 522-526, 529, 534-535
relating units of, 158–159
Midchapter review, 18, 64, 100, 140, 184, 230, 270, 314, 356, 396, 438, 470, 508, 552
Mile (mi), 232, 282–283
Milligram (mg), 74–75, 80
Milliliter (mL), 74–75, 80
Millimeter, 72–73, 80
Mixed applications. *See* Problem solving, applying skills for.
Mixed numbers,
addition of, 226–229, 240, 246-247
division with, 280–281, 325
fractions, decimals and, 200–203
multiplication of, 268–269, 325
subtraction of, 236–241, 246-247
understanding, 198–199
Mixed review, 11, 15, 25, 45, 51, 55, 63, 71, 73, 75, 91, 109, 127, 129, 135, 137, 147, 149, 153, 177, 179, 189, 193, 197, 199, 221, 223, 241, 257, 261, 267, 281, 283, 285, 309, 323, 325, 327, 349, 353, 389, 395, 409, 429, 443, 475, 493, 507, 515, 541, 559

I N D E X

Möbius strips, 315
Mode, 10–11, 13–15, 34–35, 71
Models, making, 312–313, 512–513, 526–529. *See also* Problem-solving skills and strategies.
Models, using, 104–105, 190–192, 222–224, 226, 236, 276–277, 430–431, 436–437, 542–548, 560–562
Money, 32, 56–59, 65, 72–77, 79, 95–99, 102–103, 107–108, 110–113, 118–119, 183, 203–207, 257, 260, 268–269, 286–289, 352,390–395, 424–453, 459
More to explore
　adding integers with a calculator, 545
　adding ratios, 387
　another way to divide fractions, 279
　area of trapezoids, 499
　calculating pi, 505
　changing rates, 393
　complementary and supplementary angles, 303
　curved graphs, 347
　density property, 53, 203
　divisibility by four, 173
　double stem-and-leaf plots, 27
　estimating and adjusting, 219
　estimating products using compatible numbers, 93
　estimating tips, 435
　events and their complements, 467
　histograms, 9
　more metric relationships, 159
　multiplying by changing fractions to decimals, 269
　percents and banking, 437
　permutations, 479
　properties of addition, 229
　repeating decimals, 157
　simplify fractions by using a calculator, 195
　skew lines, 305
　slicing 3-dimensional figures, 521
　solving two-step equations, 371
　subtracting integers using a calculator, 549
　using properties to add mentally, 59
　volume of a cylinder, 525
More to investigate, 21, 67, 103, 143, 187, 233, 273,317, 359,399, 441, 473, 511, 555
Multiples,
　common, 180–181, 185, 208-209
　least common, 180–181, 185, 222–223
Multiplication/multiplying
　applying, 102–103, 272–273
　associative property in, 88–90, 100, 101, 271
　by fractions, 262–265, 270
　commutative property in, 88–90, 101, 271
　decimals by decimals, 104–109, 114–115
　decimals by whole numbers, 96–97, 100, 114–115
　distributive property in, 88–90, 100–101, 271
　division and, 148–149, 158–159, 276, 368–371
　equations, 368–371
　estimating products, 92–93, 96–97, 114–115, 118–119, 266–267
　fractions, 258–261, 270
　identity property, 88–90, 100–101, 271
　in measurement, 158–159
　integers, 553
　mental math for, 88–90, 92–93, 100, 108, 114–115, 148–149

　patterns, 88–90, 148–149
　whole numbers, 88–95, 100, 114–115
　zeros in, 88–90, 100–101, 135, 271
Multiplication equations,368–371
Multiplication expressions, 134–135
Multiplication properties, 88–93, 100–101, 271
Multistep problems, solving, 98–99, 410–413. *See also* Problem-solving skills and strategies.

Negative coordinates, 556–558
Negative integers, 538–543, 546–547
Number line, 216-217, 538–541
Number sense, developing
　diameter, 323
　estimating with percents, 439
　front-end estimation, 65
　measurement, 309
　multiplication of integers, 553
　using properties to multiply mentally, 101
Number theory
　common factors and GCF, 178–179, 184–185, 194–197, 208–209
　common multiples and LCM, 180–181, 185, 208–209
　divisibility rules, 172–176, 208–209
　prime factorization, 174–177, 180, 184–185, 208–209
Numbers
　compatible, 93, 125–126, 164, 266–267
　composite, 174–177
　expanded form of, 46–47, 137
　exponent forms of, 42–44, 64
　factor forms of, 43–44
　greater, 68–69
　means of, 12–15, 18, 34–35
　median/mode/ranges of, 10–11, 13–15, 34–35, 71
　one-digit divisors, 128–129, 140. 164-165
　ordered pairs of, 344–349, 556–558
　percents, 424–443
　prime, 174–177,
　sentences, 543–544, 548
　standard form of, 42–44, 46–47, 64, 80–81
　two-digit divisors, 130–133, 140, 164-165
　understanding, 46–47
　whole, 42–61, 88–109, 124–137, 144–159
Numerators, 188-202, 216-228, 236-240, 262-265, 276-279, 388-389, 400-401, 426-427

Obtuse angles, 300–303, 314
Obtuse triangles, 306–309, 314
Octagons, 298–299
One-digit divisors, 128–129, 140, 164–165
Operations
　inverse, 364–369, 376–377
　order of, 136–137, 225, 264, 279
Opposite integers, 538–539, 546–547
Order of operations, 136–137, 225, 264, 279
Ordered pairs of numbers, 344–347, 556–558, 567
Ordering integers, 540–541

Organized lists, 182–183
Origin, 344–345
Ounce (oz), 284–285
Outcomes
　certain, 466–467, 470
　equally likely, 462–467, 470
　favorable, 462–465, 470, 476–477
　impossible, 466–467, 470, 502–504
　less likely/more likely, 466–467, 470
　possible, 462–467, 476–479
Overestimates and underestimates, using, 110–113

Parallel lines, 304–305, 521
Parallelograms, 306–309, 404–405, 496–499, 502–503
Parentheses in expressions, 136–137
Patterns, relations and functions, 42–45, 58, 71, 88–91, 124–126, 140, 148–150, 152, 234–235, 247, 267, 269, 275, 309, 330-333, 335, 426, 427, 495, 503, 545, 553. *See also* Algebra.
Pentagons, 298–299, 330-331
Pentominoes, 509
Percents
　applying, 440–441
　banking and, 437
　decimals, fractions and, 426–429, 432–434, 454–455
　discounts and, 442–443, 454–455
　estimating with, 430–435, 439, 442–443
　game, 429
　meaning of, 424-425
　of a loan, 437
　of numbers, 430–435, 454–455
　one number is of another, 436–437, 454–455
　probability and, 472-473
　problem solving, 444-445
　renaming, 432-433
　understanding, 424–427, 454–455
　using models, 430–431, 436–437
　writing, 426–434
Performance assessment, 37, 83, 117, 167, 211, 249, 293, 337, 379, 417, 457, 487, 533, 571
Perimeter
　and area, 492–493, 510–511, 530–531, 541
　applying, 510-511
　in enlarging rectangles, 494–495
　of a rectangle, 492–493, 530–531
　using formulas to find, 492–493, 530–531
Permutations, 479
Perpendicular lines, 304–305, 318–321, 518–521
Pi, 505
Pictographs, 2-5, 7, 51
Pint (pt), 284–285
Place-value, 46-53
Plane figures, 514–515
Planes, 514–515
Polygons, 298–299, 306-314
Portfolio work, 1, 21, 37, 41, 67, 83, 87, 103, 117, 123, 143, 167, 171, 187, 211, 215, 233, 249, 255, 273, 293, 297, 317, 337, 341, 359, 379, 383, 399, 417, 423, 441, 457, 461, 473, 487, 491, 511, 533, 537, 555, 571
Positive integers, 538–543, 546–547
Pound (lb), 284–285, 294-295, 419
Powers, 42–44, 46–47, 64–65, 80–81, 148–149, 151, 154–155

Practice strategies, 32–33, 78–79, 112–113, 162–163, 206–207, 244–245, 288–289, 332–333, 374–375, 412–413, 482–483, 528–529, 566–567

Pre-assessment, 1, 41, 87, 123, 171, 215, 255, 297, 341, 383, 423, 461, 491, 537

Predicting, 21, 67, 103, 143, 187, 233, 273, 304, 317, 357, 359, 399, 441, 471, 472–473, 474–475, 511, 526, 534, 555, 567

Prime factorization, 174–177, 180, 184, 185, 208-209

Prime numbers, 174–176, 177

Prisms, 514–515, 522–529

Probability
  applying, 472–473
  computer simulation, 471, 483, 529
  counting principle and, 476–479
  experiments, 462–465, 471, 472–473, 567
  frequency tables, 462–465
  making predictions and, 474–475
  of injuries, 488-489
  outcomes, 462–466, 476–477
  permutations, 479
  simulations, 468–469, 471, 483, 529
  tree diagrams and, 476–479
  understanding, 466–467 *See also* Outcomes,

Problem formulation, 9, 15, 17, 45, 59, 69, 77, 91, 99, 111, 127, 133, 139, 147, 157, 159, 163, 173, 179, 183, 193, 205, 219, 225, 229, 265, 275, 279, 283, 305, 313, 355, 367, 371, 373, 387, 393, 403, 411, 428, 435, 445, 449, 451, 467, 479, 513, 525, 527, 541, 545, 549, 550, 562, 565

Problem solvers at work, 30–33, 76–79, 110–113, 160–163, 204–207, 242–245, 286–289, 330–333, 372–375, 410–413, 450–453, 480–483, 526–529, 564–567. *See also* Problem-solving skills and strategies.

Problem solving, applying skills for
  consumer math, 32, 56–59, 65, 76–77, 87–119, 183, 203–207, 257, 260, 268–269, 286–289, 352, 390–395, 424–453
  decision making, 15, 21, 25, 45, 55, 67, 71, 75, 76, 91, 95, 99, 103, 108, 133, 143, 179, 187, 193, 233, 269, 273, 283, 317, 323, 359, 363, 371, 375, 387, 393, 395, 399, 403, 410, 441, 445, 450, 473, 480, 483, 499, 511, 515, 555
  mixed applications, 5, 11, 15, 17, 25, 27, 35, 45, 53, 55, 59, 63, 69, 71, 73, 75, 81, 91, 93, 95, 97, 99, 108, 115, 127, 129, 133, 135, 137, 139, 147, 149, 152, 157, 159, 165, 173, 176, 179, 181, 183, 184, 189, 193, 195, 197, 199, 203, 209, 221, 223, 225, 229, 235, 240, 257, 260, 265, 267, 269, 275, 281, 283, 285, 291, 303, 305, 309, 313, 321, 323, 325, 327, 335, 346, 349, 355, 363, 367, 371, 377, 387, 389, 393, 395, 403, 407, 409, 415, 428, 435, 437, 443, 445, 449, 455, 465, 467, 469, 475, 479, 485, 493, 499, 507, 513, 515, 521, 525, 531, 541, 545, 549, 551, 563, 569
  problem formulation, 9, 15, 17, 45, 59, 69, 77, 91, 99, 111, 127, 133, 139, 147, 157, 159, 163, 173, 179, 183, 193, 205, 219, 225, 229, 265, 275,

279, 283, 305, 313, 355, 367, 371, 373, 387, 393, 403, 411, 428, 435, 445, 449, 451, 467, 479, 513, 525, 527, 541, 545, 549, 550, 562, 565

Problem-solving skills and strategies
  act it out, 468
  alternate solution methods, 444–445
  choose the appropriate graph, 30–33
  choosing whether to use fractions or decimals, 286–289
  do a simulation, 468–469, 483
  express quotients, 204–207
  find a pattern, 234–235, 330–333
  guess and test, 68–69
  interpret data, 450–453, 564–567
  interpret quotients and remainders, 160–163, 204–207
  make a diagram, 512-513
  make a model, 312–313, 512–513, 526–529
  make an organized list, 182–183
  make a table, 16–17, 480–483
  missing or extra information, 242–245
  multistep problems, 98–99, 410–413
  simpler problems, 354–355
  underestimates and overestimates, 76–79, 110–113
  use estimation, 76–79, 110–113
  use a formula, 138–139
  use logical reasoning, 550–551
  work backward, 274–275, 372–375
  write an equation, 402–403

Products
  of decimals, 96–97, 100, 104–109, 114–115
  of fractions, 258–261, 270, 292–293
  of whole numbers, 88–97, 100, 114–115

Proportions
  scale drawings and, 408–409, 414–415
  similar figures and, 404–407, 414–415
  understanding, 400–401, 414–415
  writing equations using, 402–403, 414–415

Protractors, working with, 300–303, 310–311, 318–321

Pyramids, 514–515

Q

Quadrilaterals, 298–299, 306–311, 314

Quart (qt), 284–285

Quarter inch, 282–283

Quotients
  decimal, 128–132
  division with zeros in, 135, 140–145, 155, 172-173
  estimating and rounding, 128–132

Quotients and remainders, interpreting, 160–163. *See also* Problem-solving skills and strategies.

R

Radius, 322–323, 500–504

Random sample, 28–29, 474–475

Range, 10–11, 13–15, 34–35, 71

Rates, 390–393, 396, 414-415

Ratios
  adding, 387
  applying, 398–399
  better buys and, 394–396
  combining, 387
  equal, 388–389, 396, 398–401, 414–415
  rates, 390–393, 396, 414–415
  understanding, 384–387, 396, 414–415
  unit prices, 394–395

Rays, 300, 318–321

Reading, Writing, Arithmetic,
  Ask Questions, 1, 4, 30
  Draw Conclusions, 171, 173, 204
  Make Generalizations, 123, 139, 160
  Reread, 87, 93, 110
  Sequence of Events, 341, 355, 372
  Steps in a Process, 461, 468, 481
  Summarize, 215, 218, 242
  Use Diagrams, 297, 315, 331
  Use Graphs, 423, 441, 450
  Use Tables, 41, 63, 77
  Visualize, 491, 521, 526
  Write Advertisements, 382, 395, 410
  Write: How to, 255, 278, 287
  Write: Paragraph, 537, 538, 565

Real-life connections
  art and design, 297–339
  average sixth graders, 1–39
  buying and selling, 423-459
  careers
    architect, 300
    automobile road tester, 154
    cordwainer, 278
    dance academy director, 190
    engineer, 494
    marine biologist, 74
    market researcher, 12
    marketing executive, 436
    meteorologist, 556
    mountain biker, 220
    speleologist, 408
    treasury analyst, 106
    veterinarian, 364
  earth science, 537-573
  entertainment, 171–213
  games and sports, 461–489
  getting it built, 255-295
  interesting buildings, 491–535
  leisure time, 215–251
  money, 87–119
  science and the world around us, 341–381
  transportation, 123–169
  travel, and vacations, 383–419
  water, water, everywhere, 41–85

Real-life investigations
  applying
    addition and subtraction, 66–67
    algebra, 358–359
    divisibility, 186–187
    division, 142–143
    fractions, 232–233
    geometry, 316–317
    integers, 554–555
    multiplication, 102–103, 272–273
    percents, 440–441
    perimeter and area, 510–511
    probability, 472–473
    ratios, 398–399
    statistics, 20–21

Reasoning. *See* Logical reasoning; Spatial reasoning.

Reciprocals, 278–281

Rectangles, 174–175, 306–309, 407, 492–495

Rectangular prisms, 514–515, 522–525, 526–529

Reflections, 316–317, 326–327, 334–335

Relating perimeter and area, 492–493, 541

Repeating decimals, 157

Representative sample, 28–29

Rhombuses, 306–309

Right angles, 300–303, 304, 314

Right triangles, 306–309, 314

Rotations, 324–325

Rounding
in measurement, 272-273, 504, 508, 519–520, 524
money, 106-113, 442-443
to estimate products, 92-93, 100
to estimate quotients, 128–132, 154-157
to estimate sums and differences, 54–55, 216–219, 230
to tenths and hundredths, 144–147, 154–157
to zero/one-half/one, 216–218
Ruler, 282–283

Sale price, 442-443
Scale, 6–8, 22, 24, 37, 272-273, 390–392, 408–409, 494–497
Scale drawings, 408–409, 469
Scalene triangles, 306–309
Scatter plots, 20-21
Science, integrating with math, 38–39, 84–85, 118–119, 168–169, 212–213, 250–251, 294–295, 338–339, 380–381, 418–419, 458–459, 488–489, 534–535, 572–573.
Sides, corresponding, 404–406
Similar figures, 404–407
Similarity, 404–407
Simplest form of fractions, 194–195, 202, 208–209, 262–263, 268–269, 278–281, 426–428
Simulations, 468–469, 471, 483, 529.
Solve a simpler problem, 354–355.
Solving a multistep problem, 98–99, 410–413
Solving equations
addition and subtraction, 364–367, 376-377, 560–563
multiplication and division, 368–371
Solving real-world problems, 16–17, 20–21, 30–33, 38–39, 66–69, 76–79, 84–85, 98–99, 102–103, 110–113, 118–119, 138–139, 142–143, 160–163, 168–169, 182–183, 186–187, 204–207, 212–213, 232–235, 242–245, 250–251, 272–275, 286–289, 294–295, 312–313, 316–317, 330–333, 338–339, 354–355, 358–359, 372–375, 380–381, 398–399, 402–403, 410–413, 418–419, 440–441, 444–445, 450–453, 458–459, 468–469, 472–473, 480–483, 488–489, 510–513, 526–529, 534–535, 550–551, 554–555, 564–569, 572–573
Spatial reasoning, 33, 63, 69, 112, 113, 127, 163, 183, 189, 260, 265, 275, 289, 303, 309, 333, 363, 403, 413, 435, 453, 465, 469, 483, 507, 513, 545
Spatial sense, developing,
Möbius strips, 315
pentominoes, 509
spatial visualization, 231
Spheres, 514–515
Spreadsheets, 113, 119, 141, 163, 169, 213, 251, 295, 357, 375, 381, 413, 471, 529
Square feet, 294-295
Square pyramids, 514–515
Square units, 492–493
Squares, 306–309, 330-331, 509
Standard form of decimals and numbers, 43–50, 64, 80

Statistics
applying, 20–21
bar graphs, 6–9, 34–35
choosing the appropriate graph, 30–33
circle graphs, 446-449
collecting, organizing and displaying data, 2–5, 34–35
databases, 19
line graphs, 22–25, 34–35
make a table, 16–17
mean, 12–15, 34–35
range, median, mode, 10–11, 13–14, 15, 34–35, 71
relationships between two sets of data, 20–21
sampling and predicting, 28–29, 34–35
scatter plots, 20-21
stem-and-leaf plots, 26–27, 34–35
tables, 16–17
Stem-and-leaf plots, 26–27, 34–35
Straight angles, 300–303
Subtraction/subtracting
applying, 66-67
decimals, 60–64, 75, 80–81, 221, 285
estimating differences, 54–55, 60-62, 216–219
fractions with like denominators, 220–221, 230
fractions with unlike denominators, 224–225, 230
integers, 546–549
mental math, 45, 216–221, 240
mixed numbers and, 236–241, 246–247
Subtraction equations, 364–367, 560–563
Subtraction expressions, 70–71
Sums
estimating, 54–55, 64, 216–219, 230
of angles, 310–311, 330-331
Supplementary angles, 303
Surface area, 518–521
Surveys, 2-5, 16-17, 28-29, 176, 233, 267, 309, 407, 428, 436-437, 450-451, 474, 489
Symmetry, 326–327

Table of measures, 650
Tables, using, making, 2–5, 9, 16–17, 79, 85, 342–347, 459, 462–465, 480–483, 498, 544, 556–558, 567, 573
Talk it over, 2, 6, 12, 22, 42, 48, 56, 60, 88, 106, 124, 130, 144, 150, 154, 174, 190, 200, 216, 238, 258, 262, 300, 306, 318, 344, 350, 360, 364, 368, 384, 390, 404, 426, 432, 446, 462, 476, 496, 502, 522, 542, 546, 556, 560
Technology, integrating with math, 38–39, 84–85, 118–119, 168–169, 212–213, 250–251, 294–295, 338–339, 380–381, 418–419, 458–459, 488–489, 534–535, 572–573. *See also* Calculators; Computers.
Technology sense, developing
comparing graphs, 19
using graphs to make predictions, 357
using a computer to do a simulation, 471
using a spreadsheet, 141
Temperature, 350–351, 538–541, 545, 552–555, 562–567, 572-573
Tessellations, 328–329
Three-dimensional figures, 514-527
Translations, 324–325
Trapezoidal prisms, 514–515

Trapezoids, 306–309, 320, 404–405, 514–515
Tree diagrams, 476–479
Triangles
acute, 306–309, 314
area of, 496-499
equilateral, 306–309, 314, 330-331
isosceles, 306–309, 314
models using, 312–313
obtuse, 306–309, 314
right, 306–309, 314
scalene, 306–309
sums of angles of, 310–311, 314
Triangular prisms, 514–514, 521
Triangular pyramids, 514–515
Two-digit numbers, 130–133, 140, 164–165
Two dimensional figures, 298-299, 334-335

Underestimates and overestimates, using, 110–113. *See also* Problem-solving skills and strategies.
Unit price, 394-395
Units
cubic, 522–523, 526–527
square, 518–519

Variables, 70–71, 80, 271, 350–352, 360–370
Venn diagrams, 513, 550–551
Vertex/vertices, 300–303, 310–311
Vertical axis, 6–7, 348–349, 350-351, 437
Volume
cubic centimeters in, 522–525
cubic units in, 522–525
determining on a computer, 529
of a cylinder, 525
of a rectangular prism, 522–525
of a skyscraper, 534-535

Weight in customary units, 284–285, 418-419
Whole numbers. *See* Addition, Decimals, Division, Estimating, Fractions, Multiplication, Subtraction.
Word names of decimals and numbers, 46-50
Work together, 2, 12, 21, 28, 42, 66–67, 104, 110–111, 150, 153, 174, 190, 204, 226, 236, 242–243, 258, 276, 286, 298, 300, 310, 316, 328, 330, 342, 347, 360, 372, 384, 398, 400, 404, 410, 424, 430, 450, 462, 480, 494, 500, 502, 509, 516, 518, 522, 526, 538, 542, 546, 560, 564
Working backward, 274–275, 372–375. *See also* Problem-solving skills and strategies.
Writing equations, 402–403.
Writing problems, 9, 15, 17, 45, 59, 69, 77, 91, 99, 111, 127, 133, 139, 142, 147, 157, 159, 163, 173, 179, 183, 186, 193, 205, 219, 225, 229, 265, 275, 279, 283, 305, 355, 367, 371, 373, 387, 393, 403, 411, 428, 435, 445, 449, 451, 467, 479, 513, 525, 527, 541, 545, 549, 550, 562, 565

INDEX

Yard (yd), 282–283

Zero pairs, 542–543, 546–547, 560–562
Zeros
  in division, 130–131, 135, 140, 144-
    149, 154-155
  in factors, 88–89
  in integers, 542–543, 546–549
  property of, 88-90, 101, 271
  relating to exponents, 42-44
  rounding to, 216-218, 266-267